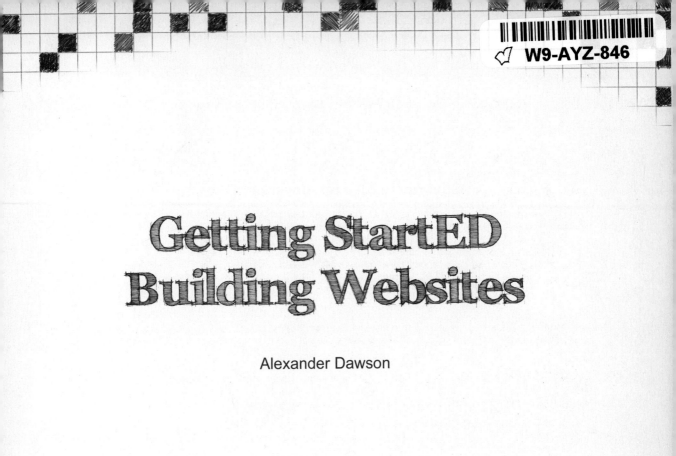

Getting StartED
Building Websites

Alexander Dawson

an Apress® company

GETTING STARTED BUILDING WEBSITES

Copyright © 2009 by Alexander Dawson

ISBN-13 (pbk): 978-1-4302-2517-1

ISBN-13 (electronic): 978-1-4302-2518-8

Printed and bound in the United States of America 9 8 7 6 5 4 3 2 1

Trademarked names may appear in this book. Rather than use a trademark symbol with every occurrence of a trademarked name, we use the names only in an editorial fashion and to the benefit of the trademark owner, with no intention of infringement of the trademark.

Distributed to the book trade worldwide by Springer-Verlag New York, Inc., 233 Spring Street, 6th Floor, New York, NY 10013. Phone 1-800-SPRINGER, fax 201-348-4505, e-mail orders-ny@springer-sbm.com, or visit www.springeronline.com.

For information on translations, please e-mail info@apress.com, or visit www.apress.com.

Apress and friends of ED books may be purchased in bulk for academic, corporate, or promotional use. eBook versions and licenses are also available for most titles. For more information, reference our Special Bulk Sales–eBook Licensing web page at http://www.apress.com/info/bulksales.

The information in this book is distributed on an "as is" basis, without warranty. Although every precaution has been taken in the preparation of this work, neither the author(s) nor Apress shall have any liability to any person or entity with respect to any loss or damage caused or alleged to be caused directly or indirectly by the information contained in this work.

Credits

For the long-suffering professionals who work tirelessly to make the Web a better place, especially those individuals who continue to strive for a more accessible and standards-compliant Internet.

Contents at a Glance

Contents

About the Author

Alexander Dawson is a freelance website designer and recreational software developer specializing in web standards, accessibility, and user-experience design. When he is not busy running his own one-man consultancy firm HiTechy (www.hitechy.com), he spends much of his time assisting others in the field and those who are just starting out as a mentor on the SitePoint forums. His aim in life is to share his knowledge so that others can be energized rather than intimidated by the constant flow of new technology.

About the Technical Reviewer

Kristian Besley is a Flash and web developer currently working in education and specializing in games/interactivity and dynamically driven content using Flash, PHP, and .NET (not all at the same time, obviously!). He also lectures in interactive media.

Kristian has produced freelance work for numerous clients including the BBC, Heinemann, and BBC Cymru. He has written a number of books for friends of ED, such as working on the Foundation Flash series, *Flash MX Video* (ISBN-13: 978-1-59059-172-7), *Flash ActionScript for Flash 8* (ISBN-13: 978-1-59059-618-0), and *Learn Design with Flash MX* (ISBN-13: 978-1-59059-157-4). He was also a proud contributor to the amazing *Flash Math Creativity* books and has written for *Computer Arts* magazine.

Kristian currently resides with his family in Swansea, Wales and is a fluent Welsh speaker.

Acknowledgments

Before we get started, it's only fair that I should give thanks to the many people who have given me support and assistance, or have just inspired me, on this journey of writing a book for those starting out in building websites.

First, my thanks have to go out to the team at Apress and friends of ED, who gave me the opportunity to get published. It's been a real pleasure getting to know you all. Some of the names needing a shout out here are Ben-Renow Clarke (for giving me the opportunity and tirelessly working to get this book released), Kelly Moritz (who, like Ben, gave me hours of useful Skype and e-mail assistance when it was needed most), and Kristian Besley (who gave his wise advice to help make this a better book). Also praise needs to be given to Patrick Meader and Heather Lang, who took my scary grammatical skills and helped this book evolve into something worthy of reading!

Next, I need to give a shout out to my friends on the SitePoint forums. Without your longstanding presence of helping others with technical questions about web design and development, the Web would be a much darker place. Giving your free time to help anyone who joins the community really does make a difference.

I also need to shout out to all my friends on the koach.com network and elsewhere (like MSN Messenger) who have put up with (or are secretly cheering at) my absence for the months I spent writing this book.

Finally, I need to give thanks to anyone who decided to give this book a read. It covers a wide range of subjects, so I hope that no matter your interests, some information in it will help you better understand the web design process. If this book helps a single person, it will have been worth the effort I put into writing it.

Introduction

So you want to build your very own website? That's awesome! By picking up this book you have taken the first step in making your wish come true. A lot of stigma exists about the difficulty of building websites, but you can take comfort in the fact that almost anyone with a computer and access to the Internet can produce a website! It might take you a while to get through this book, because it goes into more depth than some other beginner books to equip you better for all possible scenarios. Hopefully, once you finish this book, you will want to learn more about the subjects discussed, but if I can offer you a single piece of advice before starting on your quest it is "stay calm and don't panic." After all, creating a website can be a lot of fun!

Your Expectations

You probably have a number of expectations for this book based on what you want to learn. Basic details of what you should expect are provided within each chapter of this book, but the following general rules apply and state exactly what kind of experience you should get as you begin reading. From this book, you *should* expect

- A comprehensive guide to website design and development
- Easy-to-follow steps provided whenever possible and always in a logical format
- Advanced subjects covered in simple terms to reduce confusion

You *should not* expect the following from this book:

- This book is *not* a reference manual, and you will find no detailed language tutorials. For that, you should look to related titles like *Getting StartED with CSS* by David Powers (ISBN-13: 978-1-4302-2543-0) or *Getting StartED with JavaScript* by Terry McNavage (ISBN-13: 978-1-4302-7219-9).
- This is not a quick-start guide, as quality and depth are more important than speed.
- This book will not dive straight into coding but underlines what you need to know first.

Book Conventions

This book is a great resource if you are building a website for the first time, and it uses some cool methods to structure the content to make things easier to read. The following conventions have been used to try to break down some of the stuffy subjects into easy-to-swallow segments. The book also makes use of screenshots and examples throughout to help you see how technologies interact, visualize your web designs easier, and generally show you how to organize all the bits and pieces in your design without leaving you puzzled. As a general rule, when you see "Try It Yourself" sections, you should take the opportunity to pause reading and follow the instructions to achieve a goal that will assist you in your development process. These sections provide important exercises for this book. When you find a "See for Yourself" section, you can look at the example, play around with it, or even adapt the provided code or information when making your own website. In short, these are the examples in this book:

- **Try It Yourself**: Step-by-step tutorials you *should* follow to achieve a goal
- **See for Yourself**: Examples that you can use or adapt for your website

The following sidebars are also included for your use:

- **LinkED**: Useful website addresses related to the subject
- **ExplainED**: A basic explanation for something being talked about
- **NotED**: Details that more-advanced readers may find interesting

And here are some other useful sections you'll find:

- **Tips and Tricks**: These sections explain things to take into account that could affect your website.
- **Questions and Answers**: These sections offer simple answers to questions you may have.
- **Chapter Checklist**: Measure your progress by marking off your achievements.

You are about to embark on a journey of learning, creativity, and hands-on skills that will test your mind to the limits. At times, you might wonder if you can swallow all of the information available, but just keep picturing the finish line and remember that learning never has an expiration date. Everyone has a own unique way of learning, and you can decide for yourself when you feel that you are ready to take in some new information. Before we get into the meaty aspects of web design (that is, creating something), the following section has been included to give you a crash course in understanding how the Web works, in case you don't already know.

Understanding Some Basics of the Web

Can you picture a world without the Internet? There would be no access to the mighty Google, no information stored inside Wikipedia, and no ability to instantly contact people through e-mail, social networking, and instant messaging. We, as members of a modern society, depend on the Internet for everything from making new friends from all over the world right up to delivering high-quality savings on the kinds of goods we once bought at a premium in brick-and-mortar stores. Some businesses are entirely run through the Internet without having a physical presence! When producing websites, you should have a basic understanding of the history and technology that goes into keeping the Web running to give you perspective on the bigger picture.

What Is the Internet?

The Internet and the World Wide Web are different things. The **Internet** is made up of hardware (think of your computer) and has lots of cables streaming out of the back leading in different directions keeping in constant communication with other machines that are hooked up to the Web. The Internet supports everything that you choose to run on it. The **World Wide Web**, on the other hand, is the software and goes through a series of processes to send and receive information, which is controlled by the behavior of the people who use it. Because we are going to build a website, rather than focus on all the behind-the-scenes stuff (which the majority of us leave to the people who keep our websites running), we will focus entirely on the World Wide Web.

ExplainED

For future reference, the World Wide Web may be referred to as the Web or WWW, which is where you get the www at the start of a website address.

Information is transferred around the Web using a variety of methods; each method of transferring information has its own specific purpose and is commonly referred to as a **protocol**. You don't need to know the technical lingo, but you already make use of these protocols on a regular basis (see Figure 1). Whenever you go to your favorite website, you make use of the

Hypertext Transfer Protocol (HTTP), which basically means that you request information and a website sends it to you. If you upload your design onto the Web, you use the File Transfer Protocol (FTP), which lets you take stuff from your computer and place it online. Finally, if you buy something off the Web, the website will keep everything secret from prying eyes using HTTPS (the "S" stands for "secure").

When these are in use you can see them working their magic. If you have a web browser window open, just take a look at the address bar. You will notice (perhaps for the first time) that before the ://www, which shows your website address, there will be an acronym like http, https, or ftp listed before it, which indicates the protocol your web browser is using. Fairly simple, right?

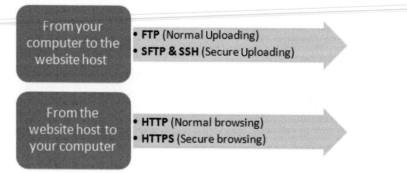

From your computer to the website host
• **FTP** (Normal Uploading)
• **SFTP & SSH** (Secure Uploading)

From the website host to your computer
• **HTTP** (Normal browsing)
• **HTTPS** (Secure browsing)

Figure 1. This diagram explains the direction in which several protocols send information.

The place where your site will be hosted is, not surprisingly, called the **host** or the **server** (that is, the machine that serves information to your computer). Likewise, the computer that accesses the website through a web browser is called a **client** (like being a customer of the Internet). Information is sent, upon request, down your telephone line into your computer so that the web browser can look at it and start making use of it. Figure 2 how the computers interact with each other, much like two people having a conversation on a telephone; information is exchanged by your computer and the place where the stuff you want to look at is hosted. Things get really interesting (as we will look at next) when browsers spice up the conversation and make elements appear on your screen!

Your web browser requests permission to view a website such as www.google.com.

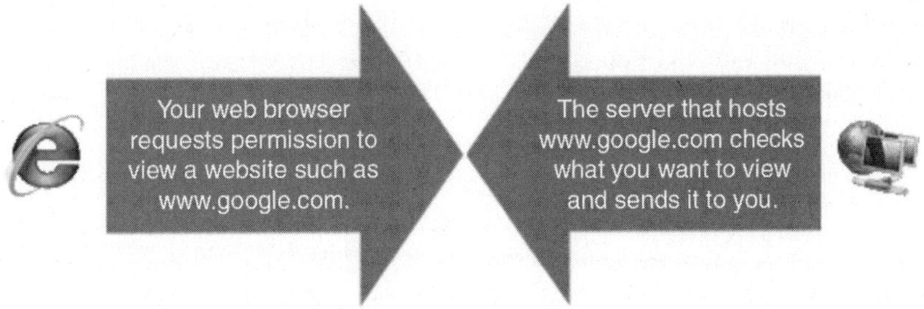

The server that hosts www.google.com checks what you want to view and sends it to you.

Figure 2. This basic model shows a representation of your computer (left) and the place that hosts your site (right).

Websites and Browsers

A **website** is a collection of documents, images, and other digital media that have been written specially for the Web so that they are suitable for viewing within a browser. All websites are summoned through a website address, which will direct the end user to the place where the site itself is held. Websites are made up of pages that are joined up by **hyperlinks**. You click these links to navigate from one page to another as you browse the site. You have probably use hyperlinks hundreds of times without really thinking about it. Links can either refer you to another page within the same site or link to another external website. For example, you could have a link in your website to one of your favorite places on the Web or some cool product on Amazon.

Website addresses exist because they are easier to remember than IP addresses. The IP address is the "real" address that computers use for a website and is just a series of numbers. The friends of ED home page has the IP address 66.211.109.45, but remembering www.friendsofed.com is much easier than remembering that seemingly random series of numbers, right?

You have almost certainly used a web browser before, whether it is Internet Explorer, Mozilla Firefox, Opera, Apple Safari, Google Chrome, or one of the many other website browsers that have appeared. The **web browser** is the piece of software you use to visit websites, and browsers normally have a wide range of tools and support for the different technologies on the Web. Without a browser, the Internet certainly would not be as rich and contextual as it is today. There are many different kinds of web browsers (as discussed later in the book), you will find that the vast majority of your visitors will make use of one of desktop browsers named previously or a mobile browser on a cell phones or portable device.

Browsers take text documents that have been specially formatted for the Web and use that formatting information to decide how the page will appear visually. Here's a simple way to view this in action: Go to any website of your choice (just pick one at random). Right-click the screen when the page loads, and select the View Source menu option to see what is going on behind the scenes (see Figure 3). What you will see is a page of code.

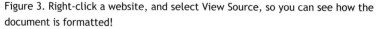

Figure 3. Right-click a website, and select View Source, so you can see how the document is formatted!

Code is defined as the elements of the document that explain and decide how the page should appear. When we talk about web development, most code is referred to as **markup** because it marks elements of a page to have special formatting applied to them. When you first look inside a website's source code, you will probably think it looks pretty alien and confusing (see Figure 4). With all those weird bits and pieces placed throughout the document, the code probably makes no sense to you at all. However, when you get used to seeing this information, you will notice that everything has a purpose (which we will discuss later).

Now that you know what a website is and how everything gets shuffled between your computer, the browser, and the place that holds the documents online, we will look at what exactly makes a perfect website. After all, you don't want to make your site look horrible; you want it to look exactly how you may have pictured it in your imagination!

```
<body class="" onload="">

<ul id="navbar">
  <li id="articles"><a href="http://www.alistapart.com/articles/"
title="Articles">Articles</a></li>
  <li id="topics"><a href="http://www.alistapart.com/topics/"
title="Topics">Topics</a></li>
  <li id="about"><a href="http://www.alistapart.com/about/"
title="About">About</a></li>
  <li id="contact"><a href="http://www.alistapart.com/contact/"
title="Contact">Contact</a></li>
  <li id="contribute"><a href="http://www.alistapart.com/contribute/"
title="Contribute">Contribute</a></li>
  <li id="feed"><a href="http://www.alistapart.com/feed/" title="Feed">Feed</a></li>
</ul>
```

Figure 4. This code may look confusing, but it explains to the browser how everything is laid out.

The Ten-Step Guide to Zen Creativity

The steps involved in creating what could, perhaps, be the ideal homepage are quite simple and straightforward. However, creating websites is a skillful and artistic process because it takes practice, time, and effort. You need to not only learn to adopt these skills but to be able to implement them in such a way that your website will have longevity over the years to come. To help you understand the book's method of teaching, I have devised what I call the ten-step guide to Zen creativity, a series of ten words written in order that define the very essence of what producing the perfect website requires. The questions provided for each element in the "Try It Yourself" sections are to help look at other people's websites (and eventually your own) to see where they went wrong or where they did well. If you want to apply these steps to your own website, you can refer to this section once yours is completed.

The ten steps are as follows:

1. Capability
2. Productivity
3. Simplicity
4. Desirability
5. Functionality
6. Compatibility
7. Flexibility
8. Accessibility
9. Usability
10. Expandability

The following poem is easy way to remember them:

I'm capable of being productive, simple, and desirable too.

I function on multiple levels, compatible all the way through.

I can flex to my users demands, being accessed and used just right.

And when I'm updated and expanded, I make for a very good site!

Capability

What makes an individual capable of creating a website, or what makes a browser capable of showing that website correctly and easily? The answer is as simple: standards, rules, and history. Without a basic understanding of what goes into making a website, neither the creator of the site nor the creator of the browser can ever hope to make things look and feel as intended. The pinnacle of most sciences is experimentation and education, and producing for the Web is no exception to this rule. By learning about a wide range of subjects, you gain a very powerful insight into the way things work, what mistakes have been made in the past, and how to avoid falling into those traps. An endless wealth of knowledge is available to someone wishing to make a website, and understanding the standards that exist will allow you to become more experienced as an individual and able to match the professionals.

Try It Yourself: Checking for Capability

- Do you understand how the web browser makes a site appear the way it does?
- Have you learned enough about the different languages to decide which to use?
- Are you keeping your knowledge up to date beyond just what this book offers?
- Do you feel comfortable at the end of each chapter with what you have learned?
- Are you aware that you can get support for most of your questions online for free?

Productivity

The last things anyone hoping to build a website wants to come across are sudden lacks of ideas or motivation to put plans into action. Many people would like to just jump straight into the process and get down to making a website, but problems soon arise if they do not know where they want to go with their projects. To give you the best possible start before you actually get down to coding, a few chapters in this book talk about what you need to do before you physically start putting the website together. You may want to get busy right away, but knowing what you are building is important before you put your site together. This book takes that approach because you do not want to end up with a "build now, think later" philosophy that come back to bite you when you try to get your ideas into the design. Nothing beats having a good plan of action that you can use as a reference (or starting) point in your project. It will give you the added benefit that you can track your progress and reduce the chances you will forget something important. After all, what kind of architect would build a house without knowing how many rooms or floors the building requires?

Try It Yourself: Checking for Productivity

- Have you decided what kind of site you would like to build throughout this book?
- Are you aware of other websites that are competing against yours for visitors?
- Do you know and are you equipped to deal with your visitors' requirements?
- Have you spent any time considering how your want your site's pages laid out?
- What ideas do you have, and are they written down so you don't forget them?

Simplicity

Nobody likes mess, and nobody likes tasks that are overcomplicated or frustrating. Simplicity is the key to avoiding trouble when building a website. Now, I do not mean that your designs themselves should be minimalistic, far from it. When you start building, your intention should be to keep to the bare minimum the amount of effort you require to achieve the effect you want. For example, if you have two equal designs and one is half the size and requires less effort to produce, why would you want to do more work and more maintenance for the website than absolutely necessary? Later in this book, you will learn how to manage everything you build, and by doing so, you may actually avoid some of the more annoying quirks that can occur when large amounts your design and the stuff that goes into making it become hard to maintain.

Try It Yourself: Checking for Simplicity

- Do you know how to reduce errors on your site by validating your pages?
- Can you decide which languages for the Web will meet your website's needs?
- Are you able to separate the layers of your design to improve maintainability?
- Do you know which elements of a language will best explain its contents?
- Do you understand enough about your chosen languages to do a good job?

Desirability

Everyone (secretly) loves a beautiful website. It is entirely possible to go over the top trying to make your design outstandingly sleek, but even some minimalistic websites can achieve the element of beauty that will make other people jealous. Getting your website looking good is a key factor, but the look certainly should not be the only reason people visit your site.

The key to any website's success is its inner value, made up of services, content, and products you offer through it. After all, the majority of people do not visit a site with the intention of ranking it on "Hot or Not." They visit your website to learn more about what you have to offer them and read the contents of your website that enticed them there in the first place.

You may, therefore, ask why desirability is so important if it cannot attract visitors. Well, the simple answer is that a well-structured and good-looking design may help increase the enjoyment someone gets out of viewing and browsing your site, which can be essential to gaining regular visitors for the websites you build. However, you should be extremely careful to remember that you cannot please everybody. You should try as hard as you can to make your website the kind of place where people will feel at home, but there will always be a small group of people who just cannot be satisfied. Sometimes, you just have to let go of the criticism you get to avoid being sucked in by obscure requests and feature ideas that might drive away other visitors. After all, some individuals (and potential visitors) unfortunately enjoy being rude to website owners.

Try It Yourself: Checking for Desirability

- Does your website look pretty to you, your friends, and people who visit?
- Have you received any complements about how good your design looks?
- Are you always making minor tweaks to ensure things stay looking fresh?
- Do you feel there are areas where your design could improve over time?
- Have you given any thought to how your site looks to people who are color blind?

Functionality

Most websites fall into one of two categories: **static** sites contain no flashy interactive behavior, and **dynamic** sites let visitors do more than just click and be sent to a page by offering special effects, customized content, and much more. Static websites serve their purpose as a baseline for what visitors should expect when taking their first trips to your website (and we will start off building a static website). However, you should not underestimate the value of extending the functionality of your website when you are given the opportunity, such as in the discussion of scripting basics later in this book.

Functionality can come in many forms and be implemented through many technologies (as you will find out later on in this book), but remember that functionality must fit the purpose of the website. Any additions to the interface that will interfere with the user experience or draw attention away from the purpose of your site should be left out of the final design. The key to being functional is to be consistent, so you should use your best judgment to decide what should be put in or left out, which means you will spend a fair amount of time making decisions.

Try It Yourself: Checking for Functionality

- Does your website actually need interactive elements like a member system?
- What kind of interactivity do you think would be really useful to your visitors?
- Have you thought about what might happen if functionality is unavailable?
- Are you willing to use existing software to simplify adding site functionality?

- What methods does your website provide to let visitors get in touch with you?

Compatibility

Don't you just hate it when things start breaking without notice? I certainly do! When building your website, you will find that many factors can influence how your design comes out. Unfortunately, no easy fix can resolve the problems that different browsers, users, and needs will bring you in the long run, but you can learn to cope with problems by minimizing the chances of anything going wrong in the first place. That way, when something does go wrong, you can clean up the mess with as little hassle as possible. Cleaning up messes is the one step that most people would love to be able to do without, but the advantage of ensuring compatibility does mean you will find yourself able to better appreciate your finished website. More importantly, you will be able to deal with potential problems that may occur in the future with minimum effort.

Try It Yourself: Checking for Compatibility

- What happens when someone encounters an error on one of your pages?
- Does your website work on browsers like Firefox, Chrome, Safari, and Opera?
- Are you aware of the browser wars and how they affect building websites?
- Are all of your website's pages written correctly, and do they remain free of errors?

Do you know how to check, fix, and resolve any problems with your website?

Flexibility

This step in the process does have a lot in common with the previous one (compatibility), but some genuine differences should be taken into consideration. To define flexibility, the important thing is to simply ask yourself the question, "Do I feel lucky?" It may be cliché, but the question is a valid one. Flexibility in every sense of the word defines the website's ability to degrade with grace. Degrading gracefully means that if a certain technology is not available, rather than all of your hard work falling apart in front of your users' eyes or simply locking out those users, the site simply stubs its toe, grumbles a little, and carries on. Think of the process as giving your website and visitors a bit of dignity: the site may not display all the frills and excitement of the full thing and may take a less-picturesque route, but the important thing is that it continues to work!

Try It Yourself: Checking for Flexibility

- Have you ensured that plug-in reliant elements, like Flash animations, have alternatives?
- If style, scripting, or images are disabled, will your website still work properly?
- Does your website take into account people who use older browser versions?
- What happens to your website if someone looks at your site on a cell phone?

Can anyone using your website find any problems with the way it works?

Accessibility

The perfect website is hard to achieve, but the perfect visitor is impossible to find partly because everyone is different (in every respect of the word). Users have different requirements, needs, expectations, and abilities. All of this adds up to a complex situation that many people feel uncomfortable trying to address. The process of making your site accessible deals explicitly with taking care of your visitors who may have some impairment that could hinder their ability to browse your website. As you will find out later in this book, it's shocking just how many people are affected by these issues. When creating a website, there are so many things to take into account that it can make your head spin, but with a little practice and some understanding of what is relevant, you can make your site easy to use for almost anybody.

Try It Yourself: Checking for Accessibility

- Are you aware of the various types of disabilities that affect users of your website?
- What steps have you taken so disabled people can browse your site?
- Do you know anyone with a disability who may be able to test your site?
- Is there a method where people can get in touch with any issues they find?
- Have you checked the site does not use frames or other damaging features?

Usability

When you visit websites, do you sometimes wonder why their creators made them so difficult to use? This concern has existed for many years and plagues the World Wide Web to this very day. Usability is an incredibly important step to take in your learning experience. Every individual expects something different from an experience, but you need to consider what will be most convenient to the largest majority of your visitors. Understanding how people make decisions and learning about conventions will allow you to be empathetic toward the people who you are trying to attract to your website and hopefully provide a website that has common and recognizable functions so people can navigate effectively.

The key to effective usability is to make everything appear where people expect it to appear and always use the terminology that people expect. For example, you would not call a contacts page a "communication resource center"—well, you wouldn't if you wanted people to actually contact you. People need to be able to use as little brainpower as possible, because split-second decisions determine whether someone will stay on or leave your site.

Try It Yourself: Checking for Usability

- Is your website easy to navigate? Can users quickly find relevant content or features?
- Have you ensured the design does not interfere with usability?
- Do you provide your visitors with multiple ways of navigating your website?
- Exactly how (upon reflection) do you think the website could be easier to use?
- Have you conducted a usability study to see if there are any navigation issues?

Expandability

Finishing the design and coding will not be the end of the process. Your website will be an ongoing process of adding new content, making new sections, and trying to get as many new visitors as possible. The success of a website is defined literally by the amount of people who enjoy visiting your website on a consistent basis, and therefore you are always in a battle against your fellow competitors to get more people looking at what you offer and making them want to visit your website instead. Expansion, therefore, comes in two forms: The first is to improve both the design and content of your website on a regular basis fixing any bugs and adding new functionality all of the time. The second form covers the art of marketing and search engine optimization, which deals with not only expanding your sites focus but also the amount of visitors you get, especially when a website with no visitors is pretty much considered nonexistent!

Try It Yourself: Checking for Expandability

- Are you aware of social networking and ways you can market your website?
- Does your website appear in search engines with a moderately high position?
- What plans do you have for the future to improve the website you have made?
- Have you received any feedback about users' wishes for future versions of the site?
- Are there any other ways you could market your website to get more visitors?

ExplainED

Remember that these questions are only intended to get you thinking about completed websites. You are making your very first website, so these questions will be really useful to consider after the site is complete, especially if you intend on revisiting any parts of the book to see if you missed anything useful.

Summary

This ends my quick overview of the elements that go into making an ideal website. You will learn the specifics of these steps throughout this book, but the overview you have just read can act as a measuring stick for the principles you should keep trying to apply as best as you can when you begin coding. By answering these checklist questions as you go through the process of building your website, you should be able to rate your website to see how effective and how close to possible perfection it really is! Therefore, you may want to return to this section at the end of your website creation process to see if there are any areas you could improve on in the future, as these questions should certainly help you see if you put everything into practice effectively.

Are you ready to start building your very first website? If the answer is yes, let's get started!

What Kind of Website Should I Make?

Before you can sit down and start publishing your website, you need to have an idea in your mind of what you want to achieve. Many different types of sites exist out there, and each has its own reason for being. Some sites are personal and have the sole aim of providing solutions to common problems or sharing experiences with the world. Other sites are business oriented, with an emphasis on making money by providing goods and services. Before learning the code that will physically bring your design together, you need to flex your creative muscles and come up with the ideas, layout, and functionality that you want to include in the final product. Even if you are not the most creative person, you can define your project's aims and goals quite easily with the aid of various development models and inspirational resources (don't worry, it's not as complicated as it sounds).

In this chapter, you will learn about the following topics:

- How to mold your initial idea into something potentially useful
- Where to find and draw inspiration for your design and site features
- The basics of *information architecture* and producing a design

Who Are You?

The first step in understanding what kind of site you want to produce is to gain an insight into the reasoning and motivation behind your choices. When you undertake any project that involves creativity, each decision you make will impact a series of factors that you need to consider. This section of the book is not philosophy 101, and it certainly does not deal with the big questions of the universe, but it does focus on the way you see yourself and others to help you determine why you should choose a particular method over another.

Understanding this can help you create something that appeals to the needs and views of other people around you.

Your Inner Processes

While you might come into the creative process believing you have an open mind, there are already a series of variables at work in your brain that will affect your ability to make decisions. Sometimes, these variables are as simple as having preconceived ideas about your users. For example, many people have make incorrect assumptions about the needs of disabled users; in other cases, people might believe that integrating a particular service will benefit the end user, when in fact it will have the opposite effect and drive them away. It can help you to keep an open mind if you remember that everyone sees things differently.

Who Are You?

Self-analysis is something that many people creating a site overlook. By questioning your motives, you can integrate yourself more tightly into the decision-making process. Sometimes you make choices based on nothing more than personal preferences. While this might work if the site is for your viewing alone, you should put that reasoning to the test, as other people will judge for themselves if they like what you have created. The purpose of this task is to allow you to decide if the idea you have for a site is worth pursuing. Building a site is a great opportunity to be creative, make something you can show off, and potentially have something you can enjoy for years to come; however, a poorly conceived idea could hurt you in the long run, especially if your site is hard to navigate or if you include a lot of time-sensitive information but then never update your site. You certainly should not be defeatist about this prospect, but understanding what is unique about your idea will help you conceptualize your ideas better. It will also give you something specific to write about when you begin writing content. Doing this will enable you to engage all of the people who will visit your site better!

Try It Yourself: Self Analysis

If you already have a few ideas you want to put to the test, ask yourself the following questions. Even though it might start getting tiring the more often you do it, critiquing yourself can help you avoid wasting time on something that ultimately will be of no benefit, counterproductive, or just downright silly! So stop what you are doing, take out a pen and a piece of paper, focus on your site idea, and think deeply over the questions that follow:

- Why do I think this site is a good idea?
- What reason do I have to support this?
- Do other people agree with me?

You want to end this activity by considering the justification for your idea and whether it is likely to be successful. When you encounter activities like this one in this book, you should pause your reading and try out the exercise whenever possible. The knowledge that you gain from undertaking activities will assist you in your website building process. So let's take a quick look at the preceding questions and see how you might answer them. The examples that follow relate to your site, so keep this in mind because this is not a philosophy lesson, and you don't want to overthink the questions. I hope the following examples will show you the kinds of answers you could give and will help you decide for yourself where to take your idea next (see Figure 1-1). We'll now use the example of a site for stamp collectors, so you can see what kind of things might be important. Note that we'll build on this example throughout the chapter, so you can see how everything comes together.

ExplainED

Remember to think about all the pros and cons of making a site for your idea; you want to go into this book knowing that your site will be able to offer everything you want and to become a great success (with lots of people visiting)!

Q: Why do I think this is a good idea?

- **A:** Using this site, I could potentially expand my own collection of stamps!
- **A:** My stamp collection might interest people whom I have never even met before.
- **A:** I have always wanted to build a site but never got the chance before.

Q: What reason do I have to support this?

- **A:** There are lots of stamp collectors out there, so public interest should be high.
- **A:** There have been requests for the service I am going to offer on this site.
- **A:** Another site that buys and sells rare stamps made a fortune!

Q: Do other people agree with me?

- **A:** Well other people interested in stamps have given their support for the site.
- **A:** Having a dedicated site could get more people involved in this hobby.
- **A:** My friend has a blog on this subject and gets plenty of visitors every month.

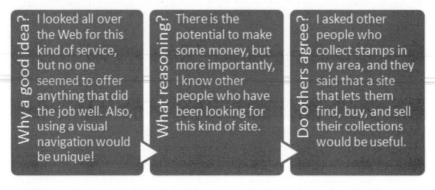

Figure 1-1. You should ask yourself these three questions when deciding on a site idea.

If my answers or any of the answers you came up with yourself make you think "this site has real potential to be something great," then you're ready to carry on. If not, you might want to reconsider the idea. If you just want to make a personal site for yourself and your family, which is a perfectly valid reason to create a site and doesn't require a large number of visitors, then you can continue, regardless. Next, you'll learn about this subject in-depth, using what you have written down to good effect. So pay attention and keep these notes handy!

ExplainED

Interestingly, we often ignore positive analysis when we critique our own work, yet show tremendous enthusiasm when it comes to piling on criticisms of our efforts and skills!

How Do You Think?

Every decision you make in the process of creating your site will derive from various questions you have asked yourself. You can break these down into short summaries, and these simple questions-and-answers can help you make decisions when you find yourself unable to choose whether one of your ideas is a good one. By taking into account the following and weighing the pros and cons for each, you can follow through each thing you set out to do, without having to fear that a choice or decision you have made was unjustified or unexplainable in the future. So put aside the book again for a short period of time and answer the following, more in-depth set of questions. Be sure to write down your answers on your ideas pad, which I assume you've been updating as you read this book and walk through the exercises laid out. After you answer these questions, you should have decided what you want to do with your site, which is useful as you start cultivating ideas for your site's functionality.

Try It Yourself: Thinking Theory

You should ask yourself several questions when considering potential ideas for your site:

- **Who?** Ask yourself who will benefit (other than you) from your idea.
- **What?** Consider what made you decide that this would be a good idea.
- **Where?** Determine whether—and where—your idea has been successfully implemented.
- **When?** Determine how long you think it will take the implementation of your idea to show results.
- **Why?** Ask yourself why you should use this method over any other in existence.
- **How?** Contemplate how you should implement your idea.
- **Huh?** Try to determine whether your idea makes sense; if not, you should reconsider its implementation.

This exercise will not only help you make decisions about which ideas you should implement on your site from the outset, but it will also aid you in making design decisions and coming up with ideas on how you can improve the site when you make updates. It's also important that you base each decision you make on your visitors' needs as opposed to your own needs (especially if the site you want to create a business-oriented site). Even if your sole goal is to create a family site, you still need to consider the other people who will visit the site. The Internet is a public place; once you put your site out there, it'll be available for anybody to see, so you want to make the best impression possible. Let's put this into practice by taking into account the first bit you looked at under self analysis. I hope you kept those written notes handy because now you need to decide what to do with your idea and finalize your plans for creating your exciting new site! Grab your piece of paper or document, and let's continue the same idea of showcasing someone's stamp collection (see Figure 1-2).

Idea?	• To showcase my stamp collection!
Who?	• Avid stamp collectors and experts
What?	• To share my collection with the world
Where?	• Other stamp sites that buy and sell stamps
When?	• Once word gets out about my cool website!
Why?	• To let visitors search by image rather than by name
How?	• A gallery of stamps you can click for details
Huh?	• A unique idea, so let's go with it!

Figure 1-2. Answering some basic questions can help you finalize your plans.

What Type of Site?

You know what subject matter you want to cover on your site; now you need to decide what type of site you want to create. For example, do you want to create a commercial site for selling products, a blog for discussing your point of view with the world, or maybe a gallery site that shows off your photographs? You have a lot of different options; I'll walk you through these options to help you decide. While this is a big decision to make, remembering what you have learned in the previous section of this chapter should help you come to the best conclusion. You want to choose a type of site that will best meet the needs of your visitors based on your idea. For instance, if you want to have a place where you can sell scarves you have knitted; you might go for a commercial site. I'll cover 15 examples of site types that showcase different areas of the Web you might wish to target. If all you have at this stage is the idea "I just want to make a website," then now would be a perfect time to decide on a direction. You'll have the chance to revisit the choice you make later on in the book when it's time to add the functionality that people expect to find. Not only that, but you will learn about some of the most popular packages out there you can use for things like blogging and adding other unique features to your site without having to become an expert in scripting. Remember that this book is intended to help get you started, rather than force you to lumber through a complex bunch of reference manuals (although some technical detail is given for your benefit! I hope the transition between stages will prove useful to you.

LinkED

For more details about the kinds of people who create sites as part of their profession, the A List Apart survey 2008 results are both in-depth and interesting from a statistical point of view. You can see them at http://aneventapart.com/alasurvey2008/.

Blog

A blog is a website that has the sole aim of allowing an individual or group to express particular points of view or opinions. These kinds of sites often include articles or features tailored to a user's interest in a particular subject. These articles or opinions might tackle real-world questions or try and bring up new fresh perspectives on a given subject (see Figure 1-3). While personal blogs that are based around an individual's life usually don't gain much widespread attention, blogs that are based around professional skills such as tips or sharing specialized information will often gain a large user base, sometimes matching the number of readers that might subscribe to a real-world magazine (imagine having millions of people reading your opinion on a subject!).

Commercial

Sites that have the sole intention of selling goods or services are described as commercial sites. These sites are usually aimed around a core selection of services and contain features such as technical support information, product descriptions and screenshots, and the ability to purchase the goods online. While some commercial sites focus their offerings on products they have made themselves, some large chains offer a wide variety of goods and services from various manufacturers or providers (see Figure 1-4). Most commercial sites simulate the feel of being in a real store by having a shopping basket that allows you to store goods you either intend to purchase or want to come back and look at later. These sites usually let you add items to your basket to see how much everything will cost and calculate any taxes you would have to pay—all before you click the *Buy* button!

Figure 1-3. Jonathan Snook's blog focuses entirely upon web development and his own projects.

Figure 1-4. Amazon sells a wide variety of goods, including books, entertainment, electronics and computers.

Community

Sites that are primarily focused around a group of active users who are interested in contributing to the overall success of a site are known as a community-powered network. These projects usually consist of interactive functionality that lets people share or express themselves and their knowledge over a wide scale. Such sites include social-networking sites or sites that provide powerful user-generated services, such as wikis, forums, chat rooms, and other interactive functionality, which I'll cover greater detail in Chapter 8 (see Figure 1-5).

Figure 1-5. Wikipedia is an encyclopedia project that allows anyone to contribute freely.

Content

Content-driven sites focus purely on providing articles or snippets of information that answer a particular question or will interest people who wish to learn about a particular area of expertise (see Figure 1-6). These sites usually come in the form of online magazines (known as e-zines) or question-answering services. Note that these services are more professionally organized and orientated than blogs, which are usually more focused on portraying pieces of news or information than full-blown articles on a particular subject.

Corporate

Corporate sites have much in common with commercial sites in that they are focused around a particular project or service; however, unlike commercial sites, they tend to act more like an information booth by providing useful information about a business or individual, as opposed to trying to sell you goods or services (see Figure 1-7). Dedicated sites usually offer such functionality as contact information and details about the type of work undertaken by the individual or group, and they are focused on bringing developments about that brand to public knowledge. These types of sites sometimes contain services for existing customers or those who are already involved at some level with the individual or business.

Figure 1-6. A List Apart is a web-design magazine that publishes professional articles.

Corporate

Corporate sites have much in common with commercial sites in that they are focused around a particular project or service; however, unlike commercial sites, they tend to act more like an information booth by providing useful information about a business or individual, as opposed to trying to sell you goods or services (see Figure 1-7). Dedicated sites usually offer such functionality as contact information and details about the type of work undertaken by the individual or group, and they are focused on bringing developments about that brand to public knowledge. These types of sites sometimes contain services for existing customers or those who are already involved at some level with the individual or business.

Intranet

Intranets are a more unusual type of site because they aren't usually available to the public through the Web. The purpose of an intranet is to hold a special localized site that is intended to serve only computers that have access to that network, such as those you would find in a library or school. Many educational institutions, corporate businesses, government offices, and large consumer networks have their own dedicated intranets for the purpose of providing information that is only relevant to (or for the consumption of) the people who use the computers or services provided by that organization.

Figure 1-7. Microsoft's homepage provides detailed information about its goods and services.

NotED

While intranets are generally aimed at employees of a particular service, extranets exist in a similar capacity for the use of those who aren't localized to the machines that connect to the service. Users of extranets might include customers, suppliers, or important individuals who need external access to the secure network.

Microsites

Microsites might sound funny, but they have a serious purpose: to provide a small but relevant amount of information on a dedicated topic. This kind of site (or subsection of an existing site) could provide information about a particular product or service (such as how the BBC offers small sections of its main site to individual television shows as if they were their own, dedicated sites). Generally speaking, these sites are less common than other types of more fully fledged sites (as you often see on the Web), although many providers of services and products maintain individual microsites to showcase individual services or products.

One popular function for microsites is to display online business cards. For example, these sites can give "brick-and-mortar stores" that currently do not have a method to sell their goods and services on the Internet a way to provide basic location and contact information. You can even find domain extensions dedicated to creating microsites of this type. The .tel extension lets companies provide basic contact information about themselves without needing to have a comprehensive site that offers more than general information (see Figure 1-8). As a result, microsites remain popular for dedicating a segment of a site to a particular subject.

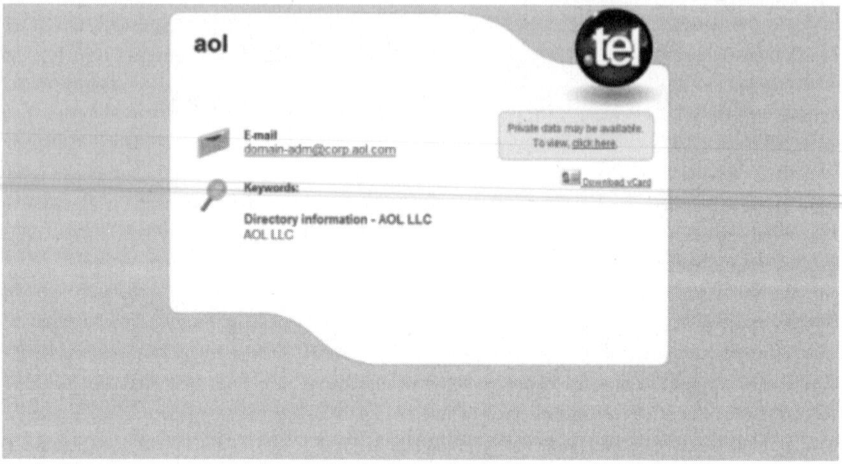

Figure 1-8. The media and Internet giant AOL maintains a .tel domain to give its basic contact details.

Mirror

The point of a mirror site is to act like the reflection of an existing site (see Figure 1-9). These sites usually function as an alternative site that can be accessed in the event that the original source of information is unavailable; however, sometimes these mirrors act as digital archives for referencing and maintaining old sites that might have some use to someone on the Internet. Mirrors are most commonly found in reference to software, where they act as an alternative location for downloading files. For example, large-scale projects can have huge file sizes, which can severely tax a site's resources. Also, search engines such as Google keep a "cached" (alternative) copy of your site on their servers, so that if your site is unavailable for any reason, people can still check out the results of a search (stripped of style and any behavior or functionality the site originally had). It's important to be aware of these mirrors if you're worried about who keeps tabs on each new version of the pages you place online. If information appears on the Internet; it will probably remain somewhere forever!

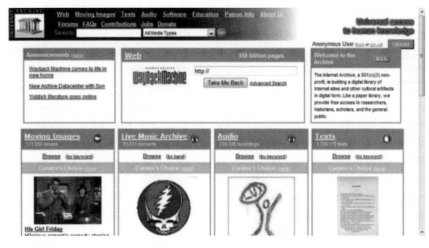

Figure 1-9. The Internet Archive project allows you to view stored archives of sites.

News

One of the most common types of sites on the Internet today is that of a news site. Since the creation of the Web, the public media has flowed onto the Internet with ease, as people from around the globe share what they have heard or seen going on around them (see Figure 1-10). In recent years, the number of sites offering alternative perspectives on current events has surged dramatically, and many newspapers and other methods of communicating local events (that charge money to gain access to services) are disappearing as a result. The Web offers the ability to acquire live updates at no cost to the consumer, and this is slowly killing the old forms of print media that cannot compete with free.

Sites like Twitter offer a method for ordinary members of the public to talk about news events live, and such sites are quickly growing as the most cutting-edge way to receive news even before it reaches more traditional news outlets, such as television and radio stations. Many news sites do more than post blogs; they also provide everything from collaboration between normal people who simply catch a video of something important on their cell phone right and want to share it, to consumer journalism where people can submit their own stories to members of the press or news-hosting sites such as the Web aggregator, Digg. You can trace much of the rise in news-based sites to the rise in social-networking sites, which I'll cover in Chapter 10.

Figure 1-10. With news, entertainment, television and radio listings, the BBC offers a wide range of services.

Niche

Sites that are described as "niche" have highly focused content for a particular audience (see Figure 1-11). While many niche sites find themselves struggling to gain widespread appeal due to their highly specific natures, they can be a valuable source of information relating to a specific individual, subject, or item. Examples of niche sites include fan sites for celebrities or people in the media, fans of a movie or recording artist, and even sites targeting a particular religion, gender, single individuals, or a political audience for a certain party.

Personal

One of the most common types of sites (apart from a commercial site) is a personal site. Generally, these places are focused towards the individual who is creating them and usually the people that they know (see Figure 1-12). Such sites often contain pictures and details about a particular person, as well as his interests. They can resemble a blog, but on a much more personal level. Often these kinds of sites are built so that friends and family can keep up-to-date with the goings-on of a particular person; however, these sorts of sites have started to disappear in recent years in favor of using existing social-networking sites. Many well-known individuals, including pop stars, have their own dedicated "personal spaces" on the Web, but there is no reason why you can't have your own personal site if you're an interesting individual!

Figure 1-11. The hello world collection allows you to see the words "Hello World" in various programming languages.

Figure 1-12. Professor Stephen Hawking has his own personal site!

Portal

Many sites link to other sites (see Figure 1-13). Because there are no limits to how many sites any individual or group can launch, some people choose to create what is known as a portal. The purpose of a portal is to offer a single site that links to other places that are owned or managed by an individual or group. These sites offer a simple yet effective method of keeping track of the different properties or locations on the Web that are associated or networked together by some means. You often find portals on large sites where individual products or services are broken out discretely to reduce confusion and increase the site's ease-of-use.

Figure 1-13. The homepage of the W3C brings all of the various working groups they run together.

Portfolio

Many freelancers, businesses, and individuals who want to show the array of skills they have choose to produce an online portfolio that serves as the online equivalent of a resume or *curriculum vitae* (CV). These sites usually consist of information about a person, including any experience she has. For example, such sites offer details about where the person has worked previously, alongside examples of her work. The site also includes methods for contacting an individual if some person or organization wishes to employ her services. These sites typically function like commercial sites, except they sell the skills of an individual or business, rather than goods and services (see Figure 1-14). For example, a student might want to put all of his experience online for teachers and other students to see, or a professional might want to get people interested in working with her by offering a snippet of the work she have done in the past, so that organizations and individuals can decide if she is the right kind of person to work with.

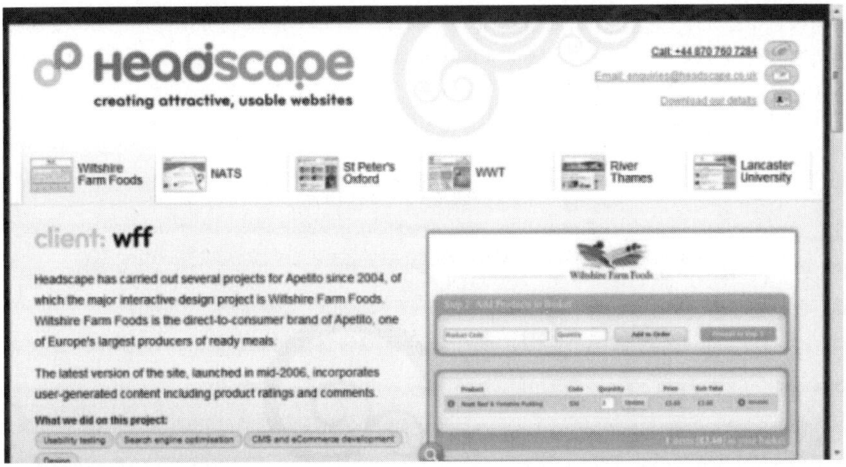

Figure 1-14. Headscape is a web-design business with an attractive portfolio that shows off the various services offered.

Review

The review site is another common form of site (see Figure 1-15). Often these sites review a specific area of interest, such as movies, goods or services, or even books and music. While these sites tend to be community driven and rely on people who have used the said product or have experienced the business being reviewed, it should be noted that some review sites focus on in-house (self tested) reviews, as opposed to relying on the viewpoints of others. These sites enable people who want to know whether they should purchase or subscribe to something to get advice from real-world consumers of the goods or services.

Targeted

Finally, targeted sites are aimed at a particular type of audience user, such as mobile-phone visitors (see Figure 1-16). Some targeted sites, such as the dot mobi domain-name project (which allows you to produce a special site for mobile devices), have arguably little value attached to them going forward because more powerful mobile phones such as the iPhone are increasing in popularity and give users the ability to see a "normal" site rather than one of reduced functionality. However, the cost of browsing over newer phones mean viewing normal sites exclusively isn't the ideal solution yet! Such devices no longer need a dedicated site to deal with the previously poor support for the Web on cell phones (which actually forced you to make another version of the site), This is a good thing because the visuals and functionality of those old-style sites were less-than-pleasing to the eye!

Figure 1-15. The Internet Movie Database offers detailed reviews about movies and television shows.

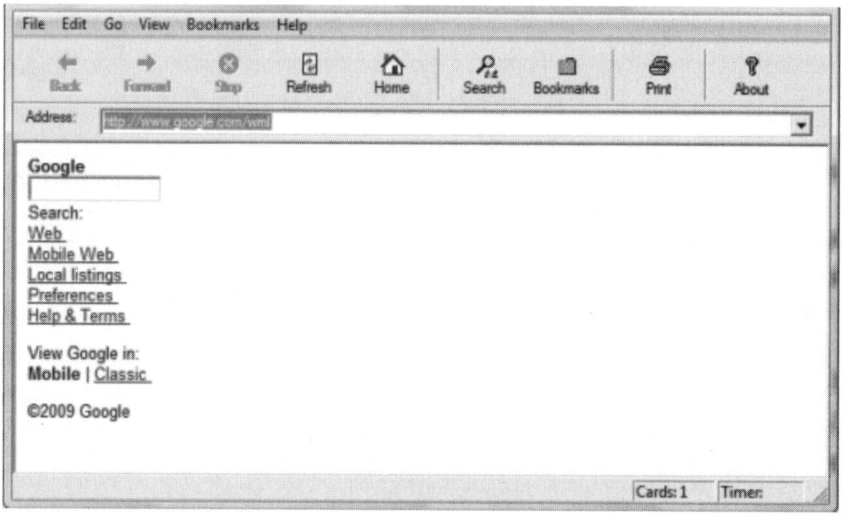

Figure 1-16. Google's dedicated site for mobile browsers allows small handsets to gain access to the powerful search engine.

LinkED

You can find a more extensive list of the various types of sites that can be produced at http://en.wikipedia.org/wiki/Website#Types_of_websites.

Try It Yourself: Website Type

Now that you know what kind of websites exist, you need to take the idea you have decided upon and choose what kind of site you want to use for that idea. The following bullet points (and the example that follows) should help you decide which site type(s) you should choose. Begin by determining the people you want to target, whether you want to earn income from the site, and what will drive the content creation of your site. Be sure to put the book to one side while you make these decisions. After you do this exercise, you will be ready to form an identity for your site based on the answers you gave.

First, you need to determine whom you want to target with your site:

- **Personal**: Niche and Personal
- **Business**: Commercial, Corporate, Intranet, and Portfolio
- **Both**: Blog, Community, Content, Micro, Mirror, News, Portal, Review, and Targeted

Second, you want to determine whether you want to make income as a result of the site:

- **Yes**: Commercial and Portfolio
- **No**: Corporate, Intranet, Mirror, and Personal
- **Maybe**: Blog, Community, Content, Micro, News, Niche, Portal, Review, and Targeted

Finally, you need to decide whether you want the site to be content, user, or service driven:

- **Content driven**: Blog, Content, News, Portal, and Review
- **User driven**: Community, Intranet, Niche, Personal, and Targeted
- **Service driven**: Commercial, Corporate, Micro, Mirror, and Portfolio

You don't need to finalize your choices right now because you can expand your site's scope as you develop your ideas, but it's worth noting that some sites fit multiple categories. Looking at the various types of sites, you probably want to know how yours will fit in to the greater scheme of things, so let's take a look at an example where you put the preceding questions to use in the service of the stamp-collection site we looked at during the questioning process earlier (see Figure 1-17). The following example is only one possible way of looking at how your site will eventually turn out, but you will want to consider what is best for your needs as you review this example; after all, the goal of this book is to implement your own site. Using the example given, ask yourself this: "Which of the site types best describes what I am after?" You will have plenty of time to go over the details later; this is simply a way of working out how best to describe your site when it's time to research other sites that do similar things (so you can see how different your idea is and who your competitors will be).

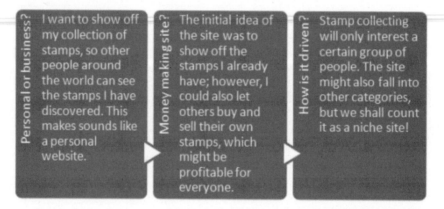

Figure 1-17. This example helps you decide logically which of the categories a stamp site falls under.

This is your first site, so you probably want to create something simple. While each of these sites can be made as simple or as complex as you like, it doesn't matter which one you choose, as long as it fits into the general ethos of what you want to end up with. For example, a stamp collection site would be a niche site (it has a highly specific target audience), even though it has the potential to be both commercial and personal (see Figure 1-18). These examples aren't the pinnacle of what you can achieve because you can adapt most sites to perform various functions. In any case, the focus of this exercise is to refine your idea further. Once you have an idea of what best describes your site, write it down so that you can use the information later on, when you need to make some more comprehensive choices for your layout.

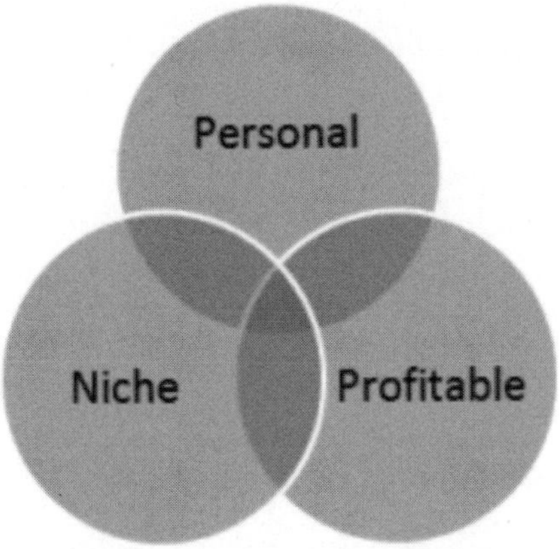

Figure 1-18. This stamp collecting site falls into multiple categories, but that isn't a problem!

ExplainED

It should be noted that the categories mentioned are a fair representation of the types of sites that exist, but exceptions do occur. You should not use this list of site types as a replacement for common sense in the decision process, especially as sites can contain multiple site types!

Form Your Identity

At this stage, you should have a general idea of the type of site you would like to produce. You should also know what timeframe you have available if you want to have your site completed by a certain date. The next stage is probably the most important step you will take: forming an identity. While this might sound simple, creating a brand name or identity you wish to use on the Web will dictate how you are referenced and known in the years to come. Just think how the world would be without having the brand names Google or Microsoft! Your identity is much like your real name; it is the label that is applied to everything you do. If your site becomes popular, it will be referenced all over the Web.

ExplainED

Remember that you as an individual will become a brand, and your name will represent what you achieve online. Therefore, you should be careful if you choose to use your own name for your identity because any failings on your site's part could directly reflect on you as a person.

Avoid Confusion

When creating an identity for yourself, you should be aware of a couple of things. First, you want to avoid confusing the customer with your chosen brand name, so make sure that your name reflects what you aim to provide. Second, avoiding confusion means that you should make your name as unique as possible. Remember that trying to fool customers into thinking you are an existing business could infringe on copyright and trademark law (depending on the name), so the best thing you can do is avoid trying to replicate another identity. Imitation might be the sincerest form of flattery, but trying to clone an existing service could get you in a lot of trouble.

ExplainED

You would not want to call a site that has pictures of different types of flowers "Chocolate central"—well not unless you have come up with a formula to produce edible flowers that taste like chocolate—in which case, congratulations!

Brand Name

The first stage in producing an identity for yourself and your site is to come up with what is commonly known as a *brand name* or *online identity* (now that you understand its importance). To create a brand name for your site, you have three routes available: you can use your own name (representing yourself online), you can use a small phrase (representing the content or the feeling you would like to emote from the process), or you can pick a name you would like to reference a business, product, or service. You should think about this carefully because this will effectively dictate how people recognize your online ventures in the future. Many people with multiple sites choose to brand each component uniquely, so that each venture acts independently, without impeding or relying on existing brand names; however, it's entirely up to you whether you choose to do this.

Tips and Tricks: Choosing a Brand Name

The following advice will help you choose a brand name for your site. Using your own name is perfectly acceptable, although your identity should remain something short and easy to pronounce and remember. Also, you could find that someone else with the same name as you (poor John Smith!) might already be using that name for his own specific brand, which could confuse your visitors—you should avoid such confusion at all costs.

- If you choose to use a phrase or word-based name, keep it easy to remember.
- Some businesses choose their brand name to be their entire web domain name. This means people never need to guess what the actual web address is, because it's the company name.
- Get ideas for your brand by looking for available domain names (you will learn more about this in Chapter 4).
- Be creative with words; look through the dictionary or an encyclopedia for ideas.
- Some people like to prefix their brand with characters such as *e* or *i* to make them sound more technological.
- Names that relate meaningfully to your content are preferable.
- Try to make your choice as unique as possible to avoid infringing on existing names.
- You can use multiple words together, as long as they make sense in context.
- Fun names or words that have feeling or power associated with them are useful.
- Never create a brand name that people that find offensive or crude.
- It's fine to use your own name, but giving it context such as "Stan Software" is better.
- You should not use hard-to-spell or nonsense names because it makes things harder on your end users.
- Use only A-Z and 0-9 characters to be consistent with domain-name conventions.

LinkED

For additional tips and ideas on how to produce a brand or business name, it is worth checking out the fantastic article available at http://entrepreneurs.about.com/cs/gettingstarted/ht/business_name.htm.

Try It Yourself: Finalizing Your Choice

Now that you know exactly how brand name selection works, let's go about making one for your site. Ideally, you want to have a name that relates to what you plan to offer, so in our example of a stamp collection site, you could perhaps call the site eStamps. This gives the impression of it being digital, with the *e* prefix signifying the site has a digital component. And of course, including the word of the thing you want to showcase on the site is always helpful, especially if you want people to remember what your brand and site. It's important to make your brand as easy to remember as possible, which almost always means making it short and easy to spell!

Brand Identity

Your brand's identity is the second aspect of your brand. The identity of a brand is how people refer to the name itself. While this is based on reputation, the products, services and content you offer will form the basis of how people perceive your site on either a personal or professional level. This means that a brand identity is something you build up over a period of time rather than acquiring it; you'll learn more about this later in the book, when we cover the post production aspects of your site, such as marketing and providing real services to your visitors in Chapter 10.

At this point, you should have a basic idea of what kind of site you would like to produce and perhaps some early ideas about what you would like to do with your site once it goes live. Next, you'll learn about where to find inspiration and how to start gathering and structuring ideas for your site. From there, the creative process will end, and the hard work of producing the site itself will begin.

Inspiration for the Masses

Inspiration can come in many shapes and sizes, whether you want your site to achieve goals or provide solutions to your potential visitors. What matters is that you take a multidirectional approach when you implement your site. By expanding your offerings, you can attract a larger audience to your site. After all, a site with a single function can be perfectly fine, but implementing your finished site in various ways will likely make it appealing to a wider audience. By doing so, you will have a much better chance of competing with sites that offer similar services. This section of the chapter aims to help you achieve just that by providing you with methods to choose what your site will need before and during the design stage.

Sources of Inspiration

Do you ever have days where you just cannot get inspired? Do you ever feel that you have hit a wall and cannot seem to come up with any unique ideas of your own? Everyone gets these mental blocks, and of course, depending on whom you ask, you will be given a different cure for the problem. Some people like to sleep, take a walk, watch a movie, meditate, listen to music, or talk to someone else. All these techniques can be helpful, but if you find yourself in a state of frustration, and you don't have the time to get inspired, you might find the upcoming information helpful because it provides some general places where you can find quick inspiration.

Natural Inspiration

We live in a world filled with naturally inspiring things that can help you come up with design concepts such as architecture, natural events, weather, and more through color, shape, and visual representation. Ask any budding photographer, and she will tell you that if you want to be inspired, there's nowhere like the great outdoors. Sometimes, people who want to be inspired will go for a walk (or drive) and visit places that might hold some meaning to them. In this case, you might visit a place that evokes emotions similar to what you want to convey on your site. You can use a place you visit as a source for colors, layout, and typography ideas.

For example, assume you want to create a site for a restaurant. You might choose to take photos of the inside of the establishment for use on the site, you might also base your site's color palette on those used in the restaurant to carry that feeling across onto the Web. Specifically, you might choose to use wooden beam images (if it is a rustic style restaurant) for the site header to show off the history of the building. This is only one example of how inspiration from the natural world can be used with ease to impact your design choices and help give you some ideas for how to approach the visual style of the design itself.

The Media

Another medium where people can experience a wide variety of inspiring visual representations is known widely as the media. Whether you watch something on TV, view a movie, listen to the radio, read a newspaper or magazine, or read blogs and online forms of media, you can find a wealth of inspiration to draw from the high-quality content available (especially if those sites have images and video footage). While this kind of inspiration is more conceptual, it can serve as a springboard to new design ideas if you look at the way things are portrayed or how things are expressed, as long as you have a good imagination.

Friends and Family

When you have no ideas for your web design, who you gonna call? Nope, not the infamous Ghostbusters! When you find yourself unable to come up with a design mock-up that matches your ideas, why not show your ideas to your friends and family, and ask them for ideas? Different perspectives on an idea can help bring across fresh inspiration. Because family and friends will usually offer their advice for free, it's always worthwhile to ask them about potential design choices, as long as you don't keep bugging them until they throw you out!

Software Design

As with web design, a lot of time and effort goes into the design and usability of software products. While some products can be downright ugly, many conventions used in software design or on the Web can also be downright beautiful and more straightforward than traditional menus. For example, consider the Microsoft Office 2007 Ribbon (see Figure 1-19). While the color scheme and the typography at work within it are fantastic, the notable use of tabs for the workspace to organize and display blocks of functionality is a great example of user-interface design for software. It should also be noted that, using the right code, the ribbon effect can be implemented on the Web, although using a ribbon-like interface for navigation is something that only you can decide based upon the other elements of your site's structure (including whether you need something that complicated).

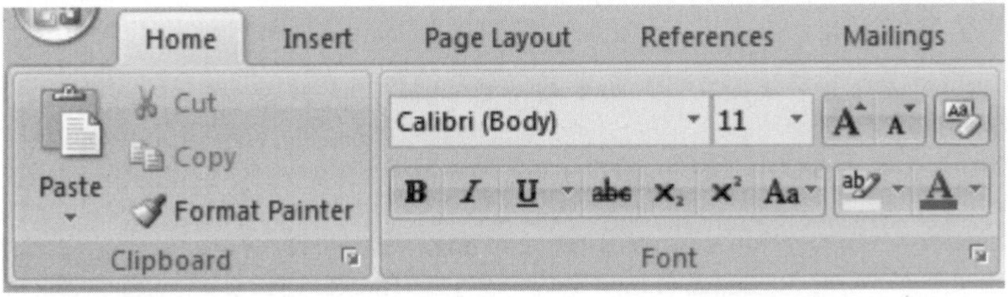

Figure 1-19. The ribbon in Microsoft Office 2007 ribbon is simple, yet beautiful.

StumbleUpon

While I don't generally show a preference or disposition towards a particular social network, I think you might find StumbleUpon's service extremely useful when performing research or trying to inspire new ideas. StumbleUpon works much like Google's *I Feel Lucky* button, which directs you to a site that has high relevance to a given topic; however, in the case of StumbleUpon, the resulting site is random, based on topics or categories you choose to subscribe to (see Figure 1-20).

Figure 1-20. The StumbleUpon toolbar sits in your browser, ready to rate sites you like and dislike.

You can use this social-networking tool to find a wide variety of information, as well as many sites worthy of mention. Because this service filters out a lot of the junk on the net, you can also be sure that the results of searching for a particular type of site will only return recommended, high-quality results. This is in contrast to many social networks that show sites that are bookmarked to other people. In StumbleUpon's case, the results you get can be inspiring, and due to the random and quirky nature of how it works, you never know what you will find next, which gives it added value, especially when you're looking at the design and layout of those sites.

LinkED

To start using StumbleUpon to see how sites around the world choose to design their sites (for your own inspirational adaptations), please visit www.stumbleupon.com/.

Design Blogs

If you want to think like a web or print designer, it makes sense to check out some of the useful blogs, sites, and resources that are provided at no cost on the Web. Many of these blogs showcase existing design or provide insight into how design can be achieved with ease with tutorials for working with graphics and other related material. However, it should be noted that, out of all the inspirational regions of the media, those exclusively aimed at people in the design community should always be your first point of reference for worthwhile examples (see Figure 1-21).

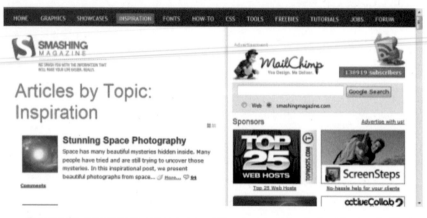

Figure 1-21. Smashing Magazine is one of the more popular design blogs and galleries on the Internet.

ExplainED

There are many design and development blogs that are worthwhile to read on a regular basis; you can learn about many of these (with some useful links attached) in the appendix at the end of the book.

Web Design Galleries

Site galleries are my personal preference when I'm looking explicitly for design ideas for how to make a site more visually appealing. These sites are basically showcases of design. Sometimes they contain cutting edge use of modern standards, lots of flourishes and special effects, and even the occasional minimalistic site; however, they all show that beautiful design is possible and achievable without making unreasonable sacrifices. While these galleries do not offer tutorials or details about how to recreate these kinds of effects they employ, the ideas and thoughts behind them should be enough to satisfy (or at least whet) your appetite when coming up with your own design ideas.

Some of the many galleries and showcases you might visit include the following:

- **9Rules Network**: http://9rules.com/
- **Best Web Gallery**: http://bestwebgallery.com/
- **Creattica**: creattica.com/
- **CSS Beauty**: www.cssbeauty.com/
- **CSS Drive**: www.cssbeauty.com/
- **CSS Elite**: www.csselite.com/
- **CSS Heaven**: www.cssheaven.com/
- **CSS Mania**: http://cssmania.com/
- **CSS Remix**: http://cssremix.com/
- **CSS Zen Garden**: www.csszengarden.com/
- **CSSline**: http://cssline.com/
- **Command +Shift + 3**: http://commandshift3.com/ (see Figure 1-22)
- **Design Shack**: http://designshack.co.uk/gallery/all/
- **Pattern Tap**: http://patterntap.com/
- **SiteInspire**: http://siteinspire.net/
- **Smashing Magazine**: www.smashingmagazine.com/category/showcase/
- **The Best Designs**: www.thebestdesigns.com/
- **The FWA**: www.thefwa.com/
- **Unmatched Style**: www.unmatchedstyle.com/
- **Web Crème**: www.webcreme.com/

Figure 1-22. Command + Shift + 3 takes a unique approach to galleries by using a "hot or not" system.

Idea Development Techniques

What you should do with any inspirational bits and pieces you find, such as ideas, screenshots of other sites, and any bits and pieces you think will be useful in the future (as mentioned previously), is store them in a product such as Microsoft OneNote, EverNote, or another note-taking application (or even a word processor). All of these "samples" you build up (such as when choosing how to decorate your house) will form your ideas pad, which will serve as a reference for your project over the entire building period. The purpose of looking around and gathering ideas is to see exactly what is possible. Keeping them in a handy place will help you achieve that. Perhaps you might also want to take some photographs of places you visit or write down conversations you have; later, you can review all of this information, which can help you out if you ever become stuck for design ideas.

NotED

If you require software for note taking or word processing (to store all of your wonderful ideas and the creative activities you are involved with), please check out the back of the book in the second section of the appendix, where I have made recommendations for various products you could try!

So far you have gathered together ideas that might serve as inspiration when developing ideas for your site; all these ideas should be in one location, where you can refer to them as needed. There are four types of idea development techniques that I believe are essential to maximizing your creativity and getting yourself organized along the way, all of which I'll cover in detail in the course of this chapter, including instructions you can follow to implement them successfully. While these techniques will aid you in expanding your project so it becomes something more structured than a simple idea, be careful not to overcompensate by trying to achieve too much with the project—you don't want something that is physically impossible to produce!

Mission Statement

A mission statement is a sort of proposal that explains what your intentions and goals are for a site. While you might only have a few ideas floating about, it makes sense to put down everything into a format that you can refer to as you develop your site. This enables you to track which goals you have managed to succeed at following, as well as to measure to what extent the ideas you have developed have been completed using progress reports. Many people developing sites choose to create a mission statement to help them stay on track and reduce distractions.

While you might feel silly writing this statement when you will probably be the only person to see it, you can come back to this document and remind yourself of your aims and goals when you have coded your site. The process of making a site can be confusing, and it's easy to get distracted with all of the "what ifs" and end up with a site that doesn't fit your needs (as mentioned in previous sections). This memory tool can help keep you on track.

See for Yourself: Example Mission Statement

Name: Silly sausage site

Slogan / motto: Organic hotdogs at an event near you!

Description: John Smith is a dedicated food fan with four years experience farming pigs and producing high-quality sausages for several restaurants in his local area. Through his site, John provides free recipes and includes a form where you can make requests to take his food to other locations.

Mission Statement: My aim is to create the largest database on sausage recipes on the Internet to promote the use of them during mealtimes. I shall allow people who share my passion to contribute to the site and be able to talk about sausages through a forum. I'll also provide a "chart" of the top sausages you can buy around the world, based on user-generated votes. This will enable more people to benefit from the knowledge that I have acquired.

LinkED

For some good examples of existing mission statements that have been produced, please visit www.missionstatements.com/.

Try It Yourself: Create Your Own Mission Statement

Assuming you've already come up with a brand name, open your chosen note-taking application (or word processor, if you prefer) and create a header with your brand name, followed by an indication that this document will apply to your site. Next, follow this information up with your slogan or motto for your site (if you happen to have thought of one). The earlier example used the name eStamps, so a perfect motto for that site might be, *"The place to be for avid stamp enthusiasts!"* Because the example site we looked at earlier was for stamp collecting, both the name and the motto make sense (of course, you want something that works for you with your own site).

Next you want to provide a description about who you are, what kind of site you want to produce (and why), and what kind of information you would like to offer on your site. Remember that all through this chapter you have been learning about what kinds of sites you can make and how important it is to come up with ideas that will make a high-quality site. Well now is the time you can go wild and start talking about them. Returning to the stamp collector's site example discussed from the outset, a good description might look something like this:

> *Description: Jane Doe is a dedicated stamp collector with a collection of more than 5,000 different postage stamps that have been collected over a period of ten years. Through her site, Jane provides scanned copies of her stamps for people to see. Her site also includes descriptions that accompany each stamp, which users can select based upon a stamp's year, color, and country of origin to make browsing the site more fun.*

Finally, you want to produce a statement that describes how you plan to turn your ideas from something you have thought about into a site (remember that at this stage this statement should be simple, straightforward, and to the point). This can include such things as writing high-quality articles and content, providing a blog to allow other people to share in your experiences, or even saying that you want to create a site that sells wrist watches. While your example (again) will be unique to you, let's take another look at the stamp example to round things off:

> *Mission Statement*: *My aim is to create the world's largest online collection of postage stamps. I would like to create a marketplace where people can buy, sell, and trade stamps. It would also be a future plan of the site to support auctioning rare stamps. With this catalog I hope to help people involved in stamp collecting find the stamps they are missing from their collections and complete them.*

Market Research

Are you looking for ideas for stuff you can include in your site? In that case, there is no better place to look than your opposition. Those of you who have problems trying to come up with ideas of your own will breathe a sigh of relief at this idea; in fact, it might become your favorite choice for deciding what should be included in your site because it requires no original or creative thought. However, you want to do more than work out what makes a particular site more successful than others when you research other sites; you also want to look at ways to improve them. If you choose only to copy a site, you will be seen as a less popular clone; however, if you create something that is superior and includes improved features, you can become more popular than the service you were inspired by.

Try It Yourself: Performing Market Research

The first stage in performing market research is to find sites that offer tools and services you want to provide, so start by coming up with some words that describe your idea. Using the example of a stamp collecting site, I have produced four key terms to go along with stamps, all of which describe the areas that describe the content the site would end up producing (see Figure 1-23). Now that you have seen what constitutes popular terms, you should put down the book and go to your favorite search engine (Google, anyone?) and enter each of the phrases you want to try.

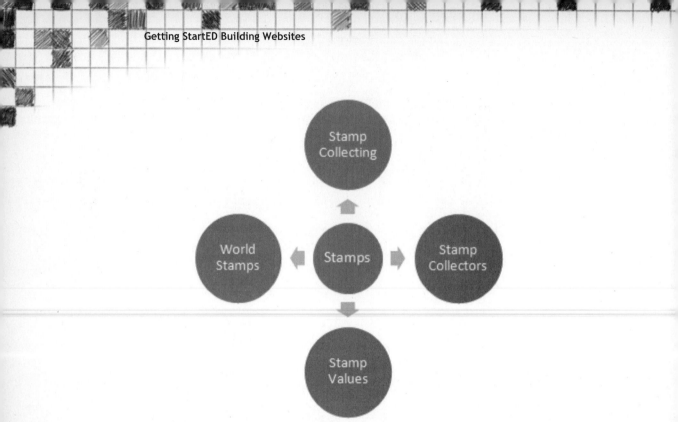

Figure 1-23. This list includes possible words that describe the stamp-collection example.

Now that you have done around five searches each using the key phrases in the diagram one at a time, you should find a whole bunch of sites in the results (I know I did, as you can see in Figure 1-24). Next you want to go to each site in turn and see whether it offers the same thing you are going to offer, or at least something similar. If you find the site is doing something identical or similar to what you plan to do, save the site to your browser favorites or bookmark list and move along (you shall return to each site you save to see what you can grab from it at a later stage). The key to this exercise is to gather information, not analyze it.

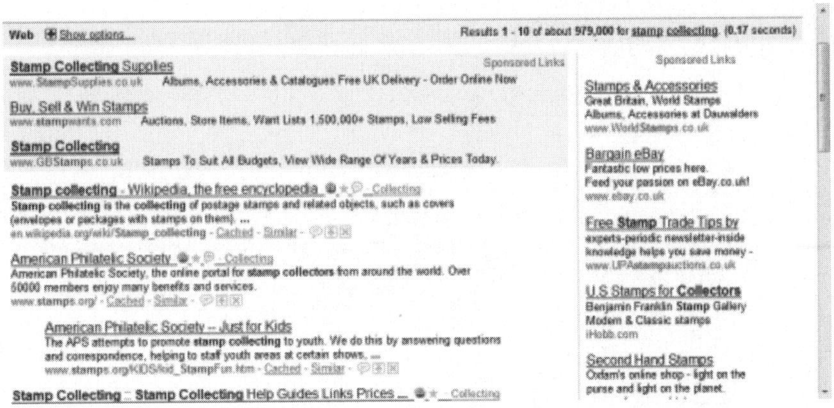

Figure 1-24. Here you see lots of results, all from searching for those related terms.

ExplainED

You will probably find that there is already a blog or site or service that covers what you want to produce, but don't let that put you off! There is no shame in remaking existing concepts into something better and more usable. After all, where would Google be if it had simply decided not to create a new search engine that would improve on existing technology?

Once you have gathered a collection of sites that fall into similar categories and could be sources of inspiration or competition, you should take a few minutes to look at each of saved sites in your favorites or bookmark list—at this point, you should have a small collection of possible related sites (see Figure 1-25). Your next step is to decide if they are really related to what you want to offer. If the sites you have looked at include some *fluff*, or low-quality sites that offer nothing to the end user, you should throw them out because you can classify them as junk. What you are looking for are quality competition and market leaders that might have the kinds of visitors you want to attract. Remember that any site you find that relates to what you are offering could also be useful for providing services that enhance your own site's experience. Potential visitors could use offerings on both sites (such as a blog about news stories), rather than having to choose between the two.

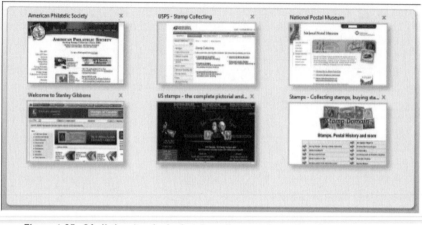

Figure 1-25. Of all the sites looked at from the search results, these six appear to be the best.

ExplainED

If you don't want to clutter up your bookmarks or favorites folder with lots of links (even though you can place them in categorized services), just open each result in a new tab in your browser, so you can hold them open, enabling you to take another look at later on.

At this point, you have completed your job and found all the best-quality sites that relate to what you want to do. You want to continue performing this process until you have enough competitors to make the search worthwhile (or until you cannot find any more quality results). The stamps example produced only six results because there wasn't anything too similar to the gallery of stamps idea. It's possible to move to the next stage, which is great because it means that the stamps site would be original. Once you have all of your high-quality sites, you can try the "word association" technique described in the following example (see Figure 1-26). Afterward, you should be ready to move onto the next stage of the process.

Try It Yourself: Word Association

This list should help you search for possible leads on your competition:

- Take a piece of paper and think of at least five words that describe your site's purpose (ten words would be even better); these words should be descriptive, not words like *and* or *the*.

- Once you have these words, try typing them into a search engine, and then take a look at the results by selecting sites that look promising (first-page results might be more accurate).

- If you run out of results, try putting the words in a different order or remove some and add others. Remember that even if you have ten words, typing four into a search engine will yield results.

- Briefly check the quality of the site links to see how they relate to your own ideas and whether they might be useful or offer something you might like to include when you start coding your site.

- Remove all of the low-quality sites you find that either don't relate to your site or have nothing to offer in terms of ideas (such as a generic site with no unique functionality).

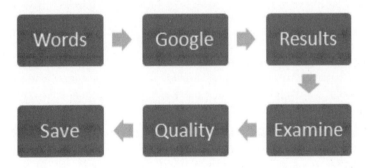

Figure 1-26. Here you can see a simplified version of the word-association process.

This job is a lot like being a detective, as you are on the hunt for information that might be useful for your site. You might find ideas for additions to your site, or you might simply find more reasons why your site idea is unique and would benefit people who visit other sites on the Internet. Market research is not about trying to steal the work or ideas of other people, but to see what is already out there, so you can determine what kind of standard you should be working towards to help ensure your site is a success. To get the best results, you want to have as many high-quality examples as possible (a minimum of five sites) that relate to what you would like to have upon completion; however, it would be preferable to have 10 or 15 to work with—the more choices you have, the better. So give this technique a try with your site ideas and see what you come up with! Once you have a list of potentially useful sites, you can take a quick breather because we have finished the first part of the research. Once you feel ready to move on from doing your searches, you can attempt to categorize the results you found and determine what purpose they might serve in your project.

Tips and Tricks—Websites to Research

You should consider researching three types of sites (see Figure 1-27):

1. **Rivals**: These are sites involved in the same (or a similar) area as your own site that you can use for future service ideas, ways to expand or improve your site, and as a source of potential visitors and customers when your design goes live.

2. **Relations**: A site that has foundations to improve upon that might be seen as a service you could form a relationship with (and possibly work together or share your customer base with). Sites that fit this description include social-networking sites that hold your favorite bookmarks or services that extend a rudimentary service that exists on the Web.

3. **Sources**: These sites contain useful information, products, or services you could use to enhance your site. These sites can include news sources, article providers, resellers of goods, or even niche sites that aggregate information on a particular subject to make things easier to find.

Once you have performed the required searches, you need to take the information you have gathered and put it under a microscope to determine what can be learned from it (see Figure 1-28). You want to see how other people have adopted using services similar to the ones you want to provide. Even if you're making a personal site or a blog, this step is essential if you want to gain users and make sure your site will not fall short of its goals when you eventually get it listed on search engines. Even personal sites compete for attention on the Web because there is so much "noise" with every individual trying to pull potential visitors (whether a few or a lot) in her direction.

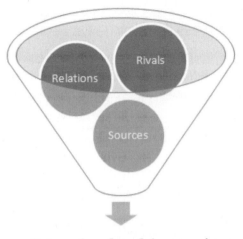

Categories of useful research

Figure 1-27. These three components can help you decide whether a site you've found is useful.

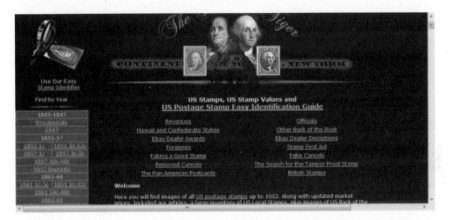

Figure 1-28. This site closely matches our stamp idea with a complete identification guide.

Try It Yourself: Analyzing Your Research

There are many different ways to go about this, but I feel that the easiest way to make sense of the information you collect is to look at each site individually and ask a series of questions that you can use to draw some important conclusions from. I provide a template that lists the kinds of things you should be asking, but you should feel free to add any additional questions you think might be useful. The purpose of this exercise is not to detract from your mission statement, but to expand your ideas of what is possible. It will also help you determine what is common to similar sites (that you should include), as well as suggest a few ideas that you might never have thought of otherwise!

You should ask yourself the following questions when visiting these sites:

- **What does this site offer?** Look for functionality, content and features.

- **What makes this site successful?** Describe the unique, fun, and quirky attractions it offers.

- **How easy is this site to use?** Browse around and rank it based on your other browsing experiences.

- **What do the site's customers think?** Read forums, check feedback, and look for reviews!

- **Is the site a friend or foe?** Your site might share, give, or take visitors from the site or the services it offers.

- **Do I have any unique ideas left?** Ask yourself whether other sites already employ your ideas.

- **How is the site laid out?** Take notice of any interesting design choices you like.

- **What is missing from the experience?** Both you and your customers might have ideas that could improve the user experience.

- **How are the site's services offered?** Determine whether the site's pricing, registration, and other details can help you plan your site.

- **What does the site interact with its users?** Look for social networks, blogs, and contact details.

Next, you want to take all of the preceding questions and apply them to all the sites you found that you thought were high quality and related to your site. In the stamp example, you will remember there were six sites worthy of further analysis in Figure 1-25. To continue the example, I looked at each site from top to bottom and answered each of the preceding questions until I was satisfied they were answered properly (see Figure 1-29). I quickly found some great features on each site that I had not previously thought about adding to the stamp site! You should do the same as this for each site on your list. At this point, you want to put the book down again and nose around the sites you found; with any luck, you'll find some useful ideas there!

Website address	•www.theswedishtiger.com
Offerings	•Visual reference (by date and image)
Success	•High placement in Google
Ease of use	•Simple picture navigation
Customers	•Unknown (no feedback forms)
Friend or foe	•Foe, offerings very similar service
Unique ideas	•My idea is much simpler to use
Layout	•Too many navigation links on pages
Missing	•Fairly bland; needs spicing up!
Service offers	•Static, generic web pages
Interactivity	•None (we can do better than that!)

Figure 1-29. Answering these questions illustrates ways to improve stamp finding significantly!

If your research came up with many answers, fantastic! However, if you found your market research rather light on information, don't worry because the next stages will expand upon what you have, giving you something you can use to generate a site structure. If you're looking for a specific way in to lay out the information you have collected, you might organize the information into the previously mentioned ideas pad. This pad helps you ensure that you don't forget anything, and it might consist of pieces of paper or note taking or word processing software (which is easier to organize).

Tips and Tricks: What to Include in the Ideas Pad

The previously mentioned ideas pad might include several different kinds of information that will come in handy when you structure your site's functionality, including:

- Bullet point answers to what the questions posed in this chapter (plus others you might have formed)
- Notes or snippets of information based on what you found on reviewed sites

- Screenshots, images, or drawings based on elements of site layouts you like
- Links to useful information you have found that explain ideas you have
- Direct quotes of feedback from your competition on requests for features

LinkED

The preceding tips will get you started with search-engine research, but the following site holds some useful details about how to conduct research to learn about your the needs of your users, as opposed to what existing sites provide: www.businesslink.gov.uk/bdotg/action/layer?topicId= 1073901910.

You've now finished reading about market research for your site. At this point, it's possible you're suffering from a headache as you try to get your brain around everything discussed so far. However, it's possible to sum up the topics discussed in a few simple sentences. Basically, you want to search the Web for examples of how sites like the one you plan to build and then apply the best ideas you find on your own site. After all, if your rivals offer something useful, it seems only fair that you can offer something similar to people who visit your site. Just browsing the Web for ideas can be a real lifesaver when you don't know what people expect from a site. Of course, when you find all of these useful ideas, you need to write them down, take screenshots, and keep notes about them so you don't forget important when you get around to building your site. Once you have noted everything you want to remember and got your ideas in order, it's time to move onto the next stage in the process.

ExplainED

At the end of this session, you will have an ideas pad filled with things you might want to include in your own site. These ideas might consist of screenshots (for things you like the look of), site addresses, and even just bullet lists of sections of a site you have discovered that you think might be useful.

Brainstorming

Now that you have a few basic ideas, you want to expand upon them to decide how best to use them—a process commonly known as brainstorming. While this is usually a group activity (and it's often more effective when practiced by more than one person), but it's perfectly acceptable to brainstorm by yourself. That said, the more people you can get involved, the more unique ideas you will end up with. Perhaps you might want to get a few friends or people who are aware of the site to give a few minutes of their time to help you out. It generally doesn't require a large amount of time to conduct brainstorming sessions. However, the process can help you organize the information, which is the most intensive and complicated part of cultivating an idea at the development stage.

While brainstorming can produce a variety of results, the overall effectiveness of this method has not been found to be productive, according to studies. Nevertheless, I've included this method because it helps you prepare the results of your research for mind mapping.

The method of brainstorming I'll describe differs from traditional forms of brainstorming because you already have some ideas and structure to work with, as opposed to a traditional problem you need to solve. Whether you use "solo" or "group" brainstorming, you need to take the method applied to standard brainstorming sessions and use it to build upon your ideas. This will enable you to sprout additional concepts around the ideas generated by your market research. So put down your book (again) and get either a sheet of paper or a note taking program, and then use the ideas you uncovered during the market research section or any ideas you have for your site's functionality, scribbling down anything that comes to mind. In the following example (which diverts slightly from the stamp site), you can see an actual brainstorming session I undertook when designing a portfolio site. Notice how I used images, text, questions and just basic doodles: the point of this exercise is to make a note of anything useful that you don't want to forget, so go ahead and scribble (see Figure 1-30)!

See for Yourself: Brainstorming at Work

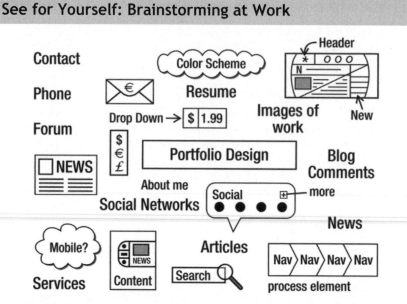

Figure 1-30. This diagram shows the results of a sample brainstorming session.

Try It Yourself: Brainstorm Your Ideas

The only preparation you should make before starting this process is to dedicate a piece of paper (or related material) for each piece of information or idea that resulted from researching he sites you looked at. While this might seem like a lot of things to look at, you could simply select the most interesting or potentially useful ideas to expand on. Using this piece of paper to brainstorm is easy: simply create a page for each question, using each question as a page heading, and then write down anything that comes to mind in relation to each subject. Your brainstorm can be made up of words, phrases, ideas, drawings, or anything else you believe will be relevant during the session.

You can get the most out of your brainstorming by adhering to the following guidelines:

- Remember to focus on quantity, as the idea here is to throw any potential idea about.

- Do not critique or think about how good an idea it is at this stage, just get it written down!

- No matter how quirky or unusual the idea is, it might end up becoming something useful.

- Start with each item as a separate brainstorming session and expand as you see fit.

- Spend anywhere between ten minutes to an hour on each item (or until you run out of ideas).

- Wait until you have finished "storming" ideas for each item before you evaluate the results.

Once you complete the brainstorming session, you will want to look at the results. The first thing you should do is remove anything that makes no sense, repeats another idea or is too closely related to other ideas or things that cannot be implemented, and anything else that falls apart under criticism. Throughout this process, you should use your best judgment (or ask someone else to look at the ideas and see what stands out). The process might seem quite lengthy, but the majority of the ideas you come up with will probably fail due to one of the aforementioned reasons or due to something else. You might wonder why you should bother. It's sometimes the case that the most unique and clever ideas can come out of the ether when you're simply placing an "idea flood" onto the page, so it's worth coming up with the brainstorm even if you return with only a few gems.

Once you select the highest quality and freshest ideas and attach them to your existing research (your ideas pad must be getting quite big by now!), you're ready to use the final method of attempting to produce new ideas, which is less erratic than brainstorming, but also less productive in many ways than market research. However it's still something that has been known to produce results, so why not give it a try! Take a look at how a computer-based brainstorming session for this stamp collection site could look; using the ideas I had for its features. This approach certainly isn't as messy as the preceding, paper-based brainstorming session, but it still produces a written list of the basic ideas that were intended as possible features of the stamp site, some of which prove to be good ideas (see Figure 1-31).

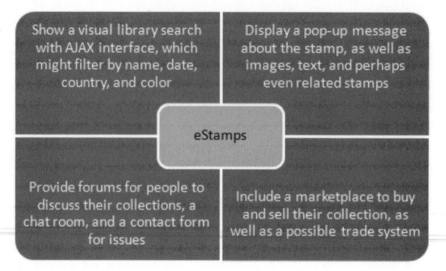

Figure 1-31. This computer-produced brainstorm is much better organized and has four "idea" sectors.

Mind Maps

Mind maps have a lot of similarities to brainstorming, but they come with their own unique set of advantages for idea classification and grouping. While brainstorming works best with a group of people who need to solve a problem or create possible enhancements for a service, mind mapping works well for individuals who want a simple way to expand on a particular subject. In the case of the ideas pad that you put together, you have two ways that you can use mind maps to enhance what you already have to produce improved results:

- **Keyword expanded structure:** Under each item within your ideas pad, you create a bulleted list of expanded information that you believe is relevant to a feature or how you should integrate it into the site (this is similar to the brainstorming method, except this approach focuses on implementation and functionality, rather than on questions and ideas).

- **Traditional tree structure:** This is probably the most familiar and usually the most fun way of approaching mind maps. In this instance, you have each question in the center of a piece of paper with the ideas you have made from brainstorms branching out from the question itself. Finally you branch out from each idea to indicate how you think you could implement the idea or any related functionality that might result or prove beneficial as a result.

Most people use traditional, tree-based mind maps because you can read them more easily; however, some people might prefer to use bulleted-list mind maps because they let them keep their entire project digital, but without having to use a drawing or painting package or a specific piece of software aimed at producing mind maps or technical diagrams. Let's take a look at a pair of example mind maps. The first is for a portfolio site that builds on the example for the brain storming session (see Figure 1-32); the second relates to the stamp collection site idea (see Figure 1-33). Once you look at the examples and read the instructions, put down the book (again) and start making a mind map for your idea. All of the materials you gather throughout this chapter will become part of a detailed plan that you can refer back to as you write content and code your site, so it's important that you participate in these activities, even if you only spend five minutes on each one. The amount of new, useful ideas you can get out of this walking through these examples can be amazing.

See for Yourself: A Mind Map Example

The following example shows an *inward out* mind mapping session where you explore ideas for the various pages of a site. The session also includes words that describe the various elements you might include on your site's pages.

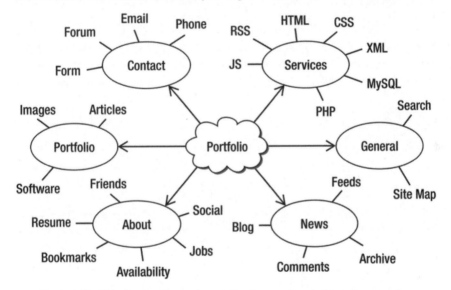

Figure 1-32. This diagram shows the results of a sample mind-mapping exercise.

Try It Yourself: Map Your Mind

It's easy to integrate both brainstorming and mind maps one after the other into a process that you can follow. First create your usual brainstorming session on a large piece of paper, spreading lots of ideas spread all over your brainstorming document. After you complete that step, convert your existing brainstorm into a loosely structured (in terms of layout) mind map.

Following four simple steps can help you produce a mind map:

1. Put the site you wish to expand upon in the center of the page.

2. Branch out with a series of pages to include within the site.

3. Branch out further with specific functionality or content to include.

4. Finally, branch out again if required to give specific details or references.

The result of whichever mind mapping technique you choose should be vast and specific, and it should give you tons of ideas for both the content and features you should provide on your site. If you feel later on in the development process that you need to further expand on your ideas and come up with some new ones, you should feel free to repeat the process as required until you get a sufficient number of ideas for site updates. Let's revisit the stamp-collection example and builds a list of possible pages and ideas (see Figure 1-33). Note that you can make the mind map as simple or as complex as you like, I prefer to use the hand-drawn method, but you should do whatever works for you, as long as you now take the time to produce one for your site.

LinkED

If you would like to use software to generate and manage your mind maps, rather than drawing them or creating lists on paper, you can find a wide variety of programs to help you achieve this task. I recommend the free (cross platform) product XMIND, which you can acquire at www.xmind.net/.

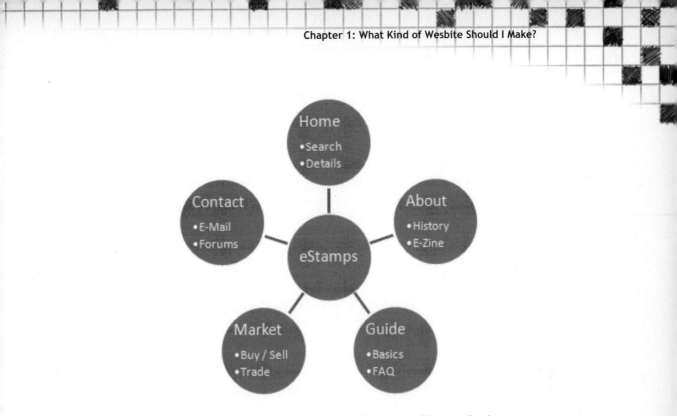

Figure 1-33. This simple mind map shows possible pages and features for the stamp-site example.

Information Architecture

The field of information architecture dedicates itself to the expression and modeling of information that requires explicit details for portraying complicated information. If you look at the ideas pad you have developed, you'll notice that it contains a large range of items that you can implement and refer back to at different points of the project. The complexity of the items in your ideas pad fully qualifies the pad and elements that comprise it as a kind of information architecture. Information Architecture itself allows you to structure information and ideas effectively to build a model that describes how a resulting site should look as you develop it.

Information Architecture is a process that does not end at the initial concept and the method you use to model your ideas and design will change as you begin producing the site. This might be due to inherent limitations of language or the way visualizing something on a page can differ from how you see it in your head. Because of this, I'll cover only the areas that occur before coding begins at this stage. As you progress through the book, you will realize that many factors affect design, and you'll employ many techniques to structure your designs and enable them "leap off the page" when you come to sections where can take advantage of them. You should take the opportunity to produce all of the mentioned elements for your site as you read about them. However, you can also find a handy step-by-step guide at the end of this chapter that can help you quickly and easily pull together a useful series of information architecture doodles for your site; once you complete these doodles, simply attach them to your ever-expanding ideas pad for later use.

Layout

When providing the information architecture for your design, layout models can be highly effective in allowing you to take a visual approach to structuring your site. Many visually minded people choose to take this approach, but it can be helpful for anyone because it can give you a good, general look-and-feel for your design as you create it. You want to try and achieve a professional look, so at this stage you need to remember that change is inevitable, and even if you enter the process with a visual layout and some inspirational elements of the site that you want to provide, what makes web design unique is that, in many cases, the visual appeal of what best suits the end result will be determined piece-by-piece as you code the site. It is in that spirit that I'll cover several layout methods. These approaches can provide a rough guide for initially representing your site.

Concept Artwork

This stage in the process of creating a site is most often thought of as the fun part! Yes, boys and girls, it's time to get your paint out and start designing how your finished site will look. Unfortunately, this is the one thing this book cannot help you with. Why? Because only you can design the physical appearance of a site to meet whatever standards you have, and only you can know your personal views on how you want everything to appear. You might initially view this as a flaw of the book or a huge missing component of the site-creation process, but it's important to realize that everyone has different tastes, and only you understand the levels of navigation, content, functionality and other elements required to put the plan for your site into action. There are simply too many variables to consider when deciding how your site should look (aesthetically) for me to walk you through this part. Even so, feel free to look at my own concept sketch for inspiration, which shows one potential feature you might implement on a site (see Figure 1-34).

See for Yourself: An Example of a Concept Sketch

The following sketch concept sketch outlines a button that will appear in the bottom of a page on the right-hand side. The page you place it on pops up a list of social-networking links (that you can use alongside the site). The sketch itself reflects this by showing the position of the element, what it might look like, and how it might function on the page.

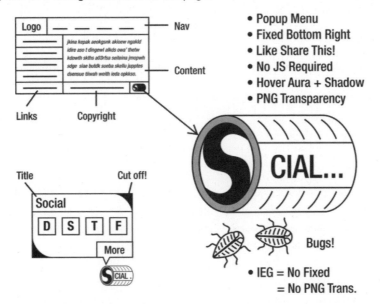

Figure 1-34. This concept artwork shows early ideas for a social-networking button.

Try It Yourself: Concept Art

When you begin coding, you should have a visual model to work with; even if the design is only roughly drawn out or incomplete, the design itself will evolve with the site. Unless you have a graphically prebuilt mock-up you wish to use, concept drawings rarely remain the same over time, and letting the design evolve will produce a more natural and graceful *worn in* appearance. Trying to create a complete package might seem rather daunting, so I recommend designing individual features of the site; these can be much easier to make alterations to and do not require you to rethink the site design itself. Use an image-editing package or a blank sheet of paper to create basic drawings of the ideas you have and to get a feel for how things might look.

The whole point of this exercise is to pull your general ideas and design skills together. You want to come up with a physical representation of the idea you have in your head, which you can use to map out generally how you want things to appear when you begin coding the site. While you might want to produce some sketches that represent your entire site's look and how it all might fit together, sometimes creating simple concept artwork for individual elements can be just as useful when trying to decide on how your ideas should eventually look on the page. These concept drawings of your potential site should be attached to your ideas pad; eventually, you will assemble the ideas contained in your ideas pad as you would the pieces of a giant jigsaw puzzle.

Tips and Tricks! Producing Concepts

You can use this list of tips to help you draw possible design elements:

- Keep things simple; fancy designs often complicate the concept beyond the point that you can execute them.

- Remember that the colors you use on paper will not look the same on computer screens.

- Annotate your diagrams with short but descriptive text for ease-of-recollection.

- Try out alternative versions of the same design to see what looks best.

- Do not use software to convert concepts into code because the tools to do this don't do it well.

While it will be your job to design your site and mold that design around your content and functionality based on your research and your instincts, you don't have to go through this process alone! This book cannot decide for you what physical structure you should choose (for the reasons mentioned earlier), but you should have gained some ideas for how to organize your content from your review of potentially competitive sites. For example, I'll bet you found some great visual and functional elements you can incorporate in your own design. Later chapters on coding your site will also offer helpful advice on the design process, as well as tips on how psychology, conventions, accessibility, and usability should factor into the complete design and its general appearance.

Structure

While the structure of a site is determined mainly by the code you use, structural mock-up in information architecture can help you implement the jigsaw-puzzle model mentioned earlier, by enabling you to make some early decisions on how your design should appear. The layout model of design allows you to give a potential feature, element, or page some form before you decide how it should be implemented, which spares you the irritation of throwing away your hard work in later chapters). The structural model of design allows you to place the elements of the site around the page and helps you decide how you want to tie everything together.

Sitemaps

Do you remember when you were in school and you made those family trees that showed how you were related to each member of your family? Well, the purpose of a sitemap is identical to this in the method that it tries to structure your site and calculate how each page relates to other pages or files (see Figure 1-35). In most cases, you produce a sitemap when your design has been approved or decided upon. You should now have plenty of ideas based on what you have discovered in your research of other sites, and you might have come up with some potential navigation thoughts when you built a mind map, which I demonstrated in the examples that show how to organize your thoughts into groups. These groups would be ideal for pages of your site because they let you place multiple pieces of information and functionality on one page. By organizing your site's content into categories you can assign pieces of information to a page, thereby determining how many pages you actually need (and even what each page should cover in terms of content).

Most people recognize that having too many links on a single page can be an issue. Therefore, you should generally restrict that each menu (and subsequently each submenu) to a maximum of eight links.

See for Yourself: A Structured Sitemap

The following sitemap takes the ideas from the mind-mapping sessions and groups them into related categories; thus, each of these groups of information ends up becoming a page of the design.

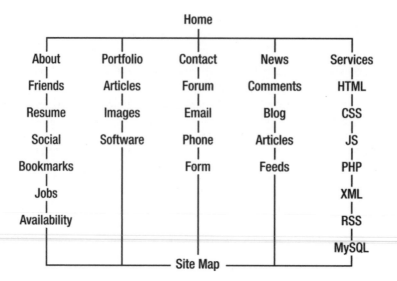

Figure 1-35. This sitemap shows how you might structure a basic site in the form of a family tree.

You head the start of a sitemap with the site or index page name, with branches that split off beneath it. Each branch represents a page that users can reach by clicking or following an internal link (not an external resource or site). For this reason, it's highly recommended that you wait to create your sitemap until you complete writing your site's content and functionality (or at least until you are sure about what pages you will require for your site); otherwise, you might find yourself with holes in your site's navigation once you place all the information (with additional links) within the flow of your pages. With each descending level in the sitemap, the child of the parent it is linked from has children of its own; in other words, each child has additional links that aren't declared in a parent or an ancestor of that child or any other page because you want to avoid repetition). Forming a sitemap helps you see the structure of your site more clearly; it can also provide insight for where to place new content or content related to existing content.

Wireframing

Website wireframing is a well-documented form of information architecture that provides benefits similar to those of concept artwork, which describes how elements should look; and prototyping (which requires coding or an environment to test the design). However, wireframing comes at the problem differently from most models by focusing more on how to arrange the visual elements on the page (see Figure 1-36). A wireframe is a based around a series of grids and blocks that represent the way the content will be laid out in your completed work.

See for Yourself: Wireframing at Work

The following wireframe could represent any site. It has all the standard conventions people expect, including a logo, search box, navigation bar, footer, and links (plus content) for articles and news.

The vast majority of cases require only a single wireframe model; however, you do find exceptions, such as when the homepage needs a different design than the rest of your pages. Note that whether you want to create such a design boils down entirely to your personal tastes). You can implement either a basic or complex level wireframe. A basic wireframe consists of referencing where to place elements such as navigation, and you should use it only as a rough overview of a design. In a complex wireframe model, you would also provide details about the navigation element, such the number of navigation links that you can squeeze into the header of a site without causing overflow in a fixed-screen resolution. Such an approach is more complex, but it also provides some added value.

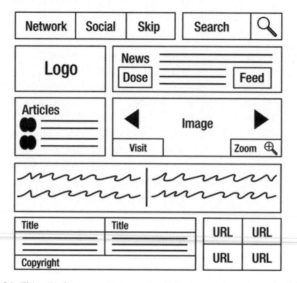

Figure 1-36. This wireframe portrays a simplistic two-column layout with navigation, a logo, and a footer.

Tips and Tricks: Wireframe Defaults

A wireframe includes several default components:

- **Header**: Logo, Search Box, Header (Navigation), Callout boxes.
- **Sidebar**: Category (Navigation), Adverts, Important Details.
- **Content**: Adverts, Feature Blocks, Content / Category listings.
- **Footer**: Copyright, Footer Links, Site Maps, Badges (Awards etc)

In Figure 1-36, the header navigation contains "Network, Social, and Skip" elements, as well as a search box on the right-hand side. Below that, you can see the logo with a News *callout box* beside it, which has a link to the site's feeds (you will learn more about syndication feeds in Chapter 09). The Articles box is a sidebar navigation link with an image gallery callout box on the right-hand side that contains a few functions inside it. The box with scribbles under that is basically a content block; this block has two columns where you can place all the text. Finally, at the bottom of the page, you can see the footer links to the right, space for some footer text, and a copyright message on the left. Simple!

A basic wireframe conveys several benefits: it places any specific requirements upon the individual implementing the code, and it provides a flexible way to address your layout needs along the way; however, a built-in downside to them is that they provide rather limited control of the overall appearance of your site. A complex wireframe provides more control over specific details of your design, so it lets you account for basic issues and decisions that might apply later on in the process; however, it provides a less *flexible* for controlling your site's appearance due to the way explicit details can evolve in a prototype. The more things evolve, the more your page loses its generic structural value, which is the main benefit of using a complex wireframe. It's up to you to determine which wireframe suits your needs better. However, under many circumstances, you might want to start out with a basic wireframe model and add in any detail that might be relevant when you transition from designing to coding. This will prove helpful when you begin producing prototypes (such as basic working models as you code the site).

The Vision Quest

You can use concept artwork, visual prototypes (if you have any built already), wireframes, and sitemaps to help you take your mental image of your site's look-and-feel and turn that into something that others can see, comment on, and appreciate. You can optimize the design process by using the models discussed to impose a well structured order for your site. The purpose of this vision quest is to take into account every element of information architecture you have and put it all together as a series of quick examples that you can literally complete in a matter of five minutes each (or longer, depending on how quick you are with a computer or pen-and-paper). By following this vision quest, you should end up with some schematics that will help you immensely when you begin writing content and code because you will know what pages you need to create, as well as the functionality that you need to refer to.

Try It Yourself: Bringing Everything Together

The process of choosing and working with information architecture can be quite complicated (as you might have noticed), but you can simplify things by undertaking things in this order:

1. Break down your ideas pad regions into grouped site sections.

2. Produce a sitemap to represent the hierarchy based on the preceding sections.

3. Create a basic wireframe to represent the sections of the generic web page.

4. Use your concept art to convert the basic wireframe into a complex wireframe.

Step 1

Begin optimizing your use of information architecture by looking at your ideas pad and organizing all of your information. This might seem rather daunting based on all the research you have done, but you can use your old friend, the mind map, to accomplish this. You need to build a mind map that will suit the needs of your individual site, rather than using the examples noted previously. Create a central element called *My Website*. Next, branch off this element by indicating the names of the pages you want to include (branching off from these, as required). Next, attach labels for each of these page elements that indicate where your research results would best fit in. For instance, including a contact form, feedback form, and message board would fit well in a page labeled *contact*. After you complete this step, you will have a structure that, if you look carefully, will provide an accurate representation of how you will lay out your site (in terms of content and features that you don't use across multiple pages—don't worry about content or elements that would span multiple pages for now).

Now let's return to the stamp-collection example, so you can see how you might follow the first step. This step combines the brainstorming session created initially in Figure 1-31 with the mind map generated in Figure 1-33 to extend what is possible with information architecture. If you haven't already done so, you should set the book down and do this exercise for your own site. You should refer back to relevant parts of this book as you produce your diagrams if you require assistance or a recap on the details of how they work; however, I cannot stress enough how important it is that you complete the steps described for your own site to ensure you have all the materials you need when you're ready to create your content and produce the code to implement everything. Finally, you should refer back to the figures included in this chapter to see the kind of information included in the stamps site example. You're now ready to move onto the second stage of the process.

Step 2

In this step, you take your recently created mind map and brainstorming session and convert them into something that is easier to read and work with later on. This step is almost identical to the first step, with one significant exception: rather than organizing your research into a map of what should go where, you turn this information into a sitemap that gives you a visual reference of what pages your site will require.

You can combine the details about the sitemaps you created earlier with your page details (including any references they make to other pages) to give yourself a visually complete structure of your site's hierarchy. Note that you need to retain your mind map because the sitemap will show only the structure of pages based on the mind map, not the functionality details of your pages. You can see an example of this for the stamp-collecting site in Figure 1-37, where you outline the pages and their possible content. While you might not know what pages you need at this time, having a general idea of your required pages based on your mind map session could prove useful).

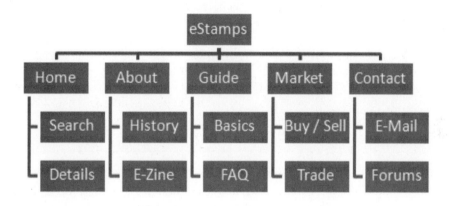

Figure 1-37. You can produce a sitemap by listing your site's pages and functionality.

Step 3

Now you need to create a basic wireframe that encompasses all of the global elements that will exist on your web pages, such as a logo, navigation, footer, and content, and then arrange them on the page as required (see Figure 1-38). Alongside this, you should begin creating some concept artwork for functionality that you need to integrate onto specific pages. As you do this, use the artwork you create to determine the basic wireframe structure. Note that this step requires you to have the visuals for each page roughly mapped out, which shouldn't be an issue now that you know the structure of your site (based on the initial sitemap you created in Step 2.

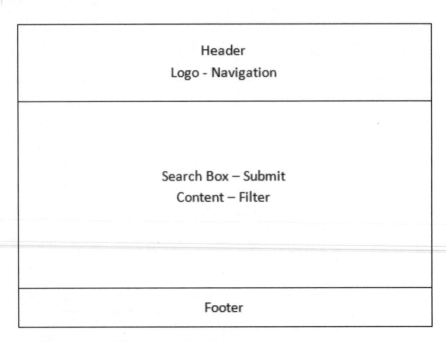

Figure 1-38. This basic wireframe takes into account the segments of the site, as well as its contents.

Step 4

Now you're ready to place your concept art for any elements you want to include on every page within the basic wireframe model (see Figure 1-39). This enables you to account for any modifications for height, width, or positioning. Doing this transforms your basic wireframe into a complex model. Be sure to label things appropriately and provide details about specific functions you want to include, such as a *search* box or *dropdown* menu. In the example of the stamp-collection site, you can see the difference between the early wireframe model and the more complicated (but more visual) layout.

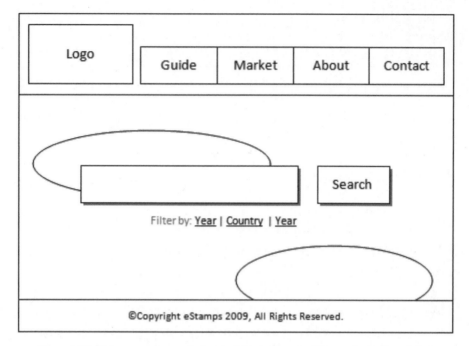

Figure 1-39. This more advanced wire model takes some of the more visual aspects of the site into account.

At this point, you should have an ideas pad full of research, plenty of screenshots of sites to draw inspiration from, useful snippets of information, lists of pages you want to include, bulleted lists of items on your to do list, and anything else you think might prove useful to remember. The ideas pad allows you to pull everything you could possibly need (along with all of your models and representations) into a single resource. This means you can take a quick flick through your ideas pad if you forget something, or you want to get some inspiration for your site and its content.

Summary

In this chapter, you learned how to factor in your needs and ideas to understand what kind of site you want to create, how to form an identity and gain inspiration for what your site should include, and how to take advantage of the basics of information architecture. You also learned and how to use the models associated with information architecture to create both a design proposal that gives you a physical representation (whether you used pen-and-paper or software to create this) of the look-and-feel you want your site to have, as well as how it should be structured. You also organized your ideas and developed some concepts that lay out a plan of action for your site. This will prove useful when you're ready to stop theorizing over the cooking instructions and get on with mixing your site's ingredients together. In the next chapter, you will begin writing and publishing your content. This will give you something to fill up your site's pages when you start coding your site you will have something to fill up all of those pages you outlined in the sitemaps and wireframes you just built.

Chapter Checklist

You should accomplish the following tasks before leaving this chapter:

- Get an idea which will form the basis for the site.
- Decide how much time can be given to the project.
- Choose the type of site that would fit your idea best.
- Produce a brand identity to represent you online.
- Create a mission statement for the site's purpose.
- Perform market research to determine the functionality you should include.
- Brainstorm and create a mind map to expand your ideas list.
- Prototype your ideas and produce concept artwork.
- Create a basic wireframe and sitemap for your site's structure.

Questions and Answers

Q: *How do I create a wireframe for dynamic content, such as dropdown menus?*

A: A wireframe's static nature doesn't lend itself to describing dynamic interactions (especially if they are on paper). If you draw out your wireframe on paper, the simplest way to do this is to cut pieces of paper (literally!) that represent the *before* and *after* elements. You can then layer these elements at the appropriate place on your wireframe; this approach lets you extend the functionality of your wireframes.

Q: *What if I want my site to use elements from multiple site types?*

A: It's fantastic that you want to enhance your site in as many different ways as possible, but you should remember that you need to focus your intentions clearly for each "part" of the site's structure when you produce a sitemap, as well as when creating any prototypes or working models of your design. If you incorporate multiple site types (such as a blog and a niche site), the design should be well balanced and reflect the needs of your visitors, adhering to the type of content and pages your users will expect to find in such sites. This means that you should be consistent with your design and always ensure your design is relevant for the audience you wish to receive.

Q: *What exactly is the point in producing an ideas pad?*

A: The main purpose of this chapter and the ideas pad is to get you thinking and looking at what is possible, so you can decide what you want to achieve with your site before you set out on your journey of putting it together. Remember that if you start churning out code without considering your fundamental goals, then you might end up wasting your own valuable time by deleting the stuff that doesn't make the cut; it will also take you longer to write your code as a result. Creating an ideas pad can help you avoid walking into this long-term commitment blind and to prepare you for the real-world issues that you face when you begin building the final result.

Where You Are Now

By the end of this chapter you should have the following:

- A finalized idea for your sites main aims
- An identity to go with your sites goals
- An idea's pad full of really useful snippets and images
- A mission statement declaring your aims
- Some primary research on your rivals
- Some brain storming and mind mapping to place in your ideas pad
- A vision quest to produce a concept design

How Do I Write Good Content?

You have your site all planned out now, and you know the functionality you want, as well as having plenty of initial concept doodles that describe how you think it could end up looking. But the most important thing about your site is still missing: the content! Before you can begin learning HTML and coding all of the functionality in your site, you need to flex your creative muscles again and start creating your content. Content is the most important element of a site. People will visit your site to learn what you have to say or offer on certain subjects, as well as to find out answers to their questions. Content does more than define the purpose of your site; it's also what search engines use to rank your site, which can be valuable in gaining a consistent stream of visitors.

In this chapter, you'll learn about the following topics:

- How to sort out the types of content you might produce
- How to write, edit, and create fantastic reading material
- How to prevent other people stealing your content

Content Is King!

Here is an unequivocal fact: content is the king of the Internet. Many people think that the most important element of a site design is how pretty and engaging it is. Unfortunately, these people often overlook the quality of their content and wonder why their site subsequently fails to succeed. People visit sites to learn, have their questions answered, or simply to help them achieve a goal—and none of this would be possible without content. The written word is the primary method humans use to communicate when verbal interaction (talking) is no longer possible. The Internet focuses entirely on the ability to allow people to put across their ideas, opinions, research, and information, whether it's writing a romantic novel right or telling your friends how funny your cat looks when his eyes mysteriously cross for no reason.

What is Content?

Content usually comes in three different forms: text, images and multimedia. When most people think about adding content to a site, they usually assume that text is what is required. While text is the most common form of content on the Internet, content can take many forms other than writing. For example, content can be images (which, as the saying goes, could well be worth 1,000 words!) or forms of multimedia such as video and audio. You have many ways to express yourself on your site; I'll walk you through how each content type can influence your audience.

Text

Text is the most common form of content available on the Web. When you portray your view on a subject, putting it into words is one of the most descriptive methods you can use. Writing content does have its own unique set of challenges, such as the barriers of language (try reading Russian if you only know English) and the need to follow conventions such as spelling and grammar to ensure that your audience can understand you. When producing a site, it's important that you provide content that your visitors will want to read.

Tips and Tricks: Benefits of Text

Using text as a vehicle to deliver content confers several advantages:

- Text is highly descriptive and can explain subjects in depth.
- Most people are familiar with seeing and reading text online.
- Text-based content can be as simple or as complicated as you like.

However, text also confers several disadvantages as a vehicle for delivering content:

- Large sections of text can be hard to read (or even boring!).
- There is little inherent attractiveness in blocks of text-based content.
- Reading can be a slow process, so people tend to scan text.

ExplainED

Another disadvantage of text is that it can be hard to read on screens (especially small mobile devices), so it can be more tiring to look at over a long period of time (in contrast to a printed page).

See for Yourself: A Text-Based Approach

One great thing about text-based content is that it can help you explain topics quite easily (see Figure 2-1).

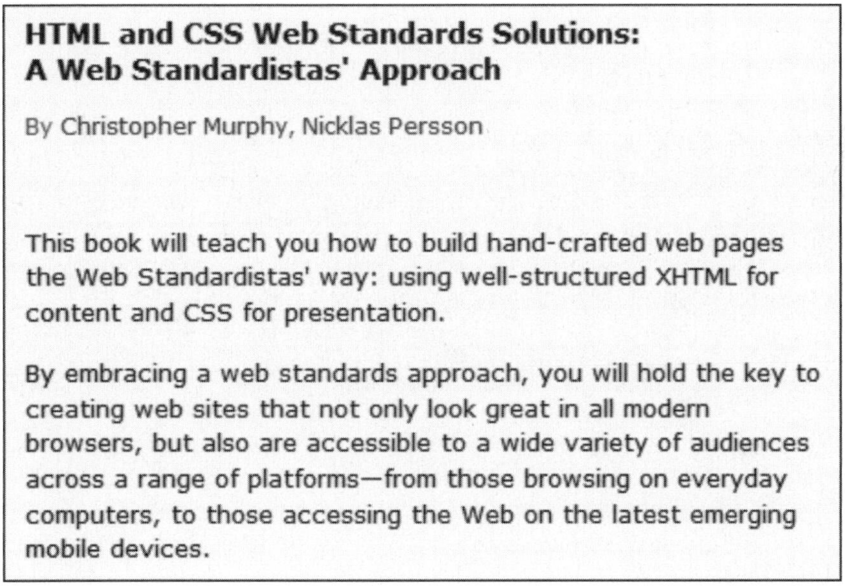

> **HTML and CSS Web Standards Solutions: A Web Standardistas' Approach**
>
> By Christopher Murphy, Nicklas Persson
>
> This book will teach you how to build hand-crafted web pages the Web Standardistas' way: using well-structured XHTML for content and CSS for presentation.
>
> By embracing a web standards approach, you will hold the key to creating web sites that not only look great in all modern browsers, but also are accessible to a wide variety of audiences across a range of platforms—from those browsing on everyday computers, to those accessing the Web on the latest emerging mobile devices.

Figure 2-1. This example illustrates how text-based content can explain topics easily.

Images

Images can express emotions and feelings that few other content types can trigger. They catch the eye and involve the audience, enabling a site to feel more engaging than that relies only on large blocks of text. You can use images to give articles more emphasis and to try to soften (or break down) those long lines of words and letters that can bore users.

Tips and Tricks: the Benefits of Images

Images confer several advantages as a method of content delivery:

- Emotion, psychology, and art can be portrayed more easily.
- Colorful graphics can make sites beautiful.
- Recognizable symbols can trigger specific emotions.

Images also confer several disadvantages:

- Web browsers can disable images, which can make the design look unwieldy.
- Visually impaired users can be impacted negatively by poorly served images.
- Images can sometimes distract your users by drawing their focus away from the text.

ExplainED

Search engines have problems understanding images because they don't have eyes! When indexing your site, search engines have to rely on alternative information provided about the images you have.

See for Yourself: An Image in All Its Glory

The often-heard cliché is that an image is worth a thousand words. In the case of a great logo that reinforces your brand for the entire world to see, it can be worth decidedly more than that (see Figure 2-2).

Rich Media

Video, audio, and other forms of rich media have become an integral part of the Web that has evolved quickly over recent years as the amount of on-demand services that offer television and radio broadcasts have gone through the roof. Being able to watch your favorite movie, television show, music artists, or even create your own content such as podcasts and video blogs have become all the rage, and such elements are easier than ever to include on your site.

Figure 2-2. MailChimp's logo and site are an iconic vision of beautiful graphics.

Tips and tricks: Benefits of Multimedia

Using multimedia content confers several advantages:

- You can use both text and visual information together.
- You can visually pack more content into a limited space.
- You can interact with visitors more easily with video content.

Using multimedia content also confers several disadvantages:

- You must account for audio and video hardware and software requirements.
- Downloading multimedia requires a fast Internet connection.
- Disabled users can have restricted access to multimedia.

ExplainED

Some requirements of rich media can include sound cards, codecs, and plug-ins (drivers for video formats); some rich media can even require certain software products in order to play.

See for Yourself: Video Tutorials

One increasingly popular content-creation option is to embed multimedia from other sites onto yours, such as a video from YouTube (see Figure 2-3).

Figure 2-3. YouTube offers the ability to watch videos directly over the Internet.

Decision Making

So you need to get some content ready for your site: which out of the three content types will you end up using? The more variety you can add to your content, the better off you will be as a result, so your best bet is to include some images, plenty of text, and possibly the occasional bit of multimedia content. However, you should use your common sense to determine where this content should be placed (see Figure 2-4). While creating images and multimedia is largely something for another book (as it requires understanding different software packages such as Photoshop or Flash), you will learn the basics of adding images and multimedia to your site later in this book (see Chapter 6 for more information). In this chapter, you'll primarily learn about writing text content because it's the easiest thing to do, and it requires no complicated software.

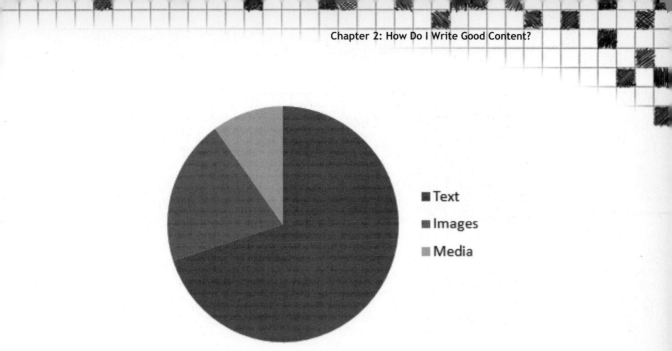

Figure 2-4. Most sites are composed primarily of text, with lots of images and some multimedia.

See for Yourself: Content Types

Let's return to the stamp-collection example. In that site's sitemap and wireframe, you can find some basic pages like About, Guide, Market, and Contact; let's take a closer look at how each content type (text, images, and media) could be implemented within the example sections (see Figure 2-5). When producing your own site, you should think about how you use these three content types; this can help you decide how you want everything to appear once you start coding later. For the purposes of keeping things simple, you probably won't get any benefit out of recreating the stamp-collection example in your own design because it's exceptionally easy to decide, for example, when an image might work better than text when you create your content.

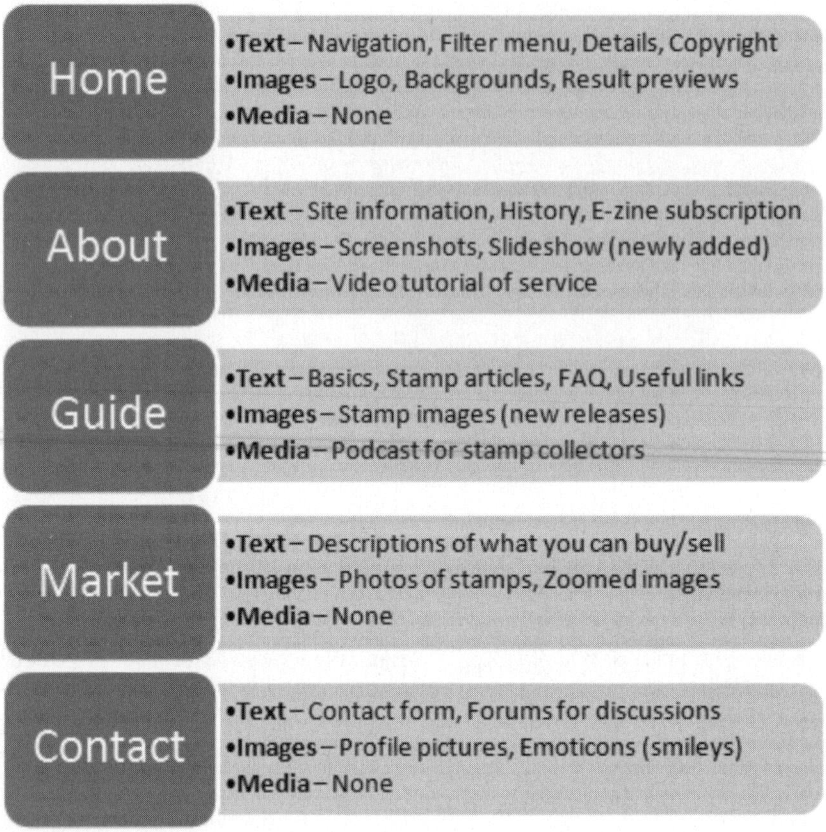

Home
- **Text** – Navigation, Filter menu, Details, Copyright
- **Images** – Logo, Backgrounds, Result previews
- **Media** – None

About
- **Text** – Site information, History, E-zine subscription
- **Images** – Screenshots, Slideshow (newly added)
- **Media** – Video tutorial of service

Guide
- **Text** – Basics, Stamp articles, FAQ, Useful links
- **Images** – Stamp images (new releases)
- **Media** – Podcast for stamp collectors

Market
- **Text** – Descriptions of what you can buy/sell
- **Images** – Photos of stamps, Zoomed images
- **Media** – None

Contact
- **Text** – Contact form, Forums for discussions
- **Images** – Profile pictures, Emoticons (smileys)
- **Media** – None

Figure 2-5. Here are some basic details about the kind of content that might be used on the eStamps site.

Information Design

The focus of information design is to ensure that your content is written to a standard in which people can use it effectively and easily. The purpose of having a site is to put forward information about something, whether you want to put together a personal site for your family, or you want to make a site that the whole community can access. That said, you want the content you include on your site to reflect a certain level of professionalism, especially if you have concerns over how easy your site will be to read, view, and hear.

LinkED

For more information and a useful overview of the types of information design that people employ, see the following Wikipedia page at http://en.wikipedia.org/ wiki/Information_design#competencies.

Content Comes First

You might be wondering why I want you to produce content before you even have a site. The simple answer: Content is the most important part of the site, so you should try to focus your attention on producing some high-quality content for the site before you build the design that will hold it. One of the biggest mistakes people make when building sites is to create the initial content around their design ideas (to make it fit into the pretty boxes), rather than fitting the design around the content. Remember that what people will visit your site for is the content; the design is there to make that content easier to navigate and more pleasant to view. This may sound harsh, but you will find it much easier if you write out what you want to appear on the page, and then wrap the code around that content as required. Even though you will still need to add content after you create the site's design, getting the initial content down early will help you work out the majority of your site's structure and style before you get to the design; doing things the other way around means you must preemptively guess how things will need to appear before you define them.

The best advice you can take from this section is to generate all the basic content you require to get your site started first, and then design your site using that content. Then, when you complete the design, you can add any labels or bits of information to improve the way the content works with the design. By following this *content-out* approach you learn to structure your site more carefully, and you won't need to write so much code (always a good thing!). It also means the code you do write will be cleaner, more efficient, and easier to maintain. By placing content only within *tags* that accurately describe its purpose (which you'll learn more about in later chapters), you can reduce the amount of guesswork needed, which in turn reduces unnecessary code or styles that repeat themselves. This advice might not make much sense at this time, but you'll thank me for it later.

ExplainED

When you get around to writing code, you can literally copy-and-paste your lovely, well-written content into the code editor and start building around it to keep the quality focus on what visitors care about!

Audience

The most important element of information design is to understand your audience. You want the material you write to be understood by the users you want to become part of your online, extended family. For instance, if you want to aim your site at children, you don't want to use the same kind of content you would find on a site aimed at academics. Many different types of audiences exist, and it can be hard for you to please everyone; however, before you begin, you should be aware of the audience demographic that might come across your site when it goes live.

See for Yourself: Audience Types

You should ask yourself the following questions about your intended site audience because all these issues could affect how you shape your site's written content:

- **Age**: How old is the majority of your intended audience, and what level of writing would it require?
- **Gender**: Is your content aimed particularly at men or women, or is it gender neutral?
- **Location**: Which countries do your intended users live in, and, do they have language needs?
- **Experience**: Will your users be aware of technical content or jargon terms you will likely use?
- **Education**: Can your audience understand the language you use on your site?
- **Ability**: Can your audience use the Web effectively, or should you use visual aids on your site?
- **Social**: Do your intended visitors like participating in activities; if so, what can you offer them?

- **Religion:** Do your intended users have any cultural needs; for example, will local festivals conflict with your site events?

- **Political view:** Do your visitors have any reforms or viewpoints they support that you should keep in mind (or cater to)?

There are literally hundreds of different types of audiences you can target, and you should only attempt to target those who best represent the kind of users your site is likely to attract. For example, trying to target t-shirts with cartoon characters at elderly visitors probably won't succeed.

Try It Yourself: Audience Thoughts

At this point, you have an idea of what type of content your example site might have; next, you need to decide what kind of audience your site will address. Let's take a look at each audience type with regard to the stamp collection site (see Figure 2-6); this can help you understand how to answer these questions for your own site. After you look at the eStamp example, you should put down the book and make any required notes for your own site as things you might want to consider. This will help you keep in mind exactly who you think will use your site, enabling you to shape your content to connect with their expectations!

Website Writing

The time has come to begin writing the content for your site; rather than leaving you to open your default word processor and come up with what you will require on your own, I'll help you choose what content you need for your site and how to determine the types of information you should include in your site's pages. While some people prefer to write content as they need it, you will find that almost all sites have certain pages in common. You should create these pages in common before you begin coding your site; this will give you something to place within the pages before you make your site live.

Age	• All ages, from children to adults
Gender	• Stamp collectors mostly male
Location	• Worldwide audiance (translation useful)
Experience	• Specialist subject and jargon
Education	• People interested in history or communication
Ability	• Visual aids extremely useful for identification
Social	• Sharing information (e-commerce possible)
Religion	• Not applicable
Political View	• Not applicable

Figure 2-6. These answers outline the expected demographics of the eStamps site.

Common pages

Knowing your site's purpose allows you to determine what pages you will require for the site. For example, if you want to produce a personal blog, you know you will need to produce some content for the initial blog posts that will greet your visitors. These posts will need to explain to visitors why your site exists. While your site's purpose will dictate some of the content you should include in your design, you should remember that each site has different requirements. While this is your site, and you are perfectly entitled to create or remove some of the established types of pages people expect, you should be aware there might be consequences for not including expected information.

Refer back to the sitemap you created in the first chapter. In conducting the research about your intended site, you have already determined many of the pages you will need to include in your type of site, such as *about*, *news*, and *contact*. Based on this information, you should begin the writing process by opening up your word processor and creating a document for each page you feel the site should include. Doing this will keep each page's content separate and help you avoid getting confused about what goes where. One positive: The large amount of sites out there means that a series of conventions has already been established, and certain expectations exist for what each type of site should include, such as contact information for the author of a site).

Try It Yourself: Choosing Pages and Content

You can pick as many elements as apply to your site type from the list of items that follow. This list can help you decide what pages you think your final design should include content for; note that you can (and should) also use your sitemap as a reference point to denote the basic pages you will require for your site:

- **About:** Gives information about the site and its author
- **Accessibility:** Explains useful information for disabled visitors
- **Advertise:** Shows details for people who might want to pay for advertising space
- **Archive:** Provides a directory of previous articles or posts
- **Articles:** Include any comprehensive writing, such as documentation
- **Blog:** Includes a constantly updated source of writing and articles
- **Community:** Provides information about ways visitors can interact socially
- **Contact:** Provides details for contacting the owner of the site
- **Contribute/Donate:** Provides details for people who might want to help or give to the site
- **Download:** Includes links to software or files that are relevant to the site
- **Event:** Provides dates, times, and important information about upcoming events
- **FAQ:** Includes a list of frequently asked questions for products and services
- **Features:** Gives a detailed look at the functionality of your products and services
- **Gallery:** Includes pictures, multimedia, and other visual materials for viewing
- **History:** Includes details about the site's history, including release dates
- **Lab:** Provides a place where you can show off what you're testing or working on
- **Legal:** Incorporates copyright, terms of service, and privacy information
- **Links:** Includes URLs to sites that you think are useful or worth browsing to

- **Members**: Denotes areas of the site that people have site membership to view
- **News**: Shares the latest information about the site, including new features and content
- **Homepage**: Gives brief details about the site; note that this is usually the front page of the site
- **Portfolio**: Provides a place to showcase work, projects, or anything else you have undertaken
- **Press**: Gives you a place to mention any awards or good reviews your site might receive
- **Privacy**: Typically provides a statement that says what personal data you might collect
- **Projects**: Details a list of things you offer through your site
- **Resources**: Provides a place for information that does not fit in other categories
- **Resume**: Where you can show off your abilities and skills, as well as list your qualifications
- **Services**: Gives details about professional (paid) work you offer over the Web
- **Subscriber**: Lists the feeds and e-zines that people can choose to read
- **Support**: Provides help files, feature requests, bug reports, and other assistance

Remember that you can always add to your sitemap if you think any of these items could benefit your site.

Also, note that some pages cannot appear on your site until you have enough information to support them. Because of this, you should only produce content for pages that you can write about with ease. No matter what happens, all sites should contain *about*, *contact* and *news* (or *blog*) pages at the top of the homepage, which acts as the launch pad for everything a site has to offer its visitors. You also want to ensure your visitors can quickly see what is new, as well as whether anything interesting has occurred since a user's last visit. With that in mind, let's refer back to the eStamp sitemap (from the previous chapter) and try to determine what pages from the preceding list and the research for the site conducted earlier should appear within the stamp-collection site (see Figure 2-7). For your own site, you can either use your research (Ideas Pad), your sitemap, or the preceding list to pick out some pages you should write content for.

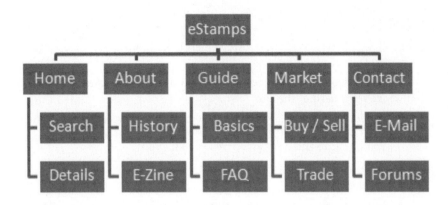

Figure 2-7. The sitemap for the eStamps site shows a mixture of *common* and unique pages.

Content Examples

Next, you should go through the documents you have created one-by-one and decide what content you should include for each particular page. It's almost time to open up your word processor and start typing in your content. However, first, you should take a look at some examples of those common page templates and see exactly what kind of information you could include in your version of them. Using the information provided in these examples will help you address many of the possible questions and needs your visitors might have.

See for Yourself: An About Page

Figure 2-8 shows you a typical about page.

Figure 2-8. This figure (http://green-beast.com/about/) shows a working about page.

Try It Yourself: What to Include on the About Page

Answering the following list of questions can help you provide the necessary information your about page should include:

- Details about what your site will offer
- Information about your target audience
- The benefits of using your site
- Your job title and other information about you
- Your interests, hobbies, and experience
- The inspiration behind the site's creation
- Any relevant *claims to fame* you might have
- Interesting facts can you share about yourself

See for Yourself: an Archive Index

Figure 2-9 shows you a typical archive index page.

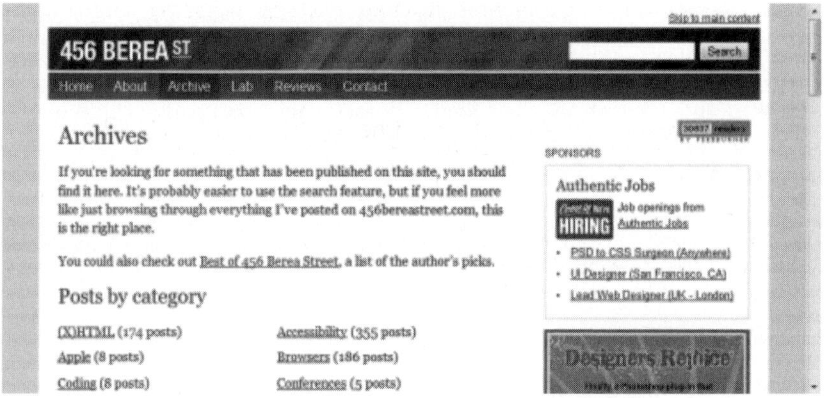

Figure 2-9. This figure illustrates a site archive page.

Try It Yourself: What to Include on the Archive Index

You can create an effective archive index page by including the following information:

- The categories your site's pages fall into
- Information on published dates and categories
- A list all of the pages that exist in your site

See for Yourself: An Article Index

Figure 2-10 shows you a typical article index page.

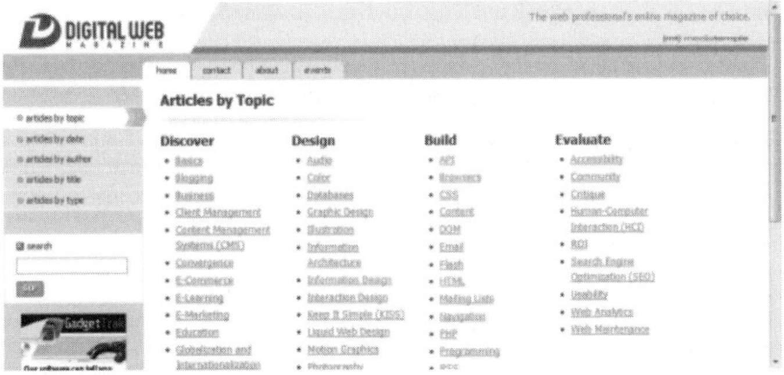

Figure 2-10. This figure shows an index of articles.

Try It Yourself: What to Include on the Articles Index

You can create an effective articles index page by including the following information:

- The title of the article being referenced
- The date and author of the published article
- Notes in the footer after the content
- Useful links to related articles

See for Yourself: A Blog

Figure 2-11 shows you a typical blog page.

Figure 2-11. This figure shows a blog page with content.

Try It Yourself: What to Include on the Blog

You can create an effective blog page by including the following information:

- A list the most recent entries to the blog
- The blog post titles and their date of release
- The website address of the URL posts

See for Yourself: A Community Page

Figure 2-12 shows you a typical community page.

Figure 2-12. This figure diplays a community page.

Try It Yourself: What to Include on the Community Page (Site-Related Links)

You can create an effective community page by including the following information:

- The location of friends to the site
- Links to user-involved areas such as events
- User-powered sections such as forums
- A list of social networks people can join
- Other sites you own that relate to this one

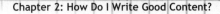
See for Yourself: A Contact Page

Figure 2-13 shows you a typical contact page.

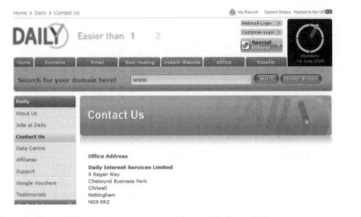

Figure 2-13. This figure shows a page with a contact section.

Try It Yourself: What to Include on the Contact Page

You can create an effective contact page by including the following information:

- Email forms for people to contact you
- Any telephone numbers (if a business site)
- Addresses or PO Boxes (if a business site)
- Instant-messaging account details
- Links to forums, chat rooms, and so on

ExplainED

Placing your email address directly on a site can be a bad move because software exists to browse sites for email addresses and harvests them for spam. The best way to avoid this is to use a contact form, instead; this will prevent your email address being uncovered by products that are built to autonomously search the Web for email addresses to spam.

See for Yourself: A Contribute Page

Figure 2-14 shows you a typical contribute page.

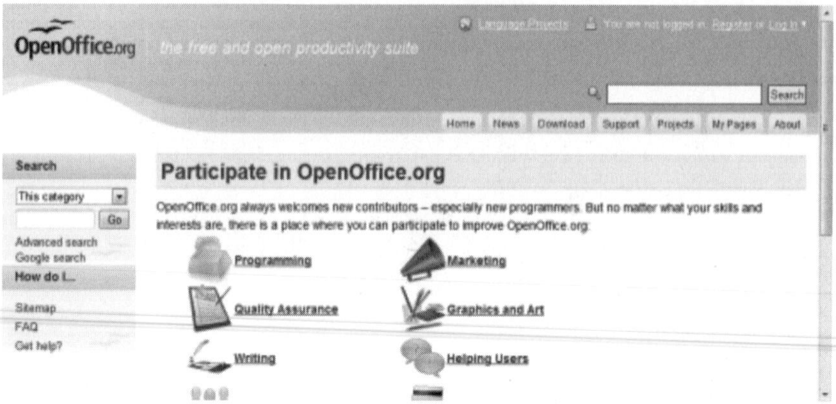

Figure 2-14. This figure shows a page with an example of a user-contribution section.

Try It Yourself: What to Include on the Contribute Page

You can create an effective contribute page by including the following information:

- Information on how to submit articles to your site
- Methods for your visitors can get involved
- Details about donations (if required)
- Advice for how to help promote your site

See for Yourself: A Download Page

Figure 2-15 shows you a typical download page.

Figure 2-15. This site shows a download page in action.

Try It Yourself: What to Include on the Downloads Page

You can create an effective downloads page by including the following information:

- Details about any system requirements
- Information about whether the product is free or commercial
- Links to mirrors of the download location
- Notes or other useful release information
- Installation and usage advice (if required)

See for Yourself: An Events Page

Figure 2-16 shows you a typical events page.

Figure 2-16. The above shows an example of a list of site events.

Try It Yourself: What to Include on the Events Page

You can create an effective events page by including the following information:

- The name of the event that is occurring
- The location and time of a specific event
- The individuals involved and event details
- Information on previously successful events
- Links to blog articles that relate directly to the events listed on the page

See for Yourself: A FAQ

Figure 2-17 shows you a typical FAQ page.

Figure 2-17. This page shows a list of frequently asked questions (FAQ) .

Try It Yourself: What to Include on Your FAQ

You can create an effective FAQ page by including the following information:

- Well-categorized questions that you get asked regularly
- Strong and clear answers to the questions you list
- Questions that enable you to provide other useful information

See for Yourself: A Features Page

Figure 2-18 shows you a typical features page.

Figure 2-18. The page shows a list of product features.

Try It Yourself: What to Include on the Features Page

You can create an effective features page by including the following information:

- Details about your product or service
- Unique selling points for promotion
- Comparisons with other services
- Bullet lists that describe the product's functions
- Why people should use your offerings

See for Yourself: a Gallery

Figure 2-19 shows you a typical gallery page.

Figure 2-19. This figure shows an image gallery.

Try It Yourself: What to Include on the Gallery

You can create an effective gallery page by including the following information:

- Categories that separate images and multimedia
- Thumbnails and links to full-size images
- Media that you show without playing automatically
- Captions for each item in the gallery

See for Yourself: A History Page

Figure 2-20 shows you a typical history page.

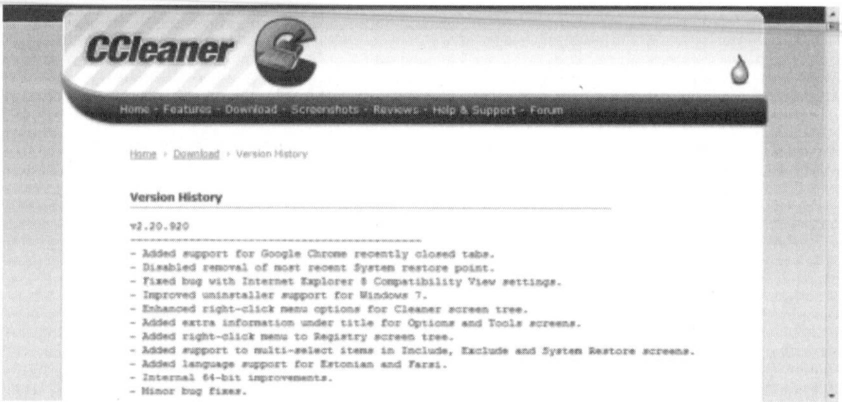

Figure 2-20. The figure shows a history document.

Try It Yourself: What to Include on the History Page

You can create an effective history page by including the following information:

- The length of time the site has been running
- Details about site improvements over time
- Site growth and progress information
- Useful statistics and charts (if required)
- Information about any planned improvements

See for Yourself: A Labs Page

Figure 2-21 shows you a typical labs page.

Figure 2-21. This figure shows an example of an experimental lab page.

Try It Yourself: What to Include on the Labs Page

You can create an effective labs page by including the following information:

- Details about what you are working on
- Fun, interesting, or new projects going on
- Whether people can test or see your work
- Any expectations visitors should have
- Details about the project-completion dates

See for Yourself: A Links Page

Figure 2-22 shows you a typical links page.

Figure 2-22. The figure shows a list of useful site links.

Try It Yourself: What to Include on the Links page (Non-site Related Links)

You can create an effective links page by including the following information:

- Any websites you recommend visiting
- Links to the sites of friends and associates
- Details about other sites you might own
- A link to the community page
- A list of sites you subscribe to or visit regularly

See for Yourself: A Members Area

Figure 2-23 shows you a typical members-area page.

Figure 2-23. The above shows an example of a members only section.

Try it Yourself: What to Include on the Members Area

You can create an effective members-area page by including the following information:

- A login form to verify a user's identity
- Special features for members only
- Advanced access to new material
- A list of members-only services and tools
- Registration codes and member profiles

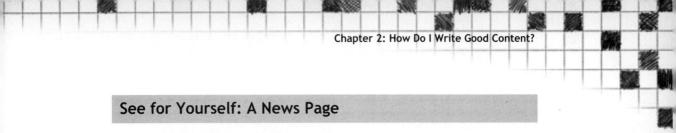

See for Yourself: A News Page

Figure 2-24 shows you a typical news page.

Figure 2-24. This figure shows an example of a news desk.

Try It Yourself: What to Include on the News Page

You can create an effective news page by including the following information:

- Anything that you want to report on
- Links to any RSS feeds available
- Announcements for your site
- Any events occurring on the site

See for Yourself: An Overview Page

Figure 2-25 shows you a typical overview page.

Figure 2-25. The example shows the front page of a site.

Try It Yourself: What to Include on the Overview Page

You can create an effective overview page by including the following information:

- All front page content
- An explanation of your site's purpose
- The most recent blog posts
- Links to common site areas
- Basic contact information
- Other important details

See for Yourself: A Portfolio Page

Figure 2-26 shows you a typical portfolio page.

Figure 2-26. This page shows an example of a freelance work portfolio.

Try It Yourself: What to Include on the Portfolio

You can create an effective portfolio page by including the following information:

- New projects you've undertaken, with links to the finished work
- Information on when the specific work was undertaken
- A list of ongoing projects and projects under construction

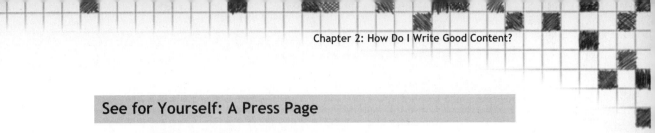

See for Yourself: A Press Page

Figure 2-27 shows you a typical press page.

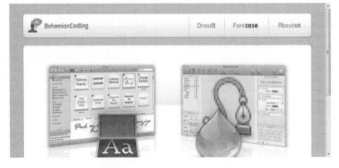

Figure 2-27. This figure shows an example of a press page.

Try It Yourself: What to Include on the Press Page

You can create an effective press page by including the following information:

- Awards you have won from other sites
- Links or excerpts from professional reviews your site has received
- Feedback from visitors about projects and services
- Details about linking to your site externally
- Press releases or promotional materials

See for Yourself: A Projects Page

Figure 2-28 shows you a typical projects page.

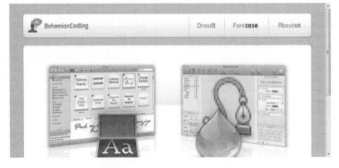

Figure 2-28. This figure shows an example of a product-listing page.

Try It Yourself: What to Include on the Projects Page

You can create an effective projects page by including the following information:

- The name of the project you're providing information about
- A brief description of the project
- Costs (including discounts and tax)
- Links to dedicated project pages

See for Yourself: A Resource Page

Figure 2-29 shows you a typical resource page.

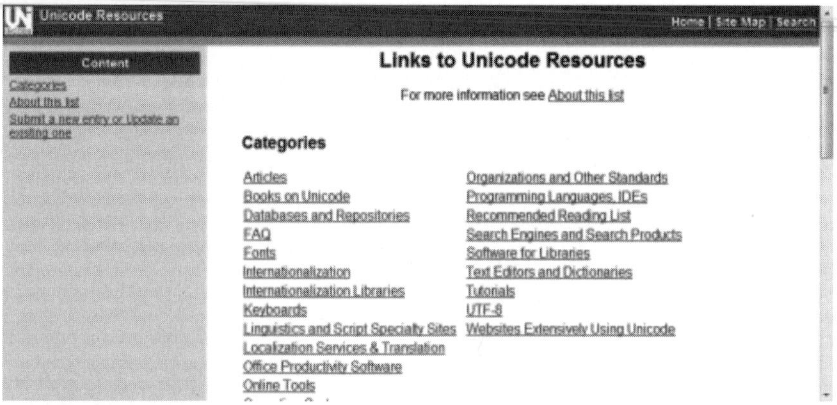

Figure 2-29. This figure shows a list of useful resources.

Try It Yourself: What to Include on the Resources Page

You can create an effective resources page by including the following information:

- Links to and information about third-party products and services
- Links to books or multimedia you have produced
- Any orphaned links or pages that aren't referenced elsewhere

See for Yourself: A Resume Page

Figure 2-30 shows you a typical resume page.

Figure 2-30. This figure shows an example of an online-digital resume.

Try It Yourself: What to Include on the Resume Page

You can create an effective resume page by including the following information:

- Who are you and what your job title is
- How you can serve your visitors
- Any hobbies and interests you have
- Your qualifications or experience
- Any relevant employment history

See for Yourself: A Services Page

Figure 2-31 shows you a typical services page.

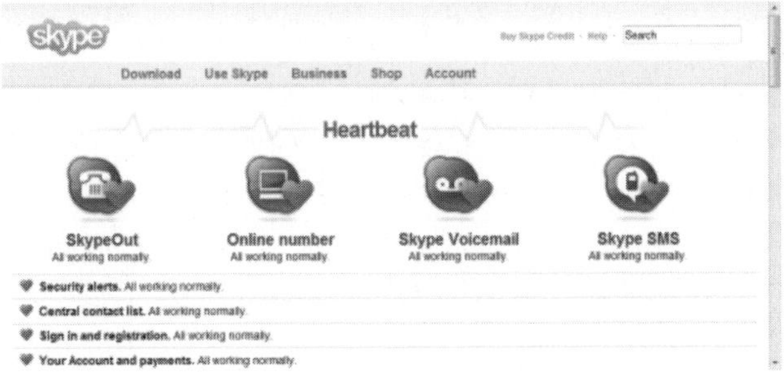

Figure 2-31. The page shows a list of services and their status.

Try It Yourself: What to Include on the Services Page

You can create an effective services page by including the following information:

- A list of individual services you offer
- Details about your packaged components
- Comparisons of the products and services you sell
- An estimate or total price for the services offered
- What your customers can expect if they use your services

See for Yourself: A Subscriber Page

Figure 2-32 shows you a typical subscriber page.

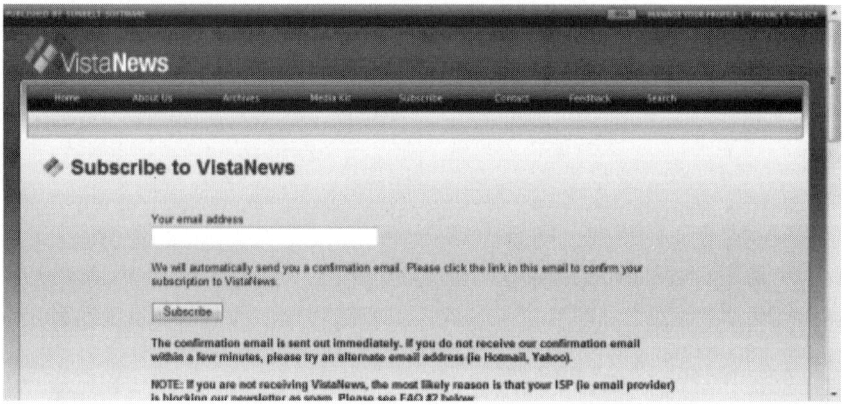

Figure 2-32. The above shows an example of a subscription area.

Try It Yourself: What to Include on the Subscriber Page

You can create an effective subscriber page by including the following information:

- Any feeds a visitor can subscribe to
- A link to any archived email newsletters you provide
- Details on how people can join and unsubscribe
- Any special software needed to subscribe
- A list of any podcasts or videocasts

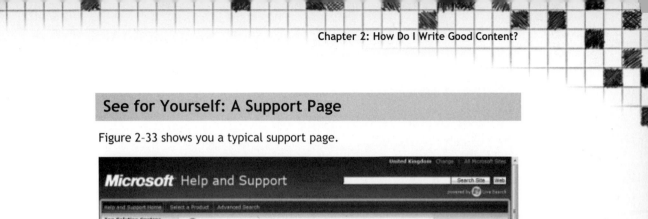

See for Yourself: A Support Page

Figure 2-33 shows you a typical support page.

Figure 2-33. This page shows an example of a technical-support section.

Try It Yourself: What to Include on the Support Page

You can create an effective support page by including the following information:

- Help documentation for a specific project
- A form to submit feature requests for your site or projects listed on it
- Bug reports for issues with the site
- Other related technical information

Now that you understand exactly what each page you have chosen should contain (except for pages that are unique to your site, such as information for a particular product or something not covered in my list of page types), the next step in the process is to begin writing the content for your pages. You can use my list to address some of the requirements for your written content. Next you will learn the basics of writing and what issues you should address, as well as some guidelines you must follow to ensure you create high-quality content.

> ## NotED
>
> *Following conventions in design is just as important as following conventions in content writing. While the examples provided give a basic guide to what you should be providing, it is essential that you try to give visitors what they expect. Information about design conventions is covered extensively later in the book, where I will detail what users expect from your design and how to keep them coming back!*

The Basics of Writing

You now have a basic understanding of the pages you want to include and the type of content you should think about including in your pages. Before you get down to putting pen to paper (or finger to keyboard), you need to ensure you follow some basic principles that can help you make sure your content is optimized for ease-of-reading. After all, a long-winded site that is full of typos, long and complicated technical jargon, and abused capital letters is enough to drive even the calmest of us to the brink of insanity! The following information is a good overview to the subject of what constitutes high-quality content. Heeding the information that follows will help you ensure that people will want to continue visiting your site to read what you have to say.

How to Write Effectively

What we need to do now is to start building pages. Begin by opening your word processor open of choice if isn't already open. (If you don't have one, check the appendix for some examples of word processors you might use.) Before you start going through the following list, you should probably put the book down and start writing content for each of the pages of your site. Note that you should restrict yourself to no more than a page's worth of content (perhaps two or three if you have a lot of images to include); once you finish this process, you can go through each of the best practices that follow and ensure that your content meets the requirements specified. Following these guides can help you ensure that your content is well structured and easy-to-read. Be creative in your writing and don't forget that you can use headings, bullets, and lists to format your text (but don't overuse them).

ExplainED

While you can choose fonts, sizes, colors, and styles (such as bold, italic, underline, or align), remember that when you paste the content into a code editor it will lose all of that formatting information (you might find it useful to play around with the text a bit, so you know how you want it to look upon completion).

If you have completed writing your content (and have a good amount of it), welcome back! I hope you had fun being creative. If you find it hard to come up with some content (knowing what people expect from the previous samples given), perhaps you can browse the Internet and take a look at your favorite sites to see how they put across their message. Next, you can easily reproduce what they say without copying them. You should now have some good, raw content that is ready to be put through the writing filter that follows to try and make it stand out better! Next, you need to run your pages through each of the steps that follow and use the tips to improve the general quality of your content. What you should end up with is something tweaked to perfection. By considering all of these steps, the edits you make to your content should really boost the overall level of what ends up on your site. Once you have read each section mentioned below, you need to put down the book (again), look over what you have written, and make the changes as required. The steps that follow form a simple but effective guide for improving your content. Good luck!

Spelling

Spelling is one of the most fundamental parts of what makes high-quality writing. The ability to put your thoughts across accurately in words enables other people to understand what you want to express. While different countries have their own rules on spelling (such as *color* in the U.S. vs. *colour* in the U.K.), you should always choose the spelling rules that best suit your target audience. While spelling can be tricky, most word processors and web editors include spell checkers, so you can quickly correct errors in your content to improve readability.

Grammar

Grammar is another key area of importance for readability and high-quality writing. While spelling looks at the formation and order of the letters that make up words, grammar focuses more on the order of readability and the use of punctuation. While grammar checkers exist in word processors, they sometimes have a higher error ratio because context plays a huge part in how a sentence should be structured.

Readability

People do not want to read content that leaves them confused or bewildered; the easier it is to brush through your content and pick up the main points, the better. The single biggest issue that can lead to poor readability occurs when sentences are too long. Many websites have huge paragraphs of text that cannot be digested at once. Readability can be improved by breaking up long sentences and offering lists (where appropriate) to show key points and highlighted information. Looking at your target audience is the best method of determining what is readable, as it can differ depending on the audience. As a general rule, many of us have short attention spans, especially on the Web, where we're used to reading shorter articles and varied amounts of text!

Structure

Most content follows a similar method of separating text using headings and images. The structure of your content will help readers distinguish what they want to read, as well as help them navigate through it. An example of poorly used structure occurs when content is split over multiple pages, forcing visitors to break their reading pattern. In extreme cases, readers might decide to look elsewhere for a site that gives the same information, without the need to keep loading new pages rather than scrolling naturally.

Layout

When laying out your design, you should take the use of color, size, spacing, and even the page position into account to ensure that the content is as easy to read as possible. This does not mean you should be using an insanely huge font size, but it does mean that you should determine what the most readable solution is for your site, especially as you want to encourage visitors to take notice of what you offer them.

Chunking

Chunking is the process of taking large pieces of information and grouping them into pieces of easier -to-read and understand blocks. This can include using bulleted or numbered lists; short subheadings; and the use of charts, graphs, and visual models to direct the user's attention. Chunking makes your content easier to read and can enable visitors to understand concepts quickly, but you shouldn't use it as a substitute for trying to keep the content free of technical jargon and overly complicated sentences.

Legibility

Try to keep your content easy to read. If you use colors that make the text appear faint in comparison to the background color (with little contrast), it can become almost impossible to read your content. Also, keep in mind that your readers might not have the same quality of vision as you, so don't make your font sizes too small.

Fluff Posting

Fluff posting is the act of writing content that doesn't add anything useful to a site; it's also synonymous with online forums and social-networking websites (quite possibly due to the amount of spam that exists). When you write your content, make sure to include only information that is necessary. No one wants to read pointless statements and endless jargon, so this comes down to trying to keep your content as interesting as possible.

Wasting Time

Wasting your visitors' time is one of the cardinal sins of producing content and dong this will often drive people away. When I speak about wasting people's time, I mean that you don't want to make them read through marketing talk or legal jargon before they can get to the information they want.

Reductionism

Reductionism is the act of reducing something to its simplest form. This rationale can be applied to web content by using the *50% reduction rule*. No matter how much content you have over a certain length, you should take what you have written and reduce it by a whopping 50%. This is possible to achieve by reducing the number of words needed to explain something. The 50% rule doesn't apply to every kind of document, though; legal information (for example) must retain its full depth and structure to ensure its integrity.

Iteration

Repeating yourself can happen when writing content. While you can use this technique to *drum* information into memory as a sign of importance, problems occur when repetition happens on a large scale. Read through your document and highlight any points where you have repeated yourself, determine if it is really necessary to restate your point, and if not, remove the additional reference(s) from the content entirely.

Complexity

Technical jargon: Geeks love it, but most of us hate it! Sites can contain words (or acronyms) only certain people would understand. Most people are of two minds about technical jargon because, as much as we hate it, the words were created to describe something that could not be explained otherwise. While technical terms are relevant because they correctly reference a subject, you should always provide a clear definition and meaning for such terms when you use them in your content.

Personal Bias

One psychological aspect of writing is accounting for any personal biases you might hold on a particular subject. While opinion pieces can benefit from expressing your viewpoint objectively, you should try to keep to the facts and not get personal. When people put across their opinions in a negative way, it can lead to online arguments called *flame wars* when they discuss controversial subjects. The key with personal biases is to know when your opinion is useful and adds to the discussion vs. when it gets in the way. Think before you type!

Empathy

You write sites for your readers; never forget this. If you want to convince people to use your site on a regular basis, you should always try to see things from the point of view of the people reading and connect with them emotionally. Try and picture yourself as first-time reader. How will people interpret what you say? Should you alter the way you write to help your audience understand you? How should the content be laid out to ensure that everyone will be able to enjoy the experience? You should ask yourself this same set of questions when it's time to implement your website's design.

Emotion

A key part of writing web content is to avoid creating content that feels dry and dull. Several factors can cause this, but what really makes text feel more involving and interesting is emotion. Leveraging the psychology of emotional triggers can help you achieve this goal because appearing friendly, quirky, funny, and entertaining can *break the ice* between you and your visitors. Essentially, you should inject a bit of yourself into what you write, so your enthusiasm for the content will leap off the page.

Context

Providing context for various scenarios can help people understand complicated pieces of information. For example you could explain that a search engine works like a phone directory (as it contains detailed, categorized listings of various places and where they are located). You should attempt to relate as much of your content as possible to examples your visitors will understand, so that people can empathize with your viewpoint.

Scanning

When you visit sites, you rarely read every single item on the page. People scan through the content of a site searching for key terms, images, conventions, or *landmarks* that can help them identify what they are looking for. People visit a site with the sole intent of finding information quickly; by scanning a page (which the human brain is very good at), people can identify what they need without having to read everything on the page. This is normally something that can be achieved naturally (and should not be inhibited), but problems can occur if the usability of a site is dramatically altered, making it harder to navigate.

Language

While English is a popular language and the majority of Internet users understand it, there are many who do not. As the site creator, it is your job to ensure that language needs of your visitors are met because people will simply abandon your site if they cannot understand what you say. The problem is that translating a site into different languages can be expensive (if you hire someone), and online translation services (such as Google Translate and Babelfish) lack accuracy when translating large amounts of text.

Free Will

Every person has the free will to choose whether he continues to view your site. If your content isn't engaging, easy to understand, and comprehensive, your visitors might go elsewhere; never forget that competition on the Web is fierce! Your content should reflect what people are looking for, and one of the best ways to achieve this is to keep your material relevant and up-to-date. Also, make sure that you talk only about subjects that you are entitled to hold an opinion on. For example: do not talk about medical advice if you are not qualified.

Plagiarism

One of the biggest crimes on the Web is the act of plagiarism or copyright theft. If you steal someone else's work, articles, images, multimedia, content, or anything else, and then claim it as your own, you not only violate the law, but you compromise the rest of your site's credibility. Never take someone else's articles and repost them on your site (although you can talk about what other people write in your own contributions or opinions). People want unique content and exclusive information; providing copied work will have consequences. For example, it can provoke distrust from readers, possible lawsuits from the content owner, and even get your site banned from search engines!

Conclusion

You have finally completed running your content through the writing-tips filter, so there is nothing more you need to add to your content! Everything discussed in this section is based on the idea that, when writing your content, you should focus on quality rather than quantity. While a quality article will undoubtedly take longer to write, the effort will show its worth in terms of the amount of visitors you are likely to receive in the future. Even if you do not provide any articles or offer other services such as software or online web applications, and even if the site is nothing more than a homepage for your business (rather than a personal blog, for example), making your content unique and worth reading will help you build your reputation, and people will be more likely to trust you (or respect what you offer) in the future. Before completing this chapter, let's take a quick look at the legal implications of creating original content and how you can protect what you produce online.

NotED

Some people make a good living rewriting content, especially with the purpose of making search engines give you a higher position in the index (PageRank). You will learn more about the process of search-engine optimization (SEO) when you're ready to market your site in Chapter 10.

Lorem Ipsum

So what should you do for places where you just don't have any content ready, and you won't be able to create it in time? Well, the standard method is to use

Latin text (see Figure 2-34). You might have come across sites on the Internet (especially templates for site designs that you can download or buy) that have strange text starting with the words, "*Lorem Ipsum.*" Text plays a vital role in the design of a site, so you can see how the style and structure of its sentences might affect the visual elements of your site. People who have no content to place on their site use what is known as *Lipsum*, or *dummy* text. Because you're writing your content before you implement your design, you don't need to rely on *Lipsum* text to achieve the feel of having something worth reading on the pages. Nor do you want to have *coming soon* plastered all over the design! However, you can use *Lipsum* text to fill in the gaps if you do have some sections of a site that you cannot produce content for before you complete the design. For example, you might do this if your content is dependent on some in-page functionality. Essentially, *Lipsum* text is the industry standard for marking imaginary content!

LinkED

It's easy to include some Lipsum *text on your own site; simply visit the site at* www.lipsum.com/ *and state how many words, lists, paragraphs, or bytes you require for the page. The site will generate some* Lipsum *text you can use.*

See for Yourself: Lorem Ipsum

Figure 2-34. Lorem ipsum dolor sit ametit's more than dummy text!

Lorem Ipsum has been used in writing and publishing as the industry standard for dummy text since the 1500s, when an unknown printer created a specimen book from scrambled type. After five centuries, it remains in popular use, and it has found a place on the Web for providing the same placeholder documentation that it has since being introduced centuries ago. *Lipsum* text can itself seem like random words just scattered in a sentence; however, it was discovered that the origin of *Lorem Ipsum* dates back to 45BC (making it more than 2,000 years old!) from a book on ethics by Cicero called, *The Extremes of Good and Evil*. Because *Lipsum* text has an even distribution of letters and words, yet also forms structured sentences, it makes sense to use it to get a feel for how content will appear within a site, rather than just using generic blocks of words such as "content here."

ExplainED

Dummy text such as Lipsum *is great for placing text in areas where the content doesn't exist yet; however, best practices that you try to place proper content into the design, if possible. This is especially true when you upload the site because you don't want Google to think your site is filled only with fluff.*

Cover Your Ass(ets)!

A common problem with the Internet as it stands is the issue of people stealing content. Copyright theft is big in the news (especially with digital media). And as someone who will be spending time creating and publishing content, art, and other media to your own site, you want to know that you will be covered as much as possible against people who want to take advantage of you. I'll list some methods you can use to license your creations, but you should always seek advice from and consult with a registered-legal professional to ensure you are as covered as possible in cases where your interests are affected by the law. For example you should seek a proper legal opinion if you offer products, goods, or services, and you make money from your site. So you the information that follows as a basic guide, but be aware that I do not intend it as legal advice or for you to use it as such; I am not a lawyer, and I cannot assist you beyond providing some basic tips I have gathered and used over the years.

Copyright

One of the fundamental ways you can protect your content is through copyright. The act of copyrighting protects creative works, ensuring that the producer of the work is entitled to a reasonable amount of protection to prevent people from claiming your works as their own. It also prevents the use of your creative works for uses that you do not consent to. In some cases, copyright gives more rights, such as the reasonable request to be accredited with the produced creative content when referenced elsewhere. In the field of web design, copyright is applicable to any written works (including content) and creative works (such as multimedia and images); however, copyright itself rarely covers the physical design of a site because, in the majority of cases, sites follow conventions and are similar enough in their appearance that you cannot protect the designs as unique works.

LinkED

For more information about the myths surrounding copyright and what your legal rights are in terms of what you have produced, see this useful site: http://www.templetons.com/brad/copymyths.html

In the majority of the world, copyright is automatically assigned to the author and/or publisher from the date of creation; however, this might be something you need to check the applicable laws your country. Some countries also allow the registering of copyrighted works with a place such as the copyright office; this can help strengthen the copyright because it provides proof of the date of creation, based on the time of submission. This can be useful if you ever have to back your claims in the pursuit of legal action against a violator of the copyright. While this is recommended, you could also print the document, mail it to yourself, and place it somewhere safe. As long as no one tampers with the date stamp provided by the post office, this can serve as reasonable proof of the date of creation because it's backed up by an individual not associated with the creator of the works (known as a "poor man's" copyright). This act is accepted in quite a few countries, but it's not as effective as relying on an official copyright registration.

Generally speaking, most people provide a statement of copyright on the site, so no others can claim they were unaware of the copyright in effect. Basically, providing a message in your document that says the site is copyrighted gives the visitor no excuses for violating the ownership of the material.

It strengthens your defense even further against potential abusers because it removes the excuse of ignorance on the part of such abusers.

Try It Yourself: Copyright Statement

When you produce your site, you will want to include a brief statement of copyright in the bottom of the page (typically as part of the footer). You can change the required elements of this statement to suit your site's needs:

© Copyright *Year, Name*. All rights reserved.

Remember that the copyright statement should appear by default on every page of your site. You replace *Year* with the year of the site's creation and place your name or brand in the appropriate section, *Name*. By including the copyright statement at the bottom of each page, you remove the excuse of claiming ignorance when stealing your content. In other words, they lose the ability to argue that they were not aware a copyright existed!).

While you can include a copyright statement that explains the details of the copyright (if you want to make it explicit), most people tend to provide only the notification and let the content speak for itself. Usually, a copyright statement appears in terms-of-service documents.

Impressum

Impressum applies in the majority of cases only to German websites, if you do come from Germany, and you produce a site, you need to include an *Impressum* page on your site that gives details about your site (see Figure 2-35). It is considered a legal requirement for German site builders to include details about their name, address, telephone number and email (businesses might also provide VAT or trade-registry numbers). This gives rise to privacy concerns because you're required to make so much public information available; however, if you live in Germany, the law requires you to provide an *Impressum* page that contains these details, notwithstanding how controversial it is to require this kind of information is for personal sites). Websites in the UK, USA, and other countries don't need to give such information, except in cases where it is a site for an LTD company or PLC (basically an official business), in which case you need to disclose effectively the same information.

Figure 2-35. It is a legal requirement to include an Impressum page for all German sites.

LinkED

If you want to see an example of what you need to include for German websites, the KDE site has a perfect example of an Impressum *document at* www.kde.org/contact/impressum.php.

Creative Commons

Sometimes you might want to allow your visitors to share certain (or even all) parts of your site's content, especially if you provide public information. Until a few years ago, doing something like this required a lengthy terms-of-service agreement (of dubious legality because such notices were usually written by the site owner rather than a lawyer) or that you give up your copyright claim and put the information into the public domain. A relatively new system of licensing your copyright called *Creative Commons* was produced to allow you to license your content, so that other people could make use of the information, but with certain conditions that you define to ensure your work is only used and shared in a way of that you approve of (see Figure 2-36). A wizard on the organization's site asks you a few questions to determine what kind of license you require and what conditions should be expressed within the license agreement. The Creative Commons scheme has become extremely popular, and it is recognized worldwide as a legal license that content publishers can use to protect their content to the extent they feel is necessary.

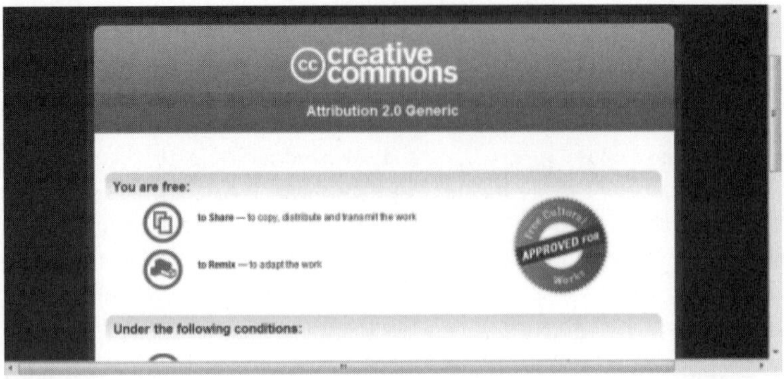

Figure 2-36. Creative Commons has become the rock star of content licensing.

LinkED

To learn more about what Creative Commons is and to see some video tutorials explaining what benefits the scheme can offer you, visit the following site: http://creativecommons.org/about/what-is-cc

Try It Yourself: License Content Using CC

You can use the Creative Commons wizard to produce a custom license that explains to your visitors what their rights are. The process is simple, free, and you are given the code to insert at the bottom of your site in place of the usual copyright message. Once you start writing the code for your site, you can find the tool that produces this code at http://creativecommons.org/license/.

Dealing with Theft

Let's assume you have produced the perfect content for your site, and you find that someone has pilfered it, even though you added a copyright notice, terms of service agreement, and a Creative Commons license for the site design itself. What can you do about it? Most cases of copyright infringements where someone takes your content and puts it on her own site without permission don't need to go to court or be pursued with the aid of a lawyer. Before you start phoning the cops and your legal advisor to chase the perpetrator out of the country with a pitch fork and a chainsaw, you should calmly deal with the issue by taking the following steps:

1. Save a copy of the offending pages for evidence, in case you need to take additional action. Also, make sure that you find some witnesses to see the offending material in case you need to take additional action. This paper trail of evidence will be of vital importance if the case ever goes to court or if the offender tries to cover his tracks. Never seek revenge against the site owner, start harassing him, or try to damage his business or site to try and get them back at him. This will reflect poorly on you, and it can become a legal issue of its own you should always take action in a calm, effective manner when trying to rectify disputes!

2. Send the offending site an email that explains it is using your content without permission and to remove it instantly. Again, you need to write this message calmly and professionally; you want to appeal to the better nature of the site's owner. In the majority of cases, sending this friendly email will get the copied content removed, and you might be able to strike a deal with the site to link back to the original article or to pay a license fee if the offending site doesn't want to remove the content from the site. Remember that people might not even be aware that the content is copyrighted, and you should always give them the opportunity to explain their actions.

3. If after 24 – 48 hours you do not receive a response, or the site's operator responds by exclaiming he won't remove the offending material for any reason (offenders will often misquote the law, proclaim you are harassing them, lie, or do other things to avoid responsibility—remember that ignorance of the law does not work as an excuse), you should step up to the next stage in the process, which is to file a cease-and-desist letter that basically explains that if they don't immediately remove the offending material, you will begin taking action through international copyright legislation. This aim of this stage is to give the respondent one last chance to do the right thing before you start pursuing heavier action.

4. After five days, if you do not receive a response or the site's operator tells you he won't remove the content, the next step to take is to file what is known as a *DCMA takedown notice*. Essentially, this is a letter (or email) that points out that you are the copyright holder; indicates where the infringing material is; states that the document is a takedown notice; and explains that if reasonable action isn't taken, you will pursue the matter through legal action. This letter or email also shows proof that you are the owner of the content. Your best way to prove this is by sharing your registration with the US copyright

office, but the Internet Archive (see Chapter 1) also serves as a reliable timestamp as a third-party source that proves your site's origin and date. Finally, your letter or email should mention that the site itself is violating the law by keeping the information you own on the site without permission.

5. If the site's operators still refuse to assist you, the next step is to take the DMCA takedown notice to Google and other search engines, which have a zero-tolerance policy for copyright violators. In many cases, these search engines will remove that site from search listings (which will encourage the site owner to remove the content or risk being banned from search results). You could also file the notice to the site's host (if you know this information), and the host will in many cases suspend or disable the site until the offending content is removed.

6. Finally, if you follow through on all these steps, which can take a week or two to see all the way through, and the content still remains, then it's time to get some legal advice about whether it would be worth taking legal action against the site owner. You might be able to claim compensation for the theft, have the site taken down completely, or even have the offender gain a criminal record if they are exceptionally malicious towards respecting the rights you have over your content and articles.

In the majority of cases, contacting a site owner about the issue in a friendly manner is enough to prompt the site owner to remove the offending content; often, it is not the site owner, but one of his users that uploads the stolen content). Offending the owner and starting a fight will do no one any good in the long run. Even many of the most stubborn violators will remove content after a DMCA takedown notice has been issued; however, taking legal action might be the only way to influence people who knowingly break the law into removing the offending material. Unfortunately, this can be expensive and lengthy to pursue, and ultimately it might not be worth the hassle and stress of seeing this option through.

LinkED

Google has an excellent guide to filing a DMCA takedown notice at www.google.com/dmca.html. *This document is aimed primarily at explaining how to report offending material to Google, so it can be delisted from the search engine. You can alter this document to suit your own needs.*

Summary

In this chapter, you learned about the different sorts of content that you can add to a site; you learned how to pick which pages you require for your site; and you learned what information your visitors will expect to find on your site, as well as some basic rules every content writer should understand for improving the quality of her work. You also learned about the different methods you can use to protect your content when it becomes available to the public. In the next chapter, you will move from producing high-quality content to coding the site and getting it published on the Internet. You will learn to take the content you have produced and mark it up in such a way that every web browser around the world can take advantage of it. Learning to produce code might sound like a daunting process, but if you take things one step at a time (which is exactly what you will learn to do), you should quickly get used to the idea of building a site and seeing it work at a basic level.

Chapter Checklist

The following things should be accomplished before leaving this chapter:

- Choose the pages you want your site to include from the list of examples.
- Produce high-quality, text-based content while following the rules of design.
- Protect your site's content by selecting the appropriate license your site requires.

Questions and Answers

Q: Can I use other people's content on my site?

A: Generally speaking, it's best to avoid using other people's content, except in cases where you quote or otherwise reference the work from another site. Under copyright law, there is a clause for fair use that allows you to take a text excerpt to reference or use; however, in any case where you want to repost a substantial amount of content (such as more than 10% of an article), you should gain the written permission from the content's author or publisher (as appropriate) to use it. While you do have certain rights in terms of producing content based on the works of others, you should intend to make your content as fresh and original as possible. This can help you avoid any unflattering comparisons that might be drawn (as a direct rip-off from someone else's work). The act of integrating pieces of information into a fresh, new, and unique piece is commonly called a mashup.

Q: How does user-submitted content affect copyright?

A: Whenever someone posts content to your site, she gives you a non-exclusive (unless stated otherwise) right to display the work on your site for the purpose of public (or private) consumption. In the majority of cases, permission cannot be revoked once someone grants it (unless something has happened to violate the original agreement); however, in all cases, copyright is maintained and owned by the person who produced the work. Essentially, the site can display the information, but it doesn't take ownership of the copyright unless expressly permitted by the author / creator of the content in question.

Q: What do I do when I run out of ideas for content?

A: The worst thing that can happen is you hit a wall and realize that you have no fresh ideas left for your content. The best way to find fresh ideas is to follow the same principles you used in the creativity chapter and research what you want to talk about (or at least the subject you want to cover). You can then create your own content and discussions, based on what has been mentioned on other sites. You can also share your own opinion and perspective on a topic. For example, all of the bullet points that cover what people expect in different sections of a site are based on conventions used across the Internet. Following those general principles can help re-inspire you to create the content your site needs.

Where You Are Now

By the end of this chapter you should have the following:

- A series of high-quality documents ready to publish
- Plenty of ideas for pages to include in your first site
- Enough information to deal with any content thieves

How Should I Start Coding My Site?

The time has come to build your first website. Excited? If you've skipped straight here to dive in and see how tough it's going to be, then read on and use some dummy content for now. Once you you've made your first page (or you know you can do it), then head back to the start of the book and get your real content worked out before you get too far into the coding. It will help you tremendously to get the content down first—trust me on this!

If you've been following the book through and trying the exercises described, then you now have plenty of ideas stored in the ideas pad and a ton of well-written content from the first two chapters ready to be placed on the Web. You should be feeling excited at this stage, as you can now take all of these materials you have produced and put them into a format that others can viewed in a Web browser. Once you have your hosting and domain set up (which you'll learn how to do in Chapter 4), you'll be able to put your site online for the world to see. But let's not get ahead of ourselves. The first thing you need to do is come to grips with the idea of what code is and how you can take advantage of it to assemble the basic elements of your site. You'll spend this chapter looking at the structure of your brand new site; the end result probably won't look very pretty, but we will be adding plenty of style and imagery later on in the book so don't worry about the visuals for now.

In this chapter, I'll cover the following topics:

- What code and HTML are and how they affect your site
- The semantics and standards of web design that you should follow
- Constructing the initial pages (the template) of your website

Back to Basics

Before you start building your first website, you need to familiarize yourself with a few of the basics involved, so that you know exactly what is being discussed in this chapter! You might encounter a lot of strange terms that you you've never come across before that people use to describe the process of building a site; so let's spend a little bit of time covering the ones that you're most likely to encounter. This will help you understand how the Web works behind the scenes. In the sections that follow, you'll learn what code is and the different kinds of code that will impact you. Then you'll take a look at what you need to do before you can create the first page of your site, as well as what you need to avoid doing. Of course, I know you are eager to get building something, so I'll try to keep this section as simple and easy to follow as possible.

Under the Hood

When you look at a site inside your browser, you probably don't put much thought into how the cogs work behind the scenes. Web browsers are built to view sites. That's what they do. They do this by examining how the site is coded (which you'll learn about next) and then interpret that code to display the site on your screen. If you have ever used a product such as Microsoft Word, you know that you can apply formatting to a document, such as changing font sizes, italics, and so on, and the document will remember those settings when you save it and open it up again. From that point on, no matter who opens the file and no matter what computer the file is opened on, these formatting will always appear in the document. Word stores these formatting settings in the file, and it knows how it should display that formatting when the file is opened. Documents for the Web work the same way: they contain special formatting information that lets the browser understand how you intend the page to look, and the browser interprets your commands to reproduce your vision on the screen.

What Is Code?

In terms of the Web, code basically refers to the invisible instructions that you give to the browser to make sure it formats your content correctly. When you open a web page in your browser, you don't see those instructions, but the results of them. In fact, you can see the code instructions behind any site if you want to—you'll learn how to do this later in the book. For now, let's take a look at a single line of code. It won't mean much to you at the moment, but this seemingly random assortment of words and characters means a great deal to your web browser:

```
<p>Hello to all who read this paragraph!</p>
```

If you like, you can try typing this code in now. To do that, you need to open a text editor on your computer. If you're on a Windows machine, this will most likely be Notepad; if you're on a Mac, this will probably be TextEdit. Of course, you're also free to use another text editor or development tool that lets you write code for your site. You can find the appropriate application on your computer by typing its name into your system search box. In Windows, you can find this in the Start menu; on a Mac, you should use Spotlight to search for the file.

Once you have your text editor (or chosen coding tool) open, type in the preceding line of code exactly as it appears, including all of the strange slashes and arrows. Once you do that, you need to save the file with the appropriate file extension. The extension is the suffix at the end of a filename that tells the computer what of file it is. Click *File* ➤ *Save As*, enter `TestPage.html` as the filename, and then save it somewhere easy to find, such as on your desktop or in your documents folder. Double-click the file, and it should open in your default web browser with a page that shows something similar to what you see in Figure 3-1.

Hello to all who read this paragraph!

Figure 3-1. Check it out: that funny combination of characters before and after the text does something!

Those two p's on either side of the text in the code make up the *element*—in this case, they comprise the paragraph element. They tell a web browser that you want to display a new paragraph of text, including where that paragraph begins ends. When a browser reads this code, it understands what the element means and displays the results. See, it's simple!

You'll learn how code is written in much more detail later in this chapter. But now, let's take a look at how you can view code from within the browser to see how a site is created (once you are accustomed to working with code, you will be able to get ideas and tips by examining the work of others). Fortunately, viewing the code (or source code, as it is more commonly known) is easy. Most web browsers display source code in a special viewer. To see the code, you should be able to right-click the page and select the *View source* context-menu option (see Figure 3-2); this option is usually available under the *View* menu of your web browser as well, so it's fairly easy to locate, once the code has loaded. You can take a good look through the code your browser displays, but much of it will probably look like nonsense to you; however, this code will make sense when you spend a bit of time getting to know and understand it.

Try It Yourself: Viewing Source Code

No matter what site you visit, you can view its source code. Open up a few of your favorite sites in your browser and take a look at the source code using the instructions given earlier. The details of it will be a mystery to you still, but you should recognize the basic format of an element wrapped around the site's information (similar to the example you created using `TestPage.html`). Now that you have an idea about what code is and how to find it, you need to know how to read it (after all, as with learning any language, understanding what you see is imperative).

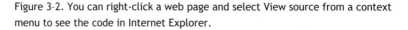

Figure 3-2. You can right-click a web page and select View source from a context menu to see the code in Internet Explorer.

Elements, Tags, and Attributes

Let's take a look at the code language you will use to create the basic structure of your site, which is commonly called *HTML* (Hypertext Markup Language). The three main things that make up those invisible instructions that browsers use to display your content are known as elements, tags, and attributes.

The elements are the central component you'll come across when examining source code. These aren't elements such as fire and water, or the sort you'll find on a periodic table of elements; rather, HTML has its own list of naming conventions that explain the contents held within. For example, img is the element that means *image*, p means *a paragraph of text*, ul means an *unordered list of items*, and a means *anchor*. The last element refers to *links* or *hyperlinks*: the things you click to navigate a site. You can find various different elements within HTML, and I'll introduce them to you one at a time later in this chapter; however, you will spend most of your time using the same elements over and over again, which will make remembering them easy.

So, elements tell the browser what it should do with your content, and they form the basic building blocks of HTML. HTML features two different types of elements, which are commonly known as *block elements* and *inline elements*. Inline elements live inside block-level elements to give added explanation. For example, you could add an anchor (linking to another page) to a few words within a paragraph of text. So an anchor is an inline element within the paragraph block element. Figure 3-3 shows a few more block and inline elements that you'll encounter.

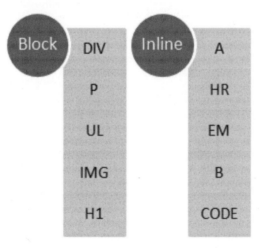

Figure 3-3. The element is a set of characters that have meaning to a web browser.

Tags are the containers that you place elements inside. When you viewed the source code earlier, you probably noticed that every instance of an element was easy to notice because it was enclosed within angular brackets (which are represented by the opening < and the closing > characters). In essence, the tags represent where the instructions to the browser start and end. For example, note how an element such as <p> (which, as you can see, has those brackets to enclose it) comes with another variant of itself at the end of the content that looks the same, except it has a forward slash (/) character that marks the end of the element. The end tag of a p element looks like this: </p>. This might sound like a lot to remember, but it's logical that you need to tell the browser both where to begin and end an instruction (see Figure 3-4). Going back to the word processor analogy, if you want to make some text italic, you need to highlight it first. The HTML tags are just like that highlighting; they tell your browser where the formatting should begin and end.

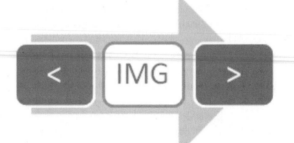

Figure 3-4. The image element is bracketed on each side by the < and > characters to produce a tag.

ExplainED

Later on, you'll notice that not all elements require a closing tag because they simply exist where you declare them. Images are a perfect example of this. You don't need to tell your browser where an image starts and finishes; it's enough to indicate where to insert an image.

You also need to understand what attributes are and how they work. Like elements, attributes are contained within tags, but where elements tell the browser what the content is (such as an image or paragraph), attributes allow you to apply properties to the element, such as telling a hyperlink where it needs to point to. Figure 3-5 shows an id attribute inside a div tag. I won't go into too much detail about it right now, but div is essentially a block-level element that you use to divide sections of your page.

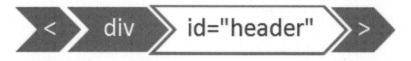

Figure 3-5. You can use an ID attribute to give elements an explicit name.

Attributes consist of two parts: a property (the attribute name) and a value. The attribute name is one of a set of special keywords that the browser understands how to interpret. For example, the id in Figure 3-5 means that you're providing an *ID*, or name, to this element that you can use to refer back to it later. The attribute name is followed by an equals character, and this is followed by the attribute value enclosed in quote marks. This tells the browser what value to apply to that property of that element. In the example discussed so far, you have a div element with an id of header. So later on in your code, you can refer back to this div element simply by using its name, header. This might not make sense to you at the moment, but with a bit more practice, it will become second nature to you. Also, you're not limited to having only one attribute reference per element. You can attach many unique attributes an element, separating them by spaces; that said, you cannot tell a hyperlink to point to two places at once (which would occur if you had two href attribute values):

```
<div id="mainSection" class="section">
```

Here, you set two attributes for your div element: id and class. You've already seen that the id attribute gives a unique name to an element; in this case, you use the class attribute to group elements together. So, you might have a number of div elements that all belong to the same "section" class, but each element has a unique id attribute. This comes in handy when you want to style your content, as you can set all members of the same class to a single style, and then apply additional styling to specifically named elements.

You can combine elements, tags, and attributes to represent a series of instructions to the web browser, giving you powerful control over how everything looks and feels within your site. The line of code that follows shows a paragraph of text that is represented to the browser using the p element (denoting a paragraph), as well as opening and closing tags that show where the paragraph begins and ends. This might have seemed an arcane mystery when you first saw this at the start of the chapter, but look again at this code, and everything should now make sense:

```
<p id="hello">Hello to all who read this paragraph!</p>
```

It is also worth mentioning at this stage that you can place certain elements within other elements, creating a hierarchy. The elements lower down the hierarchy inherit information from the elements above them. You can think of it like a family tree, where child elements inherit information from their parent elements. You can see an example of this in Figure 3-6.

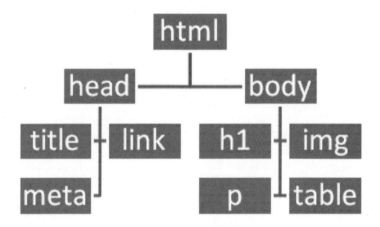

Figure 3-6. This figure shows the parent-child hierarchy that forms the backbone of HTML, where the head and body serve as the parents to many of the elements you will use.

The html element is the granddaddy of the family; in this case, it has two child elements: head and body. These two elements each have their own set of child elements, and so on. So the body element in your example is the parent of the img element, and the child of the html element. You can see the results of this if you look at the source code of an existing site. For future reference, you should be aware that not all elements can have others placed within them, and some that do allow this are limited as to which ones they can contain. This hierarchy of elements is vitally important when you must deal with subjects such as adding style to your website. Now is a good time to step back a bit and look at what this HTML language you've been learning about in this chapter really is, as well as where it fits in with the larger group of languages used on the Web.

Languages in Use

So far you've seen how to use HTML to define the structure of your site. For example, you saw how it could use elements, tags, and attributes to mark-up (describe) how you want to format your content. Thus, the p element enabled you to separate your content into paragraphs, and so on. Developers use three main markup languages on the Internet today, but it might surprise you to learn that they all work in a highly similar way; indeed, in some cases, you'd be hard-pressed to notice the differences between them! However, you will likely encounter situations where one approach is preferable to the others. Don't worry: You won't be learning three separate languages here; HTML alone is quite enough for us. However, it's good to be aware of all three main languages, so that you know what they are when you come across them later. These three languages are HTML, XML, and XHTML. Let's take a look at them in some more detail:

- **HTML:** Hypertext Markup Language is the most commonly used markup language on the Web, and it's the language most recommended for novice developers. It has support for a wide variety of elements that describe how your content should be expressed, and it's compatible with every desktop browser. The latest version (HTML 5) has recently appeared on the Web, but you should stick to the current version (HTML 4.01) until support for the new language is more widely adopted and accepted by today's existing popular Web browsers. It might seem strange to recommend that you don't learn the most recent version of the language, but that is because HTML 5 is still in the process of being created. Some parts of it are ready, and you'll find that some Web browsers already support them, but much of HTML 5 remains unfinished, much less implemented in the browsers your visitors would use. Don't worry, though, because the majority of the language is the same as the HTML 4.01 that you'll learn about in this book, so it won't take you long to switch once HTML 5 is finalized.

- **XML**: Extensible Markup Language is a general-purpose language for producing custom web (markup) languages. That might sound odd, but what it basically means is that where HTML has a predefined set of elements and attributes you can use, XML allows you to create your own elements and attributes. As long as you use the correct syntax (using angle brackets to denote tags, and so forth), you can largely do as you like. This will start to make more sense when you learn about styles later in this book. You'll see that essentially all HTML does is to split up your web page into different structural blocks. You'll see that it's the styling language that tells a browser what to do with those blocks. Given that's the case, some clever people reasoned: Why does it matter what those blocks are called? Shouldn't it be up to you to give them the name that makes the most sense to you? That freedom represents a powerful idea, and it leads to much more intuitive and readable code. For example, assume your site has descriptions of a bunch of vehicles. You might use HTML to set all of these descriptions in separate paragraph elements, enclosing them in p tags, which would make it hard to tell them apart. Similarly, you might use XML to create separate tags for cars, motorcycles, and boats; doing so lets you tell instantly which category each description falls under. Not only is it easier for you to tell them apart, but it's much easier for the browser to tell them apart. So you could instruct the browser that, when a visitor rolls his mouse over a description of a car, all other car descriptions on the page should light up. XML has seen some success in being used as an alternative to HTML, but its loose and free nature gives it a much steeper learning curve. With HTML, the browser, you, and I all know that a p tag means a new paragraph. With XML, you would need to describe manually what every single tag means. For this reason, this book will stick with HTML as its core language, although you'll learn to incorporate a little XML on your site later in Chapter 9.

- **XHTML**: Extensible Hypertext Markup Language is an evolution of HTML that takes the language in the direction of XML. Essentially, it is a way of combining HTML's structure and predefined set of elements with XML's ability to create custom own elements. It does this by slightly redefining the way you write HTML to bring it into line with the XML syntax. The problem with XHTML is that it never gained more than limited support, partly because of Internet Explorer's total lack of genuine support for the language and partly because XHTML made certain demands in how it requires you to implement things. Thus, XHTML has been discontinued, and in its place HTML5 will incorporate some of its core ideas. You'll probably see mention of XHTML on the

Web, which is why it's included here, but I don't recommend you spend time learning it now.

LinkED

HTML5 (still in production) has basic browser support and supports both HTML and XHTML modes, which mean the future of structural languages remains firmly in the camp of HTML. For more information, see this fun comic at www.smashingmagazine.com/2009/07/29/misunderstanding-markup-xhtml-2-comic-strip/.S

You can find many other markup derivatives of XML out there, such as MathML for describing mathematical notation, but you will only need to look into these under special circumstances. The low=level adoption of those other markup derivatives is a good reason not to use them on your site. For the vast majority of work on the Web, you will only ever need to know the HTML core language and have a little knowledge of the way XML works. The only things you'll need to know beyond HTML and XML are how to style your content (which you'll learn how to do in Chapter 5) and how to add some dynamic behavior (which you'll learn a bit about in Chapter 8).

Semantics and Standards

You know about the different markup languages, so you might think you're ready to begin coding your site in HTML and make it look wonderful to anyone across the world that visits it, right? Unfortunately, that's not the case (although things are improving). Web-browser manufacturers want you to use their browser for viewing sites, so they interpret the language in the way they think will give you the best experience. This might mean they change the way a certain element appears, or add their own new elements. In the early days of the Internet, this led to the *browser wars* where (for the most part) Microsoft Internet Explorer and Netscape Navigator fought for viewers' attention by releasing lots of new browser versions with new features that weren't part of existing web standards, trying to one-up each other. While this led to some great innovation and rapid progress in the capabilities of the Web, it also led to a lot of confusion, as you will learn in Chapter When developers created sites in the past, they did not know how their sites would look on the screens of different viewers because everything depended on which browser their viewers used. If a developer used a tag that worked in one browser but not another, the poor viewer might not have seen anything at all! As you can imagine, this wasn't a great situation.

Over the years, a series of standards were produced to help regulate how code is implemented within sites and displayed in web browsers. We haven't yet reached that point where our code is guaranteed to work the same in an all currently shipping browsers, but we're getting there, albeit slowly. What's important is that you follow these coding standards as closely as you can because it will reduce the chances that things might go wrong. You can find many organizations on the Internet, such as WaSP (The Web Standards Project), that promote the use of web standards to ensure that the needs of site developers are met by those in charge of setting the standards (think of them as an equal rights movement for the Web). As you're only now learning web design, the use of standards won't be such a big deal because you'll learn the right way of doing things from the start. For existing web designers and developers, though, adapting to such standards has been a big deal, and it has generated a great deal of (often heated) discussion in recent years.

See for Yourself: Web Standards Groups

The following organizations either produce or promote the use of standards that you see in use on the Web:

- World Wide Web Consortium (W3C): www.w3.org
- Internet Engineering Task Force (IETF): www.ietf.org
- International Organization for Standardization (ISO): www.iso.org
- ECMA International (ECMA): www.ecma-international.org/
- The Web Standards Project (WaSP): www.webstandards.org (see Figure 5-7)

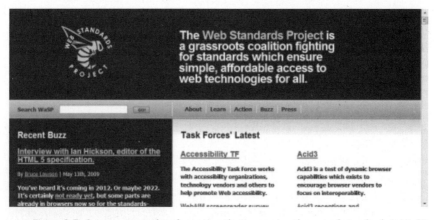

Figure 3-7. One group worthy of mention that promotes the use of standards is WaSP (Web Standards Project).

So what are web standards? Web standards are most often defined as the documents and specifications that provide guidance on how Web languages should be implemented and used. Such standards are usually written by the language authors themselves, so they are official, and often highly detailed. It is rare for a single author to come up with a language; rather, programming languages are often the result of the hard work of a dedicated team of developers, such as those of the World Wide Web Consortium (W3C). These standards act as rules you should follow, not least because breaking these standards can cause your site to not work as intended. All you need to know at this stage is that web standards exist to try and bring some order to how you present content on the web, as well as to ensure that languages such as HTML and CSS display in a consistent way across all browsers. Standards serve as guidelines for how to go about working with a language, which is a useful thing to know. Figure 3-8 shows some of the many technologies that the W3C has created for the Web.

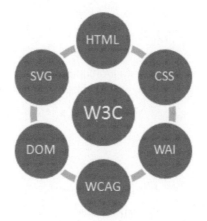

Figure 3-8. The W3C is responsible for many of the languages and standards in use on the Web today.

The W3C is most famous for creating HTML (what we use to structure content) and CSS (for styling and making things look nice). W3C is not the only standards body creating languages for the Web, though. For example, ECMA is also well known for a language called JavaScript that lets you add special effects to your sites.

Of course languages evolve over time. Thus, each new version of a language, such as "upgrading" HTML 4.01 to HTML5, adds new functionality and additional changes, which better meet the needs of modern developers (see Figure 3-9 for a list of the major versions of HTML over the years). Standards change with each new version, and you might find out in the future that a coding practice you follow is out-of-date and requires you to alter the way you go about building sites (which is why keeping your skills up to date is such an important task!). One problem with the evolution of standards and language versions is that most developers have to wait before they can implement any of the coolest new technology. Before you can put them to use, web browsers must adopt and implement the standards; otherwise, browsers will just ignore the strange, unknown elements. This presents an issue because not all users upgrade their browser, and designers and developers need to ensure any new cool stuff they use is covered with an alternative for older browsers. This issue applies especially to CSS, which you'll learn more about later in Chapter 5.

ExplainED

You can find plenty of languages with strange acronyms and various versions of each, but the content of this book has been written under the assumption that you're using a single language (and version) to make things easier.

Figure 3-9. HTML has evolved significantly over the course of various versions through the years.

There's another important aspect to understanding web standards: semantics. While standards define how the language works, semantics focus on the way in which you write each the language. Using the right element for the right job, rather than just using any element in the toolbox to get the task done, is important for ensuring that both search engines and browsers know what they are dealing with.

ExplainED

The overuse and abuse of certain elements and attributes in preference of using more semantically meaningful versions has been given nicknames to act as a friendly warning to use everything in moderation and for the right reasons. Div *overuse is known commonly as* divitis, span *overuse is known as* spanmania, *and* class *overuse is known as* classitis! *Pretty funny, isn't it?*

Of course, each language has its own rules and ways of putting across information, which you'll learn more about later in this book. More loosely, semantics can also apply to the way in which you express or display your code, such as how you choose to separate the code using new lines and tabbed indenting. Of course, how you lay out your code is up to you—you don't really need to order the code you have written in a certain way—but how you do this can affect how easy it is for someone else to read or amend your code, should that be necessary. Regardless, everything should be fine as long as the code is good, and you follow the rules.

Tips and Tricks: General Semantics

When you develop your site, you want to ensure that everything is put together with care. The following tips can help you reduce the amount of errors you receive when using the various web-related languages.

1. You should remember that code produced in HTML, CSS, JavaScript, and many other web languages rely on US English spelling for their syntax; therefore, if you come from another country (such as the UK), *colour* is spelled as *color*! This might seem confusing if you do not use American English regularly, but you will soon get used to the differences.

2. When writing code, you should try to use lowercase characters whenever possible, as code is often case sensitive and the difference between a and A can result in errors.

3. This may not affect you, but some individuals choose to improve the readability of their code by separating it using extra tab indents and spacing. This can make your code easier to understand and maintain, but it is not required, and it can increase page-file sizes.

While official language specifications are fantastic sources of information about a language, they are quite long and complicated, and this is why books (such as the one you are reading) exist: to take all that jargon and crazy talk and put it into a form that "normal" people can understand. When you are comfortable with a language, it's worth taking a look at the specification for it (available for free online). Reviewing its specification can help you learn a lot more about a language than what you will find in a book for beginners; however, you need a basic understanding of the language before you can glean much from the specification.

Your Checklist

- Now that you understand the basics of how HTML works, you can start applying it to your own site and building your first page. The first step is to decide what software you want to use to write the code. After that, you will create the folders and files required for the pages you will produce. You'll also learn about best practices when coding, including what you should try to avoid, so you can ensure your site will work as quickly and efficiently as possible. The checklist that follows in the next section will help you get organized, so you can start learning HTML with a minimum of fuss and confusion.

Editing Software

In web design and development, you can use three types of products to build and produce your first site. Of course, you only need to use one of them, but you should have some idea of the benefits and drawbacks of all of them. This list compares the various options available to you; afterward, you'll learn additional details that will help you choose the right approach for you.

- **WYSIWYG**: These are basically visual editors. Common examples of this type of software include Adobe Dreamweaver and Microsoft Expression Web / FrontPage. These editors allow you to drag-and-drop stuff around the screen, performing all of the hard code work for you! WYSIWYG stands for What You See Is What You Get. In theory, this sounds like a great plan (who doesn't want to make things easier?); in practice, such editors don't produce good code, and they don't teach you how sites actually work. You won't be able to dip quickly into the code to change the way something looks because you won't know how the language works or how to change it. By picking up this book (and getting this far through it), you've already made a critical, valuable decision: you want to build your site from scratch and to maintain complete control over it. Thus, I'll strike WYSIWYG editors from the list of potential software products to use.

- **IDE / Code**: IDEs (Integrated Development Environments) serve as a great choices for a code editor. They are fully fledged pieces of software that exist for people who work with code on a daily basis, and they offer a huge variety of features in general. For example, common, useful features include syntax highlighting (which color coordinates your code), tabbed browsing (for switching between files), and line numbering (to help you find those pesky errors). Generally, this kind of tool is a text editor that incorporates lots of gadgets aimed at improving your productivity. Examples of text editors include Notepad++ on Windows and BBEdit on a Mac).

- **Plain text**: Microsoft Notepad and Apple TextEdit are extremely basic text editors, but they are still worthy contenders. Every computer has a basic, built-in text editor, and it is quite possible to use such a text editor to create your site. You produce all sites by entering text, so products like Notepad and TextEdit allow you to get started without having to download or purchase anything, although they lack some of the cooler features you typically find in dedicated IDEs.

ExplainED

If you want to use a WYSIWYG editor such as Adobe Dreamweaver, I highly recommended that you avoid using the visual side of the product and use only its code-editing window; otherwise, the code it generates for you could make it harder for you to follow along with this book, not least because those types of editors have a bad habit of using semantically incorrect and badly formed code.

Whether you use Notepad, Dreamweaver, Notepad++ (see Figure 3-10) or something else entirely, you should pick your tool well because it will be your base of operations for the entirety of your project. This book includes a list of recommended code editors in Appendix B; you can use this list as a guide for finding a code editor that fits your needs and preferences. And don't worry: the list includes some good free options! Note that the purpose of this book is to teach you how to write the code for your site, rather than to use a piece of software. You will be typing your code by hand when following through the examples in this book; because this is the best way to become experienced enough to deal with any issues you might come across in the future. Also, coding it yourself might give you a warm and fuzzy feeling inside because you'll know that you produced everything on the site!

Try It Yourself: Install Your Editor

If you haven't done so already, please download and install your preferred editor, so it's ready to use. Each product will have a different installer, and it will come with instructions on how to use it. It might be wise to play around with your editor a little and customize it to suit your tastes because it's something you will use for a significant amount of time. It also stands to reason that you should read any manuals that come with the products you choose/ this will help you can understand better all the things you can accomplish from with a product.

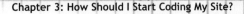

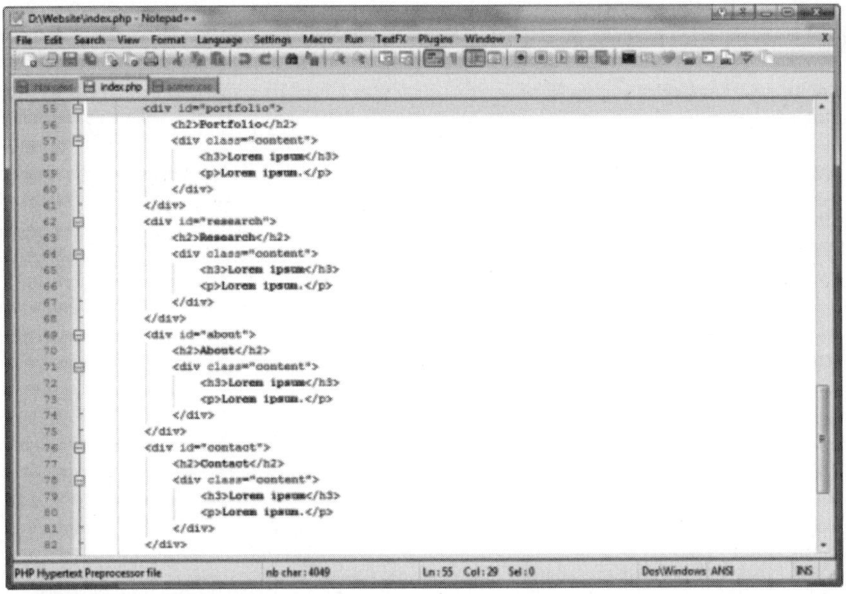

Figure 3-10. Notepad++ is a perfect example of a high quality (yet free) code editor.

Folders and Files

Next, you need to create the folders and files you will require for the entirety of your project. I'll jump ahead slightly in the chapter perspective at this point and recommend some folder names for you to produce. This will help ensure that you will have the required storage locations for all the files that that you'll end up producing for your site (don't worry if you are slightly puzzled at the reasoning behind adding these folders right now). First, you need to decide where you want to store all of your files. Some people like having a folder on the desktop; others like using the default OS folders; and still others like to store their files all over the place! For the purpose of consistency, it's probably best that you either name the created folder website or something else that you will remember over time. Once you create the folder, you will want to open it and create some folders inside it for each of the elements your site will include (you will learn more about this momentarily). The reasoning behind this approach: Your main folder will act as the *root directory*, which is essentially the place where your site will default to, and you want the structure within this folder to mirror what it will be on the site.

133

Try It Yourself: Creating the Folders

You should create the following set of folders to store all of the files you'll need for your site (see Figure 3-11):

- **style**: This folder will store your site's style sheets, which you'll learn more about later in Chapter 5. These are primarily files for defining your site's visual look-and-feel. If you don't implement your style well, your site will essentially be a dull (but well structured!) list of information.

- **images**: Of course, every website needs a few good images to spice things up. Many different formats for images exist on the Web (again, you'll learn more about this later in the book); for the moment, it's enough to create folder, where you will keep your images grouped together. This will make easier for you to track and link to your site's images.

- **scripts**: Once you build your site's structure around its content and beautify it by applying the appropriate style, you will look at JavaScript and consider how it might add some dynamic behavior to your site. You will use this folder to store any scripts you produce, as well as any existing scripts or frameworks you will use on your site.

- **feeds**: In Chapter 9, you will take learn about creating syndication feeds for your site. RSS and Atom feeds exist all over the Web; these enable people to subscribe to your site and be notified when you add new content. Most blogs have feeds, so it stands to reason that you should, too!

- **misc**: This folder is for any files that don't fit into any of the other folders; of course, you will end up with a few files that don't fit comfortably anywhere else. You'll find it useful to have a folder where you can store all your site's odd bits and pieces, so you know where they are when you need them.

Figure 3-11. Creating the right set of folders you'll need for your site is essential to keeping your site's files organized.

NotED

Some of the files that will end up in the misc *folder include Favicons (icons that appear in the address bar) and RDF files that include META data and XML files, such as OpenSearch (assuming you choose to use them). You'll learn more about these at various points throughout the book.*

You've created the folders you require, which means you have almost everything you need to start building the site. What we need to do now is create the main HTML file that will define your site. The activity that follows requires that you have your chosen editor installed and a web browser available to check your progress as you go. If you have those two programs ready to run, you can go ahead and get started by creating your front page.

Try It Yourself: Creating the Files

Open your chosen editor and create a new HTML file (or a blank document if no options are given). You do not want to use any of the predefined templates or wizards that your editor might offer because you will code this file by hand (or as I like to think of it, craft it with care). Of course, if you use something like Notepad, then the simple fact of opening the program will present you with an empty new document that's ready to go! The key here is that you have a blank document with nothing inside it. Once you have an open document, proceed to save the file (I know it doesn't make sense to save an empty document, but it does have a purpose!). You should save the file as index.html (see Figure 3-12); save it into the root folder that you call website (or whatever you chose to call it earlier). After you save the blank file, you're ready to enter code into it. You can open the index.html file in your web browser and hit the *Refresh* button each time you make changes. This means you can swap between windows to see how each thing you add to your code impacts the look of your site. This is why I recommended you save the file before you commence coding it, so you don't need to track down and open files mid-edit.

index.html
HTML Document
0 bytes

Figure 3-12. You can create the index.html file, which gives you a place to place your content and write your code.

Getting StartED

You have all the general information you need; now it's time to start writing your first site and the initial page that will act as the template for your design. The information in this section of the chapter has been organized so that you can admire your progress in your web browser as you go! The best place to start this section is by going over the basic elements every Web page requires. Next, you'll learn how to add the first page of content you wrote for the main page (plus any quirky features you might have thought of), as well as how to mark up those blocks of text. Once you do that, you'll learn how to add the bits and pieces you would like to see on every page of your site, including common functionality such as navigation, and how to break down your content into categories that make your site easier to manage. Finally, you'll learn about things you can add to the head of your document; you will also learn how to add other elements that you might find useful—exciting, isn't it?

What follows is a pair of W3C specifications (reference manuals) for HTML languages:

- **HTML 4.01**: www.w3.org/TR/html401/
- **HTML 5**: www.w3.org/TR/html5/

Your First Web Page

The time has come to build the first page of your site, so fire up your site editor and the web browser of your choice. You should have the index.html file open. This file is still empty, which is why nothing will appear in your web browser if you open the document inside your chosen web browser (whether Internet Explorer, Firefox, or something else). You need to begin by adding the elements that every single page of your site must have.

Document Type Declaration

OK, so you have your index file open and ready to edit. You need to start the document with a declaration that tells the web browser which language you will use. This is called the *Document Type Declaration*, or DTD for short. Another function of the DTD is to explain to the web browser whether the page should follow standards or quirks mode. In the earlier discussion of web standards, you learned that some older browsers didn't follow standards and interpreted code in their own special way? Quirks mode is a compatibility filter implemented by certain modern browsers to force rendering using an older version of the browser engine, so it remains compatible with old and nonstandard code. Because you'll write your site to conform to web standards, this will never apply to your site; however, you should be aware of this effect because you might see it on your Web travels.

Now let's add a Doctype declaration to your site. You can choose from among many different Doctypes for different versions of HTML (as well as different levels of standards compliance, such as *transitional* and *strict*), but you want to write a modern, standards-compliant site, so you need to know about only one: HTML 4.01 strict. Don't worry about the word *strict* here; this word doesn't make things hard on you, but merely tells the browser that you will use only standards-compliant code. In other words, the browser won't need to worry about any backwards-compatibility quirks. Transitional compliance lets you use old code that follows standards, but is less strict.

You can find a complete list of Doctypes for various implementations of XHTML and HTML at www.w3.org/QA/2002/04/valid-dtd-list.html.

The Doctype that you need to enter in the first line of your site looks like this:

```
<!DOCTYPE html PUBLIC "-//W3C//DTD HTML 4.01//EN"
```

```
"http://www.w3.org/TR/html4/strict.dtd">
```

It's not exactly an easy line to remember, but it's the same for every HTML page you'll create. Once you create it the first time, you can copy-and-paste it into your documents henceforth. For comparison, and for a taste of the good things that are on their way, take a quick look at the HTML 5 Doctype:

```
<!DOCTYPE HTML>
```

That's significantly easier! Unfortunately, many browsers don't yet support this standard in its full capacity; however, it's certainly something to look forward to, especially because this Doctype contains less jargon.

<HTML>, <head>, and <body>

Directly below the Doctype you need to add html, head, and body tags (as appropriate) to mark where the various structural elements should be placed in the natural flow. Begin by adding the all-important html element, which marks the start and end of your entire document. You can also add an attribute to this element that states which (human) language you want to use on your page. In this case, it's set it to en (English), but you can change it to whatever correctly describes the language you intend to use. Enter this code directly beneath the Doctype:

```
<!DOCTYPE html PUBLIC "-//W3C//DTD HTML 4.01//EN"


    "http://www.w3.org/TR/html4/strict.dtd">
<html lang="en">

</html>
```

Remember that you need two tags for most elements: one each to mark the beginning and end of the element. Also remember that the closing (ending) tag must include a forward slash (/). Inside the html element, you need to add your all-important head and body tags. This trio of required tags represents the places where you will store your custom structure; it also comprises the backbone of each page you add to your site.

Now add the following tags inside your html element:

```
<html lang="en">
<head>
```

```
</head>
<body>

</body>
</html>
```

The head element contains information that describes your web page (the "thinking" code), while the body element contains all of the content that makes up your page (the stuff you will see on the |screen).

Comments for Code

Before you complete this first section and begin incorporating everything required into an example site, it is worth taking a moment to raise the subject of code commenting. The line that follows is a special piece of code of code known as a comment, and it differs from what you have learned so far about elements, tags, and attributes:

```
<!--This is a comment. -->
```

You can attach comments anywhere in your source code, and the browser is trained to ignore them. Everything between the opening `<!--` characters and the closing `-->` characters is considered a free space where you can write whatever you want. Comments are useful for leaving yourself reminders in your code, or for describing how something works for future developers who might read your code. One thing to remember, though, is that they do add extra bulk to the page (larger file sizes), so many developers will ignore them (or remove them after the page is complete) to help keep the amount of resources being drained to a minimum).

NotED

Almost all web languages have some form of code commenting available, so you can use them as a tool whenever you want to remember what something does (which can be extremely useful!).

Checkpoint: Part 1

Welcome to the first checkpoint of the chapter. At this point, your document should have a Doctype, along with the basic elements that comprise the backbone of a web page. If you save where you are at and refresh the browser window with the open index.html file, you will notice that not much has changed visually (see Figure 3-13). However, your browser sees the file completely differently; your browser doesn't see a blank document, but a well-formed, standards-compliant web page. Sure, the page doesn't include any content yet, but you'll address that in |the |next section.

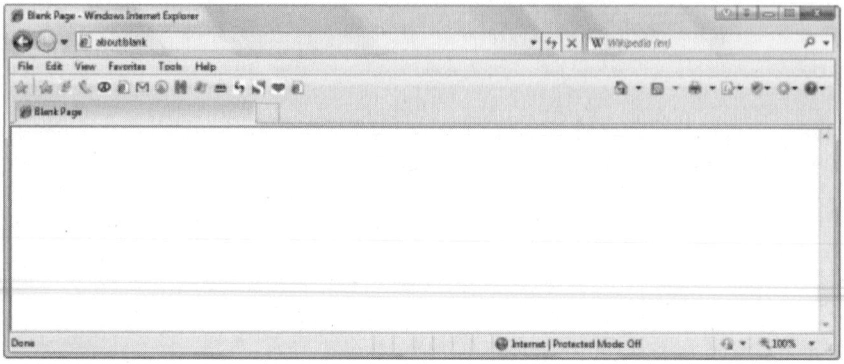

Figure 3-13. You've created a well-formed, standards-compliant page, but you still see a blank page because you haven't added anything within the body element.

From Content to Context

You've marked up all the common elements of your first page; now you're ready to inject some content into the body of the document. The great thing about this stage is that you've already written the majority of your site's content (assuming you followed the through on the exercises in Chapter 2), so you will find it relatively easy to identify where the tags mentioned in the upcoming section should be placed as you learn about them. Of course, you might find yourself wanting to add new content for a particular page at a later stage of the project. If so, you can use the wireframe you produced in Chapter 1 that described where you wanted everything to fit to help you decide where to place this information. You should expect a fairly smooth transition from your word processor (where you stored your content) to your web editor if you follow the instructions given carefully. Let's get started by adding some content to your page, which will help you understand the work involved when you need to add more pages.

Placing Your Content

The time has come to find that first page of content you wanted to appear on the homepage. You created the main homepage in index.html, and now you want to copy-and-paste anything you have written in your Word processor for use on the first page, so people will see it as they enter your site. Remember that you must put whatever content you place within the body element, and you should incorporate it in the order you want it to be read and appear on the page, from top to bottom. After placing all your new text in your editor; you need to wrap it up using the elements that best describe each segment; note that any styling you add to your content in your word processor will be lost when you port it to your coding editor because HTML doesn't permit any style other than plain text). You will probably find yourself using the same handful of elements the majority of the time, using the rest of them only occasionally (or not at all, in some cases). The important thing is that you take each element into account and decide where (if anywhere) you might use it to give meaning to your text. The better you express your content on the site, the easier you will make things for yourself in the long run (which is a good thing!).

Try It Yourself: Adding Your Content

If you have not done so already, put down the book, pick the content you want to appear on the homepage of the site from your ideas pad, and then proceed to copy-and-paste the stuff you want to use into your chosen code editor. You might think it can't be this simple to make a site (and it isn't quite this simple), but the fact that you spent time creating well-written and thought-out content earlier will make this part of creating your site a cinch. As I mentioned earlier, the point of writing the content before you start building the site is so you can take the well-written blocks of text that already exist and concentrate solely on choosing the right tag for the right job. Your job at this point is to go through each element you learn about, one at a time, and use it where you feel it can benefit your content most.

ExplainED

At the time of writing, HTML5 remains a working draft and few browsers offer support for it, so you will stick mainly to HTML 4.01. However, I will point out the exciting changes that HTML 5 will bring in the future, just as I did with the Doctype. As a site designer or developer, it's important to be aware of what the future holds, not least because it can affect how you should approach coding your current site.

Structure: <h1>, <h2>, <h3>, <h4>, <h5>, and <h6>

The most appropriate place to start when building your site's structure is with your headings. You use headings to announce new content sections, just as you do when writing. HTML 4.01 provides several different heading levels you can use to organize your site. In the majority of cases, you should constrain the text of a heading to no more than one line. You might have some headings already lined up for the blocks of text in the content you wrote. If so, you need to look at these and decide what heading level they require. You can use the following process to determine which heading works best for a given piece of content. The h1 tag (meaning heading level 1) is considered usable only for a single instance (by most developers) on a given page. In the majority of cases, you use it as the title of the page (or site) title. From that point, you need to use h2 tags to describe section headings. If you require further subheadings, categories, or any other title information inside your sections, you can use h3 tag. You can split into subsections all the way down to h6; however, you won't need to go any deeper than h3 in most cases.

This snippet shows a typical heading structure order:

```
<h1>MySite!</h1>
    <h2>Section</h2>
        <h3>Subsection</h3>
            <h4>Semi-Subsection</h4>
        <h3> Subsection </h3>
    <h2>Section</h2>
    <h2>Section</h2>
        <h3>Subsection</h3>
```

Notice the opening and closing tags for each heading element. This code indents each heading level to make the headings easier to read. Figure 3-14 shows how the different heading levels might appear on your site.

Next, you need to go through your content in your editor and wrap any headings in the appropriate tags. Remember to add an opening and a closing tag for every heading. Omitting a closing tag on any element can makes it hard for a web browser to know where to stop applying a particular style; therefore it's good for the sake of consistency to ensure that you close your tags properly. Note that you do not need quote (or any other) marks around the text; all you need is the opening tag, the heading text, and the closing tag. For example, assume you want to have the heading, "Stamps of the World". The element would look like this:

```
<h1>Stamps of the World</h1>
```

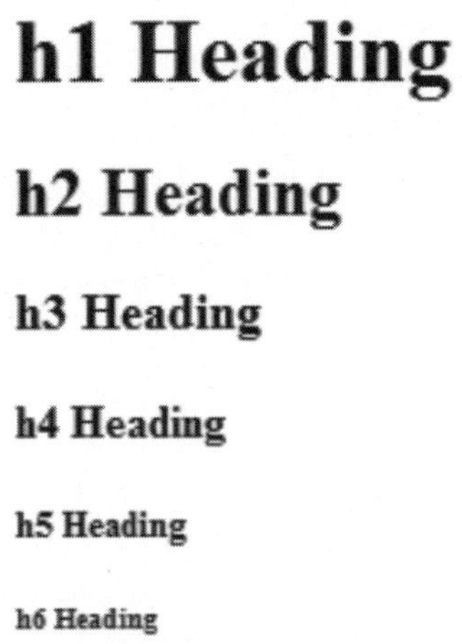

h1 Heading

h2 Heading

h3 Heading

h4 Heading

h5 Heading

h6 Heading

Figure 3-14. Various heading numbers have different default sizes, based on their priority.

Structure: <p> and

You've completed your headings; next you need to define the main body text. The most common element on the Web is the paragraph element. That little p tag you saw earlier is generally used to enclose text within a document. You will probably wrap most of your content inside paragraph tags both for long runs of text as in the example that follows and short informative messages, as shown in Figure 3-15. For this reason, you will want to wrap any blocks of text that have a fair amount of words in them in paragraph tags. This essentially tells the browser that the content enclosed is nothing more than good old-fashioned text. Run through your text now and add opening and closing p tags around suitable text blocks. Note that you want to add paragraph tags around each individual paragraph of text in your document; you cannot create an opening paragraph tag at the top of the page and a closing tag at the bottom. This is because browsers ignore any carriage returns (new lines caused by pressing Enter). If you do this, a browser will probably display all of your text in one long block. You don't want to create such an unsightly site, so you need to tell the browser explicitly where each paragraph begins and ends:

```
<p>Welcome to my stamps website! Here you will find information about
various stamps from around the world, and details of my own stamp
collection. There is also an online trading area where you can buy and
sell stamps for your own collection.</p>
<p>I started this site in order to convey my enthusiasm for stamps…</p>
```

Figure 3-15. Paragraphs don't have to be long lumps of text; they can also contain small useful messages.

At this stage, you've probably wrapped the majority of your text up in either heading or paragraph tags (because this conveys the most information). You do still have a few more elements that you might use to enclose stuff such as lists, tables, images, and other unique content. If you find that you've already added tags around all of your text, then you can go ahead and save your HTML document and test the page in your web browser (by clicking the *Refresh* button on index.html) to see what your site looks like. Don't worry if you still have some content left untagged; all you need to do is keep running through elements until you have enclosed all your content.

In addition to the paragraph tag, HTML includes a special tag for breaking text within a paragraph. The line break tag, br, is a self-closing inline element, which means that it sits within the block-level paragraph element. A self-closing tag has only one tag, rather than the usual two for opening and closing content. When you place the br tag inside a paragraph tag, you force a new line to be triggered in the natural flow of the document with no spacing (margin or padding). Many developers misuse the line-break tag for style purposes to create new paragraphs; however you know better than to do that! There are legitimate, broadly accepted reasons for using this element. For example, you should use the br element occurs when you need to trigger a new line within a continued flow of text. This might sound confusing, but consider what happens when you write an address on a letter, or even a poem (see Figure 3-15)! The address continues over multiple lines, even though it isn't technically a break or an ending of the paragraph. It is situations like these when using a line break is the best choice:

```
<p>Oh look, this text <br> has broken in half!</p>
```

Oh look, this text
has broken in half!

Figure 3-16. You can use a line break to snap the paragraph onto a new line at the desired point.

Multimedia: <img>

Images are one of the most easily recognizable elements within HTML. Alongside the paragraph tag, the image tag is one of the most popular tags on the Web. Inserting images will improve your website by enabling you to create a more involving experience for your visitors. Images have a different sort of value than text. Let's face it: If your site were nothing but text, it would look rather boring and bland. Adding an img to your site is as simple as providing a link to the image location in the src attribute in the form of a URL, then adding some alternative text to describe the image if it becomes unavailable (and for accessibility reasons) with the alt attribute. You can use this element wherever you want to place an image that relates to the content on the page.

Let's look at those attributes in more detail. The source attribute (src) points to the location of the image you want to include. When you created the folders for your site, you created a special folder called images to contain—you guessed it—the images for your site. You need to find the images that you want to include on your computer and place a copy of them inside the images folder. You might also want to make sure that you give the images a unique name, so you can remember them easily. Note that this name can't contain any spaces or special characters. You also want to make sure that your image names contain the required filename extension, such as .jpg for JPEG files, .gif for GIF files, and so on. This img element refers to a file in your images folder:

```
<img src= "/images/elephant.jpg" />
```

Notice that you include the name of the containing folder within the src attribute. This is because your index.html file resides in the site's root, and all of your images live in a subdirectory of the website folder. You need to tell the browser it can find the image it needs by looking in the correct folder. As long as you keep all of your images in the images folder, then that's all you need to know. If you start moving your images around into different folders, though, you will need to include the correct folder name in the source attribute, which can get quite confusing. You can see why it makes sense to keep all of your files in designated folders! The other key thing to note: The image element itself is self-closing. It consists of one tag that contains a set of attributes, starting with <img and ending with />.

The next step is to add another attribute to the image element: alt. You use this attribute to supply alternative text to browsers if the image is unavailable. This might be because the visitor has chosen to disable images (unlikely in this day and age, but possible), because the browser can't find the image (perhaps you didn't put it in the correct folder), or because the visitor has a disability and cannot view your image. In the last case, the visitor might have a piece of software called a *Screen Reader*, which literally reads out loud all of the text on a page. When it gets to an image, the screen reader reads the alt text you supply, enabling the visitor to understand everything that appears on your page. You might think you don't need to add alt text, but it is well worth the effort, not least because the more visitors you can get, the more vibrant your site is likely to be. You will learn more about accessibility on the Web later in Chapter 9. An image element containing an alt attribute looks like this:

```
<img src="/images/rocket.png" alt="The Saturn V rocket." />
```

You should also be aware and keep in mind that Internet Explorer mistakenly displays alt attributes as tooltips (those little pop-ups that appear when you hover over things), but you can fix that with another attribute. You use the title attribute to add a title to an image, and this title usually appears in the form of a tooltip. Adding a title attribute (blank or otherwise) fixes the bug:

```
<img src="/images/logo.gif" alt="MySite logo" title="Welcome to MySite!" />
```

Figure 3-17 shows all of these attributes in action. If the browser can't find your image, then it displays a small red cross with the alt text next to it. Holding your mouse over the image (even if the image itself isn't displaying) causes a tooltip to appear that displays the title attribute.

Figure 3-17. You need to remember to link to the correct path, or else your images won't appear correctly!

Note that you want to keep your style and structure separate, so you need to provide images in the structure only if they convey information that relates to the content. If you include the images for decorative purposes, such as for backgrounds or decorative borders, then you should handle this (like all other style-based code) with CSS.

> ## NotED
>
> *HTML5 will have support for a new tag called* figure. *One problem with images is that you are limited to using the* title *or* alt *attribute to give a meaningful description of the image, but if you can see the image then the* alt *text isn't displayed. The* figure *element includes the* legend *attribute that will enable you to provide a caption giving more details of the picture.*

Lists: <ol>, <ul>, <dl>, <dt> and <dd>

HTML lists come in three flavors: ordered lists (ol), unordered lists (ul), and definition lists (dl). The purpose of these lists is to group and pull together a collection of items. In the case of an unordered list, there is no importance or emphasis placed on any of the entries; in the case of an ordered list, the opposite is true. Definition lists work slightly differently because they consist of pairs of items, a term and a definition, for each entry. By default, items in an ordered list are preceded by a list of numbers (or letters or symbols) that suggest a specific order to the contents. In the case of the unordered list, the items are preceded by bullet points (or images). Definition lists don't have either of these, but by default the definition is indented from the term. Note that developers commonly use the unordered list in navigation menus on sites, not only for its accessibility benefits, but also because it offers tremendous flexibility when you use CSS styling to manipulate a list's position on the page. Note that using unordered lists in navigation is more semantically correct because navigation is, by definition, a list of URLs that relate to the site. You can try adding a list to your site, as well as adding an item for every page that you want to link to by giving each item a name. You'll see how to create links from them soon.

This example displays an unordered list for a navigation menu:

```
<ul>
    <li>Home</li>
    <li>Blog</li>
    <li>Services</li>
    <li>Portfolio</li>
    <li>Contact</li>
</ul>
```

Notice that the list includes two main parts: the ul block-level element and the inline li element, which denotes a list item. You wrap each item in the list

147

inside its own `li` tags, and you open and close the entire list with `ul` tags (see Figure 3-18).

- Home
- Blog
- Services
- Portfolio
- Contact

Figure 3-18. A bullet list allows you to group items together quickly and effectively.

I mentioned previously that you use the ordered list for a list of numbered items, listing them in order. This example illustrates how to implement an ordered to-do list:

```
<ol>
    <li>Get out of bed</li>
    <li>Turn on the computer</li>
    <li>Eat breakfast </li>
    <li>Go to work!</li>
</ol>
```

Notice that this list is almost identical to the earlier unordered list. The difference between the two lists: You wrap an ordered list in `ol` tags, rather than `ul` tags (see Figure 3-19).

1. Get out of bed
2. Turn on the computer
3. Eat breakfast
4. Go to work!

Figure 3-19. You can use an ordered list to display a list in order.

The final list is the definition list. This looks a little different than the other two list types because it consists of term-definition pairs. For example, you might create a list that compares three types of transport:

```
<dl>
    <dt>Car</dt>
        <dd>Travels on land</dd>
    <dt>Airplane</dt>
```

```
        <dd>Flies through air</dd>
    <dt>Boat</dt>
        <dd>Skips across water</dd>
</dl>
```

Again, you can indent these to make them easier to read, but you don't *need* to indent your code like this. Instead of using a single li element for each item, you use a pair that consists of a dt and a dd element for the term and the definition. This gives you the following output:

```
Car
        Travels on land
Airplane
        Flies through air
Boat
        Skips across water
```

You can choose whichever type of list suits your needs best.

Tables

Tables might be a good way of displaying your information if you find yourself wanting to show a comparison of different things (such as an example that compares features of several electronic goods), or if you want to show information that you might otherwise find in a spreadsheet. You can use tables to display rows and columns of data that sit side-by-side (similar to cells in a spreadsheet program); you can also use them to display complex pieces of information easily. The explanation of tables that follows is quite long, but unlike most of the other elements discussed, tables come with a multitude of elements that you can use to express various bits and pieces you might expect to find in a table, such as a caption, headings, and tabular data. If you find yourself wondering how to express your information in a table, you might play around with the example that follows. You will likely find it straightforward to adapt it to your needs by adding rows, columns, or whatever else you require.

LinkED

You might be aware of table-based design, where developers use the table element to build a site (and split it into sections). This practice has long been frowned upon, and today it's considered bad practice, so you won't learn how to implement such bad habits in this book! If you want to know more about table-based design, including why you shouldn't use it, visit www.hotdesign.com/seybold/everything.html.

A basic table consists of opening and closing `table` tags, with some rows (`tr`) containing either header information or data (`th` and `td`)—remember that rows go across the page, and columns go down it. Take a look at the following code:

```
<table>
    <tr>
        <th>Blue eyes</th>

        <th>Green eyes</th>
    </tr>
    <tr>
        <td>12</td>
        <td>15</td>
    </tr>
</table>
```

Here you have a simple table that consists of two rows and two columns. You denote rows with the `tr` elements and columns with the `th` and `td` elements. The first row has two columns that contain headers, and the second row has two columns that contain data. The result looks something like this in your browser:

Blue eyes	Green eyes
12	15

Notice that the table headers are bold by default. You can continue in this vein easily, adding additional rows and columns to this simple table.

You can group the table headers as you did in the preceding example, where the headers appear above the results as top columns. However, you can also provide headers to the side of your rows by including `th` elements before the `td` elements in each row. This might sound confusing, but it's simple to implement:

```
<table>
    <tr>
        <th>Two legs</th>
        <td>Good</td>
    </tr>
    <tr>
        <th>Four legs</th>
        <td>Bad</td>
    </tr>
</table>
```

This gives you the following result:

Two Legs	Good
Four Legs	Bad

If you want to create a table with headers on both the top and the side, then you might find that you want to add the scope attribute to your th elements to make it easier to tell the difference between the two. The scope attribute can have one of two values: col or row. You might implement such a table like this:

```
<table>
    <tr>
        <th></th>
        <th scope= "col ">London</th>
        <th scope= "col ">Carlisle</th>
    </tr>
    <tr>
        <th scope= "row ">London</th>
        <td>-</td>
        <td>306</td>
    </tr>
    <tr>
        <th scope= "row ">Carlisle</th>
        <td>306</td>
        <td>-</td>
    </tr>
</table>
```

Note that you must add a blank th element in the first row to push the second pair of headers along. This gives you the following output:

-	**London**	**Carlisle**
London	-	306
Carlisle	306	-

This might do the trick for basic tables that display tabular data, you can apply some additional techniques to spice things up! For example, you might add a caption element to the top of your table. The caption explains what the table contains (such as a paragraph of text attached to the table). Next, you might add thead, tfoot, and tbody elements to separate the headers from the data itself (note that thead and tfoot must appear before tbody!). This is the first time this book has touched on either header or footer elements. Here, the header elements are solely for table headings that sit at the top of the table and footer elements solely appear at the bottom of the table. You can see them in action in this table code (see Figure 3-20 to see how this code renders in a browser):

```
<table>
    <caption>Example table.</caption>
    <thead>
    <tr>
        <th></th>
        <th scope="col">Title A</th>
```

```
                <th scope="col">Title B</th>
            </tr>
        </thead>
        <tfoot>
            <tr>
                <th></th>
                <th scope="col">Title A</th>
                <th scope="col">Title B</th>
            </tr>
        </tfoot>
        <tbody>
            <tr>
                <th scope="row">Names</th>
                <td>Data One</td>
                <td>Data Two</td>
            </tr>
            <tr>
                <th scope="row">Other</th>
                <td>Data Three</td>
                <td>Data Four</td>
            </tr>
        </tbody>
</table>
```

Example table.

	Title A	Title B
Names	Data One	Data Two
Other	Data Three	Data Four
	Title A	Title B

Figure 3-20. A complex table with rows, columns, headings and even a caption.

Advanced Tables

I bet you thought you'd already seen the advanced tables, but you can do much more than this! This book won't go into absolutely everything you can do with tables, but there is one more technique you might consider taking advantage of. Assume you want your table items to span across more than one row or column. In this case, you can take advantage of the colspan and rowspan attributes. These attributes let you add as many rows or columns as you want an element to bridge; as long as there are enough elements to span the specified number:

```
<table>
    <tr>
```

```
        <th></th>
        <th scope="col" colspan="2">Favorite food</th>
    </tr>
    <tr>
        <th></th>
        <th scope="col">Chili</th>
        <th scope="col">Chocolate</th>
    </tr>
    <tr>
        <th scope="row">Boys</th>
        <td>32</td>
        <td>15</td>
    </tr>
    <tr>
        <th scope="row">Girls</th>
        <td>8</td>
        <td>35</td>
    </tr>
</table>
```

Here, you have two headings for the columns. The first is a general heading that covers both columns; the second heading shows a pair of headings immediately beneath the first heading:

	Favorite food	
	Chili	Chocolate
Boys	32	15
Girls	8	35

It's time to make things a bit more interesting. You've created elements spanning multiple cells, but now let's assume you want to group your columns so that you can apply a style or behavior to an entire column later. You can achieve this using the `colgroup` and `col` elements. These elements have functionality that assists you with styling your tables, but they can also help you assist your browser in rendering the table, reducing the chances you might end up with a skewed table while data loads. You can use the `colgroup` element (which you place above `thead`) to specify how many columns you want your table to have. In a similar vein, you can use the `span` attribute to target several of the columns within a single declaration, or you can give individual declarations to the columns you want to target explicitly. Note that your `colgroup` elements add up quickly. For example, if you have five columns going across and you want to target the middle column, you might have three `colgroup` elements. The first and the third could span two columns, while the second would have to span a single column. Note that you should not provide a span if your `colgroup` element targets only a single column.

The table that follows uses the colspan element to span Title B across two columns, where Data Two and Data Three are held. The first colgroup element reference acts on behalf of Title A, but the second colgroup element spans two columns, so it can apply a style and behavior directly to Title B and both Data Two and Data Three elements because this table groups them together (you can see what the following code looks like in a browser in Figure 3-21):

```
<table>
    <colgroup></colgroup>
    <colgroup span="2"></colgroup>
    <thead>
        <tr>
            <th>Title A</th>
            <th colspan="2">Title B</th>
        </tr>
    </thead>
    <tbody>
        <tr>
            <td>Data One</td>
            <td>Data Two</td>
            <td>Data Three</td>
        </tr>
    </tbody>
</table>
```

Title A   **Title B**

Data One Data Two Data Three

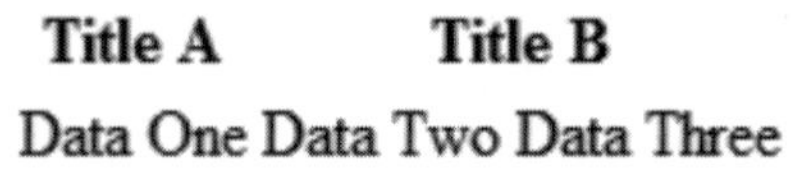

Figure 3-21. A simple table that splits a cell into two segments to show the three "data" values

This might seem confusing because it involves math and grouping. However, what might blow your mind are the possible complexities you can produce within those colgroup elements by defining secondary layers for these elements! For example, if you use the preceding code sample to target a style to Data Two rather than both Data Two and Data Three (as defined by the colgroup element), you can add col elements inside the colgroup element that you use in the same way as before by providing the correct number of columns or making one col element span several columns. You can also target an individual column instead, as in this example:

```
<table>
    <colgroup></colgroup>
    <colgroup>
        <col />
        <col />
```

```
    </colgroup>
</table>
```

That's about it for tables, and I won't be surprised if you have a headache! Tables are probably the most complicated element you will come across in terms of their scope and depth in the HTML specification. The preceding guide shows some of the ways you can work with data in tables, and you might find it helpful to look at tutorials on the Web that cover the subject in greater depth.

NotED

The HTML5 specification includes a new element called datagrid. *This element allows a site visitor to reorganize the information within the table, such as sorting by letter and number). This element will enable you to provide customizable fields that your visitors can interact with.*

Structure: <blockquote>, <q> and <cite>

Blockquote is a misunderstood element, partly because over the years many developers have abused its native ability to indent text. Blockquote is one of a handful of HTML elements where issues have grown up their use. Due to the way developers misused this element, using it to apply styles rather than for its intended function, which was to quote a block of text, some browsers today ignore its quote marks, using it as an indenting element by default. Some browsers do render blockquote as intended, but support for quotation marks remains patchy. This means you must add the quotes yourself or ignore them. One thing worth mentioning: The blockquote tag requires that you use the cite attribute to indicate the source of the quote itself. Generally a blockquote contains other block-level elements such as paragraphs to denote their content (it can theoretically span many lines of text, including, but not limited to, images and links). Note that you need reference the quote in the form of a URL, rather than a name or title (see Figure 3-22). This snippet shows you how to implement the blockquote element:

```
<blockquote cite="http://www.yoursitehere.com"><p>"Quote goes
here!"</p></blockquote>
```

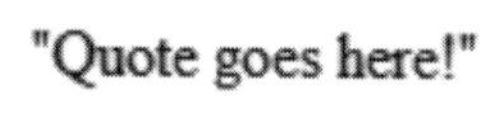

"Quote goes here!"

Figure 3-22. This useful element is offset from the left, but you might find it useful for stating quotes.

ExplainED

The inline quote element suffers the same poor browser support for quote marks that you see in blockquote*; worse, Internet Explorer doesn't support it all! This means you should probably try to avoid using the* q *element unless you use CSS and JavaScript to patch the issue.*

You know that a cite attribute exists within the blockquote element that allows you to reference where you got the statement or quote from (at the point of origin). HTML also includes an inline cite element that lets you ensure that content is properly credited (see Figure 3-23). Unlike the cite attribute, the cite element allows you to use names, locations, and other references on top of listing a site address. This useful element can help you reference the works of others:

```
<p>Check out <cite title="Getting StartED Building Websites by Alexander
Dawson">Chapter 1: What kind of website should I make?</cite>, it's
worth reading!</p>
```

Check out *Chapter 1: What kind of website should I make?*, its worth reading!

Figure 3-23. Citing sources is important for any potential content author, and the HTML mechanism for doing so works well.

Multimedia: <object>, <embed>, <noembed>, and <param>

The easiest way to include multimedia items in HTML 4.01, such as movies or animations, is to embed a browser plug-in in your page. The plug-in tells the browser how it should play the media. The ability to embed browser plug-ins and objects into your documents is one of the primary ways in which the Web has evolved over recent years. The sharp rise of people using technologies such as Flash, Silverlight, and ActiveX components (you'll learn more about these in Chapter 8) has produced some exciting and dynamic ways to experience the Web. HTML includes two competing standards for adding multimedia or additional functionality into your site. The first standard is the object element, which the W3C created to hold ActiveX and other plug-in components, such as media players, PDF readers, and other applications (see Figure 3-24).

The object element is a standard, but it's sometimes pushed aside for the better supported, but nonstandard embed element created originally for the now abandoned Netscape browser. The embed element is deprecated (so you should avoid using it); nevertheless, I recommend that you keep it in your toolbox, purely for compatibility considerations. The embed tag lets you use a sub element called noembed that allows you to provide alternative information if the embedded file is unavailable. A tag called param also exists for the object element, and it enables the coder to define properties for the element based on the application.

The following example uses both the object and embed elements to display an Adobe Flash movie:

```
<object>
    <param name="movie"
value="http://www.yoursitehere.com/video/video1.swf"></param>
    <param name="allowFullScreen" value="true"></param>
    <param name="allowScriptAccess" value="always"></param>
    <embed src="http://www.yoursitehere.com/ video/video1.swf "
type="application/x-shockwave-flash" allowfullscreen="true"
allowScriptAccess="always">
    </embed>
</object>
```

The preceding code is admittedly complex, but you can probably work out what most of its parts do if you go through it slowly. You can combine using both embed and object to provide an alternative for cases where a web browser doesn't support the object element. Doing this ensures that your site will function properly, no matter which of the two approaches a visitor's browser supports. I won't spend much time explaining how it works because Adobe's Flash product (along with many other flash-generation tools and sites) use the technology to autogenerate this kind of code for you when you publish this type of document; this means you'll rarely have to type it in code like this from 25.341 25.341 scratch.

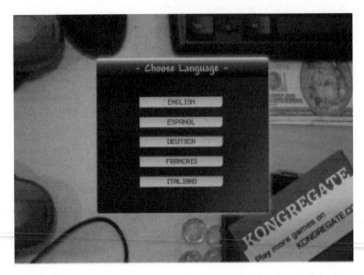

Figure 3-24. Desktop Tower Defense is a Flash game that uses the `object` element.

Structure: <hr>

The horizontal rule is one of the simplest of elements inside HTML. Basically, it creates a visible line break that separates two sections of a web page (see Figure 3-25). For example, you might use a horizontal rule to place a separator between two posts in a blog. The use of the `hr` tag is perfectly valid, but its use has declined with the rise of CSS styling. This is because the horizontal rule is quite hard to style, as browsers use their own unique default styles, and you can achieve this separation using StyleSheets and no additional markup. Don't let the fact others no longer use this element as much discourage you from using it if you feel your page requires it. For example, you might use this element to separate two paragraphs or headings. `hr` is a self-closing element, so it has a minimal impact on a site's structure:

```
<h2>Check it out!</h2>
<hr />
<p>There is a line separating the heading from this text!</p>
```

Check it out!

There is a line separating the heading from this text!

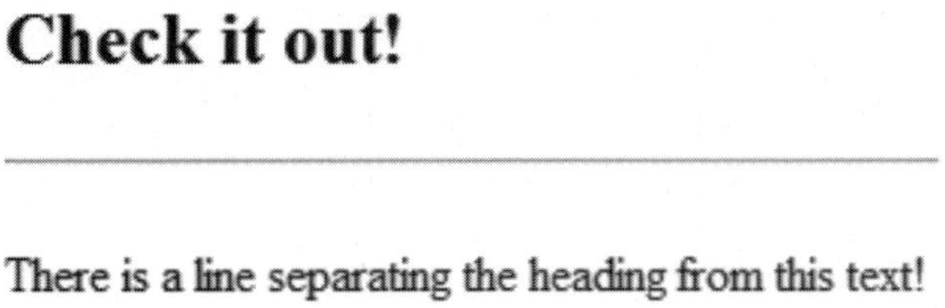

Figure 3-25. You can add horizontal lines using the hr element to represent a split in content.

Multimedia: <map> and <area>

You can add links to images by wrapping the img element with an anchor tag, but sometimes you might want to allow the image to be more interactive and have clickable regions within it. The primary method of creating hotspots for your images is to use what is commonly called an image map. The map works by producing an invisible, shaped link at a specific set of coordinates within the image known as the area. Image maps are useful because you can set the clickable area to be a custom shape. You connect the map itself to your choice of image using the usemap attribute. You use the shape attribute to indicate whether you want to use a circle, square, or polygon; and you can also use the coords attribute to specify the position of links, including the coordinates for top, bottom, left, and right of the invisible shape. Like all links, this attribute requires href and alt attributes; but you're otherwise free to produce complex image maps using as many different area locations as you like!

The example shows you how to implement an image map that creates a custom link around an image:

```
<img src ="galaxy.gif" alt="A map of stars" usemap ="#galaxy" />
<map name="galaxy ">
    <area shape="circle" coords="0,0,82,126" href="star1.php" alt="Star
1" />
    <area shape="circle" coords="90,33,3" href=" star2.php" alt=" Star
2" />
    <area shape="circle" coords="1,24,66,8" href=" star3.php" alt=" Star
3" />
    <area shape="circle" coords="33,58,0" href=" star4.php" alt=" Star
4" />
</map>
```

ExplainED

Image maps are quite complicated (and require coordinates!), so you might find it easier to create any you require using a visual (WYSIWYG) editor. This is one of the few times where I think they prove especially handy!

Structure: <address>

The address element is a slightly obscure and underused tag within the HTML specification. Its purpose is to hold contact information about the creator of the site and its content (see Figure 3-26). In addition to containing an address, it can also contain geographical information, telephone numbers, email addresses, and even a site address. This element isn't popular, and you should never use it more than once within a page. However, it is commonly used for the hCard microformat, which you'll learn more about in Chapter 9.

The following example illustrates how to place the address element on your page:

```
<address>
    This website was produced by Yoursitehere:<br/>
    <a href="mailto:admin@yoursitehere.com">Send us a message</a><br/>
    Mail us at PO Box 123, Code City, 12345<br/>
    Tel +9 876 5432
</address>
```

This website was produced by Yoursitehere:
Send us a message
Mail us at PO Box 123, Code City, 12345
Tel +9 876 5432

Figure 3-26. Your visitors might find it useful if you make your address available to them with the address element.

Checkpoint: Part 2

At this stage of the process, you have seen more than a few elements that you might want to review for potential use on your site. You'll encounter many of these elements as you add new pages of content, and as you produce common elements such as navigation elements for your site. For now, however, you should focus on adding the elements only where you deem them appropriate within your index.html file. After all, you don't want to lose your place thinking about other things you can embed into the page when the focus of this exercise is to give your content the best possible chance of being easy to maintain and navigate. Once you complete this stage and get your content housed in elements properly, save your progress, return to the web browser to hit the *Refresh* button. Notice how your site is no longer blank, but overflowing with visible, formatted content. Also, your site is much more than a block of text; it's starting to resemble something you would see on a site and includes images, lists, paragraphs, headings, and more.

See for yourself: Marking Up Content

This example shows you how to mark up text using the tags discussed in this section: (see Figure 3-27):

```
<!DOCTYPE html PUBLIC "-//W3C//DTD HTML 4.01//EN"

    "http://www.w3.org/TR/html4/strict.dtd">
<html lang="en">
<head>

</head>
<body>
        <h2>Who are we?</h2>
        <p>You have visited this sample website because obviously you
want to see what code can look like if it's placed together in a logical
order, hopefully what you are reading makes a little bit of sense.</p>
        <img src="/images/chart.gif" alt="Chart of how everything
appears" title="Pie chart!"/>

        <p>As you can see from the above image, everything may look
bland but it has a purpose!</p>
        <h2>What can this website do?</h2>
        <p>Well I am glad you asked, if you check out the below list you
can see what this site uses.</p>
        <ul>
                <li>Headings</li>
                <li>Paragraphs</li>
                <li>Images</li>
                <li>Unordered Lists</li>
        </ul>
</body>
</html>
```

You can see the differences between this example and the previous one in the highlighted code sections; the part in bold indicates what you have added since the previous checkpoint (or segment of the chapter).

Who are we?

You have visited this sample website because obviously you want to see what code can look like if it's placed together in a logical order, hopefully what you are reading makes a little bit of sense.

[x] Chart of how everything appears

As you can see from the above image, everything may look bland but it has a purpose!

What can this website do?

Well I am glad you asked, if you check out the below list you can see what this site uses.

- Headings
- Paragraphs
- Images
- Unordered Lists

Figure 3-27. The example has evolved dramatically since its last iteration!

Enhancing Content

You've marked up the majority of your content appropriately; now you're ready to add some flare and added depth to your content by using some additional elements that enable you to give your content extended meaning. Of course, this means you need to learn still more elements, but all of these apply to the text that already exists on the page, so it shouldn't be too much hassle for you to go through your content again and apply the new elements appropriately. For example, if you find yourself using an abbreviation or an acronym, you can go ahead and mark it up so that the browser knows it's an acronym, too. Adding these elements to your content will give it greater meaning for search engines and your visitors. Also, doing this will mean you can implement a bit of style later on, ensuring that things such as keyboard shortcuts stand out!

Formatting: <span>

The span tag in HTML is a generic container that can apply special style rules. For example, you might use this element to turn a couple of words from black to red. You place this element inline, rather than at the block level, but the element itself contains no semantic meaning. This enables you to apply style or behavior directly to a certain amount of text within a container. You will probably encounter situations where you want certain parts of your site to stand out, even though no semantic tag exists for what you want to portray;

the span tag proves especially useful in this circumstance. As a rule of thumb, you should try and keep your reliance on the span tag to a minimum, using it only when no appropriate HTML tag exists:

```
<p>Why does <span id="special">this</span> word get to be so
popular!</p>
```

You've learned that the span tag above doesn't do anything now, but later you will be able to target it with some additional style rules.

Formatting: <a>

One of the most popular formatting tags that exist is the anchor. Basically, this element allows you to produce hyperlinks either to external resources or to a specific part of the page the visitor is looking at (see Figure 3-28)! You can find hyperlinks everywhere on the Web, and they serve as the primary mechanism for sending visitors from one page to another. Of course, anchors also have the benefit of being able to work with third party programs, as long as the custom protocol employed is correct (Skype and iTunes are both popular examples of this). Anchors have a variety of different attributes, but href is probably the attribute that is most commonly associated with them. When you provide a value to this attribute, clicking the anchor that contains it will redirect a visitor to the path specified in the href attribute. This element is literally the life and soul of the Web because it provides the mechanism that takes users from page to page at the click of a button; without it, the Internet would probably be much harder to browse. a tags act as points of reference, and you will probably have a wide number of them on your site, especially in terms of navigating your site:

```
<p>If you are not already a member, <a href="register.php">register for
free today</a>!</p>
```

If you are not already a member, register for free today!

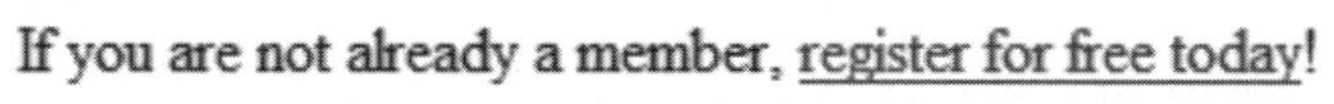

Figure 3-28. Hyperlinks allow visitors to navigate from one page to another.

Notice how the anchor tags surround the part of the text that you want to turn into a hyperlink. The default style for a link is underlined blue text.

ExplainED

Developers used to use anchors for creating fragment links (URLs to sections of a page), using the name *attribute as a reference point. Today, it's considered more semantically correct to link to other parts of the page (such as* index.php#section1*) using an* id *attribute with the value of* section1 *in an element.*

Formatting: <abbr>, <acronym>, and <dfn>

HTML includes a group of elements that can give added meaning to the words on your page. They all have independent functions, but I cover them together because they all serve a similar purpose: providing additional details about your content. You might find these tags especially useful if you need to produce academic papers or homework because they help you format the content you provide with details that might be the difference in helping a visitor understand your content.

The abbreviation and acronym element can help enhance the meaning of your content significantly. However, implementing the abbr and acronym tags can be complicated because determining the difference between an abbreviation and an acronym is fairly explicit. Abbreviations are counted as any word or phrase that is shortened. Standard acronyms occur when you create a term based on the initial letter of several other words to form something that someone can speak (such as SCUBA). However, you can also find a key exception to this rule, known as an initialism, that occurs when you need to spell the word out, rather than pronounced it as a complete word (such as HTML). When in doubt, you should default to using the acronym element. The problem with this: HTML offers no initialism tag, so you need to use an acronym element with class="initialism" or something similar to determine the difference. You can display the complete meaning of an acronym or abbreviation by enclosing it in a title attribute, which appears as a tooltip (see Figure 3-29).

This short snippet shows you how to incorporate an abbreviation, acronym, or initialized acronym:

```
<abbr title="Et Cetera">Etc</abbr>
<acronym title="Self Contained Underwater Breathing
Apparatus">SCUBA</acronym>
<abbr class="initial" title="Hypertext Markup Language">HTML</abbr>
```

Etc SCUBA HTML

Self Contained Underwater Breathing Apparatus

Figure 3-29. You should include definitions for abbreviations and acronyms that your visitors might not be familiar with.

ExplainED

Unfortunately here is another area where you come across one of Internet Explorer's failings. Internet Explorer 6 and 7 do not support the abbr *element. In this case, you might just have to live with that fact that your visitors who use those browsers won't get explanations of your abbreviations.*

One element remains from this group: the dfn element, which you use to provide extended meaning to particular words on your site. This element works similarly to the other elements in this grouping. For example, you use the title attribute to display the definition as a tooltip (as shown in figure 3-30):

```
<p>50 points if you know what a <dfn title="A method for storing and organising files and data.">folder</dfn> is!</p>
```

50 points if you know what a *folder* is!

A method or storing an organising files and data.

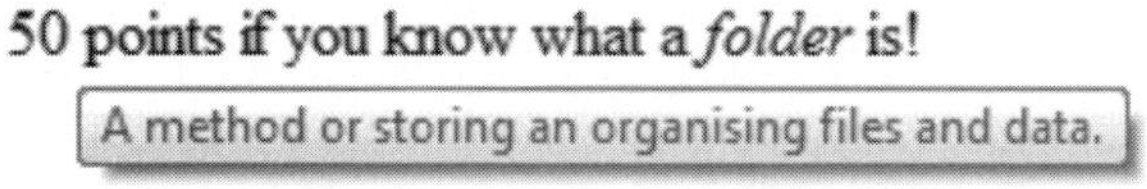

Figure 3-30. The dfn element gives you a way to provide definitions for particular words that appear on your site; this might prove especially helpful if your site contains a lot of technical or subject-specific jargon.

Formatting: \<b>, \<i>, \<big>, \<small>, \<em>, \<strong>, and \<tt>

When you're ready to come to apply structure to the textual elements of your site, you will find seven HTML elements that can give your text added punch. Many people choose to ignore these elements entirely because they view them as stylistic (and most developers use CSS for any styling); however, each of these seven elements has an important semantic value that can help you create a more effective site. When writing your code, keep in mind that you should use these elements only under the circumstances mentioned. Otherwise, you might end up using them erroneously for presentation, rather than aid your site's structure. It can take a bit of practice until you get the hang of which element will work best in which circumstance.

The bold and italic tags are good examples of elements that are in decline because of their natural presentation effect, yet still have an important role to play structurally. For example, sometimes bold and italic tags are more appropriate to use than a span tag with CSS styling. Specifically, you can make use of the b element when you require a word to be offset from the page in terms of its importance, but without having any additional meaning behind it. You could use this to highlight certain keywords in a document that might hold some semantic value to the page, but not much importance apart from the context you use them in. You will find the same rules apply for the i element, except this time you could apply the element to the name of an object, individual, or word (or even a film!) rather than words that have inherent meaning. This works because the word or phrase you apply these tags to are part of the natural reading context of the page, but they aren't things you would shout out loud when saying them (see Figure 3-31)! The use of bold for offset words or italic for subtle recognition still has a place within the coding environment:

```
<p>While searching the web is important, if you use <i>Google</i> you
may end up browsing through a lot of <b>spam results</b> which as you
will know from reading email can be quite annoying!</p>
```

While searching the web is important, if you use *Google* you may end up browsing through a lot of **spam results** which as you will know from reading email can be quite annoying!

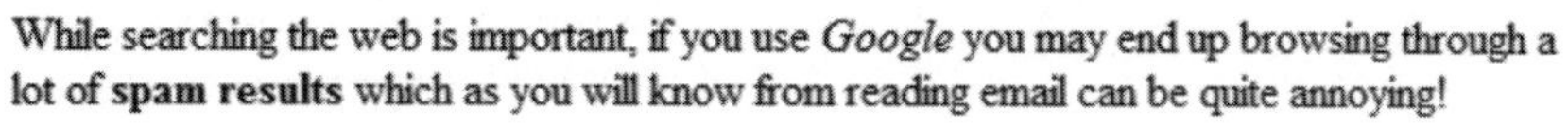

Figure 3-31. You can use italic and bold elements to bring focus to content without semantic value.

Like bold and italic elements, big and small elements are often abandoned in favor of using style elements, even though they still have a clear time and place (see Figure 3-32). You can use the big and small elements for what you might call relative measurement. You should probably use the small tag only when creating information that is no more or less important than other content, but could be less interesting to read, such as a legal disclaimer or small print in a document. In contrast to this, you might use the big element to highlight more interesting snippets of information. Sure, you might highlight such material through emphasis, but using a big element might help a discrete piece of information to speak for itself, as opposed to adding emphasis to the overall meaning of the document, such as expressing shock:

```
<p>I once saw a dolphin and it <big>jumped out of the water knocking me
over</big>, luckily I can swim pretty well <small> though it took me 15
minutes just to dry off when I got home</small>, so anyway it was a
unique trip!</p>
```

I once saw a dolphin and it jumped out of the water knocking me over, luckily I can swim pretty well though it took me 15 minutes just to dry off when I got home, so anyway it was a unique trip!

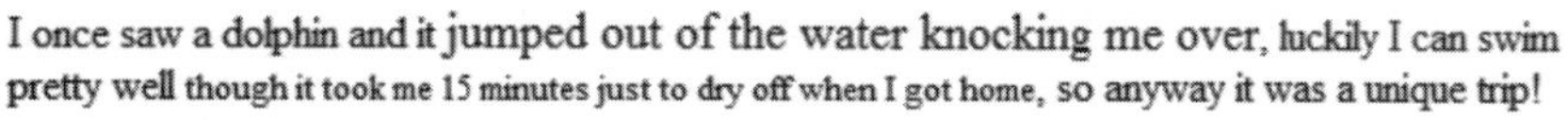

Figure 3-32. You can make your text slightly bigger or smaller by using the right elements.

In contrast to the big and small elements, the emphasis (em) and strong (strong) elements add a layer of importance and relevance to key information (see Figure 3-33). Whereas bold and italic elements offer natural highlighting for things like names; and whereas the big and small elements enable you to express the interest level of your content; the em and strong elements prominently draw attention (in terms of semantics) to the elements they enclose. Any word or phrase enclosed in these elements will be promoted in its importance in the context of the text:

```
<p>While all the <em>workers</em> are important and the
<strong>supervisors</strong> may be extra important, there is no-one as
super important as the <em><strong>CEO<strong><em> who owns the
business.</p>
```

While all the *workers* are important and the **supervisors** may be extra important, there is no-one as super important as the ***CEO who owns the business.***

Figure 3-33. Emphasis and strength elements enable you to add focus and heightened importance to your the content.

HTML's <tt> element acts like *teletype*, or marked up like typewriter text). Developers have almost totally abandoned this element in terms of CSS-imposed styles. This is probably for the best because you have few genuine opportunities to implement it, although you might employ it to highlight something historical.

NotED

HTML5 deprecates both big *and* tt, *which means you should no longer use them. You can still use them in HTML 4.01, but the fact that go away in HTML5 means you should consider using alternative tags.*

After reading this section, you know several additional elements that can you might use purely to implement style in your document, but which might also be more appropriately used for structural formatting. When you start marking up your content (highlighting elements as appropriate), you should ignore the criticism of these elements and use them for their intended purpose: they are valid, useful tools when marking up content—honest!

Formatting: <sub>, <sup> and <bdo>

The subscript and superscript elements exist to define characters that you want to display smaller than the surrounding text, but either elevated slightly above or pushed slightly below the regular line level, usually for a highly specific content goal (see Figure 3-34). As with other formatting elements, the subscript and superscript elements might seem confusing, but you have probably come across instances where both sub and sup have made an impact on a page. Often, people mistake the usage of these tags as purely presentational because they affect the text's visual appearance; however, if you need to display mathematical or scientific equations, or if you want to reference footnotes, you might find yourself needing these elements. The chemical symbol for water provides a perfect example of subscript in action: (H_2O). In a similar vein, you might use superscript to express a date, such as the 12th century:

```
<p>Please could I have a glass of H<sub>2</sub>O when I take the train
on the 20<sup>th</sup> of this month?</p>
```

Please could I have a glass of H_2O when I take the train on the 20th of this month?

Figure 3-34. You can see two elements in this example: subscript and superscript..

The bdo (bidirectional text) element exists for one extremely good purpose: it allows you to change the direction of text flow within the browser. For example, you might want to use this tag if you want to add translations for your content because some languages (such as Arabic) change the natural left-to-right reading direction. This element has limited applications, it can serve you well if you offer multilingual information on your site. The bdo element is assisted by the dir direction attribute, which either uses ltr (left-to-right) or rtl (right-to-left) as its value; the element also has a the lang attribute, which you can use when translating text. For example, you might use the lang attribute to define a language that certain text should use by default, causing the element to become a container for linguistics:

```
<bdo dir="ltr">Insert your content here.</bdo>
```

Formatting: <ins> and <del>

When you make changes to your site's content—perhaps you are as prone to making typos as I am—you might want to make sure that people can see where you have made these changes (see Figure 3-35). The HTML specification provides insert and delete elements that you can use to allow people to track changes to your site (and its content). Businesses do not tend to use these elements because they don't want to advertise their mistakes—they might fear it would impact their perceived professionalism—but you might encounter several appropriate circumstances where you might use these elements on your site. For example, you might want to use these when you provide genuine updates to your site, such as when you add new information to an existing article or new facts surface that undermine or enhance the claims of an existing article. Of course, using the ins element to show where you inserted new information and the del element for where you deleted information is great for cases where you need to track changes. Be careful not to go overboard using these elements; for example, mass changes could result in an unreadable document, with lots of crossed out content:

```
<p>Welcome to the website! <ins>Since you last visited we have fixed
some general bugs.</ins> The website itself was created for
<del>you</del><ins>both you and your friends</ins> to share your
experience with the world.</p>
```

Welcome to the website! <u>Since you last visited we have fixed some general bugs</u> The website itself was created for ~~you~~<u>both you and your friends</u> to share your experience with the world.

Figure 3-35. You can use the insert and delete elements to show the addition of new content and deletion of old information visually. Notice how the inserted elements are underlined, but the deleted elements are marked with strikethrough.

NotED

The HTML5 specification includes a new time *element that lets you reference specific times and dates; this might be useful for tracking changes and updates. Another tag that you might find useful is the* mark *element, which enables you to highlight text, such as search results or a quote.*

Formatting: <code>, <pre>, <var>, <samp>, and <kbd>

The purpose of elements such as code is to display programming or syntax on your site. For example, if you want to put some readable HTML on your site, this would be an appropriate use of the code element (see Figure 3-36). Of course, you won't need this element unless your site will show off your coding ability (or provide coding tutorials). If you do decide to show code, you might want to preserve its formatting and any spacing it uses. The preservation element (pre) comes into play at this point. You can use this element to ensure that your code appears as you see it within the source code window, and it will retain any formatting you give it.

```
<pre><code>body {color: #000000;}</code></pre>
```

```
body {color: #000000;}
```

Figure 3-36. You can display code on the screen and make it look just as it does in a code editor.

Tags such as var give you additional ways you can apply special meaning to your elements (see Figure 3-37). This tag allows you to define a variable that you want the visitor to take into account. You could use this content as placeholder text for places where the visitor must take action, rather than simply view a sample that you display. Of course, if you want to show the intended result of an action (or define the action itself), rather than allowing the visitor to choose, you could use the samp element. Technical manuals often use the samp element to provide a sample value that explains how a process works, such as stating which button someone should press or which menu someone should click in a window. These two elements work as opposing *forces*: the variable element gives you an example of what you should expect, while the sample element indicates what output will likely result from a given action. You don't see these elements often, but they are useful alongside code tags because they help you provide usable examples:

```
<p>You should go to the <samp>File</samp> menu and set your name to
something like <var>NinjaGuy</var>.</p>
```

You should go to the `File` menu and set your name to something like *NinjaGuy*.

Figure 3-37. The variable and sample elements give you even more ways of providing explicit meaning to your content.

Finally, you might find a quick note on the underused keyboard (kbd) element keyboard (see Figure 3-38). Like var and samp, kbd lets you provide a value for something within your content. In this case, the code exists to mark up references to keyboard shortcuts that the visitor needs to press, such as pressing Ctrl and C to copy text to the clipboard. This element is exceptionally useful for tutorials, but it has limited appeal elsewhere.

```
<p>For more assistance with this product press the <kbd>F1</kbd> key
now!</p>
```

For more assistance with this product press the `F1` key now!

Figure 3-38. Use the keyboard element to tell your visitors what key combination to press to accomplish a particular task.

Checkpoint: Part 3

Welcome to the third checkpoint. Your web page should have all the basics in place, including the required first elements that you learned about in stage one, and the content that you formatted with the appropriate elements in stage two. If you've been doing this book's exercises as you go, you have added all the extra bits and pieces that describe what is going on between those paragraphs and lists on your site. You have also taken the time to think about the anchor links you wish to incorporate into your content (assuming you require any, of course).In the next stage, you will build a navigation menu, along with some other common elements, such as a logo and copyright statement. You will also learn how to link to external sites and other useful pages you intend to offer (using your sitemap as a guide); and you will learn how to include more areas of interest for your visitors.

It's great to provide your visitors with interesting and exciting places to explore, but you don't want to go overboard. After all, your visitors might find it confusing if you give them too many places to go, especially if you don't provide sufficient explanation for why a visitor might want to visit a particular piece of your site. For example, I have adapted the sample code from the previous checkpoints to add some of the useful elements you learned about in the preceding sections. Once you make sure that you have marked up your content correctly, you have done all you need to do to set up your site's content. At this point, all your text should be appropriately represented, and all images should be referenced. What you should do now is pause whatever else you might be doing, save your file, and refresh your browser to see how everything looks now that your site is complete. When you're ready to continue, carry on to the next stage.

See for Yourself: Marking up Content

This example shows how you might mark up a site based on the tags mentioned in this section (see Figure 3-39):

```
<!DOCTYPE html PUBLIC "-//W3C//DTD HTML 4.01//EN"

    "http://www.w3.org/TR/html4/strict.dtd">
<html lang="en">
<head>

</head>
<body>
    <h2>Who are we?</h2>
    <p>You have visited this <a href="about.html">sample</a> website
because obviously you want to see what code can look like if it's placed
together in a <strong>logical</strong> order, hopefully what you are
reading makes <del>a little bit of</del> <ins>enough</ins> sense
<ins>for you to follow</ins>.</p>
    <img src="/images/chart.gif" alt="Chart of how everything appears"
title="Pie chart!"/>
```

```
    <p>As you can see from the above image, everything may look bland
but it has a <a href="features.html">purpose</a>!</p>
    <h2>What can this website do?</h2>
    <p>Well I am glad you asked, if you check out the below list you can
see what <em>this</em> site uses.</p>
    <ul>
        <li>Headings</li>
        <li>Paragraphs</li>
        <li>Images</li>
        <li>Unordered Lists</li>
    </ul>
</body>
</html>
```

As before, the highlighted code shows off the parts added since the previous example.

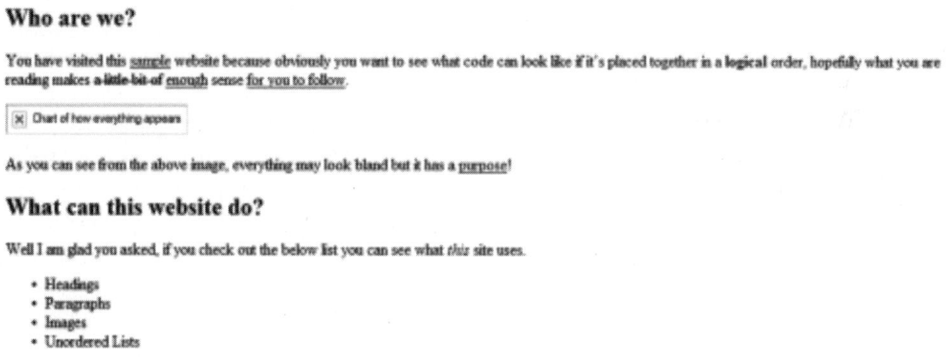

Who are we?

You have visited this sample website because obviously you want to see what code can look like if it's placed together in a logical order, hopefully what you are reading makes a little bit of enough sense for you to follow.

[X] Chart of how everything appears

As you can see from the above image, everything may look bland but it has a purpose!

What can this website do?

Well I am glad you asked, if you check out the below list you can see what *this* site uses.

- Headings
- Paragraphs
- Images
- Unordered Lists

Figure 3-39. The latest iteration fo the stamp-collection site implements some subtle but welcome additions in the site's presentation, including the addition of links to other parts of the site.

Further Learning

You're probably getting used to the idea of adding HTML to your site's content. Moreover, what you have learned will prove a good start, because your next steps will leverage the parts you've already done heavily. You probably intend to have more than one page on your site, so you need to take into account the elements of your site that you haven't written already. These are the *global*, or common, elements of the site. Most sites have a logo (or some text that shows the name), a navigation menu that contains links to important pages in the site, and a footer that contains a copyright message. Your next step is to add these common features, which will make browsing and navigating your site easier for your visitors.

Separating Sections

The most common elements of a website—in other words, the elements you find on every website—consist of the header, the navigation menu, and the footer (see Figure 3-40). You've seen descriptions of each already; now you will need to decide how you want to implement these common features on your own site. Note that your visitors will expect all of these elements; few sites have a valid excuse for not using them in their designs:

- **Header**: Generally speaking, the header is the most important part of a site, in terms of both recognition and a visitor's ability to browse a site. Headers usually contain a logo formed with text, an image, or through the use of a technology such as Flash. Your logo is an important part of your brand identity (you'll learn more about creating a logo in Chapter 6). Also, the header can include a search box which allows visitors to find pages quickly and easily.

- **Navigation**: Headers often contain some form of navigation menu, and you can place them within sidebars, content, or even in the footer, which is why they deserve their own section. Generally, consists of an unordered list that has anchor links to each page (as an item in a list). Most developers agree this is the best way to express a menu because, if you think about it, most navigation menus are basically a list of various locations within a site.

- **Footer**: The footer is a location that usually contains a copyright statement, useful links to explicit pages of a site (rather than general links to common locations), and even links to social sites such as Twitter or other useful sites. Generally, footer text is like small print, which most people look at only when they're feeling curious. It is usually comprised of a mixture of text, unordered lists, and anchor links with images.

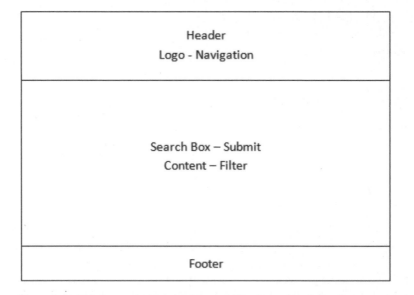

Figure 3-40. This image shows you might use div elements to layer the contents of your site.

The first thing you need to do to organize the various elements of your site is separate the global elements, such as navigation, from the content you have so neatly marked up. Before you begin building the common elements, we need to split your content from the rest of the body. HTML includes a special divider element (div) to help you do this. Because it is a generic element of little semantic value, this element works much like a span element: it allows you to group code together both for the purpose of styling and to make things more organized. One interesting thing about this tag is that it doesn't appear visually on the page; rather, performs its magic in the background.

Structure: <div>

When you start defining the structure of your HTML in the body tags, the first thing you want to do is define a series of categories to group your content. Developers typically describe these categories in terms of a header, navigation, content, and footer, but you can produce custom groups wherever you like and for any part of your site. What you want to do is to begin grouping your content, and no tag will do the job better than that of the humble div element. Splitting up your design into sections will make your life easier when you get to the stage of adding style and behavior to make your site. For example, you can almost use the div element like a folder, telling the browser to apply certain style to all the elements held within it. You use an id attribute to determine which div element represents which piece of content; , this can help you remember what each section should contain.

The following example shows you how to use a div element to split your content:

```
<div id="header">
  ...
</div>
<div id="content">
  ...
</div>
<div class="navigation">
  ...
</div>
<div id="footer">
  ...
</div>
```

NotED

The HTML5 specification includes a series of custom elements for laying out your section blocks. These custom elements are header, nav, article, section, aside, *and* footer. *Support for these elements remains minimal, but they will eventually replace* div *tags, which hold no semantic value. You will use* Section *elements to separate blocks of content (such as the* article *tag),* headers *to provide useful overviews of content, a* footer *to hold copyright and related material, and a* nav *section for navigation and menus. The* aside *element acts as a sidebar, note, or tip.*

Checkpoint: Part 4

So far you've learned about the global elements of a site and how you can organize the various sections of your code. Next, you need to add the div elements for your site's various sections, and then add the header, navigation, and footer areas to your design. At this point, you need to put down the book, fire up your code editor, and start working with this new element. When you're finished, you should have a basic, but now feature-complete design that you can enhance with any missing bits and pieces you drew in your wireframes (such as page-specific text and images that aren't part of the content). After you finish adding the dividers and the common site elements, you need to compare your existing site to the wireframe you created in Chapter 1, adding the missing pieces as appropriate. Next, you can move onto the next segment, where you will fill in that empty head element you created earlier, but have thus far left blank.

See for Yourself: Marking up Content

The next example shows you how to leverage the most recent elements discussed, modifying the existing version of the site's homepage (see Figure 3-41). As before, this code highlights the newly added sections, which is mainly comprised of div elements to place everything in appropriate sections and some useful global features, such as a heading; some navigation links to other pages, and a footer that contains a copyright message:

```
<!DOCTYPE html PUBLIC "-//W3C//DTD HTML 4.01//EN"

    "http://www.w3.org/TR/html4/strict.dtd">
<html lang="en">
<head>

</head>
<body>
<div id="header">
        <h1>Welcome to MySite!</h1>
        <h2>This website was created by me for showing you how to take
advantage of HTML!</h2>
        <p><a href="#navigation">Skip to navigation</a></p>
</div>
<div id="content">
        <h2>Who are we?</h2>
        <p>You have visited this <a href="about.html">sample</a> website
because obviously you want to see what code can look like if it's placed
together in a <strong>logical</strong> order, hopefully what you are
reading makes <del>a little bit of</del> <ins>enough</ins> sense
<ins>for you to follow</ins>.</p>
        <img src="/images/chart.gif" alt="Chart of how everything
appears" title="Pie chart!"/>

        <p>As you can see from the above image, everything may look
bland but it has a <a href="features.html">purpose</a>!</p>
        <h2>What can this website do?</h2>
        <p>Well I am glad you asked, if you check out the below list you
can see what <em>this</em> site uses.</p>
        <ul>
                <li>Headings</li>
                <li>Paragraphs</li>
                <li>Images</li>
                <li>Unordered Lists</li>
        </ul>
</div>
<div class="navigation">
```

```
        <ul>
                <li><a href="#services" title="My
Services">Services</a></li>
                <li><a href="#portfolio" title="View
Portfolio">Portfolio</a></li>
                <li><a href="#research" title="Online Articles
">Articles</a></li>
                <li><a href="#about" title="About Me">About</a></li>
                <li><a href="#contact" title="Contact
Me">Contact</a></li>
        </ul>
</div>
<div id="footer">
        <p>Copyright &copy; MySite 2009 - 2010. All rights reserved.</p>
</div>
</body>
</html>
```

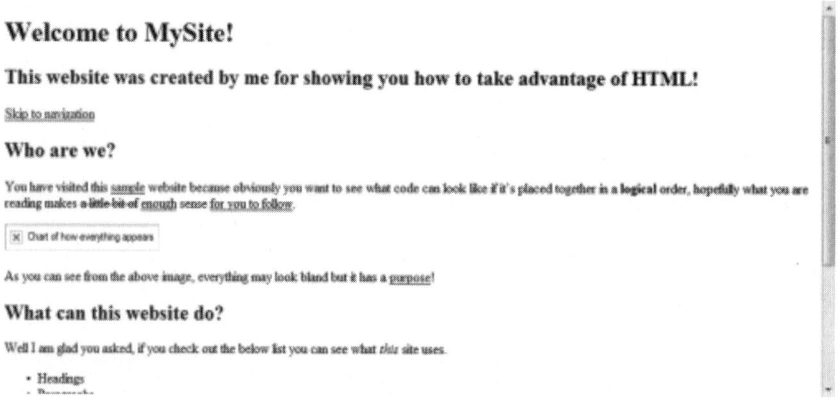

Figure 3-41. The most recent additions incorporate div and other element into your site.

Expand Your Mind

Your page now includes your content and the common elements of the site, and it's beginning to look relatively complete. However, at this point you need to turn your attention away from the body and look towards the head of the document. The head of the document exists to hold information that doesn't appear on the page, yet the information it holds is quite valuable, adding context to your site. Essentially, the code that goes in the head of the document is the "thinking code" that lets browsers and search engines extend the functionality of your site beyond what visitors can see on the page. You won't learn about many of the elements that you use in your head in great detail right now, but this book will discuss them in much greater detail at various points throughout future chapters of the book. That said, you'll still learn several useful bits of code you can add to the head of your page in the next section; the later chapters that cover this material will build on the information covered here.

Inside Your Head

Welcome to the brains of the workshop! The head of an HTML document is where you place all the thinking code you want the browser to act on. A few of these elements are mandatory, but some aspects of what you include in the head are entirely up to you. You should place all of the code in this section between the two head tags in your index.html file (this is which you left a gap there when you created this section originally). Now let's get your site thinking for itself, starting with possibly the most widely recognized and important element on your site: its title.

<title>

As its name suggests, the title tag is where you provide the brand name or site title of your site. The title tag influences browser windows because it places its contents, not only in the top of the tab you find it in, but also in the browser's title bar (see Figure 3-42). The title element also plays a role when people add your site to their bookmarks (favorites) because it represents the default filename of the item when your site appears in search engines (the search results people use to find you), and even when users submit your URL to some social networks, where the name of your site is used by default. Thus, it's important that you keep the title tag for each page unique; it's also critical that your visitors know what page they are on, not least because you want to ensure that the bookmarks visitors create for your site won't override each other by default. You can usually accomplish this by giving both the page title and the website title (separated by either a (–) or (|) character, with a space on each side).Note that this element is not optional; you *must* include a *unique* title for each page.

This example shows you how to implement a title for the front page of a site (in the head tag):

```
<head>
<title>MySite!</title>
</head>
```

This snippet shows you how to implement a title for a secondary page on a site (again, in the head tag):

```
<title>About Me - MySite!</title>
```

Figure 3-42. The information in the title tag displays in the browser window; this figure shows the title text for the Apress site.

ExplainED

Search engines and browsers can display only a limited amount of characters in a title, *so you should keep the title short but sweet, using no more than 75 characters. This will help you avoid seeing your* title *"cut off" when a browser displays it.*

<meta>

You will probably find several uses for the meta tag on your site, and you'll learn more about this subject in Chapter 9. However, this tag has a special role to play in your pages are served, as well as how they work with the browser. Most meta tags hold a name and content attribute, which exist to provide information about the content of your pages; this enables search engines, browsers, and applications to get such details as a description of your site, the authors of your pages, and much more).

A meta tag you mark with the http-equiv attribute gives instructions to the host of your site (the web server), rather than to the browser. HTML includes several http-equiv meta tags, some of which are standardized and some which are proprietary to browser makers. To keep things simple, this chapter will focus on a single implementation of this type of meta tag (the most commonly used one). Of course, as a beginner you don't need to know the specifics about http-equiv and how it functions; all you need to remember is that the these tags can give your site some useful behind-the-scenes functionality that could serve your site in a variety of different ways.

In this section, you'll learn about the content-type http-equiv attribute, which is the only required tag for this type of element you'll encounter. Your declaration of this tag provides details about the MIME type of the page, which basically indicates the file format a browser should use to display your document. You should always place the content-type meta element directly under the head element because it affects the entire page. In other words, this element takes priority over even your title element, as well as and any other references you place within the head of the document. It is recommended that you use the following content-type attribute on all of your pages:

```
<meta http-equiv="content-type" content="text/html; charset=utf-8">
```

This line tells the web server that this is a standard HTML file, and that is uses a standard character set. The character set indicates what characters your site will display. If you use any special characters, such as a foreign language, then you might need to use a different character set. For most purposes, the character set provided in the preceding line will suffice (utf-8 signifies the Unicode character set). This is the most common implementation for the http-equiv META element (which defines how your page should be rendered), but you can find other potential http-equiv declarations that can benefit the visitor, such as the ones included in this list:

- **imagetoolbar**: www.dynamicdrive.com/dynamicindex9/imagebar.htm
- **pics-label**: www.w3.org/PICS/
- **X-UA-Compatible**: http://msdn.microsoft.com/ie/cc405106.aspx

Note that the preceding implementations are more technical, so you should use them only when you feel comfortable with them and you believe they will be worth the extra difficulty of adding them to your site.

NotED

To see how the pics-label http-equiv *attribute can certify your website so that it'll register as safe on net-nanny software for children's viewing, you can check out the independent ratings systems for ICRA (www.icra.org/decode/#legacypics), SafeSurf (www.safesurf.com/ssplan.htm), and Weburbia's Safe for kids scheme (www.weburbia.com/safe/ratings.htm).*

<link>

Finally, you're ready to learn about one of the most popular elements that appears in the head of an HTML file: the link tag. This tag acts as a method of referencing external resources, such as CSS, RSS, Atom, RDF, OpenSearch, and other documents (including Favicons, iPhone, and iPod Touch icons). You'll learn about all these things later, so you have some exciting things to look forward to including in your site as you progress further into the project! The Opera web browser also uses link elements for its navigation menu, but because few other browsers have adopted its potential, so you won't take advantage of this particular use for link tags at this time.

ExplainED

You'll learn about implementing style and scripts later in the book, so the style *and* script *header elements have been omitted. Also, you want to separate your style and structure entirely from the document's content, so it's recommended that you do not use these elements, except when referencing separate files.*

Checkpoint: Part 5

You have reached the final checkpoint of this chapter, which signifies that you've learned a lot about what you must do to build an HTML document, as well as some handy information about a few unique and useful tags that you can throw in for added functionality. You should now have something similar to what you see in the code that follows, but customized for your own site.

See for Yourself: What Your Site Looks Like So Far!

```
<!DOCTYPE html PUBLIC "-//W3C//DTD HTML 4.01//EN"

    "http://www.w3.org/TR/html4/strict.dtd">
<html lang="en">
<head>
        <meta http-equiv="content-type" content="text/html; charset=utf-8">
        <title>MySite!</title>
<head>
<body>
<div id="header">
        <h1>Welcome to MySite!</h1>
```

```
        <h2>This website was created by me for showing you how to take
advantage of HTML!</h2>
        <p><a href="#navigation">Skip to navigation</a></p>
</div>
<div id="content">
        <h2>Who are we?</h2>
        <p>You have visited this <a href="about.html">sample</a> website
because obviously you want to see what code can look like if it's placed
together in a <strong>logical</strong> order, hopefully what you are
reading makes <del>a little bit of</del> <ins>enough</ins> sense
<ins>for you to follow</ins>.</p>
        <img src="/images/chart.gif" alt="Chart of how everything
appears" title="Pie chart!"/>

        <p>As you can see from the above image, everything may look
bland but it has a <a href="features.html">purpose</a>!</p>
        <h2>What can this website do?</h2>
        <p>Well I am glad you asked, if you check out the below list you
can see what <em>this</em> site uses.</p>
        <ul>
                <li>Headings</li>
                <li>Paragraphs</li>
                <li>Images</li>
                <li>Unordered Lists</li>
        </ul>
</div>
<div class="navigation">
        <ul>
                <li><a href="#services" title="My
Services">Services</a></li>
                <li><a href="#portfolio" title="View
Portfolio">Portfolio</a></li>
                <li><a href="#research" title="Online Articles
">Articles</a></li>
                <li><a href="#about" title="About Me">About</a></li>
                <li><a href="#contact" title="Contact
Me">Contact</a></li>
        </ul>
</div>
<div id="footer">
        <p>Copyright &copy; MySite 2009 - 2010. All rights reserved.</p>
</div>
</body>
</html>
```

ExplainED

This example uses several of the tags discussed in this chapter, but you should be aware that HTML includes many other useful tags you might add to the page's head *tag after you provide some basic structure to your page's* body *element.*

Before you proceed to the next step, you should put down the book again, save where you are at, and preview your site as it stands now: a complete (but single) page that is ready to appear on the Web. Of course, you aren't done with it yet because you have plans to add styles that will heighten the attractiveness of your pages! But this will occur in Chapter 5. We still have a couple of other elements worthy of mention before leaving this chapter

What Else Can You Do?

At this stage, you have basically completed your document, and you're ready to post your page live on the Web. You know almost everything you need to know about the basics of HTML, but you might find the following tips and tricks relating to the structure of your site useful. These and a couple other tips you'll learn later in the book will help you make your site easier to manage, while also giving it a bit more functionality. You will also find some useful tips for making the best use of everything you have learned so far, as well as some critical advice on how to avoid common pitfalls in the concluding segment of the chapter.

Forms

Everyone hates filling out forms, but they are a required element of the Internet. The ability to send data is useful for everything from posting to blogs to searching for information on Google. The good news: Adding a form to your site is easy. The problems tend to come when you try to apply styles to them because browsers can be stubborn when it comes to styling to form elements. You also face a significant level of complexity when dealing with information sent or received using forms (especially as a beginner). You should keep in mind that the form element exists at the block level, but it requires that you place another block-level element inside it, such as a div or paragraph tag. You might also use the container element known as a fieldset and its required child element, legend, which groups form elements (legend gives the fieldset a title to work with, though you can hide both using CSS).

The form element contains two attributes that ultimately control how the form's data is sent. First, you have the method attribute, which can either have the value of GET or POST. The GET value will append the URL with a query string that includes the results of the elements you specify. This is what enables you to bookmark the results and see the search terms in the address bar when you perform a Google search (see Figure 3-43):

```
<form method="get" action="http://www.google.com/search">
        <fieldset>
                <legend>Search this website</legend>
        </fieldset>
</form>
```

A GET value can only be of a certain length, so you might use a POST value instead if you want to process information in the background, rather than display it in the browser. You should also be aware of the action attribute, which is a URL to the server-side script that will handle the form. You need this attribute because HTML cannot do anything, except send the results. You'll learn more about server-side scripts later in Chapter 8. In any case, the preceding example enables you to create a form that performs a Google search.

Figure 3-43. Legends allow you to provide information about a group of elements in a form.

NotED

Sometimes you might want to block visitors from the using part of a form. You can accomplish this by using the disabled="disabled" *attribute, which disables form elements, even though they remain onscreen; the user won't be able to input information or otherwise interact with the element.*

The most common element you see in a form is the input element. This self-closing tag usually has two attributes: name and value. However, the most unique aspect of this element is how the attribute type can physically alter both the input element's visual appearance and the input method based on the available controls. Generally, you can precede each input with the `label` tag to give a description of the item in question. You can link this label to the object it precedes using the `for` attribute, which should have the same value as the input's ID attribute. You'll learn how to take more pronounced advantage of this technique later in the book. You can add several elements to forms that enable you to collect information from your visitors, or allow them to pass back details required to complete a transaction successfully.

The button input type is one of the most critical input elements. Without those buttons to click, none of your data would go anywhere! You can use four different types of buttons on a form. The standard, generic `button` input type has no direct usage, except that you can use scripting to customize a button so it triggers certain types of behavior (see Figure 3-44). Clicking a button to complete a form and pass the information to the server takes advantage of the `submit` input type. If you want more control over the look and feel of your submit buttons, you can use the `image` input type, which lets you select a custom picture to replace the default look of an icon. Finally, you can take advantage of the `button` element (be careful not to this be confuse this with the `button` input type) to customize your text through inline tags:

```
<input type="button" value="I do nothing but click me anyway!"/>
<input type="submit" name="form-submit" id=" form-submit " value="Send
your email now!"/>
<input type="image" src="/images/register.jpg" alt="Sign up today!"/>
<button>Please <em>sign me up</em> to your newsletter!</button>
```

Figure 3-44. You can add a range of different button types for your visitors to click.

ExplainED

There is a fifth type button type you can use: `reset`. However, you should avoid using this button because people often mistake it for a submit button and end up wiping out all of their work!

Next, let's look at the most popular form of input available: the good old text field. The ability to insert text on a form allows visitors to send emails from a webpage or add comments to blogs. Without the text field, you would simply not be able to have a decent amount of interactivity on the web. You can add two input types to a text field: `text` and `password`—it should be obvious what these do. Forms can also include a `textarea` element, which allows you to add multiple lines of information (the default input types only allow single-line entry). Determining the size of these elements consists mainly of defining the `size` attribute within input types. In the case of `textarea`, you define the attributes `cols` (letters across) and `rows` (letters down). The best way to size them up is to try them out yourself (see Figure 3-45 to see the following code in action):

```
<input type="text" name="username" id=" username " size="20"/>
<input type="password" name="password" id=" password " maxlength="12"
size="20"/>
<textarea cols="40" name="comment" rows="5">Text goes here!</textarea>
```

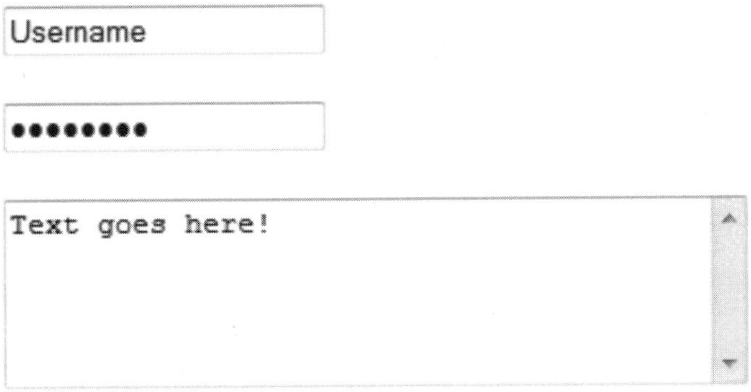

Username

••••••••

Text goes here!

Figure 3-45. Form elements let visitors type and submit information (note how the password is hidden!).

Another popular form element(apart from the `input` element) is the `select` element (see Figure 3-46). This tag allows you to create dropdown menus that you can categorize into sections. Within the select tag, you can optionally place optgroup tags with a label attribute that state what category the dropdown menu item falls into. Finally, you should use the option element to specify the available choices for each entry in the dropdown menu:

```
<select name="Computers">
        <optgroup label="Operating Systems">
                <option>Linux</option>
                <option>Mac</option>
                <option>Windows</option>
        </optgroup>
         <optgroup label="Software">
                <option>Firefox</option>
                <option>InkScape</option>
                 <option>OpenOffice</option>
                <option>Scribus</option>
        </optgroup>
</select>
```

Many developers like to use this element to let users choose from predefined options; good places you might implement this are a feedback form or a list of brands you resell in an ecommerce shop on your site.

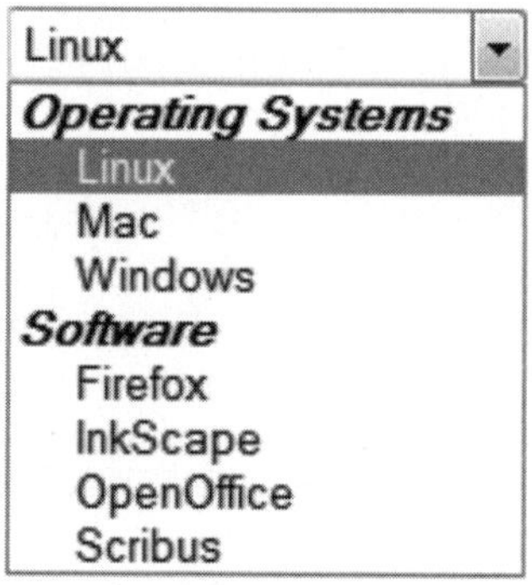

Figure 3-46. You can use dropdown menus to let visitors select an option from a list of items.

If you want to give your visitors a choice between preselected options, the select menu doesn't suit every situation. For example, you might want to present all of the possible options, so a visitor can them all without having to browse through a menu. The select system works well when you want to rate something or look through a catalog of options. However, you might want to use the checkbox or radio multiple-choice options to enable visitors to provide the feedback through a survey (see Figure 3-47). It's important to understand the difference between checkboxes and radio buttons. A checkbox can present a range of options that your visitors can checked or unchecked, as they see fit. Radio buttons, on the other hand, only allow a single selection between various options. Selecting one radio button empties the previously selected radio button to make way for the new one. If at any point you want to preselect an option in a checkbox or radio box, you can use the checked attribute, assigning it a value of checked. You should also remember to wrap checkboxes and radio buttons with meaningful and descriptive labels:

```
<label for=" agree">I accept the terms of usage</label><input
type="checkbox" name=" agree" id=" agree" value="I-agree"/>
<label for="beeb1">BBC 1</label><input type="radio" name="station" id="
beeb1" value="BBC 1"/>
<label for="beeb2">BBC 2</label><input type="radio" name="station" id="
beeb2" value="BBC 2"/>
```

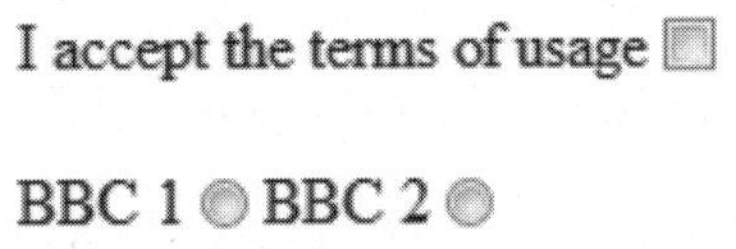

I accept the terms of usage ☐

BBC 1 ◉ BBC 2 ◉

Figure 3-47. Checkboxes allow visitors to choose as many options as they desire from a list; radio boxes allow visitors to choose from one of two or more options.

Another important input type has the attribute value of file (see Figure 3-48). You use this input type primarily for file uploads, and it comes equipped with a text field and a *Browse* button (visitors can click the *Browse* button to launch a dialog box that lets them search their computer for the kinds of files they want to upload). Few sites take advantage of this element, but it does figure prominently on sites that allow you to store files online, such as hosting-file managers, photo- and video-sharing sites and even email websites that include an attachment field. The code to incorporate a file looks like this:

```
<input type="file" name="upload" id="upload" />
```

Browse...

Figure 3-48. This input type value enables visitors to upload files to your site.

Frames: <frameset>, <frame>, <noframes> and <iframe>

Frames are one of the bad boys of the Internet. Some sites still use them (especially the iframe element), but they have been deprecated, so you should avoid using them. Every type of frame has problems that are too significant to overlook. Frames have accessibility, browser, standards (due to the fact they've been deprecated), and security issues. For example, frames can hide embedded code that is potentially malicious. The only reason I cover them here is because they remain prevalent on the Web, and you will probably come across them in your travels.

One frame element that remains in wide use today is the iframe tag, which allows you to embed one page within another. One of the significant, genuine uses of frames is to provide a sandbox environment where you can load subpages without affecting the holding page. While iframes do have legitimate uses, it is highly unlikely you will ever need to use an iframe element in favor of other, cleaner methods provided by CSS, AJAX, JavaScript, and all those other lovely little acronyms. Regardless, you should abandon and avoid using iframes whenever possible because they have the same problems that all frames have, including the potential security issues.

The following example illustrates how to embed iframes into documents:

```
<iframe src ="/files/advert.asp">
    <p>Your browser does not support iframes.</p>
</iframe>
```

The iframe *element is used today and it has been reintroduced to HTML5 for sandboxed content); on the other hand, there you can justify the use of* frameset, frame, *and* noframes.

The PVNK Approach

As in many other endeavors, less is more when it comes to web development. It helps you to avoid ending up with *spaghetti code* or *tag soup,* as it is known in the industry. I could go on for hours about the benefits you might gain from keeping your source code clean, but you will quickly learn that more code equates to more stuff you must manage, more bandwidth you must use, and slower site speeds—you want to avoid all of these things at all costs. Instead, you want to sit back, relax, and take your time when you build your website, ensuring that you keep things as easy for yourself as possible.

One way to minimize the code you create, while also keeping it as clean as possible, is to follow the conventions defined by the PVNK approach. This approach combines four different philosophies web designers commonly use for approaching site development:

- **POSH**: Plain Old Semantic HTML takes the approach that everything in your structure should comply with existing standards, meeting all recommendations that promote using the right piece of code for the right job (semantics). By ensuring that you use everything as it was intended, you can avoid the chance you will end up with content that is expressed inappropriately.

- **Vanilla**: The vanilla concept builds on the POSH ideal that code should be kept as plain as possible. You can accomplish this by reducing the amount of non-essential bits that you use to mark up the document. Don't misunderstand, please: You should use as many tags as you need to structure and style your content properly, but you should also remove any div or span elements that you don't need (or that are used inappropriately for achieving stylistic effects).

- **Naked**: Naked coding is the act of keeping your structure free from styles and behavior. Naked coding helps you ensure that your site will function for people who either do not have access to a technology (such as JavaScript) or have turned it off for some reason. You'll learn more about this in Chapter 7, where you will also learn about such topics as progressive enhancement.

- **KISS**: A well-known acronym used commonly in web design and in normal life, KISS stands for "Keep it simple, stupid!" This common phrase reiterates my earlier comments that you should make things as easy for yourself as possible. There is no point trying to build a simple that uses hundreds of lines of code, when half of that code would probably be redundant.

I know the preceding advice probably sounds rather more entertaining than you were expecting (especially expressions such as *POSH*, *Vanilla*, *Naked*, and *KISS*!), but developers often use the individual terms that comprise the PVNK approach to coding. Combining the terms gives you something to think about as you try to minimize your markup, maintain your code effectively, and stay in shape (a clean site is a happy site).

Summary

In this chapter, you learned about the semantics and standards of HTML. You learned about the various HTML tags that exist and got a few glimpses at the future with HTML 5). At this point, you should have a fantastic site filled with great content, though it probably looks visually bland and boring, if not ugly in some people's eyes! Don't worry about that, however; in later chapters, you will learn how to make your site as beautiful as any other site out there on the Internet. But you're not quite ready for that step. Instead, the time has come to buy your hosting package and domain name. You will use these to bring your wonderfully coded site online for the world to see. You have come a long way in learning HTML and content and site design, and you should be proud of what you have accomplished so far. This book has covered a ton lot of material in a relatively small amount of space. Don't be surprised if you need to refer back to this chapter as you create additional pages for your site. Before too long, the HTML elements and attributes discussed in this chapter will become second nature to you. Now you can close your editor and browser; you're ready to continue your journey by getting your site up on the Internet!

Chapter Checklist

- Learn the basics of HTML and come to grips with the idea of a site's structure
- Add your content to your code editor and add the appropriate HTML

- Take all you have learned so far and build all of the pages you require through this point

Questions and Answers

Q: *Should I start implementing HTML 5 while it remains in the drafting stage?*

A: You can find some basic support for HTML 5 in some web browsers (including IE8), but it's still too early to think about using it for your site at the present time. A draft specification means that the language in question is still under development and remains incomplete. This means elements you implement might be removed or new things might be added; this is your first site, and you don't want to worry about having to retrofit your site with new code to meet new drafts as they appear. It will probably be a few years before HTML 5 hits the mainstream, and when that does happen, you still have to account for supporting older browsers. At that point, you should feel free to have some fun and mess with the new language if you want!

Q: *Is producing and editing code complicated?*

A: This answer to this depends. You should be under no illusions that making a website is a multi-dimensional process that includes a lot of different elements. The sheer number of languages and technologies involved means some people will find the coding elements complicated, especially when it comes to remembering the different names for the various bits of code! However, this book should help take the edge off that learning curve by illustrating one critical fact: if you learn one thing at a time and layer it effectively, you can make things as easy for yourself as possible. As a result, you should be able to avoid getting bogged down in your site's code.

Q: *How do I take the template and create the other pages?*

A: At the end of this chapter, you should have (at least) the first page of your content completed and looking pretty sharp. Of course, you want to be able to adapt your knowledge to other pages (now and into the future), but that part is relatively simple. The best thing I can recommend is to that you make a copy of the `index.html` file you have produced; open it in your code editor and browser; give the page a new `title` in the `head` element; remove all of the code within the `div` element where your content is held (leaving the stuff that appears on every page intact); and then doing what you did the first time around, which is to paste your pre-written content into the editor and mark it up using the simple steps provided in this chapter. You can use this repeat this process as many times as required to produce a bunch of well-marked up and well-written HTML files that are ready to go on the Web (remember that to ensure the pages link to each other in some form!).

Where You Are Now

By the end of this chapter you should have the following:

- Folders for everything you will need on your site
- Content that is marked up carefully into HTML pages
- A site viewable in your favorite web browser

What About Web Hosting?

You've created a website; now you need to have a place on the Internet to put it! After the hard work you've done so far creating your content and marking it up in HTML, this part of your site creation will prove much easier. Until now, you've been looking at your site *locally*; that is, on your own, local computer. However, in order for the rest of the world to see your site, you have to upload it to an external computer, or *server*. Maintaining a web site requires two very different things. First, you need a host that will hold the files you create for visitors to see. Second, you must have a domain name that serves as the website address people type into their web browsers to visit you. You must have both of these vital components to publish your site, and you will need to decide on both a domain and a hosting provider. This is a critically important decision, and you must consider your options carefully. In the majority of cases, you pay for domains on a one- or two-year basis. Hosting agreements can range from monthly payments to yearly contracts (unless you go with a free host, which I will cover later in the chapter). When spending money, it behooves you to be sure about what you want because it will help you get the best service possible for the best price (within reason).

In this chapter, you'll learn how to do the following:

- Choose, purchase and protect the perfect domain name
- Evaluate your hosting options and choose the best provider for you
- Determine what functionality and features you should look for in a web host

There's No Place Like Home

Finding the perfect domain name can be a tough challenge; especially with the frustratingly high proportion of names that are already registered or taken (many of these are little more than vehicles to deliver spam vs. a proper web site). The web address you choose will appear in all search engines, user favorites, and bookmarks, and it's the address visitors will type into their browsers when they come to your site, not to mention what people will link to when referring to your site. Your web address is the visible symbol of your site for all to see. While picking a domain name is important, trying to developer a strong, unique brand on the Web in a roiling sea of competition can be the bigger and more important challenge, requiring solid research and a willingness to try different things to achieve the results you want.

The Web Site Addresses

Your online presence is dominated by a web site address; without it, your visitors would be unable to find you, which would cause all sorts of problems! The domain name you pick will give people something to type when they want to take a look at your site. The problem with there being so many sites is that it can be hard to stand out, which is why picking the right name and the extension to match is such an important aspect of making it as easy as possible for visitors to find you. Of course, you have various options when it comes to a domain name, including a wide variety of extensions you can use (there is more to the Web than .com, .net, and .org!). Some of these extensions are fairly generic, and you can use them on a worldwide basis, while others are intended for people residing in specific countries. The important thing to remember is that whatever you choose, you need to choose a domain (and extension) that mesh well with your needs.

Domains and Subdomains

Domain names are considered the primary location (central point) of a site. Whenever you visit a site that either starts with www or uses a simple site address such as google.com, you are visiting the main domain of that site. The purpose of a subdomain is to help separate different sections or areas of a site by splitting them off from the default location. The way this works is simple: Most places you visit will have a value placed between the http:// and the domain name (such as google.com). This could be the famous www that acts as the default subdomain to show the main site, or it could be something of your own choosing (such as images.google.com) that redirects users to a special area of the site you set up for a specific purpose. Subdomains are important because they can give individual sections of your site some unique branding and a sense of individualism that can help you target your audience better.

See for Yourself: Sample Subdomains

Google offers a wide range of services, and it features an assortment of subdomains to help users identify its services effectively. For example, Google uses these subdomains to make the subsections of its site addresses easier to remember:

- **Images**.google.com
- **Video**.google.com
- **Maps**.google.com
- **News**.google.com
- **Mail**.google.com
- And many more...

LinkED

If you would like to know the top 40 most popular Google subdomain, you can find a great article on the subject at www.labnol.org/internet/popular-google-subdomains/5888/.

One great benefit of using a subdomain is that, depending on your provider, you will have limitless access to creating and deleting subdomains as you need them; unlike standard domain names, they do not cost anything to set up. This is mainly because such subdomains are essentially part of the single address owned by the person who purchased the domain name. Subdomains are often provided by free hosts as a simple method to give users a unique website address, without requiring their users to purchase their own domain names. You can also find services that offer free subdomains to redirect users to a site that has a longer website address. For example, the free host might give you a domain of yoursite.freeprovider.com versus www.yoursite.com. In this case, your free host gives you a subdomain, but ultimately has its own branding visible (the free provider part) throughout your site.

Domain Extensions

The domain-name extension was born out of the need to categorize and separate different types of sites. The domain name registrars (the people in charge of adding your site's domain name to the big list of registered names) have such a wide variety of extensions available, so you might have a good chance of finding an alternative representation of your brand name if the .com domain you wanted has already been taken. Note that some extensions have limitations on them to prevent people from misusing them. For example, some country-based domains that require you live or work within the country to be entitled to register the extension name that refers to the country. The most important part of the domain extension is the part after the very last period, such as the com in www.google.com, or the org in en.wikipedia.org. This part is known as the *top-level domain* or *TLD* for short. There are two main types of TLDs: generic and country code.

- **Generic (gTLD):** The most popular domain names are known as generic TLDs. They retain their popularity because they apply on a world-wide scale, so they retain the most value in terms of public appeal and knowledge of the extension. While there are an ever-growing number of generic TLDs, three stand out as the most widely recognized, and they account for a majority of all registrations: .com, .net, and .org. You can find more details can be found at http://en.wikipedia.org/wiki/Generic_top-level_domain.

- **Country Code (ccTLD):** The country code top-level domains (such as .co.uk, .es, or .de) are used or reserved for use in a particular country (you might be required to have citizenship or business within the country to register certain domains). This usually limits the appeal or use of a domain name, but many countries have opened their domain names up for worldwide use, such as the pacific islands of Tuvalu, who have the .tv domain assigned to them. You can find more details on this subject at http://en.wikipedia.org/wiki/Country-code_top-level_domain.

The Future of TLDs

On the 26th June 2008, the Internet Corporation for Assigned Names and Number (ICANN) approved a process that would open up the amount of top-level domains, enabling organizations to register their own domain extensions. This means is that a company like Google could be entitled to apply for the extension .google. Similarly, Microsoft could register .msn as an officially recognized domain extension. In a different vein, a trade organization might register a generic domain, such as the .media TLD. The process will take a long time to implement (possibly starting in 2010), but new extensions will appear over the coming years. Note that the average person won't be able to acquire his own, unique TLD extension due to both the required expense of proposing a new name to ICANN and the restrictive measures the board will take to guarantee only suitable extension proposals get through.

ExplainED

It's easy to imagine a future where you might be able to have yourname@mail.msn *as your primary email account or* search.google *as the new home of your favorite search engine!*

What this means for you, the average person, is that the owners of those TLDs could effectively sell domains to the end consumer to expand the available extensions further. One downside of this could be that the overall domain extension pool will be further diluted because users will find it harder remember which extensions apply to the sites they want to visit. This change could make well-known extensions such as .com more valuable, while less-popular choices could simply drown in the expanding sea of TLDs.

Choosing a Domain Name

I once heard a joke on a well-known quote site that stated: "Domain names are like dates, all of the best ones are taken, but you can always find one from a foreign country." Sure this is funny, but it also holds a kernel of truth. An entire industry has appeared on the Web from people who literally spend their days buying and selling domain names just as your local-estate agent buys and sells houses. These companies reserve high-quality domains and sell them for a vast profit; this approach has become a lucrative and profitable business model for some companies. Of course, the problem is that when someone else owns that perfect name you want, it can ultimately affect your ability to take your brand to the Web and can (worst case scenario) force you to reconsider the brand name you want to use.

Brand Emphasis

Earlier in the book, you learned about choosing a brand name. Your goal was to come up with something simple, easy to remember, and unique that will serve you well during the next stage of the process. One of the first things you should do after deciding on a brand name is to use a domain-name checking service to investigate how you might represent your brand on the Web. While many domain registrars will freely check the availability of any domain name extensions, some name-checking services have been known to snatch domains searched for by individuals, forcing these people to purchase the domain from those companies at a higher price! Because of this, you should first check your chosen brand name using one of the many independent domain-checking services or registrars who are trustworthy.

The most commonly used domain extensions worldwide—and therefore the most potentially valuable to your brand name—are .com, .net, and .org. If possible, you want to use a domain checking service to make sure you can register at least one of these. Of course, using a country based domain such as .co.uk to gain higher relevance in a country is also acceptable, as is using a country-based domain such as .me to give you a clever domain name hack (I'll cover this later in the chapter). Many people who represent themselves online choose to purchase a single domain name pointing to their site, while others will buy up multiple domains in an effort to protect their brand identity.

See for Yourself: A Domain-Name Search

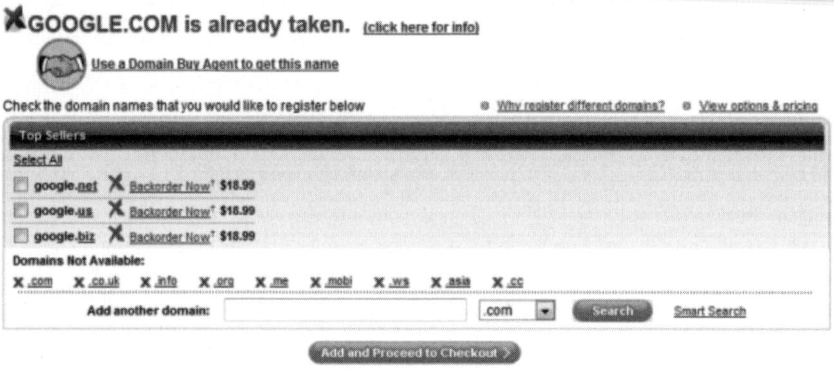

Figure 4-1. You can see a list of sites that have the domain name of *Google* if you use the extension search on www.godaddy.com.

Try It Yourself: Acquiring Primary Domains

You can follow this trio of steps to determine whether the brand name you have created is available as a domain:

1. Visit a domain registrar—the more extensions the registrar offers, the more chances you have of finding one that might work for your brand! You will be offered the opportunity to purchase whatever you search for, but you won't be required to, and you should hold off buying the domain that you search for until completing this chapter (or section on domain names). Some domain registrars you can try include www.godaddy.com (one of the leaders of cheap domains) or

101domain.com (you can register if you need a more extensive list of possible extensions).

2. Enter the address you want to purchase and perform the search results for various or individual extensions; if you find that the site you want is taken, you can always try changing your search terms, or you can go for alternative spellings of your brand or hyphen-separated words.

3. Once you know that the domain you searched for is available, make a note of it and continue reading this book for other important information about the domain-registering process. So, instead of mystamps.com, you might want to look for my-stamps.com or even mistamps.com. Capitalization is ignored in domain names, so bigredbus.com is the same as BigRedBus.com. This is handy because you can advertise your brand using the capitalized name, which can make it easier to read, but this won't affect how visitors navigate to your site.

Many businesses choose to buy up as many extensions for their brand as possible. Their goal is to remove any potential confusion that might occur if people don't remember what extension their site uses (this is especially useful if you choose to register country-specific domains for providing services worldwide in various countries). You're producing your first site, so it would probably suit your needs better if you focused on getting a single domain name, unless your brand's representation on the Web is extremely important to you (in terms of how much real estate you own on the Web). Generally speaking, it doesn't matter which extension you choose to use for the vast number of personal sites, as long as you feel the URL meets your needs. You can always purchase additional extensions later (assuming they remain available, of course).

Your primary domain name will be the focus of attention; however, you can register additional URLs as needed if you start offering services that you feel warrant a domain of their own. Most registrars will allow you to redirect these to a specific part of your site.

International (IDN)

While international domain names (IDN) have gained in popularity in recent years, it's important to take into account that these kinds of domains generally have more downsides than upsides for the English speaking and writing nations of the world. While the majority of standard domain names use the English alphabet of A-Z, numbers 0-9 and additional allowed characters such as – and _, the IDN allows the registration of URLs that don't contain standard characters. For example, you can use characters such as ☺. Figure 4-2 shows a domain that would effectively be a smiley face character—and it's taken!

See for Yourself: International Examples

Figure 4-2. This shows an example where an international character (smiley face) is a domain name!

Registering these kinds of domains might seem like fun, but problems can occur because it means visitors would have to open a character map program and find the special character to copy to the address bar, or they would have to work out the keyboard equivalent of that name. This puts added pressure on your visitors because they cannot easily type in the name of the address, whereupon they will probably give up on your site. Unless you're particular domain will serve an audience that uses an alternative alphabet such as Japanese or Greek, you should avoid using these domains.

Domain Hacks

Some people have been using an unconventional domain-naming technique since the early 1990s as a simple method of combining a domain name with a domain extension (and possibly a subdomain) to achieve a clever naming pun. This technique has been referred to as a *domain hack*, though it should be noted that it has nothing to do with security, and in this context, the word *hack* only implies a trick on wordplay. People continue to debate whether this domain convention affects both the usability and the readability of the site's name. However, this technique shows that you can reduce the amount of characters required for the domain; it also gives you a better chance of acquiring a domain name that spells out a particular word you wish to use.

To form a domain hack, you must take a word or name and ensure that the last two (or three) letters of the website address can be represented by a domain name extension. (You also need to make sure you are entitled to purchase that domain.) For example, the site inter.net makes use of the .net extension, but combines it with *inter* to form the single word, *Internet*! If you find that the word you want has been taken (provided that the word is long enough), you could add a subdomain to form the word instead. The social-networking website del.icio.us uses the domain name icio.us (note the .us extension) and adds the required del to the front as a subdomain, forming the word, *delicious*. It's quite a clever concept when you think about it!

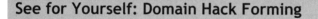

LinkED

One independent service I personally recommend is http:/domia.nr, *which can take your brand name and show you ways you could use domain hacks to achieve a particular site address.*

See for Yourself: Domain Hack Forming

The benefit of domain hacks is that it gives people a higher percentage chance of acquiring the URL they want in some form or another if the standard domain has been taken already. Some people question whether this approach might cause confusion when you give people your address because the way it separates the word. In other words, a name like this could make your users feel disjointed. Another downside of this method of domain naming is that, because of the way the domain hack is constructed, your potential visitors are more likely to misspell the domain name and get an error or end up on someone else's site.

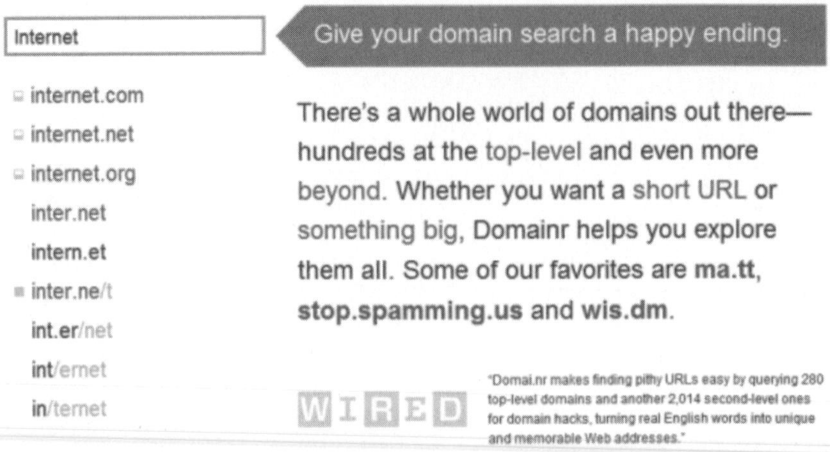

Internet

- internet.com
- internet.net
- internet.org

inter.net

intern.et

inter.ne/t

int.er/net

int/ernet

in/ternet

Give your domain search a happy ending.

There's a whole world of domains out there—
hundreds at the top-level and even more
beyond. Whether you want a short URL or
something big, Domainr helps you explore
them all. Some of our favorites are **ma.tt**,
stop.spamming.us and **wis.dm**.

WIRED

"Domai.nr makes finding pithy URLs easy by querying 280
top-level domains and another 2,014 second-level ones
for domain hacks, turning real English words into unique
and memorable Web addresses."

Figure 4-3. Domai.nr is a site that allows you to search for your own domain hacks.

The Problem with Domains

One of the many issues that exist when choosing domain names is the problem
of name infringements. When you register a domain name, you must be careful
that you don't violate any copyright, trademark, or patent laws by attempting
to knowingly register a domain name where exclusive rights are held by a third
party. IANA and ICANN—which set all of the rules for domain names-currently
have a resolution policy (UDRP) in place to settle cases when infringements do
occur. Note that even if you prevail during the UDRP, the company that alleges
infringement might still have genuine grounds to pursue legal action.

LinkED

*For more information about the Uniform domain name dispute resolution
policy (UDRP) and a copy of the rules and how they are implemented,
check out* www.icann.org/en/udrp/udrp.htm.

Holders of rights are required to protect their trademarks; otherwise, they
could potentially lose them. So it makes sense for you to take a few basic
precautions when choosing a domain name. Never register a domain name that
is identical or similar to (and could be confused with) an existing trademark,
patent, brand, product, or identity, whether it's online or offline. While you
probably don't need to do an investigation into the background of your name,
it might be worth putting the identity you have chosen into a search engine to

see whether any potential conflicts might occur based on your choice, then use your best judgment when deciding whether to use a name.

WHOIS Records

When you purchase a domain name, you will be asked for contact information by the registrar. This information is placed into a document called a WHOIS record. Essentially these records exist to provide basic details in a central location, so that site problems can be reported. Over the years, criticisms have been made over the use of this data because it is available to the public and could therefore be seen as a potential privacy risk factor. If you fail to keep your details up-to-date or provide false information, your domain can be taken away from you.

ICANN has a policy where domain registrars are required to give individuals the opportunity to change their information to keep the records up to date. Failure to do so or providing false information could result in you losing the domain. You can learn more about this at www.icann.org/en/registrars/wdrp.htm.

A WHOIS database contains four types of contact records known as the *registrant*, *administrative*, *technical*, and *billing* details. The registrant and administrative records state the legal owner of the site; this is where you provide your personal details. The technical and billing (otherwise known as the service provider) details sometimes differ, but they usually hold the details of the organization that manages the domain. That said, most registrars allow you to update your personal information (and WHOIS records) quickly and easily from their site-control panel. All of these will contain names (yours and that of your business, if provided), email, addresses, postal/zip codes, and contact telephone numbers (for both you and the provider of the service).

Try if Yourself: WHOIS in Action

Just for fun, let's do a WHOIS lookup on Google:

1. Open your browser and visit http://whois.domaintools.com/, which in this case will serve as the WHOIS lookup agent of choice (I recommend this one because it also provides extended information).

2. Type www.google.com in the large text box and press the Lookup button to perform the search.

3. Finally, read through the various sections to find some interesting information such as visitor details, server, and registrar information; however, if you scroll down to the WHOIS Record, you will get a complete list of information on the owner of the google.com domain name (see Figure 4-4 for an example).

Figure 4-4. WHOIS records can hold a wealth of interesting information.

Some registrars offer the ability to keep your personal details private (you can use the registrar's own information to protect your identity), but you should be aware that ICANN considers the details described in the WHOIS record to be the official record of the domain's owner; if a dispute ever occurs between you and your registrar (or if you want to transfer your domain to a new provider), the provider could block the transaction, and you might find yourself unable to switch. Therefore, it is highly recommended that you avoid using these services unless you trust your provider. Some people choose to keep their domains and hosting separate by using different providers, which can ease the transition if you ever need change site hosts.

LinkED

While the majority of domain extensions have a range of costs attached to them, a free registrar has existed for a few years that allows anyone to have his own .TK domain (based around the country of Tokelau located in the South Pacific). You can learn more about this at www.dot.tk/.

Purchasing Methods

In the majority of cases, people tend to register domains through a registrar. And in normal circumstances, you should be able to acquire the brand name you want through simply searching and purchasing it. If the domain name is potentially valuable (it's possible there might be many people interested in buying it), you might find that the only way you can acquire the domain is to buy it at auction. Auctioning of domain names has been around for years, and you can find some quality sources of auctions that will help sell the rights to a given site address. While there are people on the web who buy and sell these properties like houses (only selecting premium goods that will do well at auction), you might find that bidding for that domain you so badly want could be the only way of acquiring your brand name—the downside of auctions is that you could end up spending a small fortune to acquire the site address you want, especially if other people also want it.

LinkED

For a comprehensive list of what factors can ultimately affect the value of a premium domain during the appraisal process (where experts look at a domain and give it an estimate of what it could make at auction), check out this Wikipedia article at http://en.wikipedia.org/ wiki/ Domain_appraisal.

See for Yourself: Domain Auction Sites

Some of the most popular auction sites for acquiring domain names include the following:

- **SEDO**: http://www.sedo.com/
- **Afternic**: www.afternic.com/
- **GoDaddy**: https://auctions.godaddy.com/
- **SnapNames**: www.snapnames.com/
- **Pool**: www.pool.com/

Figure 4-5: Sedo is one of the world's largest domain-name auction sites.

Remember that whenever you decide to purchase something on the Internet, you need to research the company well. This same logic applies to the purchase of domain names. Seek out high-quality reviews on sites and ask people who already have sites for their own preferences. Referrals are one of the main things that keep hosts and registrars in business because, hosts and registrars were to keep receiving poor quality reviews and nobody liked them, they would be out of business quite quickly.

LinkED

You can browse Google for references if you want to research the reputation of a given site. You can also see what the site was used for in the past by visiting the Internet Archive, a project that has the sole aim of referencing old sites. You can learn more about this project at www.archive.org/web/web.php.

Tips and Tricks: Finding a Registrar

Finding the perfect registrar is easier than you might think (even though there are hundreds of them). Simply follow these tips and tricks; to learn many of the things you need to look for in a domain registrar (you can use these same tips and tricks whenever you buy goods and services from any site over the Internet):

- Make sure the registrar is ICANN-accredited (to help reduce the likelihood of fraud).
- Check review sites and *domain-award* systems that list high-quality providers.
- Test a registrar's support and send it some questions to learn how well the company assists customers.
- Ask around the Web in places such as web design forums about advice on good registrars.
- Look out for coupon codes, discounts, and other money-saving options that exist.
- Compare prices of domain extensions between providers to get the best possible deal.

Choose Your Landscape

Hosting is one of the most competitive markets on the Internet. There are thousands of different web-host providers fighting each other to gain your attention, and they provide all sorts of pricing schemes, features, services, and models. The extraordinary range of options available can make it tricky to decide which provider to use (especially when you try to gauge your future needs). The following information should help you separate the wheat from the chaff and help you choose what type of hosting provider you should look for (albeit the final decision is, of course, yours. The *best host* (subjectively speaking) changes from provider to provider on a daily basis; your job is to choose the best host for *you*.

What Is a Web Server?

According to its simplest definition, a web server is a computer that hosts a web site so that it is publicly accessible. Servers are almost always left running on a 24/7 basis, which means that someone surfing the Web can have instant access at any time of day (or night) to whatever the server hosts. Hosting companies own a large number of web servers, and every part of your website—including every HTML file, image, and movie—has to be stored on their servers for it to be publicly available. Most hosting companies will set aside a specific amount of space on their servers for each site; exactly how much space it sets aside is explained when you purchase your hosting package. In addition to *server*, you'll often hear the term *client* bandied about. A client machine is the computer that receives the information from the server—in other words; it is the visitor to your site.

NotED

You will host your site on an external server; however, some people choose to run their site from their own computer. One popular solution is the open source product XAMPP, which provides an easy way to install and use local-server environment. You can download this at www.apachefriends.org/en/xampp.html.

Hosting Types

You can find many different types of hosting packages available, and they come equipped with a wide range of functionality (and vastly differing prices). When deciding what will best benefit your site, you need to remember that hosting is a highly competitive market, so you can find some great deals out there; however, the ever-changing array of requirements make it pointless to provide prices. You'll need to do your own research to decide the best host for your site.

That said, this list details your most popular options in order of their *grade* and *cost*:

1. **Free:** While sites have the benefit of having no costs attached, free hosting is often paid for by embedded advertising on your site or limitations in its functionality. Free hosting can be good for personal websites that don't require an immediate level of professionalism or a lot of functionality, which makes them worthy of consideration for absolute beginners. If you want to start up a simple blog that relies on a freely hosted website with WordPress, then this approach might work well for you.

2. **Shared:** Shared hosting is by far the most common entry-level hosting package. While the cost is kept down by *stuffing* lots of web sites onto a single server, it has the downside that you might end up sharing with a site that drains a lot of resources, which can affect the performance of your own site (possibly causing downtime). Because of this, most providers have a policy that states if an individual puts too much stress on their system, they can be kicked off the service.

3. **Grid:** The downside of shared hosting is that multiple sites share the same server. A model known as grid hosting allows an entire network of computers to equally distribute the resources of many servers

across a series of websites (essentially this is like shared hosting on a much larger scale). Of course, this hosting type often costs more than shared hosting, but in most cases, it also is one of the more reliable methods you can use without having to pay for your own server.

4. **Cluster:** Grid hosting has the inherent flaw that it can take time to move and manage the resources being allocated. Clustered hosting overcomes this by giving every site equal access to a network of servers that allocate resources automatically when they are needed. This removes the case-by-case requirement to move customers about to ensure server stability, but it still presents problems when resources are oversold beyond their capacity.

5. **Cloud:** Cloud hosting is a relatively new concept that works on the basis that you only get resources when you need them. So if your site has very little traffic, you can rent a single server or different amount of resources. As you grow (or shrink), you can adjust the amount of power you need by adding and removing servers virtually. This can be an excellent cost-cutting measure, but only a handful of hosts implement this form of hosting.

6. **Virtual:** A virtual private servers (VPS) allows you to share a server with other people, but this type of server guarantees you certain resources and is partitioned (separated) so that each individual using it has full control of her own share of the system. Unlike shared hosting, people on a VPS do not tend to be oversold because the site host usually limits how many individuals can be allowed access to each individual server in use.

7. **Dedicated:** This is the most popular (and the most expensive) hosting package you can get. Large sites such as Google have a huge amount of traffic, so they don't want to share their resources with anyone else. Going with a dedicated package means you have an entire server (or several servers!) all to yourself. This gives you total control over your own resources, which are restricted only by the power of the machine/s used to host the site in question.

So which should you go with? Generally, as the price increases (as you go down the list), the amount of features and benefits you get also rises. For someone beginning to make a site, you should probably go with either a shared-, grid-, or cluster-hosting package as they offer great value for money and offer good levels of service. If you think your site is going to be the next Google or Amazon, you might want to consider virtual or dedicated hosting. However, at this early stage you would probably be spending a lot of extra money for too little benefit because you don't have any visitors yet! If you just want to *test drive* your site—for example, if you expect only your family or a couple of people to visit—you could go with a free package. The great thing about hosting is that it's easy to upgrade your package with the same host at a later date. If you want to move hosts, you can also do that without too much hassle. This means that you can simply *top off* your package when you need to.

Beware the Villains!

Unfortunately, not every business trying to offer you web hosting offers high-quality service. You can find many shady organizations that make promises they cannot keep, or they make impossible claims that often point to small print in the contract that can ultimately leave you with a lackluster or poor experience. While many hosts are straightforward and are open and honest with their customers, you should take into account the following advice because it will help you weed out site providers that will take your money and give you little in return. It will also help you steer clear of those hosts that spend more time trying to get new customers than serving their existing ones.

The Unlimited Lie

During your host research, you have probably seen (if you have looked around already) web hosts that offer unlimited disk space and bandwidth (this is basically the disk space and memory you are allocated—I'll discuss these terms in more detail later in this chapter). While this is common practice among hosts, it is essentially nothing more than a marketing ploy to try and win customers through dangerously misleading lies. While the idea of having no limitations can sound pleasing, you should know that nothing in this world is infinite, and as much as hosts will try and talk you around by saying any of your needs will be covered, the fact is that you would be banned in the majority of cases if you did use a lot of resources being too greedy! While the whole concept seems laughable, the problem is that hosts that claim infinite anything, yet the small print in their contracts allows them to ban people who take advantage of the promised level of service. If you do see a host offering unlimited services, your best option is to avoid this company because you cannot be sure what else the company is hiding from its customers.

See for Yourself: Unlimited Hosting Claims

- Unlimited GB's of Space
- Unlimited GB's of Transfer
- Unlimited Domain Hosting
- Unlimited E-Mail Accounts
- Unlimited MySQL Databases
- FREE Site Builder
- FREE Domain for Life
- FREE Instant Setup
- Anytime Money Back Guarantee

- FREE Domain For Life
- FREE Instant Setup
- No Hidden Fees

£4.95 Special Promo

£2.95 /month

Sign Up Now

Figure 4-6. Site hosts that proclaiming unlimited resources provide a sure-fire clue that there is a catch attached to the hosting package.

Oversellers

I've already mentioned the problem of overload on shared hosting. This can be a major problem with small hosts or those trying to maximize their income without spending on required upgrades. The problem with most shared-hosting services is that, when too many people use a specific server, delays occur in the processing of requests, which can lead to serious down-time problems. Overselling is a common practice, but it doesn't usually lead to problems when done on a small scale. If a high number of people from a host provider complain about down time and the slowness of their sites, it could be because their provider is trying to cram too many people onto a server without paying for the new hardware required to reduce the workload being placed on their servers. If you hear about a host overselling its services, you should consider whether your site's needs will be inhibited by the site's host trying to cut costs.

Too Good to Be True

You've almost certainly heard this phrase: "If it sounds too good to be true, then it probably is." This effect holds especially true in the field of site hosting. If you see a host making extraordinary claims or you get a *dodgy feeling* looking at a host's claims (such as a poorly created site), then it might be worth investigating that business further to make sure that the site you're looking at is legitimate and not trying to rip off its potential customers by making false claims. Remember that hosting is something that you pay for either monthly or annually, and this can be quite an expense in itself. Therefore you want to ensure that you sign up with someone trustworthy. The best way to determine whether something is too good to be true is to follow your instincts or investigate an offer or business as much as you can. You don't have a time limit when you need to get hosting generally, so it's worth making sure that you're happy with your choice, rather than encountering a situation where you buy something that doesn't live up to the hype.

Trusting Reviews

When researching which host you would like to go with, the first thing you will want to do is look at what other customers think of that business. You can find many sites that offer professional and independent reviews about site hosts, as well as sites that rank hosts based on how well they perform for their customers. However, you should understand that many of these rating sites are biased towards a certain provider, and the views expressed on a site might not match the overall point of view of the people who use a given provider's services. In some cases, the hosts *pay* for the positive reviews they receive. This is one reason why you should favor customer feedback over business feedback; it is also a reason you should be careful about the advice you follow.

Try It Yourself: Find Host Reviews

You can find independent reviews of site hosts at the following sites:

- **Web Hosting Geeks:** www.webhostinggeeks.com/
- **Web Hosting Jury:** www.webhostingjury.com/
- **Top 10 Web Hosting:** www.top-10-web-hosting.com/
- **Find My Host:** www.findmyhost.com/
- **Web Hosting Reviews:** www.webhostingreviews.com/
- **Web Hosting Guide:** www.webhostingsearch.com/

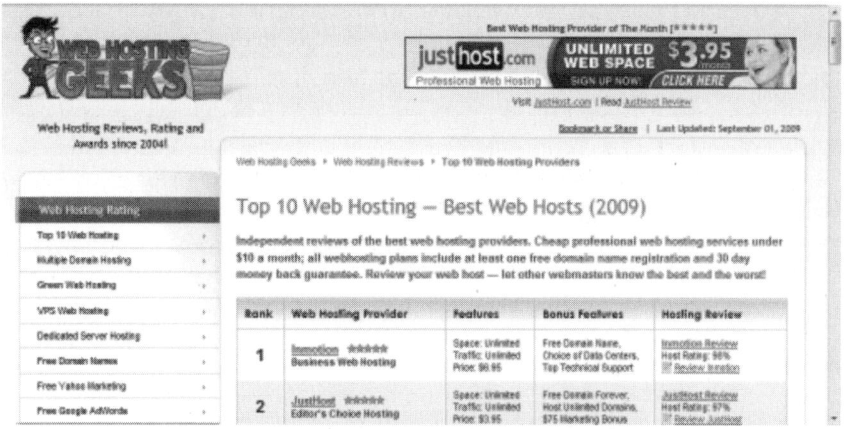

Figure 4-7. Many independent sites offer reviews for the different hosting packages.

The best way to find independent host reviews is to look for negative statements. This might seem counterproductive in terms of finding someone you *want* to host your site, but what you must keep in mind is that hosting companies will sometimes pay people to positively review their services to try and gain more visitors. Looking at the negative reviews help you get a good idea about how good a host is. For example, you can learn how that host deals with complaints; the fewer complaints a host receives, the better the host will seem. People love to complain, and there is more honesty in finding the flaws rather than the marketing hype they will try to put across during the sales process. As a side note, you might want to consider the age of the reviews given, especially as the quality of service might vary on a frequent basis, and occasional faults might result in a flurry of complaints in relation to a now non-existent fault.

Functionality Guide

You might find all of the information provided on hosting sites confusing to wade through. In this section, I'll create a quick-and-dirty guide you can use to understand some of the terminology used. My guide will also cover exactly how the information listed on sites can assist you in determining what you will need to look for when you consider purchasing a hosting package for your own site. The guide covers the most important terms a host might use to state what it can offer you. When making decisions, you might find it worthwhile to write down on a bit of paper the ideal package you want to find; this can help you compare all of the available hosts (that are trustworthy) against your ideal host.

Price

Price is often a make or break factor in finding a host. While you want to keep your hosting (and other) bills down as much as possible, you generally do get what you pay for. So when a host offers you a much lower price than a competitor, it is probably skimping in some areas of its service. You want to figure out the specific areas it skimps in—it might be you won't miss what the host doesn't offer—but it's your responsibility to sort out a host's claims before you make a final decision on which host to go with. As a beginner, you should probably look to pay somewhere between $5 and $25 a month. This difference in price might seem significant to you; what you should pay depends on your site's specific needs. Yes, you generally get what you pay for, but good deals and bargains exist, too, so watch for them!

Guarantee

The money-back guarantee should be one of the foundations of any purchase you make. If the product does not match your expectations or does not do what it you were promised, then you should have a way to back out of the agreement and get your money back on any unused portion of the service. The typical guarantee for a hosting company ranges from 7 days to 30 days, but having that guarantee in place means you can see what the host is really like, without having to worry you will be stuck with a host that won't fit your needs as hoped.

Load Balancing

The term load balancing refers to the number of people a host places on a server, as well as to how much strain a server's resources will be placed under. Generally, this usually applies only to those on a non-dedicated service. Problems caused by hosts overselling services can impact the sites they host significantly, so it's important that you try to determine the resource availability for a given host you're considering. You can't typically find this information listed on a host's site; it might be worthwhile emailing a host about its load-balancing situation, then comparing results among hosts you're considering; the idea here is to determine which site has the best ratio of users to a server. Determining this can help you decide which service will serve you best from a hardware and performance perspective.

Uptime

Is there a chance you will suffer some period of time where your site is not available? Yes, unfortunately. While you want your site to be available

24/7/365, there is always a chance that an issue might occur that will prevent your site from being online. Your down time might be caused by hardware faults, problems with DNS servers, or other issues that cannot be prevented. Most hosts will declare an uptime of 99.9%, which is a somewhat realistic figure that takes into account the 0.1% chance of something catastrophic happening that might affect your service for an extended period of time; however, your host should have measures in place—such as backups and alternate servers—to minimize any maintenance time and how it will affect your account. You want your host to take reasonable steps to keep things running while upgrades and technical problems are resolved.

Backups

What happens when things go wrong? The most frustrating issue you face is potentially losing personal data or that forum full of people who visit your site on a regular basis. One of the most important features you can have in place is either a manual- or automated-backup system that allows you to either download a complete copy of the site's content or to have an on-site (at the host's end) copy that holds a regular and up-to-date copy of your site in case you ever encounter an issue where you need to recover data from a saved, external source.

Support

If things do go wrong, you want to make sure you can get help and support for your problems. Many hosts offer a wide range of problem-resolving assistance in the forms of helpdesks, contact forms, telephone numbers, chat rooms, forums, live troubleshooters, feedback forms, FAQs, wikis, and problem-reporting systems. You can receive support in many different ways, but one critically important factor is how quickly you can get an answer to your questions. Generally, a host should return your emails or help requests within 24 hours; however, the faster a host responds, the sooner you can try to fix the problem.

Bandwidth

Bandwidth refers to the amount of traffic you can receive (in terms of how much data your site can transfer). Every host has a different policy, but hosts generally allocate a certain amount of bandwidth per month to you, just as some Internet providers do. Once you use up your allotted amount of bandwidth, your site will either become unavailable, or you will need to purchase additional bandwidth, which can become expensive. Most people find it difficult to gauge how much bandwidth they need, especially for sites that get popular and require more bandwidth on a month-by-month basis. However, your best approach is to go for a host that offers you the most for your money. For example, having terabytes (TB) of bandwidth is far better than having gigabytes (GB) of bandwidth, as 1.5TB is far more bandwidth than 60GB (1TB is equal to around 1,000GB).

Disk Space

Everyone likes storing files. The disk space a host offers gives you a fixed capacity you can fill with your files, databases, emails, and other relevant online information your site holds. When researching this factor, you want to look for a host that offers the best size in terms of disk space, which in turn means you can hold more stuff online. While some hosts have policies that ask you not to store personal files unrelated to your site, some people do choose to use their online disk space for holding nonsensitive-personal data. Overall disk space usage is a feature that plays mainly into how much bandwidth you have, but it can be useful to people who wish to hold large files online for people to download (if, for example, you want to host a lot of photos).

Operating System

When choosing a web host, the operating system will play a part in what functionality you can expect. For example, if you want to use ASP (Active Server Pages, a server-side language that I'll cover later in this chapter), you need a Windows server because Microsoft designed this proprietary technology. Site providers typically host your site on one of four server platforms. The least common server platforms are Mac and UNIX (such as Solaris). Windows is the second-most popular hosting platform, and it has its own server software called Internet Information Server (IIS), which Microsoft developed and maintains. However, the most popular server platform currently is Linux, which runs the powerful Apache software and has fewer known-security risks than Windows that can be exploited from a hosting perspective.

Languages

The more programming and syntax languages your host supports, the more choices you will have in terms of what you tools you can use to develop your site. I'll describe the basics of these languages later in the book, but it's worth noting that you should check your host for as many different server side languages and database formats as possible. Some popular examples of syntax languages for the Web include PHP, ASP, ASP.NET, ColdFusion, Perl, CGI, Ruby, and Python. These names might seem confusing to you at the moment, but for now you can assume that the more languages a site supports, the better off you will be. You might ask around to see what other people would recommend in terms of which language would provide the best deal, or you could simply learn the required coding languages when you toned them. In all fairness, each language has its own set of (upfront and implicit) costs, advantages, and disadvantages, so you might want to choose your host based on language support.

Databases

When you learn about adding behavior to your site that people can interact with, you will find that you need somewhere to save the information that users submit. For example, if someone posts a message to a forum, you need to have somewhere to store the message. This data is held within a storage container known as a database. Databases are like file cabinets that allow you to hold and organize information in an easy-to-read format. Developers use a variety of branded databases; again, you will want to do the same thing you do when looking at language support; that is, you want to go with the host that has the widest support because you might wish to use more than one database format to cope with different scripting requirements. The most common database formats currently are based on SQL (Structured Query Language), and I'll walk you through several available options later in the book.

Email

Most site owners want the ability to send and receive email through their site, not least because an address such as me@website.com has a better ring to it than me@hotmail.com, which has the email provider's brand firmly in the address. Most site hosts don't place restrictions on the amount of email addresses you can have, and the amount of space that your email account has available for storing mail is subtracted from the disk space provided with your account. Having a snazzy and unique email address can be exciting, and it can give your site additional promotion when you hand out your address to people who want to contact you!

Statistics

Getting to know your users is important because it tells you how people choose to visit your site, which enables you to cater your site to their ever-changing needs and habits). Most site hosts provide a basic statistics package that will monitor your site and give you information that includes information on any errors that occur on your site (so you can fix them); where people are visiting your site from (if they come from another site); what browser they use (which can be important for compatibility); and fun facts everyone likes to know, such as how many downloads a file got, how many people visit your site daily, and even what part of the world the people who visit your site live in. All of this information is provided in the form of numbers and percentages you can measure, and it's often displayed with pretty graphs, charts, and visual displays that you can look at to understand your site's traffic better. While this information can be extremely useful; if your host doesn't provide you with a statistics package by default, you can always use a good third-party package instead. For example, Google Analytics is currently the most used third-party statistics package, and it's completely free to use.

Applications

If you've never made a site before, your host will probably assist you in creating your sites. Many hosts have a control panel filled with applications or wizards that will help you through tasks that can seem quite complex, such as setting up databases. Some applications can be extremely useful, but sometimes you might want to avoid such wizards, especially if those wizards are page templates or site-creation packages. Most web hosting packages offer more than just applications to help you build things for your site. They also offer a control panel full of various settings and tools for managing your site, as well as the ability to install third-party tools and products that can enhance your site. I'll cover some of the applications you can add to your site in Chapter 8.

File Management

After you complete some of your site's pages, and you're ready to put them live on the Web, you will generally use an *FTP client*. FTP stands for *File Transfer Protocol*, which is basically a simple method of uploading files from your own computer up to the web server. All hosts (except some free ones) should by default provide the ability to upload your files through FTP, which is akin to copying data through folders on your computer. If FTP is not offered, you might only have the choice of uploading files through a web interface on your host, which can be a slow and frustrating process. Once you upload the files, you can use the file management tools provided by your host to perform simple tasks, such as moving files around or renaming them. Note that you will need dedicated FTP client software if you want to upload your site though FTP. Don't worry: You can find plenty of high-quality free programs for file management that are easy to use. I'll walk you through some of these momentarily, and you can also find a list of recommended software in appendix B.

ExplainED

If you have areas of your site that you want to keep hidden or permit only certain people to access, the simplest method to achieve this is through password protection. Most hosts allow you to apply usernames and passwords to folders by using a control panel.

SSL Certificates

If you ever want to sell items through your site, then you will want to look out for the ability to add SSL certificates to your site. The SSL certificate system is a measure that allows you to guarantee that any customer's information will be held in the strictest confidence. Most site hosts have the ability to install a certificate that allows you to process payments and information securely over an encrypted connection; however, this is usually a service you must pay for because certificates are sold by a licensed authority. While many hosts can sign you up for an SSL certificate and put it in place for your use, you should look around the Internet for better deals than your host might offer. A great number of places might offer you better deals on SSL certificates than your host can; you'll learn about this in greater detail in Chapter 10, which covers selling things online.

Multiple Domains and Subdomains

If future expandability for your site is important to you, then you will want your host to allow you multiple domains and subdomain hosting. As I explained previously, subdomains enable you to split your site into different areas, such as maps.google.com and news.google.com. This can be great if you want to offer a variety of services or minisites, such as a blog or a store. Having multiple domains, FTP accounts, sub domains, email accounts, and more can be extremely useful in helping you create a site that encourages people contribute to on various levels. This can be especially useful if you make a site frequented by friends, family, or colleagues, and you want to have individual login details.

Conclusion

At this point, you should do some research based on the information in this chapter, and once you are ready, choose and purchase your domain name and a hosting package that you feel best suits your needs. The process will be pretty simple because it will ask you for the address you want to register (and, of course stuff such as where you live, your credit or debit card information, and all the usual bits you need to pay for something. A site might take up to 48 hours to activate, depending on the host you select. Now it's time to upload all of your files to your new account.

Uploading Your Files via FTP

As I mentioned, the most common method of uploading your files to your site is via FTP. If you chose a host that doesn't support FTP, then you will need your host to provide you with an alternative solution for uploading files. Usually, your host will do this through a control panel. These utilities differ massively from host to host, but you should be able to follow their instructions for uploading your files. In most cases, it's a simple case of clicking a Browse button, then navigating to the file you want to upload on your computer. In this section, I'll walk you through how to use the much more powerful file-management features provided by an FTP client.

The first thing that you'll need to do is download an FTP client program. You can find a list of available software in Appendix B, but this example will rely on the free FileZilla application, which is free to download and use and has no costs associated with it. It doesn't matter if you choose something different, though, because all FTP programs operate in essentially the same way. You can download FileZilla from `http://filezilla-project.org;`click the `Download FileZilla Client` link on the site, and then pick the appropriate application for your operating system.

Once you download and install FileZilla, double-click the application to fire it up. Before you go any further, you will need to check the documentation provided by your hosting company for your FTP details. These details will consist of an FTP address, such as `ftp.yoursite.com`, a username, and a password.

1. In FileZilla, go to File > Site Manager to open up the Site Manager window. Click the New Site button, then enter a name for your site. This is simply a name for you to remember the site by, so the easiest thing to do here is provide the name of your site, such as `yoursite.com`.

2. On the left hand side of the Site Manager window, you will see a tabbed panel, with the General tab open. This is the only one that you will need to use. In the Host section of the General tab, type the FTP address that your host provided, such as `ftp.yoursite.com`.

3. Click the Logontype drop-down menu and select Normal. You will notice that the fields below this that were previously grayed out are now available.

4. You now need to enter the username and password that your host provided you into the appropriate fields. Your host might have provided you with a seemingly random string of characters here, so make sure that you enter them exactly as they were supplied. If at any time you choose to alter your username and password (this function is usually available from your host's control panel), then you will need to make sure you make the same changes in your FTP program.

5. That's all the information that you need to enter. All that remains is to click Connect! If all went well, you should now be connected to your site. You will know this is the case because some folders will appear in the Remote Site window on the right-hand side. If they did not appear, check the message window at the top of the program screen, where any error messages will appear in red. You might need to go back to the Site Manager window and check that the information that you entered was correct. If your host has provided you with any other additional information, then you might need to enter that information in this window. Another common problem you might encounter when you try to use FTP after purchasing your domain is that your purchase hasn't yet been processed yet. Domain processing can take up to 48 hours, which can be infuriatingly long when you've got your site ready to display to the world!

6. Once you have connect via FTP, take a look at the main FileZilla application. You should see two main windows, Local Site on the left, and Remote Site on the right. The Local Site is your own computer, and the Remote Site is your area on your host's web server. All you need to do is to copy the appropriate files from the left-hand window over to the right-hand window.

7. In the Local Site window, navigate to the website folder where you created your site. You should see at least your index.html file there, as well as all of the folders you created earlier.

8. In the *Remote Site* window, scroll through the available folders until you find one called www, or something similar (httdocs and html are other popular names for the folder). Your host should tell you which folder you need to place your files in. Open up this folder—and the real magic happens here—then drag your index.html file from the left-

hand side into the www folder on the right-hand side. That's all there is to it! You should now be able to visit your site in your web browser and see your first page appear in all of its glory. If you have any images linked to your page, then you will notice that they don't appear yet because you haven't uploaded them yet. To do this, grab the images folder from the left-hand window and drag it across into the www folder in the right-hand window. This will copy across all of the images that you stored inside that folder. If you have any large images, this step might take a little while. You can see the progress in the window at the bottom of your FTP client. Do the same for all of the folders that you created, as well as for any additional files that you have created. Now refresh your page in the web browser, and everything should be working just as it was on your computer earlier. The difference is that now your page is now available for anyone in the world to see!

Summary

In this chapter, you learned what goes on behind the scenes of a web site address, as well as how to choose what domain name you should go with and how to pick the right site extension. You also looked at the different types of site hosts and learned what you should look for in a hosting provider. This should have put you in a good position to pick the service provider(s) you want to use. Along with this, you have a basic understanding of how to use FTP clients to get your site from your computer to the Internet. At this point, you should have everything set up, online, and working, which is great because you can show your site off as it stands now to your friends, assuming you are not too embarrassed by the current lack of styles and other special formatting. In the next chapter, you will learn about CSS and how to layer styles over the top of your beautiful structure, as well as how to make your site look visually fantastic, yet do so in a way that ensures people won't be confused by all the exciting and dynamic visuals you plan on adding. Yes people, next you will need to get your Crayola markers out because you're going to give your site a television-style fashion makeover!

Chapter Checklist

- You should accomplish the following tasks before leaving this chapter:
- Choose the domain name you want to register for your site.
- Decide on what features you need as part of your hosting package.

- Register your domain name and select a host provider for your site.
- Upload your files to your host to make them visible online.

Questions and Answers

Q: *How can I maximize my chances of finding a domain name?*

A: If you find that the word(s) you want for your domain are unavailable, some simple ways to try and overcome the disappointment and get something similar would include using hyphens between words (such as web-dev instead of webdev), using the previously mentioned domain hacks, or trying a synonym that has a similar meaning (such as ground rather than earth). If you're desperate, you could even try using text-message "spellings."

Q: *Which is the best web host or domain registrar?*

A: This question is extremely difficult to answer. "What is best" is a relative question that cannot be answered simply or easily; there is no one-size-fits-all answer that will satisfy everyone's needs. Each person has different needs and requirements for a site; you need to research the host that provides the best fit of services for your needs at a price that works for you. As a result, you should use information from the host's own site or customer reviews to help you make such a decision.

Q: *Where can I find coupons or discounts for host providers if I'm looking for a deal?*

A: Many websites offer deals, coupons, and discounts for domain registrars and hosting providers, but three stand out: www.retailmenot.com/, a well-known site for discounts and special deals; www.couponcache.com/, which is dedicated solely to providing domains and hosting; and http://coupon.sc/,which offers similar discounts. At any given time, you can also find a provider of hosting or domains that might have special deals. Competition is fierce, with incentives to match. It's also worthwhile to check the sites of individual hosts because you might find one-day events or discounts that aren't widely publicized or referenced on the coupon sites.

Where You Are Now

By the end of this chapter, you should have the following:

- A domain name of your choice registered and working
- The HTML files you created transferred to your hosting package
- A basic but functioning web site live on the Internet

How Can I Style My Website?

You have a basic website that should have some good content and links to other pages you have produced, but your site remains fairly bland and basic at this point. And it's true that your site won't get much attention if it continues to look the way it does at the moment. So it's time we added some style and beauty to your design. Leaving the style of your site until now will help you separate your structure and style more clearly because now you can see and layer everything effectively. When you have the style handled externally, you can just tweak everything to your heart's content, until you're happy with the results. With this in mind, you should look through your ideas pad and any prototypes or other useful materials you might have generated, such as screenshots of things you found inspiring during your research, and then proceed to turn those ideas into something unique and worthy of showing off to the world! After all, a usable and well-designed site keeps visitors coming back.

In this chapter, you will learn about the following:

- What style is and how you can use it to achieve a great looking design
- The decisions and variables that can influence your design's appearance
- The style language CSS, which you can use to beautify your website

Back to Basics

Just as when you examined HTML before you began building your first site, you need to learn some background information before you dive into giving your site some color and pretty flourishes. In this chapter, you'll begin by learning the basics and useful terms before turning your attention to the process of making your site look unique. This will help you overcome a few of the tougher decisions that every designer considers when deciding how the finished product should look early on. Most of the information is straightforward, but it can be daunting if you have never come across the various layout types, measurement units, or code style before. You'll add style to your site using a different language than HTML, but don't worry: the language is constructed in a way that makes it easy to pick up. Of course, you're eager to get building something, so the goal is to keep this section as simple and easy to follow as possible, which will let you can get down to producing the all-important style of your site as soon as you complete this section.

Under the Hood

When you examined HTML, you looked below the surface of what constitutes code. Now that you have a basic website, you need to some time to consider how things change when you start adding the style to your site. The first thing you need to know is that *style* refers to the visual look-and-feel of your design, as well as the code you use to customize it. At this stage, you should have a basic understanding of what code is. Next, you will focus on how the language you use to style your site, Cascading Style Sheets (CSS), differs from HTML in its appearance.

What is Code (Again)?

CSS is the most commonly used method of expressing style on the Web, and it has no equal in terms of its functionality. For most people, starting out with CSS is the only method that this book recommends for providing style. CSS supports a variety of different elements in its various levels; one significant issue with using CSS is the lack of support for parts its specification by various browsers (especially Internet Explorer). Support for the most recent version of CSS (3.0) is very low; however most modern browsers meet much of the CSS 2.1 specification.

NotED

There is a style language called Extensible Stylesheet Language (XSL) that can help you transform a document from one format to another (such as from HTML to PDF); however, this language is aimed at a more technical audience, so this book won't address that language.

At this stage, you have a basic understanding of what code is. Each language you work with sends instructions for the web browser to interpret, and CSS is no exception to this rule. Think back to when you examined what code looked like in a browser, that strange assortment of characters that you soon learned had a purposeful meaning and told the browser what was contained within the tags. Of course, you did not spend an entire chapter learning HTML and marking up your document only to override it with another language here! The great thing about CSS is that it works in unison with other web-oriented languages; each language has its own, equally important job. So let's recap and take another look at the original example, with a couple of subtle changes that dramatically affect how the code appears when viewed in a web browser (see the results this code produces in Figure 5-1):

```
<p id="hello" style="font-family: Impact, serif; ">Hello to all who read
this paragraph!</p>
```

Hello to all who read this paragraph!

Figure 5-1. Check it out, the font for the paragraph of text has changed with the additional code!

In the preceding example, you will notice that the font is different because of the style attribute that this snippet introduced. You use this attribute within HTML to allow the insertion of CSS code directly inline within the document, although as you will find later on, it's generally seen as a better idea to keep your CSS in an external file rather than to use it with your inline code. These additional files are called stylesheets. Defining the style in one place makes it a lot easier to maintain and update your code than if you write the style inline into every element that you want it to apply to. You'll learn more about the reasoning behind this later in the chapter, but if you want to see the before and after effect, try it out for yourself and see what happens if you take away the style attribute from the source code—the effect will disappear. In the preceding example, the style you apply is a CSS property called *font-family*, this style lets you assign a typeface (font) of your choice to the document, although the font must be already installed on the visitor's computer for it to render as intended.

In the example, the font applied is *Impact* (with a family type called serif). You could even try adding the attribute to a different element, and the effect will reoccur wherever you place it, as long as there is text inside. Once you get your head around the idea that you can attach instructions for a visual style, you will begin to understand the true power of CSS. Adding some CSS code inline will give instructions to the element itself, but CSS has its own, built-in method of letting you decide which elements should have style applied to them. The method it uses is like a family tree, where when you apply a style to one element, and it applies the same style to all instances of that element and child elements within it. The full name of CSS is Cascading Style Sheets, and that is where the notion of the cascade comes in. Styles you set in your stylesheet cascade down through all of the content that you attach it to. Before you start working with CSS code on any scale, you need to be able to view the source code inside a web browser, which will help you understand exactly what CSS can does for you. As you already know, you can use the *View Source* menu item to view the source code of a website quickly and easily. This is great when working with HTML; unfortunately the same cannot be said for CSS, because browsers default to showing the page rather than attached files, such as stylesheets.

ExplainED

Most web browsers have a menu item to turn off style, (so you can see how things used to look!). With Internet Explorer 8, you can find this option under the Page *icon (View Menu)* ➤ Style ➤ No Style. *Of course, you can turn it back on with the "Default Style" option when you finish looking at the* naked *structure.*

Try it Yourself: Source-Code Viewing

You can display the source code for CSS in a text editor like notepad, but many web browsers do not show the style elements of the site because you store them separately from the structure (in different files). CSS gives you three ways to display code; you can see two of them through the standard *View Source* option, while the third requires a little bit of hunting and manually inputting the web address.

You will probably find the majority of CSS is held within a `link` element within the head of the HTML file; of course, your website doesn't have one currently because you haven't applied any style to the document yet. The `href` attribute that gives the location of the file can be either relative (as in the example that follows) or absolute (with the full site address); however, the important thing is that it exists. If no reference exists, it's quite possible that the style is either inline through style attributes (as mentioned earlier) or it's placed within the head of the document using the `style` element. To view the source code, you might need to copy the address given and place it within the browser's address bar by (navigating to the file) and then hitting the open button (if a download dialog appears) to let you peek inside! Some browsers make your life easier by allowing you to click the URL in the source code, which enables you to view the contents without having to "copy, paste, and navigate" manually to the file you want to see inside (see Figure 5-2). This feature can save you a tremendous amount of time. For example, take a look at the following code:

```
<link rel="stylesheet" type="text/css" href="/style/style.css"
media="all" />
```

If you were at www.yoursite.com, then the address you'd need to enter to reach the CSS style sheet would be www.yoursite.com/style/style.css.

```
<link rel="stylesheet" type="text/css" href="/style/tignish/template.c
<link rel="stylesheet" type="text/css" href="/style/tignish/content.cs
```

Figure 5-2. Firefox allows you to click a style sheet URL within the source code to navigate to it!

You can view some CSS within the HTML source code. Inline style occurs where you place CSS into the document in the head elements under an element called <style>. This element exists solely so you can place CSS code between the opening and closing tags; it functions much like text within a paragraph, except the browser recognizes this text as instructions. Check out this example, where the style tags include a lump of code that tells a paragraph of text (the p) to change the text color to #000000 (the hexadecimal value for black):

```
<style type="text/css">p {color: #000000;}</style>
```

You'll notice an attribute within the style element that you haven't seen before: type. The type attribute declares the MIME type of the document. The MIME type has nothing to do with street theater, of course; rather, it states what file format the content should be rendered as (such as CSS or XML). Some browsers allow you to omit the type attribute, but you should include it to ensure that the content of a style element is noticed and used properly. The type is the same for all CSS documents, so it's easy to remember.

You can also include CSS in an HTML page using the style attribute. You can apply this attribute to any element in HTML, which gives you the specific ability to provide style for a particular element without the need to target and reference it (you'll learn more about this later in this chapter).

The following example displays a paragraph of black text (in a browser), that reads, "Hello to all who read this paragraph!"

```
<p id="hello" style="color: #000000;">Hello to all who read this
paragraph!</p>
```

You'll learn more about the ID attribute later in the book because it has some special functionality. This book will ignore the style element and its attribute, and instead focus on helping you create your CSS code in a separate file. This serves two purposes: it helps keep everything organized, and it enables you to make changes to the way something looks by editing a single file, rather than having to change the reference in every file (which can be time consuming, especially if you have a few hundred pages).

ExplainED

Keeping your style separate from your structure also saves your site some bandwidth (memory), which means your pages will load more quickly. Browsers use a trick called caching to retain files they display; this enables your browser to recycle the stylesheet (CSS file) for every page that references the CSS.

The Semantics of Style

CSS has its own semantics and standards that come into play when producing a website. Like HTML, CSS is maintained by the W3C. This organization oversees the standards for the language, as well as the evolution and development of the CSS specification. The evolution of HTML has been built through stages, with each version of the language effectively overriding the previous one; however, CSS uses a different approach. Each version of CSS builds on the previous version, like a series of levels in a computer game. Everything starts at CSS level 1, which basically lays the underlying foundations of the language and includes a limited number of properties and values. CSS level 2 builds on level 1 by improving the number of things you can style; it also fixes a few of the bugs in the original version. CSS version 2.1 is the latest version of the language. Version 3 is in the works, and it will give you even more fun things you can work with (along with CSS 2.1 and 1 support), increasing your options for adding style to your site. You can see the layering of each level in Figure 5-3.

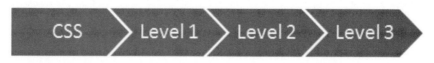

Figure 5-3. Each version of CSS builds on the previous version; it does not replace it.

It's easy to get your head around the idea that CSS layers level 3 on top of level 2 on top of level 1, with each successive level giving you more stuff to play with; however, it's important to know that this doesn't mean you need to change immediately to the latest, coolest version of the language as soon as it comes out. Your site won't be out of date (and it will still be perfectly valid) because the new version adds functionality on top of the old version, rather than replacing it. Of course, you should at least take a look at the new language because it might give you some useful new tools that will make your life easier and allow you to get around some of the limitations of the current version of CSS.

ExplainED

Throughout this chapter, you will see explicit references to new properties that exist within the CSS 3 specification; however, the lack of browser support for this standard and the fact that the specification remains in a draft stage mean that you should use version 3 only for providing additional style. You cannot rely on such features for visual consistency at this time.

As when programming with HTML, you need to be aware of several browser-compatibility issues when programming with CSS. Older browsers cannot see new languages (or new versions of existing languages) for the simple reason that they are no longer updated (such as Internet Explorer 6). Most browsers these days have complete support for CSS 2.1 (which is a great thing!); however, you should not expect every web browser to recognize or be able to use CSS 3 as soon as it is released formally. If you provide support for older browsers, you must remember you might face some issues related to this.

ExplainED

Chapter 7 covers how to resolve inconsistencies between web browsers, so don't worry if you find your site looks awesome in one browser, but fails in another. You'll learn how to patch those problems!

In Chapter 3, you learned about the basics of HTML, including how to use elements, tags, and attributes. CSS doesn't work exactly the same way, but it has a lot in common with HTML. When you write code in CSS, you will find that styling elements of your design is based on what is called a *rule-set*. The purpose of a rule-set is simple: you reference the HTML tags or other components that you want the style to apply to, using what is known as a

233

selector; and then you produce a list of style properties and values that you want to apply to that selected part of the design, known as the *declaration block*. For example, you might use img as the selector if you want to style an image; p as the selector if you want to style paragraphs; or the ID attribute as the selector, assigning it a value of hello using #hello. Here's an easy way to conceptualize this: The selector applies to the element itself, while the declaration block applies to all the goodies contained in the selector.

You place the declaration block with the properties and values being applied to the selector in curly brace {} characters. This is similar to how you enclose both elements and attributes in HTML tags. The same principle applies in CSS. These brackets let you provide information with a special value for the browser to look at and interpret. The example that follows will explain the concept of a rule-set. The selector is img (image), and any properties and values held within the declaration block will be applied directly to the element named in the selector. This means that you should only apply properties and values that are compatible with that element. For example, you should not use the font-style property (which can make text italic) to apply style to an image. This doesn't make sense because images aren't textual; thus, nothing happens if you try to do this. Figure 5-4 shows the basic format of a CSS rule-set. You see the element name, followed by a pair of curly braces that enclose a property and a value for that property.

Figure 5-4. Every CSS rule-set begins with the element (selector) that indicates the style it targets.

Setting a property in this rule-set applies that style to all img elements in the HTML page that the CSS stylesheet is attached to. Remember that rule-sets cascade throughout the document, affecting all instances of the element they target. But what happens when you want to target individual element instances, rather than apply styles throughout the document to all paragraphs or images? This is where the class and ID attributes come in.

Using Class and ID for Targeted Styling

In Chapter 3, which discussed HTML, you saw how to use the class and ID attributes to name the sections of a site. But their real power becomes evident only when you start using them alongside CSS styling, where they can act as reference points for you to apply style to elements on your page. It might be that you'll find inheritance (mentioned later)--or even targeting single elements—doesn't help you get the job done to your satisfaction as you build your style sheet. In this case, you'll probably come to appreciate class and ID, which are staples of all web designers because they allow you to target single or multiple elements.

Rule-sets do not have to specify an element (such as img). Indeed, you might use them to target an element with either a class or ID attribute value, which can use a unique name of your choosing. Class names are preceded by a full stop character, and ID names are preceded by a pound # character. For example, #hello targets an element using id="hello".

The # sign has a number of different names. In the U.S., it is commonly referred to as the pound sign. In other countries, it is referred to as the hash or number sign. This book refers to it as the pound sign.

Assume you have three div elements, but you want to apply a background color to only one of them. This is tricky because using div in a rule-set applies the style automatically to all three elements. What you can do instead is give that div a name in the form of an ID attribute (a unique name you can only give once in a document) such as id="hello" and then target that ID inside your CSS file using #hello in place of div. The pound character before the value tells the browser that you're using an ID. The result should be a unique style for the div that uses the referenced ID. It's great that you can target an individual element when trying to apply style to your site's pages; however, this might add to your challenges when you want to target several unrelated elements. In that instance, you can use class. The same idea applies: you assign class="hello" to all the elements you want, and then target the class in the selector using .hello. Notice this time you have a period in place of the pound sign. What you need to remember about CSS is that it uses the elements and attributes in your HTML document as a reference point, so that the browser knows where the styles in the external file should appear. Figure 5-5 illustrates the way the CSS cascade works, and how you can target individual elements. The body of your document contains three div elements. You target these elements using a single style rule to make them all white (#FFFFFF is hexadecimal for white, as you'll see later). One of the div elements has an ID attribute that gives it the ID of hello. At the moment, this element remains white because it is a div, and it has been targeted by the cascading original rule-set that makes all div elements white. However, it also has an ID, so now you can target that element individually using #hello {color: #000000;}. This overrides the color of that single div element and changes it to black (#000000 is hexadecimal for black). The other divs remain unaffected, so they stay white.

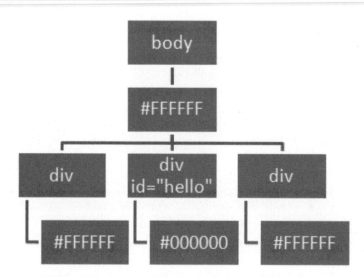

Figure 5-5. Using #hello {color: #000000;} lets you avoid inheritence of the color applied to the body element.

So far you know what a selector, declaration block, and rule-set look like. You also have an idea of how to use them. This means you can tell the browser where to apply the style, and which elements you want to target. The next thing that you need to look at is what these styles are, and how you can use them.

The answer lies within the curly braces that appear after the reference to the element you want to target inside the document. You can place a range of properties inside these curly braces that state what style to apply, such as a border or color, as well as a value to go along with it. Together, you can use these to tell the browser what color you want to turn a particular element. Using a number of properties and values, you can make every element in your design do exactly what you want (within reason and as long as the browser supports it). Assume you have the following line of code:

```
border: 1px solid;
```

This is a border property with a value of 1px solid. It sets a 1-pixel border (px is the abbreviation for pixel) around the element that it targets. Notice the colon and semi-colon after the property and value. All properties are followed by a colon character, and all values are followed by a semi-colon character. This is essential because it lets the browser know which part is the property and which part is the value.

You can see exactly how this works in Figure 5-6, and the CSS in this example should be relatively easy to understand. This code creates an image tag with a border applied to it with a width of 1 px (pixel). This border is solid (rather than being patterned, dotted or something else). Properties in CSS state what needs to be changed (such as a border or width) for an element, and the value gives all the information a browser requires to make the change. Properties are usually the easiest things to remember because CSS includes only so many of them, and they are usually things such as width, height, border, color, background, or something similarly straightforward. Values, on the other hand, can either be a single item, or a space-separated list of things you want to change. You can predefine a value with a few choices (such as the type of border in the following example—solid), or you can make it a unit value (such as a measurement unit or a hexadecimal color value). Values are harder to remember, but you can always do take advantage of trial and error to see what works best for your situation.

Figure 5-6. Between the curly braces, you can supply properties along with the values you want to give them.

Cascading Code

The *cascading* in Cascading StyleSheets refers to the way that styles flow through the document and affect the elements within. This is a simple concept at its heart, but it can become more complicated when you begin overriding existing rules to target specific elements, or you write custom rules that can affect things in different ways. Browsers take all of these different factors into account and use them to determine which style has the highest ranking. The browser uses the one with the highest ranking to render your pages. You can find three main rules that the browser uses to decide the style that takes precedence when a conflict occurs: *inheritance*, which describes how elements learn style from their parents; *specificity*, which states the most detailed reference to the element gets to win; and the *important declaration*, which gives added priority to any element you apply it to). Let's start with the most vital element of the cascade: inheriting style and value.

Inheritance

The general principle behind Inheritance is similar to what you might have learned in a biology class. For example, you're probably aware that the genes that dictate your parents' eye color influence your own. Earlier in the book, you learned that elements in HTML relate to each other through a series of parents and children that are contained within each other. In CSS you can take advantage of the relationship that elements have to each other and use this ancestral link to pass on an element's style to its children. For example, adding a foreground color to the body tag tells CSS to pass down that color to all of the elements contained within the body tag. Figure 5-7 shows what happens when you change the default text color within the body element from the browser's default (black) to gray without actually applying any style to the paragraph itself; instead, the element simply takes the style information from its parent and uses it by default.

body {color: #808080;}

Figure 5-7. Applying gray text to the body tag hasn't stopped the paragraph of text from inheriting its color.

The simple but effective tool known as inheritance enables you to save yourself a lot of time rewriting the same code over and over (see Figure 5-8). For example, you might use inheritance to specify a foreground color for all text within your site inside the body of your page, rather than stating the color you want on each manually on every element (which would take a lot of code). Taking note of what elements will inherit which pieces of style enables you to reduce your workload. Specifically, you might use a single selector that provides the default style for everything you place within the element. Of course, this does not mean you cannot override the rules for certain elements; inheritance in CSS changes only the default value for a specific property (which children naturally pick up). You can always provide a new value for a property that inherits its style, and that element and all of its children will use your new color rather than the one specified by its parents.

ExplainED

The body element is the parent of all elements that you can see on the screen (more commonly known as the canvas or the viewport); therefore applying code to the body tag causes all children to inherit the element's style by default.

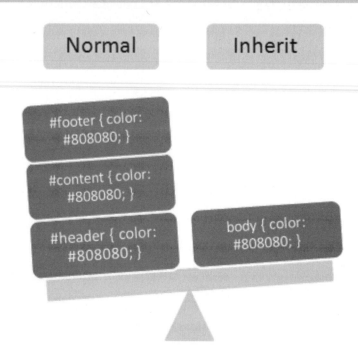

Figure 5-8. Repeating yourself is time consuming; fortunately, inheritence can help you avoid rewriting the same code repeatedly.

ExplainED

Adding style to your website is straight forward if you get used to the idea of inheritance. For example, assume you want to place an image in the background of your pages, rather than referencing the image in every element. Applying the style to the body element covers the entire canvas).

A problem that many people encounter relates to the way different browsers have different defaults for basic elements, such as margins, padding, size, or even the typeface. Because of this, many people choose to use a general purpose CSS Reset mechanism that explicitly provides default values to apply to all elements across every single web browser. This eliminates the natural discrepancies that occur between devices. This reset mechanism uses a simple set of style rules that make sure all of the important properties are set to standard values, and that your pages will behave similarly in different browsers, whatever their typical default values.

LinkED

Many sites use Eric Meyer's CSS reset mechanism, which you can find at http://meyerweb.com/eric/thoughts/2007/05/01/reset-reloaded/.

CSS reset mechanisms generally allow a beginner to overcome some of the potential glitches between browsers because they help to promote consistency in how your style is rendered across different browsers. For this reason, you might want to consider using a reset mechanism in your own pages.

Exceptions to the Rule

I said earlier that all CSS properties follow the cascade (on the matter of inheritance); however, that's not entirely true. When you think about it, it makes sense. You want to carry some things, such as a background color, all the way through your document. However, other things, such as an element's position, should not be carried out all the way through your document. For example, when you set the position of an image, you probably don't want every other image in your document to sit in exactly the same spot! Naturally, only properties suitable for inheritance use this feature. You can find full details about whether a property is inheritable on the W3C's website; specifically, the Full Property table at www.w3.org/TR/CSS2/propidx.html provides this information. Remember to use inheritance to your advantage and to use it often. Before you move onto the next element of the cascade, it might be helpful to look at some code which illustrates the principles of inheritance in action.

In the next example, the div element inherits the font-family and font-size from the body element, but you override the color. The browser (which reads CSS in order) will notice and apply the body color first; when it reaches the div element, it will see that you define another color and think to itself: "You are attempting to apply more than style of the same CSS property to a specific element, where neither has more importance than any other. So I'll apply color to the body (which all elements naturally inherit, including div elements), and then I'll override the value explicitly for div elements as requested." The code the browser must interpret looks like this:

```
body {
        color: #FFFFFF;
        font-family: "Trebuchet MS", Helvetica, Arial, sans-serif;
        font-size: 1em;
}
div {
        color: #000000;
}
```

Specificity

Specificity is the technical term for the way browsers resolve conflicting properties and values. For example, you might have two references to the same element at different points that ask the browser to change the background color of the element. When determining which value deserves to be given the highest priority, the browser takes into account and tests several factors. Basically, the browser iterates through a checklist of items. When a browser detects a conflict, it will use each item on the list below to assign a weight to the conflicting values. If a particular value is deemed more important after the browser runs through its priority checklist, the value is assigned to the element in question. This is important for you to know because you might discover that a style (value) you assign to an element won't seem to take effect; in this case, you might have a conflicting value being elsewhere in the style sheet that is overriding the style you want to implement.

Adding an !important declaration after properties in a rule-set is one of the simplest methods to give a CSS declaration to a particular element; this adds specificity and importance within the cascade to the item being given style instructions. You must write this declaration at the end of the value, before the semi-colon that separates each set of rules, or it won't count. This declaration basically gives your code a VIP backstage pass!

In this example, color has an important declaration that gives it priority over normal properties:

```
div {
    color: #000000 !important;
}
```

If one of the two conflicting values has a higher value on this list than the other, it qualifies as the highest priority, and thus overrides any conflicts that might have occurred (the list is ordered in terms of its importance):

1. An !important declaration after the value

2. More ID attributes references in the rule-set

3. More class attributes references in the rule-set

4. More pseudo elements or classes in the rule-set

If you look at any piece of CSS and add up the number of individual components (such as the ID or class attributes) in the selector using the order given, you can work out which has the highest priority a browser will assign (see Figure 5-9). The easy way to remember this is to think: ID, class, pseudo. When you count them one at a time, the value with the highest count wins the prize. Basically, if a value has importance, it's more valuable than ID, class, or pseudo references. If not, you move to the next stage in the cycle. You can calculate which of two conflicting elements holds the priority by counting these steps.

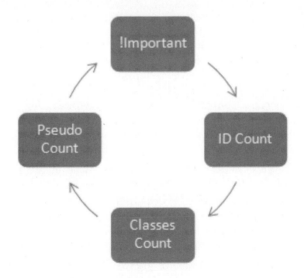

Figure 5-9. The conflict resolution policy (specificity) ensures that only the most relevent values are applied.

Let's look at an example. In the following code, the div with the "wow" ID is more explicit than its predecessor, so it takes specificity. While they both have a div reference, the second one has an ID attached to it, which you know takes priority after reviewing the preceding list. The ID gives it more explicit relevance because you indicate more directly hinted that it needs the style. It's important when using CSS that you take care to style everything appropriately, ensuring that the values that matter most overrule the generic ones. Also, if you take care to use the right references, you can also fix some bugs that occur when a style doesn't apply as you intended. For example, the following code assigns white text to all divs, except for the one with the ID value of wow. That special div gets black text instead (the black overrides the white due to the specificity value):

```
div { color: #FFFFFF; }
div #wow { color: #000000; }
```

ExplainED

You'll look at rule-sets in depth later in this book, when you learn about selectors. Basically, you can target elements within elements using code such as div p a {property: value;}. *This line targets all anchors within paragraphs inside a divider (there is no limit to the depth you can specify).*

Colors and Units

When you begin working with CSS, you'll notice that every possible style-related property you can change consists of the property title that describes what you want to change and a value that explains what the default or inherited style should be altered to. You'll learn about the various properties you can use to apply style in CSS later on (as you begin building up your style sheet). At this stage, however, you need to be aware of the possible values that you can use to alter the style of your pages. Some elements allow you to create custom text values (font, for example), while others have a predefined set of values that you can choose from (such as a cursor). The majority of elements either take advantage of color naming (which you can use to turn your black and white pages into something prettier!) or rely on units of measure that you can use to designate the size, thickness, position, or location of elements in the structure of your web pages.

LinkED

You can find a comprehensive guide that lists the various CSS units and values you can take advantage of at www.w3.org/TR/CSS2/syndata.html *(CSS2) and* www.w3.org/TR/css3-values/ *(CSS3).*

Color Values

Color is one of the most important aspects of web design. For this reason, it's essential that you know how to add color to your site, not only by using images, but also by adding solid blocks of color to your site's background, foreground, borders, and other properties that can take advantage of visual enhancement. You can use a variety of approaches to add color values to your code, such as keywords, system colors (based on the visitor's theme), hexadecimal references (such as #FFFFFF), and RGB values (red, green, blue), which can use numerical 0 to 255 values or percentages.

LinkED

You can find a larger list of different colors that you can use in your style sheets on Wikipedia at http://en.wikipedia.org/wiki/List_of_colors.

Possible color values you can take advantage of include:

- **Color keywords**: These are simply the names of colors. You can choose from W3C valid colors (there are 16 to choose from) or use named colors that many browsers have adopted as a nonstandard convention (there are many more of these). The W3C valid color keywords include: Aqua, Black, Blue, Fuchsia, Gray, Green, Lime, Maroon, Navy, Olive, Purple, Red, Silver, Teal, White, and Yellow. You can find a list of the color keywords (X11 colors) that aren't sanctioned by the W3C but supported in popular browsers (see Figure 5-10) at http://en.wikipedia.org/wiki/X11_color_names.

- **System colors**: Developers typically avoid these due to the visual differences they might cause for each visitor. This term refers to the default system colors used by a computer within its default OS theme, and these colors are supported by almost all browsers. You will notice that these words describe their use rather, than their color. So, if you have a button on your webpage, and you want it to be styled exactly the same as the buttons on your visitor's operating system, then you could achieve that using these values. The possible values for system colors include: ActiveBorder, ActiveCaption, AppWorkspace, Background, ButtonFace, ButtonHighlight, ButtonShadow, ButtonText, CaptionText, GrayText, Highlight, HighlightText, InactiveBorder, InactiveCaption, InactiveCaptionText, InfoBackground, InfoText, Menu, MenuText, Scrollbar, ThreeDDarkShadow, ThreeDFace, ThreeDHighlight, ThreeDLightShadow, ThreeDShadow, Window, WindowFrame, and WindowText.

- **RGB hex colors**: These are six-digit codes preceded by a required # (pound) character that represent color values according to the RGB color system. As you might know, colors displayed on your computer screen consist of different combinations of red, green, and blue light to produce a single color. The RGB hexadecimal system tells the computer how much of each color to use. The amount of each color is stored as a value between 0 and 255 in the hexadecimal numbering system. Normally, you use the decimal system (base 10) for counting, which uses the numbers 0 through 9. The hexadecimal system (base 16) adds the letters A through F to the mix. Hexadecimal is used because it lets the computer store the full range of 0 through 255 values using only two digits—you write 255 in hexadecimal (hex) as FF. Don't worry: You won't need to be a hexadecimal expert to use colors in CSS. So, if you want no red at all in your color, you set it to 0. If you want the full (255) amount of red, you set it to FF. And if you want a medium red (128), you would set it to 80. Remember that each color is made up of values for red, green, and blue, so each hex value is made of three pairs of numbers, which gives you a total of six digits. Thus, #FFFFFF makes white by mixing the full amount of red, green, and blue, while #000000 makes black because it contains zero amount of each color. You can write some basic hexadecimal color values like this: red is #FF0000, green is #00FF00, and blue is #0000FF. If you ever set all three colors to the same value, such as #C0C0C0, you get a shade of gray. Many people find working out color combinations in this way hard, but you can use one of the many online color charts or web- and software-based color pickers to help you find the value you need to represent the shade and color you want to apply to an element. There is also a handy shortcut that you can use. If all of your color pairs consist of digits with the same value, such as #FF22CC, then you can shorten them to one digit each, which gives you #F2C. Note that you can do this only when all three pairs consist of twin digits; if even one of the colors has a different digit, then you cannot shorten the hexadecimal. For example, you must write out the value #FF22C1 completely.

- **RGB notation**: This notation uses a similar method to RGB hex colors, except that it separates red, green and blue using rgb(0, 0, 0) where you represent each color with a values from 0 through 255. Again color pickers and charts can assist you with using this method. It also worth mentioning that RGB notation can also use percentages to gauge the amount of each color being used, such as rgb(50%, 100%, 9%).

NotED

CSS3 extends the ability to reference color by using RGBA, which adds alpha levels into the mix. You can write this as rgba(0, 0, 0, 0). You also have the option of writing it in another color model called HSL (Hue, Saturation, Lightness) or HSLA, which adds alpha support. The HSL format lets you indicate the color based on its hue, saturation, and brightness levels. This line indicates how you might do this: hsl(50%, 30%, 20%).

Figure 5-10. You can find many named color values to use in your web designs.

Measurement Values

Units of measurement comprise the second—and most common—type of values you will come across when adding style to your site. These values can be relative (to the page, device, or inherited style), absolute (where the output medium is known), or percentage-based (in the context of what space is available). Of all the various units mentioned in this chapter, only px (pixel—for fixed-width designs), em (font-size—used mainly for elastic designs that stretch and skew to meet the user's browser size), and % (percent—used for liquid and fluid designs that resize according to the available screen space) are commonly used on the Web today (see Figure 5-11). Consequently, you might want to restrict yourself to the three most common types of measurement values until you come to grips with how positioning works and how your design might be affected by such units. It's also worth remembering that most measurement units allow decimal values, such as 1.95em. However, pixels are the smallest measurement you can get, so pixel values must consist of whole numbers, such as 2px, 3px, or 4px).

Possible measurement units include:

- **cm**: Centimeters are an absolute form of measurement.

- **em**: This unit of measurement is relative to the font-size property of your parent or ancestral elements. If you apply width: 10em; to a div tag, it would search for either a font-size of the current element or any inherited font-size, then use that to determine the width used. Because this is dependent on the size of the font, it's called an elastic form of measurement; it flexes to the available (or required size), so the content doesn't overflow.

- **ex**: The ex unit is relative to the lowercase x character you would find in a font. Even if no x exists for that particular font, the estimated size will become the default unit. This unit is not generally used on the Web, but it's still a valid form of sizing that you can use in your design.

- **in**: Inches are an absolute form of measurement equal to 2.54 centimeters.

- **mm**: Millimeters are an absolute form of measurement.

- **pc**: Picas are an absolute measurement where 1 pica is equal to 12 points (points are covered elsewhere in this list). You rarely see this format used on the Web because it is hard, if not impossible, to scale print media to every possible scenario that exists online.

- **%**: Percentages always relative to another value, whether it's the available space in a parent or ancestral element or the amount of screen space available. This popular unit on the Web can scale designs according to the available space. If a user resizes a window during her visit, the page will retrofit itself to meet the needs of the design and content. A 100% wide element will fill the entire width of the canvas (screen space).

- **pt**: Points are absolute measurements that you can often find in print media, where 1 point is equal to 1/72 of an inch (this can differ depending on implementation on the Web).

- **px**: Pixels are relative to the resolution of the device you're viewing. Pixels themselves are the smallest possible element you can display (they are dots on the screen), and they cannot be cut in half (you might think of them like atoms). The density of pixels can affect the size of the element–this is often described in terms of *DPI*, or dots-per-inch). 96dpi is the standard scope for px usage on the Web. Pixels are fixed, so no matter how the window is resized, everything will stay in its place, which helps you avoid distortion in your design.

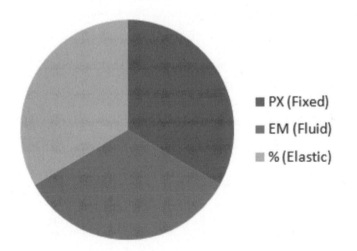

Figure 5-11. PX, EM, and % are the most commonly used measurement units on the Web.

Your Checklist

You now understand exactly how CSS works, and you're about ready to start applying it to your own site. At this point, you're ready to do a practical exercise (finally!). So get yourself organized and open your chosen editor. It might also be worth reopening your chosen browser of choice to the local copy of your index.html file (not the one online) that you created for your site's first page. When you start laying down the style for your site, you can refresh the page to see all of the cool things you have learned to implement. You'll also be adding code to the structure (class and ID attributes and a link to the style sheet in the head), so it's also worth ensuring your editor has the various HTML pages of your site open and ready to tweak. Most editors have some form of tabbed browsing for keeping multiple documents open at once. Once you have all your files open and ready to go, it's time to create the CSS file you will use.

Try It Yourself: Creating the Files

Within your editor of choice, create a new CSS file (or blank document). You don't want to use any predefined templates or wizards that your program offers because you will code this site by hand. You should have a blank document with nothing inside it at this point. Once you are ready, proceed to save the file. You should save the file as style.css in the style folder (see Figure 5-12) that you placed inside the base directory previously (website or whatever you called it earlier). After you do this, you're ready to begin adding style to your site.

Figure 5-12. Creating the style.css file will give you a place to put your content and write the code.

After you complete each task, you should save the file. You might also want to create a backup, in case you make mistakes and want to revert to using an earlier, working copy). You can then test the file in your browser. You can also upload each saved update of your files to your site, if you want to. This will enable you to see what the site looks like on the Internet, which is a good way to find any errors as you go along. CSS can be temperamental in various web browsers, so Chapter 7 helps you debug your code and resolve issues with CSS. If you encounter an error, my best advice is that you check that your code is correct and that you give some serious thought to what might work instead. Experimentation is an important aspect of solving these kinds of problems. At this point, however, you should not mess around with your HTML structure for the sake of resolving an issue with CSS because this could easily result in unsemantic and bloated markup.

Getting StartED!

You've learned about most of the things that affect the CSS language; now it's time to start layering your style over your structure and put that theory into practice. You've finished working with the structure (HTML), and you should feel free to keep referring back to the code to determine what elements you need to target for style, adding class and ID attributes to your HTML elements as appropriate. The next section of this chapter teaches you how what you can do with CSS; it covers the selectors that reference individual elements and the properties and values you can apply style to. You will learn some cool tips and tricks and some theory that will help you maximize your CSS potential. The time has come to finally take your creative ideas (and any drawings you made in your ideas pad in the creativity chapter and mold them into something that people will enjoy looking at.

You can find a list of W3C specifications or reference manuals for the CSS language here:

- **CSS 2.1**: www.w3.org/TR/CSS2/
- **CSS 3 Modules**: www.w3.org/Style/CSS/current-work#CSS3

LinkED

If you want to learn more about the different properties you can use, check out a reference guide such as the one at www.w3schools.com/css/ *or* http://reference.sitepoint.com/css.

Basics, Rules, and Selectors

Before you start adding any properties and values to your stylesheet, you need to first reference the file in your HTML head, so that the browser knows where to look. Then, you need to decide which elements you want to apply style too. The process of attaching style to segments of your page is something you should attempt on a case by case basis. Because you will find yourself referring back to various sections regularly, it might be worth putting a bit of paper or a bookmark in the pages you find yourself returning to most. If you want to test what element has been selected, you can give it a temporary background color. This is a great way to see where your style will apply because the background color will fill and highlight any elements your carefully written rule-set applies to. Plus this works whether you target a single part of the design, an inherited section, or even a combination of multiple elements that have been comma separated (and their children)!

ExplainED

If you want to add a background color, you can (for the moment) simply use this property and value combination: background-color: #808080. *This code gives the elements you selected a simple but visible gray background around everything that the style affects.*

Declaring the Style Sheet

Before you can apply any style to your site, you need to reference the CSS file in each HTML page's head element (so that your style will be applied). You might remember the link element, mentioned back in chapter 3—well, the time has come to start using it. In the next the code example, you can see two references to CSS files; the first refers to a conventional stylesheet, and the second reference refers to an "alternate stylesheet"—this is exactly what it sounds like. An occasion might arise where you want to add a second stylesheet to give visually impaired users (whom you'll learn more about in Chapter 9) a high-contrast page with plenty of large text and solid colors. Of course, you could always add an alternative stylesheet that gives your site a second theme, so people can simply swap the site's "look and feel" to one they find easier to use (or more enjoyable to look at!). Having an alternative stylesheet isn't a requirement, but it's worth being aware that they exist, in case you encounter a situation where you could use one. Most people will probably need to use only the first of the two links:

```
<link rel="stylesheet" type="text/css" href="/style/style.css"
media="all" />
<link rel="alternate stylesheet" type="text/css" title="High contrast"
href="/style/contrast.css" media="all" />
```

So let's examine this link element and break it down into its vital components, so you can see how you build such an element properly. The following example contains a basic link element with the href attribute to locate the file (you should be already familiar with this attribute). In this case, you should ensure that the link targets the right file and that the file exists (otherwise no style will be applied, and your site will look like bland HTML). This example uses two different declarations, illustrating how you might incorporate multiple stylesheets; however, you could simply use the first one at this time, for the sake of keeping things simple:

```
<link href="/style/style.css" />
<link href="/style/contrast.css" />
```

Now you have a basic link with an href attribute that tells the HTML document where to find the CSS that contains the style you need. Next, you need to declare the type of document it is. Because you link to an external file, you need to ensure the MIME type is the text/css value that browsers expect for a CSS document. This attribute instructs the browser that it is a CSS file, ensuring that the browser read its content properly:

```
<link type="text/css" href="/style/style.css" />
<link type="text/css" href="/style/contrast.css" />
```

Next you need to tell the browser that the link is a stylesheet. The type attribute allows the browser to know what it's looking at, but the rel (relation) attribute allows you to state how the file itself relates to your page. This is interesting because the rel attribute has a lot of uses. For example, you'll see this attribute in action when we examine microformats in Chapter 9. For the moment, you only need to worry about only the two values that stylesheets tend to use. The primary file should include the value stylesheet; however, if you do have a secondary file (such as in the next example), then you want to give it the value of alternative stylesheet so that browsers will know which style sheet should be used by default. Note that most browsers allow you to switch stylesheets, so you could use alternative ones to produce themes for your site, as I mentioned earlier. For example, imagine being able to switch designs with the click of a button; it's really that easy:

```
<link rel="stylesheet" type="text/css" href="/style/style.css" />
<link rel="alternate stylesheet" type="text/css"
href="/style/contrast.css" />
```

Finally, you need to add the finishing touches. In the case of alternative stylesheets, you have the option of giving the file a title attribute. This enables browsers that allow style switching to give the visitor's browser a list of any available files, each with its own, unique name (of course, the default stylesheet doesn't require a title). You can also attach a media attribute to the end that states the at-media type for the file (more on that later). It's worth mentioning here that if you specify a media type other than all in the link, you won't need to specify at-rules within the separate CSS file because the media type will have already been declared. I don't recommend doing this, though, because you wouldn't want to change a stylesheet at-rule in every page, when you can simply choose the relevant at-rule for your code within the easy-to-maintain external file. For this reason, the use of the media attribute is entirely optional (I personally use a media value of all to allow further specification of at-rules externally):

```
<link rel="stylesheet" type="text/css" href="/style/style.css"
media="all" />
<link rel="alternate stylesheet" type="text/css" title="High contrast"
href="/style/contrast.css" media="all" />
```

You're starting out, so it makes sense to stick to the first style sheet, rather than worrying about alternatives at this time—you don't want to get confused with lots of different CSS files at this early stage. So add your first stylesheet into the head element of every page you have created. Depending on the number of pages you have, this might take a fair bit of copy pasting. Once you do this, and you have your simple reference in place, with the href attribute linking to the file you want to use, you're ready to turn your attention to your CSS file and start adding some style to your design. It's time to turn your focus away from the HTML you have written and focus on the CSS file. The first thing you'll need to examine is the at-media rule that you just encountered.

Comments for Code

One thing you might not be aware of: You can add comments to your CSS, just as you can with HTML. If you find yourself wanting to maintain your code and remember exactly what everything does, you can use comments to markup your stylesheet. This enables you to keep written notes of whatever you feel needs documenting. You begin a comment with this character combination:

```
/*
```

You close a comment with this character combination:

```
*/.
```

These comments won't affect the page (or how it styles). It is worth mentioning that incorporating comments does add extra bulk to the page, so many developers tend to ignore them (or remove them after the page is complete) to help keep the amount of resources being used to a minimum. After all, you don't want to end up with a site that takes longer to load because you burned extra bytes with plain text! This following line illustrates how to create a comment:

```
/* This is a comment. */
```

Follow the @rules

@rules (or at-rules) are similar to rule-sets (which you learned about earlier), except they generally start with the @media reference, rather than a selector for a particular part of the page. CSS also includes alternative at-rules such as @import and @font-face, but this section will stick to @media. These rules let you specify a certain type of device you want to target, such as the screen or a handheld device (or even a printer). Together, these rules give you greater flexibility over how your design appears on a number of devices. It's simple to use these rules; all you need to do is wrap all the rule-sets (CSS selectors, declaration blocks, and their relevant properties and values) that you want to be read by that device inside the at-rule. Of course, at-rules are entirely optional, so you don't need to add them if you have no interest in targeting anything other than the user's screen.

Figure 5-13 highlights the way at-rules wrap around CSS code; such rules only affect pages when certain conditions are met (such as particular device types being used). In this example, the div with the color reference has an at-rule of @media. In a complete example, this would include a specific type of device to target, such as "print" for printers: @media print. Each at-rule does allow you to provide special style rules for certain devices; however, you should be aware that desktop browsers are the only devices that widespread support for this useful feature (mobile devices are a pain in this respect).

Figure 5-13. Wrapping at-rules around CSS code lets you apply their contents to an explicit device.

Of course, you might find it useful to see how all of this should come together. The following example shows some simple CSS code that uses at-rules and rule-sets (with plenty of stuff going on inside, such as properties and values). This example might seem familiar if you have looked at a site's CSS source code before. Many developers like to use at-rules to specify device-specific style, so it's quite possible you will encounter such media types in the source code of other sites. At this stage, however, you probably need a better understanding of how to put together a simple style sheet. So let's put this into action and see how you can use a wide variety of different rules, selectors, properties, and values to forge some basic style that you might use in a live scenario. The line of code that follows declares that the stylesheet should target the "screen" (this is basically your normal PC monitor) explicitly:

```
@media screen {

}
```

Inside the at-media selector, you now need to declare some elements that we want to target. To keep things simple, you use body (the document's body tag) and div (any dividers that might exist). You should remember you can always add a reference to a class attribute using a period, followed by the name of the class; or a pound # character, followed by the name for the ID (it's worth remembering that you can reuse class names whenever you want; however, IDs must remain unique—to quote the movie Highlander, "There can be only one!"):

```
@media screen {
body {

}
div {

}
}
```

You have targeted the device (your screen) and two elements (the body and all dividers). Next, you can add a few properties and values. In the example that follows, you apply a background element with a hexadecimal color value. You also apply a font-family property that references three comma-separated fonts (in order of priority) and a closing sans-serif reference that states what the element should fall back to if none of the fonts is available on the visitor's machine. This example includes a font-size reference; this indicates how big you want the font to be using the em measurement unit). Finally, this code snippet includes a color reference that indicates the color of the text (000000, or black). Essentially what follows is a complete code snippet that adds some fancy style to a page:

```
@media screen {
body {
        background: #FFFFFF;
        font-family: "Trebuchet MS", Helvetica, Arial, sans-serif;
```

```
        font-size: 1.1em;
}
div {
        color: #000000;
}
}
```

Some people choose to separate their media type information into separate stylesheets, but it's probably better in your case to keep them all organized into one file; after all, you want to make the process as simple as possible to maintain. The print at-rule is great for media-type usage is because it allows you to reduce the amount of clutter that will be printed, such as navigation (which is unnecessary on paper). This enables you to reduce ink usage when the document is printed because the non-vital components will be hidden (see Figure 5-14). One issue with this approach is that more recent devices tend to ignore media types (especially mobile devices such as cell phones), which ultimately inhibits their real-world use. Even with the possible downsides, media types are simple to use and worth including for those cases where devices do support them.

You can use the following media types in CSS, but the two you'll most often use are screen and print:

- **All**: When you use this media type, all other media types will use this style.

- **Aural**: This is a deprecated media type, and it should no longer be used (use speech instead).

- **Braille**: This media type is intended for tactile devices (such as Braille feedback readers).

- **Embossed**: This media type is intended for paged Braille readers.

- **Handheld**: This media type is used for mobile and handheld devices (discussed later in the book).

- **Print**: This media type is used to target style for printers; it enables you to describe how your site will appear on paper.

- **Projection**: This media type is used for large-scale projections and paged media.

- **Screen**: Whatever is placed in this style sheet will appear in a conventional browser.

- **Speech**: This media type replaces aural style sheets, which is intended to aid screen readers.

- **TTY**: This media type is intended for teletypes, terminals, and other display-limited media; it is rarely used.

- **TV**: This media type is for users with low resolution, television-style devices that have sound available.

LinkED

CSS3 allows designers to target devices beyond conventional media types. By stating the width, height, color, aspect ratio, and other variables, you can create style sheets aimed explicitly at devices you know will support the design. You can learn more about this at www.w3.org/TR/css3-mediaqueries/.

You know what media types are; now you're ready to add some to your document. Inside your empty CSS file, you should type @media, followed by the device you want to target (you can use comma separation for multiple devices if you want certain styles to apply to more than one device). Remember that the style you include in each media type will only apply to that media type. If you want certain elements to look the same, you either need to group them (comma separated), or you need to re-add the relevant CSS to that specific media type (you can also place them under the media type all, which targets all devices). It might help to think of the contents of each media type as a separate stylesheet because a device will only see the CSS at-rule that applies to itself.

Figure 5-14. Websites can be optimized for printers, so they don't waste a visitor's ink.

The next example would be perfect in your own CSS file because it shows you how to target a user's screen and printer. This example includes one media type that targets all media types, one media type that only applies to people who view the page using a screen (what you see on your browser), and a final media type that will be used only by printers (visible both on paper print outs and in the print preview screen of a web browser). If you add the following media types to your blank CSS page, you can customize how your structure looks on a printer and a screen. The all reference will (of course) target both screens and printers; fortunately, this isn't as difficult as it might have seemed at the beginning:

```
@media all {

}
@media screen {

}
@media print {

}
```

Super Selectors!

Selectors are what allow you to target particular elements or actions that affect them, such as applying a style when someone hovers over the hyperlink in an anchor tag. You have already learned about the basic structure of a CSS file, but it is important to understand what specifically adds style to your structure. So next you will walk through a simple, step-by-step example that shows you how each part of a rule-set (involving selectors) will let you apply those useful CSS properties to your pages, giving you a beautiful design.

You begin with the element selector. The example that follows assumes that you want to target a paragraph of text using the p element. This means that all paragraphs in your structure will have a gray background. Element selection will work on any recognized tag in the HTML specification, and it's great for applying the default style to all instances of that structural tag. You can recognize the element selector quite easily because it sits outside of the curly braces, and it has the name of an HTML element. The example uses p, but as you know, you can find many other elements to choose from. Figure 5-15 illustrates how applying this style changes the background color. Try adding this code in the @media all block in your CSS file, and see what difference it makes to your HTML content. Remember that you need to save both your CSS and HTML files (and upload them if you want to view your site online) before you can refresh your browser and see the difference:

```
p {
    background: #808080;
}
```

This is a styled paragraph of text!

Figure 5-15. You can use an element selector to apply a background color to a paragraph of text.

ExplainED

You can style multiple selectors by using a comma-separated list. For example, you might use h1, h2, h3, h4, h5, h6 { font-style: italic; } *to make all heading tags use italic styles. Of course, you can use this approach for more than element selectors; you can also use it for class and ID selectors (comma separated), as well!*

Next you will learn about class and ID selectors. Earlier, you learned that you could link to an element using both the HTML class and ID attributes to specify explicit style; you also learned about the power this gives to specificity. In this section, you will learn how you to implement this selector. In the example that follows, you will see two different styles within a rule-set. You place a period (dot) before the name of a class selector; similarly, you place a pound (#) character before an ID selector in CSS. The point of a class and ID is to state explicitly what elements require a unique style in your document (see Figure 5-16). You can use classes multiple times throughout your pages, but you should never have more than a single instance of an ID because they are intended to be unique. You can also link to an ID in your document by using the pound (#) character, followed by its name in the href attribute (such as index.html#hello). The great thing about this is that, when a browser loads the page, it will jump the user down to that part of the document. This gives the ID attribute both a stylistic and a functional purpose.

Remember that you will need to add the appropriate attribute into your HTML structure for the selector to hook onto. You can apply a class or ID attribute to any element. For example, these attributes might take this form in your code: class="name" or id="hello". The ability to assign unique style to elements is useful, but you should try not to go overboard. Yes, you *could* apply ID attributes to every element in the HTML document, but it would require far less code (and effort) to reference an element or use inheritance, instead.

After all, littering your HTML with class and ID attributes adds up quickly and results in a larger page size that could make your site take longer to load. Use your common sense to decide when it makes sense to apply style in this manner, rather than through some alternative means:

```
.name {
        background: #808080;
}
#hello {
        background: #FFFFFF;
}
```

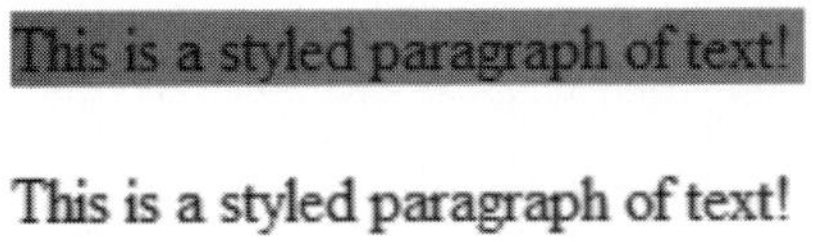

This is a styled paragraph of text!

This is a styled paragraph of text!

Figure 5-16. You can use an ID selector to can apply a background color to a single paragraph of text.

The example that follows (see Figure 5-17) uses the universal selector. You reference this selector with an asterisk (*) character before the declaration block that hold the background property. The * character basically acts as a generic declaration that targets every element at that level (you can think of it as a wildcard character). In the example that follows, this character helps you assign a gray background to all HTML tags within the body (including all children that inherit from these tags). You can also use the universal selector in simple CSS resets to create default padding and margins for your elements:

```
* {
        background: #808080;
}
```

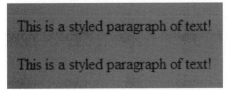

Figure 5-17. You can use the universal selector to apply a background color to every base element.

Attribute selectors are slightly more complicated to use than class or ID selectors; they are also used less commonly because IE6 doesn't support them. These selectors let you target your structure quite efficiently, partially removing the need for class and ID attributes in your structure. Attribute selectors allow you to target any attribute within an HTML structure. For example, you might use them to target the alt attribute within an img tag. You enclose all attribute selectors within square brackets [ ], and you either include the attribute name or the attribute followed by a value. You can find examples of both approaches in the code that follows.

In this example, your default rule for images with an alt attribute asserts they will have no border. The code also asserts that any images with the alt attribute "MySite!" will have a border. This works because the first reference targets any image with alt attributes; you don't provide a value, so CSS will simply reference them if they exist). Your second reference includes a value (and therefore added specificity), so it overrides the initial statement:

```
img[alt] {
        border: 0;
}
img[alt="MySite!"] {
        border: solid 1px;
}
```

You can spot the attribute name in the example easily because it's enclosed within the square brackets. If you provide a value, you precede it with the equals sign and provide the value itself in quote marks. You can provide additional details about the elements you want to target by using a special character before the equals sign. CSS provides several special operator symbols (characters) you can use to manipulate your elements:

- *a[lang|="en"]*: The | pipe character operator in this example applies style to hyphen-separated values with the lang attribute if they partially match the initial value. In this example, you might include values such as en-gb or en-us. CSS will recognize the en and style your text properly, even though it's joined to something else by a hyphen character.

- *a[class~="post"]*: The ~ character operator in this example indicates that you want to apply style to space-separated values. If you had multiple classes, such as class="news post", this instruction would apply style to all your text that contains the word, "post."

- *img[src^|="http://"]*: The ^ character operator in this example indicates that you want to style image attributes that start with http:// differently than links that do not contain it. (This is a CSS3 operator.)

- *a[href$=".pdf"]*: The $ character operator in this example lets you target all anchors that have the file extension .pdf; this means you can provide unique icons for file types! (This is a CSS3 operator.)
- *a[href*="downloads"]*: The * character operator in this example indicates you want to apply style to all anchors that contain the word "downloads" anywhere in the URL. (This is a CSS3 operator.)

Targeting with Combinators

Combinators let you place multiple, space-separated selectors next to each other. This enables you to target a sibling or a child of a certain element. For example, div p {} targets paragraphs of text that are children of a div element. The great thing about these combinators is that you can use them to apply a style to a potentially infinite level of depth. Another great thing: You can create them using any number of varying selectors (such as element, class, or ID):

```
#header div p acronym
```

The preceding code targets all acronyms within paragraphs that sit inside a div inside an element with an ID called header—whew! The following code example illustrates how to use the different types of combinators in coordination with the combinator reference (you can also see this at work in the bulleted list that follows):

```
<div>
    <div>Item 1</div>
    <div>
        <div>Item 2</div>
            <div>
                <p>Item 3</p>
            </div>
        <p>Item 4</p>
        <h2>Item 5</h2>
        <div>Item 6</div>
        <p>Item 7</p>
    </div>
    <span>Item 8</span>
    <p>Item 9</p>
</div>
```

Combinators let you target, not just elements or selectors, but the children and siblings of these elements. Unfortunately, you can't use them to target the parents of elements in CSS. The next example shows you might use combinators to target elements from the preceding example. Developers commonly use four types of combinators: *descent selectors*, *child selectors*, and *general* and *adjacent sibling selectors*:

- **Descent selectors**: These space-separated combinators let you target all instances of children inside a particular element, no matter how many other elements exist between them (see Figure 5-18). For example you might have three levels of `div` tags and still target all paragraphs that occur everywhere between them. In the following code example, you use this code `div p {property: value ;}` to target Item 9.

- **Child selectors**: These combinators replace the space with a `>` character to target only immediate children of the element. Even if the initial `div` contains paragraphs (but they are inside other `div` tags), the child selector notice because it isn't one of the immediate children. In the example that follows, you use `div>div {property: value ;}` to target Items 2, 4, 5, 6, 7, and the `div` of Item 3.

- **General sibling selectors**: These combinators replace the space with a `~` character that target only elements that share the same parent, but appear after the selector itself in the source code. This lets you target every paragraph following an `h2` element, but not the paragraphs before it. In the example that follows, you use `div div~h2 {property: value ;}` to target Items 6 and 7.

- **Adjacent sibling selectors**: These combinators replace the space with a `+` character and only targets elements that follow directly after the combinatory itself in the source code. This works a lot like a general sibling selector, but it targets only the first tag that follows it. In the example that follows, you use `div div h2 {property: value ;}` to target only Item 6.

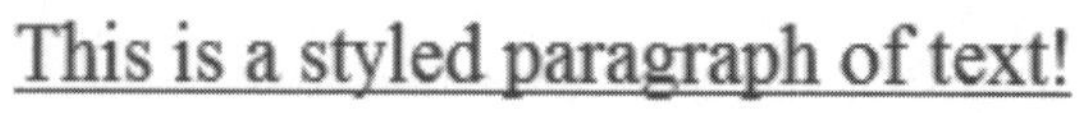

This is a styled paragraph of text!

Figure 5-18. You can use descent selectors to style a unique anchor's font-size without a class or ID.

LinkED

You can find more details about combinators (including some examples that show you how to use them) by visiting www.w3.org/TR/ CSS2/selector.html. You can also read the following, easy-to-understand article at www.456bereastreet.com/archive/200510/css_21_selectors_part_2/.

Pseudo Classes

The final selectors you'll look at are *pseudo classes* and *pseudo elements* (see Figure 5-19). You can use these virtual extensions to your selectors to apply a unique style to part or all of an element based on a certain event (such as hovering over an element or applying style to the first letter). This helps you further reduce the need for class and ID references within your document, as long as the visitor's browser supports the pseudo item. Implementing pseudo classes is easy: You add a colon (:) character and the name of the pseudo item you want to trigger (right after the selector and before the opening curly brace).

Developers use pseudo selectors most often in anchor links to apply style when a visitor hovers over the element or to indicate that a user has already visited a link. Most developers use pseudo classes with anchors to change the color of the link based on its state; however, you could also be creative and do something unique with the anchor links you use on your site's pages. The interesting thing about pseudo selectors is that they can perform a function based on the behavior of the user (this kind of action is normally reserved for scripting languages). In the example that follows, you'll begin by assigning a hyperlink a color value of FFFFFF (white). When a user hovers over the hyperlink, you will change the color to 808080 (gray):

```
a:link {color: #FFFFFF;} a:hover {color: #808080;}
```

Pseudo selectors essentially allow you to apply basic behavior functions or apply special formatting to a certain component of an element. This selector is what enables you to produce rollover effects on your hyperlinks, change their color when clicking them, or even produce a dropdown menu using anchors and unordered lists.

This is a styled paragraph of text!

Figure 5-19. You can use pseudo elements to style an anchor so it looks entirely different to the default hyperlink.

ExplainED

The order in which you provide pseudo classes for anchors is important. You need to use these properly to ensure a style you choose does not override other styles in the document for the various states of a link. You should provide them in this order: a:link, a:visited:, a:focus, a:hover, and a:active (you don't need to declare all five pseudo-class selectors in your CSS code).

You can use the following pseudo classes and elements to assign style to key parts of your site:

- **link**: This pseudo class applies style to anchors or links the user hasn't visited yet.

- **visited**: This pseudo class applies style to anchors or links the user has already visited.

- **active**: This pseudo class applies style to the active selection event of a link or anchor.

- **hover**: This pseudo class applies style to anchors or links when a visitor hovers over them.

- **first-letter**: This pseudo class applies style to the first letter of text in an element.

- **first-line**: This pseudo class applies style to the first line of text inside an element.

Properties and Values

CSS includes many properties and values. Indeed, most of the power of CSS derives from the way it lets you combine properties and values with rule-sets you create to affect the style of your design. The ability to select elements you want to reference is important, and you learned about them first because you cannot apply properties without understanding how to do this, but it is your ability to leverage properties and values in CSS that will truly make using this language fun to use. This book organizes each of the various principles (and styling methods), so you can quickly reference what approaches affects text, color, positioning on the page, and so on. You can work through each of these, exploring how you can make them work best for your site. As with other aspects of scripting, this is a process of trial and error, and playing around with the results can help you tweak your design to suit your needs. If you find that your elements don't style as you expect them to, you should review Chapter 7, which covers debugging (it would be nice to avoid bugs entirely, but that's difficult when browser makers implement code that doesn't always follow the specifications correctly).

Fonts and Text

Text will (likely) make up the majority of your site's content, so you want to get your text customized, sized, and presentable to your visitors (see Figure 5-20). You can start by using the existing fonts and typeface properties already available to you. The first property you'll learn about, `font-family`, lets you declare a comma-separated list of fonts that you want to apply. This element is called a `font-family` because it lets you provide a list of alternatives, in case a typeface is not installed on the end user's machine (a common problem with modern web design). All the fonts contained in each family will match a certain style of typography, such as sans-serif.

This is a styled paragraph of text!

Figure 5-20. You can cause a dramatic change in the readability of your text by selecting the right (or wrong) font.

Ideally, you want to make your the fonts look similar enough that visitors won't see too much difference between them. Also, you want to avoid mixing fonts that are serif with sans-serif (or other family types) within the same font stack (a stack is just another name for a font-family) because it will result in more unwanted differences if one of the primary fonts is unavailable. Font families should relate to each other by appearance and style. You can see the anatomy of a font stack in this line of code:

```
font-family: <ideal>, <alternative>, <common>, <generic>;
```

You begin most font families with the ideal typeface that you want to use. This might be something you would like people to have, but you should be aware that your visitors might not have it installed by default. Next, you can add an alternative choice that closely matches the font you prefer. Your alternative font should be something more common and should have a similar feel). Next, you add a well known-font that everyone is likely to have. This is a fallback option; it's better to use a common font than to rely on the default font. Finally, if all else fails, the browser can use whatever font is available; this part of the generic font-family declaration tells the browser what family type you want (such as serif)). You can see a list of common typefaces in Figure 5-21.

Andale Mono
Arial
Arial Black
Bookman Old Style
Calibri
Cambria
Candara
Century Gothic
Century Schoolbook
Comic Sans MS
Consolas
Constantina
Corbel
Courier New

Georgia
Impact
Lucida Console
Lucida Sans Unicode
MS Sans Serif
Nyala
Palatino Linotype
Segoe Print
Segoe Script
Segoe UI
Tahoma
Times New Roman
Trebuchet MS
Verdana

Figure 5-21. This list of typefaces includes the most common fonts people have installed on their computers.

LinkED

You can find an online wizard that helps you produce you a customized font stack at www.codestyle.org/servlets/FontStack. *You can also see font-stacks that have already been produced by visiting* http://font-family.com

You can't count on the fact that your visitors will have a font just because you do. Fonts such as Arial, Courier New, Georgia, Times New Roman, Verdana, Trebuchet MS, and Lucida Sans are usually safe choices, but nothing is ever certain. This issue has become a matter of contention among web designers because it makes trying to give everyone the same visual experience an almost impossible task. Commonly installed fonts are classified as *web safe*, and methods have been developed to help designers try to allow for unique typography on the Web.

LinkED

If you would like to find a list of common fonts found on computers that you can consider fairly web safe, visit www.speaking-in-styles.com/web-typography/Web-Safe-Fonts/ *or* www.codestyle.org/css/font-family/ sampler-CombinedResultsFull.shtml. *You can find a list of fonts installed by default on different Operating systems at* www.apaddedcell.com/web-fonts.

Note that some browsers prefer that you enclose fonts with spaces in their names with quote marks (like this: "Times New Roman"). This happens because some older browsers thought that a space in a font family constituted a new filename. This doesn't affect modern browsers these days, but rendering your font names that way it's still considered good practice to follow this convention. For the sake of being safe, you should do the same. A typical font-stack might look like this:

```
font-family: Georgia, "Times New Roman", Times, serif;
```

In the preceding example, you see a list of font types after the font-family declaration (serif in this case). You learned previously that you should include a font type at the end of your font stack, for cases where a computer returns that the user has none of your preferred fonts installed (although this shouldn't occur if you have a good stack). The visual appearance of a font determines what family it belongs to. There are five basic font types that make up the *rainbow* of typography: serif, non-serif, cursive, monospace, and fantasy.

Serif fonts feature small flourishes on the edges of their letters; examples of serif fonts include Baskerville, Cambria, Garamond, Georgia, Palatino, Rockwell and Times New Roman). Sans-serif fonts omit the *edge work* at the edges of their characters; examples of sans-serif fonts include Arial, Calibri, Century Gothic, Geneva, Gill Sans, Helvetica, Impact, Lucida Sans, Myriad, Segoe UI, Tahoma, Trebuchet, and Verdana). Serif and sans-serif are the most commonly used font-family types, but they aren't the only font-family types you can use on the Web.

Cursive fonts use more circular and rounded style text, rather than straight lines. Cursive fonts popular are popular among many in the Web 2.0 design movement, but they remain far less common than the serif/sans-serif duo. Examples of cursive fonts include Comic Sans MS, Monotype Corsiva, and Zapfino). *Monospace* fonts space their characters out equally, regardless of their widths (an *i* and a *w* use the same amount of space in a monospace font). You see such fonts frequently in code editors (for readability), as well as in books (code is often rendered in a monospace font) and on the Web. Examples of monospace fonts include Andale Mono, Consolas, Courier, Fixedsys, Lucida Console, Monaco, and Terminal). Finally, *fantasy fonts* include all other fonts that don't fit into the aforementioned categories. Fantasy fonts include *pixel* and *symbolic fonts*, such as Apple Symbols, Wingdings, Webdings, and Zapf Dingbats).

You might wonder what happens when you want to display a font that your visitors don't have installed. The most common mechanisms for dealing with this issue are to provide alternatives in a font stack (and hope the visitors have one of those typefaces on their machine); provide an image with the text printed on it (and use that in the background of a heading with the text offset, so only the image is visible); or use Flash to embed the font and the displayed text on the screen (using scripting to *swap out* the normal text alternative). The last technique is known as sIFR (Scalable Inman Flash Replacement—see Figure 5-22). None of these methods is especially clean, but all can help you pull in some unique typography to your site, at least for headings that do not have reels of text you need to replace.

Figure 5-22. sIFR allows web designers to make use of any font they like on the Web.

You can alter more than the type of font you use; you can also change its size using font-size (see Figure 5-23). This property lets you specify how big or small you want a font to appear. The general rule with font sizes is to ensure that your fonts are large enough to read and that headings are larger than your body text. The font-size property can use any measurement unit type, but it's highly recommended that you use em measurements rather than px because Internet Explorer has a bug that causes text resizing to fail if a typeface has a fixed-font size. This can cause accessibility problems if you have visitors with poor vision because they won't be able to see the tiny text, and they can't resize the fonts in the browser effectively enough to meet their visual needs.

Plus, the tiny fonts look bad even if you have good eyesight! This line sets the size of a particular font:

```
font-size: 2em;
```

CSS3 introduces the ability to embed fonts in your site using the @font-face at-rule; however due to its inconsistent implementation, legal restrictions on typefaces, and the requirement that the reader install the font (which can be burdensome when a font has a large file size), this approach isn't worth considering at this time. Services are starting to appear that will overcome some of these issues, so might be worth considering in the future.

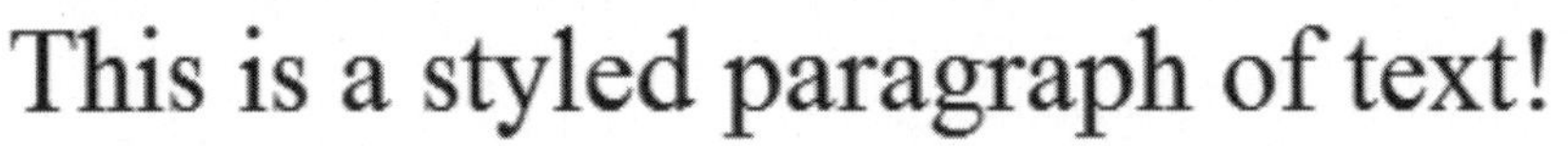

This is a styled paragraph of text!

Figure 5-23. You can change the font-size and the line-height to improve the readability of your site further.

You can also specify a font's `line-height` to provide appropriate spacing between individual lines of text (known as leading). You can do this as either numeric (such as 2.2em) or as a percentage value. The amount of space between each line can be an important tool in improving readability; whitespace makes things look at lot cleaner. Ensuring that you have enough space between your lines of text can help you turn cluttered text into something far less cramped and far more appealing visually; this has the added benefit of making your content easier to read, as well. You set the `line-height` with this line of code:

```
line-height: 1.2em;
```

The `font-weight` element allows you to determine whether text is displayed as normal, bold, or something else (see Figure 5-24). While you have several choices other than `bold` and `normal` for `font-weight`, but you should generally stick with those two because many fonts do not support other values. You can use `font-weight` as a replacement for the old `b` element in HTML, but you should also remember that the `b` element continues to have its uses. Your needs will dictate whether you decide to use the element or the CSS style (you might even use the `strong` tag). Ultimately, it's a matter of semantics and what best meets the needs of your content. More important than which approach you use is making sure that you are consistent in whichever approach you adopt on your site. This line of code sets the `font-weight`:

```
font-weight: bold;
```

What holds for `font-weight` also holds for `font-style`, which enables you to apply italic style to an element. Bold and italic text have both been severely misused through the years. This CSS replacement (for cases where `em` or `I` are not applicable) has two possible values: `italic` or `normal`. Italics slant your text, and they can help you emphasize names or objects that you want to give a bit of priority. This line of code applies italic text:

```
font-style: italic;
```

This is a styled paragraph of text!

Figure 5-24. Bold and italic text enable you to apply strength and emphasis to your content.

You can pull all of these style aspects together using the single `font` property. You do this by declaring (optionally) `font-style` and `font-weight` (space separated). Next, you provide the `font-size`, followed (optionally) by a forward slash and the `line-height`. Finally, you round off your style instructions with the `font-family`:

```
font: italic bold  1.5em/1.2em Georgia, "Times New Roman", Times, serif;
```

Figure 5-25 shows you exactly what a combined list of font changes can do to your text. This image shows what happens when you apply italics, bold, sizing, and a font-family. Using the `font` property enables you to avoid having to reference every single one of the previous properties individually (unless, of course, you want to change only one property for a particular element).

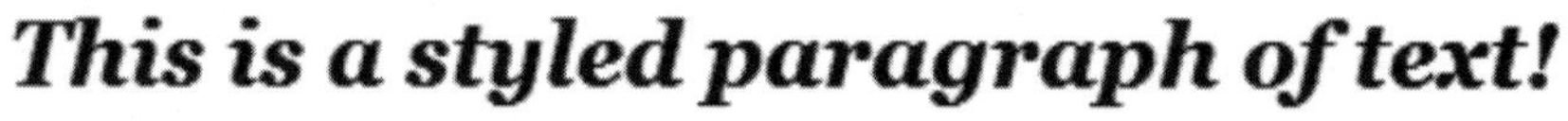

This is a styled paragraph of text!

Figure 5-25. You can tie all the different properties for specificying font characteristics into a single, neat CSS statement.

NotED

CSS3 adds some additional font properties called font-size-adjust, font-stretch, font-effect, font-smooth, *and* font-emphasize; *unfortunately, browser support for these properties is weak and you shouldn't use them at this time.*

Another text-related CSS property, letter-spacing, allows you to add extra spacing between your characters (see Figure 5-26). This process is sometimes referred to as *tracking*, and it behaves similarly to the line-height property. This line of code lets you change the spacing between your letters:

```
letter-spacing: 2px;
```

If adding spacing between letters makes your content *less* readable (and you want to give your content a bit of extra breathing space), you can also add a bit of whitespace between words using the word-spacing property, like this:

```
word-spacing: 2px;
```

Note that the white space between your letters can be affected by text justification, which automatically spaces out your words to ensure that all of the lines of text line up and are of equal width.

This is a styled paragraph of text!

Figure 5-26. Changing the letter and word spacing allows you to pad out your text to suit your needs.

You can also use the white-space property to state that text should not collapse onto another line using the nowrap value or that you want to preserve formatting using the values of pre, pre-line, or pre-wrap. You don't see this often on the Web because, without line collapsing, your text will overflow the space available to the text, which can look quite unprofessional. However, this technique does have some uses. For example, you can use it if you need to ensure that the full line is preserved, no matter what the design states (think of this element as overruling the specified width). You implement the property like this:

```
white-space: nowrap;
```

ExplainED

Other CSS properties include font-variant, *which produces small capital letters (that aren't supported by Safari, unfortunately; and* text-shadow, *which gives the WebTV style shadow. This property was removed in a past version of CSS, but then reintroduced in CSS3; however, neither Internet Explorer nor Mozilla Firefox supports it at the present time.*

Other ways you can alter your text include text-align, which lets you specify an alignment as left, right, center, or justify. This feature behaves just like similar features in popular text editors and word processors, enabling you to align text to a certain part of the screen. The left and right alignment properties make your text gravitate towards the side walls of your content box, the center property situates the content of your element in the middle of the area it occupies, and the justify property uses a sort of word-spacing effect to calibrate your text so that it takes up the same width (in space usage) for each line. This effect gives a fullness to your text, ensuring that it doesn't have the ragged opposing edge you see when aligning to the left or right of the screen. One interesting thing about the text-align property is that early versions of Internet Explorer (6 and earlier) required that you use center text alignment on a parent element to get a child to appear on the middle of the page. This stemmed from the fact that Internet Explorer 6 and earlier didn't apply equal margins to center your content. This line of code aligns your text to the left margin:

```
text-align: left;
```

You can also use text-decoration to give flourishes to your text with values such as line-through (aka *strikethrough*). The line-through value lets you achieve a *crossed-out* effect; this style is the equivalent of the del element in HTML; of course, the CSS version exists purely for applying style to your text, so you aren't restricted to using it for deleted content, The overline value draws a line above the content, although this could be confusing for some people, who might mistake such a line for a hyperlink because it will appear directly beneath the line that precedes the one you are creating an overline for. Similarly, the underline value draws a line beneath your text; it's commonly used on links to show where the clickable area is). While useful, the text-decoration properties can lead to confusion unless you take care in how you use them. This line enables you to underline a bit of text on your page:

```
text-decoration: underline;
```

You can also use the `text-indent` property with a numerical value to push the first line of text further into the line. You can see this effect at work in Figure 5-27, which displays an image where the left spacing is slightly bigger than the spacing on the right-hand side. You see this because the text has been indented. Some people use indenting on paragraphs to leave space for inserting a background image. This line of code indents your text:

```
text-indent: 10px;
```

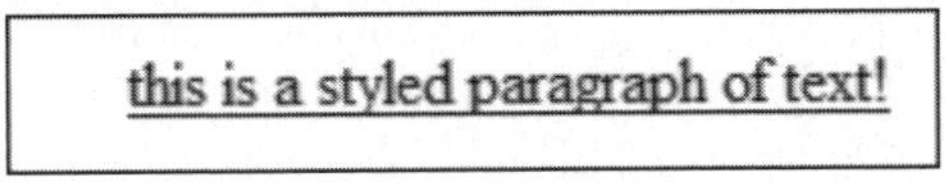

this is a styled paragraph of text!

Figure 5-27. You can use an indent to offset your content from the left-hand side. This image also illustrates the effect caused by underlining your text.

You can alter your text using the `text-transform` property, which lets you alter the characters or words to either `capitalize` (each word) or set all of the letters `lowercase` or `uppercase` (caps). It might seem like a good idea to set all the letters to uppercase, but you should use this technique in moderation; a lot of people consider the use of capital letters for everything quite invasive—it is widely believed that all caps equates to shouting in email and on the Internet. This line of code enables you convert your text to lower-case letters:

```
text-transform: lowercase;
```

CSS also includes a `vertical-align` property that lets your position elements like images within inline boxes. This property uses numeric and percentage values to set properties for the `baseline`, `bottom`, `middle`, `sub`, `super`, `text-bottom`, `text-top`, and `top`. For example, assume you have a single-line paragraph of text and an image that sits on that line. You could use the `vertical-align` property to ensure the image is balanced anywhere from the bottom right to the top (or anywhere in between). This property can help you balance the position of your images, especially if you don't want a lot of whitespace in a certain part of the page. It should be noted that the vertical-alignment property does not work for children of a block-level element. If you want something to appear in the middle of the page, `vertical-align` will not place your image an equal distance between the top and the bottom of the canvas—it's not designed for such use! This line of code enables you to balance your image in the center of the designated area in relation to the text that surrounds it:

```
vertical-align: middle;
```

Finally you can also change the direction of your text using the `direction` property. You do this by assigning it the values of `ltr` (left to right) or `rtl` (right to left). You will probably find this property of limited usefulness, but it does have its place: rtl is often used in languages such as Arabic. The direction property is easy to understand and implement:

direction: ltr;

NotED

CSS3 adds some additional text-direction related properties, called text-overflow, word-break, text-wrap, word-wrap, text-align-last, text-justify, punctuation-trim, ext-emphasis, text-outline, *and* hanging-punctuation; *unfortunately support for these properties in browsers is weak, and you should avoid using them.*

Colors, Backgrounds, and Borders

So far you've learned a great deal about how to manipulate your text; next, you will look at one of the most important parts of CSS: adding color to your design, adding images to the background of elements, and applying borders around the edges of elements. This task serves as the cornerstone of all graphic designs you place on the Web (with the exception of the img tag in the HTML specification). The first and simplest thing you will look at is the color property. By applying one of the many color values in CSS (mentioned earlier), you can give text a wide range of foreground colors on a style-by-style basis. For example, you could even use a span tag to highlight text with a color. This line of code uses a hex value to change your text color to blue (see Figure 5-28):

color: #0000FF;

Of course, you probably remember that you're not limited to hex values; you can also use color names (both standard and non-standard), RBG color values, and even system colors. That said, most people tend to use hex values because they are the most widely supported convention when working with color values.

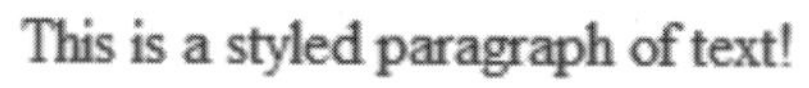

This is a styled paragraph of text!

Figure 5-28. It's easy to change the color of your text; simply use the color property and decide upon a color value.

The background property lets you affect the appearance of the space behind the element in use (see Figure 5-29). CSS lets you apply various different properties that affect the way your background appears. The first is background-color, which behaves like the standard color property (that affects font colors), except that this property can apply a flat color for the background for an element. This means you could use it to create white text on a black background, or vice versa. Generally speaking, it's worth defining a background color even if you want to place an image in the background. For example, the user might have images turned off or the images might be unavailable. Unlike the HTML img element, CSS won't display a red cross if your images are unavailable; instead, it will appear as though nothing exists in the background. Under the wrong circumstances, this can make your text unreadable. No one will be able to see your text if you're using a light color for text and the default background color of white, (well, no one without amazing vision, anyway!) Defining a background color explicitly gives your design a fallback that will be less pretty when invoked, but still highly readable:

background-color: #000000;

This is a styled paragraph of text!

Figure 5-29. You change the background color, in addition to the color of the text.

You can also assign a background value of transparent if you don't want any background to be applied or if you would prefer to use the background of the parent element rather than inherit or overwrite it. In addition to a background color, you can also add a background-image. The great thing about background images is that they enable you to give your site a bit of texture. For example, you might use this property to give your design a tiled wooden effect, which might make your site feel much more organic. When you add a background image, you need to fill the value of url( ) with a direct link to the image; you place that link between the brackets:

background-image: url(/images/banner.gif);

As is the case when you fill out the image element's src attribute, you need to make sure the address you supply for a background image is valid and in a format that is compatible with the Web (such as .gif or .jpeg). Background images can greatly enhance the appearance of your site, but you should also make sure that your site looks fine with images turned off. Until CSS3 hits the mainstream, you cannot attach multiple background images to an element.

Now assume you have a background image (such as a seamless tile) that needs to repeat itself in various directions, until it spans the entire width and height of the screen. In this case, you can use `background-repeat` property, which can have the values of `repeat` (both directions), `repeat-x` (repeated left to right), `repeat-y` (repeated top to bottom), or `no-repeat` (for a single image). Being able to repeat a background is great for creating a seamlessly infinite and "edge free" design; however, you can't take a single image and stretch or skew it to fill the whole screen until the CSS3 specification goes final. This is something that many web designers have been hungry to do for ages, and this limitation impacts how you can use backgrounds. As things stand today, repeating an image in a direction is the only way you can enable a single image to span beyond its natural borders to fill an area. This line of code repeats an image from left to right:

```
background-repeat: repeat-x;
```

LinkED

If you would like to produce a seamless tile for your site with no effort required (apart from clicking a couple of buttons), check out the site at http://bgpatterns.com/.

CSS also includes a property called `background-position` that has two values on an axis. You can use these to determine the location of the image. The property takes either numerical values such as 200px or uses values such as `left`, `middle`, `right`, `top`, and `bottom`. You use one value to determine the image's vertical position, the other to determine its horizontal position. If you want to align and position a background image explicitly, this property allows you to ensure that the background image appears only where you want it (rather than at the default, the top-left position). You should be careful when you state the image's position that the space you place it in is large enough to host it, or it will simply overflow and be cut off or hidden. You'll learn more about positioning later in this chapter; however, this method of positioning provides the simplest way to affect the visual placement of an image in your source code:

```
background-position: top left;
```

Finally, CSS includes the `background-attachment` property, which indicates whether an image should remain fixed in place or roll as a user scrolls the window. Possible values for this property include `fixed` and `scroll`—and they behave exactly as you'd expect. If you add a background image to a body element, it takes up space on the page (filling the browser window's background). This code fixes the background image in place:

```
background-attachment: fixed;
```

Like other CSS properties, the background property itself can represent a combination of other properties that you group into one single statement. For example, this statement combines several instructions in a single line:

```
background: #FFFFFF url(/images/banner.gif) repeat-x top left fixed;
```

You usually assign background references a background color value: a link to an image. You also indicate whether you want the image to overlap the top of the background color); state whether you want to repeat the image; state its location on the page; and indicate whether it should scroll or fixed in place. How you use it is up to you, but squeezing all the preceding background properties and values into a single line can save you a lot of space in your code.

CSS3 adds support for multiple backgrounds and other border-related properties called background-clip, background-break, *and* background-size. *Unfortunately, support for these properties is weak, and you should avoid using them (it is worth noting that Safari supports multiple backgrounds).*

The border property does exactly what it sounds like: it gives you a method of applying a styled line around the outside of an element. The border property, like the aforementioned background and font properties, can be combined into a single statement. This code shows how to give the border a width, style (such as solid or dotted), and a flat color:

```
border: 2px solid #000000;
```

You'll learn about all of these properties in greater detail momentarily. As things currently stand, you cannot add an image as a border (which might be useful), although it's something that might appear in browsers in the future, when CSS3 has been more widely adopted. For now, let's celebrate the fact that you can add a border to make your elements have visible boundaries that will clue people in to how you have split your content.

The first element of the border property you'll look at is border-color. This property uses a hex color value to assign a flat color to the border:

```
border-color: #000000;
```

If you want to create a basic visual frame around an element (that takes into account any padding the element has), you can use a flat color that achieves this basic effect. You can also use border colors when you develop your site (along with a background color) to help you see how much space particular elements take up on your page. This approach can also help you see the dimensions of your page's elements or find a positioning quirk. You'll learn how to do all these things later in the chapter.

Of course, you can do much more than create a flat border. You can't create a custom image at the moment, but you can apply a few basic effects to your flat border to give it a bit more punch. For example, the border-style property allows you to achieve some of these effects by using values such as none (which removes the border), hidden (not supported well by Internet Explorer), dotted, dashed, solid, double, groove, ridge, inset, or outset. Trying out some of these different styles might serve as inspiration to add some flair to your design. Note that you need to define what style a border uses for it to become visible in some browsers; simply giving it a border a color and stating a width might not make it display properly (or even at all!). This line sets the border-style property to solid (although, as already noted, it's not a complete code example because you would still need to add color, style, and width in your declaration:

```
border-style: solid;
```

CSS also includes a border-width property, which uses a numeric value to determine how thick the border should be. Typically, you define the width of a border in terms of pixels rather than em or percentages because most borders on a website employ subtle effects to outline the edge of a segment. If you used another unit that is relative or fluid, your border's width would literally expand and contract based on the space in the window, possibly creating an inconsistent appearance for your site. People with low resolutions would barely see a border, while people with high resolutions might see a border as thick as a tree (well maybe not that big, but you get the idea!). Most borders on the Web fall to something like one-pixel wide, which is a wafer-thin line. How subtle or how visible you make your borders is entirely up to you and the requirements of your site. This line of code sets the width of a border:

```
border-width: 2px;
```

Finally, the border property provides an interesting set of subproperties that let you define the explicit borders for each side of a box. This means that that you can define the borders for the top, bottom, left, and right sides of an element separately. This might prove useful if you want to create a border on one only side of the element. You might even add a dash of additional style, defining separate width, style, and color properties). If you choose to give different border properties to each side of an element, you cannot define these using a single reference. Instead, you would need to give four separate declarations (one for each side). This following example shows how to provide separate declarations for each of the four borders in the image shown in Figure 5-30. Also, notice that each side has the same width and style, but different colors; this gives the border a cool rainbow effect:

```
border-top: 2px solid #000000;
border-bottom: 2px solid # 0000FF;
border-left: 2px solid # AAAAAA;
border-right: 2px solid # FF0000;
```

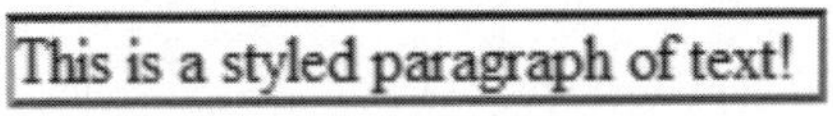

This is a styled paragraph of text!

Figure 5-30. You can create borders for elements either individually or as a group.

The preceding code can be a great space-saver. If you want to attach a single piece of style to a single side, you can use one of the following references that edits a specific property for a specific side of a specific border. The code to do this is a little verbose, and it won't be for everyone; however, it's one more option you have when applying style to your site. You can be as efficient (or as explicit) as you feel is necessary. This code block produces exactly the same effect as the preceding example; what it illustrates quite well is how much space the *combination* properties can save you:

```
border-top-color: #000000;
border-top-style: solid;
border-top-width: 2px;
border-bottom-color: # 0000FF;
border-bottom-style: solid;
border-bottom-width: 2px;
border-left-color: # AAAAAA;
border-left-style: solid;
border-left-width: 2px;
border-right-color: # FF0000;
border-right-style: solid;
border-right-width: 2px;
```

Before you move onto the next section, it's worth mentioning that something similar to border called the outline property exists. This behaves similarly to border, except all sides must be identical, and, more importantly, it does not take any space away from the CSS box model. As we'll see later, the outline property is great for highlighting inline elements. Like the border property, the outline property provides subproperties that let you assign width (outline-width), style (outline-style), and color (outline-color) to your outlines.

CSS3 adds some additional border-related properties called border-radius, border-break, border-image, and box-shadow. As with other properties introduced in CSS3, support for these properties remains weak, and you should avoid using them.

The effects are similar enough that it's not worth spending an extended amount of time on the outline property; however, it is worth saying that you could use this property to place a border around an acronym. This might be a better option than using a standard border because outlines are like a background property in the sense that they do not add any width or height to the overall element (the border property's borders do add width and height to the element because it's a physical effect). Like the border property, the outline property lets you combine the color, style, and width references into a single property:

```
outline: 2px solid #000000;
outline-color: #000000;
outline-style: solid;
outline-width: 2px;
```

NotED

CSS3 adds some additional outline-related properties called outline-offset, outline-radius, box-sizing, nav-index, nav-up, nav-down, nav-left, nav-right, resize, appearance, and icon. As is the case with other properties introduced in CSS3, the major browsers don't yet support these features, so you should avoid using them at this time.

Choosing the Right Color

Let's take a break from CSS code for a minute and take a look at color. You've seen multiple ways that you can apply color to the various items on your site, but you haven't looked at why color is useful, or how you can pick the right colors for your site. I can't tell you exactly which colors to use because that comes down to personal preference, and the choices you make will be a function of your site's requirements. That said, I can give you some hints and tips for how to go about finding the best colors for you. The first thing you need to know is where you can find appropriate colors.

Wheels and Charts

Have you ever seen a color on another site that you wanted to use, but didn't know what it was? Or have you ever wanted to try and work out what combination of colors would work best for your design? You can go about this in several different ways, but many artists and designers attack this problem using what is known as a color wheel. A color wheel for websites is comprised of a palette that displays an entire spectrum of colors you can use, illustrating how they relate to each other (see Figure 5-31). Color scheming software can simplify the process by offering you examples of colors that would complement your default choices. By examining a range of different colors, you can build up a palette that ensures your site has enough contrast and complementing colors.

You can find a range of free color wheels online:

- **4096 Color Wheel**: www.ficml.org/jemimap/style/color/wheel.html
- **Adobe Kuler**: http://kuler.adobe.com/
- **Almsamim Color Picker**: www.almsamim.com/color-picker.html
- **Color Scheme Designer**: http://colorschemedesigner.com/
- **Colorotate**: www.colorotate.org/

Figure 5-31. This image shows a complete color chart that spans the entire spectrum of colors, including web-safe and web-smart colors.

You have probably seen examples of color wheels, either in the form of an actual wheel or through a box filled with various shades and tints. For example, you don't have to make use of these kinds of programs, but you might benefit from their ability to visualize colors next to each other before you put them to work on your site. If you want to use one of these schemer programs, you can find some recommendations in Appendix B. Note that you can also find websites that boast long, lists of different colors you can choose from, organized into tables that show which color combinations work best together.

ExplainED

The evolution of display technologies means that you're no longer confined to using a selection of 256 web-safe colors (once upon a time, this represented the highest number of colors most computers could display. this was the most many computers could display). The selection of potential web-smart color values now runs to more than 16 million different options—you probably feel spoiled to have so many choices!

Harmony and Meaning

Color can have a significant influence on people's emotions. The most important area of color psychology in terms of the Web relates to trying to understand how people react to the use of color within websites. Unfortunately, this is a tough task because different people have wildly different preferences when it comes to what they like. Consequently, you hear many different and sometimes conflicting theories about what a color represents and whether the effect it causes is calming or something to the contrary. One classic example of this: Genders are often said to experience color differently. For example, many people associate the color blue with boys and pink with girls. Regardless, it's important to consider what colors remind you of when you start implementing them.

ExplainED

The concept behind people associating color with emotions is fairly well recognized, but psychologists have yet to prove conclusively a link exists or even gauge a meaning that does not differ on a person-to-person basis. Therefore, you need to take into account the fact that people might have different emotional reactions to the colors you use.

People often associate color with temperatures, where blue and green represent cold; red, yellow, orange, and brown represent hot; and gray acts as a neutral force. This association is probably where the terms *icy blue* and *red hot* come from! Other color associations relate to the colors signified by certain objects (such as with traffic lights or even the measurement between daytime and nighttime).

Different cultures often associate colors with different emotional states. For example, some people see red as a sign of passion or love, whereas others see it as a sign of danger—perhaps it's both?). Ultimately, the factors that convey meaning through color are so diverse that you need to take into account how the people you intend to target with your site will respond to your use of color. Determining this might be difficult, but the rewards are potentially significant because the right color choices could help you connect with your visitors on both emotional and psychological levels.

LinkED

For more information about evoking emotion with color, read the following article at http://thethemeblog.com/tutorials/evoking-emotion-with-color.

See for Yourself: The Meaning of Color

The following section lists common choices and the emotional states commonly associated with them:

- **Black:** Death, rebellion, disease, mystery, emptiness, evil, darkness, fear, anarchy, and sorrow
- **Blue:** Security, tranquility, coolness, technology, nobility, strength, trust, wetness, and depression
- **Brown:** Richness, dirtiness, common, roughness, heaviness, comfort, depth, stability, and appetite
- **Gray:** Decay, pollution, dreariness, age, pessimism, boredom, balance, mourning, and shadow
- **Green:** Nature, fertility, wealth, jealousy, greed, growth, earth, creativity, stability, and festivity
- **Orange:** Energy, balance, vibrancy, animation, enthusiasm, glowing, comedy, and softness
- **Pink:** Love, tranquility, admiration, feminism, health, flirtatiousness, sympathy, and sexuality

- **Purple:** Spirituality, luxury, wisdom, bravery, sensuality, creativity, enlightenment, and envy
- **Red:** Luck, passion, sex, energy, romance, love, excitement, heat, blood, danger, war, and anger
- **White:** Purity, neutrality, snow, peace, hope, light, cleanness, innocence, sterility, and coldness
- **Yellow:** Happiness, friendship, annoyance, mellowness, warmth, sunlight, illness, and cowardice

Here's a concrete example of how you might use this list: Let's assume you intend to produce a website aimed at children. The use of vibrant, solid colors promotes a sense of fun and makes a bold attempt to hold a child's attention. This is in contrast to calming pastels, which children would be more likely to find dull and boring. In this case, using vibrant colors that do not clash might be a fantastic way to appeal to and capture the attention of your target audience. Colors that work well for a children's website might include yellow, blue, orange, and white; this color combination would convey a sense of calmness, yet also add a touch of vibrancy and light-hearted fun.

ExplainED

The previous section mentioned the fact that you should not choose colors that clash. For example, you do not want your visitors to go blind looking at neon yellow text on a white background; that combination induces a visual effect known as simultaneous contrast. *This effect causes heavy visual conflicts to occur—think an eye burning color that fights for priority!*

Tables and Lists

You have some color theory under your belt; now it's time to return to the code, and your journey through the available CSS styles you can apply. Next, you will tackle styling tables on your site. You can find some specific CSS properties that are intended to help you provide styling for tables and their cells. Table-based design itself is generally frowned upon by the web design community, but that shouldn't stop you from using and styling tables for their correct semantic purpose (such as for displaying spreadsheet data). CSS includes a property called table-layout; you can use this property to tell the browser to render a table dynamically or to render the table's cells with fixed lengths. If you set the table-layout to auto, a browser will read through all the content and use a built-in algorithm to calculate the width and rendering of table items. This is as complex as it sounds, and it can slow down how quickly a browser renders your table. This is one reason why many developers set the value of table-layout to fixed. Doing so dictates the width of the table's cells by basing them on the overall width of the table (rather than the contents of each cell). This line of code sets the table-layout property to auto:

```
table-layout: auto;
```

The point of most tables is to display content in each cell so you can compare it with the content in the table's other cells. However, sometimes a table will have empty cells (this occurs often in spreadsheets). In some circumstances, you might want to hide a cell with no value. You can accomplish this by using the empty-cells property, which you can set to the values of hide or show. Assigning one of these values to this property has exactly the effect you would expect: the cell will either appear on the screen with nothing inside it, or it will be hidden entirely. This line of code tells the browser to display empty cells when rendering your table:

```
empty-cells: show;
```

Most tables include a caption, which are basically blocks of text that describe the contents of a table. A caption can be as simple as a name or as complex as a detailed description of what the table measures or compares. The caption-side property indicates whether these textual descriptions for tables should appear at the top or bottom of the table. Setting the property to one of the two values will alter the position where the caption appears. This code tells the browser to display the caption above your table:

```
caption-side: top;
```

The final table-based properties you'll look at involve borders. Earlier in this chapter, you learned how you can provide a line that surrounds an element, giving that element an enhanced visual emphasis. Tables can have cells that have their own border properties. The first of these is called border-spacing; this property enables you to specify an equal amount of padding (on each side) between the borders of various cells that make up the table. For example, you might indicate that a cell should have 2 pixels of whitespace on each side of a border. The second border-related property for tables is border-collapse; this property enables you to determine whether border-spacing and empty-cells are acknowledged (with a value of separate) or ignored (with a value of collapse). The border-spacing and border-collapse properties allow you to pad tables. The purpose of this padding is to make your tables more readable by giving the text in their cells a bit of extra breathing room. As you learned earlier, whitespace is quite important for readability. This code tells a table with borders how each cell should collapse and be joined together (rather than appearing independently):

```
border-collapse: collapse;
border-spacing: 2px;
```

NotED

CSS tables exist that can potentially use the benefits of table-based layouts with semantic markup by using the display property with values such as inline-table, table, table-caption, table-cell, table-column, table-column-group, table-footer-group, table-header-group, table-row, *and* table-row-group. *However, Internet Explorer 7 and earlier don't support it, so this functionality is typically avoided.*

Next, let's take a look at CSS and lists. When you examined HTML elements earlier in Chapter 3, you saw three types of lists: ordered lists, unordered lists, and definition lists. You need to be aware that definition lists, despite being in a list themselves, are unaffected by the following discussion. The CSS properties that follow prove useful only for ordered and unordered lists. The first style that you can apply is a list-style-type that affects the bullet you see next to a list item. You can find many predefined types of list bullets you might include with a list; these range from pictorial bullets (dots) to numerical counting bullets that automatically count the number of items in the list as you add new items to it. The different values you can assign to the bullets in list-style-type (see Figure 5-32) include circle, disc, square, armenian, decimal, decimal-leading-zero, georgian, lower-alpha, lower-greek, lower-latin, lower-roman, upper-alpha, upper-greek, upper-latin, upper roman, and none. This line of code assigns disc-style bullets to your list:

```
list-style-type: disc;
```

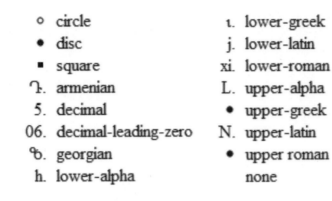

Figure 5-32. You can assign your bulleted and numbered lists a basic default style.

Specifying predefined bulleted or numbered list items might sound perfectly adequate for most lists; however, you might find yourself wanting to add an image in place of the predefined-bullet points. For example, you might want to create a custom bullet or icon of your choice. CSS includes the list-style-image property, which you can use to set a url ( ) that points to the custom bullet or icon you want to use. Of course, as with any other URL reference, you need to ensure that the URL points to a valid image, or nothing will appear on the page. As a rule of thumb, most bullets tend to be images no larger than 16 x 16 pixels; however, you can always use something bigger and make use of the text-indent property to offset the required space. This line implements a custom bullet for a list:

```
list-style-image: url(/images/bullet.gif);
```

CSS also includes a less commonly used property called list-style-position. This property lets you indicate whether the marker (read: the bullet) is positioned inside or outside the container box. If the bullet is positioned inside the container box, any overflowing lines will appear directly below the bullet; however, if the bullet is positioned outside the container box, you will see a clearly delineated margin where no text will be positioned below the marker (this is the default option). Generally speaking, which you use depends more on your personal preferences; however, you might find placing the marker outside the container box makes your content more readable. This is because the bullets are easier to identify if you separate them visually from the content. This line of code places the marker inside the container box:

```
list-style-position: inside;
```

Like font and many other CSS properties, list-style can be used as a single property that edits all of the available list-item values, such as type, url, and position. This can be a useful space saver; it also lets you assign an element with the full range of available style properties. The example that follows gives a list the default disc bullet as a fallback for the custom bullet that has been defined. The bullet itself is held inside the element, which makes it appear as though it has no space on the side.

```
list-style: disc inside url(/images/bullet.gif);
```

Next, you'll learn how you can use CSS to define the position of the content on your page. This is a much more complex topic than the simple styles you've learned about so far. For this reason, the text that follows serves as more of an overview rather than a definitive guide for walking you through the entire process. The main reason for this complexity is that you need to understand how CSS calculates where each item should be positioned. This is done using the *CSS box model,* and you'll get to see how it works in due course. However, let's take a step back and begin by looking at the main design types you fit your site into.

Using CSS for Design

Grids serve an important role in helping you lay out your site with CSS. When you look at your structure, you should think of everything in terms of grids. In CSS, everything is represented in terms of a rectangle. When you add style, color, images, and other flourishes, one of the biggest issues that affect your design is that everything is placed into rectangular containers. This can give your site a boxy look; it can also feel restrictive in some cases. You can often help your site overcome this feeling by replacing CSS's standard borders and incorporating curves into your images. For example, you might add effects such as 3D-style buttons and other elements used commonly within the Web 2.0 design convention! Having your design look like a bunch of grids can work just fine. However, if you want to make your website look visually unique from most other sites, breaking away from grid-based design can be an important step toward gaining visual independence (see Figure 5-33).

Figure 5-33. Elan Chicas breaks out of the default grid layout by using a clever mixture of images and positioning.

When producing CSS, you can choose from several different layout models. The form of measurement you decide to use will ultimately determine what kind of layout you end up with. All of the common approaches have advantages and disadvantages, and all have been used successfully on a variety of sites. Which you should choose depends on your own preferences and the needs of your site. Before you begin adding style to your site, you will need to decide which design style you want to use to position and spread out your site elements.

LinkED

For more information about the different layout models that you can use, check out this website: http://green-beast.com/blog/?p=199.

The rest of this section will walk you through the various layout styles you can choose from, as well as the unit measurement implications of choosing a particular design:

- **Fixed:** This layout style is one of the most common on the Web (see Figure 5-34). As you might expect from its name, this layout uses a fixed width and will not resize, regardless of how much spare real-estate the screen has available. One of the upsides of using this layout type is that it lets you avoid gaps that occur from stretching when you use a lot of images that require specific dimensions and sizes. Of course, a downside of this is that visitors with higher resolutions might see a lot of whitespace in their browsers. Similarly, if a visitor's resolution is too low, she might need to scroll from side-to-side to view your content, which can causes accessibility issues if your text cannot be resized (as is the case in Internet Explorer).

Figure 5-34. The essentials of Buddhism website leverages a simple example of a fixed-width layout.

- **Elastic:** This layout style is what it sounds like (see Figure 5-35). Rather than using pixels as the unit of measurement, elastic layouts focus on using em, which is sized relative to the parents of each tag. Thus, an element will stretch and shrink to meet the requirements of the page! Elastic designs are less common on the Web, but they provide a genuine advantage for users who want to exercise control over the text region, rather than letting it just fill up all of the available screen space. Advantages of this type include much better visitor control over text resizing, a more flexible way of meeting the needs of the content, the ability to resize your site's text without breaking its basic design. This provides a solid alternative to fixed-width layouts.

Figure 5-35. One of the most famous and original elastic layouts comes courtesy of the elastic garden design from the CSS Zen Garden.

- **Liquid:** This layout style is often grouped with the fluid-layout style, but it differs from that design in several important ways (see Figure 5-36). The liquid layout works much as its name suggests. It features a flexible form that fills up the areas of the available space it is given (like water in a cup). This design uses the measurement of percentages, which ensures that everything will appear in proportion with the screen size given. One of the upsides of this layout method is that it never breaks in terms of maintaining its grid because everything will flood the available space needed to fit everything in. The downside of this layout is that it can include tons of whitespace if you have a high resolution (everything will look stretched), or everything can get squeezed together if you don't have much screen space (everything will look skewed). For this reason, developers tend to incorporate the fluid style as part of a hybrid-layout style, which ensures that it will work, but with restrictions to stop everything from spilling out over a wide surface area!

Figure 5-36. The technology news site Slashdot uses a liquid layout that flows across the full width of the page.

- **Fluid:** This layout style behaves a lot like the liquid style, but has a couple behavioral characteristics that help distinguish it (see Figure 5-37). Rather than being like water (where it pours everywhere to fill up the maximum available space), a fluid site uses the same consistency of liquid (percentages) but with limits you apply using `min-width` and `max-width` properties. Using these CSS properties lets you guarantee that the content will not get cramped or too flooded outward, removing the problems most often associated with liquid layouts. The fluid layout is also more flexible than elastic layouts (it is like jello in the way it sits within its boundaries), so it is almost a perfect choice. So what keeps it from being perfect? It still has the problem of needing fixed-widths for images, and it will not work in Internet Explorer 6 or lower, which presents a compatibility problem that you must overcome using a normal width property.

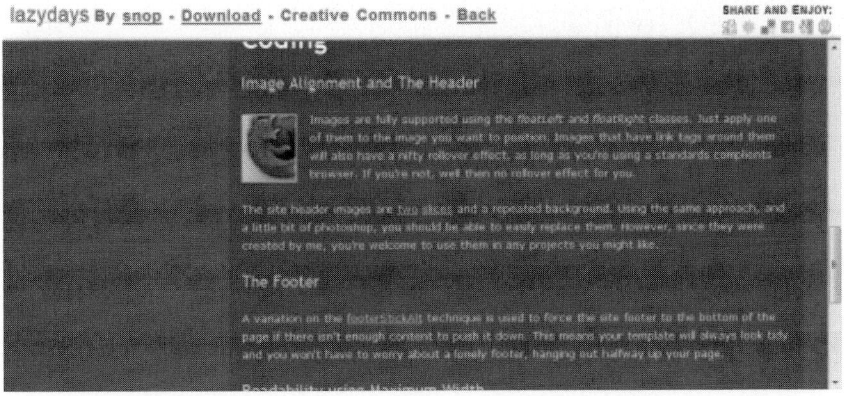

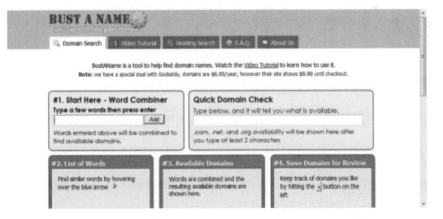

Figure 5-37. This template illustrates how a fluid design can give your site more flexibility than a traditional liquid layout.

- **Hybrid**: The final layout type essentially combines elements from two or more other design layouts see Figure 5-38). For example, you might mix various measurement units, such aspects of a fixed site with other aspects of an elastic site, to achieve a particular structure for your layout. Some people might describe fluid as a hybrid of liquid, but I prefer to list it separately because it doesn't use a mixture of relative measurements, so much as it uses a different method to implement the percentages (to overcome the inherent limitations of a liquid site). The goal of a hybrid site is to create a flexible, easily controlled layout using a mixture of set dimensions.

Figure 5-38. Bust A Name makes use of a hybrid layout to ensure maximum visitor compatibility.

You now know the different types of CSS designs available to you; your next step is to take a look at how CSS calculates the position of the elements on a page.

The CSS Box Model

When you begin positioning elements on a website, it's vitally important that you are aware of the CSS box model. Having a solid understanding of what the box model is and how it affects you can make all the difference when it comes to building a successful layout. For example, it is critical that you appreciate that every single element on a page, from a paragraph to a divider, is composed of a rectangle. Like a rectangle, every element on a page has four sides commonly known as the top, bottom, left, and right sides. Given that each element is rendered as a rectangle on the page, you can guess how the modeling and rendering of these elements on the screen became known as a *box*. Like any box, the containers on your site must be tall and wide enough to hold all of the contents you place in them.

This brings you to a critical question: how wide and how tall does a given element need to be? When you produce a design, you need to understand that the parent container is the first thing you need to consider carefully. For example, try picturing a giant warehouse in your mind. Inside that building, you will find a ton of boxes (each of which contains an element). If you find yourself with too many boxes, you will need to stack them outside the warehouse or move them to another location. If the width of a child element exceeds the space given to it by its parent, it might try one of three things. First, it might try to give you more space by making the parent taller—a bit like adding a new floor to a warehouse. Second, it might cut off the flow of information and say, "Nope, no more room. You'll just have to lose everything that doesn't fit." Third, it might provide some scrollbars that let you go up and down the element, so you can read the stuff that didn't fit. For example, consider the screen of a browser itself. When you begin making a website, you don't see a scrollbar (usually) because you have no need for one. Once you place enough content on the page, you will pass a threshold where you can no longer see all the content on the page. In this case, the browser will add scrollbars to allow your visitors to navigate below the available space and read the rest of your text. You've already seen how elements inherit from their parents, so the amount of space available or even the width and height an element can attain (if you use percentages) can be dictated by an element's inherited space.

Now that you get the idea that all elements are like boxes that you stack in a warehouse, you need to know what steps you can tale to change the box's shape and appearance (to meet the needs of the item the box holds). Figure 5-39 displays a box (which could be of any element, but you might think of it as a paragraph of text). Outside the box, you can see several other words, such as *border* and *padding*. The contents of an element will have a standard width and height, but this doesn't mean there isn't extra space taken up by other things. Let's return to the analogy that an element is like a package. Not all packages are tightly wrapped items with paper over them. In a similar vein, you need to take into account for the effects introduced by the border (wrapping paper), padding (foam or bubble wrap that keeps the package safe), and the margin (any space inside the box). Thinking of an element as a package takes you only so far when contemplating your web design, but the analogy itself puts across the idea that the amount of space available you need inside a box depends on more than the size of a given item you might place in the box. It is these extra items that you must be certain you consider when you calculate the space you will require for your elements.

See for Yourself: Calculating the Box Model

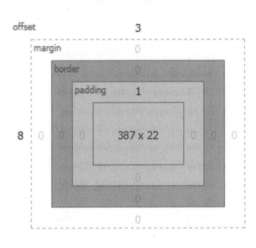

Figure 5-39. You can use the Firefox extension Firebug to see the package and all of its contents.

Before attempting to calculate the size of your box, you need to take a moment and acquaint yourself with what each of the "layers" in your package does, and how you can manipulate these layers to make all the packages fit together nicely in the box. You begin by accounting for the general width and height of an element. These two elements let you define how big the box should be (either explicitly or based upon the available space). Together, these properties represent your content area, including the physical amount of space required to display the box's contents (such as all the text in a paragraph), as well as any inline elements (such as hyperlinks or anchors that might have unique requests of their own!). As you now know, the width and the height only go so far in explaining how big the box itself needs to be. You also need to take into account the size of the border that visually outlines an element's general shape. A border might be only a few pixels wide, but it still adds to the overall dimensions of an element. You also need to take into account the whitespace that occurs outside both sides of the border, which people commonly call the margins, or the space outside the box. Next, you need to account for the padding, or the space inside the box. Finally, you need to account for the offset. The offset itself isn't a CSS property; it simply refers to any special positioning rules (such as a rule that pushes an element 10px away from the left-hand side of the page). You'll learn more about this in the section on absolute positioning, which allows you to control the location of an element on a page.

It's important to know all this because most people think that the box's width and height are the only things that matter when considering a box's size. However, failing to take into account the margins, padding, borders, and any offset you give an element can cause your content to overflow the amount of available space. For example, assume you have a 100% wide paragraph that has a 1px border on either side. This would mean your element is 100% + 2 px wide, not 100%). So you need to add up a few bits and pieces on either side—what's the big deal, then? Unfortunately, and as you have learned in previous sections of this book, Internet Explorer 6 and earlier have some problems with how they implement CSS that might cause you some issues. Fortunately, the problems it causes are relatively minor. It's not worth going into the complexities of what goes wrong and why, but it does go wrong. If you ensure that you do the math right, and you take into account all the bits that make up the height and width of a box, you should end up with a perfect design that fits together beautifully!

Now you know about the various bits that make up the overall height and width of an element (see Figure 5-40); next you need to know to do the math that works out the total size. You can see that math in the example that follows; it works by determining the sum of the offset, margins, borders, padding, width, and height for each side of the box. The equation looks like this because you need values for all of the relevant variables:

- **Width:** LO + LM + LB + LP + W + RP + RB + RM + RO = Total width and position
- **Height:** TO + TM + TB + TP + H + BP + BB + BM + BO = Total height and position

In the preceding example, L, R, T, and B (the prefixes for each of the elements) refer to left, right, top, and bottom, respectively. The second part of the variables, O, M, B, and P refer to offset (absolute positioning), margin, border, and padding respectively. Finally, W and H refer to a box's width and height.

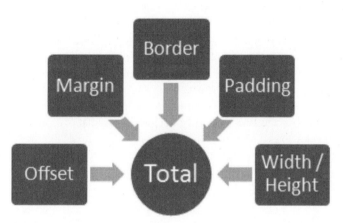

Figure 5-40. You add each of the values (left and right for width, top and bottom for height) to get the box-model size.

Let's assume that you want to work out the information for the box in Figure 5-39. That box is 22 pixels high, with 1 pixel of padding on either side. That gives you a box that is 24 pixels high. Adding in an offset of 3 pixels takes the box up to 27 pixels of space. The reason it takes 24 pixels, rather than 23, is because is the box has padding on both sides of the element—this is why you need to take into account each side of the shape). If you put all of this together, you learn how big the box is and how much available space you need to prevent overflow from occurring. Performing these calculations can also help you ensure that don't accidentally introduce scrollbars or "cut off" content. It also lets you take advantage of the screen space (relatively or explicitly) the viewer might have.

NotED

Internet Explorer 6 in quirks mode, and Internet Explorer 5 (and earlier) sometimes encounter the broken box model effect. When this bug is triggered, it causes the browser to take borders and padding away from the content (reducing the content size), rather than to increase the size of the box that contains it. This often leads to inconsistent visual rendering that can break your layout! To avoid this, never do anything to trigger quirks mode (you will learn more about this in Chapter 7).

Something else you need to take into consideration is the more complex topic of collapsing margins. This subject can be rather confusing, so I will try to describe it in the simplest terms possible. Assume that you have two elements that are positioned outside of the natural flow of the document. Now assume that you have a margin around these two elements, where one sits on top of the other, so that the two margins meet. What will happen naturally in most browsers is that the smaller (or equal) margin will collapse and merge with the other one. This means you will no longer have two visible margins, but a single margin that sits between the two elements. If you have nothing between two elements (content-wise), the height will default to zero, and the collapse will merge the margins between the elements.

LinkED

For more information about the box model and collapsing margins (with examples attached!), check out the box-model section of the CSS specification at www.w3.org/TR/CSS2/box.html.

This might seem confusing, but think of it like a jigsaw puzzle, if you have space on the sides to fit the pieces together, they will collapse into each other, causing the pieces to fit together. However, if they do not fit in the existing space, they take up more space because the bits that stick out won't be able to push their way into an available gap. One problem with margins collapsing is that (as in the case of the box model), you face numerous issues with Internet Explorer and how it deals with margins collapsing. IE7 and earlier iterations of that browser refuse to honor this standard, so, rather than sliding the jigsaw pieces together when appropriate, these browsers leave them disjointed, which can break your design or cause visual inconsistencies between different web browsers. In many cases, you can avoid this by using borders to separate margins visually. This will cause other browsers to render the box identically to Internet Explorer, even though it is IE that renders it incorrectly (see Figure 5-41)!

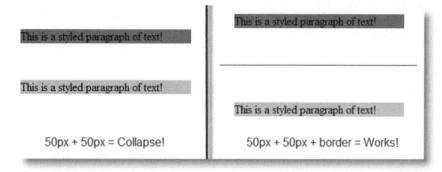

Figure 5-41. Collapsing Margins can be a real problem, but adding a border fixes this issue in Internet Explorer.

ExplainED

Because of its inherent problems, Internet Explorer receives a fair amount of criticism. While bashing IE is one of a typical web designer's favorite pastimes, it should be noted that more recent versions (especially IE8) support CSS standards to a much higher extent and have fewer quirks.

Dimensions, Margins, and Padding

Now that you know how to calculate CSS position, you can begin to plan the dimensions, margins, and padding that influence the whitespace (the areas with nothing in it) of your design. This can have a dramatic influence on the appearance of your site because whitespace conveys an impression of cleanliness and relaxation (space to breathe). Dimensions in this case refers to the height and width properties. These are straightforward: height allows you to state explicitly how tall an element should be, while width allows you to determine how wide the element should span in your design. Developers use height and width regularly in their web designs to define the space that elements can take up, so it's definitely worth being aware them. Both height and width can use measurement units of your choosing, although it should be pointed out that early versions of Internet Explorer do have a tendency to act funny around height and width properties defined in percentages (due to the way those versions of IE incorrectly calculate percentages). Typically, you overcome these issues by ensuring that the total widths of elements positioned next to each other add up to 99%, rather than 100%. This often gives those browsers enough breathing room to compensate for the way they miscalculate the space available. This code enables you to state the height and width of a given element:

```
height: 100px;
width: 300px;
```

Many people are aware of the width and height properties themselves, but not everyone is aware that you can also set the minimum and maximum values for both width and height (Internet Explorer 6 does not support this). Specifying the max and min width and height enables you to create a fluid design (which is different to a liquid design because there are limits to the size a liquid design can expand to). Of course, the lack of support for this feature in Internet Explorer 6 and earlier means that you want to take care to define the width and height explicitly; this can help you ensure that your site looks equally good without using max and min (see Figure 5-42):

```
max-height: 150px;
min-height: 50px;
max-width: 400px;
min-width: 250px;
```

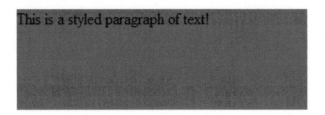

Figure 5-42. You can give the paragraph a height and width value to display the box at an explicitly specified size.

At this point, you have an idea of the dimensions you can add to your elements. This means you can begin using margins and padding to give your elements some whitespace (see Figure 5-43). Margins determine the space between the border and outside elements. Unlike padding, margins can have negative values. This means you can decrease element sizes (taking away from width and height to arrive at the size you want to achieve). Margins can be tricky to work with (due to the possibility of a margin collapsing), but they can also be useful for adding space between a border and other elements, not to mention the fact that they permit you to apply negative values. You write the code for a margin much as you write the code for a border. You can declare all four values individually, or you can combine them into the single property (covering all sides) that you declare in this specific order: top, right, bottom, left. You need to use this specific order to account for the default behavior of the CSS parsers that apply your properties. This example puts the principles described into effect by applying unique size rules to each of the four sides of the element:

```
margin-bottom: 25px;
margin-left: 35px;
margin-right: 30px;
margin-top: 20px;
margin: 20px 30px 25px 35px;
```

The code you write to create padding for an element looks similar to the code you write to add margins. Specifically, you can target the top, right, bottom, and left values, but you must apply them in that explicit order if you choose to combine them into one line, because browsers parse these lines in this order. You cannot use negative values for padding. Margins affect the space between the border and outside elements, but the padding determines space between the content and borders (essentially the inside). You can (and should) use a mixture of both margins and padding to create your site's required whitespace because each provides a different way of giving an element some breathing space. The example mirrors the code you saw in the margin example; it provides a list of the four corners of padding that you can apply, and then proceeds to show a combination of all four properties in one line:

```
padding-bottom: 25px;
padding-left: 35px;
padding-right: 30px;
padding-top: 20px;
padding: 20px 30px 25px 35px;
```

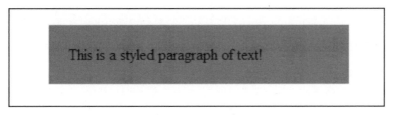

Figure 5-43. You can apply margins and padding to manipulate the dimensions of an element.

303

Position, Visibility, and Behavior

The ability to place different pieces of content next to each other or in a specific position on a page is one of the most important benefits of using CSS. The position property can take values of absolute, relative, fixed, or static. A value of absolute removes the entire element from the natural flow of the document and places it where you want it on the screen. You effect this placement using top, bottom, left, and right properties. Assigning a value of relative ensures that the element inherits its default position from its parent. Assigning a value of fixed causes the element to stay put on the page, no matter where the user chooses to scroll. You can specify its exact position using top, bottom, left, and right properties; in other words, the code you apply fixed positioning to remains on the screen at all times, as though it were glued to the screen. Finally assigning a value of static makes your content appear where the browser says it should, rather than relying on inheritance or explicit positioning. IE6 doesn't support fixed positioning, which is a shame because it can be useful. However, you can implement it for browsers that can take advantage of it. For example, you might use fixed positioning to keep a navigation bar in view as a visitor scrolls down the page; this will keep handy links visible and always in view. You just need to make sure that you check how your site behaves in IE6 (with and without the scrolling), so your IE6 users don't suffer too much! This line of code assigns the value of absolute to the position property:

```
position: absolute;
```

Setting position to a value other than static enables you to define how the element itself is offset (if you set position to relative) or where it is positioned (for absolute and fixed positioning) by using the top, bottom, left, and right properties. All of these values enable you to define the position of the element, so you can offset the element's position from the page. In this example, you offset the content of an absolutely positioned element from the top left hand side of the page by 10 pixels on each side (positioning documents within the document is that easy):

```
top: 10px;
bottom: 0;
left: 10px;
right: 0;
```

Positioning elements precisely can be a useful and handy tool, but it's better in many cases to use floats to position tags next to each other (side by side); otherwise, you might have problems getting the elements to stack next to each other and expand when the browser dimensions change. This is because absolutely positioned elements ignore everything that goes on around them, including siblings, parents, and even inheritance.

Floating which allows you to have two pieces of content float next to each other see Figure 5-44). As we mentioned previously, floats (unlike positioned elements) stack themselves next to each other, so they recognize both the parent element (so the available page width can be taken into account) and siblings (which balance themselves against their closest relation). Possible values for a float (taken out of the document flow) include left and right (to indicate where the stacking should start) and none (to indicate that no floating occurs). You can use the clear property of a float to make content appear directly underneath (and remove) existing floats above it; you should apply this to the topmost element. You can clear any existing floats for other elements using the values of left, right, none, or both; essentially this tells the element to counterbalance the float effect, so that it repositions the document flow directly beneath the element that you floated previously. This snippet illustrates how to use the float and clear properties:

```
float: left;
clear: both;
```

This is a styled paragraph of text!   This is a styled paragraph of text!

Figure 5-44. You can use the float left and right values to position text so it appears side by side, rather than on opposing sides of the screen.

If you want to stack positioned elements on top of each other in order of priority, you can use CSS's z-index property. This is especially useful if you use absolute positioning and have elements that overlap each other. You can give them a z-index where the highest number value has the highest priority and the lowest number has the lowest priority. The value of a z-index can go into the thousands, which can be useful if you have far too many elements to play with; however, you typically assign every item in the document a default value of 0. This causes the elements to stack on the same level; they overlap because no priority is given except for their position in the flow. For example, assume you assign an element a z-index value of 99:

```
z-index: 99;
```

This code places the element 98 times above a normal element, which means it will stack on top of any element with a value of 0 through 98). The ability to prioritize elements is useful, but z-index only works if you have an element positioned to something other than static. You can take advantage of this element to balance elements and overlap them. For example, you might layer text above a heading so the elements interweave.

The useful `clip` property is also worth mentioning; it gives you the unique ability to cut a hole in an element and display the content that lies underneath. If you use the z-index priority order and you have overlapping elements, you could use the `clip` property to cut a porthole and literally peek at the element hidden beneath. Of course, using positioned elements in conjunction with the z-index isn't as common as using floats. The `clip` property has relatively few uses on the Web. However, this doesn't detract from the usefulness of this property. The clip property requires a `rect ( )` value that uses `top`, `right`, `bottom`, and `left` values (again, in that explicit order) to cut out a rectangle and reveal what sits underneath. You can't use any other values, but you can use all four of these values to indicate the region you want to cut out. Note that you can use any measurement units; both fixed and relative units work for describing the hole you want to create. This code cuts a rectangular hole in an element that is 10em tall and wide; this makes anything positioned behind it visible.

```
clip: rect(5em, 5em, 5em, 5em);
```

Another property worth mentioning is `overflow`. If you declare a height and/or width for this property, an interesting thing will happen when content overruns the area it is allowed to inhabit. Rather than expanding, it will either be `hidden`, in which case it is cut off and is no longer displayed from the point where it goes outside its acceptable `width` or `height` values; or it will be `visible`, which will cause a scrollbar to appear when the content exceeds its allotted space goes. The body tag uses the `visible` value to enable the page to scroll down and see how much content you have. Of course, you can also use the value `scroll`, which will produce scrollbars (similar to what you see in an iframe) to allow your visitors to read within the confined area, except that the visitor will be able to scroll up and down to read more content within that element of your page and without scrolling the entire page. CSS3 also contains `overflow-x` (left to right) and `overflow-y` (right to left) properties that don't work in IE6. If you want a scrollbar to appear in a particular direction, you might have to wait until that old browser finally disappears. The diagram shown in Figure 5-45 uses the `overflow` property's `hidden` value, which chops down the size of that paragraph! You use the overflow property like this:

```
overflow: hidden;
```

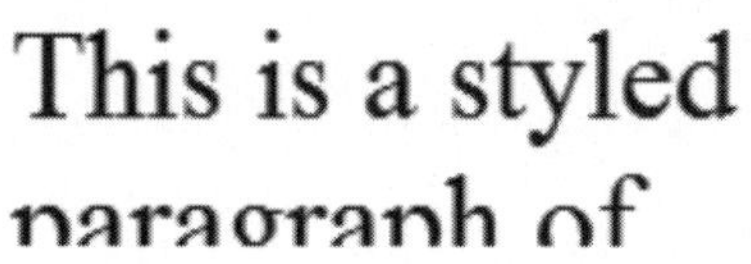

This is a styled

paragraph of

Figure 5-45. The overflow property's hidden value lets you set an explicit height and width for an element, causing overflow to be hidden; note how some of the text in this paragraph is cut off!

You can also use CSS to alter the type of box created (in terms of how it appears in the document flow) using the display property. This property lets you set the element as block, inline, or block-inline—you can even do this against the display property's initial value. For example, you might make a blockquote inline, or you might make a span a block-level element (you might remember from Chapter 3 that this goes against a span element's natural inclination). You might want to do this so you can give an inline element such as an anchor a visible margin or pull it away from its container element. You might also want to add padding to an anchor to increase the clickable area or make a bunch of items in a menu *fold*, so they stack against each other (as shown in Figure 5-46). Other values you can set include run-in, which creates a box that is either block or inline style depending on the context); list-item, which gives it the appearance of a li element; and none, which lets you to hide the element entirely from the document. You use the display property like this:

display: inline;

Figure 5-46. You can use the display property inline to take an unordered list and place items next to each other.

In addition to being able to use display: none to hide content, you can use the visibility property with the value hidden (to make content disappear entirely) or visible value to show an element, such as the child of a hidden parent. The difference between display and visibility (when hiding content) is that visibility hides the element but leaves a placeholder where the element once existed; it's invisible, but it's still there. On the other hand, display removes the element entirely from the document flow, leaving nothing in its place. Note that some screen readers are unable to read text you hide with the display property display (temporarily or otherwise); this might be one reason to use visibility or some kind of overflow instead of display: none. You assert the visibility property's hidden value like this:

visibility: hidden;

The only one other behavior-related CSS properties you'll find of particular benefit is called cursor. This property lets you set a cursor for cases when someone rolls over an element. You can do this by pointing to the cursor through a url ( ) value—again, the path you use to point to this custom cursor must be valid, or the cursor won't appear. Or, you can specify one of the cursor property's predefined selections, such as default, crosshair, help, move, pointer (hand in IE 5.5 or lower), progress, text, n-resize (north), ne-resize (north east), nw-resize (north west), e-resize (east), w-resize (west), s-resize (south), se-resize (south east), or sw-resize (south west). You can see example of all of these in Figure 5-47. One thing which should be mentioned is that some browsers do not support setting a custom cursor through the URL value, and those that do might require a valid cursor file (rather than a .gif). You'd have to store such a cursor in the form of an .ani file (for an animated cursor, as annoying as they are!) or a .cur file (the default file extension for cursors). Unfortunately, you cannot typically create these files in a conventional image editor unless it has icon support. This means you might require a special icon / cursor editor to do the job; fortunately, you can find quite a few free and commercial editors for such a task.

cursor: pointer;

Figure 5-47. CSS's cursor property includes a variety of different cursors you can leverage: just take your pick!

NotED

Other properties exist, but you won't you them use often. If you want to learn more about the generated-content properties, be sure to check out content, counter-increment, counter-reset, *and* quotes. *Or, if you want to control paged media (line printing), check out these properties:* page-break-before, page-break-inside, page-break-after, orphans, *and* widows. *You can check find many online reference manuals that discuss these properties.*

Checkpoint!

Congratulations; you have reached the finish line for CSS! Before you move onto the next chapter, I recommend that you put down the book and work through everything you have just learned (if you have not done so already). Then I recommend that you take some time and add some great style to your site. You should remember that some style might be unique to each page, so you should take the time to ensure the style you use on your website is applied successfully to every page. Also, you should ensure that any elements you place on a single page match the style of the rest of your site's theme. If you feel the need, you can return to previous sections of this chapter and keep tweaking your design (for all your pages) until you have them looking exactly how you want them to look (or as close to that as possible). Once you do this, you should have a website that looks great and is more aesthetically pleasing than it when it consisted only of bland HTML. As ever, you should save your progress and upload all changes you make to your site, so you and others can see them implemented live on the Web.

Summary

In this chapter, you learned about the roles CSS and stylesheets can play in helping you create elegant designs. You also learned about the various properties that exist within the style language, as well as garnering some insight into what CSS3 will bring. You should now have the basic understanding required to produce a visually enticing website design. While many beginners books end with HTML and CSS, the rest of this book will show you there is more to life than learning how to write code (thankfully!). Indeed, you will discover there is a whole world of additional knowledge that you can leverage to improve your site for your visitors. More importantly, you will learn how to resolve any problems you encounter as you try to make your site look right in more than one browser. But it's not time to put aside those pencils and erasers yet; the style aspect might be over, but it's time to get even more artistic and learn about how to create images and multimedia. Your site might have a great layout and great text content, but images allow much more texture and beauty than CSS alone can provide!

Chapter Checklist

You should accomplish the following tasks before leaving this chapter:

- Learn the basics of CSS and come to grips with the idea of adding style.
- Add any required `class` and `ID` attributes to your HTML that your design requires.
- Take the knowledge you have collected to give your site unique visuals.

Questions and Answers

Q: *My CSS is providing strange results in a web browser' what can I do?*

A: Support for standards like CSS has come a long way from where it once was. However, you should note that even with modern browsers, some people continue to stick with their old ways, relying on out-of-date products such as IE6 for their daily browsing. Often this is not through their fault—some businesses fail to update their browsers, for example); however, this means that you cannot rely exclusively on the CSS you'd prefer to use for compatibility reasons. Sometimes, you need to add extra CSS properties or try and hack your way out of trouble. You will learn how to do this in the chapters that follow.

Q: *What do I do about mobile devices that have much smaller screens?*

A: The rise of devices like the iPhone means that browsing the Internet on a mobile device has become increasingly popular. The downside of this: Creating sites for mobile devices over the years has proved tricky for several reasons, some of which you'll learn about in Chapter 7, which discusses problem solving. In that chapter, you'll look explicitly at mobile development and learn how to test your site on mobile devices. You have two possible approaches when using CSS on mobile devices: first, you can provide a section of your style sheet that is optimized for mobile devices (this is tricky for reasons you will learn);

second, you can simply provide a separate mobile site (which you would have to create from scratch!). The latter approach might seem daunting, but it requires less work than you might think because your goal throughout is to keep everything as small as possible. This means less content per page, fewer images, less code, and so on. Basically, you want to fit everything into a cramped space. If you want your site to work on cell phones, hold onto this idea for later!

Q: *Do you have any tips or tricks for determining what qualifies as great web design?*

A: I have tons of such tips, and I've tried to fit as many of them as possible into this chapter and this book. You will also return to this subject once you finish making your images and fixing the problems you encounter. Specifically, you'll learn some additional great tips for using HTML and CSS to make your site a friendlier experience for your visitors. Of course, much of what you will learn is theoretical, but it's still worthwhile to evaluate this information for possible sources of inspiration. You will soon discover that design is about much more than making your site look pretty; it's also about creating a usable, accessible site, and that you will also have to employ some psychology and pragmatism. This might sound scary, but this book presents that information in small, discrete chunks that you will find easy to digest.

Where You Are Now

By the end of this chapter, you should have the following:

- A CSS stylesheet that is accurately referenced in your HTML documents
- Elements in your pages that are styled according to your tastes and your site's needs
- A beautiful site that can be viewed in your favorite web browser

How Can I Use Images and Media?

We have finished our tour of applying CSS to your website design, and you probably have something that looks half decent. The only problem is that we have not covered one vital element of design that gives your website a bit more depth and texture (more than a bunch of colors, anyway). What have we not yet added? Images and multimedia of course! Having images in your design can give your website a lot more visual zest, and it can also help make your design look less boxy and bland. Having images is a vital component of the web, whether you choose to use textures, tiles, background images (huge ones that cover the whole page or small ones that fit into a box), or even if you want a logo or some illustrations to accompany your text (maybe just a slideshow of pictures you took with a camera). Whether you want to create an image to make your design look unique or create a video or audio presentation, this chapter will provide an overview of the essentials.

In this chapter, we're going to cover the following topics:

- Creating and using images within your sites design
- The image and multimedia generation languages available
- The audio and video formats you can use on your website

Pushing Pixels

Working with images and multimedia is one element of web design that really stumps a lot of people. Generally, a huge proportion of individuals are really good at producing solid code (you may be one of them now that you know the basics of HTML and CSS), but producing images is usually reserved for those with the rare gift of graphic creation. I happen to be among the crowd of people with the same level of graphics-creation ability as a 6-year-old with a pack of crayons, but (just like I keep telling myself and am telling you now), do not worry if you find yourself unable to produce the images you need for your website. While those of you lucky enough to be good at making images will find this chapter pretty basic (and you may want to refer to other books for more advanced image creation), this section of the chapter explains how the rest of us, who have no or limited graphical abilities, can make our websites rich in multimedia and images without sacrificing our design to the great gods of the pixel.

Online Formats

Generally, visual media on the Web fall into three kinds of formats: images (which, of course, are great for supplementing the style and can be used either within the structure or used as backgrounds for style), audio (which is great for all you podcasting fans or for talking about something awesome you saw this week on the web), and video (handy for creating your own miniature TV station and broadcast pictures of your cat live via webcam). Because images, audio, and video all have various formats in use on the web, I am going to take a bit of time explaining the various choices and the general differences among them so, you can choose the format that best suits your needs. Keep in mind that you may end up using a mixture of formats for different tasks.

Image formats

Of |the hundreds, or possibly thousands, of existing image formats, we will focus here on the three most commonly on use on the web. The image formats we're looking at are GIF (Graphics Interchange Format), JPEG (Joint Photographic Experts Group), and PNG (Portable Network Graphics), and these are shown in Figure 6-1. All of these formats have native support within browsers. Because each of the three formats has its own unique pros and cons and is better at certain tasks than others, we'll take a look at when you should use each one, and you can decide exactly what will suit your needs best for each image you need to include.

Other formats such as APNG, BMP, JNG, JPEG-2000, MNG, TIFF WBMP, and XBM have seen varied support among browsers. However, due to inconsistencies, it is advised that you do not use them unless you have no other choice, as you will find some browsers unable to display them.

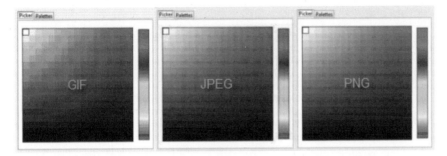

Figure 6-1. GIF has limited colors, and JPEG can have compression artifacts, but PNG looks as good as an image possibly can!

GIF

GIF (Graphics Interchange Format), an image format created by CompuServe in 1987, has become one of the primary ways of showing images on the Internet due to its ability to compress images effectively. The GIF format includes basic transparency, though its transparency is not as effective as PNG's because GIF doesn't allow partial transparency—pixels are either transparent or they are not. The GIF format also includes support for animations, which has remained to this day the primary reason to use GIF files. GIF usage has declined over recent years because better formats (namely PNG) have appeared to offer better levels of transparency, more than 256 colors (limited colors is GIF's major issue), and better compression (which means smaller file sizes). GIF would be a good choice if you want to include some basic images such as solid background colors or basic images, use bullet points, or make an animated image without having to use something like Flash; otherwise, there are better formats you should consider.

ExplainED

People still use the GIF format for producing animations, because site visitors do not have to have a plug-in installed to view the images, as they do with Adobe Flash. This means that you have a very high likelihood that your end users will see the animation you provide. The downside is that GIFs can only provide basic flip-book animations, unlike the more dynamic animations Flash can produce.

Here are a few occasions to use GIF images:

- Basic animations that do not require Flash interactivity
- Emoticons, such as a smiley face, within forums and chat rooms
- Images that use flat colors or lack of detailed texture
- Clip art and graphics that need wide product support

Animated GIFs Producing animation on the web is one of those controversial areas. On one hand, giving some animation to a website can give it that extra effect you wanted to make your website look interesting. On the other hand, animation can be distracting, annoying, and in some cases drive visitors away from your website. If you exclude the general animation provided in videos, the majority of animation on the Web is advertising (to portray a message over a sequence of steps) or enhances a website in the form of a quirky motion or event. Among the most common of these enhancements are emoticons, those little smiley faces you get in instant messengers, forums, and other social networks. While, of course, an emoticon can be static, if you actually make your face smile or wink, that subtle animation gives a little bit extra, which in essence should be the limit of your use for animated GIFs. They should be subtle, never imposing, distracting, or most important of all, annoying.

LinkED

For more information about animated GIFs, please visit http://www.animationfactory.com/en/ *for a whole bunch of examples. You can see what they are all about. Don't use them on your website unless you have a genuine reason to, as your visitors may think they are tacky!*

JPEG

JPEG (Joint Photographic Experts Group) has remained one of the most commonly used image formats on the web, with its primary advantage being in its ability to show large images with small file sizes. It has remained popular in photography ever since it appeared. While GIF has the disadvantage of supporting only a small palette of 256 colors, JPEG files can hold a complete range of colors depending on the needs of the picture. One of the downsides of the JPEG format is its compression method. Because of the way it reduces file sizes, the picture itself can be distorted or end up with a pixelated look about it. If you want to have good color support and your images do not require transparency, the JPEG format could be worth using. Also, JPEG is great if you need small file sizes and do not mind losing some of the quality to keep your images working for users with slow connections. If you need high-quality images, you may prefer to use the PNG format instead.

Pixelation is a general term for where the image on the screen tends to look rather blocky, because of the lack of shades to reduce the number of colors being used (in compression). It groups the closest shades together causing the effect that makes the images look slightly distorted.

Here are some occasions to use JPEG images:

- Graphic art you want to showcase with wide product support
- Complex designs you want to use for website backgrounds
- Photographic work that you want to optimize for small file sizes
- Gradients, line art, and other images for which no further editing will occur

PNG

PNG (Portable Network Graphics) is one of the newer image formats on the web and has benefits over both GIF and JPEG. In comparison with GIF files, PNG can achieve smaller file sizes and has a wider range of support for transparency. Unlike the GIF format, it has a wide range of colors; instead of 8-bit (256) colors, it supports 24-bit to 48-bit colors before compression. Also, it uses a lossless compression method, which means, unlike with JPEG, you will not sacrifice image quality to reduce file sizes. This feature is especially useful if you plan on editing images constantly, as you will not see the image degrade after every save. PNG does have some disadvantages though. It does not support animation like GIF, and its own alpha transparency layer is not supported properly within Internet Explorer 6. Also, unlike JPEG, it does not have nearly the widespread use within cameras, mobile phones, webcams, and other devices that can be used to take snapshots for photos.

ExplainED

There is a project called APNG (Animated PNG) that will allow you to give your PNG files the same animated effects as GIF files and thus reduce the reliance on technologies like Flash. However, for the moment, support for APNG is very low, so it's not really worth using yet.

Here are a few occasions to use PNG images:

- High-resolution photography where quality is essential
- Logos, advertisements (nonanimated), and textual images
- Transparency effects that require subtle use of shades
- Complex and detailed images that need to retain quality

As a quick preview of what has been explained in the previous sections, Figure 6-2 compares the three most commonly used image formats and an overview of their discussed benefits to help you make your choice.

	GIF	JPEG	PNG
Colors	256	Millions	Millions
Quality	Low	Medium	High
Compression	Basic	Good	Good
Transparency	Partial	No	Yes
Animation	Yes	No	Partial

Figure 6-2. A comparison of the various image formats you can use. Dark shading indicates full support, and light shading is partial support.

Working with Images

So what images are important when building a website? Well, of course, your site will need a logo of some kind, and if you want to advertise your website, perhaps you might want to produce a banner for people to link to your design. As well as logo design, we will look at favicons (which give your design a more unique identity) and how to add those little tweaks that give your website that complete feeling. We will also quickly note the rise in offering web-based graphics, such as SVG, as they will have a large part to play in the future of web graphics. Most importantly, we'll look at how to produce your own images and media even if you have limited skills and where you can go to purchase premade images. Premade stock photography and media can often be really useful if you're either lazy or want to have a professional look and feel using artwork someone else has made.

Creating and Editing Photos

Producing awesome graphics is one area of website design that eludes me, and I am totally envious of anyone who can wield Photoshop and end up with something that looks like it belongs in a Pixar movie. However, for those of you who can produce your own images, the benefits you can give your website are enormous, and the impact of producing high-quality images is well worth time and effort put into them. Using an image editor, there are a variety of different things you can build and use throughout your website:

- **Logo**: This shows off your identity (and brand) on the Internet (more details are given in the next section).
- **Advertisement**: Promote your website through banners like you see all over the Web.
- **Backgrounds**: These most common images on a website give emphasis and context.
- **Line art**: Line art generally refers to borders, separators, or other ways to break down content for easy reading.
- **Screenshots**: These pictures of applications or desktops show off products and services.
- **Photos and artwork**: Photos you have taken or images you made usually appear in galleries.
- **Icons:** Easy to spot and understand, icons are great for giving visual points of reference.
- **Special effects**: Want a flourish for your site? Make some images that draw visitors' eyes.
- **Heading text**: To get around the font limitations of the Web, you can use images of text.
- **Buttons**: Using image buttons, you can get around the boring defaults of input buttons.
- **Portraits**: These are images that represent something like profile pictures for social networks.

- **Redirects:** These are the icons or logos of social networks that link to your online profile.

- **Sprites:** These images are grouped together for rollover effects to save loading lots of files.

If you need help creating your own images (beyond the very core basics outlined by this chapter), you may want to find yourself a suitable book on using a particular software package. Image editing and using software to produce images is dependent on specialist software (image editors), and as this book does not focus on particular products, you may want to invest some time into learning how to produce and edit graphics using a different title for reference. If you have not done so already, you can find lots of great examples of these types of images on the Web. One great thing about the Internet is that there are plenty of free tutorials to guide you to producing an image of your choice (though you will still need to learn to use an image editor).

Building Logos

Of all the various types of image you can produce, the most important and recognizable is the one element you should have on all pages of your website—the logo. Since I already spent a fair bit of time explaining the importance of a brand and identity, you should be well aware that your identity is how people view you on the Web; it's what you will be associated with on a regular basis. Therefore, looking presentable and having a logo that well represents you can be the difference between looking professional and having your visitors look elsewhere due to the amateurish feeling it may project. On the Web, there are three types of logos: textual, iconized, and flourished. These are explained in this section with some examples of popular websites that make use of the various styles. Once you have looked through the various logos available, you should think about creating a unique logo of your own to place on your website (if you already have not done so), this, of course, is an activity where you will want to put the book down and get creative with how you want to be branded online.

Textual If you do not want an image in your logo and would prefer just to use styled text, this is also perfectly fine; plenty of websites have logos that are nothing more than text. Textual icons are one of the easiest to make and are used around the world by many well-known brands (see Figure 6-3). The basis of textual icons is exactly what they sound like. These logos are entirely made of text, and while this may sound boring, with good use of fonts or color, you can make this logo just as easy to remember as something with a lot of delicate work put into it. Simply using the typing tool in your graphics editor with a transparent background will allow you to make an image. To brighten it up, you could use something like a gradient or colored letters. You could even, perhaps, position the characters in a unique way.

Figure 6-3. An assortment of logos based entirely around text

Iconized Iconized logos use the same techniques as the text-based ones except they include a single image (or icon) to add a visual representation to build onto the logo (see Figure 6-4). While clip art and stock icons can be used, if you do so, you might face difficulty in getting the icon and the text in your logo to work harmoniously, so the logo doesn't simply look like you dragged something unrelated into the picture. If you want to use one of an iconized logo, start with a textual icon, and add an icon that fits in well with the design afterward (the more interesting it is, the better). If you are going to use an icon, you must ensure that the icon is not being used elsewhere, as your logo could be mistaken for someone else's website, which could be disastrous!

Figure 6-4. Logos that have a prominantly placed icon can draw attention to the brand name.

Flourished Flourished logos go one step further and require the most care and attention to produce. They take an iconized logo and add flourishes—enhancements that improve to the artistic flare of the logo (see Figure 6-5). If you are producing one for yourself, you will probably need to get a graphic designer or artistic friend to help you out if you are not graphically savvy. Most websites out there use either textual or iconized logos that are relatively simple, so you do not worry about having to keep up with the Joneses just to make your website icon look professional. Flourished logos do have a unique air about them, but they are generally used when websites need a totally unique experience or for designs which aim to go beyond the realms of typography andicons.

Figure 6-5. More interesting logos that make use of text, icons, and flourishes can also work.

If you have not already produced a logo of your own, hopefully some of these examples have given you inspiration. Remember that you do not have to have a logo if you are making a personal website; you could just have some text. If you are intending on having a highly recognized brand or running a business, however, you may want to invest some time into creating a logo of your own (or getting one made for you professionally) so that people will associate your website, products, and services with you! Be creative and imaginative with your logo, and find something that will work with your current website in terms of colors, text, and size. Once you have built the logo, no matter how it looks, people will associate you with it over time.

LinkED

For some more inspiration in creating logos, visit http://www.fuelyourcreativity.com/50-kick-ass-logos-for-inspiration/.

Stock Collections

What do you do when you aren't very good at making images, audio, or videos, but you are able to at least edit something to a basic extent? Well, one thing you should consider if you either can't, won't, or don't have the time is clip art or stock collections. Getting premade images and media is an excellent and cost-effective way to make your website look pretty without knowing how to create images, video, or audio (you will need to edit them, though). While you can usually buy packs of clip art and stock media, you should be very careful because many providers allow you to use but not distribute their creations. This limitation leaves you with an issue, because when you put images on the Web, you are effectively placing them up for distribution. While you cannot get round this restriction, you will find that your new best friends will be words like "royalty free," "public domain," or "creative commons," as they give you more flexible rights over what you can do with the items you want to use.

Various types of stock art and media are available:

- **Clip art**: These images are generally low quality and cartoonish. You can often buy huge packs of clip art containing tens or hundreds of thousands of images (perhaps even millions), and these are most commonly used in presentations or websites aimed at young children.

- **Vector graphics**: Used primarily in backgrounds, flourishes, specialist artwork, and icons, vector graphics are high-quality versions of clip art built with a specific purpose of providing an air of professionalism. These are the most common types of artwork purchased for web design.

- **Stock photography**: These images have been taken by cameras and are based in real life. For example, you could get images of buildings, sunsets, or animals—pretty much whatever can be snapped by a photographer. These are different from vector graphics, which are generally manmade.

- **Audio clips**: Of course, stock collections don't end with images; you can get audio snippets of sounds you would find in the real world. You'll find everything from bird noises or train whistles right up to full-blown Hollywood-style sound clips made using orchestras and expensive computer equipment.

- **Video footage**: Over the years, many production companies have gotten a lot of stock video of animals in the wild, people in the street, and lots of different scenes both real life and animated, and you can take advantage of this footage for multimedia presentations and videos.

ExplainED

While clip art can be fun to work with, it does not generally have the professional feel that you get from using licensed or royalty-free stock photography or professional artwork and multimedia. Stock images (unlike clip art) are generally produced by professional photographers and graphic artists.

I have already mentioned creative commons in Chapter 2 when talking about content writing, and the same rules apply to images. You are allowed to edit and use the work, just as long as other people can use it too. If you intend to directly or indirectly make any money from images or multimedia (such as using them within advertisements), you must ensure that the license (if one exists) allows you to use the image for commercial purposes.

The public domain is another great foundry of images, as stuff in the public domain is free of copyright and therefore can be used for anything without restrictions, which means you don't have any rules to follow, and you can use them for any purpose you see fit (though finding public domain images may be harder). The following websites offer free, public domain, or creative commons image content that may help you in your quest to find some nice images to use within your design (of course, licenses will apply):

- **Easy Stock Photos**: http://www.easystockphotos.com/
- **Every Stock Photo**: http://www.everystockphoto.com/
- **Free Photos**: http://www.freephotos.com/
- **Open Clipart**: http://www.openclipart.org/
- **PD Clipart**: http://www.pdclipart.org/
- **PDSounds**: http://www.pdsounds.org/
- **Photos8**: http://www.photos8.com/
- **WP Clipart**: http://www.wpclipart.com/

The final and probably most important place you can look for images is royalty-free stock photography websites. While there are free places on the Web that allow you to download and use images, the majority of good quality images are found on sites that let you buy a pack of credits, and you can use those credits to get images. This process is simple, easy, and fairly inexpensive. The following websites offer free or paid royalty free images:

- **Big Stock Photo**: http://www.bigstockphoto.com/
- **Corbis**: http://www.corbis.com/
- **Fotolia**: www.fotolia.com
- **Getty Images**: http://www.gettyimages.com/
- **iStockPhoto**: http://www.istockphoto.com/
- **Jupiter Images**: http://www.jupiterimages.com/
- **Photos.com**: http://www.photos.com/en/
- **PunchStock**: http://www.punchstock.co.uk/
- **Shutterstock**: http://www.shutterstock.com/
- **Stock.xchng**: http://www.sxc.hu/ (free)
- **StockXpert**: http://www.stockxpert.com/

You must not, under any circumstances, just take images from a website or Google image search and use them within your own website: this qualifies as copyright infringement, and you can get into serious legal trouble over it. You should also avoid hot linking, that is, rather than taking the image, you are embedding the image within your website and linking to the resource on another website. Hot linking is one of the worst practices on the Internet, because it costs websites a lot of bandwidth, and even though the image was not physically taken, using a copyrighted image via a hot link still violates copyright law as you are broadcasting without permission.

What makes royalty-free websites so great is that once you purchase the image, you have a nonexclusive right to reuse it over and over (as long as you don't try to resell it or otherwise violate the license terms of your purchase). Most professionals use stock photography if their image editing skills are not near good enough to get the sorts of results they want or if they just want a quick image. If you find yourself unable to find an image you like from these resources, you may well have to pay someone to produce the image for you instead, and that can become quite expensive. If you are looking for more than just an image (such as audio and video), the following websites offers either free or paid for royalty free media which is licensed in similar ways to images:

- **Corbis Motion**: http://www.corbismotion.com/
- **NeoSounds**: http://www.neosounds.com/
- **Pond5**: http://www.pond5.com/
- **PremiumBeat**: http://www.premiumbeat.com/
- **RevoStock**: http://www.revostock.com/
- **Royalty Free Music**: http://www.royaltyfreemusic.com/

- **StockMusic**: http://www.stockmusic.net/
- **The Music Bakery**: http://musicbakery.com/
- **Thought Equity Motion**: http://www.thoughtequity.com/

ExplainED

Some of the stock image websites also offer a variety of audio and video clips that you can use. The best thing you can do is browse around the various resources and see if you can find the perfect stock item you require for your website. Hopefully, you will end up with some good images and media.

Favicons and Apple icons

So you now know how to make a logo and have some basic ideas for what kinds of graphics you could make. One other thing we need to produce is what is commonly known as a favicon. A favicon is a 16-by-16-pixel icon file. Now, you may be wondering what this has to do with web design. A modern trend in web browsers is to allow the customization of the icon that appears both in the address bar (before the URL) and in the tab in which the website is opened (see Figure 6-6). This small image representation, by default, is just a boring image in the browser, but you can do produce your own! Once you've created your 16-by-16-pixel icon, you can link to it in the head section of your website, and the browser will notice an icon is available and will display on screen. While you may wonder how important tiny images like that are, the answer might surprise you.

Figure 6-6. Using Firefox, you can clearly see the favicon for the Google website.

Favicons, at their core, may be simple, but their effect on the end user is subtle and powerful. If you are lucky enough to have your website bookmarked by visitors, the icon will be cached with the website address, so having a unique logo will let your website stand out in the list of bookmarked sites. Not only does a favicon benefit bookmarks, it also serves a purpose when people are multitasking and have several windows open, because, of course, when they are navigating between tabs, finding your site is much easier if it has an image to identify it.

While most people are aware of favicons, not as many are aware of a similar system for adding icons to the iPhone and the iPod Touch! If you know you have visitors who may bookmark your site within their Apple devices, the process is identical except you use a 58-by-58-pixel PNG image rather than a 16-by-16-pixel icon.

Try it yourself: Producing favicons

How do you go about adding a favicon to your website? Well, the process is actually really simple for both favicons and Apple device icons. Once you have created your images all you need to do is place the following code within the head tags of your website (you will need to add this into every page you want it to appear):

```
<link rel="shortcut icon" type="image/x-icon" href="/images/favicon.ico" />
<link rel="apple-touch-icon" href="/images/apple.png" />
```

Once you have created a favicon for your website, you should save, upload, and try out the website with the newly added icons to ensure that they are functioning correctly (the favicon should appear in the address bar). While a favicon can use an extension other than ICO (if you are worried about using an icon editor or simply don't have one installed), you should take note that some browsers, including all versions of Internet Explorer, will not take notice or render other formats properly. Therefore, it's recommended you ensure it's a proper icon file. Some people also prefer to have a favicon.ico file in their website's base directory without the link reference, as most browsers will actively seek out the file without asking (though this isn't a standard, so you're better off using the code in this exercise).

LinkED

Producing a favicon is so easy that you do not even need an image or icon editor to create one. Plenty of websites, like http://www.favicon.cc/, *can make a favicon for free, which you can download and include as part of your website.*

Graphics Languages in Use

While creating images for the Web itself can be done within any conventional image editor, producing 2D or 3D dynamic graphics for the web has become something else entirely. There has been a rise in the number of these images, which are produced on demand using special structural code. Essentially, in the same way you use HTML to describe how your web content should be structured, you can use one of these languages to describe how an image should be constructed. While this concept is a fairly old for the Web, the adoption of these formats has been fairly slow. The potential uses for these graphic formats include producing on-the-fly elements like charts, graphs, and timelines that depend on user input:

- **SVG:** Scalable Vector Graphics is an open standard (and the industry favorite) that allows you to produce 2D graphics using XML code. Support for SVG is limited within browsers, but it remains the most popular of the graphical coding formats on the Web and has found success on sites such as Wikipedia. Version 1.2 is the most recent edition and contains support for some mobile devices. SVG allows drawing to be dynamic, animated, and even interactive. It is fairly straightforward to learn, and to increase support for the format, plug-ins have been produced for browsers including Internet Explorer, such as Renesis player.

- **VML:** Vector Markup Language was the original trendsetter for producing graphics for the Web dynamically through XML. While it's nowhere near as popular as SVG, it's just as straightforward to learn. VML has been supported in Internet Explorer since version 5, which means it has a fairly high market adoption rate (perhaps equal to SVG). Google, to enhance compatibility, uses VML for its map service on Internet Explorer and SVG for other browsers, though this may not be required in the future as SVG gains higher adoption.

- **X3D:** The successor of the original 3D modeling language Virtual Reality Modeling Language (VRML), X3D is the primary method of making 3D objects natively for the Web. The concept of having 3D environments may have risen in popularity through services like SecondLife, but the unfortunate truth is that neither VRML or X3D have seen much in the way of success in getting people to code with it. Browser support for VRML is basically nonexistent, so you should not expect visitors to be able to make use of your 3D content without a plug-in to enable it's functionality within the browser. See Figure 6-7 for an X3D example in action.

- **XAML**: While SVG is the modern standard for all browsers except Internet Explorer, Microsoft has released its own XML-based language capable of producing vector images known as Extensible Application Markup Language (XAML). XAML allows you to produce SVG-like vector images (as well as .NET web applications) for Internet Explorer or other browsers that support Silverlight. Because plug-in support for Silverlight is moderate and has basic support on Mac and Linux, XAML is a genuine competitor for SVG. However, XAML is sometimes considered slightly harder to get to grips with. Unlike SVG, XAML is capable of generating 3D images (an added advantage).

Figure 6-7. This example of X3D in action shows the potential of rendering 3D objects using just XML.

LinkED

For a complete reference on SVG, visit the W3C specification at http://www.w3.org/TR/SVG/. *For details about using the HTML5 Canvas element (a new graphical format which is embedded into the new version of HTML and gaining widespread support), visit* https://developer.mozilla.org/en/Canvas_tutorial.

Mass Multimedia

Now that you have images down to a tee, and you want to make something a bit cooler and lively, the obvious solution is to add a bit of animation or multimedia into your website. While you can add special effects and other cool things that make your website bounce around with fun using JavaScript (discussed in Chapter 8), the general ways in which multimedia or special effects within web design are harnessed are either through offering videos and audio directly from the website, such as linking to an MP3 file or embedding the default player into the site, or by using one of the formats purposefully created for adding multimedia flourishes into your design, such as the well known Adobe Flash format or its up-and-coming competitor Microsoft Silverlight. We will take a look at the benefits and uses of each format for providing multimedia and explain when it should and should not be used.

Languages in Use

Back in the old days, before sites like YouTube, if you wanted to add multimedia into a website, you were forced to use a specially engineered plug-in, such as those produced for Windows Media Player, RealOne Player, or Apple QuickTime. This requirement caused all sorts of compatibility issues where people were required to download and install multiple players just to be sure they could view videos on the Web. Luckily, these days, just two formats have been standardized and promoted for the use of showing both audio and video on the Internet.

- **Flash**: Adobe Flash is a multimedia platform that you will have seen all over the Web, especially on video websites like YouTube. While Flash (and its own language ActionScript) can be quite hard to learn and a special client is required to produce the files, it has the highest amount of active users of any multimedia language (with Silverlight in second place). More importantly, it has the highest market penetration, which means more visitors will have the Flash Player installed and will be able to view your Flash movies than people using competing formats. Flash has also found success in websites created entirely from it. An example of Flash providing multimedia for the BBC iPlayer is shown in Figure 6-8.

- **Silverlight**: Microsoft Silverlight is a competitor of Flash, though it is much more recent in its arrival to the Web. Like Flash, it has many features and requires a special client that is able to produce the required files. However, it has less users and a lower market penetration than Flash, as fewer people have the plug-in installed on their machines. Because it is produced by Microsoft, it's been bundled with recent versions of Windows, which helped increase adoption rates. So you could see Silverlight become as popular as Flash in the future. The language it uses is about the same in terms of difficulty, so which you choose to use will be entirely down to your own personal choice; many people choose Flash, as it is the most widely recognized player on the Web.

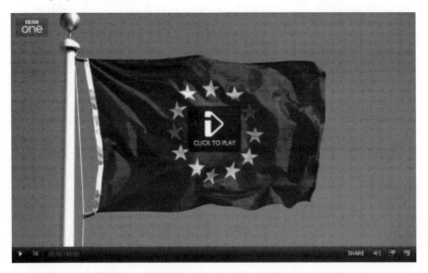

Figure 6-8. The BBC's on-demand service iPlayer allows you to watch rich media or interactive multimedia through Flash.

Audio and Video Formats

Creating audio and video on the Web is a complicated matter. Although images can be produced using anything from the expensive Adobe Photoshop right down to the Paint product that comes with Windows, and the resources that can produce simple to complex images are in their thousands (such as all those "learn how to draw" articles you find on the Web), creating video and audio takes much more skill due to its added complexity. Software for producing audio and video (and images) is easy to come by and, in many cases, basic packages are free or cost little money (some examples are shown in Appendix B). While I do mention briefly later on how to do some basic audio recording, the following formats are used commonly for the Web and are therefore useful if you do begin publishing (for a comparison of these formats, see Figure 6-9):

- **Adobe Flash (FLV and SWF):** Adobe Flash has its own popular video format for displaying and streaming media over the Web. Used on sites such as YouTube, Flash has seen a high market penetration, especially as it rides on the back of the already popular Adobe Flash plug-in. This video format is therefore compatible among most computers, but support on mobile devices and portable media players is an issue due to the lack of cross-device support.

- **Apple QuickTime (AAC, AIFF, ALAC, and MOV):** With backing from the likes of iTunes, iPod, and iPhone, Apple's popular formats have a wide spectrum of compatibility across both handheld devices and desktop media players. While native support for these formats isn't available within Windows, iTunes, the world's biggest online media store, uses AAC and the Apple lossless codec to provide high-quality media that works across their highly popular and market-dominating range of media devices. Therefore, support for this format is worthwhile as a high proportion of the browsing public will be able to make use of the format.

- **DivX and XViD (DIVX and XVID):** When it comes to compressing your media, two formats have gained widespread and popular appeal. DivX and XViD have seen an ever-increasing number of both hardware and software devices being able to make use of their codec format, which is often wrapped in AVI files (or other existing video formats). The best thing to remember about these two video formats is that they provide a very high-level of compression maintaining a high level of quality playback at the same time. It should also be noted that XViD is open source (and free), whereas DivX is proprietary, and you must buy the codec software that allows you to compress your media. DivX, though, is the more popular of the two.

- **MPEG (H.264, M4A, MP3, MPG, and MP4):** MPEG and its related well-known industry standard called MP3 are simply the most popular audio and video formats by far on the Web. While they are proprietary like many of the formats listed, they are the most commonly used on the Web and, therefore, will be the most likely to work for everyone. As my personal recommendation, if you offer audio in MP3 and video in M4A (used within the iTunes store), you will find that the formats are pretty much supported by every device and software product.

- **Real Player (RA, RM, and RV):** RealPlayer (formerly RealOne Player) is now one of the less-common formats; it used to be quite popular in the '90s and still holds a varied share of users. While the player was controversial early on because it was bundled with advertising, the player itself was successful in early streaming media for the Web. While this format is worthy of consideration for compatibility reasons, you will be better off using a different format.

- **Windows Media Player (AVI, WAV, WMA, and WMV):** While Apple's formats are obviously among the most popular because of iTunes, the iPod, and the iPhone, Microsoft has seen success with the default format that comes with preinstalled support within Microsoft Windows. The format itself is supported by many non-Apple MP3 player products and Microsoft's own player, the Zune. As a result it's well supported all over the Web and is considered a reliable format for use within websites, especially for visitors running Microsoft Windows.

- **XIPH (FLAC, Theora, and Vorbis):** The final formats we will look at are part of a collaborative effort to produce media formats that are nonproprietary (and therefore have no licensing costs for software developers adding support for the formats). These are the fairly well known lossless (large-sized but ultra-high-quality files with good compression) format FLAC and the lesser known OGG format (Theora for video and Vorbis for audio). While some people prefer these formats, which do generally have a better overall quality, they have a pretty niche audience, so perhaps add them as a secondary choice to MP3 and another format.

	Audio	**Video**
Adobe Flash	Yes	Yes
Apple QuickTime	AAC / AIFF / ALAC	MOV
DivX and XViD	Yes	DivX / XViD
MPEG	MP3	H.264 / M4A / MPG / MP4
Real Player	RA	RM / RV
Windows Media Player	WAV / WMA	AVI / WMV
XIPH	FLAC / Vorbis	Theora

Figure 6-9. A comparison of the various audio and video formats including their file extensions

ExplainED

Tutorials for how to produce animations and high-quality audio productions and even how to use the software that produces these are beyond the scope of this book. Audio can be produced using a microphone (or headset) and some free recording software, and video can be taken from a digital camcorder, your webcam, or a cell phone.

On-Demand Streaming

Video on the Web comes in two forms: video on demand, where the video is stored on the Web where people can download and view the media in their own time, and streaming media, where live events and video are broadcast and download piece by piece to allow the viewer to watch a movie without having to complete the download first. The most often used on the Web is, of course, streaming media, as over the years, being able to stream services like your favorite movies, television series, and YouTube clips have dramatically overshadowed the older styles of service where you have to wait for the entire movie to download to be able to play it. Streaming services work because they buffer the video (download a small bit before playing and then gradually download more and more as the movie has started) and continue to download the stream. This process tries to prevent interruptions in the movie by having downloaded a minute or so ahead. If the video has any problems trying to download a segment, it still has a buffer to play before the video will stop. In Figure 6-10, you will notice that the bottom of the image shows how much of the video has played, but the grey line that is further than that represents how much of the video has been buffered (downloaded) for playback.

ExplainED

While streaming is usually associated with live content (like television), streaming over the Web also functions with on-demand services to allow people to watch their favorite shows within their browsers. If you want an example of this, just look at the website Hulu; it has TV shows you can watch online!

Figure 6-10. YouTube buffers the video to allow the video to stream without interruption.

So what should you do? Well, if you want to encourage people to play the video or audio, don't force them to download a really large file. Instead, offer them a Flash-based version of the video you wanted them to see on a service like YouTube, or you can even host the media yourself using one of the many Flash video solutions. The sight of a video window in which people can click the play button, as shown in Figure 6-11, is more likely to encourage them to view or listen to your offerings than just providing a download link that they have to wait for and then find a media player that will support the format you are offering (though you should not discourage you from having a download as well for people who like to view their videos or audio offline).

Figure 6-11. You can offer your visitors a Flash-based MP3 media player.

The general theme here is to offer your visitors multimedia (if that is something you want on your site) and to give them the kind of service they are used to getting on video-sharing websites. While you may find your own website will not benefit from the addition of media (video or audio), there is a growing trend in sites offering this kind of digital media, so I thought it was worth addressing the preferred method of offering multimedia online. Publishing this media can be done in one of several ways: You can host the media yourself, which can be quite expensive due to the large file sizes associated with media. You could use a mirror or special service dedicated to hosting media; these have servers especially designed around streaming or serving media. Or you could use a video-sharing website. Of course, these video-sharing websites are fairly common and used a lot, but you should keep in mind that many bundle advertising, and possibly even restrictions and time limits, on the media.

ExplainED

While you can upload your images, audio, and video to many online services, you should make sure that you always keep an offline copy of the media in case the website should ever be shut down. With third-party services, you can never be too careful when it comes to relying on their existence.

Podcasting Basics

Podcasting is one of the Web's new phenomena, because of the advances in broadband and faster Internet connections, many people have taken it upon themselves to produce podcasts. Essentially, a podcast is a web-based TV or radio show (such as the one shown in Figure 6-12). People host podcasts for various reasons, and most of these podcasts are almost like audio or video versions of blogs; they target a specific audience, talk about various subjects, give insight and advice, and generally provide people with a method of which they can enjoy the contents of your website on the move (through their iPods, Zunes, or MP3 players for example).

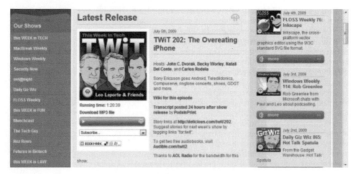

Figure 6-12. Radio host and podcast producer Leo Laporte produces a wide range of fantastic podcasts.

Sound like fun? Well, the only things you should consider before starting up a podcast are the following:

- Do you really have something worth talking about? Podcasts are not appropriate for advertising products (though you can monetize them by including advertisements), and people do not want to listen to you waffle on about how great your product is. The only exception to this rule is if you are giving reviews on products you have purchased.

- Do you have the time to create a quality podcast? Podcasts require time and effort. You should release new shows every day, week, or month, and you should always ensure that the date of these shows release is standardized. Your audience members, just like with TV or radio, should know when they can tune into your show. More importantly, it's expected that you keep the length of the podcast relatively consistent; generally, you don't want your broadcasts going on for longer than 2 hours, though the average is 30 to 60 minutes.

- Finally, do you have the resources to cope with a podcast? Because of the need for bandwidth, finding hosting with enough bandwidth (or a dedicated service) can be a challenge. Also, you need to ensure the quality of the recording is correct; make sure your voice sounds clear and that the content of your shows is like your content on your site—dynamic, interesting, and fresh (not dry and boring!).

The most common types of podcasts are

- News and recent events on various subjects
- Specialist tips, tricks, or product information
- Job-specific information (even web design)
- Topical shows (such as science or photography)
- Tutorials and learning material (such as classes)

NotED

With the rise in VoIP (Voice over IP) clients like Skype, which allow you to call people over the Web (and via the telephone), you can have discussions with groups of people all invited into the same conversation being recorded by the person running the show. Having more than one person on a podcast can make things more interesting.

So now that we have gotten that out of the way, how do you create a podcast? Well, the simplest method is to get an audio editor (recommendations are in Appendix B) and get yourself set up with a microphone to record your voice and a webcam or video camcorder if you want video. If you just want to do audio, you can just use a microphone without any additional props, as people can only hear you. Of course, with video, while you will need a webcam or a camcorder to record you, you also want to have a room in your house or workplace that is set up especially for broadcasting. Think of a studio: perhaps have a desk, some comfy seats, a laptop, and a big monitor so the camera can see what you are doing onscreen (see Figure 6-13). You could instead simply overlay some recorded screen activity or screenshots if you don't have the budget for all that stuff. Literally, how much you spend is up to you and how much of a long-term investment you want to make. Some professional podcasts spend thousands on their setups, but the average Joe can set up and create a podcast with a cheap laptop (with a webcam and microphone) and a couple of bits of free software, which is pretty great. You could become a YouTube celebrity in no time and end up with thousands of people watching you regularly!

Figure 6-13. With a full-production studio, CNET broadcasts its video shows with a professional look and feel.

When you have everything ready to broadcast, make sure you know what you want to talk about. You can make as many mistakes as you like and just retake the scene (just like on TV) by cutting up the final recording and cleaning it up. While you can do the show on your own, if you want to do some camerawork, you can make things interesting by perhaps getting a friend to hold the camera and record you doing the show. You friend will be able to see things from the viewer's perspective, though you may want to avoid someone with shaky hands! If you are using a laptop, you won't have much of a problem, as the webcam will be focused on you the whole time.

Once you have your final recording completed, you should download the video or audio files, or if they were recorded on your machine, simply save them in a high-quality format. Don't use MP3 or AVI, for example, because they will immediately degrade the quality of your recording; use a raw lossless format instead. Once this is complete, you can edit the audio and video in your chosen editor, whether it's something as simple as Audacity (as shown in Figure 6-14 and mentioned in the software list in Appendix B) or a video-editing suite that came with your DVD player like Nero or Pinnacle Studio. You should be able to play back what you have, select and cut bits that don't work, add some special effects, perhaps even write some subtitles to accompany the video for people who cannot hear, and even reorder the video and audio using the editing package of your choice. Plus, you can add in some credits, theme music, and place the advertisement breaks at suitable intervals if you want to support your podcast with advertising.

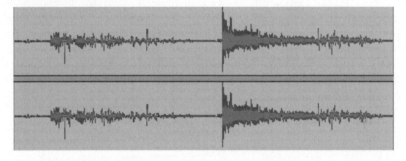

Figure 6-14. Inside Audacity, you can see how the audio looks and make edits.

Next, you should have a finished podcast (or videocast). At this point, you should save the (lossless) master copy and then export and publish the audio or video into a format of your choice. You could use MP3, which supports compression (you want the download to be as quick as possible). You can use an audio format if the podcast is just people speaking and therefore needs no visual effects. You should probably save in 64kbs or 96kbs (for higher quality if your audio editor supports editing the bit rate, as it can decrease your file size dramatically). You only need to use 128kbs and above if you are including a lot of music that requires sharp and highly focused sound. The same applies for video—use a method of compression (and a format such as M4A) to come to a compromise between quality and file size. While video files will be more bandwidth heavy, you don't want the video using gigabytes of space, as it will take visitors ages to download (unless, of course, you want to broadcast in high definition, as you won't really be able to get around the high file sizes due to the quality level).

Once got your podcast in the correct format, you can upload the files to either your website or another host like YouTube (see Figure 6-15). After that, just link to the content on your website and embed it within a media player for the web. such as one built in Flash (there are plenty of free ones out there). Flash is a great way to embed video in websites, as most people have the plug-in and you don't need a special media player installed.

Once you have the podcast up on your site and linked, you can publish the audio and video links in an RSS feed (talked about in Chapter 9) so that feed readers and software like iTunes and Miro can let people grab new versions of your show when they appear. It's also worth mentioning that once the feed has been created, you will need to get it listed within the various directories (such as iTunes) alongside your website to ensure it's visible for potential listeners (the more you advertise it the better).

While making a podcast gives you a lot of things to consider, remember that the emphasis of good podcasting is to have an interesting topic, regular shows, a high standard for quality (get rid of the fluff), and most important of all, have fun and get visitors involved! If you want more tips and tricks for how to produce a podcast, you may want to read a book like *Podcast Solutions, 2nd Edition* by Michael Geoghegan and Dan Klass (ISBN: 978-1-59059-905-1), which covers this subject in greater detail.

Figure 6-15. YouTube is the largest video sharing websites on the Internet.

ExplainED

Even if you don't want to create a podcast yourself, you could always listen to some of the great ones out there. Lots of media players, including iTunes and the open source product Miro, have podcast support and can point you in the direction of both audio and video shows.

Web SFX

You |have already seen how useful Flash can be in hosting video and audio within your website. Special effects on the Web are rampant, since the invention of technologies like Flash and Silverlight and the rise in JavaScript toolkits (which we will look at in Chapter 8). The ability to give your website some extra flare has been made easier with these special plug-ins for browsers that offer unique functionality beyond what HTML and CSS on their own can. Flash and Silverlight are so powerful that they can be used to create animations, web applications, and even games! You may have even played a couple of Flash-created games on the Web. But be warned—the use of these visual enhancers can have downsides too, and these need to be taken into consideration when you create Flash-based solutions for your website. In the following list, you will find some of the basic problems with Flash-based design (when the whole sites or components are written in Flash):

- **Accessibility:** People with disabilities who require specialized software aids may not be able to make sense of the content, because Flash does not have semantic value (in terms of its content), though this can be worked around with by providing alternatives to all Flash content.

- **Usability:** Very complex designs can be made with Flash and Silverlight. This can make the website very difficult to navigate as a result. While this problem can be major, if you offer navigation aids and make things obvious, it can largely be worked around.

- **Search visibility:** Search engines can read Flash files, however, because of the general lack of semantic value (as I mentioned in Chapter 3), a pure Flash site may not rank very highly in search results (I cover how to deal with search engines later in Chapter 10).

Of course, even with the downsides of Flash- and Silverlight-powered pages (where there is little or no HTML and CSS), you do come to a sort of tradeoff. While you are ignoring the accessibility needs of people and potentially damaging your position in search engines (both of which are very bad), you do have the gain of producing websites that are simply not possible if you are only able to use standard web languages. This question of whether to create a website that is more visually entrancing and interesting or stick with what you know will work for everyone can be perplexing, and you'll mainly find your answer in your target audience. If you do consider, like many, producing Flash-only websites or an element that is dependant on such technology, you must consider what you will be giving up and the price you could pay for doing so. As someone who has toyed with Flash, I believe that compromise is one of the website builders' best rational thought processes. And if you are keen on experimenting with Flash, you should produce a secondary website that does not require the use of the technology. Dealing with the flaws in technologies like Flash will make your site a better experience for everyone.

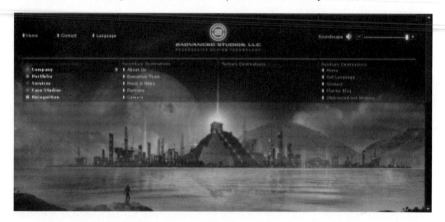

Figure 6-16. The 2Advanced Studios website is filled with stunning effects but has a downside: it's beautiful but inaccessible.

Tips and Tricks: Special Effects for the Web

So how can you use these powerful technologies to your advantage?

1. Never make an entire website in Flash. I cannot emphasize this enough.

2. Never make your website dependant on JavaScript or plug-in-based tools.

3. Always provide alternatives in case the functionality or file isn't available.

4. Always get people to test your website and give feedback on their experience.

5. If you must use Flash or a similar plug-in, layer it over HTML, like CSS, to enhance your site.

This book does not deal with the production of Flash or Silverlight content, as you are learning about the early stages of producing a website. If you want to create something like the awesome Flash website you found using Google, it is important that you try to avoid becoming too dependant on a particular technology, even one as widespread and as popular as Flash. Producing Flash websites involves a lot more work and a dedicated software product to build the project, whereas old HTML and CSS can be built using any free or commercial text editor, which is another consideration when deciding if you want to make use of the technology available.

LinkED

For more exciting examples of Flash-based websites, you can visit Smashing Magazine's *awesome showcase, which contains some examples of some of the best Flash websites that have been produced at* http://www.smashingmagazine.com/2007/10/30/65-excellent-flash-designs/.

While I am emphasizing the need for accessibility and usability within websites, it would be foolish to simply not use Flash on the basis that it has problems. The real truth of the matter is that as things currently stand, producing Flash-only websites (as damaging to some visitors as that can be) means that you can make websites that extend far beyond the reach of any conventional markup language. Also, while it is important to consider your target audience, this form of website creation is the only exception I would give grounds for use, though only on the condition that you meet the requirements of your audience and provide alternatives for those who cannot use Flash. By coming to this compromise and giving choice, I believe that in the future as and when you learn how to take hold of these multimedia languages, you can really do some wonderful and beautiful works of art.

Getting More for Your Money

So now you know how graphics, audio, and video can be used within your website. Next, you can try to produce (or buy) some of your own audio and video to use within your website. While having lots of images may give added richness, and of course, video and audio can expand the way you entertain your visitors), you may find that your website has very high bandwidth (and memory) usage, and this may impact the speed of the site when loading, and you might end up pushing the limits imposed by your web host. As a result, the guidelines in the following will give you a nice simple introduction to how you can boost the speed of your website and reduce the drain on your resources. While you want to keep your site's quality high, you can give your website a boost in performance and help those poor visitors still using a 56K modems (yes, dial-up users still exist) access your site.

Speed Tweaks

Even with broadband becoming ever faster and more readily available, one thing you need to remember is that there are still unfortunate people out there who can only get dial-up connections! Not only this, but with the demand for bandwidth going through the roof, many providers find themselves unable to afford high bandwidth charges for going in excess of what is provided by hosting packages. Also, you should consider the situation on the visitor's side, where Internet service providers give bandwidth caps that prevent them using more than a certain amount of data each month. As a result of this, offering multimedia on the Web can become an expensive business unless you take the time to tweak your site and media so that it uses as little bandwidth as realistically possible. Now, this does not mean you must cut features to save space. Making your website use standards-based code rather than table-based design, for example, will save you bandwidth, as a standards-compliant page uses less code in most cases. But more often than not, it's multimedia and high resolution images that need the fat trimmed from them to reduce high file sizes in order to reduce loading times.

Quality vs. Size

One of the main problems with using images, audio, video, and even technologies like Flash and Silverlight is the quality to size ratio. People hate waiting, whether standing in line at the post office or waiting for the taxi to show up at the door, and if there is one thing people hate doing online, it's waiting for something to download. Because on the Web, a considerable amount of file size is made up of images and multimedia, we therefore need to do something about keeping those file sizes slim. The primary two ways we can do this are by using file compression and reducing the size and quality of the files to minimize the amount of downloading that will occur (and therefore speeding up the rate at which the file will download). Most image and video editors allow you to make the adjustments needed to help come to a compromise that your visitors will find acceptable, as reducing the quality of your media too much could have a negative impact on the viewers you get. In Figure 6-17, you can see how the various elements of a website design can increase the loading time and file size.

⊞ **GET 9781430:**	304 Not Modified	friendsofed.com	1 KB		66ms
⊞ **GET 9781430:**	304 Not Modified	friendsofed.com	1 KB		66ms
⊞ **GET 9781430:**	304 Not Modified	friendsofed.com	2 KB		75ms
⊞ **GET 9781430:**	304 Not Modified	friendsofed.com	2 KB		183ms
⊞ **GET 9781430:**	304 Not Modified	friendsofed.com	3 KB		187ms
⊞ **GET book.gif**	304 Not Modified	friendsofed.com	94 B		199ms
⊞ **GET quote.gif**	304 Not Modified	friendsofed.com	152 B		212ms
⊞ **GET external**	304 Not Modified	friendsofed.com	54 B		203ms
15 requests			**45 KB** **(34 KB from cache)**		**2.21s**

Figure 6-17. Mozilla Firefox's add-on Firebug allows you to see how much bandwidth a page uses.

Caching

Caching is the method that web browsers and ISPs employ to reduce bandwidth consumption and increase the speed of pages loading. Here's how caching works: Whenever you visit a website, a copy of the files is stored in a temporary location where they can be recalled. If you revisit that page, the web browser will check with the server to see if a new version is available and if not (see Figure 6-18). Loading the locally stored copy will mean that pages do not have to be fetched every time you retype a URL. This feature of web browsers can help increase the speed your page's reload if your visitors want to navigate deeper into your website than the first page or if they choose to click the refresh button.

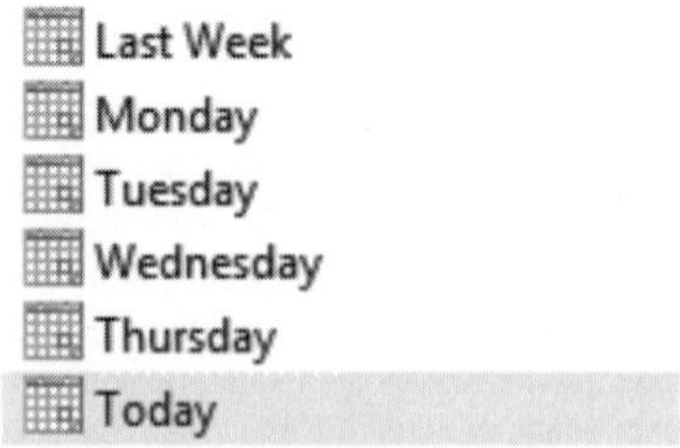

Last Week
Monday
Tuesday
Wednesday
Thursday
Today

Figure 6-18. Internet Explorer keeps a record of all the pages you have visited on the web.

The reason pages load faster on refresh is because CSS, images, and scripts are cached (a term which means that unmodified files don't have to be downloaded again). Because of the cache, as you split your design in separate files, unless you make any changes to the style document, for example, these files will be fetched from cache, and *voilà*, the subsequent pages will load faster as there is no wait for the download to occur. Reusing styles, scripts, and images in this way can dramatically increase the overall navigation experience your visitors have, and this improved experience is one of the reasons, apart from maintainability, why you should separate your style and behavior from your site structure. However, you should note that server-side includes will not be cached, because they are pulled together on the server side, not the client side.

LinkED

For more information about caching, see the comprehensive guide at http://www.mnot.net/cache_docs/.

Other Tweaks

Reducing the quality and size of the images, multimedia, video, and audio of your website will dramatically help reduce bandwidth costs and increase the speed of your website, and using CSS sprites will reduce the amount of downloading going on through the server (plus, you'll have no delay in loading the rollover. And using browser caching, with separated styles and behavior, you can also make things faster for your visitors. However, there are always other things you can do to make things faster for your visitors who suffer using dial-up Internet access.

Some other useful things you can do to help your website lose a bit of weight include the following:

- Getting rid of comments held within your site's source code will reduce the size of files.

- Removing whitespace from the code improves readability and can reduce page weight.

- Grouping your CSS will reduce reoccurrences of the same code and reduce code bulk.

- Turning on HTTP compression (if your host supports it) can also help reduce file sizes.

- Outsourcing images and scripts to other hosts (such as image hosting) can help too.

LinkED

For more performance tweaks you could implement on your website, the following guide could be helpful in getting the best mileage from your design: http://developer.yahoo.com/performance/rules.html. *This article is not meant for beginners but is certainly worth reading.*

Summary

In this chapter, you have learned about the importance of images, audio, and multimedia as alternative forms of content. You have learned about the different formats for producing your rich content and the kinds of things people produce using images and media. If you have not done so already, you should get busy being creative with these forms of enhancing your website and giving your a bit more texture and style, while keeping in mind the problems of relying on technologies like Flash and keeping file sizes low. Your website should be really coming together at this stage, and the visuals you have provided should make your site look more polished. However, there is still something we need to address. What if something goes wrong? Hopefully, your design went off without a glitch (we can dream), but there is a high probability that you may encounter issues perhaps because of to the way you coded or an inherent bug in the web browser (cue the throwing of rocks at Internet Explorer 6). Therefore, in the next chapter, we are going to look at what makes things go horribly wrong, how to get your website working across all the major browsers, and how to successfully debug your code.

Chapter Checklist

You should accomplish the following tasks before leaving this chapter:

- Understand the benefit of images, audio and video and their formats.
- Create or buy a logo and any other images you need for your website.
- Produce any materials you need and update your website as needed.

Questions and Answers

Q: *Do I need to be good with graphics and image editing?*

A: Of course not! Although many people find being able to work with images a useful skill to have, some websites on the Internet have no images on them whatsoever. Even if you do want to have images, you do not need to create them yourself (though again, having the ability would be useful). There are, for example, a wide range of stock photography websites from which you can purchase images to use within your designs. While all of this is true, being able to produce your own images will dramatically increase the complexity of web designs you are able to produce and thus give you more choice.

Q: *I am not very good with graphics, so can't I just use existing images?*

A: Many web designers are not graphic artists and have no real skill with Photoshop or another professional image editing package. Because of this, when starting out, it can be tempting (seeing all those images on the websites you like in your ideas pad) to just copy one and make it work for your website. You should not do this for two reasons: Your website should aim to be unique, and if you start taking other people's images, you are likely to end up with something that is a copy of other people's sites (like some strange hybrid). The other reason, and perhaps the most important one, is that taking and using images without permission from the creator is actually illegal; it violates international copyright law.

Q: *Why should I be interested in creating multimedia, like podcasts?*

A: The fact of the matter is that much of the entertainment industry is slowly appearing online. Most people are aware that you can buy music in a place like iTunes, and the general public is also getting used to the idea of getting television and films on demand as well (where people pay to see what they want, when they want it, without needing DVDs). While there are still many challenges with getting people used to the idea of getting everything entertainment-related on the Web, now that most people understand that you can watch media online, you have the opportunity to offer your visitors similar online content. Providing high-quality media could teach your users something or give them a convenient way to be a part of your website even if they're not at their computers. Remember that most people listen to podcasts on MP3 players, giving your site a potential offline value!

Where You Are Now:

By the end of this chapter you should have the following:

- Any images you require to enhance your design
- Audio and video if you feel your site could use it
- An investigation of the possibility of using Flash and Silverlight

Chapter 7

What If Something Goes Wrong?

It's an unfortunate fact that when you're creating a technical and precise object like a website, things can go wrong. Your issue could just be a simple case of spelling an element name wrong, or it might be something more complex, like conflicting CSS styles. Those bugs can be annoying, but they're quite easy to find and fix with a bit of patience and practice. What's more annoying is that you'll come across events when your website won't work through no fault of your own. The error might be not with your code but in the way that different web browsers interpret that code. Recognizing these problem areas and being able to fix the bugs browsers throw at you is one of the key skills of a modern web developer and will be the focus of this chapter. At this stage in this book, you've had fun playing with CSS and have a reasonably good-looking website. However, if you find your design isn't working the way you wanted or that some element is not doing as it is told in a web browser, this chapter may well be the lifesaver you have been looking for! We will take a look at the problems both web browsers and developers face with the Web and how to go about resolving any issues as they occur.

In this chapter, we'll cover the following topics:

- Some problems with the Internet and the browsers that use it
- How to investigate problems and find out their causes in code
- Methods, such as conditional comments, that you can use to fix bugs

Where Did It All Go Wrong?

Most of the problems with trying to make your website work the way you want are caused by the different ways web browsers implement standards such as CSS 2.1. Although you may be thinking to yourself, "my website looks perfectly fine in Firefox," you could find that in Internet Explorer, your website doesn't look right and things have gone downhill rather quickly. If you have not yet tested your website in more than one browser, now would be about the right time to try it, because you don't want complaints from visitors that the site looks broken (as they may just give up trying to look at your design). Websites created in Flash do not suffer this problem, as the plug-in is consistently implemented across all browsers. But if you're using HTML and especially CSS (even with JavaScript), you may just find yourself in a nightmare situation.

The Browser Wars

It has been said that laws are silent in times of war. This noble truth has proved accurate in two great battles on the Web (referred to as the browser wars) over the last few decades. There have been casualties and foul play involved both from the developer and the browser, and the scars of these epic wars have left their mark on the Internet as it stands to this day. That mark will directly affect you as you refine and continue working on your website (you may have already encountered problems needing fixing), so let me take you back in time and paint a picture depicting the fight for supremacy started between two browser makers and the rift it has left in the World Wide Web.

Web War 1.0

When the Internet became widely recognized due to media attention in the mid-1990s, a wide variety of web browsers appeared and tried to gain popular appeal among its users. The two most notable individuals who began to throw around weight to gain dominance in the market were Netscape Navigator, the most popular browser at the time (shown in Figure 7-1) and the newly released Microsoft Internet Explorer 1.0, which appeared as part of the Windows 95 Plus! pack. It seems almost poetic that both Internet Explorer and Netscape were the children of a single browser known as Mosaic, which was the first popular graphical browser and held the crown for being the most popular browser of its kind. Over the following few years, a battle had started to gained pace between the two siblings who were separated by a year of age; the new kid on the block, Internet Explorer, and the old sage, Netscape, were desperately trying to overtake each other by rapidly releasing new software versions. Unfortunately, rather than addressing critical issues with the products themselves, the updates focused more on creating new functionality in an attempt to take the lead of the browser market share.

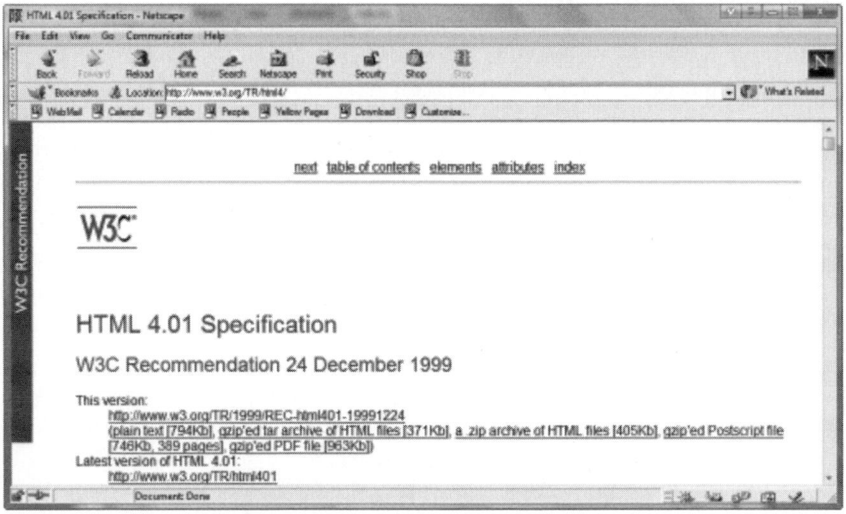

Figure 7-1. The initial competitor to Internet Explorer was Netscape.

The move that proved the heaviest blow to Netscape (and ultimately caused its downfall) was the integration of Internet Explorer 4.0 within the Microsoft Windows operating system. Anyone who made the move to upgrade to the latest versions of Microsoft Windows would be ultimately forced to have Internet Explorer pushed to them by default, as it was tightly interlocked with the operating system. This move was widely criticized as monopolistic by technology professionals worldwide (and the courts agreed, though only after a lengthy legal battle, which was very expensive and time consuming).

Other moves such as the development of a Mac version of Internet Explorer (now no longer in production) and the creation of a visual website editor (FrontPage) that focused its core functionality around Microsoft's browser helped to cause the eventual and steady collapse of the Netscape browser, and at its peak of dominance, Internet Explorer held over 90% of the browser market, a feat that has never been equaled.

Web War 2.0

To this day, Microsoft Internet Explorer remains the most dominant browser in use because of its tactics in the previous browser war to try to put down the original leader of the market, Netscape. However, in recent years, another battle has been gaining momentum, and it is strangely similar on many levels to the original browser war. As in many great battles, lessons have been learned, and the first war has shown itself to be a shining example of how things should not be done. The second browser war, which is currently underway, is what I refer to as the battle to overthrow Microsoft Internet Explorer. A number of browsers have been steadily working hard to gain market adoption while talking advantage of the fact that Microsoft has become rather sloppy in its browser maintenance and has let the time between upgrades to Internet Explorer increase, which has slowed the evolution of the Internet.

The browser that started this revolt against Internet Explorer is the now well-known and very popular Mozilla Firefox, a browser whose genealogy can be traced right back to its ancestor, the late, great Netscape. After Netscape suffered fatal blows from Internet Explorer, the choice was made to take the code to the open source community. By doing so, the Mozilla foundation was set into action to try to create a successor to Netscape that would be worthy of competing with the dominant Internet Explorer. The child of Netscape known as the Mozilla Suite was formed, but the browser failed to penetrate the market in any large proportion. However, after a couple of years work, the very first version of Firefox appeared (see Figure 7-2). Firefox was slimmer and sleeker than its predecessor (Mozilla Suite) and gained immediate recognition and rapid adoption. It has held an escalating market share ever since.

Figure 7-2. Mozilla Firefox has successfully managed to reduce Internet Explorer's market share.

In contrast to the first browser wars, the most widely adopted browser now is not necessarily the one with the most functionality (now, many of those features would be seen as bloat). Instead, the selling point is the ability to provide the most stable and standards-compliant browser possible, as the future of the of the Web and the browsers seems to be focused entirely on speed, adoption of new technologies, security, and raw power. Whether a truly standards-compliant browser will ever be achieved is a matter of debate; standards and technologies move and evolve so quickly, browser makers find it hard to keep up. Because of this, other browsers who would like to see the market share of Internet Explorer reduced in favor of their own solutions have joined forces by heavily marketing their products and providing a mixture of fixes for known security vulnerabilities and constantly updated features; examples are the browsers Opera, Safari, and Chrome.

Luckily for you, a newly fledged website creator, this second browser war works in your favor. Over recent years, these much friendlier goals for web browsers reduce the need to write yucky code to fix common flaws or independent features. The general goal is now to create a web browser that adheres to existing modern standards, which will mean more cool features we can play with. Essentially, the current situation is a case of trying to reach the finish line and end up with the most innovative, secure, and compatible browser around, which, as you can imagine, is a huge relief for everyone who builds websites on a regular basis. Just to give you a current idea of the progress made, the only old browser that currently has a dominant market share is Internet Explorer 6 (which is the version most developers tend to moan about). Once that browser has lost its battle with age, you will find that a great deal of the bugs and lack of compatibility with it will disappear, never to be seen again!

ExplainED

If you think you have been having problems getting your website to look right, just be thankful you are not currently creating HTML emails. The situation for creating HTML emails is so bad that you would probably have to go back in time 10 years in website creation to match its limitations and problems!

The Future of the Wars

Who will win this browser war? It is hard to tell, but what you should be aware of is that while multiple browsers fight for supremacy, your job, as the website maker, will be to get your site working in as many of them as possible, which is a mighty task not to be undertaken lightly. You should take into account, however, that many browsers follow the same series of standards (as mentioned previously), so trying to make your website look identical in a wide variety of browsers, in the majority of cases, has become something much easier to achieve. It is worth mentioning that, even though the second browser war is still being fought, another potential conflict is rising in the mobile device market over the next few years as Internet-capable mobile devices gain rapid popularity and a wide variety of browsers (some of whom are relatives of the desktop browsers) begin to make progress in gaining widespread use by individuals who visit the Web on the move.

LinkED

For more information about how web browsers have stood the test of time, you should check out the following timeline on Wikipedia; it details the lifespan of each related browser over the period of the web wars: http://en.wikipedia.org/wiki/Timeline_of_web_browsers.

Acid Tests

The Web Standards Project (WaSP) that I mentioned in Chapter 3 is one group who promotes the production of websites that meet industry standards. WaSP is actually involved in helping to promote this competition to become the most accurate browser possible. The group has developed a series of tests, known as the acid tests, which try and exhibit common browser flaws in how a website should be rendered and shown on the screen (see Figure 7-3). These tests score the browsers based on the level of support they have on a percentage scale. While having these tests may seem pretty cool, the great thing is that they essentially give browsers a series of goals to achieve, and the browser makers, in general, pay attention and try to deal with the problems that occur. Although using acid tests does draw attention away from the specifications, it promotes healthy competition and a clear method of seeing just how sloppy a browser is in general. To date, there have been three acid tests, each pushing the boundaries of browsers. Hopefully, there will be more to come in the future.

Figure 7-3. Because this image showed correctly in Mozilla Firefox, it passed the Acid test and conformed to standards.

LinkED

For more information about the three acid tests, visit http://www.acidtests.org/. Wikipedia also has some great articles that you can link to from the site.

Mobile Madness

The problem with mobile devices started when the old language of mobile devices (Wireless Markup Language) was overtaken by the use of HTML and CSS to make websites accessed on mobile platforms look almost as they would on a desktop browser. As I mentioned in Chapter 5, the handheld at-selector was created for the sole intention of being able to target handheld devices such as mobile phones (and in CSS3, this feature has been enhanced to target browsers based on specific conditions such as height and width). However, due to inconsistent implementation of standards, some browsers faithfully implement the selector, and others ignore it completely, making the task of trying to give mobile devices usable style sheets to make your website look as beautiful on a phone as a desktop browser has become almost impossible. Most modern mobile handset browsers, rather than use a specialist handheld style sheet, simply split the website into sections and allow you to browse around these portions of the canvas (the area where the site displays, such as the one shown in Figure 7-4) by scrolling or flicking between them, depending on whether your handset has a touch screen. This innovation started with the highly successful iPhone, which put forward the concept of making a mobile device a genuine Internet device.

Figure 7-4. On a mobile device, things may not always look the same as on your computer.

LinkED

The invention of media queries in CSS3 allows you to be more selective over what style will be applied, by specifying the width, height, aspect-ratio, color, *and* orientation *of the device, you have more control over the way you site looks. Details can be found at* http://www.w3.org/TR/css3-mediaqueries/.

Some people have managed to stem the problem by using scripts to detect the mobile devices one by one and serving them a separate style sheet. However, with the release of devices such as the iPhone and the Google Android G1, which make use of desktop rendering engines, the scripts may be unable to tell the difference between these devices and desktop machines. Also, the sheer number of devices that appear every year is a problem. The list of available devices would be impossibly long to maintain, and each could have its own browser. While the majority of Web traffic now comes from cell phones that support HTML and CSS (thankfully), some devices still use WML, which means you might have two different languages to deal with. Of course, these WML devices are becoming much less common, and you could probably just leave them out in the cold.

Now that you know the doom and gloom of the situation, what can you do about it? Well, the same applies advice to mobile devices as desktop browsers. Using emulators and actual phones (get your friends and family to test your site on their phones) and debugging as you go (which requires a level of patience) are the only realistic ways you can get around the problem if you want your main website to work effectively in mobile browsers. If this task seems huge with the number of devices out there, remember that you only really need to deal with mobile devices that actually visit your site. Consider which mobile platforms to test on a case-by-case basis—the iPhone is always a good start; it's the most popular device out there, no matter how much you love or hate Apple. Trying to prematurely deal with every device in existence isn't worth the hassle or stress as it just isn't achievable (and would be very time consuming).

LinkED

To learn more about how mobile devices cope with the use of CSS and how you can try to overcome the problem, visit this article: http://www.alistapart.com/articles/return-of-the-mobile-stylesheet.

What if you really want to have a website that is specially adapted for mobile users and don't want to go through all the hassle of making your lovely website even more flexible? Many designers are starting a trend of making a specific mobile website with a minimalist look and feel (with less graphics and faster load times because of the reduced amount of stuff on each page). The thought of making another dedicated website might sound rather drastic, but with the increase in mobile devices accessing the Web, it might be useful for your visitors.

Of course, the key to making a mobile site is to keep it simple: Don't use lots of columns and plug-ins. Don't rely on a specific width for the content. And most importantly, keep the images and flourishes to a minimum. If you own a cell phone, you probably know that handsets have data charges, which are pretty expensive, so keeping things clean and simple is the key to ensuring the best, and cheapest, experience for your visitors and also helps people with slow connections get access to your website at a reasonable speed.

LinkED

Creating a mobile-specific website is usually simpler than creating a site for a browser, as you will be keeping the design simple and streamlined. An interesting trend with these mobile sites is to list the site in a subdomain called m *(for "mobile"), such as* http://m.alistapart.com/.

Web Renderers

The most important part of a web browser is what goes on behind the scenes. To keep things simple, a rendering engine is nothing more than the code within a browser that organizes the contents of a website on your screen. Each rendering engine is developed by a different organization, and usually, multiple browsers share that engine as the basis for their own web browsers. So overall, the level of support for web standards remains relatively high. There are actually a wide variety of rendering engines, all of which have different levels of support for various technologies and standards on the Web. The ones I list in this section have the most relevance to how people browse the Web. I have included a mixture of desktop, mobile (or handheld), and textual browsers for you, so that you can understand how different browsers are actually related to each other (at the code and genetic levels), as this understanding will give you some insight into how you might go about testing your website across different systems.

Here are some desktop layout engines (ordered by popularity):

- **Trident:** Used by Microsoft Internet Explorer (versions 4-8), MSN Explorer, AOL Explorer, and Microsoft Outlook
- **Gecko:** Used by Mozilla Firefox, Camino, Thunderbird and Netscape 6 and above
- **Webkit / KHTML:** Used by Apple Safari, Google Chrome, and Konqueror
- **Presto:** Used by Opera (desktop version only)
- **Tasman:** Used by Microsoft Entourage, MSN Explorer (for Mac only), and Internet Explorer (for Mac only)

And these are some mobile layout engines (ordered by popularity):

- **Webkit/KHTML:** Used by the iPhone, iPod Touch, Google Android, Myriad, Iris, WebOS, and Nokia models 40/S60
- **NetFront:** Used by the Amazon Kindle, NetFront, PS3, PSP, cell phones and PDAs
- **IEMobile:** Used by Windows Mobile devices, Windows CE, and some PDAs
- **Presto:** Used by Opera (Mini and Mobile) and Nintendo (DS-I and Wii)
- **Mango:** Used by the Blackberry Browser
- **Lumi:** Used by Polaris, various cell phones, and some smart phones
- **SkyFire:** Used by Windows Mobile and some other devices
- **Gecko:** Used by Fennec and Minimo
- **OpenWave:** Used by WAP phones

Other rendering engines include Teashark and WebTV. You might even find some people visit your site using a text-only browser, such as Lynx, in which case they wouldn't see any of your images or multimedia. Figure 7-5 shows a breakdown of the market share of the most popular web browsers in use today. These are the ones you will most likely focus your attention on.

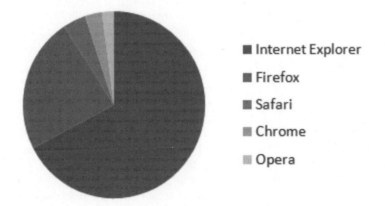

Figure 7-5. The most popular web browsers (according to Net Applications) for the third quarter of 2009

It should be noted that general browser market share data provided by Net Applications were used as the determining factor to denote which browsers were marked as popular in retrospect of usage figures.

Though a lot of devices are listed in this section, just remember that all rendering engines (depending on their version) will show graphically the same thing (with the exception of those listed as "other rendering engines"). Therefore when experimenting with web browsers or trying to understand how people browse the Web, you will require only one browser for each rendering engine with the following notable exceptions:

- Microsoft Internet Explorer has always been fairly ambiguous and troublesome with its support for web technology. Therefore, it is always worth treating each version of the browser as a separate and independent browser for the purposes of classifying each rendering engine.

- While Webkit and KHTML (the predecessor of Webkit that Apple forked into a separate project) are related in that they have evolved from the same basic rendering engine (KHTML), the rendering engines are now developed separately, so differences may occur.

- Though both Apple Safari and Google Chrome use the same rendering engines, minor differences have been spotted between their rendering choices, especially those involving JavaScript, where they use entirely different rendering models.

LinkED

If you would like to read more about the different rendering engines and web browsers available and their adoption of technology, you can read the following Wikipedia article on the subject: http://en.wikipedia.org/wiki/Comparison_of_web_browsers.

Playing the Blame Game

Who is to blame for all of the problems that exist on the Web? Is it the fault of the browser makers who tried so hard to gain popularity that they started deviating from the specifications? Is it the fault of developers who got sloppy so the browser makers had to work around their needs? Or is it the fault of the W3C for not turning around updates and newer versions quickly enough to deal with the ever-increasing needs of everyone else? In truth, the fault lies a little with all three. But now, we should take a look at where things have gone seriously wrong to the point of insanity, how we can keep up to date with the latest problems discovered, and more importantly, when we should choose to simply stop supporting older browsers in favor of new ones.

Market Shares

The importance of a web browser is entirely based on the number of active users it has. If you find, for example, that 60% of people using your website do so using Internet Explorer, you know that your browser must work in that rendering engine (Trident), and to a further extent, the concept of deciding which browsers to support branches down to individual versions of browsers (especially in Internet Explorer where rendering is inconsistent across versions). Just like the stock market, the number of people using various browsers goes up and down on a daily basis, and even some of the really old browsers can occasionally make a blip on the radar. You can determine which browsers are important to support by following the percentages of people who use those products through a mixture of what you find in your statistics package (the browser information section) and statistics gathered by independent groups who provide market research information into what people use to browse the Web. For an example, check out the Net Applications market research site in Figure 7-6.

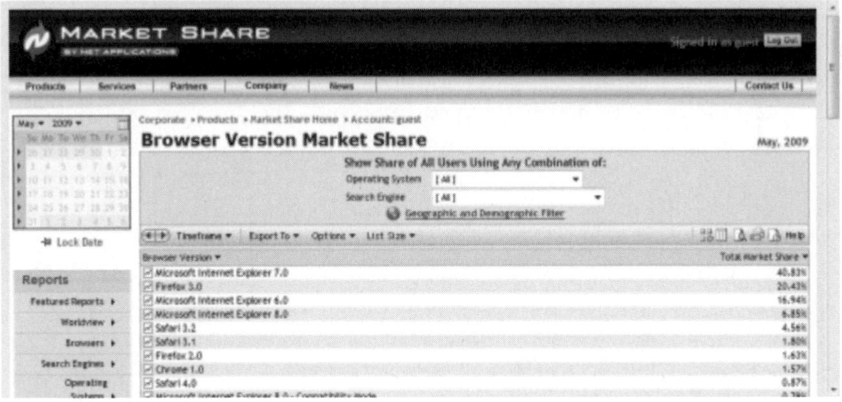

Figure 7-6. Net Applications provides one of the most well-established usage statistics websites.

ExplainED

Not only does market share apply to the browsers, but through statistic gathering, we can also determine the percentage of people using a certain resolution. That information can be useful if you're creating fixed-width layouts.

While the potential for knowing more about your visitors is fantastic, remember that a lot of factors influence a statistic. Statistics are meant to be used as nothing more than a rough guide, because the information can be overestimate (or underestimated) and skewed by the type of audience who visits websites where logging occurs. Statistics on the Web may not be entirely accurate, but they are the closest you can get to knowing exactly what browsers are in use by the majority of people who browse the Internet on a regular basis—these are the browsers you must ensure your website will work with.

LinkED

For details about web browsers currently in use, the following article keeps a close eye on the demographics for browser users at http://en.wikipedia.org/wiki/Usage_share_of_web_browsers, *though it doesn't list the W3Schools statistics available at* http://www.w3schools.com/browsers/browsers_stats.asp.

How we make use of browser-usage statistics is simple: the general rule is that, at a basic level, your website should work with the top five browsers (see Figure 7-5). As the situation currently stands, working with the top five means you account not only for the majority of in-use rendering engines but for discrepancies that may occur among individual browsers. For extensive testing, which is advised if you want to ensure maximum compatibility, the general rule is that you should ensure your website works within any browser which holds more than 1% of all visits to your website (or if you use global statistics, the Internet). The reason for this is that there are around 1.5 billion people who have access to the Internet (according to http://www.internetworldstats.com/stats.htm), and this means that 15 million people make up that 1%—that is a lot of potential visitors you don't want to ignore.

Dropping Support

Choosing the appropriate time to stop supporting a web browser can be a complicated process because of the partial fault of web browsers refusing to support standards and the continued use of those browsers by people on the Web. Many developers are left in a stalemate position: we cannot simply just stop allowing people who use old browsers to our websites, and we certainly can't try to force users to download another browser. It was once estimated that 90% of people who encounter a major problem in visiting a website (even in an old browser) will leave it immediately, and less than 1% of people who are met with a request to download or use a different browser will do so. As you are in a position where you are making your very first website, you need to look at what browsers are currently in use. As your website is new and will have few statistics of its own, you should use existing statistics from places like Net Applications. Then, use that information to check your website in the various browsers (how to do this is explained later in the conditions, quirks, and filters section of this chapter). Once you know where the errors are, it is up to you to make a judgment call of which to address (some basic guidance on how to make those calls is also given in the next section).

As mentioned previously, I recommend that you try to support browsers with over 1% of the total browser market share. However, as long as your website works well within the most recent versions of the five popular web browsers (Internet Explorer versions 6-8, Firefox, Safari, Chrome, and Opera) you should be| fine.

hasLayout

Internet Explorer contains its own property built into the rendering engine, which allows it to dictate whether an element is responsible for its own layout sizing or whether it should automatically inherit the ancestry of its parents. This idea sounds good for something that can be turned on or off, but if left unchecked, it can seriously damage your website design within Internet Explorer. When the property is set to true, the element will look after itself, but if the value is false, the element will rely on parents. In the majority of cases, it is in your best interests when problems start occurring to set hasLayout to true (see Figure 7-7). Leaving hasLayout set to false can cause missing content, content appearing and then disappearing or getting misplaced however some elements such as html, body, tables, input, img, hr, frames, object, and embed are automatically given hasLayout, which gives them immunity from the issue.

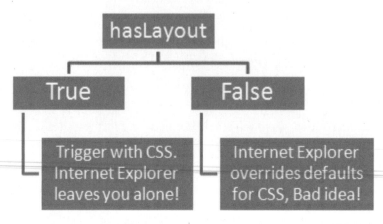

Figure 7-7. If you don't ensure hasLayout is triggered, things might go wonky!

While all of this may be confusing, all you really need to know is hasLayout is a bad boy. He rebels against the natural order of things and gets up to all sorts of trouble, and his master (Internet Explorer) makes use of him even though you, as someone building a website, will get very frustrated with what it tends to do. So how do we punish hasLayout? Well, your options are either to trigger having layout within the problematic element through giving height, width, position: absolute, float, or display: inline-block or ,within Internet Explorer 7, to give overflow, position: fixed, or minimum and maximum width and height properties to trigger the effect. My recommendation is to take into account hasLayout existence and then come back and face those issues when something doesn't work properly in Internet Explorer. Fixing bugs can be tedious and annoying but it's a necessary evil in CSS, as you will find out soon.

LinkED

For more information about the hasLayout *element of the Internet Explorer Trident engine (and a very interesting guide to the subject and how it may help you resolve basic issues), check out the following website:* http://www.satzansatz.de/cssd/onhavinglayout.html.

Conditions, Quirks, and Filters

Now, you know about the existing problems within web browsers and understand why it is important to address them, so how can you work around those problems? The first thing you will do is check that your code is valid and that everything looks consistent by testing the site within a multitude of different browsers, including various versions of each one (especially Internet Explorer). Next, you need to fix the problems affecting the way your website looks in the browsers your visitors intend on using. This section takes into account everything you have learned about CSS to help you discover, isolate, resolve, and fix your problems, and it tells you what you can do to prevent them. If you are at the stage where you want everything to look as perfect as possible across every browser, you should do your best to iron out some of the wrinkles.

Discovering Problems

Get out your magnifying glass, Sherlock, and we'll go on an adventure to see exactly how well put together and durable your website really is! Actually, this detection process isn't so much a case of what you did wrong but how some of the gremlins in the web browsers started messing with your perfectly coded design. You can take various steps, in terms of testing through browsers to validating and debugging your code manually or automatically, but the important thing here is that we uncover the issues that have appeared and work out exactly what is going wrong under the hood of your website. After all without seeking out the clues, how can you expect to solve the mystery? Once you have discovered some nasty little bugs to take a swipe at, you will be ready to move onto the next section of this chapter, which thankfully shows you how to exterminate the little pests.

The Human Touch

When checking if your website works properly, there is no substitute to getting your visitors to report bugs and issues as they find them. Much of web design is based around getting feedback from the people who use the service, and as they control the very devices you want to adapt to, their input is imperative to the long-term survival of your website. The two primary ways in which user testing sessions are carried out are through beta testing, where you get a bunch of people to find any strange, noticeable bugs, and stress testing, where you get a select group of people to try every feature and play with everything over a period of time to try and draw out any more hidden flaws that may exist. These methods are worth using once your website has enough visitors for the response to be worthwhile, so we have to rely on our own testing methods at the moment. However, keep these ideas in mind for when you want to know how you can further improve the user experience in the future.

ExplainED

You could, perhaps, get people to test your website by giving them free access to something you offer (if you are planning on selling a service) or listing their names in a page of credits for people who have assisted you, with links to their own websites!

W3C Validators

Before you start testing your website for problems, you need to make sure that your code is valid. While you have probably taken a lot of care putting your website together and checking it in your default browser, one of the most common reasons websites tend to suffer glitches is due to mistakes (however small!) that accidentally appeared in your code. Checking for mistakes could not be easier: All you need to do is go to one of the validation websites; put in your website address (or copy and paste the code, if it's not on the Web), and click the validate button. You will receive an overview of problems on that page. Note that this works on only a single page at a time; you will need to manually check each page on your site for issues using the validator. Because, in previous chapters, we took the time to look over how HTML and CSS work and how you should use tags to ensure semantic value, you should find that there are relatively few issues with your code, which is more than could be said if you used an editor like Microsoft FrontPage. However, if you do find any issues, there should be explanations of where the error is (though the results can be confusing at times) and how you should fix it.

Try It Yourself: Validating Your Website

Check out these useful online code validation services and resolve any issues as they occur:

- **W3C Validation Service**: Validate HTML, XHTML, and SVG code at http://validator.w3.org/ (see Figure 7-8).
- **Jigsaw Validation Service**: Validate your CSS code at http://jigsaw.w3.org/css-validator/.

- **FeedValidator**: Your RSS and Atom can be validated at http://www.feedvalidator.org/.

- **Validome**: WML and XML code can be checked at http://www.validome.org/.

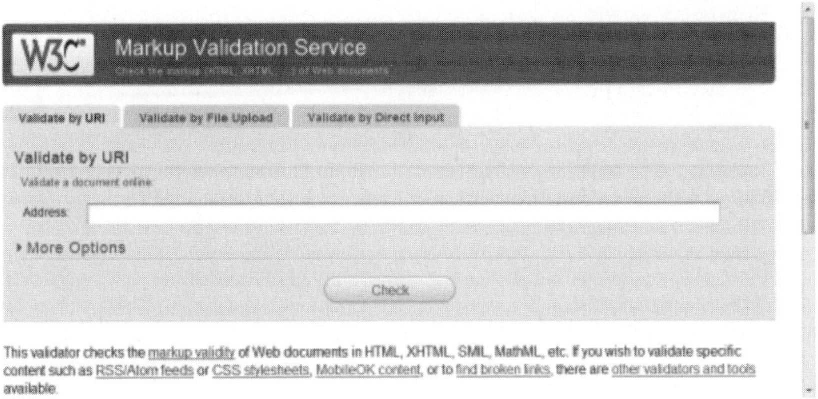

Figure 7-8. The W3C validator can check your website uses clean and semantically correct code

ExplainED

Although getting your site as valid as possible is important, in cases like opacity, using invalid code is better than risking compatibility issues. This advice may sound contradictory, but while consistency is important in design, proprietary code can be seen as undesirable but cleanly coded when implemented.

Browser Emulators

Now that you know your source code is valid (hopefully fixing any bugs the validators detected), it is time to wander into the territory of testing your site in multiple browsers. This is the primary way in which many inconsistencies in visual appearance are spotted. In the case of Windows, versions of every major browser are available to download for free on the Internet, and you can run them alongside each other to test for the majority of users. Mac users will require software such as Parallels or Bootcamp and a valid Windows installation to take care of Windows-only products such as Internet Explorer. And Linux users will need a virtualization program such as VirtualBox or Wine for the same reason. As for getting the other browsers that you cannot run alongside each other (such as multiple versions of Internet Explorer), you can use a mixture of virtual machines (created using technologies such as Microsoft Virtual PC or VMware), emulators, or online screenshot utilities that capture images of your pages. Sounds confusing? Don't worry; we'll go through each of these elements in turn.

Try It Yourself: Testing Your Website in Different Browsers

Let's get started checking your website through the variety of browsers that exist. You will want to download and install various browsers so that you can see if there are any problems and fix them until things look like as you intended (how to debug and fix the issues is explained later in this section). Visit the following websites, and follow the steps to get the browsers up and running (each of these is considered a popular browser):

- **Microsoft Internet Explorer**: http://www.microsoft.com/windows/internet-explorer/
- **Mozilla Firefox**: http://www.mozilla.com/firefox/
- **Apple Safari**: http://www.apple.com/safari/
- **Google Chrome**: http://www.google.com/chrome/ (see Figure 7-9)
- **Opera**: http://www.opera.com/

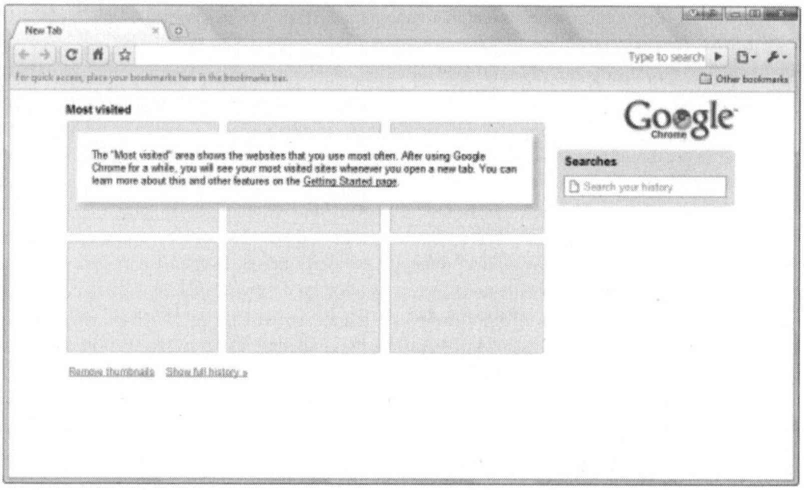

Figure 7-9. Google Chrome is one of the newest web browsers to gain popular support.

Once you have the browsers downloaded, you can open your website in them to see if things look right. If they do, awesome! If not, make a note of the problems you have found, and we will work on fixing them when we start debugging your source code a bit later on in this section of the chapter as part of playing detective and debugging gracefully (which we shall soon encounter).

LinkED

If you would like to download previous versions of well-known and popular browsers, the simplest way is to visit the browser archive at Evolt (http://browsers.evolt.org/), download the product of choice, and install it. Note that not all browsers will work happily together, so be careful what you install.

Try It Yourself: Emulating the Other Browsers

The simplest way to emulate browsers that do not work well together (like various versions of Internet Explorer) is to use a piece of software designed to allow multiple versions of the product to be used (see Figure 7-10). A few are in common use, and many of these work fairly well. However, they are in no way replacements for an actual or virtual machine environment that uses the genuine product out of the box. However, if you do not want to mess with virtual machines, choose one of the following Emulators for testing various browser versions:

- **BrowserCam**: http://www.browsercam.com/
- **BrowserLab**: https://browserlab.adobe.com/
- **IETester**: http://www.my-debugbar.com/wiki/IETester/HomePage
- **IE Collection**: http://finalbuilds.edskes.net/iecollection.htm
- **MultipleIE's**: http://tredosoft.com/Multiple_IE
- **Spoon Sandbox**: http://www.spoon.net/Browsers/
- **SuperPreview**: http://expression.microsoft.com/en-us/ dd565874.aspx

These products are easy to install and run, and they can give you a preview of your site in various available browser versions. Figure 7-10 gives you an example of IETester in action. This product enables you to see how your website will function and look within Internet Explorer version 5.5 through 8 (four generations of the browser). These make excellent additions to your testing regime so feel free to make use of them alongside conventional browser tests.

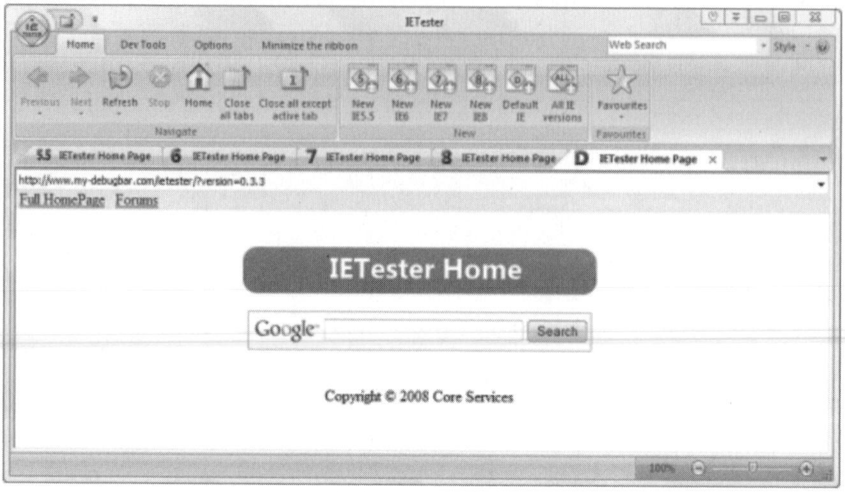

Figure 7-10. IETester is a small, compact product that lets you preview your website in various Internet Explorer versions.

ExplainED

You can actually emulate Internet Explorer 7 within Internet Explorer 8 if you use the developer tools! Select Tools ➤ Developer Tools *or press* F12 *to launch, and click* Browser Mode; *you can switch between Internet Explorer 7, Internet Explorer 8, and the compatibility mode for Internet Explorer 8 (which does have its own differences)!*

Try It Yourself: Virtualizing Web Browsers

While emulators can be a simple way of checking your website in various browsers, they are not as accurate or reliable as virtualization. Therefore, here, we will examine setting up a virtualized environment so you can test the various web browsers available in a virtual machine. The quickest and easiest of these methods is available to Windows users through Windows Virtual PC. You can download and install the product, and you can install whichever of the available Internet Explorer packs you need, or you can download the specific browser you want to be able to check your website in. These are called Virtual

CDs (VCDs), and links to both are provided in this section. Mac and Linux users have equivalent software available and can be found using a quick Google search, so the process will be more or less the same (though these systems may require a valid Windows installation disk as well).

To download the software to set up Windows Virtual PC, visit http://www.microsoft.com/windows/virtual-pc/default.aspx.

To install the virtual CDs (VCDs) for the browser software, visit http://www.microsoft.com/downloads/details.aspx?FamilyId=21EABB90-958F-4B64-B5F1-73D0A413C8EF.

Try It Yourself: Online Screenshot Services

The final way you can check your website in various browsers (if you do not want to install anything on your computer) is to use one of the many screenshot services. To use these services, type in your website address, and select a browser (or series of them), and the servers on the website will capture a screenshot of your website in that chosen web browser. Because you do not need to install anything, these services can be pretty useful if you have limited hard disk space. However, some critical disadvantages are that waiting times for screenshots can run into hours depending how busy the service is; many of the services aren't free, so there is an incurred monthly cost; and more importantly, you do not get to interact with the page, which could mean other underlying issues are not visible on first loading and are likely to be entirely missed altogether. Of course, for quick snapshots, these services can be genuinely useful, but they should not be the sole method of testing used.

Here are a few online website screenshot services that you can try if you prefer to use this option for testing:

- **BrowserPhoto**: http://www.netmechanic.com/products/browser-index.shtml
- **BrowserPool**: http://www.browserpool.de/kc/wob/portal.jsp?lang=en
- **BrowserShots**: http://browsershots.org/ (see Figure 7-11)
- **BrowsrCamp**: http://www.browsrcamp.com/
- **IE Net Renderer**: http://ipinfo.info/netrenderer/
- **Litmus**: http://litmusapp.com/

Figure 7-11. BrowserShots gives you the opportunity to see your site in various browsers for free.

Try It Yourself: Emulating Mobile Devices

While all of the previously mentioned techniques—virtualization, screenshots, and emulators—are great at assisting you in checking that your website works on standard browsers, what will you do about mobile devices? Well, there are genuinely only two realistic approaches you can take to getting your website to work across a variety of mobile phones. First, you can visit your website on the devices themselves. This option is probably not the most realistic, but you could perhaps go into your local cell phone supplier and play around with them to see how things will look (if they allow you to). Other than that, you could use one of the many emulators that exist (yes, more bits of software to install or websites to visit). Because each mobile device is different, you will find that discrepancies will occur in how your website looks on each. However by using the following emulators, you can reduce the chances of a seriously damaged website displaying as the result of neglecting testing:

- **Android SDK**: http://developer.android.com/sdk/1.5_r2/index.html
- **Blackberry Simulator**: http://www.blackberry.com/developers/downloads/simulators/
- **Dot Mobi Emulator**: http://mtld.mobi/emulator.php
- **Klondike WAP Browser**: http://apachesoftware.com/download.html (WML only)
- **NetFront SDK**: https://www.access.co.jp/english/nf/form_WAVE.php

- **Nokia Browser Simulator**:
  http://www.forum.nokia.com/info/sw.nokia.com/id/db2c69a2-4066-46ff-81c4-caac8872a7c5/NMB40_install.zip.html

- **OpenWave Emulator**:
  http://developer.openwave.com/dvl/member/index.htm?softwareId=23
  (see Figure 7-12)

- **Opera Mini Demo**: http://www.opera.com/mini/demo/

- **Opera Mobile:** Open the Opera browser and navigate to the *View* ➤ *Small Screen* menu.

- **Windows Mobile:** http://msdn.microsoft.com/en-gb/windowsmobile/bb264327.aspx

Figure 7-12. The OpenWave simulator will show your website on a mobile handset.

While the listed well-known emulators will do a good job, note that many phones like Google's Android G1 and Apple's iPhone will display your website like a desktop browser, making use of zoom functionality to look at specific sections of a website (which means less work for you).

Playing Detective

Now that you know the various ways you can check to see if everything looks fine, it is time to learn how to work out where any problems are occurring. In the majority of cases (and with plenty of practice), you can look through the source code and know approximately what region of the structure the problems are affecting. For example, if you found that a paragraph of text would not italicize properly, the issue is likely to occur in the CSS reference for that element. You can then relate that knowledge to the CSS style you have applied to reduce the amount of code you need to debug. But how do you know which of those properties is causing the problems? The aim of learning to debug code is not just using the various tools mentioned previously to know when problems occur but pinpointing the locations of problems and playing detective to discover why the problem occurred!

Possible causes of problems in how your website looks and works could be something like a conflict between two statements you made. Some rules override others, and you might have forgotten about a previous reference that is hijacking your repeat code later on. Or the culprit could be a parent with higher specificity overriding a child element. This is something we looked at carefully in Chapter 5, because it's yet another conflict that can occur. You problem could also be that you forgot to add something into the code (always something to check if you are forgetful) or simply a case of the browser in question not following the specification correctly, which is most likely if you find a strange effect being rendered.

To determine the root cause of an issue, we use a browser extension known as a developer tool, which lets us enable, disable, and edit certain styles on the fly. Using developer tools like the ones shown in Figure 7-13, we can tinker with the source code to learn how other CSS properties are interacting with the style and where the quirk started causing the inconsistency to occur.

Each of the major browsers has a different set of browser tools you can access:

- **Internet Explorer 8**: Go to the *Tools* ➤ *Developer Tools* menu, or press F12 to launch.

- **Mozilla Firefox**: Install Firebug from http://getfirebug.com/, and press F12 to launch or go to the *Tools* ➤ *Firebug* menu for more information and options.

- **Apple Safari**: Select *Edit* ➤ *Preferences* ➤ *Advanced* ➤ *Show Developer Menu*. Then press Ctrl + Alt + I to launch or go to the *Develop* menu for more information and options.

- **Google Chrome**: Go to the *Control* ➤ *Developer* menu, or press Ctrl + Shift + J to launch the developer tools.

- **Opera**: Go to the *Tools* ➤ *Advanced* ➤ *Developer Tools* menu to launch the debugger.

LinkED

It should be noted that Internet Explorer 7 and lower do not natively contain any debugging tools; therefore, you will need to download the Internet Explorer developer toolbar from the Microsoft website: http://www.microsoft.com/windows/downloads/details.aspx?FamilyID=e59 c3964-672d-4511-bb3e-2d5e1db91038.

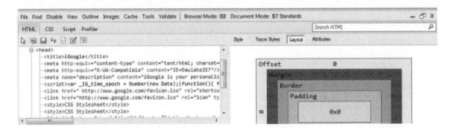

Figure 7-13. The Internet Explorer developer tools allow you to debug your code quickly and easily.

If you find a piece of code that isn't behaving correctly, the first thing you need to do is isolate the problem, so you know exactly what is causing the web browser to have a hissy fit. You can use many different methods to discover this. First, you could use one of the above tools (from the browser emulators section) and look through your source code disabling things that could be affecting your design. Think logically at this stage: if, for example, your text won't italicize, you could try disabling any code in the design that triggers font-style. That's pretty straightforward, right? Being able to turn styles on and off at your own command is a great way to see what might be making funny things happen. Of course, not everyone likes using browser tools, so another option is to wrap properties in CSS comments or remove them entirely to see if that helps. The process of debugging a website is really not so much an explicit technique as just following the simple rules of cause and effect and deciding what elements could affect that particular type of style and how this could affect the resulting web page. In other words, trial and error is a simple, effective, and popular method of debugging code.

Once you have disabled all of the possible elements that could affect your design, enable each CSS property one at a time (while previewing in each browser) to see what happens. If the problem reoccurs once you enable a line of code, you know where the problem lies. Of course, once you have spent time poking around the code to find the problem, you need to focus on fixing the issue entirely. To fix the problem, you need to first check that you are applying the code correctly—if you made a mistake, fix it. If the error isn't in the code, you can finding another way to go about the same task to remove the problem (perhaps giving added specificity or triggering hasLayout) or use a browser bug website to find out if the issue has been reported before and how to fix it. Plenty of known problems are out there, and luckily for you, some good sites document the issues and how to fix them. Think of these sites like a giant help file! Then too, you can use a browser-specific hack or filter, such as conditional comments, to resolve the inconsistency by force.

ExplainED

Do not blame yourself for issues you encounter, as the world's best developers have problems getting things to work half of the time. You are not cheapening the value of your website by using hacks and filters when they are required, because they are a necessary evil until browsers conform to standards.

Debugging your source code can be a complicated procedure, as you do not want to alter something that will break other browsers, and you certainly do not want to resort to using hacks and filters unless you have to. The truth of the matter is that much of fixing problems between browsers is down to playing detective, and while debuggers can assist you in determining the cause of the problem, resolving the problem itself can be something those who are new to building websites (such as yourself) may find it perplexing and frustrating.

Because this book has trained you to use semantic and valid source code, the number of problems you will receive should be kept to a minimum, and with the aid of website validation, the errors you accidently made can be quickly resolved. For the bugs that are not your fault, if you find that none of the information in the issue tracking section is helping and you know which browser is explicitly giving you trouble (my money is on Internet Explorer 6), just take a calm, deep breath, and I will help you address the issue.

Debugging Gracefully

Fixing bugs and issues inside CSS can be a tricky business. You want to ensure that only affected browsers respond to the treatment and keep the code as semantic and clean of bulk and mess as possible (and of course, you want to avoid code that won't validate). Therefore, the following information is provided to help duct tape that leaky drain shut and stop your code from oozing all over you otherwise glorious website. For the purpose of keeping things simple, while there are issues with other browsers rendering engines such as Gecko, Webkit, and Presto, the majority of all problems involving website design (and their inconsistencies) are typically the result of early versions of Internet Explorer. Once Internet Explorer 6 disappears permanently, the majority of bugs that need to be addressed will die with it.

Hacks and Filters

Knowing that web browsers across the board have inconsistencies and knowing which ones are popular enough that you should care how they see your website is one thing, but knowing what bugs exist within those browsers may help you recognize symptoms while you are testing within browsers. Therefore, as we start addressing the diagnosis and treatment of your website in particular, note that a variety of websites hold a database of known problems within various web browsers and solutions to overcome the issues. When you go through this section of the chapter, these resources will be extremely valuable to help you deal with the problems you may in your own website once you see it through the eyes of another browser (I have left this step until now to ensure you have the resources to deal with the problems and understand the implications of some of the fixes used).

NotED

Internet Explorer has a proprietary CSS property called zoom. *It does not work in other browsers and won't validate, but it triggers* hasLayout *and therefore may be useful for testing purposes, as it can be useful in debugging Internet Explorer.*

So what exactly are hacks and filters? As you already know, the web browser has, through a mixture of evolution and blatant faulty programming, developed all sorts of nasty quirks that result in your lovely semantically correct website getting all confused and rendering incorrectly across browsers. Through validation and the use of emulators, you have seen firsthand what your website looks like in various browsers, and by now, you are probably sick of hearing about how things have gone funky. We now need to look at hacks and filters to target flaws the way those browsers render CSS (or features that they give for the task), so we can work around the problems caused by a browser going rogue on our source code.

See for Yourself: Using Bugs, Hacks, Filters, and More

These websites contain in-depth information about browser bugs and the use of hacks and filters to fix them:

- **Centricle:** http://centricle.com/ref/css/filters/
- **CSS Discuss:** http://css-discuss.incutio.com/
- **CSS Tests:** http://www.brunildo.org/test/
- **Dynamic Site Solutions:** http://www.dynamicsitesolutions.com/css/filters/support-chart/
- **Gérard Talbot:** http://www.gtalbot.org/BrowserBugsSection/
- **Position Is Everything:** http://www.positioniseverything.net/
- **QuirksMode:** http://www.quirksmode.org/
- **Rich In Style:** http://www.richinstyle.com/bugs/
- **WebDevOut:** http://www.webdevout.com/

The problems with using hacks and filters are many, so you may be wondering why I'm providing information about them at all. It is important you know how browsers interpret code in case you ever find yourself trying to deal with a problem that is not related to Internet Explorer (Internet Explorer issues can be dealt with using conditional comments, which are discussed next). You could be quite tempted to start using a hack or filter to get a browser to behave the way you intended. But even if you keep all of your hacks separate from your main style sheets so you can eliminate them as old browsers die out, hacks are considered unstable, and there are no guarantees that they will work if a browser is updated. This debate into whether you should use hacks or filters ends with the conclusion we made earlier about using invalid or quirky code to try and solve problems: only use this trick if you find there is no other choice—and "no other choice" includes asking yourself whether having something look slightly different is bearable enough that you can live with it!

Overcoming the Double-Margin Float Bug

OK, let's put everything we have mentioned on problem solving into action with a nice, easy-to-follow example. I'll show you how a known issue in

Internet Explorer, the double-margin bug, can be overcome. The double-margin float bug is a common issue of Internet Explorer, which is still in use today. So what causes the problem? If you take advantage of the float: right; property and give it a right margin of something like 50 pixels, you should have (you guessed it) an element floated to the right-hand side of the screen that is indented 50 pixels:

```
<h3>Title</h3>
<p>Normal Text</p>
<p style="float: right; margin-right: 50px; border: 1px solid
#000000;">Indented text</p>
```

But what does Internet Explorer 6 do? If you view the preceding code in a browser like Firefox (attached to some HTML), you will notice it looks exactly how it should. But try that code in Internet Explorer 6 and the browser strangely applies twice the margin specified in your source code, as shown in Figure 7-14. Now, that isn't what we asked for, we wanted 50 pixels, not 100! After testing a page that suffers this bug, you now have the problem of inconsistent browser rendering, so what do you do?

Figure 7-14. Firefox (left) displays the page with the correct margin, but Internet Explorer 6 (right) doubles the indentation to the paragraph when it shouldn't.

Of course, at this stage, we know where the problem occurred, but what if we didn't? Say, for example, you tested the website in Internet Explorer 6 and suddenly saw this problem for the first time. You would probably be confused and quite taken aback at the serious visible difference the browsers show. To help you in that case, I'll explain the process of playing detective and finding out where the problem occurs. In our example, the difference only seems to occur in a single paragraph of text (everything else looks how it should), so by definition, we must assume that the problem is the paragraph (or at least the style applied to it). Looking inside the source code doesn't really tell us much other than the code is floated to the right-hand side (as it isn't entirely at the right, this could be the issue) and the size of the right margin (which could also be causing problems). Of course, we have two possible causes of problems, because both of the CSS properties we have declared directly influence the right-hand side of the element where the problem is occurring.

Which of the two elements is the problem, and why does it happen? As for why it happens, no one really knows but in working out which of the two elements it is, you attempt to fix your page by replacing the margin with some padding. Of course, this doesn't seem to help, especially if you have a background color or image that gets spread to the edge of the screen. You can't seem to figure out why the code isn't working, so you should next see if someone else has encountered the fault. Because this problem is well documented, after doing a Google search for "double-margin float bug," you find an article on Position Is Everything that explains the problem and how it can be solved (see Figure 7-15). While sending you to search the Internet might sound like a strange way to fix a problem, the truth is that, because we could not directly identify the problem (as the code was valid and there were no reasons why it should occur), finding others with the same problem or seeking some help, especially as your still pretty new to coding, is a simple way to resolve common bugs.

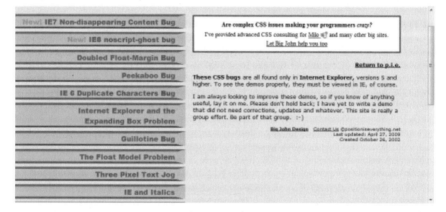

Figure 7-15. Bugs, bugs, and more bugs! Position Is Everything will help you find a fix to common issues.

How is this problem overcome then? Just like with many browser bugs in Internet Explorer, using an unrelated CSS property and value combination to overwrite the strange behavior of the browser will fix your problems. Although this solution is technically a hack, note that it's clean enough to validate and simple enough that other hacks, filters, or conditional comments are pretty pointless under the circumstances. In this case, adding `display: inline;` to the element that has the float magically fixes the issue (see Figure 7-16).

Although this explanation is probably is rather confusing, explaining the fix is quite complex, especially with the cause unknown, so if you ever come across this problem when you test your website in Internet Explorer 6 (which you really should do as it still remains one of the most popular web browsers), you now know about this unusual but fairly common issue and, more importantly, how to fix the problem if you encounter it.

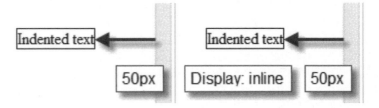

Figure 7-16. Adding display: inline; will resolve the double margin problem entirely—simple and strange but effective.

LinkED

For more details about the double-margin float bug and how it affects Internet Explorer 6, you can see the original article that inspired this example (as I have encountered this problem many times in my career) at http://www.positioniseverything.net/explorer/doubled-margin.html.

Conditional Comments

Even though the majority of browser glitches occur within Internet Explorer, we are lucky enough that a simple yet effective (and did I mention clean?) technique exists to eliminate most of the need for hacks and filters. The situation with conditional comments allows us to avoid using glitch browser bugs to target specific versions of the popular browser and simply supply CSS enclosed within a specially engineered style sheet wrapped around a set of HTML comments that give explicit instructions for which browsers can peak inside the wrapper. Wouldn't it be nice if we did not need any workarounds in the first place? Since we do, and you are pretty new to the whole concept of messing round with CSS to get things working, I highly recommend that you use conditional comments instead of hacks and filters. The only exception to this recommendation is if there is a natural (hack-free) way to resolve the problem, such as a solution using clean and pure CSS code.

Conditional comments, at their most basic, are a method of targeting browsers with code that Internet Explorer will read to solve a problem that can't be fixed naturally (or supernaturally using some of the hacks that exist).

Conditional comments let you just override the existing style with the targeted style sheet. Using conditional comments is like having one CSS file that works generically for all browsers and another directly below it for a broken browser to rewrite the style as needed.

Let me show you how to get some conditional comments running. The first thing you need to know about conditional comments is that they are a proprietary extension. While this would normally set the alarm bells ringing (as you don't want invalid markup), it is important to realize that these comments have been structured specifically using the perfectly valid HTML comment element with the ability to explicitly be recognized as more than just a comment from within Internet Explorer. In other words, Internet Explorer will take specific notice of conditional comments, and other browsers will simply see them as normal HTML comments not worthy of looking at and will carry on as if nothing happened. Not only this, but the W3C validator will see the comment as perfectly formed, and the code will validate.

Conditional comments are composed of the following:

```
<!--[if ... ]>
```

```
<![endif]-->
```

The opening comment tag starts with an `if` statement that gives the conditions of the contents being used, followed by the contents that will be applied, and finally the closing `end if` statement to end the conditions. In place of the ellipses after `if`, you can set a wide variety of conditions, though the most common one of all would be `IE` followed by a space and a version number. This declaration explains which edition of Internet Explorer should be targeted by the source code held within it. A simple example of this follows:

```
<!--[if IE 6]>
<link rel="stylesheet" type="text/css" href="/style/fixes.css"
media="all" />
<![endif]-->
```

The preceding code will attach the `fixes.css` style sheet if Internet Explorer 6 is being used—simple enough, right? You could also change the version number to any version of the browser you would like to target, such as `IE 5`, `IE 5.5`, `IE 6`, `IE 7`, or `IE 8`.

Targeting explicit browser versions may be useful, but conditional comments become truly powerful when you use a set of operators to give instructions so that multiple versions of the browser can be targeted. Table 7-1 shows the various symbols you can use.

Table 7-1. Conditional Comment Instructions

Operator	Example	Meaning
Basic if	`<!--[if IE 6]>`	Internet Explorer 6
lt	`<!--[if lt IE 7]>`	Versions lower than Internet Explorer 7
lte	`<!--[if lte IE 6]>`	Versions lower than or equal to Internet Explorer 6
gt	`<!--[if gt IE 6]>`	Versions greater than Internet Explorer 6
gte	`<!--[if gte IE 6]>`	Versions greater than or equal to Internet Explorer 6
!	`<!--[if (gt IE 5.5) ! (IE 7)]>`	Versions greater than Internet Explorer 5.5 but not Internet Explorer 8
&	`<!--[if (IE 6) & (IE 7)]>`	Internet Explorer 6 and Internet Explorer 7
|	`<!--[if (IE 7) | (IE8)]>`	Internet Explorer 7 or Internet Explorer 8
()	`<!--[if (lt IE 6) | (gt IE 7)]>`	Versions less than Internet Explorer 6 or greater than Internet Explorer 7
true or false	`<!--[if true]>`	Can be used to detect conditional comment support

Conditional comments were first introduced in Internet Explorer 5, so they have a wide scope of support, as Internet Explorer 6 and above are what the majority of your visitors will be using (less than 1% of visitors tend to use Internet Explorer 5.5 or lower, so you can safely drop support for it). Conditional comments cannot be used within CSS, because they are an HTML element. However, you can wrap a style sheet link declaration in the head of your website using conditional comments, and thus any style inside the comments will be applied only to specified Internet Explorer versions (other browsers will think the code inside is just a comment and ignore it).

LinkED

If you would like to learn more about conditional comments for Internet Explorer, you can view the MSDN article on the subject at http://msdn.microsoft.com/en-us/library/ms537512(VS.85).aspx. *It contains a much more comprehensive guide and is full of easy-to-follow examples.*

Proprietary Code

A number of CSS properties are proprietary and have been created by browser manufacturers with the sole intention of giving functionality beyond the W3C specification; these were mainly created during the browser wars to try to get a competitive advantage against others. While I highly recommended you do not use these, you could want to target a particular browser alone or implement something that cannot be done in any other way. Most proprietary CSS code starts with a dash, is followed by a vendor prefix and another dash, and concludes with the usual property name and value. Unfortunately, over the years, these extensions have changed, so many proprietary extensions do not follow these conventions. As a result, you may require more than one extension to target multiple versions of a web browser. Not only this, but some valid CSS properties have been given proprietary CSS code to use instead, due to either lack of uptake, the incompleteness of drafts by the W3C, or just plain laziness from browser makers (you really can take your pick on who to blame).

ExplainED

Proprietary code can be used to explicitly target browsers, though your style sheet will not validate properly (if you choose to check against the W3C tool mentioned later). Using proprietary code does offer a unique ability to work around some issues and give your website flair not yet in general use.

Though I still caution you against using these, a list of proprietary CSS prefixes is provided for your reference:

- `ms` indicates Microsoft Internet Explorer proprietary code, which is explained here: `http://blogs.msdn.com/ie/archive/2008/09/08/microsoft-css-vendor-extensions.aspx`.

- `moz` indicates Mozilla's proprietary code (for Firefox), which is detailed at `https://developer.mozilla.org/en/CSS_Reference/Mozilla_Extensions`.

- `khtml` and `webkit`, which indicate Safari, Chrome, and Konqueror code, are explained at `http://developer.apple.com/documentation/AppleApplications/Reference/SafariCSSRef/Articles/StandardCSSProperties.html#//apple_ref/doc/uid/TP30001266`.

- `O` is for Opera's propriety code, which you can find out about at `http://www.opera.com/docs/specs/opera9/css/`.

Proprietary code for CSS is still accepted and used because of the need for such elements from inconsistent rendering. However, HTML has evolved a number of elements over the years that have now been removed from the specification because they no longer serve their purpose. Despite lingering browser support for these elements, you should avoid using them because they are not guaranteed to work in the future and their replacements are ultimately more semantic and contextual, which means you will end up with a better website as a result. Many of the elements were wiped out as a result of the availability of CSS and the separation of style from structure, and others disappeared because of overuse or problems caused as a result of their usage. The vast majority of tags you should avoid using are provided in the following list. The general principle to work by is that if you see any of the following elements, do not include them as you may break your website and invalidate your code!

- `<animate>`: Replaced with animated GIFs
- `<applet>`: Replaced with HTML `<object>` element
- `<audioscope>`: Replaced with Flash, SVG, or Canvas
- `<basefont>`: Replaced with CSS body `{font-size: value;}`
- `<bgsound>`: Removed with no replacement
- `<blackface>`: Replaced with CSS `font-weight;`
- `<blink>`: Replaced with CSS `text-decoration: blink;`
- `<bq>`: Replaced with HTML `<blockquote>` element
- `<center>`: Replaced with CSS `align: center;`
- `<comment>`: Replaced with HTML comments (`<!-- text -->`)
- `<dir>`: Replaced with use of the `<ul>` element
- `<fn>`: Replaced with fragment references

- `<font>`: Replaced with CSS `font` property
- `<ilayer>`: Replaced with HTML `<iframe>` element
- `<image>`: Replaced with HTML `<img>` element
- `<isindex>`: Removed with no replacement
- `<keygen>`: Being reintroduced into HTML5!
- `<layer>`: Replaced with HTML `<iframe>` element
- `<limittext>`: Replaced with CSS `width` property
- `<listing>`: Replaced with HTML `<pre>` element
- `<marquee>`: Replaced with CSS3 `marquee` property
- `<menu>`: Being reintroduced into HTML5!
- `<multicol>`: Replaced with CSS3 `columns` property
- `<nobr>`: Replaced with CSS `white-space: nowrap;`
- `<nolayer>`: Replaced with HTML `<noframes>` element
- `<nosmartquotes>`: Removed with no replacement
- `<plaintext>`: Replaced with HTML `<pre>` element
- `<s>`: Replaced with CSS `text-decoration: line-through;`
- `<server>`: Replaced with DOM Scripting
- `<shadow>`: Replaced with CSS3 `text-shadow` property
- `<sidebar>`: Removed with no replacement
- `<spacer>`: Replaced with CSS `padding` and `margin` properties
- `<sound>`: Replaced with HTML5 `<audio>` element
- `<strike>`: Replaced with CSS `text-decoration: line-through;`
- `<u>`: Replaced with CSS `text-decoration: underline;`
- `<wbr>`: Removed with no replacement
- `<xmp>`: Removed with no replacement

Implementing Cross-Browser Opacity

To show you how proprietary CSS functions, I will explain one of the new CSS3 properties we have not yet explored. Setting the opacity allows you to fade an element (such as a background) so that you can partially see through it. Opacity works on a numerical or percent scale, with 0 being fully transparent and 1 fully opaque. Opacity is one of the wounded in the competing browsers battle, as you require many different declarations to ensure cross-browser support, and unfortunately, the use of opacity through CSS will cause your code to fail validation (if this matters to you). The problems with opacity can be seen very easily if you try making use of the opacity CSS property in one of your pages (perhaps for an image). Firefox, Safari, Chrome, Opera, and all the other standards-friendly browsers will give you the effect you requested, but if you try and view the site in any version of Internet Explorer (shockingly even the most recent version, Internet Explorer 8), you will find the pretty effect just isn't doing what it's been told!

The reason for this glitch is because Microsoft, rather than following the convention, decided to go its own way and use a proprietary extension to declare opacity. This decision may seem reasonable on the face of it, as CSS3 is still a draft specification and not yet complete, but it means that we require the use of markup that pads out the CSS file (and in some cases is purely invalid) and makes the code seem less streamlined and uglier. While you probably do want to keep your code valid, the fact remains that someday you may find yourself wanting to add cool transparency effects into your website, and the cost of keeping your pages entirely valid against using a bit of proprietary code to ensure it works across all browsers is a tough call that you will need to make for yourself. Of course, the main problem in getting opacity to work properly in your web browser is Internet Explorer (yep, again!); it just doesn't like the idea of following the standards.

Things are even more diabolical because practically every version of Internet Explorer has its own required fix, requiring a slew of browser filters to guarantee that everyone will see your site the same. Luckily, this lack of support is possible to overcome (unlike some browser problems) and can be done using a few savvy properties and values, as shown in the following code:

```
opacity:.50;
-moz-opacity: 0.5;
-khtml-opacity: 0.5;
-ms-filter: "alpha(opacity=50)";
filter: alpha(opacity=50);
filter: "progid:DXImageTransform.Microsoft.Alpha(Opacity=50)";
```

Of course, Internet Explorer isn't the only problematic browser that needs special help in being able to make use of the property. Old versions of the Gecko and Webkit rendering engine also require their own hacks to get the same functionality (though this doesn't explain why Internet Explorer needs three different properties and values to ensure Internet Explorer 5.5 and above can actually view the effect).

The preceding code uses a mixture of various required opacity proprietary code to work. First comes the correct CSS implementation (opacity). Next, you have two statements using moz and khtml to deal with old versions of Netscape, Safari, and Konqueror. Finally, the last three statements are for good ol'

Internet Explorer: `ms-filter` works for Internet Explorer 8; `filter:alpha` works for Internet Explorer 6 and Internet Explorer 7; and the filter for `DXImage` will handle the even-older Internet Explorer 5.5 and lower, as well as Internet Explorer for Mac. That is a lot of code for one simple property. Unfortunately, as long as old browsers are still in use, compatibility will always be an issue; therefore, we need to address those problems as they occur. Arguably, with some of the previous incarnations of browsers having died (or nearly so), you could probably remove all but the correct `opacity` and the two hacks for Internet Explorer versions 6 to 8. However, with the global fix is so readily available, you may as well give the maximum level of care and ensure it will look great on everything.

Prevention Is Better Than Cure

Of |course, we use hacks and filters only out of necessity, and most of us would prefer not to even need to spend time debugging our designs when they should work perfectly. While issues do occur within web browsers, five very simple philosophical processes have been created to approach the entire realm of website design; these are backwards compatibility, graceful degradation, progressive enhancement, future proofing, and the bleeding edge. These methods of dealing with problems and reducing the chances of them occurring in the first place will be addressed one at a time in the following sections. These concepts remain an important step in ensuring your website is not only semantic, accessible, and usable but also as sympathetic as possible toward browsers that are limited or challenged in the way they implement languages such as CSS. Acknowledging errors is important, but being flexible to the requirements of your visitors and their browsers is also very important (as you can't force people to stop using Internet Explorer 6).

Ensuring Backward Compatibility

The ideology of backward compatibility states that everything you do should work with older technology of the same type. Of course, the idea of making things backward compatible also implies patching websites that use new technology to support the old. This is the purpose of conditional comments, hacks, and filters. An example of backward compatibility would be the growing trend of using conditional comments to make broken design elements pull themselves together in Internet Explorer 6 where CSS support is unstable at best. Methods of approaching design have come into play to limit the amount of necessary patching, but the whole concept of making your website the best it can be for all the shiny new web browsers and then dealing with those who refuse to play nicely afterward is still a commonly used approach to web coding.

Degrading Gracefully

Graceful degradation means that, when a technology is unavailable, the website should have something to fall back on so the design is still usable. For example, if JavaScript is suddenly turned off by one of your visitors, you do not want links to stop working or parts of the website to fall apart. Having a working website if a technology cannot be used is especially important in older browsers where certain blocks of code may not be understood by the browser. A well-crafted site will gracefully fall back onto something that may not be as good or powerful but will still function all the same. An example of graceful degradation could be a slideshow effect. If JavaScript is available, the image will pop up without the visitor having to navigate elsewhere. However, if JavaScript is turned off, the image will still load, without the flashy effects and will just load as an ordinary image within the browser.

Using Progressive Enhancement

The most recent theory and ideology of designing websites is the replacement of backward compatibility and graceful degradation with progressive enhancement. The core of this methodology states the exact practices that you have been following in this very book. Websites should first ensure that the basic technologies are taken care of and then layer each independent element of a website on the next to build up a site that enhances with each new layer of technology, while ensuring the one feature is not dependant on the last. The core concept behind this aims to separate style, structure, behavior, and content. Essentially it tries to get you starting off with HTML, then (in order) layering CSS, client-side scripting, and server-side scripting on top of each other to create a functional website that can stand the unavailability of functionality. As you're doing all that, you visually ensure each layer works to the best of its abilities before another layer is applied, so you do not have to rely entirely on patches that may fail or half-baked functionality that results from a page that gracefully degrades into a failsafe mechanism. While graceful degradation uses the practice of ensuring there is something to fall back on, progressive enhancement deals with the situation in reverse by starting off with the basics and working upward.

Future Proofing

Another modern ideology of web design is the concept of future proofing. The general idea behind this concept is to make your website as flexible as possible so that it can cope with anything the future may bring (such as new languages that can overwrite old). The whole notion of future proofing is somewhat a pipe dream, because no one knows what the future of the Web will bring. For example, I bet no one saw AJAX pushing its way onto our screens in such a rapid fashion. What you can take from this concept is the idea that if you ensure your website is semantically coded and only uses as much code as is required to achieve the needed effects, you help to reduce the chances of encountering problems when the time to upgrade comes. For future proofing, just make your website as clean and logical as possible to avoid confusion and avoid proprietary code whenever possible.

Staying on the Bleeding Edge

Another concept of web design is the bleeding edge. The "bleeding edge" refers to the idea that adopting the most modern techniques available can give your website a unique selling point for browsers that can take advantage of it. However, this is something you won't undertake at this stage in your learning, as you are still getting to grips with the basics. CSS3 is a perfect example of the bleeding edge. While the specification is still in the draft stage, browsers can take advantage of CSS3 properties, such as opacity, to give a new level of beauty to designs. For reference purposes, if you find yourself wanting to experiment, remember to make sure your website looks fine if the feature is unavailable, and make sure that your designs are not reliant on these methods. If you do this, everything should be fine, and you can experiment with fresh features to your heart's content.

Understanding 404 (Section Not Found) Errors

Have you noticed how many errors are on the Internet? Every day, pages are moved, deleted, changed, or simply forgotten about, and the links to them suddenly become redundant and lead to errors about missing files, server problems, or invalid credentials (depending on the issue). Of course, with your website, you are in total control, and it will be your responsibility to make sure that no matter how big your website grows, you keep the wheels turning and remove as many errors as possible. You need to know about how to deal with errors both planned (such as maintenance- or event-based downtime) and unplanned (such as missing files, errors, and layout bugs). By taking precautionary measures and working with your customers, you can deal with mostly everything that goes wrong and, as a result, make people more likely to return to your website.

ExplainED

Note that the majority of this segment of the chapter is aimed at those who are hosted using Apache, which directly supports .htaccess files. If you are using Windows hosting and are hosting on Microsoft IIS, you can skip this section of the chapter, as the information will not be relevant to you.

.htaccess

The .htaccess file, which only works on Apache servers, is an important and powerful element of building websites. It allows you to send configuration changes to the server that hosts your website on a directory-by-directory basis. One thing you need to be aware of is that, although the basics of working this file to your advantage can be pretty easy to pick up (and really helpful in making your website better), the results of messing with this file could potentially be damaging to your website's overall ability to function. Therefore, everything you will read in this section should be done with care. This caveat may be worrying to you, but the simple truth is that anything you do to the .htaccess file can be reversed by uploading a fresh copy of the file overwriting the last one (with the mistake corrected), and the results will be instant. In this section, I cover some of the more common (and genuinely useful) things that .htaccess can achieve that most people starting out want to learn how to do.

ExplainED

In the following examples, you will see very basic implementations you can literally just copy and adapt to your own needs. However, for security reasons, some web hosts do not support editing the .htaccess file, so you may not be able to take advantage of these useful features.

Building Your .htaccess File

Before we can get started using .htaccess, you need to make the file. To do so, open your code editor, and save a file to the base directory where your index document is called .htaccess. Depending on your operating system, you may need to enable viewing hidden files or you may encounter problems trying

393

to name the file, as some operating systems see .htaccess files as having no filename, which is technically true. This unique filename has only an extension, not a complete filename—nothing should precede the dot in this instance. The workaround I recommend for Windows, Mac, and Linux is to open a blank text editor window (for example, Notepad), and save that file as .htaccess rather than trying to create a new file to your desktop or folder with the extension.

Remember when you created a blank document and saved that with the HTML and CSS files? Doing the same for .htaccess should let you achieve the task. You may want to ensure the save dialog box is not set to save with a default extension such as .txt and is set to view all files (if that option is given), as this will not force the application to try to apply an extension to your file once you click the save button. Once you have saved the file to your base directory (where index.html is), you can place any .htaccess code inside it to send commands to the server. Manipulating this technology, as previously mentioned, is normally reserved for more advanced users, but you should be able to do some very basic things that genuinely benefit your visitors.

Creating Friendly Errors

All the cool websites have custom error messages, whether they present a picture of Homer Simpson yelling "D'oh!" or just a friendly screen which lets visitors know that they have ended up in a nonexistent space. The point is that providing customized error messages is much more useful than simply using the default 404 or 403 errors, as most people have absolutely no idea what those errors mean. By adding a couple of lines of code to our fresh .htaccess file, we can define a custom URL where all errors of that nature will be sent.

LinkED

For examples of custom "file not found" errors, check out the 404 research lab, which has made a name for itself in showcasing some of the more unusual error message responses created for the Web: http://www.plinko.net/404/.

The markup of friendly error messages in .htaccess is made up of ErrorDocument followed by a space, a number (such as 404 for file not found), another space, and the URL to the file itself:

```
ErrorDocument 404 /notfound.php
```

With this in the .htaccess file, upload the file to your website, and create a file called notfound.php with your chosen server-side extension. Make sure the file uses your page template, and contains a message, such as "You picked the wrong door; this page doesn't exist!" Place the notfound.php file n the same folder as everything else, and *voilà*!

If users type a page that does not exist on your website, they will magically be transferred to your custom error page rather than the ugly default one everyone is used to seeing. You can include all sorts of useful information on your 404 page, such as places users might have been looking for or in the case of a 403 (forbidden) error, a login page. But the important thing is to ensure that the content reflects the type of error visitors have received to best meet their needs. Each one of these ErrorDocument pages should always appear on a new line of the .htaccess file and the URL you use to link to the file can be either relative (like the one in the example) or absolute (a full http address).

LinkED

For a complete list of different error numbers, you can use to redirect users, visit http://www.askapache.com/htaccess/apache-status-code-headers-errordocument.html. *Not all of these numbers will be useful to you.*

Redirecting Users

As you saw with the friendly error pages, you can take control over a website address that is entered to help customize where your website sends visitors who receive an error. Of course, it would be nice if there was no error at all. Perhaps you have moved a page from one location to another and want to redirect visitors from the old location to the new but do not want to have a page sitting on the server just to redirect visitors. If so, you are in luck, the .htaccess file can perform redirections as well.

In essence, you simply need to prefix the command with Redirect 301 (the 301 tells search engines that the move is permanent). After the prefix, provide the relative path to the page's location in respect to the base folder and follow up with a space and the full URL to the file's new location:

Redirect 301 /old.php http://www.yoursitehere.com/new.php

You can literally use as many of these as you feel will do the job, but if you inch your way up to 50 different 301 links, you may want to consider using an alternative solution such as httpd.conf (not covered by this book) as lots of .htaccess requests will slow down access to your website, because the server has to check the file for each page request.

Using Friendly URLs

Just like the with redirection, you can produce what are commonly referred to as "friendly URLs" to overcome the inherent difficulty people have in remembering where certain pages are located (so users can type them directly into the address bar). An example of this could be taking something like yoursitehere.com/news.php?date=may&id=1 and replacing it with something like yoursitehere.com/news/may/1/, which looks much cleaner! Redirecting from server-side languages is a little bit trickier and is not covered in this book, but you can produce a friendly URL from any file even if it is static rather than dynamic, such as an HTML file. In the following example, the code is prefixed with Options and RewriteEngine On (which should only appear once at the very top of your .htaccess file) to get things started. After that you can make use of the RewriteRule setting as many times as you want inside the document. The following code uses a caret (^) to signify the start of the address and ?/?$ to signify that the URL is allowed to end with a training slash character (/). Apart from that, it has the address to which it should redirect and the [NC] to keep the actual address hidden.

```
Options +FollowSymLinks
RewriteEngine On
RewriteRule ^products?/?$ /news/products.php [NC]
```

If you type yoursitehere.com/products or yoursitehere.com/products/ (notice the slash at the end), the preceding code silently redirects to yoursitehere.com/news/products.php, but the visitor sees only the friendly address (without the .php), as the [NC] keeps it hidden from the web browser. If that doesn't quite makes sense yet, give it a try using your own website and see what happens.

You can take any URL structure you want and get it to redirect within the site's internal structure. You can also do the same thing with an entire directory rather than just a single file to be redirected. An example of this is follows:

```
RewriteRule ^images/(.*)$ /default/images/$1 [NC]
```

In this case, all links in files to /images/ will be redirected to the images folder on the base directory. This is really useful if you like moving all of your files into subdirectories and don't want to have to use ellipses to go up a level on pages. The difference in this link is that the end of the images folder is followed up by (.*)$, which gets the filename of the requested file and redirects whichever is chosen to the end of the second URL, where $1 is listed. If none of this makes sense to you, don't worry; this level of redirection is a rather advanced subject. Simply put, you can edit the URL used to meet your needs and be able to take advantage of friendly URLs yourself!

Relative linking can be a problem if you use server-side includes, because you cannot alter the URL on a page-by-page basis. Therefore, many people use the full URL to reference files. This technique may be overkill for your site, but you can use the RewriteRule *technique to overcome the problem entirely, as in the preceding images example.*

Protecting Yourself

Now you have all your website addresses set up with friendly URLs and some custom error pages in case something goes wrong. The next thing we need to address is protecting your website so that you will be able to ban visitors who try to do bad things. Let's hope that never happens, but you need to be ready just in case, so you can deal with the issue directly. Do you have someone following or stalking you? Is there some person trying to attack or disrupt your website? In that case, you need to do is find that person's IP address (in your server logs or statistics) and add it to the deny list using the following method:

```
order allow,deny
deny from 123.45.6.7
deny from 98.76.54.32
allow from all
```

Each line can have a unique address, and anyone using that address will be blocked from visiting your website! While this sounds fantastic and a solid way to keep the weirdoes out, people can get around it. For example, some ISPs will assign a dynamic IP address that changes, or some people will use a proxy server (basically a fake IP address). Also, sometimes ISPs recycle IP addresses, so if you ban someone, you could also be banning other people who happen to be unfortunate enough to end up with the IP of someone you previously banned. So while you can ban people from your website, you should not treat this method as a foolproof and guaranteed security solution.

Checkpoint: An Example .htaccess File

Now you know how to do a few things using .htaccess, but you've only seen the tip of the iceberg, and you should remember that .htaccess is not a subject for the faint of heart (or people who suffer typo fever). Plenty of additional resources are available on the Web if you want to find out some more cool and clever things you can do with the .htaccess file, but to recap what you have learned here, I have compiled an .htaccess file based on the information we've covered, so you can get a general idea of how everything should end up looking together.

Here is an example of a complete .htaccess file:

```
# The basic functions to redirect some relative links
Options +FollowSymLinks
RewriteEngine On
# Where to go when an error occurs
ErrorDocument 403 / forbidden.php
ErrorDocument 404 / notfound.php
#The friendly URLs this website wants
RewriteRule ^news?/?$ /archive.php [NC]
RewriteRule ^products?/?$ /products.php [NC]
RewriteRule ^support?/?$ /support.php [NC]
RewriteRule ^images/(.*)$ /default/images/$1 [NC]
RewriteRule ^scripts/(.*)$ /default/scripts/$1 [NC]
RewriteRule ^includes/(.*)$ /default/ includes/$1 [NC]
```

ExplainED

Remember when we looked at HTML and CSS? You could add comments to your code to make things easier to remember. Well, the same is true of .htaccess files. To add comments to a line of code, you just need to precede the comment with a hash character (#), as in the example given.

Dealing with Issues

Most problems that occur can be fixed without disrupting people who are visiting your website, literally by uploading a new copy of the affected CSS file. However, if you ever get bored with the design you have made and want to totally revamp your website (who knows what the future may bring!), you should schedule some time where the website will be unavailable to give you the opportunity to upload the new site and ensure everything works before you let everyone gather around your new design. Dealing with downtime or the need to turn off the access to a particular service is very easy, but many people fail to bother following the steps that could quite easily keep your visitors in the loop. Hopefully, you will never need to follow these steps as your website should be getting better on a daily basis, but the information is provided in case you need it.

Error Reporting

When things go wrong, you need to know about it. Error logs can help in discovering when entire pages are made unavailable, but you need to have a system in place so people can contact you with general issues they face on your website (see Figure 7-17). To keep the visitors you have coming back, they need to feel that their opinions and needs are considered by you. Therefore, you need to offer a way to report any problematic elements of the user experience, so that you can see to what extent the problem is occurring and how you can resolve the issue. That way, users will feel happy to continue using your website in the future. Giving visitors an error-prone website can be traumatic, as some bugs can literally cause a browser to crash. Although not all bugs are as high-profile as those, getting notified about issues your visitors spot should be as simple as a few clicks of the keyboard and could include instant messaging, email, or even an HTML form for reporting bugs.

Figure 7-17. Give your visitors a way to let you know about problems with your website.

Scheduling Downtime and Maintenance

Downtime and maintenance are two of the main causes in a sudden loss of traffic, because if the website is not available, for all intents and purposes, it doesn't exist. Therefore, you need to address this issue by providing information if downtime is scheduled for something significant (or over a significant timeframe), like a complete revamp of your website or a coming soon page on a website where construction is still in progress, as shown in Figure 7-18. You can inform users by creating a holding page that contains general contact information, the reason the website is having issues (if any), a brief statement about what the website aims to achieve, and the timeframes for the fixes. Giving frequent updates on this page is imperative to helping people understand where you are in the process of making updates or resolving issues. If at all possible, you should avoid the need to use these kinds of mass fixes by applying updates in small doses to avoid interfering with the overall user experience. However, there are occasions when issuing downtime can give you the chance to deal with a large update or potentially dangerous issue that may affect your website visitors.

Figure 7-18. "Coming soon" messages are another form of website maintenance commonly found on the Web.

Providing Alerts and Notices

Do you have an announcement that will affect your visitors? You could place this information on your news page or in your blog, but a more effective method is to have an alert system on the website that gives the status of any services you run. Most websites will not often need this functionality, but if you are planning on hosting an online service, giving notice or details about things that may affect users is a good approach to take. Many alerts and notices appear in their own status pages, but some people choose to have dynamic pop-up messages (possibly using lightbox effects) on the screen when something needs to draw the visitor's attention away from the main content of the website. Of course, these alerts should be issued only when things are bad enough that there is a genuine possibility that your visitors may lose information or complete access to a service they pay for (see Figure 7-19), for example, if your website's forum suffered a meltdown. Therefore, you should take care to only issue notices when they are needed; otherwise, people will see them all of the time and learn to ignore them.

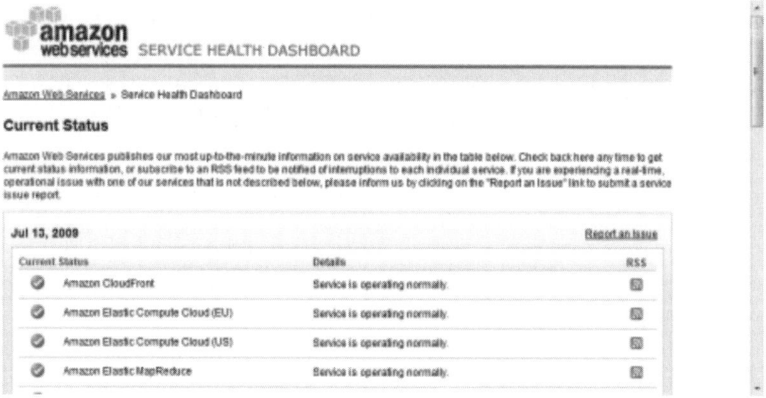

Figure 7-19. Amazon offer a clean and simple status page for all of their services.

Maintaining Support

When people encounter errors while they visit websites, many often choose to report those errors (especially the annoying ones) to help the owner of the website deal with the issue and make things better for everyone involved. With your website, you want to encourage people to take an active interest and report issues they find, because without this feedback, you probably will remain unaware of problems that could stop people from entering your site. There are a few things you can implement to assist people who visit your site with getting in touch with you and to help you deal with their complaints and issues. This section also contains information about how to deal with people who contact you and the correct procedure for dealing with any messages you receive. While the very idea of having people critique you via email can sound like something you would prefer to ignore, this core area of aftercare will help the social aspects of your website evolve.

Reporting Methods

You need to ensure that the method of reporting the errors on your website is quick, simple, and direct. Visitors do not want to go out of their way to receive assistance through technical support to get past some issue inhibiting their experience. The general rule of thumb here is to have a single link on the website for support that will direct users to a location where they can choose the method they wish to interact with you. Some people like to talk face to face; some people prefer email, and others prefer more direct methods such as chat rooms or forums—the important thing is variety. You want to show your visitors that their feedback and input is so worthwhile that you have taken the care to allow them to get in touch with you. While many websites choose to have a single method of communication, such as an email link or comments within a blog, the general perception is that as long as there is flexibility and you take into account your visitors needs, the overall rate in which they will let you know of what will make your website better will be increased. Having different types of support also helps increase your productivity; for example, a list of frequently asked questions to reduces the number of time you must repeat answers to those questions. In summary, the best process to take is to offer users a method to contact you (such as a support button) and list the ways they can get support.

Assistance Methods

Many different types of assistive methods are commonly found on websites. The following list contains various assistive methods you can provide and choose from; including any of these in your website will be a great way to help your visitors give you feedback that you can use constructively:

- **E-mail support**: Email support could either be text-based or linked to an HTML anchor.
- **Contact form**: Allowing users to complete a form to sending an email to a particular person can be quick and easy.
- **Social networking**: Joining Twitter, MySpace, Flickr, Facebook, or other networks gives users another way to get in touch with you.
- **Blog comments**: You can also allow feedback to direct posts with short descriptive messages.
- **Knowledge base**: Frequently asked questions about a website or service can save time for you and users.
- **Support forums**: You could also offer users the ability to join a community of people interacting with the site.
- **Chat rooms**: These offer a way to letting people chat directly with you and other site users.
- **Instant messaging**: Person-to-person direct contact can be useful for immediate resolution.

- **Voice Over IP**: Skype and other services allow web-based conferencing.

- **Telephone support**: You could certainly offer users old and respected method of picking up the phone to chat.

- **Glossary**: Terms and definitions in pages that require explanation can be collected into a glossary.

- **Feedback form**: A feedback form functions like an email form, except it's used for general questions and not direct support.

- **Bug tracking**: If you provide a page listing issues, bugs, and the status of your services, it should be easy to follow.

- **Faxing**: Although also an old method of communication, faxing is still a popular way to get in touch.

Offering users a choice is a good thing, but some methods of support clearly aren't going to suit everyone. Therefore, you should make use of a method only if you feel that it will serve a purpose and is worth the time it takes to maintain a high standard of support for that particular contact option.

Customer Relations

The final thing we need to address is how you communicate with people who talk to you. Although it may seem obvious that you want to come across as friendly and forthcoming with relevant information, you may sometimes find it hard to know how to should express yourself when talking to certain types of people, such as those who are rather temperamental or impatient. The general rule when speaking to people is to empathize with them and try to see things from their perspective. Understanding why people have contacted you and their frustration could be a lifesaver when you come across someone who has visited your website and sent you a rude email about an issue. On the Internet, you will find that not all feedback is pleasant, and there are a lot of rude people out there, but don't feel disheartened by what they say. Obviously, not everyone will be complementary, and you will meet unreasonable people who have expectations that can never be satisfied. The best thing you can do is be yourself. Remember to stay calm, and whatever you do, don't take what they say to heart as something personal. Dealing with clients and visitors is all part of the customer relations process, which can be stressful if you end up getting a whole bunch of feedback over the course of a short period of time.

Showing interest in your visitors is important, and you should reply to as much mail as you can, but you are only human, and your visitors cannot expect you to spend all day opening mail and thus neglecting the website itself. Therefore, once your website is in the public view and you have methods for people to get in touch with you, you need to set aside some time every day (perhaps an hour) for checking the forums, responding to any comments, email, or messages you have, and then dealing with any genuine issues which arise. Keeping your content up-to-date is important, but the process of making your visitors feel welcome and giving that personal touch is just as important to the overall health of your website. If you find yourself getting really nice feedback, perhaps ask if you can showcase the glowing review on your website (everyone loves a good testimonial). For any negative feedback, you can take the criticism with a pinch of salt, analyze it for any truth that may exist, and use it to make your website better. Negative feedback is usually the most useful kind.

While plenty of people send replies like "I could do better," the fact is they are still on your website and have not produced anything to back up their assertion, so you should just ignore these comments altogether as they are unconstructive and generally produced by people who have an ulterior motive for posting. When it comes to starting a reply, try to keep things professional and avoid throwing around insults. After all, if a comment is just plain rude, you don't need to bother to respond to that user again (or you can ban that person from the site). While the idea of getting negative feedback may sound like a bad thing, the good reviews, feedback, and friends you make as a result of producing a website far outweigh the cons. As long as you are fair, honest, and treat your fellow web visitors with respect, you should have no problems running a successful website. Hopefully, the problems on your site will all be minor, the regulars your site gets will be friendly, interesting people, and most importantly of all, what you get out of the website will have been worth all your effort!

Summary

Through this chapter, you have learned about the browser wars and the scars they left on the web design industry and how mobile devices have entered the fray now that browsing the Web on a handheld device has gained popularity. We also discussed the different web browsers that now exist, how many people actually use them, and some of the major considerations in tackling the development process. We looked at the cool things that can be achieved through the .htaccess file, how to deal with issues on your website, and how to handle visitors that are affected. Finally, we discussed validating and debugging your code, working around issues, and the preventative measures you can take to help reduce the chances of problems happening in the future. In the next chapter, we are going to look at how you can start using client- and server-side scripting to increase the level of interactivity on your website and the frameworks, packages, and tools available to help you get started. I'll also mention the security problems that could potentially burn you and the basics of online software and its benefit to your site.

Chapter Checklist

You should accomplish the following tasks before leaving this chapter:

- Understand the problems surrounding modern web development.
- Come to grips with the various web browsers and devices people use.
- Learn how to control your site through the raw power of .htaccess.
- Get a process in order to deal with issues and your customers.
- Learn to resolve issues with your design across various browsers.

Questions and Answers

Q: *How do search engines factor into the discussion of error handling?*

A: Search engines, as they currently stand, do not take very much notice of CSS, as the presentational value of your pages isn't as important as the content and the semantic structure itself. Of course, if you have broken and orphan links on your website, or if you suffer some errors that interrupt the rendering or the visibility of the pages in your website, the search engines may be unable to index your content and, therefore, would be unable to list your site properly in search results (getting your website listed is dealt with in Chapter 10).

Q: *Should I place all of my browser-specific code in separate style sheets?*

A: Many developers choose to separate any style that is browser specific into a dedicated CSS file for the purpose of maintainability and to ensure that the main style sheet remains pure and validates effectively. However, some people keep all of their styles in a single file (with the browser-specific code at the bottom of the file) to reduce the need for additional CSS documents being referenced in the HTML. The choice of which you go with is entirely your own, as both have inherent advantages and disadvantages. Personally, I choose to use a separate CSS file called fixes.css, because each time an old browser disappears (which is rare but noteworthy), I can remove some of the code that has accumulated in there to serve it. Of course, it would be best if you do not require any patches or fixes to get your lovely designs working correctly, but the chances are high that at some point or another you will encounter one of the many browser quirks.

Q: *What happens if I cannot find the root cause of my website breaking?*

A: Playing detective and hunting down the cause of problems to fix them can be literally a game of cat and mouse. Although encountering an error you cannot seem to resolve on your own is very frustrating, you can call in the cavalry. There are many places on the Internet where you can ask questions and get free help and advice with your designs. The web design forums out there are run by individuals who give their free time to answer questions to help out their fellow professionals and hobbyists. Isn't that nice? All you need to do is find a place you think can assist you, join the site, post your questions. and be patient for a response. Paid services can offer a faster response, but in all honesty, the free places are as good as any. Because the industry of making websites is so diverse and always evolving, the need for assistance has grown considerably, and you should not feel ashamed about needing help. Many thousands of people require some advice on some aspect of building websites every single day, so getting outside opinion can be helpful.

Where You Are Now

By the end of this chapter you should have the following:

- Checked your website works in a wide variety of web browsers
- Validated and fixed any problems using mentioned techniques
- Gotten to grips with the .htaccess file to improve your website's flexibility
- Thought about how you will deal with issues and user feedback

Chapter 8

How Can I Add Interactivity?

Static websites are the bread and butter of web design. Being able to pull HTML and CSS together to produce an elegant but attractive website is essential to drawing visitors into the content you offer. But what if you want more than just a pretty face? What if you want to give your website and its visitors a more tailor-made design with interactive elements, special effects, and customized functionality to meet the needs of the visitors? Well, it is time to start enhancing the site's behavior by looking at the various available scripting languages and packages, both client-side and server-side, that make your site react to the actions of your users. We'll also go beyond simple scripting to take a look at plug-ins for providing rich interactivity and web applications, such as Flash and Silverlight. Scripting is tricky, and some tasks could be slightly beyond your skill level right now, but it's not an essential addition to your website, so you can skip this chapter and come back to it later if you would like. There are some very cool things you can do to enhance your existing website, though, and languages like JavaScript can be of serious benefit to your website and how it functions. This chapter will give you a good solid idea about why scripting exists and how you can get started, but to learn more, you should check out a dedicated book, such as *Getting StartED with JavaScript* by Terry McNavage (ISBN-13: 978-1-4302-7219-9).

In this chapter, we're going to cover the following topics:

- The basics of client-side scripting like JavaScript and using cookies
- Existing server-side packages and how you can use them
- Frameworks, scripting security issues, and rich Internet applications

Back to Basics

Here we go again! I expect the prospect of learning yet another language is rather daunting. Hopefully, at this stage, you have a website that works perfectly fine, and while it may not have all of the pizzazz of some of the other sites you probably frequent, you should be proud of what you have accomplished. First, I think the good news should be given to you: the content within this chapter can enhance your website but is not actually a requirement! Many websites work perfectly fine with a mixture of HTML and CSS without a single line of script, and even if you do want to add some interactivity to your site, there are so many excellent premade packages and applications that you can plug into your site that you probably will not need to do any additional coding unless you really want to. You've already learned the compulsory languages. Of course, there are limits to what you can achieve without the use of scripting, and if you want to deviate at all from a prepackaged solution, you're going to have to learn a little scripting, which can be a daunting task because scripting languages are complex. But never fear! I will start at the beginning and bring you up to speed with what's out there.

Under the Hood

After all the hard work you've put in learning HTML and CSS, you should be well equipped to deal with the basics of scripting and seeing what goes on behind the scenes. Also, in the previous chapter on problem solving, you gained the rudimentary skills required to understand the process of isolating basic issues and working out where a mistake occurred. Unfortunately, with scripting, as you will soon find out, things are a little more technical, but so much work has been done in making things easier for the average user that the amount of work you need to do can be drastically reduced. But before we even come to looking at scripting code, you need to get to grips with the various languages involved. You can choose among lots of different scripting languages (unlike HTML and CSS where your choices are pretty standardized) especially at the server-side, and each has its own applications, tools, and communities to support people who make use of them, so let's go back to basics!

Understanding Interactivity

Before I can describe what scripting is and how it works, I need to first discuss interactivity. Since the Web was created, the idea that content could be more than just text has been at the base of its evolution. While CSS (as you now know) gave website owners the opportunity to give their designs a greater level of detail than HTML alone could offer, the combination of the two languages never really gave websites the notable level of interactivity we see today, whether a website allows you to sign up for an account (and therefore remembers your details) or some exciting animated special effects go off all around your screen to make browsing around a more enjoyable experience.

This could include a carousel that spins around showing movies you can rent or a gallery of images that can be given a closer inspection upon clicking (see Figure 8-1). Interactivity gives a website something HTML and CSS on their own could only dream of, thereby making the transition from a static design, which simply reads as pages of content, to a dynamic site with features you can manipulate on the screen.

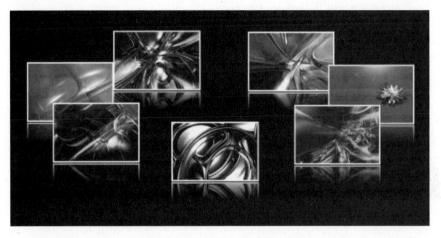

Figure 8-1. A 3D carousel that spins and has clickable links is just one example of interactivity.

ExplainED

While CSS does have a couple of interactive components, like the ability to change a website's style based on the action of hovering over a link, its interactivity is pretty limited, especially in comparison to the wide array of event's and actions a language like JavaScript can perform!

The need for such interaction and behavior within the browser gave rise to what we now know as scripting languages. The essence of scripting languages is based on behavior (not the way you act but the way the browser reacts). For instance, events may arise where you want the browser to do something upon rolling the mouse over an object, clicking, double-clicking, loading, or something else entirely. With scripting languages, you can change everything from how an element appears in the window to editing the style of a website based on the way someone interacts with the page; for example, perhaps you want the ability to move items around the window or create a pop-up message that takes priority over the rest of the visible page. While lots of examples of interactivity at work are out there, the essential thing you need to remember and understand is that when you create a website, if the effect cannot be produced using HTML and CSS alone, a scripting language may be the technology you need to give your site extra functionality. The two types of scripting languages are *client-side*, which allows you to make something happen on the user's screen (directly), and *server-side*, which allows you to interact with the place which hosts the website to do something like send and retrieve data).

License to Thrill

Scripting itself is an interesting subject, as it allows you to turn an average static website into something with a lot more interactive components. While immediately wandering off to learn one of these languages could seem like a good idea, scripting does come with its own set of problems, so the first thing you need to do before you decide to use a scripting language is ask to yourself whether you actually need it. A lot of first-time web designers tend to make the mistake that their website needs to use every technology in existence just to make it compete with the other great sites out there. Scripting is very useful if you find yourself needing (or wanting) your website to accomplish a task based on how the user interacts with the page, but in all seriousness, many websites happily prosper on the Web without a single line of client- or server-side scripting. The more complicated your website and its code become, the more you need to question whether the functionality will really benefit the end user. But you want to avoid just adding needless extras that may slow the website and subsequent pages down. As the saying goes, "with great power comes great responsibility." Scripting is an awesome force on the Web and can do a lot of different things, but deciding whether you need scripts is a different matter (see Figure 8-2).

Because this book is aimed at individuals wishing to create a website for the first time, this chapter will explain the benefits of such languages but will not go into a lot of detail for a few good reasons. Whether you decide to learn one of the languages mentioned in this chapter is entirely up to what you feel is best for your website. The thing you should remember is that scripting is a more comprehensive type of language that requires a lot of hard work and skill, especially if you want to build something from scratch. While there are tools (like frameworks) and prebuilt applications out there to make your life easier, you will find that learning one of these languages is quite a bit more complicated than you might have initially expected. Scripting at the client- or server-side is the closest thing a website developer will get to programming (in the sense of producing applications), and while there are lots of languages to choose from, not all are well suited to beginners.

Figure 8-2. The Coda website uses JavaScript to add a simple and nonintrusive fade effect when you rollover buttons.

ExplainED

This chapter offers plenty of links to prebuilt applications and frameworks that allow you to bypass many of the complex areas of scripting. But here's a piece of useful advice: learning languages like JavaScript and PHP is worth the effort, so that you can maintain your website and tweak it for your needs.

Client vs. Server

We are really spoilt with the wide array of scripting languages we can learn. The possibilities of what we can produce are almost endless because several different technologies have emerged to allow us to code using a system that best makes sense for each of us, which is lucky, as it promotes healthy competition among the language authors. Before we actually look at each of those languages, we first need to separate the two types of scripting, client-side and server-side, as each has its own unique part to play in the evolution of a website. When you produce a dynamic website, you will probably find yourself using both to encompass all the various needs your site may have (Figure 8-3 shows their relationships to the website). We also need to look at the ways in which the scripting languages store data, so you can decide which will be most efficient for your needs, as the chances are that you will find yourself using one type of storage over another depending on your scripting choice.

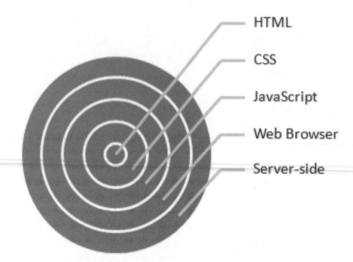

HTML

CSS

JavaScript

Web Browser

Server-side

Figure 8-3. The various layers of the Web show how JavaScript and server-side scripting are incorporated within the browser.

NotED

Depending on the language you choose to script in (generally in the server-side scripting region), you may find that the range of premade applications you can add to your website is limited. Therefore, it's best to take the popularity of the language into consideration before you settle on a language.

The first scripting language type we can make use of (as web designers) is client-side scripting. A script designed to run at the client side normally involves live interaction with the web browser that the visitor is viewing your site from. Client side scripts are usually coded in a language, such as JavaScript, for which each browser has its own special rendering engine to tackle the task of executing the commands given. The browser reads through the HTML file with the script inside, and upon noticing that there are scripts embedded in the page, the browser starts working through the scripts' contents, following the commands given to perform an action (see Figure 8-4). To react to special events, such as clicking on an element, the browser will refer to the script to decide what action (if any) should take place. As a result, you can give your website some more complex levels of interaction.

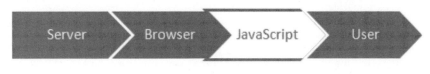

Figure 8-4. Client-side scripting only occurs after the data has been passed to the browser.

The second scripting language type that can be used is server-side scripting. Unlike client-side scripts, these lumps of code are launched and run by the web server hosting the files, and the results of the script are sent to the web browser your visitor is using (see Figure 8-5). For example, assume you wanted to customize a profile page (perhaps on Facebook). When you fill in the information Facebook requests, it gets sent to the website to be stored and saved for future reference, so you can access the information from any computer before another page loads, and when you view your profile, the information is sitting there waiting to be viewed as it is retrieved from the place it was originally stored. This process works because the request to view your profile is sent to the database where it's held, and upon receiving the request, the sites database sends the relevant data back so the whole page, with the information requested can be returned in a complete package, ready to be viewed! Because all server-side scripting is done behind the scenes without user intervention, none of the source code is visible.

Figure 8-5. Server-side scripting occurs before the data has been passed to your browser.

Generally, when learning web design, most people learn a client-side scripting language before they attempt to use a server-side scripting language, purely because client-side languages like JavaScript are bolted onto the document and run in the browser and thus can interact with a page in the same way that CSS does. Server-side scripting languages require a bit more technical know-how, because they literally can influence the place where your website is hosted. Therefore, something that goes wrong could seriously affect the website's ability to be viewed. While this may be a scary prospect, you should remember that taking one step at a time is the best way to approach learning any new skill. Even if you want to dive right into adding functionality to your website, you may want to consider starting with some of the great existing scripts before you move on to making your own.

Data Storage

Now that you know what a script is, we need to place the final piece of the puzzle into its rightful place: once you get all this great power to can make changes or send and receive information, how do you save the results? This question can simply be answered with data storage. Both client- and server-side languages have their own methods of remembering things. Client-side scripting languages like JavaScript use something you've probably heard of before called *cookies*. These small text files temporarily store information that can be used to save and retrieve settings on your visitor's computer. Cookies are only stored for a set period of time; after that, they are thrown out by the browser, making them an ideal choice for user preferences. Server-side scripts, on the other hand, need to remember things over the long term, as the results of these customizations (like your Facebook profile if you have one) need to be available on any machine you choose. The method of storing this information is known as a database. A *database* is like a huge file cabinet or hard drive filled with information that needs to be remembered, and it is kept with your web server by your hosting company. Databases are usually more secure than cookies as databases can have passwords and other security tools to stop unauthorized access.

Figure 8-6 illustrates the differences between cookies and databases in a nutshell.

NotED

Some sites store user preferences in a database rather than cookies because the user's settings can then be taken with the individual wherever they go, making everything look the same across different computers. Whether you choose to use client or server-side scripting for saving information is up to you.

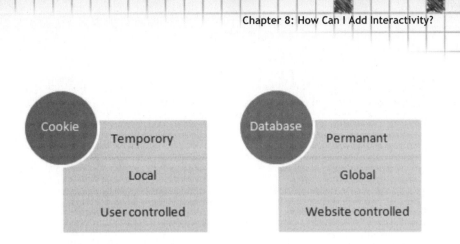

Figure 8-6. Data can be stored either as temporary cookies or in a permanent database.

LinkED

If you would like to learn more about cookies and the potential security risks they pose, you can visit the following Wikipedia article at http://en.wikipedia.org/wiki/HTTP_cookie.

Applications and Packages

As you can imagine, producing an application that stores millions of records and can do lots of interesting stuff, like communicating between members, is quite a task! Because scripting can be quite a complex job. To help developers avoid reinventing the wheel, a series of packages and applications (see Figure 8-7) have been produced for specific tasks. If, for example, you wanted to add a forum to your website so people could communicate with each other, you wouldn't want to spend hours slaving away over your chosen code editor only to come up with something that barely matches someone else's in functionality. To save yourself hassle, a whole bunch of free and commercial premade scripts and products are available for you to install on your own website or have hosted elsewhere. These tools allow you to have all that functionality without the hassle of learning to script! The great thing is that, like software, web applications tend to be very well maintained and have regular bug fixes, patches, upgrades with new features and security against people who might want to try to hack your website.

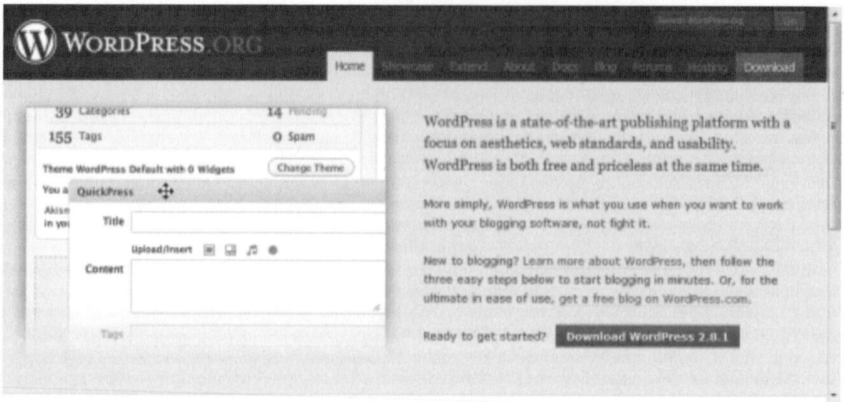

Figure 8-7. WordPress is one of the most popular web applications and blogging platforms.

These scripting packages and web applications come in all shapes and sizes, and you can shop around to see which product best meets your needs. A variety of solutions exist, such as content management systems, blogging platforms, social networks, forums, and e-commerce shops, and many of these products are given away for free (out of the kindness of developers' hearts). However, you shouldn't eliminate the paid ones just because they cost money, as they tend to have better technical support and occasionally more feature-rich functionality. Server-side languages, like PHP and ASP.NET, tend to have more applications written for them than other scripting languages because they are more popular (and therefore have a greater number of developers writing for them), which may be worthy of consideration if you are interested in using plug-in applications or scripts.

ExplainED

Client-side scripting languages have premade scripts available, but these tend to be based on adding some cool effect or functionality to your website rather than being a full-blown application. This limitation is due simply to how the two types of scripting languages function rather than popularity or preference.

Fantastic Frameworks

Of course, while applications and prebuilt packages have the explicit task of helping you achieve a specific piece of functionality (such as allowing people to talk to each other through a forum), there are packages out there with the sole intention of making your scripting life easier (if you choose to do any scripting on your own). Scripts are often laborious to write, and unless you are a code monkey who loves spending you day spewing out endless reams of code, you probably want to make things as easy for yourself as possible. I've told you about scripts that can lighten your workload, what do you do if the script you want has not been made? Spend hours writing from scratch? That's good if you have plenty of time, effort, and patience, but why would anyone want to make things more complicated than necessary? Powerful frameworks have emerged that are filled with libraries of code to simplify the process of adding scripting capabilities to your website. For many of them, you simply add a file reference to your HTML head section, add a couple of class names, and everything will work itself out! So now we will examine the world of frameworks. We'll look at which ones exist and talk about the possibility of building your own framework full of useful code snippets you have produced.

In web design, there are four types of frameworks:

- CSS frameworks to simplify the process of making complex designs
- JavaScript client-side scripting frameworks for browser functionality
- Server-side language-specific frameworks to create web applications
- RIA frameworks for making online applications that rival offline software

ExplainED

*"RIA" stands for "rich Internet application." Generally, the term is used for web applications that go beyond simply responding to clicks and actually rival the power of desktop software; for an example, check out the Aviary suite of graphic tools (*www.aviary.com*).*

Frameworks are essentially bundles of prepackaged scripts and libraries of code which can be called upon to achieve a desired effect. For example, a simple animation framework might include scripts for moving objects around the screen, responding to user clicks, and making pop-up windows fade in and out. A framework gathers all of this functionality together into one easy-to-use package (see Figure 8-8), so you only need to attach one file to your webpage to enable all of that functionality. Of course, you still need a basic knowledge of how the language works before you should add a framework to your website, because you might need to know how to code in order to use the functionality provided. Think of frameworks as handy time savers: they provide prebuilt blocks of functionality so you don't have to write them yourself, but you still need to know how to apply that functionality to your page. You add frameworks to your website like you would any other file of the same type, such as a link in the head of your HTML for CSS or a script reference for JavaScript. Of course, if you decide to use these frameworks, you will need to learn their individual methods, and these will usually be described in detail on the framework's homepage. Benefits of frameworks include having had a long period to iron out all of their bugs, being highly streamlined, and the ability to cache them for speedy loading. Also, in the majority of cases, they have been put together by individuals with years of coding experience.

Figure 8-8. jQuery is probably the most popular and well-known JavaScript framework in existence.

Because of the rise in the use of frameworks to achieve animation or dynamic interaction with the website, you may find that, while you are still required to know code, you can achieve more functionality with fewer lines of code being added by you to your website. Taking all of this into account, the first list of frameworks that I will mention in this chapter are the CSS frameworks. The reasoning behind showing you this is that, at this stage, you should be well equipped to deal with CSS code. These allow you to build complex designs with greater ease of coding; you can literally save yourself a lot of hassle if you decide to use a framework. With that in mind, you may want to see what some of the following offer you (personally, I recommend Yahoo Grids, S5, and Blueprint):

- **960 Grid System**: http://960.gs/
- **ACF**: http://www.contentwithstyle.co.uk/content/a-css-framework
- **Blueprint**: http://www.blueprintcss.org/
- **Bluetrip**: http://bluetrip.org/
- **Clever CSS**: http://sandbox.pocoo.org/clevercss/
- **CSS Reset**: http://meyerweb.com/eric/thoughts/2007/05/01/reset-reloaded/
- **Elasticss**: http://elasticss.com/
- **Elements**: http://elements.projectdesigns.org/
- **EMastic**: http://code.google.com/p/emastic/
- **MCF**: http://www.thatstandardsguy.co.uk/blog/2006/11/23/my-css-framework/
- **S5**: http://meyerweb.com/eric/tools/s5/
- **Tripoli**: http://devkick.com/lab/tripoli/
- **Yahoo Grids**: http://developer.yahoo.com/yui/grids/
- **YAML**: http://www.yaml.de/en/

ExplainED

CSS frameworks help you achieve those complicated multicolumn grid layouts and help resolve bugs with browsers by resetting the browser's natural inclination to set its own unique defaults.

Code Snippets

You can make use of code snippets as well as prebuilt frameworks. These are pretty much what they sound like—a premade function for a website that you can copy and paste into your own code. In fact, you can think of a framework as a collection of code snippets. Over the years, a vast array of websites has appeared that promoted code snippets, and this led to some pretty poor-quality code being bandied around. Luckily, these days quality is not so much of an issue as the bar has been raised due to the increase in the number of websites competing to get developers' attention. Though as a precaution you should only use snippets from sources you trust to reduce the chance of having a damaged user experience. Snippets of code can be really useful in helping you achieve an effect that has already been created in the past, and again, limit the need to reinvent the wheel.

Many software products for web development (especially WYSIWYG editors) come with code snippets to help you achieve certain tasks, such as building a navigation menu quickly and easily. The benefits of these can be great if you want to prototype a design or if you want to experiment and play around to see what you can make happen, and they are excellent for learning from as you can see how code should look like when put together. Therefore, if you find yourself unable to work out how to build something, just check out some of the great examples on the Web. While there are too many websites to list, Appendix B lists useful websites, all of which are blogs or related to web design so they will be extremely helpful in this respect.

LinkED

To find some great snippet resources, you can always visit the following Smashing Magazine *article:* http://www.smashingmagazine.com/2009/07/ 21/45-excellent-code-snippet-resources-and-repositories/.

Summary

In the coming sections of this chapter, we are going to examine both client- and server-side scripting, and I will point out the various languages in use, how the code semantics differ from languages like HTML and CSS, and the various frameworks, applications, technologies, and other useful pieces of information that make up the vast array of website-enhancing features through scripting. While this book does not teach you the specifics of each language, from the guide that follows, you should have enough information to make an informed decision as to what language will best suit your needs, what that language can offer you, and the general mechanics of how it works, so that when you do decide to take the time to learn it, you have a general idea of the implications of its true nature and power. So now, let's drive straight into the pool of client-side scripting and how it can be used to manipulate the browser through small snippets of code intended to extend or enrich your visitors overall experience; perhaps you might even find a few useful cut-and-paste scripts from the given resources!

Client-Side Scripting

The use of client-side scripting has come a long way in recent years with the realization that it can actually provide genuinely useful functionality and enhance a design in ways previously not considered. The release of frameworks also assisted the evolution of this technology's usage, because it gave people with no scripting experience the opportunity to create basic interaction with little knowledge of JavaScript's fundamentals. In this section of the chapter, we will focus purely on the JavaScript language and how it has transformed the way we can give added flexibility to our designs, achieve things previously unseen with structure and style, and how client-side scripting can let us draw on the ability to produce plug-in-free animations and special effects.

At this stage in the process, you should have a website brimming with awesome HTML and CSS code that looks great but may feel slightly flat. While CSS does allow a limited amount of behavior (such as applying hover links through anchors), the amount of dynamic interaction you can provide is hindered by the limitations of a language produced for styling content rather than altering the way it reacts. Because of this, languages like JavaScript were invented to take hold of the browser's ability to dynamically render and get information from a visitor's browser to enhance the experience. Now that you are aware that there is more to life than basic structure and style, let's start by taking a look at the most popular client-side scripting languages on the Internet.

Languages in Use

So how can you make the process of web design a little bit more dynamic, and what languages are available? Well, it is entirely possible to achieve using client-side scripting. Many people use the wonders of modifying the website's behavior to give visitors special effects, useful functionality (see Figure 8-9), and a more streamlined experience. Because scripting is a powerful way to improve your site in browsers that support it, its use has become widely accepted. Because of the raw power that it offers, you need to be careful of the consequences for the visitor in what you do. Client-side scripting that is abused and overused becomes obtrusive, and considering some people have client-side scripting turned off or unavailable, you cannot rely on it for essential functionality.

- **JavaScript:** JavaScript (which is alternatively and less commonly referred to as ECMA-Script) is the industry standard for producing client-side behavior on the Web. While it has mass market support, JavaScript can be quite a difficult language to get the hang of. Version 1.8 is supported within almost every web browser (though mobile platforms have their issues), but most problems occur due to patchy support for elements of the Document Object Model (DOM), which is the primary method of how CSS interacts and targets HTML. One disadvantage of JavaScript is that people can easily turn off support for it entirely, some do so because malicious use of scripts in the past ultimately undermined trust in the language.

- **Visual Basic Script (VBScript):** VBScript is the less common of the two main behavioral engineers of the Web. The reason for VBScript's lack of widespread adoption is that it allows a greater level of control over a person's computer than JavaScript and, therefore, is more open to the risks of malicious scripting. The only browser that actively allows the use of VBScript (independently) is, of course, its creator's browser Microsoft Internet Explorer. As a result, JavaScript would be a better choice of invoking behavior and providing a more dynamic user experience, even though VBScript, on the surface, is an easier language to learn in terms of its syntax.

Figure 8-9. This lightbox, which focuses attention on the pop-up image, was produced using JavaScript.

The Trinity of Interactivity

For the purposes of this book, we will focus our attention on JavaScript and its related components, as they are the most widely supported client-side scripting elements of the Web. The components that make up this trinity include JavaScript, DOM scripting, and AJAX, which will each be explained in turn. The first thing I need to mention about JavaScript is that it has similarities with plug-ins like Flash and Silverlight (mentioned in Chapter 6) in that, while it is powerful, not everyone has access to it. This means that, just like CSS, you should take the effort to ensure that your website still works correctly even if JavaScript is turned off. Ensuring your website functions in this manner is often referred to as *unobtrusive scripting*, which means the visitor isn't reliant on or forced to enable scripting just for your site. After all, the visitor is the one who needs satisfying.

JavaScript

JavaScript has a higher level of standardized support within web browsers than much of CSS. The majority of browsers have access to some form of JavaScript, with the exception of some mobile platforms. Even though a number of people choose to disable scripting for security reasons because it's powerful enough to be troublesome if abused (see Figure 8-10), there is a good chance that people who visit your website will be able to take advantage of some JavaScript. Scripting is turned on by default, so most people will see sites using it. Of course, relying on its implementation within browsers can be difficult at times, as Internet Explorer (who else!) uses an alternative version of JavaScript known as JScript, which has slight differences in its implementation and was created back during the days of the browser wars, along with VBScript, to directly counter Netscape's format.

Figure 8-10. Remember that not everyone has JavaScript enabled; Firefox users can disable it with a plug-in!

The DOM

How exactly does JavaScript target the correct elements of your source code? Do you remember back in Chapter 3 when we talked about inheritance and how every element relates to each other like one big family of code? JavaScript uses a mixture of element names, the type of element you want to target (such as paragraphs or images), and the relative nature of the element (such as an acronym that is a child of a paragraph) to explicitly target an element for behavior. This method of filtering down the elements is commonly known as the Document Object Model (DOM). At this stage, you are probably experiencing *déjà vu*, because the method JavaScript uses to hunt down elements is identical to using CSS to target elements for style (using a mixture of inheritance and specificity). The main difference between JavaScript and CSS is that JavaScript can actually filter down the results through a series of statements asking questions like if, while, or for (as in "for each time something appears, do something"). Think of it as CSS with the power to play "Guess Who?" It can ask questions and decide on the answers given! To keep things simple, the DOM works on the same principle that every element is related to each other through a vast family tree of parents and children, as shown in Figure 8-11.

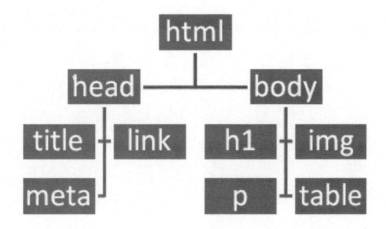

Figure 8-11. The DOM treats all elements within your HTML like a family tree.

The purpose of DOM scripting is to filter through the results you have and find the tags you want to edit. Of course, it would be boring if the DOM only worked on HTML, as you would be limited to making content move around the page. The DOM also has a CSS style model that navigates through CSS in the same way, except using the `style` property of the DOM (which affects inline style) or through the much more complex `document.styleSheets` property (which edits external style sheets). We will look at this later, but the important thing to remember is that manipulation of both HTML and style is possible and can be done without messing up your semantic code. As with CSS, the DOM has several versions which layer on top of each other improving upon the previous level in opposition to entirely replacing the language. Currently there are three active DOM layers.

AJAX

We've already considered the first two elements of the client-side scripting trinity: JavaScript, which allows us to manipulate the web browser's behavior, and DOM scripting, which allows us to manipulate the web page and its contents. The newest child to enter the market is AJAX (Asynchronous JavaScript and XML), a technology that is rapidly gaining popularity. AJAX blends the behavioral elements of DOM scripting and JavaScript with server-side languages to allow you to send and receive information to the page without refreshing or being directed away from what you're reading! Figure 8-12 shows an example of how AJAX is being implemented to make use of the ability to avoid refreshing or redirecting the window of a browser.

Figure 8-12. A completely web-based instant messenger powered by scripts—who would have thought it?

AJAX uses a process known as XMLHttpRequest to send and receive information at the same time (here is the exciting bit) without refreshing the page! With AJAX and a cocktail of languages like HTML, XML, XSLT, CSS, the DOM, and JavaScript (oh, the acronyms), you can do cool things like logging into a website without the page needing to refresh, making for a much smoother transition. One of the main uses for AJAX has been in web applications that allow developers to overcome the need to reload the document by using AJAX to fetch and send information for that application in the background (see Figure 8-13). Some of the best things about this technology are that it is in widespread use, well documented, and supported in most of the major web browsers including recent versions of Internet Explorer. You can use AJAX to accomplish tasks like sending filled in forms and even retrieving information from a database (or another file). Not only this, but you can give websites the ability to drag and drop, show and hide, and interact with its surroundings. While much of the power of AJAX is beyond your experience level right now, the technology definitely has its uses in creating dynamic web applications.

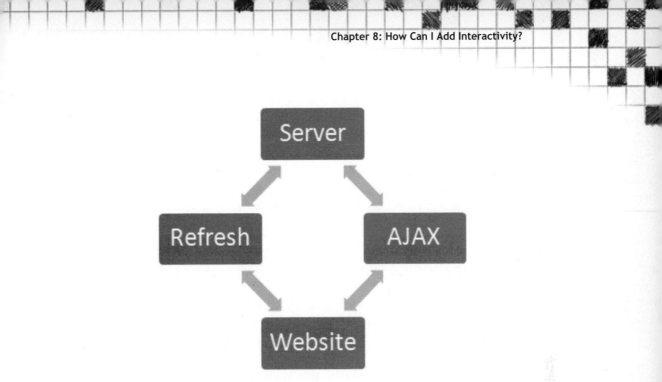

Figure 8-13. AJAX avoids the need to refresh the page by requesting information directly from the server.

LinkED

The AJAX introduction at http://www.xul.fr/en-xml-ajax.html *covers the basics, and the JavaScript and DOM skills you gained will be useful in helping you grasp the concepts there!*

Scripting Semantics

Now we have come to that stage in the book that usually references how the new language you have read about is produced and coded. Because scripting (both on the client and server sides) is more of an intermediate or advanced subject, depending on how you go about implementing it, this book will not teach you the active skills to create fully fledged scripts of your own. However, it would be foolish not to talk about the basic mechanics of how JavaScript works, as your existing knowledge of CSS will have prepared you for the general concepts of layering code over the top of HTML with the intent of extending what you can accomplish with the language. Besides, so many websites and applications make use of scripting that you should at least be aware of its purpose. Even without learning these languages, you can still embed premade scripts that give basic functionality to your website. Anyone can accomplish that, so let's get started!

A list of W3C specifications and reference manuals for JavaScript languages follows:

- **DOM Level 1**: http://www.w3.org/TR/REC-DOM-Level-1/
- **DOM Level 2**: http://www.w3.org/TR/DOM-Level-2-Core/
- **DOM Level 3**: http://www.w3.org/TR/DOM-Level-3-Core/

LinkED

If you want to learn more about the different JavaScript and DOM objects you can use, you could check out a reference guide like http://www.w3schools.com/js/ *or* http://reference.sitepoint.com/ javascript.

Try It Yourself: Creating a JavaScript File

If you want to embed JavaScript within your website, the method I would recommend is the same as creating the initial CSS file. First, you want to open your chosen text editor and create a new JavaScript (.js) file or just a blank document if no options are given. You do not want to use any of the predefined templates or wizards that the program offers, as we are going to be hand-coding this. Once you have your file, you want to save the empty document in the scripts folder we created right at the beginning when we got our structure organized. A good filename to give your document would be global.js (see Figure 8-14), and once you have saved the file, you can finish the process by adding the required declaration to your HTML document (like we did for CSS). The main difference here is that, while you can add the reference to the head of the HTML file, many people choose to place scripts at the bottom, right before the closing body tag. Placing the scripts at the end means they will only execute when the whole page has loaded (reducing the possibility of errors). Of course, just as with CSS, the declaration for the script needs to appear in every page it's required to function in. To make use of the file you have created, enter the following line in your HTML code (just before the closing body tag would be perfect):

```
<script language="javascript" type="text/javascript"
src="/scripts/global.js"></script>
```

Now that you have a file dedicated to JavaScript code, when you get the basics of what it can accomplish, you can literally paste in premade scripts into the global.js file to your heart's content, avoiding the need to clog up your HTML with references to JavaScript. Using the external JavaScript file will ensure maintaining any scripts you use will be much easier, not to mention you can use it for testing what you learn in the future if you do decide to take up JavaScript as a language to improve your website.

global.js
JScript Script File
0 bytes

Figure 8-14. Creating the global.js file will give you the ability to place scripts into an easy to manage area of the site.

Remember that you will need to upload the new .js file and update all the existing HTML files that reference it in order for the script to function properly. JavaScript can also be viewed offline if you open the HTML file in your browser, which means that you can play around with your code before it goes live.

At its core, JavaScript allows you to interact with a page, enabling you to do things like sending messages to your screen (like those dialog boxes with OK and Cancel buttons that you probably see a lot) and adding content to your page dynamically. One thing to remember is that JavaScript is generally case sensitive (uppercase characters may be seen differently to lowercase characters), so you want to be very careful how you type. If you take a look at the following example (or even try it out for yourself), you will notice that the browser posts some information to your screen using alert, prompt, and confirm—three functions of JavaScript that create different types of pop-up messages. As result of the response the dialog box is given, it will post a message to the browser window. This is one of the simplest examples of JavaScript's abilities.

```
if (confirm("Do you want to continue?")==true)
{alert("Yes!"); var name = prompt('What is your name?','John');
document.body.innerHTML = "<p>Hello, " + name + "!</p>";}
else {alert("No!"); document.body.innerHTML = "<p>Hello, whoever you
are!</p>";}
```

The preceding code displays a dialog box on the screen asking if the visitor wants to continue. If the answer is true, the second line of code will run, which alerts the user of the choice (Yes) and prompts for a name (see Figure 8-15). We supply a default name of John, so that users will know what to type. The code then saves the name as a variable called name and proceeds to write that name inside a welcome message. If, of course, the user doesn't want to continue, the script will skip the second line and go directly to the third line, which says "No!" and writes a generic welcome without the user's details.

You don't need to understand the details of exactly what's going on here, but you should be able to follow how the script works in general. I recommend that you have a go at changing the messages in this code to see what result it has on the final output. Remember to save the JavaScript file before previewing your changes.

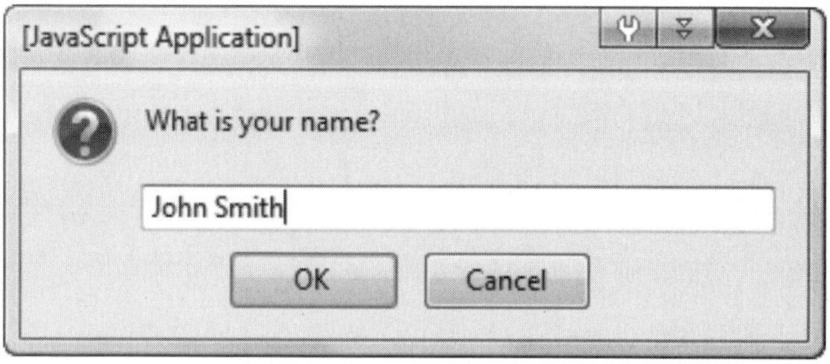

Figure 8-15. The script will ask for the visitor's name before displaying the result onscreen.

Of course, JavaScript can do more than send messages to a visitor and write stuff for all to see. As you will have noticed in the preceding example, it actually asked a question to the browser! The code says to the browser that if the result within the brackets has a certain result (in this case, if confirm equals true), it performs whatever lies within the curly braces (just like with CSS). However, if the result doesn't match the true value, it goes to the else section instead, as this best meets the criteria. Part of the power of scripting is that you can set specific conditions for running code. Examples of this include the if condition that lets code run only if it meets a certain value or criteria and the while and for conditions that force a script to keep running in a loop until something happens to trigger the reaction to occur and pause the script until it's needed. Here's an example of a simple if statement, and it's illustrated in Figure 8-16:

```
if (1 + 1 == 2){alert ("Did you know I can count!");}
```

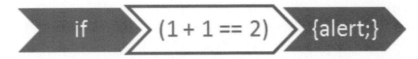

Figure 8-16. The alert appears because the result of the if statement was correct.

The preceding example shows how simple conditional statements can be: by using a basic mathematical sum, it decides what to do. The browser checks to see if 1 + 1 is equal to 2; note that you need to use double equals sign (==) for checking equality. Because the statement is true, the code in the curly braces runs and displaying the alert box shown in Figure 8-17 on your screen.

Figure 8-17. When an alert is produced, the visitor to the website will see a message box.

Try changing the line to this:

```
if (1 + 1 == 3){alert ("Did you know I can count!");}
```

This time, nothing will happen, because the condition in the if statement is never met. 1 + 1 does not equal 3, so the alert is not displayed. Because JavaScript can add (+), subtract (-), multiply (*), and divide (/), you can use this to your advantage in creating useful snippets of code that can work out things such as the sales tax for an item you are putting on your website (very useful for customers).

With operators, you can do more than just calculate and pulling variables together; you can also compare them! JavaScript operators provide the ability to check if two variables have the same value using two equals' signs (==), as you've already seen. You can also determine if one value is different from another using greater than (<), less than (>), greater than or equal to (>=), less than or equal to (<=), and even not equal to (!=). On top of these, you can pull together multiple operations using double ampersands (&&) for the AND operator (meaning both values have to work out right, otherwise nothing will happen) and double-pipe (||) OR operators (so that one or the other needs to work out properly) or simply use an exclamation mark (!) NOT operator. While all of those operators seem like a lot to learn, they will make more sense when you look at some source code!

Another thing you might notice from the original code example is the var name reference. One thing which you won't have yet found out about JavaScript is it actually has its own built-in short-term memory (see Figure 8-18). You can assign pieces of data to a named item; it's like assigning values to a CSS property, but the only difference being the property is preceded with the word var which is short for variable! There's a whole assortment of information you can hold, which JavaScript will recognize; these include strings of text, number values, Booleans (a value that can either be true or false), and arrays (which contain multiple values that are comma separated). Once JavaScript has been told to remember them, such as in the original example where the name is stored, it can be recalled by referencing the property name. This means that you can reuse and keep hold of useful snippets of data in scripts!

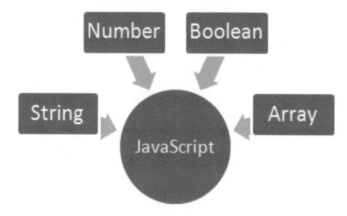

Figure 8-18. JavaScript can store different types of information for future references.

So how are scripts launched anyway? We've been looking at simple test cases so far, but browsers simply can't run through every script in order and then stop. Otherwise, all the functionality would be given to the browser upon reaching the page and that would be the end of it. That would be pretty anticlimactic, as we want visitors to be able to interact with the page itself at specific intervals. Each of these timed actions occurs as an event. *Events* are just as they sound—referenced points in a script that invoke a certain part of a script only when an action, such as clicking something, has occurred. While the event itself has to be defined (such as using an `if` condition to say only run the script `onclick` if the user clicks the H1 element), you can be very explicit in what occurs. Not only can you give the condition of launch (such as the mouse moving or clicking) but you can also use conditions to say that something should happen only when they move the mouse on a certain area!

LinkED

For a complete list of the various events you can make use of in JavaScript, check out the comprehensive Wikipedia article at `http://en.wikipedia.org/wiki/DOM_events`.

Now, you have almost everything you need to create a functioning script. But what if the whole point of the script is to target a particular element, to perhaps add some style to the document? JavaScript has a solution for that as well. To keep things simple, it has two properties called `getElementById` and `getElementsByTagName` that allow you to target a specific element. If you added, for example, an ID attribute for applying style, you can hook into that ID and apply the script's manipulation power directly to it. The same goes for the tag name (of course), though if you have lots of paragraphs on a page, targeting a specific one might be a chore! Luckily, just like with CSS, JavaScript has its own form of specificity that allows you to navigate around the DOM and pick specific parents, children, siblings, and attributes for editing (just like with what you learned about selectors in Chapter 5). While the method of writing the script may be different, the methodology behind it is identical: you can target the child of a paragraph that has the parent with an ID value of "content". By being able to browse around the DOM with conditions, events, and operators and set lots of cool variables, you can pretty much do anything! Some handy selectors for JavaScript are shown in Figure 8-19.

Element	Result	Element	Result
parentNode	Targets parent	childNodes	Targets child (index)
hasAttributes	True / False	hasChildNodes	True / False
firstChild	Targets first child	lastChild	Targets last child
previousSibling	Target previous sibling	nextSibling	Target next sibling
getAttribute	Get attribute value	setAttribute	Set attribute value
nodeValue	Get text value	createTextNode	Set text value
createElement	Create new element	insertBefore	Create sibling element
appendChild	Create child element	removeChild	Remove child element

Figure 8-19. A quick reference guide to some of the various selectors for JavaScript

If you want to apply a style to your source code (such as changing the color of a paragraph once it's clicked), you could set an event, like onclick, against the element in question by targeting it using the DOM. Then, you give the event handler the value you require to be changed. It really is that simple. For a style, you could use something like:

```
document.getElementById("eraser").style.color = "#E0E0E0";
```

to accomplish the task.

NotED

Microsoft has created a special set of JavaScript properties called expressions that you can embed within CSS files to manipulate your style. While expressions sound like a good idea, they only work in Internet Explorer and are slowly being phased out. More information about using these properties can be found at http://msdn.microsoft.com/en-us/library/ms537634(VS.85).aspx.

Try It Yourself: Erasing Content on a Page

To round off this look under the hood of JavaScript and the DOM, the following piece of code will show you how you can achieve funky behavior using the onclick event to change the color (and strikethrough) of a paragraph ID called eraser (that is, eraser is the name assigned to the paragraph in the attribute ID). The following code added into your JavaScript, therefore, only takes effect

434

if you add the ID to the paragraph in your HTML, and once you have added the ID attribute, all you need to do is click the paragraph once the page is loaded and *voilà*, the paragraph marks itself as "deleted." If you refresh the page, the paragraph returns to its original style.

```
document.getElementById("eraser").onclick = function() {
    document.getElementById("eraser").style.color = "#E0E0E0";
    document.getElementById("eraser").style.textDecoration = "line-
through";
}
```

LinkED

For a list of the various CSS properties you can implement through the DOM, you should check out the comprehensive Mozilla developer page at https://developer.mozilla.org/en/DOM:CSS *(though you should note that DOM scripting can also be used to apply proprietary CSS if required).*

JavaScript Frameworks

Earlier on in this chapter, I mentioned the benefits of frameworks and how they can simplify the task of creating interactivity on your website. The most common frameworks in use today use JavaScript. The rise in these prebuilt libraries of reusable code has allowed thousands of developers with little or no knowledge of scripting or producing client-side scripts to come up with beautiful websites with functionality only the best JavaScript gurus would have been able to produce in the past. Because this chapter focuses on getting you equipped for a time when you may wish to give your website some interactivity, it seems only fitting to highlight the most popular JavaScript frameworks in common use. Take a look at these and decide what will best suit your needs:

- **Atlas:** http://www.asp.net/ajax/AjaxControlToolkit/Samples/
- **BBC Glow:** http://www.bbc.co.uk/glow/
- **Dojo:** http://www.dojotoolkit.org/
- **Ext** (a JavaScript library): http://extjs.com/
- **IdentEngine:** http://identengine.com/
- **jQuery:** http://jquery.com/
- **jQueryUI:** http://jqueryui.com/
- **MochiKit:** http://www.mochikit.com/

- **MooTools**: http://mootools.net/
- **OverLib**: http://www.bosrup.com/web/overlib/
- **Prototype**: http://www.prototypejs.org/
- **qooxdoo**: http://qooxdoo.org/
- **Rico**: http://openrico.org/rico/home.page
- **script.aculo.us**: http://script.aculo.us/
- **Spry**: http://labs.adobe.com/technologies/spry/
- **Yahoo UI Library** (YUI): http://developer.yahoo.com/yui/

LinkED

While Spry has been included in this list, it is worth mentioning that the framework itself is integrated tightly into Adobe's own web development platform software, such as Dreamweaver.

We're not going to go into the details of the functionality of each JavaScript framework here, but you will find full details for each framework on its project page. Generally, using these involves linking the framework to your HTML page and referencing its functionality as required within your script.

Bookmarklets

Next, you are going to see a technique of employing JavaScript on your webpage called **bookmarklets**. These are hyperlinks that actively contain JavaScript to carry out a function or task of your choice upon clicking. Using bookmarklets is the only time when the use of the JavaScript: pseudo protocol is considered acceptable within an anchor link. Bookmarklets can be very simple JavaScript tools that function purely by clicking a link and redirecting the user to another website with some instructions to carry out a task. An example: taking the current website address and putting it through a service like www.tinyurl.com, which makes a shorter redirection link!

Try It Yourself: Detecting Your Browser Mode

The following JavaScript bookmarklet can be used within an anchor on your HTML page as the href URL, or you could simply put it in your address bar on any website and the action would be invoked:

```
javascript:(function(){if(document.compatMode=="BackCompat"){alert("Oh
no! You are running quirks mode!")}else{alert("You are running in
standards mode, congratulations!")};})();
```

Try it now. An alert box should pop up to tell you whether the page you are visiting is rendering in standards or quirks mode (see Figure 8-20). Bookmarklets allow you to potentially create a shortcut to a function, add it to your browser favorites, and use it to, say, remove a style or check which mode your browser is running in by simply selecting the bookmark you have produced. As you can imagine, being able to manipulate the page on demand dramatically increases the potential uses for these cute little functional pieces of JavaScript that have a simple but effective purpose. There has also been interest in the production of bookmarklets for the iPhone, as these simple snippets of functionality can be used directly from the handset to extend the basic functionality of the built-in web browser, Safari. Of course, being JavaScript-based, they will not work if the language is disabled!

Figure 8-20. Congratulations for Google, it doesn't trigger that naughty quirks mode!

LinkED

To find some more useful bookmarklets that individuals have created, you could visit one of the many directories such as http://www.marklets.com/.

437

Additional Resources

You have a general idea of how JavaScript is formed, and if you took a bit of time, you could probably look at a JavaScript file and get a general idea of what's going on (which is useful for debugging). But what can you produce with just the basic knowledge in hand? As mentioned previously, this book isn't a technical guide to learning the complete inner workings of JavaScript, but with the handy snippets of information given previously, you should be able to recognize some of the components that make client-side scripts tick. Of course, this isn't enough to write your own, so the following list of useful resources may be of use. It is a collection of various JavaScript websites with prebuilt solutions you can literally just download (or copy) and put right into the JavaScript file (unless the instructions given say otherwise!). There are other websites out there, but these are pretty well trusted and safe to use. Hopefully, this brief introduction will whet your appetite to learn more:

- **Dynamic Drive**: http://www.dynamicdrive.com/
- **JavaScript Kit**: http://www.javascriptkit.com/
- **JavaScript Source**: http://javascript.internet.com/

ExplainED

Be careful when installing scripts on your website. Because JavaScript is a pretty powerful language, you could potentially add something that could harm your visitors' overall experience (or even hinder their browser). Therefore, only use scripts that you have previously tested offline.

Server-Side Scripting

The web browser offers a multitude of different behavioral options in terms of client-side scripting, but you can also improve your website in an even more substantial way using server-side scripting. Languages like PHP allow commands to be given to the server to perform an action, render a specific piece of content, or perform queries and requests to a database. In essence, server-side scripting allows you to perform actions such as sending email, saving and requesting member information from a database, and much more! Just like with JavaScript, the things you can do with server-side scripting are pretty much limitless. This time, though, rather than the language applying to behavior in the browser (as JavaScript does), everything you do with a server-side script is processed before the page is served to the visitor. This also means that none of your precious code will be visible if people view the source, except for the end result and the relevant HTML, CSS, or other visible code generated. You should make the decision to learn server-side scripting only after you have learned client-side scripts, and as the level of complexity goes up yet another notch, I will focus only on providing real-world examples you may encounter and resources to help you learn at your own pace (rather than a complete guide).

There and Back Again

Now, we'll once again go on a path of discovery, taking everything you have learned so far into perspective and showing you that the universe is so much bigger than HTML, CSS, and JavaScript. You can provide much functionality that isn't possible any other way through server-side scripting, which is the final layer of what makes a website. Of course, as you will soon find out, you have many scripting language flavors to choose from, and this final piece of the jigsaw puzzle will give you everything you need to enhance your basic website, with its flourishes and simple scripts, and its ability to produce great tools like forums, content management systems, and blogs. Not only that, it will allow you to see what goes on under the hood of your favorite social networking websites and even how the big operators like Google manage to create wonderful applications.

Server-side Languages in Use

Server-side scripting is most often used when there is a requirement for interaction between the visitor and the website, such as sending an email through a form or creating a web application (Figure 8-21 shows a popular example of this). The script takes the necessary steps to respond to each request for information that is made by ferrying data back and forth between the web server and the visitor's computer (the client). Due to the increasing number of RIAs and the desire for enhanced web functionality, this area of web development is rapidly growing. Let's take a look at some of the most popular server-side scripting languages; the URLs provided point to the user manual for each technology, so you can learn more about the language if you wish:

- **PHP** (http://www.php.net/manual/en/): The PHP Hypertext Preprocessor (PHP) is among the most well known server-side languages in use on the web. It's an open source platform, which means anyone can contribute to the project, and has wide support within Linux and Windows servers. It is quite possibly the most popular scripting language in use today. PHP, like all of the other scripting languages, is harder to learn than HTML and CSS, but for those wanting to add dynamic features and interactive components or the ability to connect and save to a database, PHP 5 (version 6 is in development) has become a popular choice for server-side development.

- **ASP.NET** (http://www.asp.net/learn/): Active Server Pages .NET (ASP.NET) is an evolution of the classic version of ASP. ASP.NET itself is based on Microsoft's .NET platform, and with a lot of use on Windows servers, it has become one of the top choices for enterprises and organizations who are less trusting of open source software. If you come from a programming background or have written any software, you may enjoy the fact that ASP.NET can use Visual Basic, C++, C#, and other supported syntax and convert it to ASP.NET on the fly using its common language runtime. ASP.NET is a very popular language, and version 3.5 (the most recent) is another fine choice for learners of server scripting.

- **Classic ASP** (http://msdn.microsoft.com/en-us/library/aa286483.aspx): Before there was ASP.NET, there was Active Server Pages (ASP). ASP is supported by Windows servers, and is proprietary (in terms of how it functioned), so classic ASP has been a firm favorite of enterprises and businesses alike for many years. While ASP has seen a decline in use since ASP.NET was released, version 3.0 still has a following, and some people prefer it over ASP.NET due to the reduced system resources it needs. Most ASP pages are written in VBScript, and ASP is on par with PHP in terms of ease of learning.

- **Python** (http://www.python.org/dev/): Python started off as a fully fledged programming language and was later adapted for server scripting on the Web. Fairly recently, it has seen a sharp rise in the amount of people who use it to produce web applications (rather than small scripts for which other languages are better suited). With framework solutions such as Django to help manage complex applications and projects and the ability to place Python scripts within containers, the language has become a firm favorite among programmers coding for the Web and the information security industry. It should be noted that this language is better suited for applications than for websites.

- **Ruby** (http://rubyspec.org/): Ruby is the rock star of the bunch. While it has been around for a very long time, its place on the Web has only fairly recently (over the last few years) become a rags-to-riches story. The most popular method for using Ruby on the Web is Ruby on Rails and essentially provides an entire framework to help reduce the complexity of scripting large applications. Because of this rapid development environment, Ruby and Rails have become commonplace within web servers, and like Python, they support containers for managing complex projects. Ruby is well known for being fairly easy to pick up and is an excellent choice for individuals who want to learn to produce web applications with little programming experience. It should be noted that this language is better suited for applications than websites.

- **Perl** (http://perldoc.perl.org/): Perl has been around for a long time. It's currently at version 5.1 and has seen few updates over recent years. However, it has maintained a cult following among hardcore developers who want to be free of the bulk and mess that comes with other server-side languages. I would not recommend this language for beginners, because many people new to scripting have stated that it is tricky to learn and the language itself has gone into decline in terms of usage. Perl does have wide support on all platforms and may be worthy of investigation because of its lightweight nature.

- **ColdFusion**
  (http://help.adobe.com/en_US/ColdFusion/9.0/Developing/index.htm
  l): Adobe ColdFusion is another well-known server-side language that
  has its own dedicated user base. The language itself is considered
  fairly straightforward to learn and in many ways is simpler than its
  counterparts. However, any ease of use is inhibited by two facts:
  ColdFusion is limited in its support across platforms, as many hosts do
  not offer direct support for it like they do for other languages. Also, a
  ColdFusion server is very expensive to implement, which prices it out
  of reach of average consumers. Therefore, it probably isn't what you
  will want to learn as your primary server-side language.

- **JSP** (http://jcp.org/en/jsr/detail?id=152): Finally, JavaServer
  Pages (JSP), as you may have guessed, is directly related to both Java
  (which drives those little applets you see on pages) and JavaScript
  (mentioned earlier). While JSP has seen limited success in terms of
  usage across the Web, it has seen a moderate increase in use since Sun
  Microsystems (its creator) was bought by Oracle (though this deal is
  still pending). Like ASP, JSP has been fairly popular in enterprise-level
  environments, where its backing by well funded organizations (Sun and
  now Oracle) has created a level of trust. Because JSP is so broadly
  supported across platforms, it is definitely worthy of consideration.

Figure 8-21. Google Docs is a web application powered through server-side scripting.

Laws of the Playground

There are plenty of examples of server-side scripts in effect such as forums,
blogs, content management systems, social networks, and all of those other
wonderful types of websites that allow you to sign up for an account, interact
with the website, and even participate online. Ideally, I want to be able to get
you involved in this kind of scripting, because then you can let your visitors

become part of the website. However, as you may be aware, the level of difficulty has gone up even more than with JavaScript, because server-side scripting involves more complex programming languages and a much wider variety of scripting. As a result, we will (again) not focus on creating anything with the language but on equipping you with the basic knowledge to be able to make a decision on which language to chose (from the vast array of server-side languages out there) and point out some of the excellent premade and already written applications that you can install and plug into your website!

There are plenty of different ways you can learn a server-side language such as books, media, tutorials, specifications, and more. As with anything else beyond the scope of this book, you can find a wealth of excellent high-quality resources on the Internet to supplement your learning.

Because you started reading this book with the intention of making your website the best it can be, it would be foolish to completely ignore these languages, as they comprise everything that takes a website from static (or if using JavaScript, static with some behavior) to something radically dynamic and better able to handle tasks like setting up an online store or community or even just assisting you in controlling your content better. As a result, you will find the website address that contains a languages specification besides each listed item earlier, and if you want to learn through a tutorial, I can recommend you can either purchase another book (if you find yourself wanting to learn more) or use one of the many free online guides to languages, which are also fairly good.

While there are other server-side languages, the ones mentioned are by far the most commonly used and therefore will have the widest amount of support and documentation attached to them.

The Importance of Storage

A database is simply a storage container for collections of information related to each other or for data structured and organized in such a way that they can be used to save or access information placed within them. On the Web, the majority of databases make use of a common format called Structured Query Language (SQL), which has been in use in one form or another for a great many years. Again, because this is one of those topics that promises only headaches to those just getting started, I will skip over the gory details. However, many premade server-side scripts make use of databases for storing information. In this chapter, you will learn about these scripts, frameworks, and applications, as all of the hard work of scripting has been done for you! Of course, with databases, one thing to remember is that personal information stored in a database needs to be kept secret and private, especially if you hold financial or identifiable information about someone on record!

ExplainED

We will discuss the issue of privacy in Chapter 10, when we talk about selling your services (if you choose to). However, note that if you store any personal information (or cookies), you should include a privacy policy in your website explaining what information is collected and how it will be used.

Databases in Use

Websites have an awful amount of stuff to remember: content, information about users (if registration is required), individual settings for visitors, or even details about categorized items! While most people's heads would probably explode at the site of thousands of reviews on a website like Amazon or IMDB (see Figure 8-22), computers have to be able to work with information they are given, and this is the task of a site's database. Because of the clear need for databases to remember things, you should know how to work with them.

The following list of database formats could be used to store server-side script information:

- **MySQL** (http://dev.mysql.com/doc/): MySQL is the most popular of database management solutions with reportedly over 6 million installations worldwide. Many popular services, such as Wordpress and the phpBB message board make use of the open source and cross-platform MySQL project (currently on version 5). While MySQL has held its popularity due to many PHP users making use of it by default, it has been criticized about slow response times for fixing bugs and adding missing SQL features. While these may be of concern, MySQL is a solid choice and works with various languages well.

- **Microsoft SQL Server** (http://msdn.microsoft.com/en-gb/sqlserver/): Microsoft SQL Server is another popular database format commonly found on Windows. At version 10 (2008), it has an established history and, like ASP, remains a popular choice for those who distrust open source solutions, prefer to go with a solution backed by a large corporation, or want to use the default database that comes with Microsoft IIS (the Windows server platform that supports ASP and ASP.NET).

- **PostgreSQL** (http://www.postgresql.org/docs/manuals/): This alternative open source database solution has gained the attention of developers as a possible alternative to MySQL. MySQL continues to dominate the market because of its fast adoption rate by users and the large amount of documentation that supports it, and PostgreSQL has yet to push past the two mentioned previously due to lack of exposure and slowness to turn cross-platform; it's also seldom installed by default by web hosting providers, which tend to prefer MySQL instead.

- **Oracle** (http://www.oracle.com/technology/documentation/): Oracle, while one of the less-frequently used database formats, is a clear competitor with IBM's DB2, Microsoft SQL Server, and other commercial or enterprise-level database systems. However, for average people who are learning to produce websites, using Oracle would simply be overkill. Like ColdFusion's, Oracle's price of implementation is very high, and it's hard to find hosting packages that contain it by default, which prices it out of the range of most people getting started.

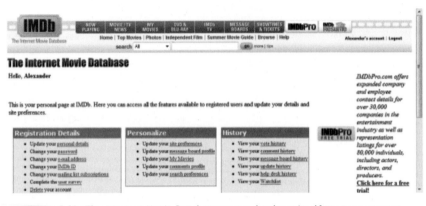

Figure 8-22. The Internet Movie Database uses a database itself to store account information for members.

Powerful Packages

You can use the languages and database formats listed in this chapter to produce your own powerful scripts, but you are only just getting into the idea of messing with scripts, so you may well want to use some of the fantastic software that exists on the Web (free of charge in many cases!). A benefit of using these well-established packages is that you are using something that has been tested to destruction and has made a name for itself as the standard in its chosen field. Most packages allow you to edit the source code, so they can be adapted to your layout with ease. And you can download themes, plug-ins, and more to enhance your site with additions that have been made by the community of developers who use the software. Therefore, you are not restricted in how you take the carefully built software and adapt it to your needs, though you should be careful to remember that you may find yourself needing to debug the code to resolve any errors that arise as updates for the packages appear. This is a good reason why you should eventually learn a server-side language rather than just relying completely on a software package. Listed throughout the following sections of the chapter are of some of the most popular pre-made tools and applications in use that you can trust for use on your website.

Despite the fact that server-side scripting is the subject for another book (due to its inherent complexity), it would be foolish not to mention some of the great things you can get out of scripting. So many wonderful products already take advantage of scripting, and you can either buy them or use them for free by downloading and installing the packages. They also normally come with plenty of instructions and help files along with a supportive community of people who are generally willing to help you out with questions you may have. So now, let's look at some of the most popular things you can achieve using server-side scripting and some packages to go with. Most of the packages listed in the following sections of this chapter have a wide range of functionality and extensibility which are created by the community of people who use the product and the developers who actively enhance it.

The packages featured in this chapter were chosen on their popularity and high regard in reviews. Whether a particular product will suit your needs is up to you to research. If you encounter problems using the products, you should either contact the makers or seek support on a related forum or website.

Content Management Systems

Managing a website can be a tricky task, if you find learning HTML and CSS complicated you may find yourself in a position where you cannot deal with the day-to-day maintenance of running a website, such as adding new content and marking it up correctly. While websites that provided a basic interface to pull a design together without knowing how to write any code have existed for a long time, which took the complexity out of owning a website (such as the famed but now-dead Geocities), more sophisticated systems have been needed at an ever-growing pace. A *content management system* (CMS) is a server-side platform meant to simplify the addition of new content and functionality as the website design is completed, but it is not intended to replace the website building process. A content management system acts as a backbone, providing structure, style, behavior, and scripting functionality all ready to use, but because of the system's open source nature, you can customize the layout, semantic value, and style of the product (with a lot of time and effort!). While these products can be useful in giving noncoders a functional website, they are intended for people with sites running into the hundreds (possibly thousands) of pages where maintenance and management becomes difficult.

A sampling of the content management packages available follows:

- **CushyCMS**: http://www.cushycms.com/
- **DotCMS**: http://www.dotcms.org/
- **DotNetNuke**: http://www.dotnetnuke.com/

- **Drupal**: http://drupal.org/ (See Figure 8-23.)
- **ExpressionEngine**: http://expressionengine.com/
- **FrogCMS**: http://www.madebyfrog.com/
- **Joomla**: http://www.joomla.org/
- **Mambo**: http://www.mamboserver.com/
- **MODx**: http://modxcms.com/
- **MovableType**: http://www.movabletype.org/
- **PHP-Nuke**: http://phpnuke.org/
- **RadiantCMS**: http://radiantcms.org/
- **Refinery**: http://www.refinerycms.com/
- **Silverstripe**: http://www.silverstripe.com/
- **TYPOlight**: http://www.typolight.org/

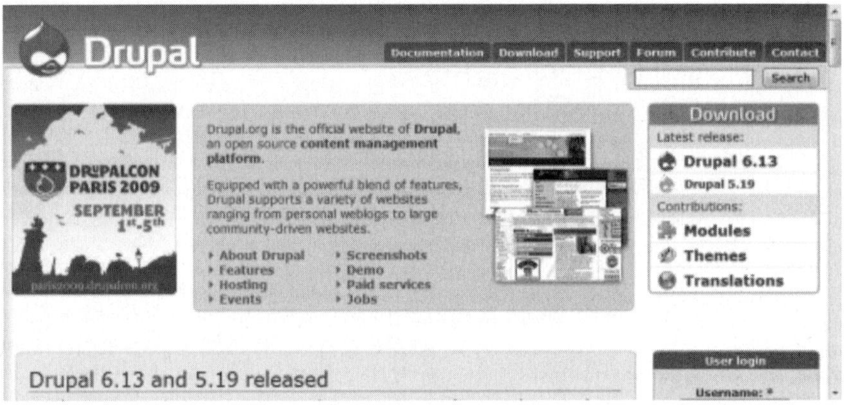

Figure 8-23. Drupal is one of the most popular open source and customisable CMS platforms.

Blogging Platforms

The |social networking craze that turned everyone into a freelance journalist is, of course, *blogging*, which offers the ability to say whatever you want (within the law) and have people visit your site just to read your opinion (making you the equivalent of an online journalist). While some people have become famous because of blogs, others have become infamous! The general idea behind blogging platforms is the same as a CMS, except these help people intent on keeping an online diary for themselves or their businesses. While blogs aren't considered traditional websites (as they're focused on topical content rather than articles, services, or other functionality), they are still a force to be reckoned with, especially if you consider the craze of the microblogging website Twitter and it's short-but-sweet method of allowing everyone to know what everyone else is up to. The general perspective behind blogging is that individuals update on a regular basis to ensure people continue to subscribe and read in the same way a newspaper needs regular editions to keep readers interested.

The following list contains some of the blogging packages available:

- **Blogger**: https://www.blogger.com/ (See Figure 8-24.)
- **LiveJournal**: http://www.livejournal.com/
- **LifeType**: http://lifetype.net/
- **TextPattern**: http://textpattern.com/
- **Tumblr**: http://www.tumblr.com/
- **TypePad**: http://www.typepad.com/
- **Vox**: http://www.vox.com/
- **Windows Live Spaces**: http://spaces.live.com/
- **WordPress**: http://wordpress.org/

Figure 8-24. Blogger may not be as popular as WordPress, but it still has plenty of users!

Wiki Packages

Nearly everyone has heard of or used Wikipedia at some point in their online lives. So what is a wiki? While "wiki" does sound like a strange word from an exotic location, the intention behind wiki applications is to offer a knowledgebase or encyclopedia of information that is easy to search, cross reference, and update. Generally, wikis are collaborative projects in which multiple people become involved in the editing process and, like blogging, the concept behind wikis is content-focused material rather than a general website that probably has more images, media, and other elements to give it contrast. However, wikis still have their place; they are excellent for creating user manuals, frequently asked question lists, and other informative multipaged resources.

The following list offers a sampling of the wiki packages available:

- **DokuWiki**: http://www.dokuwiki.org/
- **MediaWiki**: http://www.mediawiki.org/ (See Figure 8-25.)
- **MoinMoinWiki**: http://moinmo.in/
- **TikiWiki**: http://info.tikiwiki.org/
- **Twikiwiki**: http://twiki.org/

Figure 8-25. Wikipedia is one of the most well known wikis and is powered by the MediaWiki platform.

Forum Software

Message boards have been around for a long time. They are (along with chat rooms) one of the earliest methods of social media on the Internet, and they allow people to collaborate and have discussions in an environment that can be moderated and grouped into sections of appropriate discussion. Forums tend to work on a hierarchical model, where administrators and moderators control the content to remove spam and junk material manually. What makes forum software interesting is that the environment, unlike many social networking platforms, isn't technically live: you post a message and wait for other people to respond, rather than knowing who is contributing at any one time in real-time, though you may know who is browsing the forum. One common use for forum software is in technical support, where people can post problems with purchases or things they found on the website and those who run the site can take appropriate action.

The following is a sampling of the forum packages available:

- **bbPress**: http://bbpress.org/
- **FluxBB**: http://fluxbb.org/
- **FUDForum**: http://fudforum.org/
- **Invision**: http://www.invisionpower.com/ (See Figure 8-26.)
- **myBB**: http://www.mybboard.net/
- **Phorum**: http://www.phorum.org/
- **phpBB**: http://www.phpbb.com/
- **SMF**: http://www.simplemachines.org/
- **UseBB**: http://www.usebb.net/
- **Vanilla**: http://getvanilla.com/
- **vBulletin**: http://www.vbulletin.com/
- **YaBB**: http://www.yabbforum.com/

Figure 8-26. While it may be a commercial product, Invision Power Board is a very popular forum product.

Online Services

In addition to the great number of examples of scripts you can place directly within your website, a variety of free services that make use of server-side scripting are available to enhance your website (an example of this could include an online email client like Gmail). Relying on third-party services can be quite controversial, as you are relying on other people and your website suffers if their code isn't maintained. However, you should not dismiss the fantastic free services out there that have been running for a long time and have gained a reputation for being trustworthy. These are likely to be worth investing your time in using either on a single-use or long-term basis. Essentially, when using a service that will be embedded within or will have associations with your web site, you simply need to ensure that the service is quality, the product is reliable, and the brand name is well known and trusted (to avoid con artists). Some likely candidates for use in your websites follow:

- **Mapping services**: Bing Maps, Google Maps (see Figure 8-27), MapQuest, and Yahoo Maps
- **Reference websites**: Encyclopedia Britannica Online, Encyclopedia.com, and Wikipedia
- **Weather services**: AccuWeather, BBC Weather, Weather Channel, and Yahoo Weather
- **URL shortening**: bit.ly, go.to, is.gd, Tiny.cc, TinyUrl and zi.pe
- **Video sharing**: Blip.tv, Dailymotion, Liveleak, MetaCafe, Twango, Veoh, and YouTube
- **Image galleries**: deviantArt, Flickr, Fotki, Photobucket, Picasa, SmugMug, and Zoomr
- **File hosting**: Amazon S3, FileDropper, FileFactory, File Savr, and MediaFire
- **Email services:** Google Gmail, Windows Live Hotmail, and Yahoo Mail

Figure 8-27. Google Maps allows you to browse the world from the comfort of your computer.

Try it yourself: Add Google Maps to Your Website

Do you want a pretty Google Maps feature added to your website? Perhaps you want to show potential visitors where you live or give directions to a place you are recommending they go for pizza. Whatever the reason, you can embed a map quickly and easily using Google Maps. The first thing you need to do, of course, is visit maps.google.com. Once you have made it to the website, you need to type an address or location for where the map should point. At this stage, you can scroll and zoom in or out until you have the map looking just as you want it to, and all you need to do is get that snapshot from the website into your own. Click the Link button, next to Print and Send (see Figure 8-28). Then, select and copy the text in the "Paste HTML to embed in website" box; this is the source code you will need. If you want to customize the map's appearance further, you can click the "Customize and preview embedded map" link offered below the box on the Google site, and a pop-up window should appear, if you have them enabled, allowing you to edit the map size. Once you are finished, copy the source code and paste wherever you want the map to appear within your site

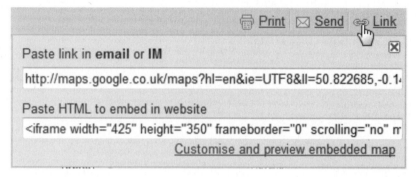

Figure 8-28. Getting the code to embed a Google map into your website couldn't be easier.

ExplainED

You will probably notice that the Google Maps uses some really yucky but necessary code, such as iframes, and some not-so-required code. You could strip out all the stuff that shouldn't be there (like the width and height) and place those values in your CSS for a semantically pretty map! Of course, Google does it this way is for simplicity, so users only need to copy and paste a single piece of code. But with our knowledge, we can take apart this code and put all its pieces into their proper places.

Server-Side Frameworks

JavaScript isn't the only language with a variety of frameworks. Many of the server-side scripting languages have their own frameworks to help produce agile and flexible websites. While these generally have features you would commonly find in a content management system, they are often built for the creation of web applications and online software solutions. If you are interested in server-side scripting, the time when you choose to employ a framework is slightly different to that of JavaScript: JavaScript frameworks are designed to avoid the need for writing scripts in the first place, but the general consensus is that you should consider using server-side frameworks only when the time comes that you feel you are going to undertake a large project. The reason for this is because server-side frameworks are often fairly bulky, have quite large file sizes (due to the sheer scale of the languages involved), and generally aren't intended to replace small scripts or general server-side interaction.

Here are some potentially handy server-side frameworks:

- **Agavi**: http://www.agavi.org/
- **CakePHP**: http://cakephp.org/
- **Catalyst:** http://www.catalystframework.org/
- **CodeIgniter**: http://codeigniter.com/
- **DotNetNuke**: http://www.dotnetnuke.com/
- **Django**: http://www.djangoproject.com/
- **Google Web Toolkit**: http://code.google.com/webtoolkit/
- **Grails**: http://www.grails.org/
- **Kohana**: http://www.kohanaphp.com/
- **Pylons**: http://pylonshq.com/
- **Ruby On Rails**: http://rubyonrails.org/
- **TurboGears**: http://turbogears.org/
- **Struts2**: http://struts.apache.org/
- **Symphony**: http://www.symfony-project.org/
- **Web2Py**: http://www.web2py.com/
- **WebObjects**: http://www.apple.com/webobjects/
- **YII**: http://www.yiiframework.com/
- **Zend**: http://www.zend.com/en/

Head in the Clouds

The field of producing RIAs is one of the fastest growing in the web industry. The whole concept of Web 2.0 allowed us to make more feature-rich applications (see Figure 8-29) through innovations like AJAX and tools and frameworks that let us carry our web software offline as fully fledged applications. Desktop PCs have a similar method of achieving this type of offline environment for web applications through software-based toolkits such as Adobe AIR. Products like the iPhone also allow you to produce applications that can interact directly with the Web or products that require no active Internet Connection. The ability to turn something like a word processor into an online package (or a web based word processor into an offline application) that works regardless of operating system and can be upgraded from the side of the maintainer of the products has a lot of appeal in an industry where one of the critical flaws (as you learned in our discussion of the browser wars) was that many users failed to keep their software up to date; perhaps even you are running some out-of-date software!

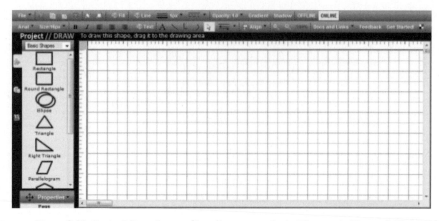

Figure 8-29. Project Draw is an online diagram product. Who needs Microsoft Visio anymore?

This kind of application is described as *software as a service* (SaaS); the essence behind this is that the product is no longer a physical piece of software on your desktop computer but a floating entity that exists on the Web through the web browser, which acts like a portal. When software no longer has a physical presence on the hard disk and exists purely on the Web in a virtual capacity, this situation is commonly referred to as *cloud computing* because the software is floating freely for anyone to connect with. The software can also be qualified as a service because many people running commercial services online charge a subscription fee rather than a single cost with upgrade costs for each new release. This pricing structure benefits visitors who only pay for what they are using and the period of time they use it, which makes SaaS a virtual product.

As you are still fresh to the whole concept of building a website, cloud computing services are something you do not have to worry about achieving any time soon. Just take from this discussion that scripting for the Web has become so powerful with server- and client-side scripting, Flash, Silverlight, and others that the potential to build a fully fledged application for which you could charge money is entirely possible for a seasoned scripter.

LinkED

If you want an example of SaaS in action, you just need to look to Adobe, who has made a basic version of its Photoshop product available for free on the web at https://www.photoshop.com/?wf=testdrive.

Plug and Play

Of course, when you create an RIA, it doesn't need to be created using AJAX or a server-side language—far from it! Many web applications, like the one shown in Figure 8-30, are produced using technologies you learned about earlier in this book, specifically Adobe Flash, Microsoft Silverlight, and Java. The self-contained Flash and Silverlight products have their own dedicated scripting languages (ActionScript and XAML/.NET respectively) and allow you to create highly functional applications and services that run from within the plug-in-based environment. Of course, the problem with using such languages is that you cannot guarantee that people will have the players installed or available. However, because Flash and Silverlight (and to a point Java) have high market-penetration rates, this lack of a guarantee for the products being available probably shouldn't stop you from trying to create your site using them if you feel it would help the visitors of your website. The great thing is that if the plug-in is installed and available you are guaranteed the application will work across every browser it's supported in, because unlike general scripting, you don't need to worry about the browsers' rendering engines.

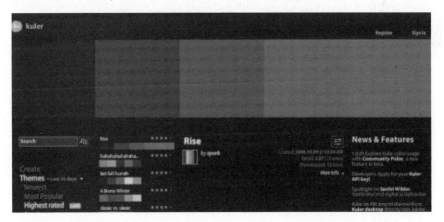

Figure 8-30. Adobe Kuler is a Flash-powered color-scheming service and a RIA.

ExplainED

The technology which allows plug-in's like Flash, Silverlight and custom written web-based tools within Internet Explorer (and to a lesser extent, Google Chrome) is called ActiveX. While this technology has helped evolve the web it's worth steering clear of writing ActiveX components as they tend to have a lot of security implications, mainly as a result of enabling the application to do anything to a visitor's PC!

RIA Frameworks

Now, we are at the final bunch of frameworks; the only ones we have yet to cover are the frameworks to aid the development of RIAs, and the following list will not disappoint you. The exciting thing about these frameworks is that, using them, you could actually create a proper piece of software that can have functionality like anything you see on the shelves at your local PC retailer, even if you just know the basics of HTML, CSS, and JavaScript. This ability to cross over between online and offline technology means that budding web designers can create software and take their creations to the average consumer. This portability is exciting for the future of the Web (and also for the software market), as you will have more options as to where your site-creation hobby takes you next!

Here are some RIA frameworks for you to investigate further:

- **AIR**: http://www.adobe.com/products/air/
- **Cappuccino**: http://cappuccino.org/
- **Curl**: http://www.curl.com/
- **Flash**: http://www.adobe.com/products/flash/
- **Flex**: http://www.adobe.com/products/flex/
- **Gears**: http://gears.google.com/
- **JavaFX**: http://javafx.com/
- **Prism**: http://labs.mozilla.com/projects/prism/
- **Silverlight**: http://silverlight.net/
- **Titanium**: http://www.appcelerator.com/

ExplainED

Web application frameworks produce software based on existing scriptable languages (both server- and client-side), whereas RIAs are independently powered by third-party plug-ins (such as Adobe Flash). Either of these two methods can be used to produce web applications that function online and offline.

Additional Resources

Now that you have a general idea about the kinds of products that can be produced using server-side scripting languages, the frameworks that exist, and the actual languages you can choose, it's probably best to offer you some useful resource websites that can help teach you the basics of these languages (of course, you could always buy another book on the subject). Whether you choose to learn server-side coding is entirely up to you. Many people happily survive using third-party products and web applications that have already been created, so if you don't feel the need to learn scripting just yet, feel free to hold back until you reach the limits of what already exists—then you know it's time to learn! So, for the last time in this chapter, here are some useful resources:

- **ASP 101**: http://www.asp101.com/
- **ASP.NET**: http://www.asp.net/learn/
- **Developer Hell**: http://www.developerhell.com/
- **Tizag**: http://www.tizag.com/
- **W3Schools**: http://www.w3schools.com/
- **Web Programming**: http://webdesign.about.com/od/webprogramming/
- **Web Reference**: http://www.webreference.com/
- **Zend DevZone**: http://devzone.zend.com/article/627

Security Issues

The last topic we need to talk about is the danger of poor security. With all this scripting we are doing, it is almost too easy to forget that, when you allow code to interact with software or make changes to a system, a potential risk is born: someone may try to take advantage of your website and try to trick your site into performing something that will compromise its security. Of course, security is something you should always be concerned about, as you don't want your website getting taken over by a bunch of pirates! The Internet can be a seedy place with a dark side filled with individuals who want to take advantage of your website and its visitors. Some of the most common potential forms of security issues you will probably encounter are cross-site scripting (XSS), SQL injection, spoofing (which includes phishing attacks), and brute force attacks, which are all pretty scary!

ExplainED

While the very thought of security problems is uncomfortable, as long as you are sensible with what code you do produce (in terms of scripting) and follow the prevention advice below (within the website links), you should find yourself less likely to be attacked.

The following security issues may be encountered on your website:

- **Cross-site scripting** (XSS): If someone responded to a post in a forum, that user could enter text (possibly code). In an XSS attack, scripts are inserted and used to hijack information about someone else using the website, for example, a cookie containing login information. The attacker could then make the information publically available (or record it for pick-up later). XSS could also be used to steal your cookie and mask the attacker as you, which could grant access to all sorts of information through the exposed account. The main way to prevent XSS attacks is to sanitize your code if you allow people to enter text that will be added to your website; essentially, you need to strip text of HTML elements that may pose a threat, such as the `script`, `object`, `embed`, `iframe`, `applet`, or any other code executable tags. By doing this, you wipe out the threat, as the XSS attempt will just result in plain text rather than active code! For a detailed guide, visit `http://www.cgisecurity.com/xss-faq.html`, and for more on preventing XSS attacks, visit `http://www.owasp.org/index.php/XSS_(Cross_Site_Scripting)_Prevention_Cheat_Sheet`.

- **SQL injection**: This is where commands that were not intended to be passed by the application developer are sent to a database with the intent to gain access to information not publicly available. The method of using such commands commonly results in a *buffer overflow*. Because SQL will execute any commands that are semantically correct, you need to ensure that no malicious user input can be injected. Otherwise, the code could allow the attacker to access private records, control information held in the database, and even make administrative changes! One of the basic ways you can prevent injection is to ensure that the SQL commands cannot be tampered with and, more importantly, ensure that the database is not connected as an administrator or the database owner. For more information about SQL injections and how to prevent them, visit http://www.sitepoint.com/article/sql-injection-attacks-safe/.

- **Phishing**: Phishing is less of a problem in relation to the security of your website but is of critical importance to the security of your visitors. The act of *spoofing* is when an individual pretends to be someone else to take advantage of that person, and *phishing* is the method in which such attacks are carried out. Phishing is very commonly seen on the Internet in the form of scams that try to extract money from people through email or a website set up to look and act identically to another to prompt visitors to enter sensitive information, such as their usernames and passwords. If you find that someone else is trying to take advantage of your visitors in this way, you should make users aware that a spoof exists and contact either the host of the spoof website or ICANN (who settles disputes with domain names) to take action to have the mimic site forcibly taken down. While, scam artists exist online as well as offline, you can still do everything possible to protect your visitors. For more details about phishing, the following Wikipedia article has plenty of useful information: http://en.wikipedia.org/wiki/Phishing.

- **Brute force attacks**: Essentially, a brute force attack is a method of trying to bypass security or affect a website by following a repetitive task over and over, each time trying to achieve a goal, for example, trying to bypass your website's security using dictionaries of common passwords. In this attack, the account of someone who doesn't have a solid password could be breached. Luckily, brute force password attacks are fairly rare due to the time they require, and most servers and login processes have protection methods against them. The other really well-known type of brute force attack, which is still very common, is a denial of service (DoS or DDoS) attack. In this attack, the only intent of the bad guy is to take your website down by making thousands of requests for your pages, stressing the servers and draining your bandwidth until the site becomes too slow to visit, the server crashes, or your site is taken down because it exceeds its bandwidth limit. For more information and prevention tips, read the Wikipedia article at `http://en.wikipedia.org/wiki/Denial-of-service_attack`.

ExplainED

The issues mentioned are a very basic overview of potential security problems. However, many more vulnerabilities can occur, so you should learn to secure your scripts properly if you are producing anything from scratch. While existing scripts carry protection, it does not mean they cannot be exploited!

Summary

In this chapter, you have learned about the basics of scripting, how to add behavior to your website, and the various different types of scripts, libraries, and frameworks that exist. You have also learned about server-side scripts and the languages that power them and using databases and interactive components to give a more customized experience, as well as being introduced to web applications. You will also have gotten to grips with the concepts of web security (for behavior) and have a general understanding of the concepts behind cloud computing. In the next chapter, we are going to examine the subject of accessibility and usability and how you can improve the user experience of your website even further by taking into account the needs and methods people use to browse the Web beyond the basics of the most common web browsers. While this chapter will contain plenty of theory, you will also be confronted with various conventions relating to how people browse the web, which will hopefully get you to adapt your site to meet these very important needs and gain a few tips on why some sites look better than others. As a result, you could potentially improve your existing website.

Chapter Checklist

You should accomplish the following tasks before leaving this chapter:

- Learn the basics of client-side scripting and how to use it in your site.
- Get to grips with server-side scripting languages and their applications.
- Learn about the various frameworks you can make use of within your site.
- Be aware of security risks and the basics of rich Internet applications.

Questions and Answers

Q: *Should I use an existing framework or learn to build my own scripts?*

A: Well, this comes down to your own skill level and how much you want to learn about a particular language. Really, many people choose to use frameworks, because they require a lot less effort, and much of the hard work has been taken out of the implementation process. Also, many frameworks have been tested in such a way that you know any potential bugs are likely to have already been resolved ensuring that your website is going to break less often and will degrade gracefully for browsers that do not have scripting enabled. Of course, being able to script on your own without relying on third-party frameworks does have benefits, as these packages often are built with multiple functions that may not be used by your website, and therefore, the increase in file sizes may be considered unnecessary bloat. Take time to weigh the pros and cons before you make a decision.

Q: *Is one server-side language any better than another for making sites?*

A: This question is asked probably more often than any other in terms of website development. These days, the idea that one server-side language is better, or worse, than another is not really a factor. All of the well-established scripting languages have had years to mature and have their own benefits and pitfalls, but ultimately, the decision you make will be based on factors such as the type of hosting you have, the kind of scripting you intend to use, and the complexity of the project involved. Because this book is aimed at novices to the web development process, you will not find much in the way of coding here, as this subject is too dense a subject to walk into without getting lost in the jargon and the various different languages. Therefore, you should use your language profile and the capabilities of your host along with some research (take a look around the web to see what each language can offer) to decide where to focus your energy. It's unlikely you will need to know more than one server-side language, which probably is a relief.

Q: *How many different languages should I learn when building a website?*

A: As you are already aware, the most important languages you can choose to learn are HTML (for structure) and CSS (for style) to at least have a basic website up and running. If you want to give your visitors more than just a static website, you can offer dynamic flavor by adding to the mix one client-side scripting language (like JavaScript), and for even more functionality, you can top off those skills with a server-side language (such as PHP or ASP.NET) and a database format (like MySQL or Microsoft SQL Server). While the thought of learning more languages may sound like a lot of effort, you should remember that learning is a never-ending process, and as you become more comfortable creating websites, the additional functionality scripting languages can offer will help you make even better sites in the future. Apart from learning those mentioned here, you could potentially learn a syndication language, like RSS or Atom (mentioned in the next chapter), or a supplemental language like ActionScript (which lets you create Flash files) or Microsoft Silverlight's scripting language. The sky is the limit!

Where You Are Now

By the end of this chapter you should have the following:

- JavaScript elements you feel would suit your website
- Considered the viability of frameworks and how they can benefit you
- Any server-side scripts and applications your website needs

Chapter 9

How Can My Website Be Improved?

If you've produced a website while working through this book, you should, at this stage, have something that looks and works great. The intention has been to equip you with skills that every designer from novice to professional should take into account when building websites, from the planning and content writing in early chapters, which help you focus your site's aim, to the chapters on building and debugging your designs using HTML, CSS, and to a basic extent, scripting to actually put the plan into action. Of course, while many people make the mistake of thinking the story ends once your site is up, there are still some useful ways you can help to increase the chances your website will get noticed and perform in such a way that anyone who does come across your website will be more likely to return. In the next chapter, we shall address the issue of getting people on your website in the first place through marketing and search engine optimization, but for the moment, we need to focus on some of the improvements you can make to your code and design to help more people take advantage of your website, including making your website accessible to enriching the overall user experience.

In this chapter, we're going to cover the following topics:

- The importance of making your website accessible to disabled users
- Improving your site with design patterns and usability testing
- Using purpose-built microformats, metadata, and syndication feeds

Accessibility with Agility

You are probably wondering how much better your code can get considering you have followed the standards and semantics of the Web as best as you can. Well, not everything that affects a visitor's experience comes down to how well the code was produced. There will always be issues that occur when someone appears on your website and cannot access all of your content as a result of certain needs or restrictions that person may have, which will ultimately problems that trip up the user along the way. For instance, people who are blind browse the Web using specialized pieces of software; visually impaired users can be a part of your website as much as anyone else, that is, as long as you have made sure there are no roadblocks for them. Obviously, at this stage, you will not know what the issues are, so continue reading to learn how to deal with this subject effectively. Plus, you can make the necessary changes to your website as you learn about these factors to ensure that your site works for as many people as possible, which is ultimately the goal of any website.

What Is Accessibility?

An|accessible website is one that works for the largest amount of people as possible, regardless of any disability or factor that may make their browsing experiences more difficult. When I talk about accessibility in this book, I do not just mean making the site available to people who may have problems trying to visit your website but to web browsers, search engines, and even alternative methods of browsing such as mobile phones. There are a lot of people out there, all using a different way of accessing the Web, and while you cannot address every need that exists, by taking into account the following information, you can make your visitors' lives a heck of a lot easier—we all know how frustrating it can be when a website doesn't work as it states.

Accessibility is closely tied with usability, as it focuses primarily on trying to improve the overall user experience (usability is something we will examine later on in this chapter). They do have their differences though: accessibility tends to look at making sure your site is available, whereas usability focuses more on how things could be improved. It is important to know that accessibility is not something that can have a 100% success rate; every condition of accessibility has its own unique elements, and as no two people are affected in the same way, flexibility needs to be encouraged rather than aiming for complete equality.

The Common Myths

The first thing we need to do when taking about accessibility is debunk a myth that exists on the web today: many people make the incorrect assumption that very few disabled people use the Internet. This myth needs to be cleared up, because it is a false statement perpetuated by those who really do not understand the scope of the problem that affects millions of people on a daily basis. Take, for example, the medical condition color blindness; a web designer needs to ensure that those affected can actually see the website. Being red/green colorblind myself, I can tell you there have been occasions where I have been unable to read content on a website because of my eyes' inability to separate certain shades of color; because of the low contrast between some colors, the text became impossible to read.

A medical condition like color blindness affects a large number of people on a daily basis (some statistics say up to 7% of the population). Taking that into account and including it along with the various other disabilities that can affect how someone can make use of your site, disabilities are not simply something that a minority of people must deal with. The truth is that the majority of people have something that can inhibit their experiences, even if their medical conditions are nothing more than near-sightedness, which might hinder their ability to read small writing on the screen. Keep this in mind when you produce your website structure, style, and behavior; it is important that you take into account the fact that millions of people may have special requirements to be able to visit your website, and not all of them will be immediately obvious to the casual individual. These people may become a part of your online family, so you should take the time to find out what they need and how their needs could be met (for example, by making sure text colors are not faint against the background), and to ensure you do as much as you can to make your site as balanced as possible.

Another common myth is the price point. Many people believe that implementing an accessible website is a costly affair that requires a lot of time and energy to put into practice. It is true that adapting an existing website (especially if it contains thousands of pages) can be expensive and fairly impractical. However, for the average person such as yourself who just wants to make a normal website, at the stage of writing pages and syntax, making your website accessible is a straightforward and inexpensive process. After all, you just need to follow a few standards, run a few tests, make a few minor tweaks, and ensure your code is valid. What is also worth remembering is the cost of not being accessible could be far greater if the result of your site not working for disabled people reduces the amount of people who can visit and browse your website.

ExplainED

If you are building a website with the intention of selling things online (or making money), the cost of not having an accessible website could be huge now that disabled people have begun suing commercial sites who refuse to meet their needs (which is a legal requirement in many countries).

Also while we are on the subject, note that accessibility is not just a case of dealing with disability. Plenty of people without disabilities but could still find solid benefits in your attempts to make your website more accessible. Let's take into account, for example, the steady rise in elderly people making use of the Web. It's fantastic that there are plenty of silver surfers out there, but alas, with getting older comes increased rates of lower quality vision, arthritis, and other problems that accessibility helps to address. Many myths surrounding accessibility exist, and there will always be people who do not care about their visitors, but I hope that you are not among them. Please take the time to try to make your web experience as happy as possible for people who perhaps may need an extra bit of help from time to time.

Accessibility Benefits

Now that you know what accessibility is and its importance, you want to know what the real world benefits are for you. While many individuals and businesses will happily implement accessibility on the basis that it improves the experience for their visitors, some people out there have the opinion that if it works for them, so what if other people can't use it? Obviously, convincing some people is downright impossible, and others may think that your website will be perfectly fine without any refinements. However, you should take a look at the following information about the results of good accessibility can be and how it can dramatically make a difference you can measure to the overall success of your website when it goes live on the Web.

The benefits of accessible web design can be huge. If you are in the process of building a website where you intend to sell things, by making sure your website loads for the widest possible audience, you give yourself more of a chance that you might sell something (after all, getting 500 people looking in your shop is better than 400). Focusing on earning money isn't really one of the major concerns for the average person wanting to make a website, but it is also noteworthy that your name and brand carry with it the foundation of your public appeal. When you show your visitors that you intend to deal with issues that arise from using your website, they are going to entrust you with their time and word of mouth promotion. You may, as a result, see a rise in traffic or perhaps more people willing to help make your website a better place. Of course, many of these benefits are based in theory. As we are producing a website from scratch, ensuring that the pages are accessible will be done from the offset to help reduce the chances that issues may occur in the future.

Assistive Devices

You may be wondering exactly how disabled people browse the Web. Well, the situation is rather complex, and while there are some useful assistive technologies available, some of those products come with extremely heavy price tags. Users of the Internet who are blind and require a screen reader, for example, can pay literally thousands of dollars for a single user license of a software product that converts all the content on accessible websites into spoken words. This makes the task of testing in the wide variety of assistive devices (to see if your website works in them) rather difficult indeed! The utilities and tools in the following sections are those you may find a number of disabled people using on a daily basis.

Screen Readers

Visually impaired users are one of the most inhibited groups when it comes to browsing the Web. Because they cannot read information for themselves as it appears onscreen, they use products known as screen readers to read aloud through speakers the textual content that appears in the web browser. Two of the most popular screen reader packages for Windows are JAWS (Job Access With Speech), which is shown in Figure 9-1, and Windows-Eyes, both of which are commercial products and quite expensive. Free and low cost alternatives are available, but they have a lower number of features and users. Because of this, it's debatable whether the number of people visiting your site using them will be high enough to be considered when testing your website (unless you have the tools available to you). Generally, as well as providing text to speech, screen readers can also provide Braille output that can be helpful for anyone who has the correct hardware to take advantage of the technology.

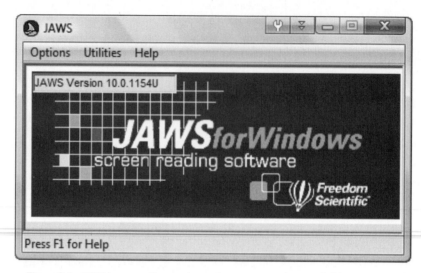

Figure 9-1. JAWS is among the most popular screen readers available to purchase.

Tactile Devices

While many pieces of software out there can assist the process of viewing a website, a number of hardware solutions can be used to aid accessibility. These include Braille keyboards and displays, and keyboard guards and switches (such as those triggered with a blink of the eyes) for those with low motor function and specially engineered mice (such as foot pedals). Many more cool pieces of technology exist for those who cannot use a standard keyboard and mouse. While these tools do exist, you should not expect your visitors to be using one of them; the cost to implement some of the hardware for yourself may be more than you can afford (this is extremely important to remember).

Magnifiers

While the zoom and text resizing abilities within a web browser do have some excellent functionality for dynamically resizing elements, some people require deeper zooming than a browser supports or want to focus on a particular element that they hover over. For these users, there are onscreen magnifiers that go beyond the limitations of the browser and enable visually impaired visitors to hone their attention on a small segment of the screen rather than scrolling through a vastly increased-scale website. Like the mouse and keyboard accessibility tools, some magnification software is built into Windows, but commercial products contain more features, such as color inversion and font smoothing.

Text Browsers

While most web browsers make use of a graphical user interface, some browsers are text based or have limited visual capacities (see Chapter 7). These play an essential role in checking your website's accessibility, as they strip away all of the style and behavior, leaving you with your website in its purest and simplest format. Even to this day, text browsers still have dedicated users, though they are considerably fewer than any other type of web browser (such as, for example, mobile web browsers). One of the most popular text browsers still in common use is Lynx, which is a free product to download and use (see Figure 9-2).

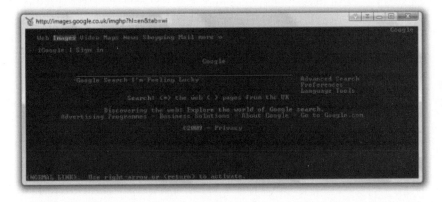

Figure 9-2. Lynx is one of the most popular text web browsers still in common use today.

ExplainED

If you would like to download Lynx to try this useful tool (and browser) for yourself, a Windows version is available for free at http://csant.info/lynx.htm. *For other operating systems, visit* http://lynx.isc.org/.

Mouse and Keyboard

Built within your operating system are several tools to help increase the accessibility of both browsing the Web and using a computer. Windows functions such as filter keys, sticky keys, the onscreen keyboard (see Figure 9-3), toggle keys, narrators, delay keys, high-contrast systems, sound sensors, selection delay, and mouse keys all play their parts in ensuring that your visitors can use their web browser effectively and therefore browse your site with ease. As many mouse and keyboard tools are provided within your operating system, you can play around with them to see how their use can benefit people with accessibility issues while visiting the site you have produced. Within Windows, you can find these tools within the Ease of Access Center within Vista or "Accessibility options" in XP, and these are free to use. You should remember, though, that these tools may assist with accessibility but do not remove the underlying causes of issues within a website.

Figure 9-3. The on-screen keyboard included with Windows assists those who cannot use a standard keyboard.

Speech Recognition

We have already mentioned software that reads text on the screen and transforms it into speech for people with visual impairments. Next, we are going to look at for speech recognition devices, which allow people who cannot use a mouse or keyboard (or those of us who want to feel like we are in *Minority Report*) talk to the computer and issue it vocal commands. Speech recognition is one of the fastest growing areas of accessibility software, and improvements in recognizing speech and accents (in particular) have meant that this tool has become something that can be used reliably when browsing and participating on the Web.

Web Browser Tools

Browsers themselves have a varied number of useful accessibility tweaks which can be used to improve the readability of website content. Some of the functions you may find within a web browser for disabled users include choosing custom style sheets, screen reading (Opera), automatic information fill-in, and of course, the customary zoom and text resizing features. While the accessibility features between each browser varies, Mozilla Firefox is worthy of mention due to its add-on support and near infinite ability to be extended to add additional accessibility features that could match commercial products. Still, you should not eliminate browsers such as Internet Explorer, as they have their own basic set of accessibility features (see Figure 9-4).

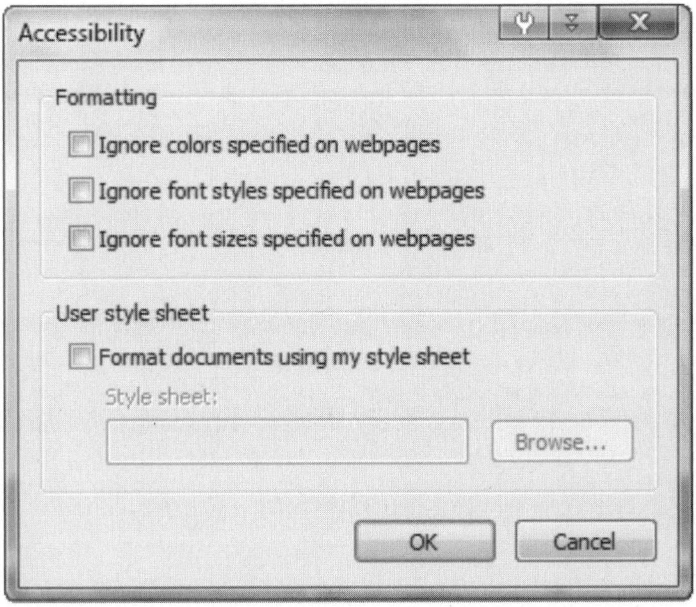

Figure 9-4. Internet Explorer contains some basic ways to ensure that style within websites will not inhibit accessibility.

Accessibility Issues

People have various types of disabilities that exist and not all of them can be easily detected, and some of them are forgotten by web and content authors. When I spoke to you about writing your content, we discussed the importance of having empathy toward your visitors, and this is never more true than when you try to make sure your website works for an audience of varied abilities. When you look over your website in your web browser, just think about how someone with a medical condition or disability may be affected when trying to make use of your website's offerings. Perhaps you could even try to replicate the same browsing conditions, for example, by turning off your monitor to test the situation that a visually impaired user might have while using as speech browser. Then, you can see for yourself how hard or easy your design is to navigate and if there are things you feel could be improved over time.

Varying Degrees

The first thing we need to establish about the different kinds of accessibility needs your visitors will have is the users are affected at various levels. Just like you should note that people with visual impairments can have a whole spectrum of different conditions, varying degrees of visual loss, and be affected in unique ways, you should also be aware that not every disability is permanent. People who have been in car accidents, for example, may lose the ability to use their limbs for a short period until they go through physical therapy. These users will need adaptations only until they have fully recovered, whereas people who have loss of motor functions from birth will most likely find that their needs are something of concern over their entire lives.

When you make use of the information in the following sections, you need to try to take into account the different variables that can inhibit the web experience of disabled users and ensure that your website can be used with the kinds of tools they use on a daily basis to access the Internet. While this does not mean you should be using every piece of accessibility software on the planet, as you are starting out, it is worth perhaps taking a look at the range of software that exists, but you can give it a try and have a bit of fun experimenting with how someone with limited vision or motor control or another condition can use the Web. If, for example, you turn off your monitor and try using a screen reader on your website, you can better appreciate others' needs, and through this, you can see potential areas for improvement that will mean that no one who comes to your site will feel unwelcome.

Physical

The most common types of accessibility concern to take into account when you produce a website are physical needs. Someone who uses a wheelchair expects to be able to enter a shop to buy goods, and users expect the same principle to apply to the Web. Of course, a wheelchair user may not necessarily have problems using a computer; a wide number of physical concerns can directly complicate the matter of browsing a website.

The following are needs that apply to this group in terms of accessibility:

- **Visual**: People with visual impairments, ranging from full and partial blindness to color blindness and even near- and far-sightedness, may find it hard to browse your website. Then too, people who have had operations on their eyes (for example, for cataracts) may have difficulty. Ensuring your website uses contrasting colors, large visible icons and that hard-to-read content works in screen readers (text-to-speech programs) and is clear and not confusing will all help to ensure that people in this group will not be rejected by your website.

- **Aural**: People who suffer from deafness, tinnitus, and other related hearing disorders may be unable to take advantage of multimedia or audio you provide. Ensuring your multimedia is well described, contains subtitles if they're relevant, and has text-based transcripts will guarantee that those who cannot hear well will still be able to interact with your website on a daily basis.

- **Speech**: Most websites do not contain the input to speak. However, if you intend on providing telephone support for your website (a good idea if you offer goods and services), you may wish to also ensure you provide other methods of contact, such as email, for people who have speech issues. For example, some visitors to your site could stutter or be mute, or they may speak English as a second language or have hard-to-understand accents.

- **Motor**: Loss of movement is a common issue. For example, people with paraplegia or other types of paralysis, multiple sclerosis, Parkinson's disease, cerebral palsy, arthritis, involuntary movement (tremors or spasms), and repetitive strain injuries may have limited mobility that affects the way they use the computer. Also, stroke or heart attack survivors, people who are recovering from injuries to limbs (undergoing physical therapy), a general lack of coordination, and even someone with a broken arm could experience movement limitations. By giving links larger click areas, ensuring a minimal amount of keystrokes or mouse movement is needed to reach something you want, and by following conventions to reduce confusion, you will give individuals with limited movement a better experience.

- **Seizure**: Photosensitive epileptics or those who suffer from other types of seizures could be seriously affected by onscreen images and multimedia. By making sure you have nothing that flashes violently, you can reduce the chances of your visitors having a seizure from the visual elements of your website.

- **Technical**: Humans aren't the only ones who can suffer accessibility problems! Computers can also have issues. Take, for example, mobile devices; with limited support for languages on the Web and smaller visual space to display site contents, they have impairments of their own. Also, available bandwidth and the speed of a website loading can have a physical impact on a site's accessibility. Making sure your website works on a wide variety of devices and browsers can help deal with specific issues that appear from the use of these platforms.

- **Health**: People with psychological conditions such as schizophrenia or those who are suffering the side effects from medications (like the ones with the labels saying "do not operate heavy machinery") may suffer physical or emotional side effects such as shaky hands or blurred vision, or they may be easily distracted by multimedia or distracting elements like Flash files, depending on the nature of their conditions. By keeping the noise in the website's background to a minimum, you can decrease the time it takes people to visit and navigate around your website. This can also impact emotional disabilities (as noted later in this chapter).

- **Age**: The young and the old can be physically affected in their ability to use a computer. Older visitors may have conditions like arthritis and could find movement restricted, and younger visitors often are still developing and may find everything a learning experience. You should be sure of your target audience and make sure you aim the website to its needs.

Intellectual

Another concern in accessibility is intellectual needs. While most developers and designers are well aware of the problems that come from using jargon and complex language when they write content, it is quite easy to forget that some visitors to your website cannot comprehend your website for other reasons that may not be as easily recognized or dealt with, especially if your website is targeted towards a certain audience niche.

The following are needs which apply to this group in terms of accessibility:

- **Cognitive**: People could have conditions that affect their short-term memory and could limit their perception, logic, practical skills, or problem-solving abilities. Examples of these conditions include Alzheimer's, dementia, and amnesia. Even those of us who just can't remember things properly can suffer the effects of cognitive disabilities! By providing visual clues in your design, following conventions, using bookmark-friendly titles, and having friendly URLs, you can help those who are less able to recall information to make use of your website with ease.

- **Lingual**: What language a person speaks isn't a disability but can still be an accessibility issue you should take into account. While English is the main language used on the Web and worldwide, if you are going to be offering content or services to those who are not from English-speaking nations, you should provide translations for their benefit.

- **Learning**: Disabilities like illiteracy and dyslexia may prevent your visitors from accessing your website. Some people with learning problems get frustrated or depressed trying to understand difficult concepts, especially if they get confused. To help these users, for example, when naming sections of your website, do not use confusing or misleading terms or jargon; these can leave visitors unable to determine where to click to find what they need.

- **Education**: People come from all walks of life. While some may have gone to college and gotten degrees, plenty of people browse the Web with a limited set of experiences and knowledge; for example, some are new to the concept of computers (especially young children or the older generations). If you want to ensure your site appeals to the widest possible audience, you should do as mentioned in other groups and keep things simple! While a lack of education is not a disability, it certainly can inhibit a user's progression through a website.

Emotional

The emotional and psychological needs of your visitors are as important as any others in this process, though they are often overlooked because trying to interpret these needs is difficult, and sometimes, the public has a negative perception of people with such needs. Even if your visitors do not have a noticeable disability in how they appear or think, their emotional and psychological states have importance in the appeal and function of your site, as frustration and the subsequent loss of visitors is a classic example of how things can go wrong.

The following needs apply to this group in terms of accessibility:

- **Nerves**: People who suffer from anxiety disorders, stress, phobias, panic attacks, and other forms of nervousness over which they have little control and can strongly feel the effects of encountering errors. This sudden rush of emotion can make visitors to your website give up rather than trying to resolve the error or ask for advice. Undue stress can potentially drive traffic away from your site, therefore resolving errors quickly and increasing the uptime of your website is vitally important, and let's face it, all of us get stressed from time to time!

- **Attention**: Holding a visitor's attention is vitally important, especially when you are trying to put across information. Conditions such as ADHD (attention deficit/hyperactivity disorder) and OCD (obsessive-compulsive disorder) can interfere with this process and may make reading long documents difficult. By breaking down information and giving a diverse experience, you can ensure that people with attention disorders can still get through your content. For people with compulsive behavior, you should ensure tasks that affect something important (such as a blog post command) have confirmation dialogs to help stop mistakes or help when people cannot resist hitting delete to see what happens.

- **Behavior**: Elements of behavior can directly influence the accessibility of your information; only rather than the behavior of your visitors, this directly implies on the way you express yourself. China, for example, is a country that blocks websites considered highly controversial or defamatory, so of course, a lot of people may be unable to visit your site if it suddenly gets added to the block list for the "great firewall." Also, many parents choose to control what kinds of sites children can visit, so if you aim to have a family-friendly website, you need to ensure you have a high level of quality control over what goes on within your site.

Social

With the rise in social networking and interaction, the social needs of visitors have become something for accessibility advisors to consider. Social needs are not something many people will associate with disability, but they are fundamental to the accessibility of a website that any forms of social interaction a visitor engages in are targeted to overcome any shyness or feelings that may cause your visitors to feel less engaged with your services. While some people are not naturally inclined to participate, encouragement could make all the difference. By overcoming social disabilities, you can give your site a greater chance of retaining regular visitors.

The following needs apply to this group in terms of accessibility:

- **Search**: The accessibility of your website to search engines (the things that crawl around your website and index everything) is vitally important to the process of search engine optimization (see Chapter 10). Search engines generally have a limited ability working with formats like Flash, Microsoft Office documents, and PDF files; therefore, their ability to index and make use of your site's content within these files can be inhibited. As a result, you should always provide alternatives to elements that rely on plug-ins or third-party components.

- **Interaction**: People who are shyness or have social disorders may have problems participating on your website. Many times, encouraging these users to become part of the process is something that many developers lose interest in, but producing a community that people can be a part of is one of the best ways you can turn the occasional visitor into a regular. By giving users the ability to stay anonymous, protecting your visitors' privacy, and asking for only required information, you can eliminate the things that often make people feel less willing to give feedback or comments or perhaps even join in your website's activities.

- **Assistance**: Guidance is something that many people look for when trying to view a website. What makes information accessible is the need for documentation and help to ensure that the visitors' questions are answered. For example, if your website has been built for your rock band, you could provide a list of frequently asked questions to reduce the number of emails people need to send you, or you could give instructions for ordering tickets for your gigs.

- **Environmental**: There are certain factors that I class as environmental. These are generally where your website's aims may conflict with people's morals or political ideals and perhaps even target the wrong audience. In terms of accessibility, your visitors may feel uncomfortable being a part of a website that conflicts with their ideals, and though this is not so much a matter of disability, like the emotional and (to a point) intellectual elements mentioned earlier, it has a very valid place in weeding out factors that could limit who will access your website.

The preceding discussion only encompasses a small number of the conditions that can inhibit users' abilities to browse the Web. Although the number of conditions listed here may be limited, the types of needs they represent provide a fairly accurate portrayal of the types of factors that affect your visitors. How should you best deal with these needs? While there is no simple fix for all, you should simply do some basic checks that your website can effectively use accessibility tools (such as those mentioned previously in this chapter). Then, determine how you could improve the overall experience from the results you gather. Finally, perhaps ask some friends with disabilities (if you have any), a disability group in your area, or perhaps even disabled people on a forum if anyone would give you a couple of minutes just to try out your site and offer some recommendations.

Accessibility testing may seem like overkill if you are just trying to produce a personal website (for commercial or business sites, it would be essential as discussed later in this chapter). However, if you just spend some time (even if it is only a few minutes) getting feedback or trying for yourself how the browsing experience will differ, you can gain some valuable insight and be able to make little changes that ultimately give you a better website. Trying to deal with the needs of disabled people is something you should take into account not only when deciding on the structure of the website but when you add style and behavior as well. Therefore, it may be worth revisiting this chapter occasionally to continue testing; you never know what you may have missed!

Accessibility Practices

There are many practices in web design and development that can act as a help or a hindrance in terms of how accessible pages are on the Web. Although some of them are explained in the following sections to make you aware of common things you will come into contact with, you should take into account that determining what could be damaging or effective depends entirely on the type of accessibility problem someone has. For instance, someone who has poor hearing (or perhaps simply someone without access to a pair of speakers or earphones for the computer) may find subtitles, transcripts, or captions on videos useful, but the same may not apply to a visually impaired user. You should not let that stop you from trying to give visitors options. Those who can make use of the functionality to help them out will often do so, and it's logical that helping and making life easier will give your visitors reason to return. We shall next examine the things you can do to improve your site's accessibility.

ExplainED

Although there are some useful hints and tips in this chapter, you should remember that you could do hundreds of different things to improve the accessibility of your website and many more potentially damaging things that could inhibit your users, so always take into account your users needs!

Logical Structure

How should you best structure your website for disabled people? This is one question that has been under some debate recently, particularly among the many visually impaired users of screen readers. While these products are fascinating to learn about and very useful, the majority of websites are full of content and text that would need to be spoken to read out everything on a page! Just think, if each time you loaded one of your pages, you had to read aloud all of the content; even the speediest of speakers would find themselves having a sore throat from spending hours reading every tiny piece of information on the page (even though some people using screen readers can listen at amazing speeds).

The debate over what constitutes a logical structure has ultimately formed into two camps: those who think (like myself) that providing content before navigation is important because having to skip over navigation on every page is a chore, and those who think providing navigation before content would be better to present the user with choices before the content of the page is read out to them. As my personal preference is content before navigation, I will explain my reasoning as to why this would best suit your structure. If you agree but your template has navigation first because you used server-side includes, you can simply swap the include from the top of the content to below it on each of your pages (luckily, you don't need to do that for every change you make, and you should ensure your CSS is altered if necessary to ensure the design still works). Here's my logic:

1. **Logo:** First things first, when people visit your website, they want to know exactly where they are. The logo should appear first in the document (even though the `title` tag will explain where users are), because the logo provides the users with a simple method of finding their way home if they get lost. Therefore, logos generally should have an anchor link directing to the home page, and this concept is more

relevant to visual consistency and user expectations than accessibility itself.

2. **Introduction**: Many people have a brief sentence that describes their websites and pages. For accessibility reasons, this quick introduction at the top of each page under the logo can be extremely useful to let people know what page they are on. By providing this information, you give screen reader users the chance to decide if the page they are on is right for them (so the text must be descriptive) without having to read the entire contents of a webpage. And using this information, they can make the next decision.

3. **Skip links**: The purpose of skip links is to pinpoint certain areas of a page by their ID attributes. Their existence allows you to link to them with an anchor using what is commonly referred to as a fragment link (basically, it would be the same as #navigation in this case). If an anchor has the # character followed by the ID of an element within that page, once you click the URL, your browser will skip over the content and jump down to the exact position of that element. These skip links are useful for screen readers, as they allow visitors to skip over the stuff in between and start reading from the start of the fragment link.

4. **Content**: This is pretty self-descriptive; content is the unique material for the page!

5. **Navigation**: I prefer to provide navigation after content for two very important reasons. First, upon loading each page within a website, the screen reader will simply say what the website is called (describe the logo), explain what the content is about (read the introduction), offer the chance to jump to the links to the site (in case the user has the wrong page or isn't interested in the content), and finally, read what is on the page. This structure best suits the natural way people read, which is to skim over the content and pick out only the parts that interest them. Second, if the navigation is at the bottom of the website, once the reader finishes reading the content, the navigation will next be spoken, giving users options of places where they could visit next. In the scheme of things, this makes sense, as people usually want to move on when they are finished reading; it's partly why footers have become so popular.

ExplainED

If your navigation is located at the bottom of the page and you want to have it appear at the top of the page, do not worry. CSS can handle this task with absolute positioning.

Text Alternatives

When you want to make your website as accessible as possible, one of the common pitfalls that people do not realize is that not everything can be read or understood on a website. If a blind person uses a screen reader to try to make sense of a website, it's perfectly fine when your website has plenty of text (as this can just be read out to the listener), but what happens when a screen reader comes across content that is not described as text, such as images or a Flash animation (see Figure 9-5)? When an assistive device comes across something that has nothing descriptive, it simply ignores it and carries on! This is a worrying thought for the majority of us, because large chunks of our websites could simply be invisible to disabled people. This is overcome is through providing alternative text (for example, an alt attribute within image tags) to describe the unavailable component.

Figure 9-5. The TurboChef website may let people know they require Flash, but what if people can't install it?

As a general rule, alternative text must represent the equivalent of the unavailable content. So if you provide a Flash-based navigation list, you should ensure the non-Flash alternative is made up of a HTML menu with the same navigation links. And if you provide an image, make sure the alt attribute contains relevant and descriptive text. As another example, if you provide audio files, make sure a text-based transcript of the conversation is available. Ensuring that your website has a text alternative for everything nontextual is probably the single most important thing you can do for accessibility (and your visitors), as this ensures that no matter what happens and no matter what needs the individual has, you can be sure that they can at least "see" your site.

ExplainED

You should ensure alt *attributes on images are not overly lengthy when they are used (which should be for most images). If, however, the image being used is portraying style, as it would not fit within the CSS without additional markup, and then you should leave the value empty.*

Most web browsers have a dynamic resize function called page zooming or text resize (see Figure 9-6). The purpose of this tool is to enlarge or decrease the size of a website's contents by a percentage, so that information can be read more easily. For instance, a visually impaired user who is unable to read small print may use the zoom function within a browser to increase the site size until it's appropriate for their needs. It should be noted that while text resize will (obviously) only make changes to the text within the website using a fixed scale, using the page zoom function will alter the entire document's dimensions and therefore is much more useful if you find yourself wanting to make things a bit clearer.

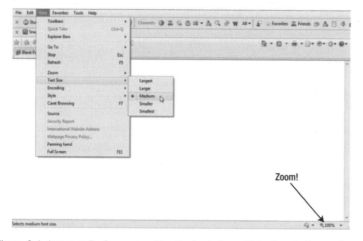

Figure 9-6. Internet Explorer can alter the text size within the window and zoom dynamically.

ExplainED

Noted that Internet Explorer (all versions) has an inherent problem with the way it resizes text. If you used a fixed font size such as px *(pixels), the ability to resize text based on your needs will refuse to work. Because of this, I highly recommend that web developers use relative sizing (such as* em *or* %*) to avoid this browser flaw.*

Skip Links

As mentioned earlier, skip links are an important accessibility tool in letting screen readers directly get hold of the section of a page they want to read without having to jump between sections in a hunt for the part they want. And let's face it, the length of some documents on the Web could make this search like trying to find a needle in a haystack. When making use of skip links, the most common convention is to have a link for both navigation and content, but you can add additional links; just try to keep the list of skip links short (see Figure 9-7).

Figure 9-7. The Web Standards Project has the ability to skip past the heading, right down to the content.

Headings

If you look at the table of contents for a book, headings play an important role as visual separators for each piece of content, which is broken down into sections. When you take accessibility into account, the point of headings is to represent marks of significance and relevance where screen readers and other software can focus (see Figure 9-8). If you provide useful headings, visitors can more accurately pinpoint the elements of the page they want to read, and in doing so, increase the speed at which they can access information.

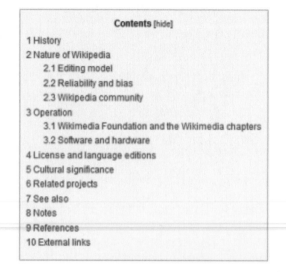

Figure 9-8. Wikipedia provides firm and well-established heading elements to maintain seperation of content.

Contrasting Style Sheets

The final major accessibility enhancement we will address here is the contrasting style sheet. While allowing your visitors to resize text, zoom, find text alternatives to everything, and be able to navigate your website, when you come to adding style to your design one of the most common issues that occurs is that people with severe visual problems cannot read your website with ease (even by increasing the text size). As a result, many web browser makers include the option to turn off all styles (or alter them specially). Although this option does exist in modern browsers, people using older browsers may be unable to make use of this feature. As a consequence, it is recommended you provide an alternative style sheet that either removes all color and style (to reduce the noise on the page), or more importantly, you can provide a high-contrast version where the text is large, the colors are vibrant (and impossible to confuse), and everything looks clean and spaced (see Figure 9-9). Yellow text on a black background is a perfect example of contrasting colors that are clearly impossible to get confused and, as a result, will make the reader's life easier.

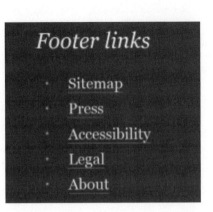

Figure 9-9. This example of a high-contrast style sheet shows no background noise and big text!

Access Keys

Of all the useful elements of accessibility, among the most controversial are access keys (see Figure 9-10). These potentially useful accessibility functions exist in an attribute within the HTML specification and can be placed within anchor links. The value of each access key will be a letter or more commonly a number that is registered for that element within the page.

Why would you want to do this? Well, the idea behind access keys is to enable people to press a combination of letters on the keyboard to activate the link, as opposed to just pressing the Tab key to go from point to point within a page. By doing this, accessing certain pages on a website can be made much easier and faster for the visitor. Support for access keys has been inhibited due to conflicts with how they function between browsers (as there has been no agreed combination of characters) and within screen readers (where keyboard shortcuts could be overridden). As a result, the W3C has deprecated their use, so for the sake of following the standards, you should probably just ignore them.

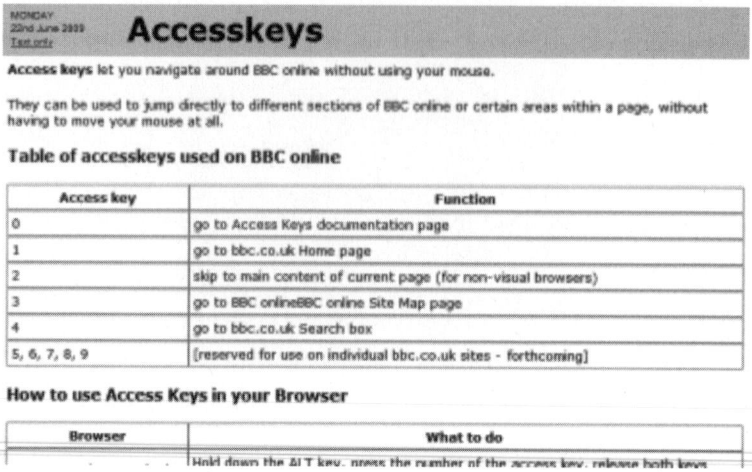

Accesskeys

Access keys let you navigate around BBC online without using your mouse.

They can be used to jump directly to different sections of BBC online or certain areas within a page, without having to move your mouse at all.

Table of accesskeys used on BBC online

Access key	Function
0	go to Access Keys documentation page
1	go to bbc.co.uk Home page
2	skip to main content of current page (for non-visual browsers)
3	go to BBC onlineBBC online Site Map page
4	go to bbc.co.uk Search box
5, 6, 7, 8, 9	[reserved for use on individual bbc.co.uk sites - forthcoming]

How to use Access Keys in your Browser

Browser	What to do
	Hold down the ALT key, press the number of the access key, release both keys

Figure 9-10. The BBC website has employed access keys to enhance the user experience.

What Can Go Wrong?

Making your site accessible takes more than just adding useful items. You also need to make sure that you avoid doing certain things that can cause problems. Most of these are common-sense solutions, but and you may have chosen to use some, such as using plug-ins, on your own site. Hopefully, you can avoid most of the following issues by being pragmatic with their usage. The following things can seriously inhibit accessibility:

- **Browser hijacking**: Never use scripting to make the browser do something that would either limit or hinder the experience of the end user. Disabling the right-click button, resizing the window, closing without permission, and breaking the Back button are examples of the nasty things that can be done. While using these methods may seem like a good idea (such as protecting your code), the results will seriously damage the user experience. Some studies have shown this can hurt your traffic, limit frequent visitors, and even stop people using your site!
- **Pop-ups**: Is there anything more annoying than pop-up windows? While you may want to make a window for the sake of advertising another website or trying to prevent a page being redirected, very few people can actually make use of pop-ups now that all popular browsers have built-in pop-up blocking, and some people have scripting disabled. As a result, even if you did choose to make use of pop-up windows

(against my advice), around 90% of people would be unlikely to ever see them, which makes them pretty pointless.

- **Obtrusive scripting**: In the previous chapter when I mentioned scripting, it was noted that forcing people to rely on JavaScript being enabled is a bad idea, as not everyone has access to client-side scripting functionality (or has it enabled). With this in mind, you should ensure that your website will function well when JavaScript is turned off. Having no scripting may sound scary if you have investigated the fun that can be had using it, but you shouldn't punish browsers and people who are missing out on the technology.

- **Plug-in dependence**: Flash, Silverlight, and Java can be truly amazing; they can allow you to produce applications, websites, and uniquely designed components that can go far beyond what HTML, CSS, and JavaScript can offer. However, it is advisable that you try not to rely on them too much (such as building Flash-powered websites). Just like with scripting, not everyone has access to plug-ins, so relying on them can break your design on top of causing a mixture of different accessibility, usability, and search engine optimization issues that damage your site! Although some of these plug-ins do have accessibility features that can be enabled to minimize problems, they're not guaranteed so use them with caution.

- **Autoplay**: Do you browse the web while listening to media? As you can imagine, the last thing you want when listening to someone else sing or talk is to suddenly have a third-party noise explode from your speakers as you surf the Net. Websites that automatically play music without asking the user beforehand cause undue stress and noise pollution, so if you choose to use media within your website, you need to make sure that nothing starts without the visitor's permission. After all, the reaction most people give to unwanted noise is to just leave the site!

CAPTCHA

The rise of products being specifically built for the Web brought an increase in people who wished to exploit them. One such case in common existence you may have seen would be the amount of spam you get in the comment sections on blogs or the advertisements you see posted on forums. One of the main ways in which individual's targeted spam on a wide scale was to produce what are commonly referred to as *bots*, which are basically robots that do work automatically. These automated robots browsed around websites adding spam, creating accounts, and doing other naughty things on a huge scale. Because of the size of this problem, a way in which humans and machines could be determined was created called CAPTCHA (see Figure 9-11).

CAPTCHA can be seen on a website where you are presented with a picture made up of distorted letters and numbers and are asked to fill what you see in the box to be able to continue. In its infancy, this technology seemed to help stem the problem, the spammers directly returned the attack by creating software to identify the characters using the same technology a computer scanner would use to turn a picture into text (optical character recognition). As a result of this, the CAPTCHA has had to evolve to try to evade these attacks with ever more distortion in characters and asking questions and has resulted in an accessibility nightmare. Even the best of us have been caught out by CAPTCHAs (both text- and audio-based) using cryptic and undecipherable checks.

Figure 9-11. While CAPTCHA has gotten more advanced, it still fundamentally fails at accessibility.

The CAPTCHA usually relies on the ability to see the screen to work out what the text says, and as bots could read the `alt` attribute of an element, it cannot provide a text version of the code. Those with visual impairments who require the use of screen readers therefore cannot make use of websites that use CAPTCHAs! Even though attempts have been made to improve accessibility, such as offering audio versions (using distortion in the sound), the issue of distortion still results in a high frequency of cases where a human will fail the test. CAPTCHA is still used even with these issues simply because it tries to tackle the problem of spam head on (as heavy handed and clumsy as the attempt may be). Unfortunately, due to these individuals who are only interested in self-promotion, we are left in a stalemate on the Web where trying to prevent spam is an uphill and losing battle.

Ultimately, the decision whether to implement CAPTCHA will be based on the balance between spam (which unfortunately is a side effect of the Web), functionality (how much people can interact), and how accessible you want to be. Speaking in terms of your audience, you are probably better off avoiding CAPTCHA and trying to find more accessible ways to get people contributing without being able to self-promote.

LinkED

For more technical information about CAPTCHAs, and their usage on the Web, visit the official website at http://www.captcha.net/.

Writing an Accessibility Statement

Some websites choose to produce what is commonly referred to as an accessibility statement, the purpose of such a document is to explain what accessibility best practices you have taken into consideration and what aids are available to assist people with various disabilities. While not all people who are disabled will read these pieces of information, I still recommend creating one if only for the purpose of providing a reference for future visitors to your website who want to suggest ways you could improve your website. Feedback is one of the most vital and important parts of both the research and cultivation of a website over time. Details of how to produce an accessibility statement are provided in the following exercise, though this statement is just an example of some of the important things you should try to include.

Try It Yourself: Producing an Accessibility Statement

Creating an accessibility statement is much easier than it may sound. Really, all you need to do is provide simple bullet points of the things you have implemented to benefit your site's visitors and regulars. While any number of elements could be included, you generally want to keep your statement as straightforward as possible. The following list of things to include can be customized to suit your own creation process:

- Indicate if the HTML, CSS, and feeds you produce (such as RSS and Atom) are validated.
- List the web browsers you have (or intend to) test your website in to ensure it works.
- Note whether your site passes accessibility standards, which are explained in the next section.
- Explain if you provide high-contrast or aural style sheets for your visitors' benefit.

- Note any conventions, such as microformats, that you have employed in your markup.
- Tell people how to get in touch with you if they are unable to navigate your site well.

Accessibility Standards

Accessibility has become a big thing both in business and mainstream culture, and various specifications have been produced giving tips, hints, and rules to follow to ensure that disabled people can make use of your website. While you should try to comply with the following specifications, there are legitimate times when you may avoid implementing certain elements to avoid causing issues elsewhere in the website. However, trying to comply with the standards should be a high priority, and passing the checkpoints should be the minimum standard of accessibility you provide. If you think of something that would improve the ease of use for your website, try it out and get some feedback from your visitors. Anything you can do to make their lives easier will encourage them to revisit your website in the future, as trust will be built between you.

LinkED

The Web Accessibility Initiative (WAI) is a working group run by the W3C who sets standards for accessibility like WCAG. For more information, visit the group's website at http://www.w3.org/WAI/.

The specifications in the following sections determine what you should do to meet accessibility recommendations and are quite long and fairly difficult to read for people who are new to the process of web design. Fortunately, there are plenty of resources out there to help you get to grips with the basic elements involved in meeting the specifications and guide you through the process. You should not feel afraid to either seek outside assistance or look for one of the many hundreds of articles out there that break down the steps. For reference, all of the following specifications are linked in some way to WCAG (Web Content Accessibility Guidelines) and version 2.0 of that specification, which coincidently has some fantastic documentation; it may be worth going with that long but worthwhile specification to give yourself the highest level of accessibility.

Section 508

The most basic legal standard involved in trying to encourage web accessibility is the US law known as Section 508. The law states that federal agencies and government websites have to ensure that disabled visitors can access information at the same level as an able-bodied person, and it was introduced to help remove the barriers that disabled people face on a daily basis when browsing the Web or using information technology. The law itself specifically applies (in part) to all websites run by government departments in the United States, but the scope of the problem of accessibility and the need to ensure that people can access your website without any inhibiting factors has made Section 508 an international benchmark for the lowest acceptable pass-rate for a website that wishes to consider itself to be accessible in the basic sense.

A checklist of Section 508 requirements is available at http://www.section508.gov/ ndex.cfm?FuseAction=Content&ID=12#Web.

Pas 78

While Section 508 was created for government organizations in the United States to meet basic accessibility standards, the British Standards Institute (BSI) alongside the Disability Rights Commission (DRC) published a good practice guide for meeting accessibility recommendations for the United Kingdom called PAS 78. Unlike Section 508 and WCAG (explained later), the BSI publication does not contain any checkpoints but outlines principles to be taken into account if you want to ensure that accessibility is paramount within your website. This document was created with the intention of targeting not only government bodies but also businesses, as antidiscrimination laws within a business environment apply both to Web and brick-and-mortar stores. With this in mind and with disability discrimination law implemented in various ways across the world, accessibility in business is a must.

If you want to download your very own free copy of PAS 78 to improve your site's accessibility, visit http://www.equalityhumanrights.com/footer/accessibility-statement/general-web-accessibility-guidance/.

It is worth noting that Section 508 and PAS 78 are both based in part or entirely on WCAG, published by the W3C.

WCAG

The Web Content Accessibility Guidelines (WCAG) are considered the industry standard of accessibility. WCAG is composed of a complete list of checkpoints; if followed as per the specifications, these increase your website's ability to be used by those who have disabilities. It should be noted that not every item on the checklists applies to every site, and some may conflict with other accessibility recommendations; therefore, you should use your best judgment. Of course, you should always try to see things from the point of the disabled individual (as mentioned earlier), and by following these guidelines, you give yourself the best chance of turning your up-and-coming site into something that can be enjoyed by everyone! Whether you choose to follow the original version of the guidelines or the second edition is up to you, but the more-recent version will perhaps meet the needs of new assistive technologies better (especially as some of the conflicting rules from version 1.0 are resolved).

Conformance with the guidelines comes in three flavors (no, not strawberry, chocolate, and vanilla); these are listed as A, AA, and AAA compliancy, which equates to levels 1, 2, and 3. Here's how this works: Once you have all the core elements you need to follow, you're at level A. The elements you should follow make up level AA, and elements you can follow are level AAA. Sounds simple, right? Well, how accessible you want to be is your choice. Plenty of people are happy with basic level A compliance, but some people like to go whole hog and ensure that their website meets every guideline (which can be quite a tricky thing to accomplish).

Here are some useful links for WCAG 1.0:

- **Checklist**: http://www.w3.org/TR/WCAG10/full-checklist.html
- **Specification**: http://www.w3.org/TR/WCAG10/

And these are the links for WCAG 2.0:

- **Detailed Guide**: http://www.w3.org/TR/UNDERSTANDING-WCAG20/complete.html
- **Specification**: http://www.w3.org/TR/WCAG20/

Samurai

Because of the major pitfalls in version 1.0 of WCAG, a group of people, lead by superstar web designer Joe Clark, decided to make an errata document to append the W3C specification and resolve some of the conflictions and issues primarily associated with WCAG shortcomings. They called their project Samurai. Because Samurai is intended to be an update specifically for WCAG

1.0, you should not use WCAG 2.0 if you choose to follow the errata provided by the WCAG Samurai, as the two are not compatible.

The Samurai errata documentation can be found at `http://wcagsamurai.org/errata/intro.html`.

> ## LinkED
>
> *To learn about what sparked the need to start a project that underpinned the flaws within WCAG, you can read the following article:* `http://www.alistapart.com/articles/tohellwithwcag2`.

WAI-ARIA

The final specification worth mentioning is that of Accessible Rich Internet Applications (ARIA). As you are just starting out your web design journey and have only thus far covered the wonderful world of HTML, you should simply skip over this specification until you come to building web applications or deeply interactive functionality. Essentially, the purpose of this specification, if you have not already guessed, is to take the principles of accessibility (already covered for standard websites in WCAG) and bring a unique set of standards and guidelines for producing web applications and scripts which are accessible to disabled users.

You can find an introduction to WAI-ARIA at `http://www.w3.org/TR/wai-aria-primer/` and the specification itself at `http://www.w3.org/TR/wai-aria/`.

Accessibility Law

Accessibility standards on the Web have precedence in law. Back in the Web of old, accessibility was the last thing on most developers' minds, but there's an ever-increasing awareness of potential legal implications that could occur from having a website defined as inaccessible.

LinkED

Possibly the most notable lawsuit in this area involved American retail giant Target. To find out more about the Target lawsuit, read the excellent article that discusses how this could affect the web at http://northtemple.com/2008/09/01/the-target-accessibility-lawsuit-and-settlement.

Most countries have some form of antidiscrimination law, and often these laws directly reference those with disabilities, such as the Disability Discrimination Act (DDA) and the Americans with Disabilities Act (ADA), though these laws were simply in place to enable individuals with various forms of disability to enter places of public interest such as retail stores and government buildings rather than websites. Other laws apart from Section 508 and PAS 78 can be applied to accessibility law such as the Illinois Information Technology Accessibility Act (IITAA), Stanca Act (Italian accessibility law) and BITV (the German Barrier-Free Information Technology legal act).

While some of these antidiscrimination laws have been directly adapted to include the brick-and-mortar locations' digital counterparts, a lot of controversy still surrounds the possibility that businesses could be sued for producing a website that does not conform to WCAG or other accessibility guidelines. In reference to your project, there is no reason why you should worry about being sued at this time. However, remember that accessibility can be easily implemented with just a bit of effort (especially as you started from scratch). The purpose of making sure your site works for everyone is beneficial, but for personal websites, such as the one you are producing, there is unlikely to be any obligation to comply with the standards or laws that exist unless you intend to sell things.

LinkED

For a list of various laws and policies around the world that tie in with accessibility (even if they do not directly reference the Internet) just visit the following website: http://www.w3.org/WAI/Policy/.

Accessibility Validation

Finally, before we move onto the subject of enhancing your structure with microformats (an exciting new element of web development), I need to briefly mention website validation. Website validation is a technique undertaken by an automated tool (such as the one on the W3C website) to look through your source code and helpfully point out errors or inconsistencies. While validation is a fantastic way to help resolve errors (as mentioned in Chapters 3, 5, and 7), you should be made aware at this point that validators for accessibility also exist. Some validators check against standardized accessibility guidelines like Section 508 and WCAG, and some custom tools use their own unique sets of standards. You are welcome to use these tools as a method of making sure your website does not have any basic issues, but you should be aware of the problems that validators have.

Accessibility involves more than just code; it is based on various components, some of which are entirely design focused. Many elements of the accessibility guidelines (such as checking for alt attributes on image tags) can be easily spotted by validators, but they often cannot validate the more visual accessibility issues, such as color contrasts and the readability of the content. And these visual elements count even more if you use any components that obviously contain no code that can be validated, like those created in Adobe Flash. When deciding to validate your website, you should use the validators as guides rather than as methods of giving yourself the all clear, because the limitations of a machine checking your website rather than a person are quite obvious and important.

It is worth also noting that various tools exist for checking additional accessibility concerns such as visualizing your website in the eyes of various forms of color blindness, testing for flashing that could affect people with photosensitive epilepsy, testing your site's speed in comparison to realistic waiting times, and analyzing various types of readability such as schemes implemented by Clear Language and Design (CLAD) and Short Measure of Gobbledygook (SMOG) guidelines and standardized readability scales such as Gunning-Fod, Flesch Reading Ease, and Flesch-Kincaid. Some examples of these types of website are shown in the second bullet list.

Try It Yourself: Validate Your Website

The following automated tools will let you check for accessibility related validation issues:

- **HiSoftware Cynthia Says**: Use this validator to test for Section 508 and WCAG 1.0 compliance (http://www.contentquality.com/).

- **ARTC**: This validator tests for compliance with Section 508, WCAG 1.0 and 2.0, Stanca Act, and BITV (http://www.achecker.ca/).

- **FAE**: This one tests for Section 508, WCAG 1.0, and IITAA compliance (http://appserv.rehab.uiuc.edu/fae/).

These other useful accessibility tools will help you test for additional hindrances for your users:

- **Wickline color blindness filter**: http://colorfilter.wickline.org/

- **Web accessible flicker tester**: http://www.webaccessibile.org/test/check.aspx

- **Website speed tester**: http://www.websiteoptimization.com/services/analyze/

- **W3C spell checker**: http://www.w3.org/2002/01/spellchecker

- **Readability tool**: http://www.eastendliteracy.on.ca/clearlanguageanddesign/

- **Extended readability tester**: http://juicystudio.com/services/readability.php

Experience Is Everything

One of the fastest growing (and in my opinion, the most interesting) areas of web design is web usability. While accessibility deals with making sure that anyone can browse your website (no matter what inhibiting factors may affect them), usability deals with the other side of the coin and looks at what happens when people are on your website: How can their browsing experiences be made to be friendlier? Or how you could improve the way the website naturally flows? Much of usability is based on testing visitor's ability to navigate a website successfully by completing certain tasks, getting hold of the content they require, receiving feedback, finding where problems lie, and dealing with them to make sure that in the future the same issues do not reoccur. Based on all of this research gathered, we, as designers, have gotten to know what makes good and bad practices, what things all websites should have, and so much more, some of which is listed in the following sections.

Design Theory

Common practices have appeared in the field of web design and continue to change on a regular basis. When you researched other sites to get ideas for your own, you probably noticed that many different websites had certain things in common—perhaps the placement of the logo, a certain style of footer, or even similar visual effects, like the Web 2.0 design movement. While these common elements may seem just like sensible choices, the art of getting the various elements of your website in a visible and sensible position is actually a science in its own right. Some people choose to study how websites look for a living as user experience designers! You will find actual benefits to taking notice of how other people make their sites and including the design decisions that are applicable to your own website, because as design practices become more commonplace, people expect the elements to be there. For example, a logo in the top left-hand corner will be easier for a visitor to find than one stuffed somewhere else on the page. Therefore, the information contained in the following sections could help you increase the usability of your design. In design theory, there are two ways you can enhance your design and bring it more in line with your visitors' preferred experience methods: design conventions and design patterns.

Conventions

First, we will look at the field of design conventions. When we talk about design conventions, we are talking about common elements within a website that meet users' expectations and have been adopted by web designers over a long period of time as an informal standard. As an example of this: over time, users have come to expect a navigation bar at the top of the screen when visiting a website, so the convention would be to do the same as other websites and include it in the position users expect to help them feel at home quicker; essentially they should know where everything is without too much effort. The use of conventions is voluntary, but by following them, you can decrease the amount of confusion that is caused when elements' positions are atypical.

Here are some examples of design conventions:

- **Call to action**: These are buttons that link to an important part of your site, such as a new product release, a contact form or even a Buy It Now button to entice users to click.

- **Abstracts**: Located at the top of the page under the navigation links and the logo is a brief paragraph of text explaining the purpose of the page (it's good for accessibility and readability).

- **Logo placement**: It's common knowledge that most websites place their logos at the top left-hand corner of the screen; this is because it's where people first look when visiting a website.

- **Title tags**: Ensuring your pages have appropriate page titles is extremely important; many websites use the convention of the page name followed and dash separated by the site name.

- **Contact forms**: All websites should have a contact form, as sending email is the most common method people use to get in touch with the owner of a website.

- **Footers**: These days, footers can have much more than a copyright message. You can place important links, a sitemap, useful information, and social networking buttons there.

- **Icon usage**: Not all navigation needs to be textual. The iPhone is a great example of a device using icons to highlight applications, and on the Web, you can use icons to attract attention.

The conventions mentioned in the preceding list are just the tip of the iceberg. Because conventions change all of the time, and this book is not intended to be an A to Z of what's cool on the Web, I will leave you at this stage to do some extra investigating if you want to know more about what conventions exist out there (an example of conventions in use is shown in Figure 9-12). One thing I will point out is that, in the ideas pad you produced in the creativity section, you should have done an analysis of the various elements that competitors' websites provide. If multiple websites in the same genre as yours implement a certain function and it is gaining adoption, you can be sure that it is a convention worth taking note of and possibly implementing.

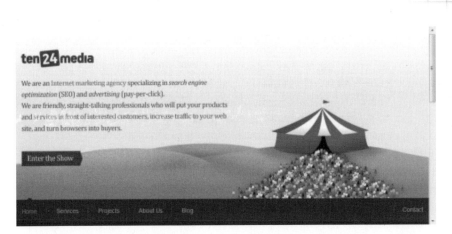

Figure 9-12. This website makes use of conventions like a big background image, a top-left logo, and a call to action.

Patterns

Patterns are different from conventions in web design; rather than focus on what the user expects to see as conventions do, the pattern covers the various ways in which functionality can be implemented. Taking the initial idea of navigation menus, you could qualify different patterns of that element as drop-down, breadcrumb, ribbon, and so on. In this example, the menu is the convention, and drop-down is a pattern. While patterns are often variations of what is commonly seen in a convention, some patterns can be simply produced out of the need for a common solution to an irregularity in design. Essentially, if you're targeting a single aspect, it's probably a design convention. If there are multiple choices for implementation, it's likely to be a design pattern.

Here are some examples of design patterns:

- **Scrolling**: Most websites scroll up and down to allow for more space than the window can offer, but scrolling from left to right can be implemented successfully (see Figure 9-13).

- **Pages**: If you have a long article, placing it in a single page can make your site take ages to load. Splitting data into multiple pages can prevent this and make finding sections easier.

- **Navigation**: There are so many different ways of producing navigation on the Web that it could have its own book. Just know that being consistent with implementation is crucial for usability.

- **Visual hierarchy:** In newspapers, the vital elements of the paper appear at the top, and the importance level reduces as you move down the page. Replicating this pattern is useful, as people usually read from top to bottom.

- **Searching:** If there's one element of the Web that's important, it's how easy information can be found. Ensuring you make results as accurate and visible as possible is vital to searching.

Of course, many hundreds of different patterns are employed within websites, from the hyperlinks we click right down to the choice of using microformats to associate structure with various important pieces of semantically informative details. The ideas in the preceding list should get you started in respect to what you want to keep an eye out for, but the majority of patterns you may want to investigate can be found simply by opening your web browser and visiting a site like Amazon that employs an army of patterns and conventions within its pages to give the feeling of familiarity. So do yourself a favor and have another look through your ideas pad to see if you can spot anything that may be worth taking into account as a pattern from the websites you visited.

Figure 9-13. With the use of sideways scrolling mixed with JavaScript (jQuery), this site is beautiful and unique.

Usability Considerations

While design conventions and design patterns are very important in giving a feeling of consistency to your visitor, you should not underestimate the power of usability alone. It is also worth noting that you can choose to ignore patterns and conventions if you want to be more unique—though being too unique can be a bad thing! In any case, there are considerations you should take into account while making usability improvements to your site. The ideas in the following sections are vitally important in the usability process, as they could potentially damage the end users experience if ignored or implemented poorly.

Screen Real Estate

As you have already learned, the viewport where your website displays in the web browser window has a limited and varied amount of space available to it, depending on the visitor's computer; therefore, any space that could encourage your visitors to check out something important qualifies as primary real estate space. This idea about treating the screen as a premium region, that is, as if it's above the fold, is not new to the Web. *Above the fold* refers to the elements of your design that are visible without making use of scrolling. It emerged back when advertisements started appearing on websites when it was worked out that commercials that appeared higher up the page were more likely to sell products. While you may or may not be offering an advertising-supported service, the real estate your website holds is still valuable when you decide which of your pages deserves to be given the priority of being placed at the top of the screen under the logo and navigation.

Three-Click Rule

One of the primary rules of the Web is to stop visitors from getting frustrated and abandoning your website because it is unusable. A good rule of thumb to maintain usability is that, at any given point in time, every page should be no more than three clicks away from wherever the user is located within your website. If you have a lot of pages to deal with, you may want to produce an intermediary page, like a well-organized sitemap, that lets both browsers and visitors find their way if they get lost among all of the fantastic content you have written since you got started on this project. Why three clicks? The simple answer is that people, in general, have a short attention span, and they will judge you on how quickly they can browse among sections. Many usability studies have found over the years that three clicks is usually the maximum of how far someone is willing to look before they go somewhere else. Of course, how many clicks users will perform can depend on how well mapped out your site is. If visitors are aware that they are very close to finding the content, such as a button to indicate it is on the next page, they will happily take the additional step to finish.

Progressive Disclosure

We have already mentioned that asking your visitors to fill in a form before they can enter your website or use your services is very annoying, but what about asking for too much information? People are very strict when it comes to what information they are willing to give out, and premature requests for information will usually be dealt with by providing either fake information or just going elsewhere. The general rule of progressive disclosure is to only ask for information when it is really needed. For example, maybe you only ask for mailing address information when the user clicks the purchase button on a shopping cart, not when items are added to the basket. Requiring membership before shopping is rather pointless, as there are no guarantees the individual wants to purchase something. Registration is something you should never trick someone into, especially as most of registrations come with legal agreements attached.

Confirmation

Making mistakes is part of the user experience, and how you choose to deal with them can literally be life and death for the work that users put into something they have spent time typing or building. What if someone accidentally closes the window or clicks the browser's Back button or even another button like delete? Making sure that the contents of any text boxes are saved to a cookie temporarily before users are allowed to change to a different URL or giving a dialog box asking users to confirm the action to delete a post they made can save visitors who have spent time participating in your website but fell sort at the final hurdle by clicking the wrong button at the wrong time (we have all done it at some point in our lives). Interestingly enough, saving content to cookies before closing the window closes or browsing away ensures that, when users return, that content can be fetched back from the browser's backup in the cookies folder (though you should note that there is a limit to how much information can be saved by a cookie). Small things like this can make all the difference online.

Connection Speed

Over the course of this chapter, emphasis has been placed on the connection speed and reliability of your visitors' Internet access. While the number of individuals who have access to broadband is consistently rising, there are still plenty of places where people are only able to receive or afford dial-up access of 56k, and some people live in areas where connections are erratic and disconnections are frequent. This means that, to protect usability, you must ensure that any multimedia you produce is optimized as much as possible without losing quality. Websites must not be bulky or fat in their source code; having a 100-page document as a single page on a website, for example, may take forever for a dial-up user. Also, for any interactive elements (for example, if you provide a chat room or other functionality that relies on an active connection), try disconnecting from the Web to simulate what may happen to the end user, and ensure that if the connection is lost, getting back on when the service resumes will be as painless and effortless as possible (a very important thing to consider).

User-Centered Design

Finally, we need to talk about the usability concept of user-centered design (UCD). This philosophy takes into account everything we have already looked at and pulls it together into a single sweeping process that should be undertaken at every step in the development of your website: Check the visibility, accessibility, legibility, and language of all your documents upon completion of each page. Then, decide if the design or content you have added meets your audience's needs (their age, ethnicity, social desire, education, and any other part of their backgrounds), the purpose it set out to do (remember that mission statement?), and the context behind the website (did it accomplish what it set out to). These elements are wrapped up together and form the foundation of what this book has aimed to teach you. UCD ensures that when you build your website, you check at every single stage how on target you are and how to deal with any issues that exist.

Studies and Testing

Patterns and conventions can be used to determine your website's usability rating. By conducting your own research through tests and studies, and by addressing the requests and needs of your visitors, you can make your website a better place. There are many different ways you can collect useful visitor information and statistics, but the methods in the following sections are some of the most common and easiest to implement. If you do decide to conduct usability studies when you produce your website (after you have a design up, of course), you should make sure, when you interpret the results, that you avoid all possible forms of bias and just consider the information as something to take into consideration rather than thinking of it as something that needs to be addressed immediately (unless, of course, the results show a large number of people complaining).

Ask Your Visitors

One of the best ways to find out the needs of your visitors is to ask them! You can produce a poll or questionnaire or simply ask people who approach your website to give their feedback on the user experience. The great things about usability testing is that it is cheap to implement and does not require much effort on behalf of your users; also in general, the people who use your website are the ideal candidates for explaining how you could improve your website in the future (as the site is intended for them). While the area of usability testing requires a lot of determination and control to implement if you want to get accurate results, it is definitely something you may want to look at in the future when you decide to make changes to your website and want user feedback.

ExplainED

If you are going to carry out research, try not to influence the results in any way or give preference to the kinds of answers you want to receive. Any forms of bias or tempting the users away from giving their true opinions will invalidate your results.

Conducting your own usability study can include anything from a simple poll on your website to a complete test of how people react to your website using webcams, software, and all sorts of strange gadgets. While big institutions can afford to put money into extensive testing, the average person will not need to go to the same extent, so do not worry if you feel that the majority of studies aren't for you. The important thing is that you interact with your visitors—get users to offer their opinions, and listen to what they have to say. Your website's potential to succeed will be increased dramatically from engaging with those kind enough to look at your site.

Research Models

Quantitative and qualitative research are used to measure and conduct the various types of studies you find to determine what usability issues and bottlenecks may exist. The main difference between them is *quantitative research* focuses on gathering hard numbers and statistics that can be analyzed to determine, for example, whether a certain feature should be implanted or whether the problems associated with a part of your website are just affecting a single person. *Qualitative research*, on the other hand, tries to look in more depth at the root causes, feelings, and perspectives of the people who visit your website, such as simply asking them what they think about your design. Both of these methods have their own inherent benefits and flaws, using a mixture of the two different research methods can help you get the best website possible.

Here are some handy usability testing methods:

- **Card sorting:** Sticky notes or cards are given to people to see what items they think should be grouped together; this allows you to decide what content belongs within which pages.

- **Questionnaires:** Sending out a questionnaire looking for feedback on specific questions you need answering can be really useful in understanding your visitors' opinions of your website.

- **Polls and quizzes:** Using a poll to grab the attention of individuals with little or no time has the benefit of collecting quick snippets of information that may help you make decisions.

- **Auditing:** The method of asking someone to go through your site and writing a comprehensive report of what could be improved can provide expert opinions and useful results.

- **Surveys:** Having people fill in a survey about their browsing habits can allow you to better target your audience by finding out what they are looking for.

- **Observations:** Physically watching someone browse your website and learn the interface can actually be very interesting and useful in finding flaws in the design.

- **Field studies:** Performing some research that could have implications with websites outside of your own can help make the Web a better place and resolve unanswered questions.

- **Alpha and beta testing:** The process of getting some visitors to have a look at the website before it goes live can help you spot any bugs or issues that you may have missed.

- **Focus groups:** Getting a group of people inside a room and have them to discuss elements of your website (like in the planning stage) can give you some ideas of possible improvements.

- **Usability checklists:** Using premade usability checklists created from existing knowledge about visitors' needs may help you overcome common flaws in design.

Existing Studies

Research is one of the key areas of usability that you may find useful. So many different studies and tests have been undertaken over the years that you may not even need to conduct your own studies if the information from previous research holds the answers you are looking for. The best place to find this kind of information is within usability websites or journals. However, a good search in Google can uncover interesting observations and studies measuring how people interact with various elements of a website. While usability is something you should consider at every stage of the process (and I hope you have been), the field itself and areas such as patterns and conventions are always changing and being investigated as people's views, likes, dislikes, and other important factors change on a regular basis. If you create your website with your potential visitor's wishes and needs in mind, the simple truth is everything should (hopefully) work out the way you intended, just as long as you are willing to learn and adapt your site to resolve any mistakes you might have made.

LinkED

One perfect example of some usability research that was carried out looked at visitor's preferences in terms of ease of use, download speed, navigation, accessibility, and customization. The results of are published at http://www.websiteoptimization.com/speed/tweak/usability-criteria/.

Analytics Software

Analytics software is one of the main resources the usability engineer has in gauging the target audience and the basic needs a visitor to your website will have. By analyzing traffic page by page and site by site, tools like Google Analytics or Webalizer can produce loads of nifty graphs, charts, and measurable details that you can use to make decisions on how to target your audience. Most web hosts provide a statistics package (see Figure 9-14), though Google makes it simple to plug their own package into your website using a snippet of JavaScript. While it is important to know that statistics are useful in helping us understand our visitors, you do not want to rely on the numbers too heavily, as they can fluctuate or be flawed (such as if the visitor has JavaScript turned off).

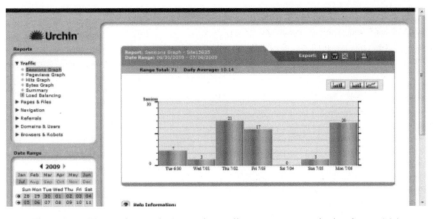

Figure 9-14. The Urchin analytics package allows you to see who has been visiting your website.

Here are some of the features you may find in analytics packages:

- **Traffic:** How do people browse your website, and how long did they stay?

- **Downloads:** What files do your visitors view, and did they encounter any errors?

- **Navigation:** How did your visitors enter, browse, and exit your website?

- **Referrals:** Where did visitors and search engines come from, and how did they find you?

- **Location:** What countries do your visitors come from, and what are their IP addresses?

- **Other:** With what browsers, operating systems, and screen resolutions are users browsing?

Mastering Microformats

Having an accessible and usable website is a great thing. It means that you have been striving for greatness and your website works for as many people as possible. It also implies that, over time, you can keep improving what you have to ensure your website eternally stays fresh and pleasurable to browse around. Of course, having a website that works for disabled people and looks pretty aren't the only aspects of your current web design you can improve for the better. This section of the chapter is dedicated to improving the semantic value of your code by enriching it with microformats (recognizable elements of a website) and metatags (those bits of information search engines recognize when indexing your site). With these, you not only have the opportunity to take your website and make it even more flexible than ever but you actually open yourself up to the potential of having a design that browsers and social networks can interact with and give visitors extra features.

Metadata Markup

Now, we come to the juicy stuff that sits in the head of your HTML documents. Metadata exists to provide your document with a description of the resource itself (basically, it's data about data). If you have ever taken a photo with a digital camera, you might be aware that each one of the files has details like the camera model that produced it, the image creation date, and even sometimes geo-tags. Information about data applies not only to images but audio (such as the duration, artist, album title, and even artwork) and video (the same as audio with other stuff like the frame rate and the size of the video). Metadata is very useful on the Web, as we can describe our pages with a whole list of information which search engines and other websites, such as social networks can make use of, in some ways it is like a MySpace or Facebook profile.

Metatags

When you use a search engine, you normally see a couple of things within the results. First, you see a title made up from the `<title>` element you produced in Chapter 3. You will also notice a snippet of text that describes the page and its contents. Many people choose to let the search engine pick the description, but give a short recommended description that may be used within search engines to state exactly what your site does you can use the following code replacing null for what you would like to see appear within search results.

```
<meta name="description" content="null">
```

The only other element used by some search engines and worthy of mention is the `keywords` tag, but this element exists to provide comma-separated keywords and search terms to help you achieve a higher rank in the search engines. Of course, this tag was created back in the day when search engines trusted people to give accurate descriptions, and as a result of consistent abuse, keywords are rarely given any notice, especially by the major search engines like Google. However, smaller engines still use the `keywords` metatag, and for that reason alone, it may be worth including some terms. I would not recommend you use more than 15 keywords in any case; otherwise, search engines might decide to ban you.

```
<meta name="keywords" content="null">
```

You may need specially engineered metatags for specific functions beyond keywords, but for the purpose of keeping this book simple, no other recommendations have been provided. You will find a combination of the DCMI (explained in the next section) and the two metatags explained in this section generally give you everything you are likely to need.

The DCMI

You can create your own metatags, but unless you want to start a new convention, you should probably just use the most widely recognized ones. Because no standard existed for metadata, the Dublin Core Metadata Initiative (DCMI) was created to provide a specification that reins in metatags. DCMI itself does have some noticeable advantages, such as a structured approach using standardized tags, but it can be separated from the structure of the site (in an external RDF file), and it can be used to more deeply explain the relationship between the site (in context with its content). Finally, note that even though standard metatags are included within the head element of every page in your website, using an external DCMI document means the metainformation for your site will be cached and therefore requires less bandwidth.

LinkED

If you would like to learn more about DCMI and the Dublin Core, you can check out the specification and user's guide at their website: http://dublincore.org/documents/usageguide/.

Microformats

You now have a clean, beautiful website that is accessible to a wide variety of people who will end up visiting your website (hopefully) on a regular basis! But take another look at the code for the site you have thus far, and ask yourself if you have found yourself using div and span tags for parts of your site structure for things that simply could not be described using existing HTML elements (divitis and spanmania can be a scary thing). Or have you found yourself marking up something (such as a business card) and thinking, "Wouldn't it be cool if there was a way for other people to know this was a business card rather than just another bunch of p elements?" Well, you have stumbled into the world of *microformats*, which are layered descriptive naming schemes for HTML elements that better describe markup so applications, visitors, browsers, and search engines can make use of it. Because standardized naming schemes are followed, as many people use them, search engines and applications know to look out for them within websites. If they are available, they can be made use of by converting them into something that offline software, for example, could import and use, which is pretty exciting.

ExplainED

A microformat lives or dies much like a social network: it all depends on how widespread its use is and how many people are making use of it, as conventions are entirely based on group behavior.

Released Microformats

A wide variety of microformats are in existence and being developed all of the time. These purpose-built conventions work from the principle that if everyone marks up an element the same way, other software and sites can recognize and use that element's information. For example, if all sites mark a business card as hCard, when search engines or software packages find hCard references, they know that a business card is contained, as both the spiders and the software have been set to recognize the hCard format. By using these naming conventions, you can give extended third-party functionality to people who visit your website and individuals who make use of tools that understand these conventions. For example, many email clients can use the vCard format produced using hCard. Using microformats offers users yet another way to experience your content. Microformats are fantastic because they require very few additions to your code (perhaps a bit of restructuring to describe the content better). Generally speaking, most microformats work by adding meaningful class and ID attributes to elements, and using span elements or other relevant markup when needed to wrap up pieces of useful information for that convention.

The following list contains all the released microformats at the time of this writing. The websites give full details about how to use each microformat on your site:

- **FOAF (Friend of a Friend)**: http://www.foaf-project.org/
- **hCalendar**: http://microformats.org/wiki/hcalendar
- **hCard**: http://microformats.org/wiki/hcard
- **hSlice**: http://msdn.microsoft.com/en-us/library/cc304073(VS.85).aspx
- **Rel (License, NoFollow, and Tag)**: http://microformats.org/wiki/rel
- **VoteLinks**: http://microformats.org/wiki/vote-links
- **XFN**: http://gmpg.org/xfn/
- **XMDP**: http://gmpg.org/xmdp/
- **XOXO**: http://microformats.org/wiki/xoxo

Draft Microformats

While the previous microformats are already released and in common use, some up-and-coming formats are worthy of mention, as they will eventually become another standard you can use to properly mark up your content so that your visitors can better understand it. If you do choose to implement the following microformats, you should do so with the knowledge that it may take some time before browsers and applications are upgraded to make use of the new conventions you have decided to adopt. The great thing about microformats is that anyone can produce their own unique extensions to HTML; if you submit your ideas (with a new specification attached) to the microformat community, they may become something that other people use on a regular basis!

The following list contains unreleased microformats at the time of this writing:

- **Adr**: http://microformats.org/wiki/adr
- **Geo**: http://microformats.org/wiki/geo
- **hAtom**: http://microformats.org/wiki/hatom
- **hAudio**: http://microformats.org/wiki/haudio
- **hMedia**: http://microformats.org/wiki/hmedia
- **hProduct**: http://microformats.org/wiki/hproduct
- **hRecipe**: http://microformats.org/wiki/hrecipe
- **hResume**: http://microformats.org/wiki/hresume
- **hReview**: http://microformats.org/wiki/hreview
- **Rel (Directory, Enclosure, Home, and Payment)**: http://microformats.org/wiki/rel

- **Robots:** http://microformats.org/wiki/robots-exclusion
- **XFolk:** http://microformats.org/wiki/xfolk

NotED

In HTML, there are three attributes you can apply to an anchor to help explain the relationship between pages. Rel *explains the relationship between the target (the current page) to the resource (the page it links to).* Rev *shows the relationship of the resource to the target, and* Role *explains the anchors relationship to the target, which is particularly useful in fragment links.*

Syndicating and Integrating

The next thing we need to examine in this chapter is the benefit of syndicating your content. Providing feeds of information for your visitors to keep up to date with recent events (or content) at a click of a mouse has become an expectation of users for the last few years. The technology has taken off to become something that almost all web browsers can take advantage of. As you have content, and perhaps some news (such as a message stating that the website has launched), it would be worth getting a feed up and running so that when people find your site, they can immediately subscribe and become part of your extended family of regular visitors!

Generating Feeds

When most people browse websites regularly, they are interested only in what is new to the website rather than in reviewing or looking over the same content. Because information in a website is normally provided in a list format (such as a list of recent news items), updates can be easily tracked by visitors. The purpose of feeds is to take those new pieces of information on a website and place them in a format that can be monitored and tracked by software or a web browser. This saves time for visitors, as they can subscribe to your site (like a newsletter) and visit only when content that interests them is added. Software that can make use of syndicated feeds is referred to as an aggregator and often contains functionality like the ability to hide already read posts; sort content by date, title, or keywords; and in the case of podcasts or media feeds, automatically download the files ready to be watched or heard. These tools are often integrated into web browsers for convenience.

Creating a syndication feed is, in many ways, the same as creating an HTML document. You pull together a series of tags, elements, and attributes in a specially formatted document (XML, in this case) that can be taken advantage of by web browsers. The two main standards for syndicating content on the Web are RSS and Atom. Both have their own advantages and disadvantages, so I highly recommended that you provide feeds for both formats to ensure the widest amount of compatibility among browsers and syndication clients. Only slightly different code is required to turn one format into another, so creating both them should be straightforward!

LinkED

*If you want to have your syndication feed created for you and hosted elsewhere, the free service Feedburner is an excellent alternative to producing your own code (*http://feedburner.google.com/*).*

OK, so now that you know what feeds are, how exactly do you go about adding them to your website so people can take advantage of them? Well, the following guide gives a quick-start crash course into getting the hang of producing some basic RSS and Atom feeds. The following instructions are in no way comprehensive, and I have pretty much repeated the example for RSS in the example for Atom so that you can compare how the two languages work on a very basic level. However, as with all of the web languages you counter, the specifications provided on the independent websites are simple to work with, so you can always extend your learning by taking a stroll across the Web to find out more useful elements you can include inside your syndication feeds.

LinkED

If you are into podcasting and want to produce an audio show on the Web, knowing about RSS and Atom feeds is important, so your visitors can get hold of new episodes automatically. iTunes, which is the biggest online music and podcast provider, has its own syndication format that you can learn and adapt your existing feeds to at http://www.apple.com/itunes/whatson/podcasts/specs.html.

Languages in Use

The idea of syndication is a relatively new concept to the Web, even though it is already a popular and convenient way of using the Web. If you browse websites on a regular occasion, you have probably come across links that allow you to subscribe to content or updates known as feeds. These feeds provide a simple but straightforward method to let people avoid revisiting a website all of the time to see what's new. Visitors can get instant notifications as you publish about new events on your site. The most common syndication formats are listed here. These formats are easy to learn, and they can sit next to each other so you can make use of both of them to ensure maximum compatibility; think of them as competing formats which can be used at the same time.

- **RSS**: Really Simple Syndication (RSS) is an XML-based language that has become the industry standard method of allowing people to subscribe to content or site updates. Most web browsers have support for RSS, and many have built-in clients to let visitors subscribe to feeds produced using the language. RSS 2.0, along with its previous versions, has wide support, and many of the software and web-based clients that syndicate feeds for stuff like podcasts widely adopt the RSS format. The language itself is actually relatively easy to learn, and feeds can be built extremely quickly. An example RSS feed is shown in Figure 9-15.

- **Atom**: Every language needs a competitor, and Atom serves that purpose for RSS. With many languages, people tend to pick one or the other, but this is one of those occasions where you are better off supporting both RSS and Atom. Don't worry; supporting both is exceptionally easy to do, as they will work alongside each other through references in your HTML header. Atom supports more tags than RSS, but this standard's adoption rate is lower and amount of users are fewer than those of RSS. However, like with RSS, Atom is widely supported by both browsers and separate clients, and the language is as easy to learn as its competitor. Because of user preferences that may occur, it is therefore recommended that you provide both feeds.

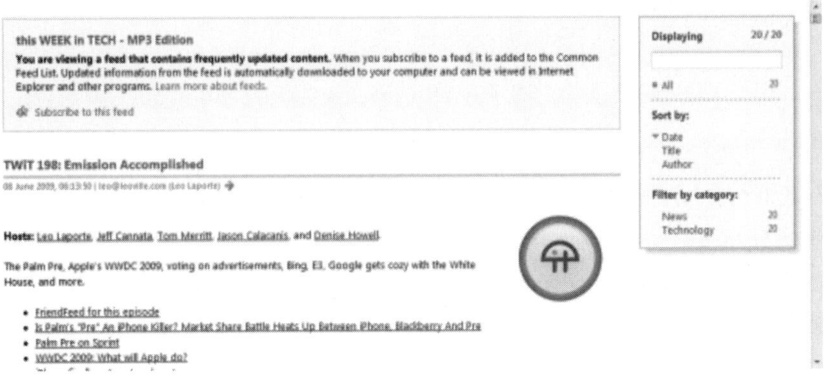

Figure 9-15. With its own RSS feed (shown in Internet Explorer 8), Leo Laportes pocast keeps visitors up to date with new episodes.

RSS and Atom

Before we get down to coding, we, of course, need to create the file where the code will be stored. For the purposes of keeping naming conventions, I recommend you save the document as rss.xml (you could save it as an .rss file, but most clients automatically assume .xml in preference for feeds so we will avoid using the .rss file extension). You should save the file to the feeds folder, as its purpose is to hold your syndication documents.

Next, we need to add the XML declaration for the file and the document type definition (DTD) it is going to use:

```
<?xml version="1.0" encoding="utf-8"?>
<rss version="2.0">
    <channel>

    </channel>
</rss>
```

Now, we have the outer wrapper, so let's add the main properties to the channel. With syndication feeds, you will find it is a lot like HTML: you have an opening tag, the element name, and then a closing tag. You are required to add some elements to your feed, so let's work through those first of all. The <title> element provides a name that will appear in the top of the document, much like the equivalent element in HTML). The <link> tag should provide a URL to your main website, where the feed was directed from. And finally, you need to provide a <description> tag to give a brief explanation to what the feed contains, such as news stories or blog posts.

```
<channel>
    <title>MySite! Latest News</title>
    <link>http://www.yoursitehere.com/</link>
    <description>All of the latest news stories from
MySite!</description>
</channel>
```

So now we have a basic feed with some heading information—excellent! Let's add our very first post to the content. Each post needs to be added within the channel under a block level element called `<item>`. Just like the main document itself, each post is only required to make use of the `<title>`, `<link>`, and `<description>` tags to function. You should remember that the heading information we provided earlier was included for the feed itself, and each item should have a title that matches the story. The link should go to that story, and the description should overview what users will find within that website. Also note that you can provide an unlimited number of items within the channel, so feel free to start playing and producing your very first RSS feed. Once you are ready to add this feed to your website, read on. The following example shows the possible content of a news story as it would be represented (in code) within an RSS feed:

```
<item>
    <title>The new website has been launched!</title>
    <link>http://www.yoursitehere.com/news/001/</link>
    <description>&lt;p&gt;My new website has been released, how awsome
is that?&lt;p&gt;</description>
</item>
```

You have all the basic components (the container, the feed, and the items) now, so you can put your very first feeds on the Web. Just like with the CSS style sheets, you simply place a link to the document within the head of your HTML, and you will find the browser will detect the feeds when you launch the website (try it yourself!).

```
<link rel="alternate" type="application/rss+xml" title="MySite! Latest
News (RSS)" href="/feeds/rss.xml" />
```

If you produced the file according to the preceding code snippet, using the relevant elements to your own feed's needs (with the item inside the channel) and have linked to the file in the HTML properly, you should be able to see your RSS feed showing perfectly in your browser! The preceding example will produce a very rudimentary syndication feed, but you do not want to limit yourself to just what has been included in this brief introduction. Why not check out the specification for the language and use their easy-to-follow guide to enhance your feed and make it even better? The great thing with these languages are that they are very straightforward and have a limit to the types of information you can enter, so mastering RSS is fairly simple.

The following are optional elements that can appear within the `<channel>` tags:

- language
- copyright
- managingEditor
- webMaster
- pubDate
- lastBuildDate
- category
- generator
- docs
- cloud
- ttl
- image
- rating
- textInput
- skipHours
- skipDays

The following are optional elements that can appear within the `<item>` tags:

- author
- category
- comments
- enclosure
- guid
- pubDate
- source

The RSS specification can be found here: http://www.rssboard.org/rss-specification.

Next, we are going to produce an Atom feed (so that we have an identical feed for each syndication format). We first need to create the file where the code will be stored, and for the purposes of keeping naming conventions, I recommend you save the document as atom.xml (you could save it as a .atom file, but most clients automatically assume .xml in preference for feeds). Like RSS, Atom code is probably is best stored inside the feeds folder.

Next, we need to add the XML declaration for the file and the DTD it is going to use:

```
<?xml version="1.0" encoding="utf-8"?>
<feed xmlns="http://www.w3.org/2005/Atom">

</feed>
```

Now that we have this outer wrapper, let's add the main properties to the feed. For the Atom feed, you will need a <title> element, which will provide the heading that appears at the top of the screen like in the RSS feed. You also need an <id> tag, which should point to your main homepage like the RSS link tag. Finally, you will require an <updated> element to describe the date the feed last acquired new information.

Unlike the RSS format, Atom has a few recommended tags you should add in to ensure your feed is as complete as possible. The first of these is an <author> element, which should contain a name for the person who put the feed together (of course, if you do not want to provide this information you do not have to). The other recommended element is a <link> tag that links back to the main Atom feed itself.

```
<feed xmlns="http://www.w3.org/2005/Atom">
    <title>MySite! Latest News</title>
    <author><name>John Doe</name></author>
    <link rel="self" href="/atom.xml" />
    <id>http://www.yoursitehere.com/</id>
    <updated>2009-12-16T18:30:02Z</updated>
</feed>
```

Now that you have a basic feed with some heading information, you can add your very first post to the content. Each post needs to be added within the feed under a block-level element called <entry>. Just like the main document itself, each post is only required to make use of the <title>, <id>, and <updated> tags to function. Again, the heading information is included for the feed itself, but each item needs a title and link to match the story and a description to overview the information.

Just like before, there are a number of recommended elements you can add into your feed: <author> and <link> we have already discussed. <content> is the equivalent to the RSS summary element, which provides a URL to the source of the item. You can provide an unlimited number of entries within an Atom feed too, so feel free to start producing your very first Atom feed and then read on to add it to your website.

```
<entry>
    <title>The new website has been launched!</title>
    <id>http://www.yoursitehere.com/news/001/</id>
    <updated>2009-12-16T18:30:02Z </updated>
    <author>John Doe</author>
    <link rel="alternate" href="http://www.yoursitehere.com/news/001/"
/>
    <content type="xhtml" xml:lang="en">
        <div xmlns="http://www.w3.org/1999/xhtml">
        <p>My new website has been released, how awesome is that?</p>
        </div>
    </content>
</entry>
```

Now that you have the container, the feed, and the items, you can put your very first Atom feed on the Web: simply place a link to the document within the head of your HTML, and the browser will detect the feeds when you launch the website. The steps, as you have now noticed, are very similar to those for RSS, luckily as you only need one of each file format for your website, it shouldn't be too repetitive for you to accomplish.

```
<link rel="alternate" type="application/atom+xml" title="MySite! Latest
News (Atom)" href="/feeds/atom.xml" />
```

If you produced the file according to the instructions in this section (with the entry inside feed) and have linked to the file in the HTML properly, you should be able to see your Atom feed showing perfectly in your browser! These instructions produce a very rudimentary syndication feed, but you do not want to limit yourself to just what is included here. Just like for RSS feeds, the specification for the language provides an easy-to-follow guide to enhance your feed. The great thing about these languages is that they are very straightforward and have a limit to the types of information you can enter, so mastering Atom is fairly simple.

The following are optional elements that can appear within the <feed> tags:

- category
- contributor
- generator
- icon
- logo
- rights
- subtitle

The following are optional elements that can appear within the <entry> tags:

- category
- contributor
- published
- source
- rights

The Atom specification is available at http://www.atomenabled.org/developers/syndication/.

Integrating Extensions

The combination of accessible HTML and microformats will pump up the levels of adrenaline in your website, but there are a couple of other exciting little functions you can embed within your homepage to help you to further integrate your design within the visitor's browser. The features in the following sections will add an additional layer of useful functionality within the web browser. These features are not directly associated with your HTML, but they might benefit visitors who can take advantage of them. You may find that some of the functions provided will not be of use due to the type of website you have chosen to build, so you should take the time to read each of the options and decide for yourself whether it will be worth implementing.

OpenSearch

Worthy of mention before we round out this chapter is the OpenSearch specification (see Figure 9-16). Have you ever found yourself wondering how websites manage to add themselves to your favorite browser's search box in the top right-hand side of the window? This useful functionality lets people remember your website and perform a search without having to look for your website's search box and gives your visitors yet another way they can experience what you have to offer. You, too, can add search functionality into your website, which also give you your first piece of interactive behavior. And the best thing is that it doesn't require much effort at all!

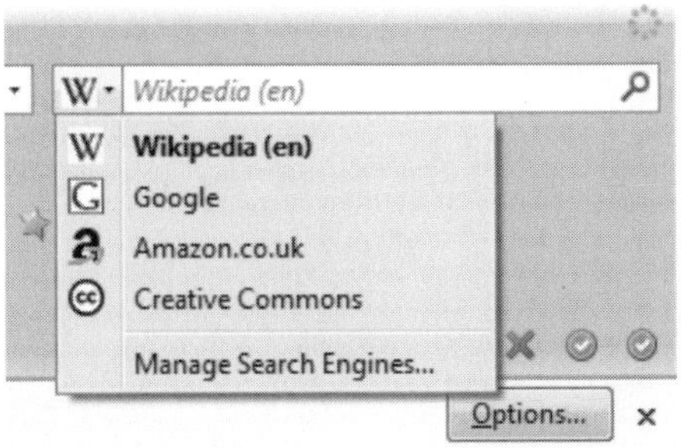

Figure 9-16. The OpenSearch standard allows you to add your website to a browsers' search box.

LinkED

Did you know OpenSearch was created by Amazon? If you want to learn more about OpenSearch, you can visit its website and see how you can give the example in this section more bells and whistles: http://www.opensearch.org/Home.

It is actually very easy to produce a basic search engine for your site, and because you have lots of content and several pages, you can make use of it right now. It's something nice and fun you can add to make your website a bit more professional. Like with the syndication formats, I will not go into too much detail to prevent you from getting bogged down with a minor part of the web design process. But I know you are probably anxious to turn all those bland, empty documents into something pretty and very stylish, and using the following exercise, you can literally plug the sample code into your website and instantly have a Google search box for your site.

Try It Yourself: Add Your Site to a Browser's Search Box

Create a file called search.xml, and place it within the misc folder where you have been dumping all your unique bits and pieces. Next, place the following code into the file, so you have everything you need to get set up:

```
<?xml version="1.0" encoding="UTF-8" ?>
<OpenSearchDescription xmlns="http://a9.com/-/spec/opensearch/1.1/">
    <ShortName>MyName!</ShortName>
    <Description>Search my website.</Description>
    <Contact>http://www.yoursitehere.com/</Contact>
    <InputEncoding>UTF-8</InputEncoding>
```

```
    <Language>en</Language>
    <Attribution>Copyright &#169; 2009, MySite!. All rights
reserved.</Attribution>
    <Image width="16" height="16"
type="image/png">http://www.yoursitehere.com/misc/favicon.ico</Image>
    <Url type="text/html"
template="http://www.google.co.uk/search?sitesearch=http%3A%2F%2Fwww.
yoursitehere.com%2F&amp;as_q={searchTerms}"/>
</OpenSearchDescription>
```

Now, you need to change <ShortName> to your website's name or brand, and replace yousitehere in <Contact> and <URL> with your own web addresses. If you have a favicon, you can replace the URL to the icon. This should be all fairly straightforward stuff, as you are now well versed in writing basic markup.

Finally, you need to reference the file in your HTML, so yet again, fly back to the head element and add another link tag (surprise!). Like with syndication feeds, the browser detects the OpenSearch support and places the link within the search bar, which visitors can add to their favorite search locations. Once a visitor searches in the box, that URL you constructed will use Google's Site Search (which is entirely free) to find any indexed content on your website. Note that the search box will not find any results until your website is listed with Google, so it's worth adding the functionality now. That way, when your site is picked up by Google, your visitors will have instant access to search your website quickly and easily with barely any effort.

```
<link rel="search" type="application/opensearchdescription+xml"
title="MySite!" href="/misc/search.xml" />
```

ExplainED

If you have been putting your pages online at each stage of production to see how the site looks, your site may already have found its way into Google; after all, we used semantic, clean, HTML! If it isn't listed, don't worry; you will learn how to get your website placed in search engines later in this book.

Accelerators

Along with the microformat hSlice, Internet Explorer 8 added a brand new way of extending the reach of your website to your visitors—accelerators (see Figure 9-17). To cut a long story short, accelerators are added to a submenu when you right-click any website (or if you select something within a website) within Internet Explorer 8, these accelerators act as shortcuts to perform a web-based function. As an example, a dictionary website could produce an accelerator to search the dictionary for a definition. Anyone with the accelerator installed could select a word in a website and right-click to opt to look up its definition on the dictionary website. This example is fairly simple, but you can see the potential for being able to run a URL or an hSlice to offer a web-based service to anyone who wants to use the functionality provided by your website.

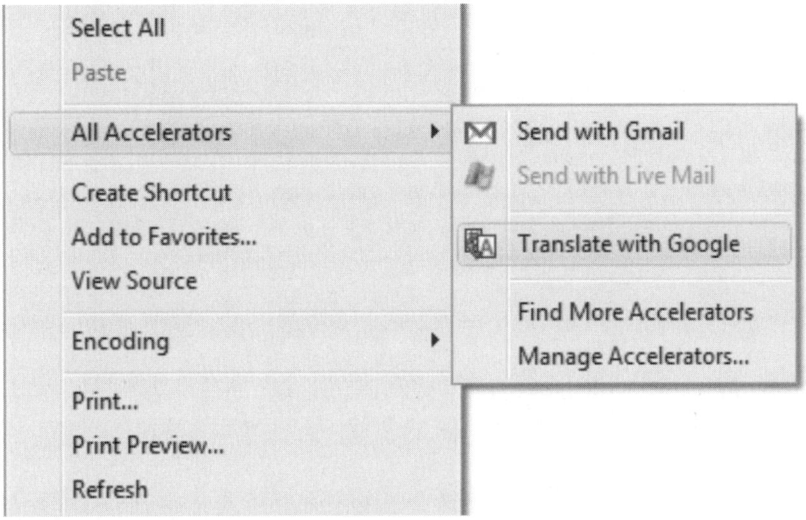

Figure 9-17. Internet Explorer 8 has the ability to use accelerators that run web-based commands.

LinkED

While accelerators are more advanced functionality than you probably want to go with now, I have included the reference to this exciting new technology, as you may find yourself wanting to take advantage of it in the future. To learn how to make an accelerator, visit http://msdn.microsoft.com/en-us/library/cc304163(VS.85).aspx.

Summary

In this chapter, you have learned the importance of accessibility and considered taking any precautions that will ensure that people with disabilities or special technological needs can access your website. We also looked at why good usability and design is important to make your visitors' experiences as enjoyable as possible. Finally, you should hopefully have learned the value of purpose-built microformats and syndicated feeds. At this point, if you have not made improvements to accessibility, usability, or the semantic value of your HTML and CSS and you want to do so, put down this book, enhance your website, and return to the book once you're finished. In the next chapter, you are going to finish off your web design road trip, and I'll explain how you can make your code perfect (or near perfect), and get people to visit your website! We will look at the murky world of search engine optimization, the basics of marketing both through conventional and new techniques (like social networking), and finally, I provide you with a section dedicated to selling products and services if you want to make your site profitable.

Chapter Checklist

You should accomplish the following tasks before leaving this chapter:

- Understand how your visitors browse the web and are affected by design.
- Take the time to consider how accessibility and usability may help your site.
- Implement microformats, metadata, and syndication feeds when applicable.

Questions and Answers

Q: *Will my design suffer as a result of being accessibility friendly?*

A: Accessibility is one of the most important parts of a website. As invisible as these features may seem, sometimes, if you take steps to increase the way your website works for disabled users, the website may suffer a less visually appealing design. Generally, there are ways to get around this issue, such as providing alternatives as opposed to trying to make everything fit or work well for everyone—because let's face it, "everyone" is far too many people to think about! It has been proven time and again that paying attention to accessibility, usability, and web standards certainly does not mean the design will be ugly; it just means you need to give a bit of thought before you act.

Q: *What should I do with a well-researched usability test?*

A: If you conduct a well-put-together usability study that has a lot of participants, making the results more widespread than if you'd surveyed just 20 or so people, and if the study found some surprising results, perhaps you should share your results with the rest of the world and publish the study on the Web! You could submit your findings to one of the many usability websites, or you could post them on a web developer forum for other professionals to see. You could even show them on your own website with your accessibility statement. The important thing to remember is that usability is structured on learning about how people use the Web and what their expectations are, so your results (if unique) could be very useful in changing the way websites are made or how certain features are implemented.

Q: *Are microformats really worth the time it takes to implement them?*

A: Yes! Recent statistics show that microformats are rapidly gaining popularity, and literally billions of websites currently make use of one or more microformats. With the increasing numbers of social networks, browsers, and search engines that can make use of them, you can guarantee that they enhance the way your visitors can use the information you provide. If you remain unconvinced about adding extra code to your already perfect mark-up, you should research the subject further to gain a better understanding of the potential these useful code enhancements can add to your very own website. If you want your code to be as semantically rich as possible, microformats add an additional layer of purpose to your tags.

Where You Are Now

By the end of this chapter you should have the following:

- A website checked for accessibility that implements any required changes
- Any changes to your design that could improve the usability
- Microformats and syndication feeds (as appropriate)

Chapter 10

How Can I Get More Visitors?

Welcome to the final chapter in this book. At this stage, you should have an exciting website packed with features that's ready for your audience to dive in and start using. You've done enough to get your fantastic-looking website functioning beautifully. Before I round off this book and leave you to your own devices, there is one more area we need to look at that's imperative to ensuring your website is a success. We need to consider how to actually get visitors to your website (after all, a party with no people is a failure!). The fields of search engine optimization, promotion, and e-commerce are increasingly important parts of the website-building process, especially with the rise in social media—those cool places where you probably hang out like Facebook, Twitter, and MySpace. We will examine the various methods you can use to get traffic to your sites (naturally and supernaturally), how to market both your brand and your content through the medium of self-publishing, and how to approach selling goods and services at a very basic level on the Internet.

In this chapter, we're going to cover the following topics:

- How to get a good position in search engine rankings
- Marketing with content, advertising, and social networks
- The basics of selling goods and services over the Web

Search Engine Optimization

One of the most common ways people get visitors to their websites is through the murky world of search engine optimization (SEO). This field of the web industry is filled with mystique, confusion, and downright bad information due to the shady characters who try to use all sorts of dodgy methods to try to get the edge over the competition. So what is SEO? As you already know, Google is the king of finding information on the Web, and a pretty fine job it does too, but what if you are a website owner rather than a casual surfer? How do you ensure your website is listed, and more importantly, listed above your competition? Well, the general premise is to use SEO to try to target search engines, through the presentation of your content and the information you disseminate on the Web. With SEO, the sole aim is to be the most recommended result by placing first in the search results when a potential visitor looks for something, of course this isn't very easy to accomplish with all the websites out there.

We will first examine organic SEO—the natural ways to get traffic. Then, we'll move onto how to assist the search engines more directly by manipulating search engines like Google by giving some pretty definite hints about what you offer. Finally, we'll look at some of the dirty tricks that have been played in the past in the battle for supremacy on the Web. While the information in this section is useful in getting to grips with the basics, you should remember that if your website has high-quality content and a good audience, it should have little problem finding its feet and a voice among the masses that occupy the search engine rankings. By the end of this chapter, though, you should have your site listed on various websites where people can find you for the very first time!

Organic SEO

Organic SEO is a healthy and natural way of getting traffic to your website without resorting to tricks or performance-enhancing tactics to improve your ranking. It generally relies on good clean markup and well-written content, which luckily you already have! Basically, you cultivate the website naturally and allow search engines to place your website as a result of how well you treated your content and source code. This leads to traffic (visitors) that naturally appear without you directly influencing the search engine. Organic traffic (those naturally occurring visitors) is the most ethical method of getting traffic, because it is entirely based on substance rather than methodology. You should consider it your primary method of getting a good placement within search engines. In this section, we look at what comprises an organic rank and dispel some of the common myths associated with SEO—a number have cropped up over the years! Hopefully, your website is already well optimized (in respect to code and content), which will improve your overall rank with minimum effort.

Arachnophobia!

Search engines seem scary when you first hear about them. Often, they are referred to as spiders, crawlers, or robots, which make them sound like something fresh from a sci-fi horror movie! These monsters roam around the web looking for new content to index or update and literally churn through millions of pages an hour. Because of the size of the Internet, they have really complex systems of filtering through all the junk and making sure high-quality websites (like yours) get the positions they deserve. When a search engine visits your website, you want it to feel at home and for things to be as easy for it to browse and as fresh as possible, because then the quality of your site is likely to be noticed more readily. You should be aware that search engines read normal HTML pages and make decisions based on what they see—just like your visitors. Therefore, inaccessible or stale websites may affect both search engines and visitors alike, so ensuring your website is accessible is very important.

Although a number of different spiders exist, the most common belong to the search engine Google (see Figure 10-1). The reason for this is primarily because Google is the most popular search engine on the market, with around 90% of all searches going through it! This means that you should ensure that your primary focus is on getting your site noticed in Google, though other search engines like Microsoft Bing can be useful they do not have nearly as many users making use of their website. It is also worth mentioning that Google is also the largest distributer of online advertising. When we come to look at the ways you can advertise and monetize your website, I'll focus on Google's own system (AdWords). When it comes to marketing your website and getting your name out there for visitors to find you, aiming at the biggest exposure points for advertising is the best starting position.

We will examine how to get your website listed on the various search engines later in the "Search Engine Submission" section. For now, let's take a look at which search engines get the most amount of traffic. In the "See for Yourself" exercise, you'll find the four most common search engines listed in order of statistical number of users. You should pay close attention to getting your website listed within these four. Google owns a vast majority of all search traffic, but other search engines still have millions of potential visitors and are therefore worthy of note. However, they usually will yield fewer results (in terms of successful visits). To ensure you keep up to date with the search engines you can use to your benefit, you should keep an eye out for new ones that appear!

Figure 10-1. Google is by far the world's most popular search engine and is used by millions daily.

See for Yourself: Searching the Web

These are the four major search engines:

- **Google Search**: http://www.google.com/
- **Microsoft Bing**: http://www.bing.com/ (This was formerly known as MSN Search.)
- **Yahoo!**: http://www.yahoo.com/ (This search engine will be replaced by Bing.)
- **Ask Jeeves**: http://www.ask.com/

LinkED

For an up-to-date list of the popular search engines (only four have a majority share of Internet users) you can check the constantly updated website at http://www.seoconsultants.com/search-engines/.

What Is SERP?

A search engine results page (SERP) is basically the list of results that appear when you perform a search on a website like Google, and this is the page where you want your website to appear. Your position on a SERP is determined by a variety of conditions, and different result types can appear within the listings such as images, maps, definitions, and even videos (see Figure 10-2). Of course, we are mainly interested, at this stage, in getting your site listed under the normal textual results. These can be broken down into sponsored results (which are paid to get promoted on the front page) and natural listings that had no assistance from the search provider in being positioned in one of the pages. The higher your website is positioned on the SERP, the more likely it will be noticed by people looking for what you are offering (the top five natural positions are coveted like gold).

Within the natural search rankings, you generally get ten links per page, which gives each link adequate space to get some attention from the person searching. Placement within the highest ranks is considered the most valuable. Generally, fewer than 50% of people will go beyond the first couple of pages, and the chance of getting your website clicked reduces tremendously beyond the third page. People tend to restate their search terms and try again if they cannot find what they want within the first few pages of results. Also, having a natural SEO rank is more likely to get you visitors than using a paid sponsored link. In fact, some studies show the chances are over double! Perhaps this is because people have become trained not to click advertisements (due to the general dislike of them) and because relevance may not be as accurate.

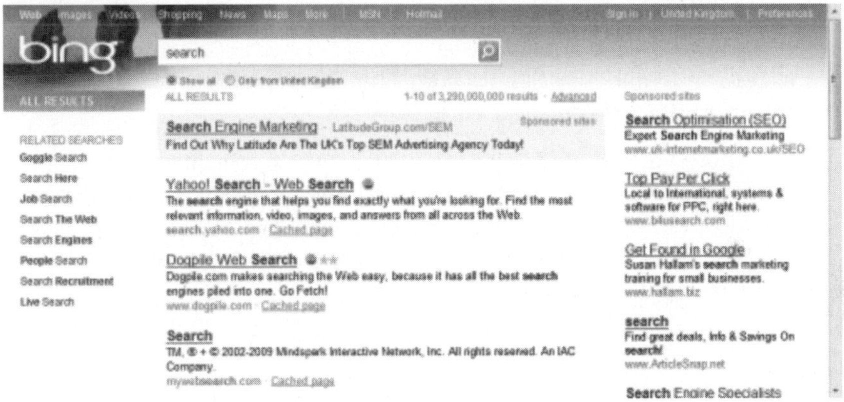

Figure 10-2. Microsoft's newest search engine Bing displays results using various conventions.

ExplainED

You are more likely to get a high position if your site has a unique name and offers a service that no one else offers (as there are fewer competitor links to compare yours against), but for common and popular terms, trying to get to the peak of Google is very difficult!

Shades of Gray

Three common terms in SEO are "white hat," "black hat," and "gray hat." They refer the range of techniques to get you listed in search engines. These terms are buzzwords that hold little meaning, but they do point out that depending on your morals (and ethics), some techniques for getting a search engine's attention are perfectly innocent where others not only sound deceptive but can get you banned from search engines. Most search engines like Google have a policy to deal with unethical search optimization. The terms descended from the days when hackers used to use these words to represent if they were virtuous hackers who let security teams know about flaws or unscrupulous hackers who simply wanted to do damage. Of course, some also fell in between. While these terms are still in use for hacking, I will use them to define the different approaches in SEO:

- **White hats**: These individuals focus on clean semantic markup, fixing problems directly with sites, natural and progressive listing in search engines, and generally accepted techniques to increase visitors through advertising, social media, and clean but effective publicity schemes.

- **Gray hats**: These individuals focus on a mixture of both aggressive and subtle marketing and are often willing to put a bit of risk (such as the potential of getting banned from search engines) into an SEO strategy. However, they usually exercise more restraint than the black hat SEO experts, who use more brutal methods.

- **Black hats**: These individuals focus on aggressive forms of marketing, heavy use of metadata, getting large numbers of back links, and generally pushing the boundaries of the search engine. These tactics are much higher risk, but the result can be higher placement.

For more information about the differences between ethical and unethical SEO, check out the article at http://www.searchengineguide.com/jill-whalen/black-hatwhite-hat-search-engine-optimization.php.

Natural Ingredients

Now that I have briefly mentioned search engines and the kinds of people who perform SEO, we need to examine the relationship between your source code and searches (and how to keep things natural). One of the key factors to anything organic is the use of natural ingredients. In web design terms, this means you want to make things as purely and simply as possible to allow search engines to find their way around your content quickly and easily; you need to make sure your code is semantically correct and as minimalistic as possible in respect to bloat. You are already aware of the importance this has in accessibility, and search engines fall into a category of disabled visitors as they are limited in what technologies they can make use of such as CSS, JavaScript, and Flash, though some search engines, including Google, are getting better at understanding this technology. As a result, only using technologies as you need them will help reduce the complexity and let your website's relevant content stand a better chance of being indexed properly.

It is hard to tell what extent search engines understand technologies like Flash, JavaScript, and CSS (and the semantic value they add to the content), because searching algorithms are closely guarded secrets; competition is fierce in the search engine market, especially among the top providers!

Try It Yourself: Fixing Minor Issues

Check through your source code and see if you can find anything that doesn't validate or isn't semantic or if you made any other mistakes. Fixing these small things can be a fine balancing act in terms of how search engines will react. You might get a higher rank for being semantic, especially if search engines notice important information easier, but accessibility for search engines is also a key factor. Perhaps after using the W3C validator (mentioned in Chapter 7) you find that some of your code doesn't validate properly? If this is the case, you may want to ensure the bugs are ironed out, as they could harm your ranking (especially because certain HTML elements like headings have a lot of relevance and priority in results and of assigned value overall).

If you have followed the recommendations earlier in this book about keeping your code clean and semantic, your website should pass this test fairly easily, but it's always worth checking to see if there are any tweaks or improvements you feel you could make to your website. Any reduction in file size can improve the speed of the site. Smaller files can be useful when search engines attempt to index your content, because pages over 100KB may cause the spider to time out or delay the addition of the page to the index. The natural ingredients apply to not only the code of your website but also to the domain name and URLs you possess. Ensuring you have a domain name that is easy to remember, is unlikely to be a victim of constant typos, and makes use of friendly URLs helps spiders and visitors recognize the contents by the address rich in keywords and context.

ExplainED

Most new websites are automatically discovered by Google, but it can take anywhere between a week to a month before anything happens. Therefore, you may wish to submit your website manually if you are impatient. You will need to repeat this task for every search engine, as each uses its own database of websites! I will explain how to manually submit your website to a search engine later in this chapter.

Busting Myths

As you are aware, organic SEO stands on the principles of making your website as clean and efficient as possible. We already know your website is semantic and valid; therefore the natural SEO ranking of your website should be optimized already! While making your website work as well as possible is perhaps the simplest form of SEO and requires no actual contact with the search engines to achieve (unlike what we are going to be working with later on), a lot of myths have appeared in reference to SEO, and we need to address these before we start doing anything more than simply optimizing the source code of your website.

The first myth we are going to bust is that people seem to think extensions (whether the file type such as .php and .html, or the domain name extension) will affect your search engine rank. While popular extensions such as .com, .net, and .org are often taken, you do not need to worry about another extension performing poorly in rankings, as the only time that domain extensions play a part in the rankings of search engines is when your visitors search using local listings (it will not make a difference to the average person who wants a global audience), such as the google.co.uk website. And in cases such as these, the United Kingdom-based extension will hold more weight than the generic top-level domain (if your hosting is also located in that country, it makes a difference too!). So take the locality into account when getting your site indexed. This rule also applies to the location of your hosting company's servers. For example, if you went with a server located in the United States and you want your website to perform well in the United Kingdom, even with a British domain name (.co.uk), you may find yourself being affected in terms of your overall raking in the search engines as a result of the server's locale.

The second myth is one of the most popular and incorrect ones out there—that metadata will help give you a good spot in search engines. The use of description and keyword metadata is of limited importance, and while description is considered by Google and others, the keywords tag is totally ignored. Due to abuse in the past, the keywords tag has been all but abandoned by the major search engines so it will hold little value except to the niche search engines that serve a very tiny proportion of web searchers. However, the use of microformats and Metadata that is served correctly can have additional benefits. For example, rel="nofollow" is a microformat that allows you to state that an anchor should not be listed as linked to from that page. This can stop spam links from being counted when the quality of the links is considered by search engines.

ExplainED

If you do make use of metatags, you should ensure (just like with the title *element in HTML) that each page has a unique set of keywords and a unique description. If every page uses the same keywords, the usefulness to your site will be reduced, as spiders won't target your pages by their subjects.*

The third myth we are going to look at claims that SEO software will get you banned from Google. While there are some bad products out there that could potentially get you blacklisted due to their outdated methods of getting you noticed by search engines, you should not be deterred from trying out some of the good products that can be useful for getting some ideas to further boost your ranking within search engines. All you need to do is make sure the product you choose is using acceptable optimization methods (you can check user reviews to see how well it worked for them), and products with positive reviews should be fine for use.

The fourth and final myth we will debunk is a classic mistake people seem to make; some people have the false assumption that the amount of traffic (visitors) their website gets will give them a better position within search engines. This isn't the case for one very simple reason—search engines can visit your website just like any other, but they can't see your statistics (and I am unaware of any research to show that Google Analytics use will affect this). Essentially, Google simply doesn't have enough information about what kinds of visitors you get (outside of its own search results) to be able to factor in your traffic.

ExplainED

There are so many myths associated with search engine optimization that I could probably write an entire book on the misconceptions. The ones in this section are very common issues, and you should be skeptical of SEO tips you read online unless you can be sure of the information's authenticity.

White Hat SEO

If you want to be considered the "good guy" of SEO, using the methods contained in this section will help you improve the rank of your website by looking at the approved methods of gaining a better position in search engines. We will examine how you get your site listed in the first place, doing keyword research and link building (with high-quality resources). We'll also cover building sitemaps and `robots.txt` files to assist the indexing of your content as effectively as possible. All of the methods contained in this section are considered good practice, are safe to use as long as you do not abuse them, and could boost your performance. So now that you have a general awareness of the search engines and your design is organically ready for the search engines to find, we'll look at some simple ways you can positively influence the SEO rank of your website. Let's get started with some performance-enhancing tweaks to get the best rank for your money (that is, if you choose to spend any).

LinkED

Google also offers a simple but easy-to-understand guide to SEO. Google's own advice is worth a quick read and is available for free at http://www.google.com/webmasters/docs/search-engine-optimization-starter-guide.pdf *(you will need a PDF reader such as Adobe Acrobat reader to open it).*

Keyword Research

When we use a search engine, the primary way we look for information is by entering some relevant keywords to describe what we are after and clicking the search button. The search engines do the rest and check their records to see what we are most likely looking for. When we perform search engine optimization we therefore need to ensure your website is appropriately making use of keywords within the content and the other information processed by websites (such as metainformation and headings as appropriate). Because the process of choosing keywords can be fairly complex, you will find a much-simplified step-by-step process through the ordeal in the following "Try It Yourself" exercise. Remember that once you have this information and research, you need to ensure that your content appropriately reflects the keywords (or vice versa); otherwise; you could end up being detected as a spammer by accident, which could result in being banned from Google!

Try It Yourself: Researching Keywords

Use the following step-by-step guide to build a keyword profile. The results of this research will give you some words and phrases you can make use of throughout your website not only within the keyword metatags, if you choose to use them, but also within any content you write. Hopefully, with those keywords in place, your site should be well listed in search engines because of the number of times these words were used and mentioned.

1. Make a list of words that best describe your website and its contents (look at the content you have produced for ideas). These will be your primary keywords, though you should remember not to just use one- or two-word combinations, because three- and four-word options like "free web design" often better cover what a regular person using a

search engine will look for. Remember also to include your brand identity into the keywords; this is particularly important.

2. Next, you need to add some more possible words to your list. You do not want to just look for synonyms of your previous words (they can be useful for getting ideas), as there are no guarantees visitors will search for those freshly worded terms. Instead, open your ideas pad and look at the details of competitor's websites; visit the sites, view the source of their pages, and add any relevant keyword terms to your ever-growing list. These are known as commonly used search phrases (CUSPS), as they are keywords that you share in common with your competition. The more sources for CUSPS you use, the better, because you will get a much better idea of what keywords are the most popular with and coveted by your competitors.

3. Now, you have original and competitive keywords, you want to find some relational keywords; these are keywords that spiders suggest as alternative search terms. To get these terms, visit your favorite search engine (e.g., Google), enter some of your current keywords, and see what alternatives appear in the "Did you mean" section on the results. You should add all of these ideas to the list, as they show the terms that people looked that relate to your keywords. These I tend to call equivalent search terms (ESTs), as they relate to the searches of the average user, as opposed to CUSPS, which are simply replications of existing website entries.

4. Now, you probably have close to a few hundred words. You cannot use all of those, so you need to weed out the results that will not hold as much importance or may not get any visitors to your website. Do this by searching each keyword one at a time (this may take a while). See how many results each gets in search engines. Then take that list and split it in half. As a result, you will have two lists comprising half of the keywords that are overexploited (the ones with the most hits which are hard to get a high rank in) and half that are underexploited (fewer hits means you will be more likely to get a high rank). You want to use a mixture of popular and less-popular search terms within your marketing to guarantee a level of success.

5. Next, you need to narrow down the words in these two categories. First, you should remove any words that are ignored by search engines like "and," "the," and "I"—they are a waste of potential keywords. Next, you should look at the trends in what people search for (using something like Google Trends) to see how hot your exploited search terms are. Basically, pick out the best of the bunch (for both

combinations and singular words), and keep eliminating words as you see fit until you end up with about 25 key overexploited words and 25 underexploited ones. With this information, you finally have your premium keywords to target.

6. Finally, you need to apply your research to your site. Because you have already written your content, you could perhaps target some of the key phrases used for your keywords or edit your content to include a few references here and there to keep them relevant. You can distribute them through your site in content, headings, alternative text, metadata, and more. With these well-researched keywords for your website having been discovered through the investigation and analysis you have done, you should attempt to use them when a genuine opportunity arises. The result of this is that your website will appear in the search terms you have chosen.

LinkED

To understand how Google Trends can be of benefit in researching keywords, you may find the following article useful: http://www.google.com/intl/en/trends/about.html. By searching for each of your keywords, you can literally see how your potential visitor's use of the terms has changed over the years.

Creating Sitemaps

While appearing in search indexes' some relevant keywords is important, ensuring that all of your pages are linked together so that no orphan pages exist is also a high priority. **Orphan pages** are those with no links to other pages on your website, and these can often be troublesome as search engines can't usually find them.

Keeping your pages indexed used to be the job of submission software that gave a directory of links and then indexed them on a case-by-case basis. However, these days an open standard XML format known as a sitemap has become all the rage, as it literally provides a contents page of where everything on the website exists, with information such as the date the page was last updated and how often it changes in context with the whole site. A sitemap allows search engines to display more relevant results, as everything has been categorized effectively. The sitemap document is simply a file that attempts to point to every single file location within the website (see Figure

10-3). You can put one together, of course, either through software or by hand (like most other syntax).

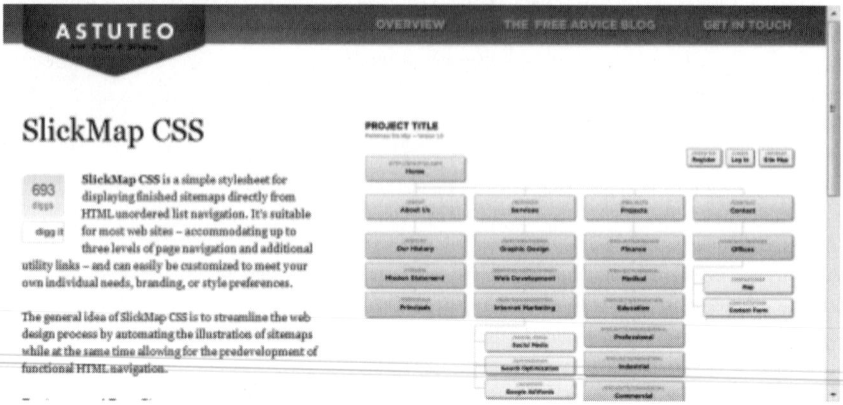

Figure 10-3. Sitemaps do not have to be ugly; the SlickMap CSS tool (at http://astuteo.com/slickmap/) is proof of this.

ExplainED

I will show you how sitemaps can be produced using XML, but you could always make one quickly and easily using HTML and CSS (using unordered lists for each layer of the hierarchy of the website design). Note, though, that search engines will look for an XML sitemap by default.

So you want to produce a sitemap to list all of the pages of your website? Excellent, because it can certainly improve your ranking, and if you submit the sitemap to Google, you will find that it is used as the primary resource for determining what needs to be reindexed. The following information may seem a little confusing at first, but when we get to the "Try It Yourself" exercise, you will see how it all comes together quickly and easily.

You'll start by producing a file called sitemap.xml, and place it within the base folder of your website (so it can be detected by search engines natively). Next, you need to add the code used in the following exercise into your file, as it contains an XML declaration and the following required elements: <urlset> to declare the DTD for the file, the <url> container element for each file to be indexed, and <loc> to state the location (URL) of the file that needs to be indexed. Those three elements are the only required ones, but you also have some cool optional tags that you can use, such as `<lastmod>` to contain the date the file was last modified (in the format YYYY/MM/DD). You can also try using `<changfreq>` to explain how often the document is updated (note that you should not use this on archived pages); possible values for `changfreq` are `always`, `hourly`, `daily`, `weekly`, `monthly`, `yearly`, and `never`. Using this tag gives spiders an estimate for when pages need to be reindexed. Of course, most people would look at setting the value to `always`, because it will offer the fastest results. Finally, you have the optional `<priority>` tag; it won't give you added weight in search engines, but it describes how important the page is in comparison to the rest of the site. The default is `0.5`, but this value can range from `0.0` up to `1.0`.

In XML files, you need to use character escaping to ensure the page works. Escaped characters essentially act as replacements for characters that the browser would naturally assume are part of code: use & instead of & for an ampersand, ' for ' to indicate an apostrophe, " in place of a " for a double quotation mark, < in place of < for an opening tag or less-than symbol, and > in place of > for a closing tag or greater-than symbol. Escaping these characters ensure that they appear as text rather than being mistaken for code, which makes escaping an essential skill to learn. This is also important if you are using RSS or Atom feeds to ensure the correct characters appear as they were intended within your syndication feeds.

Try It Yourself: Building a Sitemap

The following example shows a sitemap in action. Using the preceding information about what each tag represents, you could replicate the following example and make any alterations you require, and hopefully, this will make the task easier for you. The important thing to remember is that each page in your website should have the relevant tags (as shown) held within the URL element. The general rule about using XML sitemaps is to keep them simple. Luckily for you, there are only a very small number of tags (and most of them are optional), so you can put together a basic sitemap to be indexed in no time at all!

This example basically points to three separate links: one for the main page, one for a movies section, and one for a music section. Each reference has a date indicating when the file was last modified, so search engines know when an update has been made, and each has the frequency with which the pages should be reindexed. If you do choose to build a sitemap, you should (as mentioned) place it in the base folder along with the `robots.txt` file (mentioned at greater length in the next section of this chapter), as this is the primary location where most search engines will attempt to look for it!

```
<?xml version="1.0" encoding="UTF-8"?>
        <urlset xmlns="http://www.sitemaps.org/schemas/sitemap/0.9">
        <url>
                <loc>http://www.yoursitehere.com/</loc>
                <lastmod>2009-12-22</lastmod>
                <changefreq>monthly</changefreq>
                <priority>0.7</priority>
        </url>
        <url>
                <loc>http://www.yoursitehere.com/catalog/movies/</loc>
                <lastmod>2009-12-22</lastmod>
                <changefreq>weekly</changefreq>
        </url>
        <url>

                <loc>http://www.yoursitehere.com/catalog/music/</loc>
                <lastmod>2009-12-21</lastmod>
                <changefreq>weekly</changefreq>
        </url>
</urlset>
```

LinkED

If you want to learn more about sitemaps, you can visit the specification website to see how you can use them to have more control over what pages on your site get indexed: http://www.sitemaps.org/.

robots.txt

When we examined microformats back in Chapter 9, I mentioned that search engines use microformats and metadata, which is intended to allow us to explain whether search engines should index, follow, or ignore pages. One of the most widely recognized and reliable methods of determining what a search engine can browse is the robots.txt file, which is just what it sounds like—a text file that sits in the base directory (it does not need to be declared in the head of your HTML) and explains to search engines what won't be worth trying to index. Of course, the major search engines support the robots.txt file, but you should be made aware that it certainly isn't foolproof, as there is no actual requirement for search engines to make use of the robots file, so they could ignore it and index pages you want blocked (this is unfortunately a common practice from malicious spiders who steal people's content). Use the file anyway, because for the majority of search engines (and therefore for most people), the robots.txt file does the job of filtering the search engines well, and it's really easy to produce.

Try It Yourself: Creating a robots.txt File

Let's produce a `robots.txt` file and save it (as mentioned) to the base folder of your website. Then, you need to add details for each `User-agent:` (search engine) you want the commands to apply to by the spider's given name. If you want a command to apply to all spiders, you can use the global wildcard `*` character. Next comes the `Disallow:` statement with the relative path you want to stop search engines from indexing. While this is how the basic standard works, a new standard has some support from the big search providers, and it includes some other useful rule sets. Note that, in the following example, I also included a reference to the sitemap file so that the spider knows where to find it (this is one of those new commands that has partial support in search engines).

```
User-agent: *
Disallow: /members/
Disallow: / cgi-bin /
Sitemap: sitemap.xml
```

The following partial and unsupported features have been included in this section because support is expected in the future. You don't have to wait for browsers to support them (it's all about the search engines), though it probably won't take very long before they are supported by browsers too.

- **Partial support**: `Allow` (provides an exception to the disallow rule, allowing you to put a file or folder back on the index list again), `Craw-delay` (measured in seconds, this asks search engines to hold off indexing for a set period of time), and `Sitemap` (links to the sitemap you created).

- **Unsupported**: `Robot-version` (specifies only a certain version of a search engine to index content), `Visit-time` (requests for any indexing to occur between certain times of the day or night), `Request-rate` (denotes how quickly a spider can request a page in seconds), and `Comment` (asks the robot to send info back on the actions it performed).

LinkED

For more information about the `robots.txt` *file, you can visit the best resource on the Internet in terms of producing and managing these files for search engines at* http://www.robotstxt.org/.

Search Engine Submission

Now that you have a sitemap and a robots.txt file to deal with the search engines, you need to get them actually visit and index your website. An effective method of getting your website initially listed within search engines is to have your website featured or linked to from someone else's website. Search engines will naturally browse the listing site, and they will notice your link and subsequently follow it to see what exists at the new unknown location, though this method can sometimes take a long time get your noticed. You could also submit your sitemap to the search engines directly using services like Google webmaster tools, or you can simply use the spiders' own submission pages to get your website listed by visiting one of the following websites and entering your URL (in the case of Ask Jeeves, edit the address after sitemap= to put in your URL):

- **Google**: http://www.google.com/addurl/
- **Bing**: http://www.bing.com/docs/submit.aspx
- **Yahoo!**: http://search.yahoo.com/info/submit.html
- **Ask Jeeves**: http://submissions.ask.com/ping?sitemap=http://www.yoursitehere.com/sitemap.xml

Google's webmaster tools are more powerful than you might imagine. As well being able to list your website using a sitemap, you can also use tools for finding keywords, buying advertising space, and integrating with Analytics (Google's powerful and popular statistics package). And it will help you diagnose issues with your browser by getting the search engines to explain where your website is falling short of the ideal mark. By making use of the tools in this productivity suite for your website, you could help resolve any immediate website issues.

LinkED

If you want to manage your website using webmaster tools and indexing, you should sign up for a Google account and visit https://www.google.com/webmasters/tools/. *Type in the website address you wish to manage by clicking the "Add a site" button.*

Rankings

How high your website ranks (its position within search results) depends on various factors. Different kinds of rank exist, and a few online services even offer their own ranking schemes. Though they are not as accurate as standard search rankings, they are still popular. Ranking was invented by the search engines as a sort of digital voting booth to get people the best results possible. Ranks are affected by the quality of the content (spam will be removed from the indexes), and a site's reputation is made when high-quality reputable websites cite that page. These reputable websites are ranked highly themselves due to the quality of their content and general authority (the BBC is an example of a reputable news source), and their links to your site show that your website was deemed important enough to warrant reference.

Rankings especially come into play when you are link building (as you will find out when we begin the process later in this chapter), as you are essentially trying to build reputation points with other websites. First though, we will examine the various ranking schemes employed by the search engine and the weight each holds in determining how highly ranked your site is. Even age can deflate your site ranking, as newly indexed sites could be used for spam, so the search engines put less trust in the SEO value of websites under a year old by default.

- **PageRank**: This is built through the voting mechanism mentioned earlier. A website with a high PageRank (PR) often has been given votes (links to the website) from high-quality sources and therefore is deemed important and worth citing. PageRank ranges from 0 (basically unlisted) up to 10 (outstanding). Most websites fall into the 3-5 PR value if they have been around for a while and constantly post new content. To check the PageRank of your website, you should install some software like Google Toolbar, which has a built in rank checker.

- **LinkRank**: This measurement is taken from the address of the website itself, which, when indexed, the spider performs a relevance search based on whether information relating to the keywords appears in the domain name or within the URL structure. This is why it is important to get a domain that makes sense for your brand and why using friendly URLs will assist you; you can convey more meaning through /news/google/search/ than something like `article_3343.php`.

- **TrustRank**: This factors into the quality and the trustworthiness of websites who link to yours. Websites that have established trust and a high-quality reputation for links they post (as compared to directories that let you spam their index or blog comments) will contribute to you getting a higher PageRank as a result (like a stamp of authority). Well-known directories that index high-quality content like DMOZ (www.dmoz.org) or Yahoo Directories (dir.yahoo.com) and even government (.gov) and educational (.edu) websites and Wikipedia are considered of high internal value, because they have a reputations as quality sources.

- **LocalRank**: This subsidized format of PageRank works out the relevance of information on a geographical status; the location of a host, domain extension, content language, and various other factors are pulled together to compose a ranking index that gives results higher positions in local search results (for each country). The normal PageRank applies to global search results that do not have a need to factor in geographical location results.

- **BuzzRank**: This relatively new factor works on the concept of popularity of articles, people, subjects, and anything else measurable. BuzzRank itself works using a hot-or-not ratio that fluctuates based on what people search for. While this ranking will not technically affect the PageRank itself, a noticeable trend in **viral marketing** (a term that denotes an explosion of success through a mass "word-of-mouth" campaign to which the popularity of something is denoted by the short term appeal) has shown that websites that get a lot of buzz through social network sites like Twitter immediately receive free referrals of visitors from websites who pass on the link. Essentially, the viral "buzz" rank effect is a form of self-perpetuating fame that generates traffic on the basis of attention. As an example, a news story that goes viral could gain a higher position on some websites if the results are based on the number of page views or thumbs-up received rather than on relevance. A fair number of sites (like Digg) list popular articles based on the amount of attention (buzz) they receive over a period of time. A similar tool for Wikipedia articles exists called the WikiRank, which uses the same methodology of making front-page news based on articles that have received high numbers of visitors.

- **Alexa**: Provided by Amazon, the Alexa toolbar is a controversial system for ranking websites based on their popularity with the small number of users who participate in the program. Like TV's Nielsen ratings system, a small group of individuals rank websites as they browse (the results are measured automatically) to gain an idea about how people are browsing the Web. While the concept itself is sound, the problem is that too few people use the service for its rank statistics to be considered even remotely reliable (even if you weigh it in as a cross-section). To get listed with Alexa entirely for free, visit http://www.alexa.com/help/webmasters#crawl_site.

- **Quantcast**: In much the same way as Alexa, the Quantcast model measures the success rates of visits to websites. Like Alexa, it has the flaw of a low volume of general users. As a result, if you're using services like Alexa and Quantcast, which do not get their information from a majority source like search engines do, remember that their measured results are interesting to look at but do not hold very much value for either you or your website in terms of popularity rank. The ranking system has never properly been able to be introduced at this time. However, unlike Alexa, Quantcast does not require a toolbar to be installed (it uses scripts embedded in pages). To get listed with Quantcast for free, sign up at http://www.quantcast.com/user/signup.

LinkED

For more technical information about PageRank, its variations within Google, and the algorithm itself you can read this interesting Wikipedia article on the subject at http://en.wikipedia.org/wiki/PageRank.

Link Building

Now, we need to move into the final stage of the process known as link building. Because you are listed in the search engines (or are in the process of doing so), you want other websites to link to you to not only increase public awareness of your existence but to help send you up the PageRank system as effectively as possible (not as quickly as possible). When link building, I prefer a less aggressive approach; I find that submitting to every directory, forum, or location on Earth is counterproductive, as it dilutes the quality of the people who link to you.

When a website with a high PageRank includes a link to your website, you inherit some of the credibility that website is offered by association. As search engines build up trust with websites, your PageRank increases, because PageRank is primarily about trust and how good a website is. Once a highly trusted website links to you, the search engine immediately knows that the website gave your site a stamp of approval. The search engine assumes that by linking to your site, the other site is recommending yours (this effect is commonly referred to as **link juice**). As a result your website is effectively squeezing out a bit more PageRank with every link posted.

Of course, you do not want to go as far as spam, and you should not post on websites that use nofollow (as search engines ignore those referrals). Your site can do pretty well for itself encouraging some friendly websites to get involved in your site marketing by placing a reference to your website somehow. In contrast, a website that posts lots of links (or sells them to make money) will usually gain a low PageRank, because the search engines think that the sheer number of links means they are not based on quality. Link-swapping services, like the one shown in Figure 10-4, that often have very little quality control and are unfocused are called **link exchanges**.

ExplainED

You need to be careful where you post links. Many sites including forums and blogs use the microformat rel="nofollow"*, which means that the link you have posted may bring physical people to your website but it will in no way count for your search engine optimization (this limitation is to help reduce spam).*

As you want to get only the highest quality links, using link exchange websites is a bad idea. They work by putting a link to your site when you put an equal link to theirs. Because your websites are unrelated and exchanges have very little quality control (generally), the value of your website will be diluted by placing it there.

Figure 10-4. While sites like LinkMarket aim to offer a swapping service, their effectiveness is debatable.

Another method of link building is through social networking in the form of social bookmarking websites like del.icio.us, StumbleUpon, and others that allow you to store not only your own website but also list your favorite websites on the Web so people can see them. You store a site by tagging it, reviewing it, and submitting the review. Bookmarking sites can be useful in your campaign, as you can share link juice with other websites and give your visitors some insight into how you browse the Web, as well as cite places you recommend.

Another commonly used method of link building is by posting links to directories. This can be a very good move if you use a trusted directory, like DMOZ (shown in Figure 10-5), that gets rid of all the spam links, but you may be able to get a higher PageRank for yourself. Arguably, being listed in the trusted resource websites pays off, because the link is simply to your homepage among many others, but the real value is diminished somewhat.

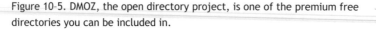

Figure 10-5. DMOZ, the open directory project, is one of the premium free directories you can be included in.

The real secret to getting your website linked to and getting some extremely high quality link juice is to do things like write articles on the subject that your website deals with and get article websites who request high-quality content to publish you. Not only could you get paid but you generally get a link back to your website, which will do your site the world of good. People will see what you offer, and by giving something to another site, you will instantly achieve status. This basic publicity technique also applies to producing Wikipedia content (which cites information from your website or perhaps an article you wrote on a related subject—as long as it's factual). Contributing to forums, other communities, and social networks can also help get your name, brand, and website out there as having your website mentioned can bring in some quality leads. Nothing gives you such a massive boost in promotion like genuine links for offering something other people find useful. Unfortunately, many people prefer to spam their way to the top, which is ineffective and degrading to the quality of your website as a resource. If you have good-quality content, you will be fine without resorting to spamming as people will be naturally inclined to link to you and effectively do the hard work for you—as far as giving you free recognition.

Black Hat SEO

Now that we have looked at the legitimate ways to get your search engine ranking up, it is time to look at some of the ways people have tried to get a better position that may get you banned if you are unlucky enough to get caught out. It is important to note that everything mentioned in this section should never be replicated by you, as these tactics could result in your site getting removed from the search engine results (yes, you can get banned from Google or any other search engine!). If you are banned, your website might as well not exist, as research shows that around 70% of all traffic comes through search engines rather than other methods such as directly typing the website address or being redirected through another website you are listed in. Therefore, it is vitally important that you stay on the good sides of the big search engines, and do not try to scam them for a position!

SEO Techniques to Avoid

There are many black hat techniques out there, and they all have consequences for your website and its rank in search engines. To help you avoid taking on any of these potentially dangerous techniques, they have been listed in this section, along with what they do to your site as a result. While I cannot stop you from implementing these techniques, the best thing I can say is that if you are an honest person simply trying to make your website well known, you certainly do not want to degrade your brand using anything you see in the following list.

- **Keyword stuffing** means overloading your `keyword` metatags (or content) with far more keywords than is necessary. You should observe caution when adding keywords into your website. One reason I had you to write content before learning SEO is that you can target a small number of relevant keywords from your high-quality content instead of building content around your keywords, which can often result in a spamfest! Keyword stuffing will be considered spam by Google and will get you unlisted and possibly banned.

- **Link saturation** is when you have far to many links in your pages to external websites. If the links are relevant and within your website, they are probably fine. However, spamming third-party websites (especially if any of the links your pages reference point to a site with a low PageRank) dilute the quality of your website. Too many links may cause the search engines to think you are just spamming. Although you should feel free to advertise other websites, you should use the `rel="nofollow"` attribute and microformat on specific links if you want search engines to know you do not endorse or want that link considered in your PageRank.

- **Content cloaking** occurs when you use CSS or JavaScript to hide keyword-rich content from visitors with the intention of boosting the number of keywords you use without anyone else being aware of it. For example, you could use `display: none;` on a paragraph full of nothing but keywords. Or you might use of frames and iFrames to inject hidden content or use JavaScript to spam keywords using `document.write` and `innerHTML` objects. Search engines do not take much notice of CSS and JavaScript, so they will see what you are trying to hide, and like keyword stuffing, content cloaking may result in you being banned or unlisted.

- **Spamming** is the bane of the Internet. Whether through e-mail or website links posted in blogs, forums, or other places, it is simply unacceptable to participate in this activity. Going to websites and setting up accounts just to post a website address is the sign of a true amateur. The same rule applies to social networking websites: while they can work for you and your website, you will only see success if you participate in the networks on a regular basis.

- **Pharming** is the process of adding your website to those free directories with no quality control simply to get as many links as possible. While Google will often unlist any pharming sites it comes across, your website will not get any benefit from being included in them because the link juice of those websites has already been sucked dry. Adding your website to websites with thousands of links (unless they're high-quality directories) will be a waste of time as they will have effectively suffered the same problem which occurs in link saturation.

- **Landing pages** are specially engineered pages to greet visitors who click advertisements or links to your website. In my personal opinion, they are annoying and a pain to navigate around. When people visit your website, they want to be able to reach all of the content; they do not want to find themselves at some big advertisement screen trying to get everyone to buy something from the outset. Landing pages are mainly used to bombard visitors with what you want to sell, and the hard sale does not work online. People want to see what you offer, what it does, possibly a few demonstrations and screenshots, and then decide for themselves.

- **Buying links** is, in some ways, quite a bit like buying advertisements. However, it is more subtle and considered a shady practice by Google. Essentially, you pay a high-ranking website to link to your own site in a place where it does not look like an advertisement. If Google suspects you are buying links with a website both your site and theirs may end up having their PageRanks dropped and being classified as spammers, which is no good for either of you!

- **Duplicate content** is a problem that occurs over the Web and dilutes the quality of what started off as a high-quality article. When you produce content, you want to try to keep people from reposting your articles as their own (because of copyright laws and because you don't want your hard work going unnoticed). So duplicating content, even if you do quote the article and link back to the original website, is a bad idea unless you have permission to do so. Generally, you are entitled to use up to 10% of an article before it qualifies as an act of plagiarism, and search engines may refuse to index parts of your website if they believe it is simply a duplicate source, you may even be unlisted if you are found to have stolen content.

- **Stealth redirects** use the `refresh` metaelement or other well-known redirection methods to redirect spiders and visitors away from a page filled with keyword-rich content to a page that may not be related to the dummy content. This is considered one of the most underhanded methods of SEO, because it essentially tries to fool the search engine into believing a website contains information relevant to a certain subject when it's just a spoof to send visitors to an unrelated page or resource, usually with the intent to spam people or provide irrelevant junk.

- **Element overuse** is simply a case of abusing the semantics of HTML to better serve the search engines. This is the most common form of SEO abuse, and examples are adding extra unnecessary headings, filling alternative text for images with keywords, and other underhanded and generally unsemantic methods of displaying content to the search engines. If element overuse is detected, your website could have its PageRank dropped.

As you can see from this list, people will go to all sorts of lengths to try to take advantage of the search engines. While most of these techniques are acts of deception and may get you punished, many black hat SEO experts like to push the envelope and try to get away with them.

Penalties

So what will happen if you use any of the black hat techniques? Well, the search engines may choose to employ a wide range of punishments to respond to your use of deceptive techniques. While you may think it is unfair that the search engines can tell you what to do, instigating some rules to keep the overall quality of search results up makes sense for them. They want to provide the best possible service for their visitors not only because it is the right thing to do but because competition in the search engine space between the big four is literally visible all over the Web as Microsoft, Yahoo!, Google, and Ask Jeeves try to get a bigger share of the market.

ExplainED

As long as you are sensible about how you choose to market your website and do so using the white hat methods listed, such as involving yourself in other communities, building a reputation, and having your links available for others to find you, the result should be that you never encounter these issues!

Here's a list of the possible consequences of using black hat techniques:

- **Sandboxing:** The Google sandbox is said to be a place where new websites appear. Its objective is to help reduce the chance of spam from newly launched websites appearing at the top of search results. An imposed PageRank is assigned until a period of time has passed to which maturity trust can be given (you can't just start a new site filled with spam immediately and have it rank highly). While being in the sandbox is deemed normal for new sites, yours may not be lifted from the sandbox if you fail to pass Google's spam filtering system. This particular penalty seems to have some credibility but it's unofficial and isn't proven to exist, because exactly how the sandbox works (if such a thing exists) is known only to Google.

- **Deflating**: If you start breaking rules and saturating your website with keywords or links that do not belong in the content, your site's PageRank may be deflated (dropped heavily) to try to counteract the imbalance occurring from pharming, spam and other devaluing factors.

- **PageRank 0**: One of the biggest weapons the search engines have to vex those who try to spam the system heavily is to reset their PageRank to 0, essentially making the quality of their website drop through the bottom into something considered untrustworthy and low quality.

- **Restricting**: As well as restricting your PageRank, if your website is found to contain worms or malicious scripts (through being hacked or otherwise), Google may suspend your position in the index and block visitors from visiting your website through a Google referral (search result) or through their advertising scheme until you prove that your site is clean of infections and vulnerabilities. Potential visitors will be met with a warning saying your site is dangerous!

- **Unlisting**: If none of the preceding techniques work or if you are a serious offender, Google may remove your website entirely from the index and unlist you to help avoid visitors to your website getting caught up in the mess you have made for yourself. Unlisting doesn't occur unless you have done something seriously underhanded or malicious.

- **Banning**: Finally comes the worst thing of all. If you are a repeat offender and continue to flout the rules and violate Google's requests, you may simply be banned. Since 70-80% of all traffic (estimates differ) come from search engines, if your website is banned it will literally disappear off the map, and your future traffic and visitors will be significantly reduced.

LinkED

For a wide range of details about the factors that can affect your search engine position, and plenty of other useful statistics that may help you improve your website to get a better ranking, you may want to check out the excellent study at http://www.seomoz.org/article/search-ranking-factors.

Mastering Marketing

Now that your website looks good for the search engines, you can layer on an additional level of promotion in the form of conventional marketing. Advertisement on the Web is one of the most profitable industries going, and with major players like Google leading the fight for getting promotion to your website, it is something that you should consider. Unlike SEO, marketing often cannot be done for free, but its rewards are more instantaneous. You have already done some basic marketing through link building, so you understand how getting your site listed on other websites can be important. In this section, we will examine how your campaign for visitors can be both online and offline, how to make use of social networking and social media to get your website some followers, and the benefits of e-mail campaigns. We'll also consider, as a result, what should hopefully be a good amount of visitors you can get out of employing these techniques to increase not only page views but potential sales and revisits.

Advertising

The most popular way for professionals to get visitors to their websites is through the conventional form of marketing known as advertising. This method of getting visitors to your website has existed for a very long time and is one of the earliest forms of traffic generation. While advertising can be taken to the limits with radio and television, we will primarily focus on ways to get your site noticed online. Of course, conventional media can get you a high amount of notice and visitor awareness, but the costs of those methods are far too high for a beginner like yourself. When we talk about advertisements, we are not just going to be covering those banners you see on websites to try to get you to click and visit another site. We will also look at other methods of promotion that may seem more ambitious, but they will definitely get you noticed and possibly raise awareness of your site with individuals and groups who are not naturally inclined to visit websites through advertisements.

Using Offline Marketing

Let's start by advertising your website using offline marketing techniques now that we have given people the best chance of finding it naturally. Your website certainly is already housed on the Web for all to potentially see, so word of mouth and getting people to notice the site offline is part of the battle. People talk about Google, Wikipedia, YouTube, Facebook, and Twitter when they are away from their computers and in conversation with people they know; perhaps it's because they saw something funny or read something interesting. The important thing to note from this is that you want to take your brand from a virtual entity into something people perceive to be real. Talking to people about your website, promoting it offline—perhaps by placing an advertisement in the paper, mentioning it at work to your colleagues, or even telling your friends and family—contribute to the grand scheme of making awareness of your site as widespread as possible among those who may be interested.

LinkED

For more ideas about taking your brand offline, you can visit the following website: http://www.allfreelance.com/freelancing_blog/2008/01/24/60-unique-ideas-for-marketing-your-business-offline-locally/.

Of course, using offline media such as advertising through the television and radio (beyond simple word-of-mouth marketing) is a pretty expensive affair, so you probably will not want to engage in that unless you have a lot of money, which is partly why I have advised you against considering it in the past. However, assume you are making a website dedicated to your favorite music group. Perhaps if you visit one of their gigs, you could pass out some free leaflets or business cards with the link to your website. That way, other fans know your site exists and is looking for people who want to talk about the band! If you are a coffee lover and are looking for people to talk about their favorite brands, perhaps get your local café to advertise your site in their window. Perhaps you want to offer tutoring services over the Internet for people wanting to learn how to write professionally; you could have a leaflet posted at your local community center. Marketing and advertising are something big companies do often, but that doesn't mean that you should just ignore it in favor of online media only. After all, the things I mentioned are pretty easy and relatively cheap things to accomplish, and if you somehow manage to get a few people you wouldn't have otherwise found, your ideas for getting people on your site will have been worth it.

Pay per click

Search engine marketing (SEM) is the professional-level method of advertising on the Internet. The largest providers of paid advertising on the web are Google AdWords (see Figure 10-6), Yahoo! Search Marketing, and Microsoft adCenter. Each of these offers the ability to put paid advertisements within the search pages. You pay for a certain amount of visits to your website, which is counted through a pay-per-click (PPC) scheme. When someone clicks the advertisement and enters your site, this click is subtracted from the amount of clicks you paid for. While paying to receive visitors seems pretty fair, you should note that paid advertising often has a lower chance of getting traffic than natural referrals through websites (link building), and usually the amount of people who end up staying a member or buying something through paid advertising is quite low. This technique can be worth using, though: if the advertisements are fairly priced, you can see some boost in traffic, and it gets you more immediate exposure than you may be able to get naturally within the generic search engine result listings.

If you don't want to use a conventional pay-per-click model, you could always pay to be advertised in podcasts or online media forms. Usually, you will see a good return on the number of people who take notice (if you have a good deal or product to offer), though this method tends to be much more expensive than conventional text or image advertising. And you will actually be paying for advertisement based on the average number of listeners for the podcast, which can literally run in the hundreds of thousands with popular shows. While standard pay-per-click schemes are more likely to be the kind of system you will use (due to their relative inexpensive structure), the use of new media and viral marketing through things like podcasts and social media could be useful to you.

Advertise With Google
Find Customers With Google AdWords
Get Your Ad Online In Just 15 Mins!
< >

Adsense Alternative
Increase Site Earnings /w Infolinks High
Rev Share, 1 Min Integration!

Ads by Google

Figure 10-6. Google AdSense advertisements (called AdWords) that appear in relevent websites look something like this.

ExplainED

Google offers another advertising product called AdSense, which allows people to get paid for placing advertisements on their pages (sort of the reverse of paying for advertising). This is one of the most popular ways to monetize websites by simply adding in some nonintrusive advertising.

Marketing Ideas

If you are looking for some free ways that do not require as much effort as campaigning on the streets or paying Google for a premium spot on the front page, there are still plenty of other nonsearch-related marketing techniques you can employ. You could think about getting your website sponsored by another one if you feel like working in partnership. The other site may offer you some traffic or links in return for the service you bring their customers. You could also run a competition to win a prize (though you need to be careful with this, as gambling laws in some locations may prevent this) and thus entice people into being a part of your website or participating for the chance to win something. Your prizes could be Amazon gift vouchers or something you intend to offer commercially. Other ideas involve paying someone to professionally review your services and get the review published somewhere potential customers will read, such as a magazine or another related website.

Campaign to Conversion

While some of these ideas may get you started, the real key here is your imagination. Look for inspiration all around the Web in potential places you could gain a reputation (you want a good one!), and involve yourself with those services to potentially get links back to your website so that visitors who get to know you can find your website and participate there too. You are only limited by your imagination, as almost every service could become a method of getting attention, and perhaps a few more visitors or customers, for your website. While you do not want to put all of your eggs in one basket (using multiple services is the key), whichever method you choose to employ will need a good amount of time and effort invested into it to see a decent return.

While you want to do your best to market your website, remember to consider everything you do with care, because once you do something online, that action becomes a permanent fixture (in most cases), and you could end up regretting any serious mistakes you make.

Now you have a bunch of ideas and potential marketing schemes, and you want to build a profile of what sites you have signed up with, what schemes you have signed up for, and who you are networking with—keep track of all your memberships and affiliations. One really useful thing you can do for this profile to get more visitors involved in your websites various social activities is to integrate the profile within your About Me page by adding a list of all the places (such as social networks) where you are a member and how people can follow what you are doing; you want to hopefully get them subscribing. By spreading your potential for gaining visitors around, you can ensure your website sees moderate flows of traffic with a blended mix of methods and link building.

Content Delivery

People mainly browse a website for content (as well as for products and services, which we discuss later), so you may want to deliver content in a format where people can share a multipage document you have produced. When you get used to blogging or writing content, there may come a time where you want to bring traffic or money to your website through the written word! Perhaps you want to write an e-book (basically a digital copy of a self-published work) or a really in-depth tutorial, or maybe you just want to write your life story and put it online for everyone to see. Whether you intend on using content for profit or making it available for free, the great thing is that you can use a whole selection of different file formats to publish your documents and content, so your visitors can download it and read what you have to say offline using the default reader they have installed.

While most content is probably suitable for viewing online, really lengthy articles might benefit if you use on offline format and distribute it for free with a link back to your website to get some bonus traffic or sales. Of course, if you want people to be able to download and save a copy of a multipage document to read offline, or if you simply wish to publish something that can be distributed or self-contained without needing access to the Internet, using a standardized file format could help you publish your work on your website to enable such functionality.

Why would you want to publish your document in a file format not typically viewed within a web browser (or at least is a separate application)? Well, magazines are a prime example! People who subscribe to magazines may want to be able to read the articles and informative reviews that they pay for as a subscription without having to get a thick printed book, especially if that reading material is several hundred pages thick and has new editions each month! With the world seeking to be as green as possible and saving resources, it's beneficial to offer a version that can be read on a computer that may have hundreds of pages but is protected from being redistributed and can be downloaded at the user's wish. This is a rapidly evolving market for digital media, especially with the rise in e-book readers!

The advantages of publishing to file formats rather than directly onto a website follow:

- You can protect your content from being copied or accessed by individuals without rights.

- Documents that span even hundreds of pages can be self-contained without navigation.

- Other distractions, such as navigation or advertising, do not interrupt the reader.

- The published work has a more book-like glossy feel to it as readers navigate the chapters.

- Devices, such as e-book readers, can allow readers to access the files offline and on the move!

- Document files can be easier to print than a collection of linked website pages.

With the rise in genuine publishing for the Web, four formats for documents have a high number of active users and have proven themselves suitable for putting content online:

- **PDF**: Adobe's Portable Document Format

- **XPS**: Microsoft's XML Paper Specification

- **ODF**: Sun Microsystems's Open Document Format

- **DOC**: Microsoft Office Word format

These formats are in common use and are deemed suitable for publishing content. However, in many cases, you require special software to allow your word processor to publish in one of these formats, and the end user will need certain software to read the end result, though these four are well supported. Luckily, there is a great wealth of free and commercial software that you can search for and install to accomplish this task.

PDF is the most common format used on the Web for publishing and is usually associated with Adobe's own PDF reader called Acrobat (see Figure 10-7). PDF files have high market penetration, and a lot of different technology supports them, but do not take as a given that support for this or any other format is guaranteed on the end user's computer. PDF files supports a large number of features including text, graphics, and multimedia to some extent and have a wide range of features to protect the document such as digital rights management (DRM) to prevent copying just like for DVDs, document signatures to prevent malicious edits, and even the ability to password protect and block copying and printing of the document. This last feature makes it very popular among web professionals and content publishers alike. One thing that holds PDF above many of the other formats is that it does contain a lot of features aimed at helping disabled users read and search the contents of the document. PDF is, in essence, the industry standard for web publishing and is highly recommended.

Microsoft Office 2007, OpenOffice, and other products have native support for publishing PDFs, but other products out there will freely convert (or print) your document to PDF format quickly and easily.

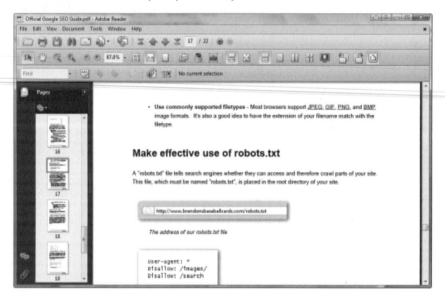

Figure 10-7. Adobe Reader allows you to browse multipage documents with ease such as the Google SEO guide!

XPS was invented recently by Microsoft to provide a more open competitor to Adobe's own PDF format. This more open format allows individuals to produce their own web documents that are protected but can also be opened natively within their browser (see Figure 10-8), giving the impression of viewing a book through the Web, even though it can be saved offline (while PDFs can be viewed natively within the browser, if saved to the desktop they will open in your default PDF reader). In essence, the XPS file is a web document compressed into a ZIP archive to reduce file size, and only a single file is needed to view the document. While adoption rate of this format is limited because it's only been recently released and few products support it, you should keep an eye on this format, as it has the potential to be just as popular and widely used as the family favorite PDF.

Microsoft Office 2007, Windows Vista, and Windows 7 natively support the XPS format, and Windows XP users can take advantage of the .NET runtime 3.0 download from Microsoft's website to get the XPS printer for free.

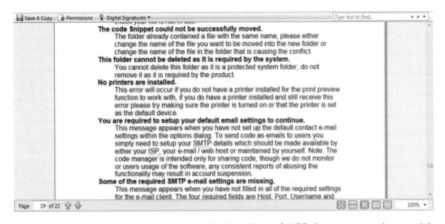

Figure 10-8. This document presented using Microsoft XPS shows some real potential as a PDF competitior.

NotED

If your word processor does not support exporting or publishing to one of the formats mentioned in this section, there are virtual printers you can download or purchase that use your Print dialog to convert the document into a file using that format.

ODF and DOC are different to the other two formats, because they were not designed for use online. They have both been mentioned, because they are used extremely commonly in the workplace and in the home, so visitors will usually be able to read documents provided in these formats. While these are less than ideal because users are able to edit the document upon receiving it (and it doesn't natively show within the web browser), the sheer flexibility and power of these formats make them worthy of consideration if for any reason you believe that the PDF or XPS formats will be unsuitable for your website (and your visitors' needs). ODF is commonly found in the open source word processor provided as part of OpenOffice, and DOC is, of course, the default format provided within Microsoft Word. They both contain powerful editing, viewing, and security features, and if you want to provide a document that visitors will give inline feedback to or be able to edit for their own use, these two popular industry standard document formats will be worth using in preference to the two viewer-based formats.

Social Networking

Of all the methods of promotion, social networking has grown from strength to strength to get people involved in a community. Social networks are exciting places to interact with your visitors and build a community of friends who will visit your website as a result of being made aware of its existence through these communities of millions of people. Many different social networking opportunities are available on the Web, each with its own purpose. By looking at each one and building yourself a reputation in those you choose to explore, you can convert a high number of people who become emotionally involved with your community into regular visitors. Before looking at the phenomenon of social networks, which are taking the world by storm, we will look at how you can use conventional communication methods such as e-mail to put the word out about your website to gain some traffic.

E-mail

Before we round off the quick start guide to marketing your website, we need to talk about a couple more things. The first is the popularity of e-mail marketing, which has become an extremely big thing over the years. The most common ways of using e-mail to market websites are through providing press releases (such as special offers on your site), newsletters, and e-zines to give details about what is new on your site. You may think, "Great, so how do I get started?" But you should use caution with e-mail marketing. Having an e-mail system to send people newsletters is a great thing to include on your site, but before you can start sending people e-mail on behalf of your site, you need to first have their permission. Obtaining permission also implies that you probably should not buy lists of e-mail addresses and start sending mail to them advertising your website, because let's face it, your site, e-mail content or newsletter is probably better than a Viagra advertisement, right?

While sending e-mails from person to person is perfectly fine, if you are acting in a capacity of a business or even just on behalf of a website with multiple members involved, you have to ensure newsletters or advertising e-mail are opt-in services: you shouldn't send e-mail unless users agree to receive it. While this may sound silly, the problem is that, due to the high amount of spam we get (90% of all mail is now spam), the sending of unsolicited e-mails has become something considered of the upmost importance to people trying to keep the Web free unscrupulous characters. Sending spam e-mails (especially through bought e-mail lists) is actually a criminal offense in many countries (including the United States and United Kingdom) and can be met with legal action, though admittedly such cases are rare. In any case, before you send e-mail, ensure you have permission!

LinkED

To see more tips about producing HTML e-mail and how different it is to producing a standard HTML file (in terms of how you can design), read the article at http://www.anandgraves.com/html-email-guide.

So you have decided to set up a newsletter and you want to know the basics of what you are getting into. Well, the forming of an e-mail newsletter is much like writing a website. The first thing you need to do is write the content and ensure it is of high quality so that people will be interested in reading it. Although you can include images and media, you need to be careful because e-mails over 10MB may have issues with some e-mail clients. You also need to write the code to represent your content (if you're not using plain text) just like with a web page, as this will represent the visual appearance of your e-mail, though HTML e-mail is somewhat limited.

When sending e-mail, your choices are to send it in a plain-text format (just text), which is easy to do and will probably be the quickest way to achieve a good e-mail format, or rich text format made up of HTML embedded within the e-mail. While you should be equipped to mess with HTML, you should be aware that e-mail and HTML have a poor history of compatibility (even worse than Internet Explorer 6!). While I really hate to say this, if you intend on making an HTML e-mail (rich text), the rules of standards-based design almost take a back seat due to the issues that clients encounter. Table-based design and inline style (using style attributes) are usually frowned upon, but often the only way of getting your e-mail to look exactly the way you want. With e-mails, you should try to reduce the amount of attachments used (such as images) to keep the file size down for the recipients benefit.

ExplainED

Did you know you can track when people read your e-mails by embedding a web bug, which is essentially an invisible image embedded within the e-mail to which the `href` links to your website? As the image is requested from the website, the server will log hits and the IP address of the reader!

Networking

Finally, we are going to talk about the explosion in the use of viral social media (social networking) and what it means for you as someone wanting to promote your website. We need to examine social networks, because they are quickly becoming the world's premium method of communication. Of course, where there are people who share common interests and want to engage with each other, a unique business opportunity is given to allow you to target your audience where they can interact with you. Through these online networks visitors can become friends with you, recommend what you offer (to people they know), or simply keep a watchful eye on your profile for updates because they decided to subscribe out of genuine interest (rather than e-mail, which is mainly spam).

Viral media is based around the concept of something on a social media website becoming so popular and widespread that it appears on every inch of the Web from personal blogs right down to e-mail and word of mouth! In fact, viral marketing has become such a force to be reckoned with that news that hits the viral buzz can shoot up in popularity to the point that entire websites can go offline due to the heavy flows of traffic trying to find out more information. This effect of social media is often known as the Slashdot effect after the technology blog that started this trend (see Figure 10-9) and has spread over into sites like Twitter (which uses the word "Twitterpated" to imply that something has gone viral). While I don't know if what you produce will be cause a major collapse of services, the infectious buzz of social website will seriously help your promotion.

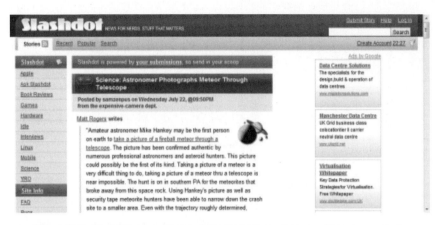

Figure 10-9. Slashdot.org was one of the first places that could topple a website through the popularity of its articles.

One popular use for social networking websites is to get other people to rate and review you, and thankfully, two services to allow people to do just that: AddThis (http://www.addthis.com/), which is shown in Figure 10-10), and ShareThis (http://sharethis.com/). Both websites have demonstrations on their front pages to explain their functionality. By adding one of these widgets to your website (typically at the bottom of every post on a blog), you offer a quick and recognized method for people to directly vote for your website with a large number of the social networking websites, allowing you to take all of the effort out of either producing social media links or having your visitors manually recommend your website. I highly recommend adding a widget, as it lets some of the marketing of your website occur naturally, and it will get your visitors actively participating in your campaign.

If you want to be more involved in the social networking process than simply including one of the two previously mentioned widgets, you will need to join some social networks, produce a profile for your website (or brand), and start actively participating. While AddThis and ShareThis will help with link building if you want to really immerse yourself in the social media circle and potentially get yourself a higher number of visitors, joining friendship circles is a great way to get involved in the communities and get yourself noticed (with your website). Just like it is worth setting up a blog to discuss recent events on your website, by being a part of sites like StumbleUpon, Twitter (see Figure 10-11), and Flickr to share your favorite links, news, discussions, and photos, you can really expand your reach across the Web and find new visitors in the people who use those services regularly.

Figure 10-10. Sharing your articles and content with the world couldn't be any easier than this!

LinkED

For an awesome list of over 400 social networking sites that you can investigate and consider making use of to market your own website, please visit http://traffikd.com/social-media-websites/.

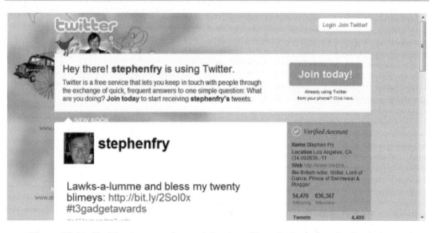

Figure 10-11. Twitter is a popular social networking platform for sharing information snippets.

There are a few rules you should follow if you want to market through social networking websites. First, never spam your website on the networks' indexes; you will quickly get yourself banned from the service for violating their terms of usage. Second, as mentioned previously, you want to ensure that you participate regularly and often to get people interested in what you have to say. Next, you want to try to build some history to your social network account by getting a good reputation as a high-quality user, so that when people make friends with you and your brand, you can offer them your website (for more cool information). Finally, if you do participate in a social group, try to follow the rules and enjoy the experience; you want to befriend these people, not irritate them and make them want to block you or report you as an offender (no getting into fights!).

Measuring Success

Now that you have involved yourself in the process of social networking and SEO, the time has come to work out how to measure the success of your campaign and, if necessary, determine the next course of action. Making your website successful is key, as a website with no visitors simply does not exist on the radar of the Internet. Unfortunately, too commonly, people simply think that making a website will instantly get results. This isn't the case, and maintaining a website is a consistent process of refinement, to which you need to be willing to invest time (and possibly money if you want it to be extremely successful). Ensuring you have a well-oiled machine of updates and improvements on top of a good foundation (how good your code is) is important in getting people to want to be involved in what you offer. If your website is simply for friends and family, it should be very easy to market your website (by simple word of mouth), but getting people you don't know to take a look is one of the biggest challenges that face both business and hobbyist alike. Hopefully, you will see some good results!

You have many ways to measure the success of your website and any campaigns you have produced. Although this book is only a brief guide to marketing (as its main focus is to get your first website up and running), we have now covered the general principles of getting ranked in search engines, marketing the traditional way, and making use of social networking and e-mail to boost your promotion techniques. It sounds pretty obvious to state that the amount of people who visit your website is a form of success. While that is true, the real success of your website is not in the click-through rates or hits your website receives but in the social community and loyalty you get from your visitors. These repeat readers and visitors are the individuals who keep your site alive in a world where loyalty to any brand or to any individual is rare and in many cases superficial.

To know whether your website is successful in terms of its visitors, you can use information from your analytics package, feedback from interaction with your visitors (see Figure 10-12), and the rank in search engines. You can also talk to the very people who make use of your website (its customers). If you run a commercial website, the return on investment (how much money you make) can also be a factor used to measure success. We have covered how you can address each of these needs in turn through this book, from user experience to accessibility and from social networking to advertising. As a result, I hope you have a good-looking website, have learned a few things, and know the Internet (and the stuff that goes on behind the scenes) a bit better. In the final section of this book, I provide some quick details about the methods of making money through your site. If you are making a personal website, you may want to skip over the final section, but if you want to make a website to sell something, promote your business, or otherwise make some extra cash, you may want to keep reading!

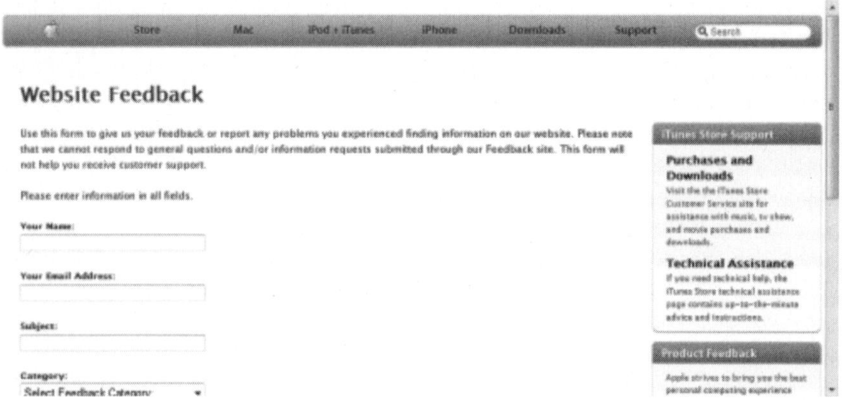

Figure 10-12. Apple wants to know what its visitors and customers think, so should you!

Selling Your Services

This section may not apply to you right now, but there may come a time where your website has become successful and you wish to turn it into a profitable business! Of course, some websites naturally will remain free for viewing but have money making methods like advertising to support them (perhaps you want the website to support itself so you don't incur any expenses for hosting and domains). If you are reading this book to make a website for your business or want to launch you own Internet start-up, now that you know how to build the site itself, this section will be extremely useful in giving you the basic concepts of e-commerce along with buying and selling online. I'll also cover some of the implications of e-commerce legally and in your responsibilities to your customers. While the advice in this section may be useful, it is only intended as a basic guide and certainly is not a replacement for a solid business plan or business advice from other professionals!

The Bizarre Bazaar

Buying and selling online is much like a busy market or shopping mall. Thousands of retailers, all available at a click, fight with each other to get customers and offer many unique services with their own selling points. If you want to get in on this area of the Internet, you need to be aware of the basics of selling online, the types of money making services on the Web, and the rules you should follow to ensure that you won't get in any trouble (legal or otherwise) for selling or providing something on the Web at a cost to the visitor. Because of this industry's nature, it is important that you know what you are doing and aren't trying some get-rich-quick scheme. When you start making money from the Internet, your hobby turns into a part- or full-time career that needs even more care and attention to ensure that your visitors and customers are satisfied and supported.

Knowing What to Offer

If you want to make money with your website, the first thing you need to know is what you plan on offering to monetize. Are you offering content that is advertisement supported? Will your website be powered by donations and helpful contributions by the sites regulars (see Figure 10-13)? Are you offering goods and services that are subscription based, or are you selling physical items that require a single one-off price, such as software or knitted scarves? The point is that you need to be aware of what you plan on selling before you can add the items to your website and process the payments. Before we move onto the next stage, you should think carefully about how you portray your items on the website. Many technology start-ups and blogs start off entirely free with no advertising until they get a regular audience, so new visitors aren't initially bombarded with advertisements. Then, advertisements can be introduced slowly later as the amount of traffic increases the site's potential costs.

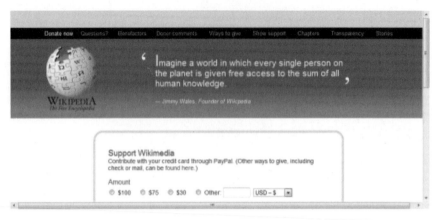

Figure 10-13. Wikipedia is powered by donations to keep the service free of advertising.

ExplainED

If you don't know what you want to offer but just want to make money, you need to realize that too many people try, and subsequently fail, attempting to make a fortune online. You won't make a fortune quickly or easily, and it takes a lot of hard work to make a web success (no matter what the advertisements say).

Rules of Engagement

So, you have your products made and they are ready to ship to the customer (digitally or physically), and you want to get on with adding a store to your website. Before you do this, you need to consider a few basic rules for selling anything online; these are essential to the web retail process! First, you must ensure that you show your prices (see Figure 10-14). Prices could be your hourly rates if you tutor people or sell custom goods and services (like website designs), fixed rate prices on your home-printed t-shirts or singular items you plan on selling, or an itemized price list for your huge online shop that will carry hundreds of goods and services at greatly differing prices. If you don't declare your prices in exact figures that are easy to read, people will be unlikely to sign up for anything you are offering. These days, people are very much aware of online fraud and will not hand over any financial or personal details until they know what they are getting and how much it will cost.

Figure 10-14. The WinZip website offers price listings in a simple and easy-to-read manner.

While we are talking about selling items for money (even if it is advertising space), you need to take into account taxes (see Figure 10-15). Everyone hates taxes and wants to keep all of the profit themselves, but you have a legal obligation to declare any money you make and factor in tax rates for your prices. Setting up a successful online business is a process that can be pretty simple, but you need to ensure that the tax people are aware of your source of income on the Web. Although I certainly would not want to tempt you out of attempting this franchise affair, I'd advise getting some further business advice before you get started. You may well want to register yourself as self-employed or freelance or get your business name registered properly, so you can turn this small secondary job into a legitimate brand that people can trust their money with. Depending on where you are, there may be some excellent free local and online business advice resources if you search on the subject.

Assuming you've clear up any possible tax questions and have gotten some business advice you will soon be ready to get your store set up and taking payments using a merchant system and shopping cart software on your website. You want to ensure that you keep receipts for everything you spend and make. Managing your accounts and finances properly, and ensuring that items are delivered to the customer is one of the most vital elements of running an online store, the last thing you want to do is lose control of your money. Getting a notebook ledger or simply printing off custom-made invoices showing what people will pay you (see Figure 10-16) and filing them away until you need to look back at your profits and expenditures are simple but easy ways to track how much money you make through your website. Perhaps you want to get a free piece of accounting software to enter all expenses and money made relating to your website to track its progress for your own ease of access.

Figure 10-15. The Corel store not only shows prices clearly but mentions tax inclusion.

Product	Version	License	Quantity	Price
My Online Product	1.00	Full Version	X2 (Single User)	$50.00
			Subtotal	$100.00
			Total Price	$100.00

To register your copy of the products listed above you will be required to enter the below information when requested to activate and begin using the product.

Product	Version	E-Mail	License Key
My Online Product	1.00	None@None.com	NONE

If you have any questions about your purchase or have any billing enquiries, please visit our website. The below reference number will be required for premium technical support requests.

Reference Code: #000000

John Doe
Manager of MySite

Figure 10-16. This invoice example gives details about the product purchased for the customers reference.

These tips only scrape the tip of the iceberg, and I certainly wouldn't want to pass myself off as an expert at business, but maintaining accurate records, ensuring you keep on the good side of the tax people, and trading fairly are pretty much half of the battle. There are so many great resources for people buying and selling online you can use to get more information, but as we were talking about selling goods, I needed to mention a few key business points, because any form of income you make is taxable. It would be a mistake to think the Internet was any different, so research your obligations well before you move to the next stage of setting up your store.

LinkED

Whether you are designing websites as a freelancer or want to make your brand a business, the following United Kingdom website is helpful when understanding the basics of business: http://www.businesslink.gov.uk/. *The site is informative even if you are reading from another nation, though other countries will have their own business sites.*

Payment Systems

There are many different ways you can take money over the Internet. Some of them are offered in exchange for goods and services, and some are simply given in form of support for the website itself. In this section, you will find a guide to the various ways you can take payments from your visitors and the trusted merchants who offer services to take credit or debit card information (to receive and hold the money for you) allowing you to focus on providing a good website rather than dealing with processing orders (though you still need to be involved in this), and the various shopping cart packages that can be used to simplify the process of adding e-commerce solutions into your website. Using these, you can let people place orders without having to worry about producing some server-side code to deal with the orders. There is some great online store software out there you can use!

Choosing a Sales Model

So what model do you want to use to sell stuff online? You could sell goods through a shopping cart or accept advertising on your pages. You could get people to subscribe to a service you offer or even have a donation button so people could give you a bit of money in return for what you offer (though returns on this can vary depending on what you choose to offer). While advertising may seem like the best option, in many respects, advertising will only get you a very limited income unless your website offers some extraordinary content, goods or services to the visitor. This is the case because each click of an advertisement on your page will only earn you pennies. You may think this is unfair, but this low cost of entry is how advertising on Google can be a good investment for advertisers which means you're more likely to get the adverts in the first place. Whichever method you choose to use, as long as your website is high quality and well publicized, there is no reason you could not make a fair amount of money from it. And if you invent something special you may become the next Google!

Working with Merchant Services

You see all of these online stores on the Web and want to get in on the action. So how exactly can you allow payments on your website? Well, you want to go with a merchant service to act as a middleman between your website and your bank; the merchant service (such as the one in Figure 10-17) will process the credit card payments and the various other bits involved. This sounds great, but even better, most of the big names out there offer free services. For free services, they take a very small amount of money from what you make to cover the costs of the service. Because rates differ from provider to provider, you want to ensure that you pick a merchant service that will do a good job for you, so trying to get the lowest rate possible may not be in your best interest.

Figure 10-17. 2Checkout may not be as popular as PayPal, but it is still a very realistic e-commerce solution.

Within the list of commonly used merchant services, I have provided solid mixture of those that are simple and flexible like PayPal and those that are powerful but expensive like WorldPay. Your bank may offer its own merchant account system as well, and you may wish to check it out.

Most merchant services fall into two categories. You have the enterprise services like WorldPay who are excellent if you need to deal with many thousands of transactions and are passing around thousands of dollars at a time. Enterprise services are a solid option, but they tend to charge monthly costs and have quite high rates. The second and more commonly used category includes the other big names that work on the business model of a free or low cost service. These services are simple to set up and use but the downside is that even the big names like PayPal are less protected against fraud than enterprise systems. Services like PayPal, Amazon Flexible Payments (AFP), and Google Checkout all offer competitive services that are trusted around the world. One of the great things with these services is that your visitors do not require an account with them to make a purchase!

Here is a list of the most commonly used merchant services:

- **2Checkout**: http://www.2checkout.com/
- **AlertPay**: https://www.alertpay.com/
- **Amazon Flexible Payments**: http://aws.amazon.com/fps/
- **Authorize**: http://www.authorize.net/
- **Cleverbridge**: http://www.cleverbridge.com/
- **ClickBank**: http://www.clickbank.com/
- **Google Checkout**: http://checkout.google.com/
- **NetBanx**: http://www.netbanx.com/
- **NoChex**: http://www.nochex.com/
- **PayPal**: https://www.paypal.com/
- **PayPoint**: http://www.paypoint.net/online-payments
- **SWReg**: http://www.swreg.org/
- **WorldPay** – http://www.worldpay.com/
- **Yahoo! Small Business**: http://smallbusiness.yahoo.com/ecommerce/

ExplainED

You want to be sure not only of what rates are offered by merchant services but also that the system you choose can be integrated within a website shopping cart easily using an API. The reason PayPal has remained the choice for many is because of its simplicity and ease of integration with carts.

Adding Shopping Carts

If you have a merchant service and want to include it into your website, you will need a package that can deliver the shopping cart you want simply and easily. While there are literally hundreds of different stores out there with plenty of shopping software (such as the one shown in Figure 10-18), if you want to keep things simple, your merchant package will come with a payment processing method itself either in the form of an actual shopping cart or a simple "click to buy" button. This simplifies matters, as you do not need to install anything on your website, and more importantly, with the merchant handling the transaction, you do not have as many privacy worries (on your end).

Figure 10-18. ZenCart is a high-quality (and completely free) method of selling goods online.

If you do want to use a shopping cart other than the one provided by your merchant service, I have included a list of some of the more popular shopping cart software solutions. The prices vary, and there are some good free ones you might consider using. You can take a look at these if you want to have a store front on your website:

- **CS Cart:** http://www.cs-cart.com/ ($265)
- **Cube Cart:** http://www.cubecart.com/ (Free to $110)
- **Magento:** http://www.magentocommerce.com/ (Free to $1,000+)
- **OpenCart:** http://www.opencart.com/ (Free)
- **osCommerce:** http://www.oscommerce.com/ (Free)
- **X-Cart:** http://www.x-cart.com/ ($115 to $575)

- **ZenCart**: http://www.zen-cart.com/ (Free)
- **ZeusCart**: http://www.zeuscart.com/ (Free)

When using either a store or a script to process transactions, you want to ensure that you can make use of you merchant service's API (application programming interface) system to allow you to control your payments and to specify what happens upon receiving a successful payment. You could, for example, automate creating an account or send an e-mail with a registration key. By using these APIs, you literally automate your website into a finely tuned machine. Of course, explaining how to use these services, such as PayPal's Instant Payment Notifications (IPN), is well beyond the scope of this book, but in short, you can use server-side scripts to process these actions. If you use IPN (see Figure 10-19), PayPal will talk to your website about what is going on through scripting to let you know when payment is successful. A range of scripts are out there to help you take advantage of the IPN system but doing so will require knowledge of a server-side language.

If you have chosen to use PayPal as your merchant provider visit https://cms.paypal.com/us/cgi-bin/?cmd=_render-content&content_ID= developer/home_US *for information about getting your online store (or website) up and running. Setting up stores can be complicated!*

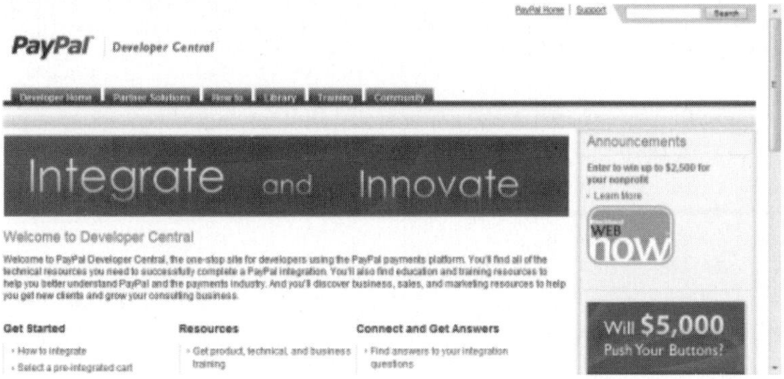

Figure 10-19. Using PayPal's IPN system, you can literally automate your payment system.

Self-Defense

Before we complete this chapter, we need to look at how you can protect yourself online. You need ensuring that your visitor's credit card details remain secure (so they won't be hacked or stolen, as this would lead to identity fraud). You should also know how deal with theft of your services and products (we already dealt with content theft earlier in Chapter 2). And you need to be aware of the importance of privacy and security when you have members (both paying and nonpaying) on the website. Security is paramount if you want to avoid being sued for not providing the level of privacy required to ensure your customers' personal and financial details are safe!

While you cannot prevent all forms of piracy, hopefully some of the self-defense tips in this section will help promote good business practice when you do exchange any sort of correspondence or financial information with individuals who choose to shop with your site. Your visitors are the most valuable assets your site has (even more important than the content!), so you need to ensure that you keep hold of as many repeat customers as you can.

Sale Security

Now, we move onto the serious matter of securely handling money and people's information. Having a merchant service like PayPal process orders through its website is really useful because you don't have to question the security of your own site to the same extent (as the payment takes place on their own territory). However, there are a few things you can do to your website to benefit your visitors greatly. The most obvious thing you can do is produce a login system for your members. Most forum software and other packages that can build accounts already make use of one of these systems, but getting people to sign in to an account helps ensure only one person has access to that area of the website, and it forces users to identify themselves as those who are entitled to see the personal information within (as long as the visitors don't let someone else in, of course).

If you do implement a login system or method of signing up for a service (see Figure 10-20), you should never store the passwords in plain text format; these should be encrypted in case someone manages to break into your website's database (that way, the passwords will not be visible for them to see). Encryption is, of course, beyond the scope of this book, but there are many good guides online. While having login details is useful, you should provide a method of retrieving a lost password via the e-mail account provided by the user, as people are often forgetful, and with all the login details we collect, it's no wonder everyone has issues keeping track of information!

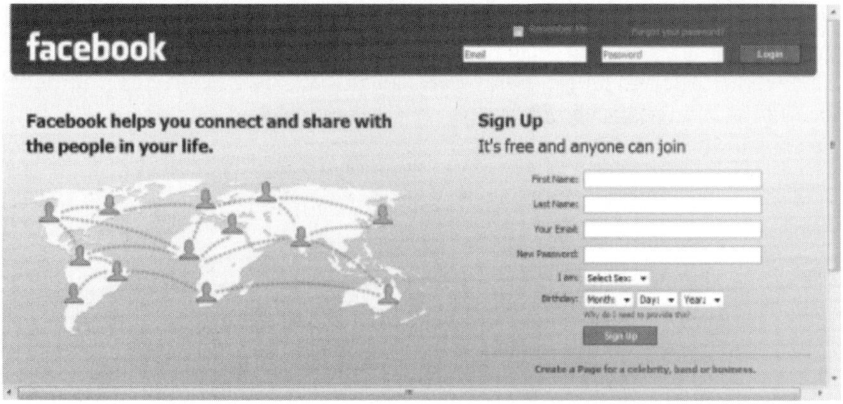

Figure 10-20. Facebook combines the login system with a sign up form for new members.

NotED

An innovative system has been produced called OpenID that allows people to use a single username and password across a variety of websites that support it. OpenID has seen widespread adoption with Facebook, Google, Yahoo, BBC, PayPal, MSN, and many others. For details, visit http://openid.net/.

Having login information for sections of your website might seem pretty obvious, but other security-related things we need to discuss may not be so visible to the end visitor, such as site encryption that goes on behind the scenes. All websites that process payments have some form of encryption and a certificate to say that the connection has been protected so that no one can intercept what visitors send to the website. Visitors know their transactions are secure, because they see a padlock on the screen (which says it is encrypted) or in some cases because their address bar turns green (in more expensive packages). If you intend to process any personal information for money or otherwise, I highly recommend you pay for a Secure Sockets Layer (SSL) certificate for your website (prices differ among providers). SSL certificates encrypt and secure a website's transactions, giving you and your visitors more peace of mind that personal details are safe. If you have issues enabling SSL, you should contact your host. When you have SSL enabled on your site, for each page that either asks for information or processes it, you should simply replace the http with https in the anchor href to trigger the SSL and make the connection secure for those pages to help ensure that no one intercepts the information. The result of which should be visible by clicking the padlock icon wherever it appears in your browser (see Figure 10-21), as the individual involved in the transaction should be able to see a signed certificate with your sites name on it.

Here are some of the trusted providers of certificates:

- **Commodo**: http://www.instantssl.com/
- **GoDaddy**: https://www.godaddy.com/gdshop/ssl/ssl.asp
- **RapidSSL**: http://www.rapidssl.com/
- **Thawte**: https://www.thawte.com/ssl-digital-certificates/
- **VeriSign**: http://www.verisign.com/ssl/

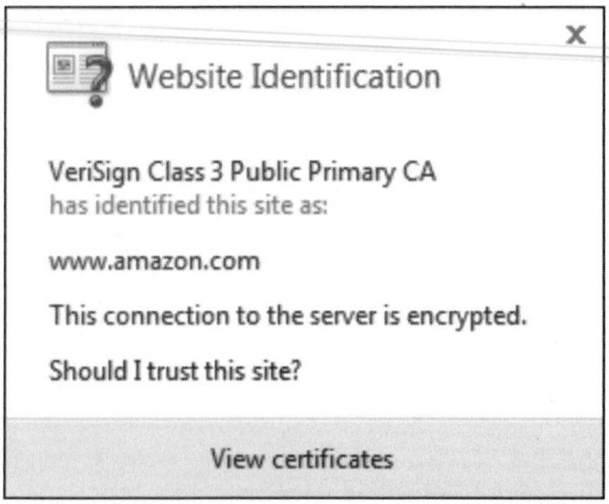

Figure 10-21. When the padlock icon is clicked, details about the website's encryption status are shown.

There are two types of certificate for encrypting an Internet connection: a standard SSL certificate puts the padlock on the screen, and an EV certificate turns the address bar green (see Figure 10-22). EV certificates are more expensive and provide better coverage, and (of course) your visitors are more aware the connection is secure. However, if you simply have a forum or members area for your website (or even just a small store), you can use a normal SSL certificate and not feel any worse off. EV certificates tend to be used by large businesses and enterprises who want the extended coverage. Most SSL providers offer some form of insurance as part of the cost, so if someone fraudulently breaks past your secured site, you will get compensation to deal with the mess, which is always a good thing, and all SSL certificates are paid for on a yearly basis like domains.

Figure 10-22. Facebook has an EV certificate, which shows the padlock and turns the address bar green.

Online Privacy

Finally, before we close this guide to e-commerce and making a bit of money online, we need to look at privacy. All forms of information collection—from a full financial record as part of a payment notification scheme all the way down to storing cookies or having a statistics package—have potential privacy implications. While privacy and security go hand in hand, the difference is that security is about ensuring that the sending and receiving (communication) of information is secure; having login information and securing transactions helps address security. Privacy is more focused what you actually do with the information you have. Privacy not only matters when we talk about the process of collecting information but in what you choose to do with that information after you have a large number of registered users in your website's databases.

While you are obviously not going to give out people's credit card information, even giving out their e-mail addresses could be seen as a breach of privacy, and selling e-mail address lists could potentially be helping criminal organizations (such as spammers, phishers, and scam artists), who obviously you do not want to aid. Your visitors trust you with their information and are loyal to you because they know you treat their privacy and security with the upmost respect. When large organizations lose information (such as AOL a few years ago), the ramifications can be an entire lack of trust from customers who will move elsewhere. When people have been burned by a company, they will not stay loyal, so you want to follow a few simple steps to ensure that what information you do collect is held properly. You should talk about the steps you take on your website in the form of a privacy policy that explains how you treat privacy and what you do to ensure security.

Tips and Tricks: Privacy Tips

Use these pointers to help protect the privacy of your site's visitors:

- Do not sell your visitors' information, no matter how much money people offer you. Anything you collect from a user should stay between you and that individual. Remember that you want to be as ethical as possible, and you want to keep your visitors protected as much as possible.

- If users requests their accounts be closed down, you should remove their accounts entirely. There is no reason why anyone should store information after such a request has been made unless the removal of that information would damage the site (such as large numbers of forum posts that would fragment discussions) or if you are required to hold such information by law.

- Make a note in your privacy policy if you record analytics to help understand your users' needs and if you store cookies to improve their experiences. Explain what these technologies are and be honest with your visitors. If there is a good reason for the information collection, your visitors will understand and will approve of it more readily if they know exactly why you need the data.

- If you ever change your privacy policy, ensure that your visitors are made aware of it and given at least 30 days to comply with changes. That way, they will not suddenly realize they have agreed to something they were not even aware of. This rule counts for any terms of service agreements, contracts or other legal documents you may have produced too!

- The Children's Online Privacy Protection Act (COPPA) is a U.S. law with some International recognition that requires adult websites or sites aimed for individuals over 18 to identify or verify the age of the individual entering the website. Therefore, if your website is aimed for adult audiences, you should make the website private, meaning that no visitor can see any pages before entering a date of birth and being verified as of age! While verifying ages can be done through a credit card transaction, some sites just choose to ask the visitor's date of birth.

- Finally, never collect any more information than you actually need. If users want to sign up for a forum, they do not need to give address, phone number, or other personal details. A user really needs only a username, password, and e-mail address (except where you are selling something and a delivery address is required). Harvesting unnecessary personal information is unethical, and many people will avoid the signup process entirely if too much is asked of them.

ExplainED

If you have a shopping cart on your website, do not ask for a user's credit card information or even name until a purchase is made. Use of a shopping cart does not require an account, especially if people simply want to window shop and get ideas for future purchases.

Summary

In this chapter, you have learned how the search engines index your website and what you need to do to ensure you hold a good place in the ranks (as well as how to avoid getting banned). You also learned how to promote, advertise, and market your website through placed advertisements and e-mail and social marketing campaigns. I showed you how to measure the success of your website and the various methods you can use to make money on the Internet (along with the responsibilities you have to your visitors if you do sell products or services). I also provided some information on what to do if you find people stealing your stuff! Now you have come to the conclusion of this book, and you should have the basic knowledge to not only build a website but make it the best thing you possibly can! While you may be about ready to close this book, you still have more opportunities to learn. If you want, you can continue by reading the appendixes, which contain some really useful snippets of information too bulky or complex to talk about elsewhere. Plus, at the back of this book in Appendix B, I have put together a list of useful reading material (such as websites worth reading) and a comprehensive list of software like image editors and code editors that you can take advantage of to make your life easier. I hope this journey has been a useful learning experience and look forward to you perhaps making the next big thing!

Chapter Checklist

You should accomplish the following tasks before leaving this chapter:

- Understand how search engines work and make use of them.
- Start a marketing campaign to promote your website in various ways.
- Get some regular visitors to build up a community of friends.
- Learn how you can turn your site into a money making machine.

Questions and answers

Q: *Can I trust any of those SEO companies who guarantee a Google rank?*

A: This is a tricky question to answer. A lot of shady dealers out there make claims that are too good to be true. When you decide to outsource your marketing to a professional group who has experience in promoting websites on the Internet, you need to be realistic about what you are going to achieve. On the Web, there is a lot of competition and plenty of people trying to sell similar or identical products, as well as people who are fighting for the same top spot in the search engines (rankings literally re an ongoing battle among websites). The best ways to get some assistance are to ensure your website is relatively unique, to have a selling point, and to choose a company that has experience in the field you want to advertise and can back up its claims with existing (or previous) customers and successful campaigns in the past.

Q: *How long does it take for a marketing campaign to show results?*

A: Marketing is not a science. Depending on what methods you use and the quality of your website, you may well see results fairly quickly. Perhaps you may actually get indexed naturally without needing to submit your website. Often, though, it can take a few weeks or months for a campaign to build up enough steam to show any real difference in the traffic you are getting. What you need to do is experiment with as many different methods of promotion as you can. Putting all of your eggs in one basket will not work on the Web, and getting involved in as many different techniques as realistically possible will help get your name out there quicker, though you should not resort to spamming your message.

Q: *Why isn't my website making very much money compared to others?*

A: There are many reasons why a website does not become a success story. Perhaps the products or services you offer are not as high quality as a competitor's. Perhaps there was simply not an audience for the site, or perhaps you tried to penetrate a market that had too much high-quality competition already. The sad fact is that making money on the Web is not as easy as people make out. There are plenty of people willing to scam you with guarantees of making income that simply isn't possible (or are out of the ordinary), and you should avoid these kinds of sites. The truth is that probably 90% of all Web start-ups aiming to make money end up either not making as much as they anticipated or not making any money at all. You need to examine your business model and spend time improving what you offer until the customers see you as a viable business. Making money does not happen overnight, and achieving a website that can be considered truly successful can take years!

Where You Are Now

By the end of this chapter, you should have the following:

- A website optimized using organic SEO and keyword research
- Any content or services you wish to sell published and prepared
- Involvement in social networks to ethically promote your website

The Ten Commandments for Websites

Welcome to the appendixes! At this stage in your learning, you should have all the basic skills you require to build a high-quality website with insightful consideration given to aspects such as accessibility, search engine optimization, usability, and all the other concepts that web designers and developers think about on a daily basis. Hopefully with all the different elements covered in this book, you now have a solid understanding as to what goes into building a website (much more than code!). The main thing you should take from this book is that you don't need to be an expert at everything but ensuring that you take the time to notice what's out there and deciding what will best help your site are among the most important elements of the process.

As you leave this book and go on to updating your website over time and perhaps learning new skills, always remember to be brave, take risks (through trial and error), and never feel that things are getting too hard. If you choose to learn skills that were only briefly mentioned in this book, like scripting, or to get involved in using content management systems and web software, go at a pace that you feel comfortable with. With that in mind, let's go over the 10 most important messages I would personally recommend. After that, I'll give you some useful resources like important websites for people learning to create for the Internet and handy software.

Advice is something many professional designers and developers give out in spades after learning some harsh lessons from what their own bitter experiences. I know from experience that all the rules, specifications, laws, conventions, guides, and other methods of trying to get you to do something can be overwhelming and, at times, rather depressing, so next is a simple list of rules which help define the most important elements of the website building process. However, even though many of you are now probably thinking "rules are made to be broken" (and in all fairness they often are), let me impart ten simple rules that are easy to remember and if you follow them through, you may have a less stressful experience which can only be a good thing!

Follow the Specifications

Over the years, a series of specifications and standards have been produced for people creating websites. Though these are often quite detailed and hard to understand at first, they can be extremely useful, when you are more comfortable with building websites, in helping to expand your knowledge and assisting you in implementing certain language functions within your source code. Think of a specification as similar to a lengthy instruction manual. Luckily for you, this book covers the basics you will need to get started without requiring to do any heavy reading (beyond what you are already undertaking, of course). However, when it comes to creating a website, the specifications are the ultimate reference (and the first port of call) to any language or best practice scenario.

Think of Your End Users' Needs

No matter what you are doing when you start making your website, the main things you should always keep at the top of your mind are you visitors' needs and wants. When you make a site to be published to the Web, you have the intention of having an audience of people who are willing and ready to read what you have to say or be involved in your creation. While trying to get into the mindset of the people you want to visit your website might seem like a scary thing to do, one of the main things that makes a website successful is that the customer is always perceived to be right, just like when you go shopping. Generally speaking, websites are not made for personal consumption; they are almost always functional or informative places that the author wishes to share with others. Because of this, you should always take into consideration what other people may want to get out of the experience so that the final product will entice them into being a part of your creation.

Have Realistic Goals and Intentions

If you are trying to make a get-rich-quick Internet venture, you may want to think again. Unfortunately, some people choose to approach website building with unrealistic intentions or expectations of what the finished site will be able to achieve. Now, I am certainly not saying that you should have a negative view of your website or that you should just give up; you should just make sure you do not come into the process with the intention of becoming a multimillionaire the same night that the project goes live (unless of course you have an amazing idea planned that is guaranteed success—in which case, share it with the rest of us!).

The fact of the matter is that the majority of fly-by-night schemes on the Web fizzle out at the first stage of the process, and success is something you have to work hard to achieve. Many of the most successful websites on the web exist purely out of the author's wish to be creative rather than to make money from it. Even if you are not trying to make money from the website, the rule is still relevant to you: the last thing you want to do is start making a website that explodes into an enormous project and grows out of control. While all of this information may sound a bit gloomy, the pitfalls can easily be overcome by making sure you do not reach too far and keeping your goals clear, simple, and concise to reduce the chances of going off track.

Have a Pragmatic Approach

Pragmatism is the art of common sense, which in some respects does not always reach the realms of making websites. Sometimes, even the best of us make mistakes and do something that, in retrospect, we realize we should have been given a firm kick over. Luckily, the art of common sense allows you to take the most obvious things into consideration when you make a website. It is obvious that having a site that does not work properly will be bad for business, and therefore we fix it. It is also obvious that if you write all your content in Russian with no translation available, the English-speaking world will have problems trying to decipher it. Trusting your instincts and common sense and, most importantly, being practical when you decide to put something into action will help you to no end to making solid choices that will see instant or fruitful long-term results.

Think Outside the Box

There are two kinds of people in the world, those who choose to be adventurous and those who prefer to play it safe and stick with what they know. Making websites is, in many respects, a creative process that requires the ability to use your imagination. In many situations, you may wish to stick with techniques, layout styles, and existing conventions, which is perfectly fine. However, one of the main elements that make a website exceptional is when something truly unique and creative comes along. But be warned, while you want to be creative and try to make things as interesting as possible, you should always make choices with care as occasionally our choices in design can actually make things less usable or, even worse, inaccessible.

Know Your Subject Well

Nothing is worse, when browsing the Web for an article on a subject, than realizing after you have finished reading that the information within the article was irrelevant or incorrect. While the Web does have a fairly high margin for error (as can be noted from the question over the reliability of websites with user contributed content such as Wikipedia), you should consider that when you pass wrong or potentially harmful information, your website will lose trust and respect, which will cause visitors to turn away. Always try to be as accurate as possible with information you give out. Freedom of speech allows people to say pretty much what they want, but when you have a site that relies on people visiting your pages, you should always refrain from saying or doing bad things for which you can be held accountable (legally or personally). You don't want to damage your brand and image.

Crawl Before You Walk

Innovation is one of the fun elements of producing websites from scratch. You get to show off as you learn, experiment through trial and error, and share your experiences with other people. Trial and error is a lot like playing detective, as you get to see things from a broader perspective and investigate what caused a problem and use your knowledge to try and resolve issues as they occurs. Maintaining your own website is a fantastic way to learn and can give you essential experience at debugging. The piece of advice which can be gained from this rule is to take things one step at a time—try not to dive right into a project that you are not ready for, but always push your boundaries as you code. After all, many developers will tell you that half of the battle of making a website is pretty much making it up as you go along and finding a compromise whenever you fall short of the goalpost!

Interact with Your Customers

A great number of the websites in the world, whether personal in nature or business orientated, are trying to give a personal feel to the folks who decide to give that page a visit. Giving that personal touch is vital to avoid making your website seem like a faceless organization in a sea of millions of others.

The interaction you have with your visitors does not need to be technical in nature. It could be anything from being involved in social networking (and sharing your experiences with those who go to your website) right up to having a personal blog to which you can allow people to provide feedback on the things you choose to talk about or even just a simple news section letting people know what changes have occurred since they last visited. A website that has warmth because the owner is willing to put in a few hours of time keeping visitors updated will foster a sense of belonging to the site in those involved in the process, and this will result in a greater number of those visitors becoming longstanding members.

Be an Efficient Manager

One of the hardest things in making a website is getting organized and structured. This book will give you a pathway you can follow (in a logical order) to start putting together a design of your own creation, but one rule you should try to follow is to stay organized. Many times, I have seen people pull together a website and publish it onto the Web only to realize that they forgot to make some recommended changes. The irony is that keeping organized can be as simple as creating a checklist of things you need to achieve or jobs you still have to do (maybe using sticky notes or to-do lists) before the website is published online. A benefit you may also see in following this method is that you get a small sense of accomplishment each time you manage to tick off a complete item in the list of priorities. I would not say keeping a checklist is required, many people may be benefit from this rule, especially if you find managing time hard.

Always Update Your Website

Of all the rules, keeping your site up to date should be the most obvious and is the most important. While the functions and interactivity you choose to provide will provide the incentive to return on a regular basis, the most dangerous thing you can do when completing a website and putting it online is to leave it alone or play it safe and suddenly reduce the momentum of the site's progress. With few exceptions, the reason people keep returning to someone's homepage on a regular basis is that interesting, useful, relevant, and up-to-date content has been posted that is worthy of reading. Perhaps you have added new functionality into a service you offer, or maybe you have made some important additions to the website. No matter what method you choose, the important thing is to keep giving the website you produce a regular stream of new items of interest. If left to go stale, a website will see the amount of people who visit it steadily decrease over what can be a rather short period of time.

Appendix B

Additional Materials

In this appendix, you will find some of my own personal recommendations for websites that are essential resources for anyone building websites as well as software products I have mentioned throughout this book that you will need to create your website. While these resources will hopefully give you the incentive to keep learning new skills and enhance what you already know, if you are looking for somewhere specific to go from this book, why not take a look at the friends of ED website to see what other excellent books exist? Now that you have a basic understanding of code, you can go with another beginner book or an intermediate level book to top-up stuff found in this one, or if you really want to be adventurous and tweak your website to the maximum, you might even consider a more advanced title (when you feel comfortable to do so).

LinkED

To visit the friends of ED or Apress website (to see what excellent titles are available or perhaps purchase one of those I have on my own bookshelf and personally recommend from reading), visit http://www.friendsofed.com/ *or* http://www.apress.com/.

Useful Websites

Websites are one of the most feature rich and resourceful places for getting useful information about web design, unlike books (which can become dated if they focus heavily on explicit technologies), these kinds of resources can offer cutting (possibly even bleeding) edge information about various subjects such as best practices, new products, tools, and even full tutorials and curriculums to enhance your level of knowledge beyond the basics. Whether you are looking for practical guides for examples, useful articles on specific subjects or just general web design information, the below (long!) list of websites will offer you plenty to think about and lots of useful things you can have a go at. The list itself has been broken down into several categories to give you a better idea of which websites you may want to check out (also remember the various links provided throughout the book).

- Online magazines:
  - **A List Apart**: http://www.alistapart.com/
  - **Digital Web Magazine**: http://www.digital-web.com/
  - **I Love Typography**: http://ilovetypography.com/
  - **Smashing Magazine**: http://www.smashingmagazine.com/
  - **Think Vitamin**: http://carsonified.com/blog/
  - **Use It**: http://www.useit.com/
  - **UX Matters**: http://www.uxmatters.com/
  - **Web Designer Deport**: http://www.webdesignerdepot.com/
  - **Web Designer Wall**: http://www.webdesignerwall.com/
- General web design:
  - **456 Berea Street**: http://www.456bereastreet.com/
  - **Boxes and Arrows**: http://boxesandarrows.com/
  - **Design Float**: http://www.designfloat.com/
  - **Mozilla Documentation**: https://developer.mozilla.org/en/Web_Development
  - **Net Tuts+**: http://net.tutsplus.com/
  - **Opera Dev**: http://dev.opera.com/
  - **Opera Web Standards Curriculum**: http://www.opera.com/company/education/curriculum/
  - **Vandelay Design**: http://vandelaydesign.com/blog/
  - **Web Design From Scratch**: http://www.webdesignfromscratch.com/articles-and-tutorials.php
  - **Web Monkey**: http://www.webmonkey.com/
  - **Web Resources Deport**: http://www.webresourcesdepot.com/
  - **WebAim**: http://webaim.org/
  - **WebCredible**: http://www.webcredible.co.uk/user-friendly-resources/

- Related podcasts:
    - **Boagworld**: http://boagworld.com/
    - **CreativeXpert**: http://www.creativexpert.com/
    - **FreelanceSwitch**: http://freelanceswitch.com/podcasts/
    - **SitePoint Podcast**: http://www.sitepoint.com/blogs/category/podcast/
    - **Web Axe**: http://webaxe.blogspot.com/
    - **Web 2.0 Show**: http://web20show.com/
    - **Web Designer Mag**: http://www.webdesignermag.co.uk/category/podcast/
    - **Web Dev Radio**: http://www.webdevradio.com/
    - **Web Hosting Show**: http://www.webhostingshow.com/
- Other resources:
    - **CSS Tricks**: http://css-tricks.com/
    - **CSS Discuss**: http://css-discuss.incutio.com/
    - **SitePoint Reference**: http://reference.sitepoint.com/
    - **Tizag**: http://www.tizag.com/
    - **W3Schools**: http://www.w3schools.com/
    - **Web Dev Out**: http://www.webdevout.net/
- Useful blogs:
    - **Adaptive Path**: http://www.adaptivepath.com/blog/
    - **Ajaxian**: http://ajaxian.com/
    - **Beast Blog**: http://green-beast.com/blog/
    - **FreelanceSwitch**: http://freelanceswitch.com/
    - **Mezzo Blue**: http://www.mezzoblue.com/
    - **Snook**: http://snook.ca/
    - **Tutorial Blog**: http://tutorialblog.org/

Tools of the Trade

Software is extremely useful. It allows us to automate our tasks, generate code, and basically make things simpler and easier to cope with. There are thousands of web-design-related products out there on the shelves, and you should decide what software you want to use to achieve your website building goal. You obviously need a text editor that allows you to write code for the purposes of marking up your site, and there are other tools that perhaps you may not have realized or thought about. Some of these particular products could save you a lot of added time and hassle in the future if you choose to install and use them.

These conventions are used throughout this section:

- **Industry standard**: The premium product, usually what I consider the best option available

- **Recommendation**: A satisfactory and almost as good replacement or alternative

- **Alternative**: Additional choices that are comparable to the industry standards and recommendations but not always as good

ExplainED

While features, popularity, or value for money ultimately decided the industry standard, as close to being the best package as they came, recommendations always fell short of the top spot.

Website Editors

The first piece of software you should consider investing some time in is a website editor. These products provide you with an environment to create and edit your design through graphical (WYSIWYG) or code (syntax) software. While other software in this list should be considered important, the syntax editor is by far the most important product you will ever use when making your website. There are three different kinds of syntax editors on the market and each has their own learning curve, advantages, and disadvantages. In the following sections, you will find a brief description of each style of editor and some general choices that are of my own personal recommendations. However, the product you ultimately choose should be based on what you feel most comfortable using.

WYSIWYG Editors

"WYSIWYG" may sound strange it is an acronym for "what you see is what you get." These kinds of editors are the most well known to people who start out making a website for the first time as they are entirely visual in nature. When using these products, there is no need to learn how to write code, as using a

WYSIWYG editor is usually a simple matter of dragging and dropping elements where you want them on the page.

While a WYSIWYG editor may seem an ideal choice for the project you are about to undertake, tutorials for visual editors will not be given in this book. First, there are already books that deal with specific products like FrontPage and Adobe Dreamweaver. Second, this book intends to equip you with actual skills you can make use of and therefore the focus inclines toward coding. But the main reason why WYSIWYG editors will be held at arm's length in this book is that there are some serious flaws in the way visual editors represent code that could potentially damage the ability for visitors to browse your website.

ExplainED

Adobe Dreamweaver has been listed among the editors you may wish to choose, but Microsoft FrontPage has been omitted because the product is being discontinued and replaced.

One merit of a visual editor is that using it requires no coding knowledge to begin creating websites, which of course, makes it a straightforward approach to website creating for those who wish to have a site without having to do any work. However, as you are reading this book with the intention of learning to make a website the correct way (without taking dirty shortcuts) and to create something that will have some longevity, the simple truth is that beneath the surface of visual editors (including the big players such as Dreamweaver), the underpinning code often ends up in a big wave of confusion and unnecessary code that has been glued together.

Because of the serious misgivings and the complete lack of awareness it requires to use a WYSIWYG editor, I highly recommended you do not use one. However, if choose to do so, make use of the code editing window to maintain complete control of everything that is produced within your website design.

Here are the WYSIWYG editors of note:

- **Industry standard**: Adobe Dreamweaver costs $399 new, or an upgrade costs $199, and it's available for Windows and Mac. See http://www.adobe.com/products/dreamweaver/.

- **Recommendation**: Microsoft Expression Web costs $299.95 new, or you can upgrade for $99.95. You can learn more about this Windows-only product at http://www.microsoft.com/expression/products/Web_Overview.aspx.

- **Alternatives**: The following alternative choices are free and open source options available for Windows, Mac, and Linux:

    - KompoZer is available at `http://kompozer.net/`

    - Amaya is shown in Figure B-1 and is available at `http://www.w3.org/Amaya/`

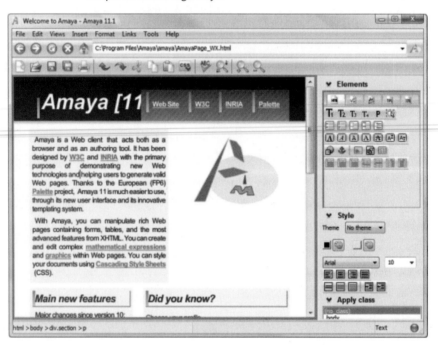

Figure B-1. Amaya is an open source browser which follows web standards.

Source Code Editors / IDEs

The integrated development environment (IDE) is quite probably the best choice of the three available options you can use. It has none of the damaging visual elements of the WYSIWYG editor and contains the same functionality as a plain text editor. It also has functionality aimed specifically at developers or people who will be working with code (which will soon be you!). Most IDEs contain useful functionality such as code highlighting for better readability, line numbering, project and code management utilities, spell checking, code collapsing to ease maintenance, and debugging tools to help reduce the number of errors.

- **Industry standard**: Eclipse is a free and open source IDE for Windows, Mac, and Linux. See http://www.eclipse.org/.

- **Recommendation**: Notepad++ is also free and open source and is available for Windows; it's shown in Figure B-2. See http://notepad-plus.sourceforge.net/.

- **Alternatives**:

  - Aptana Studio is free and available for Windows, Mac, and Linux. See http://www.aptana.com/.

  - UltraEdit can be purchased new for $49.95 or an upgrade can be purchases at $24.95. It's available for Windows and Linux. See http://www.ultraedit.com/.

  - Coda costs $99 and is available for Mac only. See http://www.panic.com/coda/.

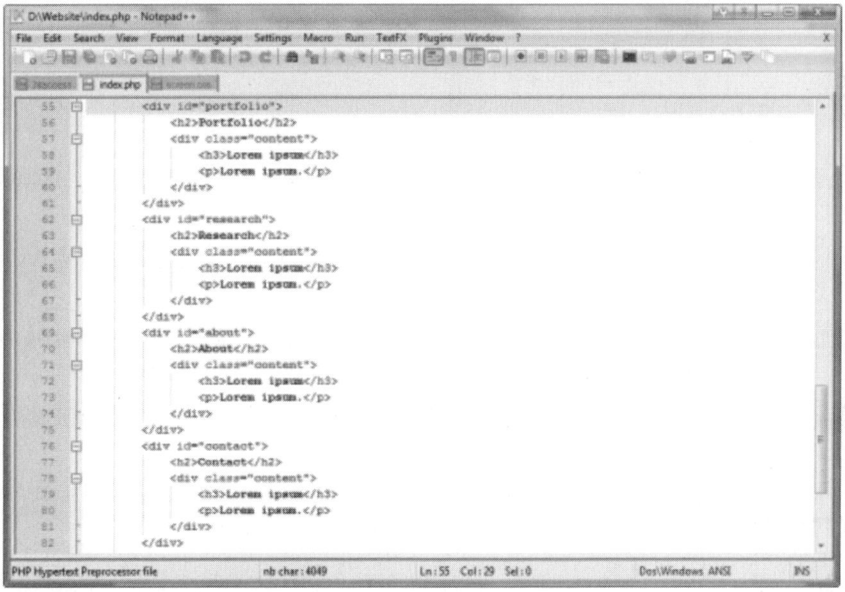

Figure B-2. Notepad++ is a firm favorite editor among web coders.

Plain Text Editors

Have you ever used Microsoft Notepad? It has been included with every release of Windows for many years. This is a simple yet effective example of a plain text editor (see Figure B-3). The nature of these products is to be able to type large amounts of text (or marked up code) with minimum features. An IDE can provide you with some quick timesaving measures (which can be really useful), but many people still choose to build websites using a plain text editor simply because of the ease of use and the minimalistic interface.

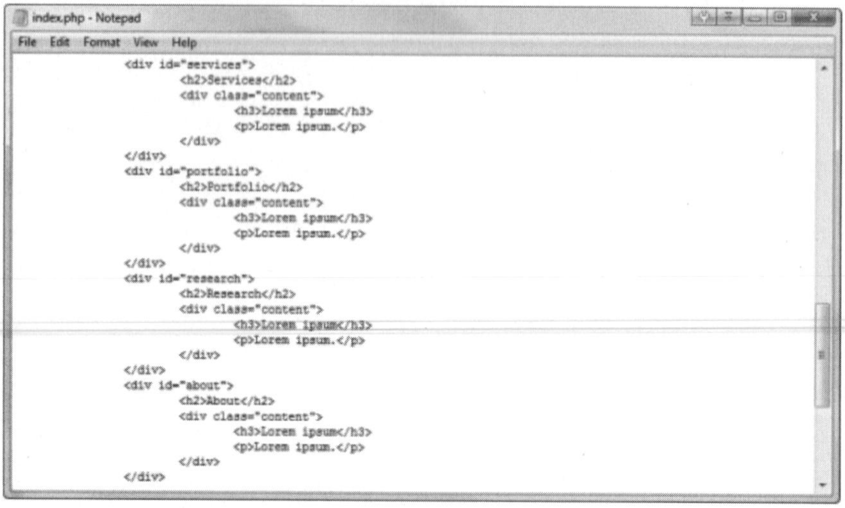

Figure B-3. Microsoft Notepad which comes as part of Windows can produce code too!

- **Industry standard**: Microsoft Notepad and Apple TextEdit are free and available within the operating systems.
- **Recommendation:** Vim is a free and open source plain text editor available for Windows, Mac, Linux. See http://www.vim.org/.
- **Alternative**: SciTE is a free and open source plain text editor available for Windows, Mac, Linux. See http://www.scintilla.org/SciTE.html.

Useful Software

While your choice of editor will form the hub of your website building experience, there are many other useful applications and browser extensions (particularly for Mozilla Firefox) that will aid the process of making a website from the ground up. The following sections list useful types of software that you should investigate to determine if you feel they would be of use to you. Then, you can make a choice based on the recommendations included here or by going with an existing editor you have, or perhaps even find something completely different altogether!

Image Editors

While you produce your website, you are almost constantly creating, editing, and working with images. Graphics are an essential part to any website design, as a simple design with few colors can ultimately look boring—and boring is not the impression you want to put across to your users. While it is important to choose an image editor that has enough features to cope with your needs, in many cases, you may not require the full feature set of a professional image-authoring package. It may also be worth nothing that for the purposes of modern web design, your editor should support as many formats as possible (including the Windows icon format) for specific reasons.

- **Industry standard:** Adobe Photoshop is available new for $699, or you can upgrade for $199. It's available for Windows and Mac. See http://www.adobe.com/products/photoshop/photoshop/.

- **Recommendation:** GIMP is a free and open source image editor available for Windows, Mac, and Linux at http://www.gimp.org/. It's shown in Figure B-4.

- **Alternatives:**

  - Paint.NET is free but available only for Windows at http://www.getpaint.net/.

  - Corel PaintShop Pro is available new at $79.99 and an upgrade costs $49.99 (Ultimate version). It's available for Windows. See http://www.corel.com/paintshop/.

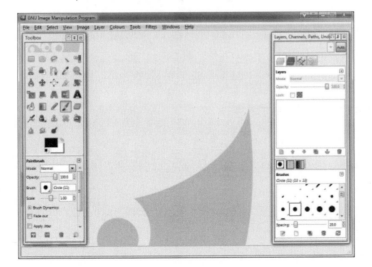

Figure B-4. GIMP is a powerful image editor with none of the costs of Photoshop.

FTP Clients

When you have created your pages, you are going to want to be able to place them on the Internet, so you will need a program that can copy the source code from your computer and place it onto you website. In terms of features, most FTP clients are very similar, but it may be worth getting a client that supports SSH (secure shell over FTP), which, as discussed in the protocols section earlier, will give you a much more secure method of transferring your files, and security is definitely a good thing.

- **Industry standard**: SmartFTP is available for Windows only, and the Professional version costs $49.95. See http://www.smartftp.com/.

- **Recommendation**: FileZilla is a free and open source FTP client for Windows, Mac, and Linux and is available at http://filezilla-project.org/ (see Figure B-5).

- **Alternative**: CuteFTP can be purchased at $59.99, or an upgrade costs $29.99. It's available for Windows and Mac at http://www.globalscape.com/cuteftppro/.

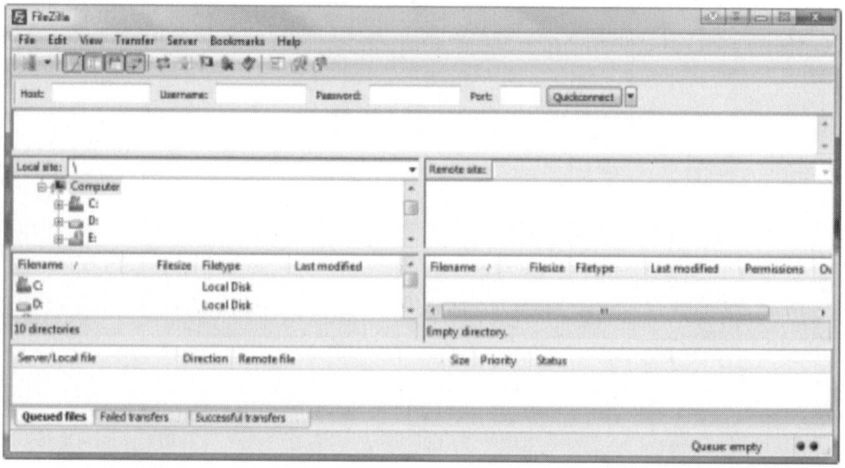

Figure B-5. FileZilla contains a vast array of features aimed at uploading files to the Internet.

Note Takers

Using a note taker may seem like one of the least obvious choices, but if you do wish to manage your projects easily, there is nothing like a good note taking application to help you organize your thoughts, plans for the website, and information you wish to include. A note taking application is basically the digital equivalent of a sketchpad; it allows you to write, draw, graph, link, and reference all sorts of information that can be organized into pages, sections, or blocks. If you have a lot of ideas, things to remember, or plans you wish to organize, these kinds of products are fantastic for the job and can reduce the amount of time you spend filing pieces of paper.

- **Industry standard**: Microsoft OneNote costs $99.95 and is available for Windows at http://office.microsoft.com/onenote/. See Figure B-6.

- **Recommendation**: EverNote is free and available for Windows and Mac at http://evernote.com/.

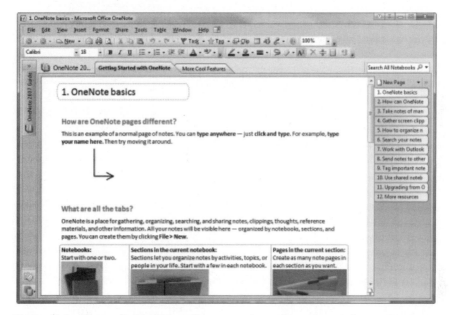

Figure B-6. Microsoft OneNote allows you to make notes and organize your ideas.

E-Mail Programs

One of the most common elements of the Internet today is e-mail; you already probably have an e-mail account of your own. As you start your own website, you will likely want to provide your visitors with a dedicated means to be able to contact you, either by giving them your existing address or providing a method of contact such as a form on the homepage. Even though nearly every website host provides a web-based interface to read your e-mail, you may feel more comfortable having a desktop e-mail client so that you can more effectively organize and work with the messages that are sent to your address.

- **Industry standard:** Microsoft Outlook, shown in Figure B-7, is available at $109.95 for Windows. See http://office.microsoft.com/outlook/.

- **Recommendation:** Mozilla Thunderbird is a free an open source e-mail client that's available for Windows, Mac, and Linux at http://www.mozillamessaging.com/.

- **Alternative:** The Bat! can be purchased for $24.56, and you get with a 30% discount on upgrades. It's available for Windows at http://www.ritlabs.com/en/products/thebat/.

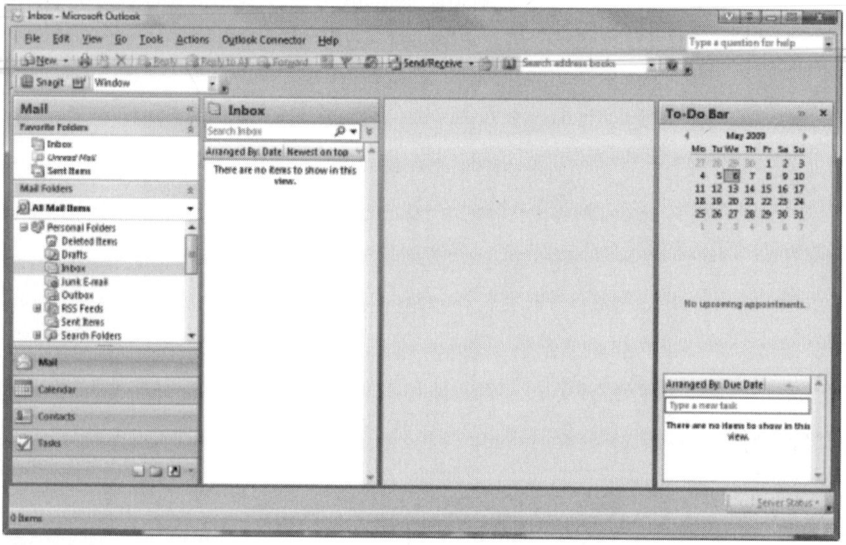

Figure B-7. Microsoft Outlook is the most popular e-mail client in businesses.

Word Processors

Writing content is a tricky business. You want to appear professional and maintain high standards, but the editor you use to build your website really is not equipped to deal with the complex needs of an individual who is going to spend any amount of time writing for the Web. Things such as spell checking, grammar checking, structuring sentences properly, and laying out your content (without the distraction of the design)—simply being able to format a document that you would like to publish online—can only come from using a rich text editor that is equipped to fit the task you are trying to achieve.

- **Industry standard**: Microsoft Word, shown in Figure B-8, costs $229.95, and an upgrade costs $109.55. It's available for Windows and Mac. See http://office.microsoft.com/word/.

- **Recommendation**: OpenOffice Word is a free, open source word processor available for Windows, Mac, and Linux. See http://www.openoffice.org/.

- **Alternatives**:

  - AbiWord is free, open source software available for Windows, Mac, and Linux at http://www.abiword.com/.

  - Corel WordPerfect Office costs $299.99, and an upgrade is $159.99. It's available for Windows at http://www.corel.com/wordperfect/.

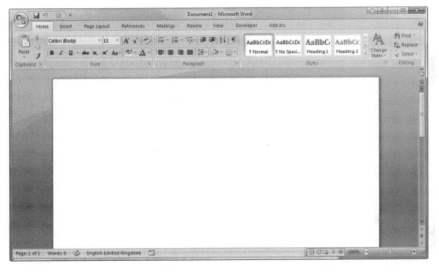

Figure B-8. Microsoft Word 2007 has a wide variety of word processing features.

Wireframe Modeling

When you start your website project, you will probably find yourself having lots of ideas but nowhere to put them. Perhaps you want to start a brainstorming session, map out your workflow, or even just create a wireframe using shapes to produce some models to help you get an idea of how everything should be organized. Whatever your choice, you will find that wireframe modeling products allow you to create technical diagrams that can be helpful when trying to get inspiration for what your potential website could end up looking like or how it could be structured. These tools are not something everyone uses, but you may well find them handy.

- **Industry standard**: Microsoft Visio Professional is priced at $344 or $245.95 for the upgrade. It's available for Windows at http://office.microsoft.com/visio/.

- **Recommendation**: Dia is a free and open source wireframing software for Windows, Mac, and Linux, and it's shown in Figure B-9. See http://www.dia-installer.de/.

- **Alternatives**:

  - SmartDraw costs $297, or you can upgrade for $129. It's available for Windows at http://www.smartdraw.com/.

  - ConceptDraw Office is $339.99, and the upgrade is $70 per year. It's available for Windows and Mac. See http://www.conceptdraw.com/en/.

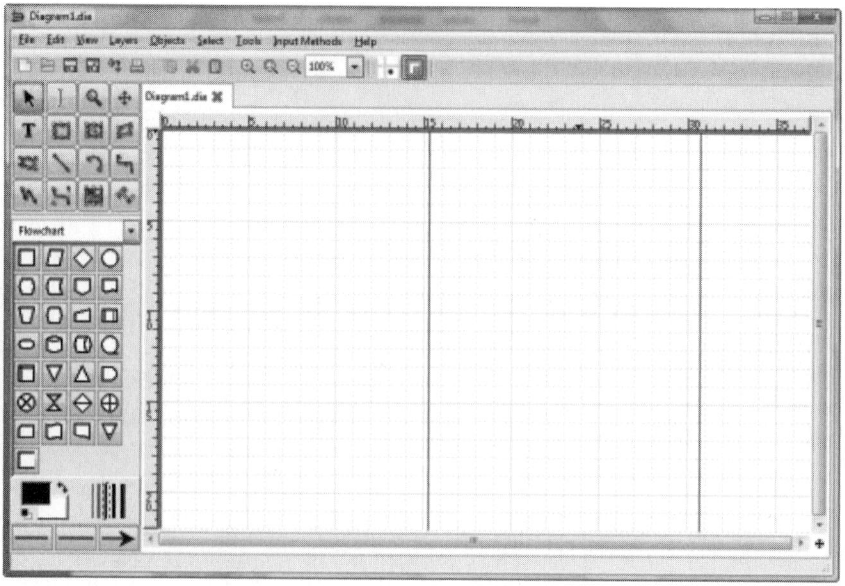

Figure B-9. Dia is an open source modeling product which allow you to create high quality technical diagrams.

File Archivers

Distribution on the Web has been made easier with the aid of file archiving tools. They act like folders to which you can insert multiple files and have them all stored within the one handy location. The technology can be useful on the Web because not only does it allow you to provide a series of files within a single download but the compression of the format means the size the downloads will be less problematic. As a result, you will not waste as many resources on your website due to the decreased file size and the reduced amount of time the file will take to download. Because of this, it's worth installing one to help manage files you wish to distribute online.

- **Industry standard**: 7Zip is free and open source. It's available for Windows, Mac, and Linux at http://www.7-zip.org/.

- **Recommendation**: WinZip Professional costs $49.95 and is available for Windows at http://www.winzip.com/.

- **Alternatives**:

    - WinRAR cost $29 and is available for Windows; it's shown in Figure B-10. See http://www.rarlabs.com/.

    - TugZip is free and also for Windows. See http://www.tugzip.com/.

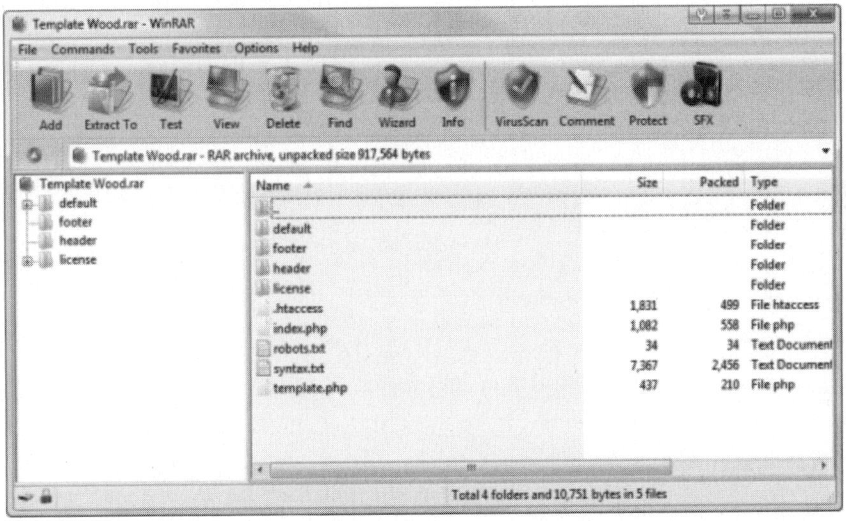

Figure B-10. WinRAR is an archiver which supports a multitude of various formats.

Backup Utilities

When you start building your website, the last thing you want to do is wake up one morning to find that your computer crashed and everything (including your website) was lost in the process. Losing important files can be devastating, and usually once you lose your data, you make sure never to lose it again. What a backup utility actually does is make a copy of everything you declare as important to you. There are many different places you can place the copy of your data onto such as a CD, DVD, floppy disk, portable memory device, or even on a private file hosting service. But the most important thing that can be gained from using this tool is the knowing that whatever happens, you can always recover what may have once been lost forever.

- **Industry standard:** Acronis True Image costs $49.99, and the upgrade costs $35.69. It's available for Windows at http://www.acronis.com/homecomputing/products/trueimage/.

- **Recommendation:** Cobain Backup (see Figure B-11) is free and is available for Windows at http://www.educ.umu.se/~cobian/cobianbackup.htm.

- **Alternatives:**

  - Genie-Soft Backup Manager is prices at $49.95 or $34.95 for the upgrade. It's Windows software available at http://www.genie-soft.com/products/gbm/us/default.html.

  - Time Machine is free software for Mac available within the operating system.

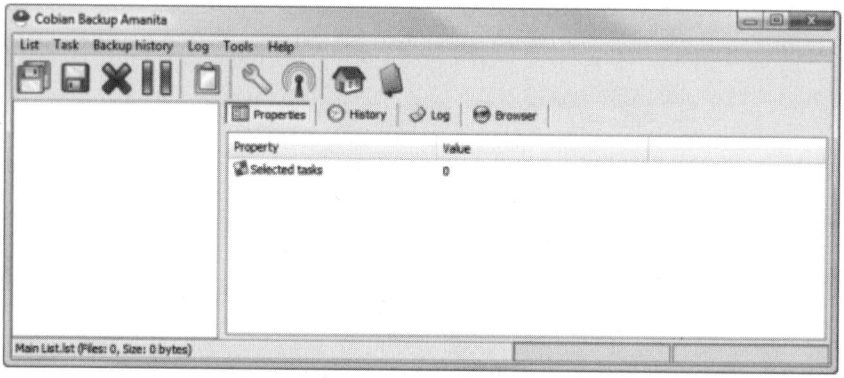

Figure B-11. Cobain Backup allows you to help guarantee your data's safety.

Color Pickers

When I make websites, the hardest thing I find is coming up with color schemes. By this, I mean choosing what colors mesh well together and what would suit my current web design needs. As someone who is beginning and will probably have no experience of the hexadecimal codes that correspond to color values, it may be worth getting a color picker or scheme creator. These tools allow you to select and create a palette of color (just like a painter), and from there, you can copy the code that represents that particular color into your documents as you require them. These tools give you valuable onscreen views of how your colors will end up looking and allow you to discover what color was used at a certain point of another website if you feel a lack of inspiration.

- **Industry standard**: Color Schemer Studio is $49.99, or you can upgrade for $29.99, and it's available for both Windows and Mac. See http://www.colorschemer.com/studio_info.php.

- **Recommendation**: Adobe Kuler is free and available for Windows, Mac, and Linux. See http://kuler.adobe.com/.

- **Alternative**:

  - CoffeeCup Website Color Schemer Studio costs $29.00 (see Figure B-12). It's available for Windows at http://www.coffeecup.com/color-schemer/.

  - Color Cop is a free Windows color picker available at http://colorcop.net/.

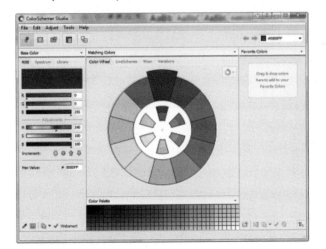

Figure B-12. Color Schemer Studio lets you create palettes that can be used in design.

Flash Developers

Creating Flash files for multimedia or creating website interfaces and components is unfortunately not one of those tasks you can do within an IDE or WYSIWYG editor. Flash is a proprietary technology that requires compilation in order to function—this means is you need to use a piece of software specifically engineered to produce these files and convert them into a format that can be used on the Web. It is worth buying one of these tools only when you start learning about the technology and only if you think it will be required or useful for the kind of website you wish to produce as a result of what you learn.

- **Industry standard:** Adobe Flash costs $699, and an upgrade costs $199. It's available for Windows and Mac. See http://www.adobe.com/products/flash/.

- **Recommendation:** SWiSHMax costs only $149.95, and the upgrade costs $74.95 (see Figure B-13). It's available for Windows at http://www.swishzone.com/index.php?area=products&product=max.

- **Alternative:** FlashDevelop is a free and open source alternative for Windows, Mac, and Linux. See http://www.osflash.org/flashdevelop/.

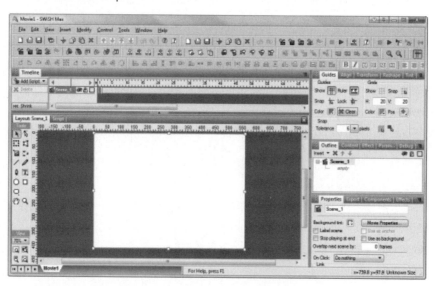

Figure B-13. SWiSHMax is a flash production tool that offers simple functionality at a fraction of Adobe's prices.

Audio Editors

Audio editors are rather specialist products for people who are creating websites. A new online experience that has been sweeping the world by storm is the notion of podcasting. Essentially, podcasts are audio files hosted on a website that are the equivalent of radio shows published by the website owner who talks about a specific subject in relation to the content of the website itself. An audio editor allows you to record your voice or other sounds that you would like to broadcast, organize the recording files into segments of a show, and then publish it in a format that people can listen to in their own time by downloading the podcast from the website. While podcasting is certainly not mandatory, it is a fun hobby that many people (especially bloggers) have found increases the value of a website's overall content and gives an added level of interaction with viewers.

- **Industry standard**: Audacity is a free, open source audio editor available for Windows, Mac, and Linux, and it's shown in Figure B-14. See http://audacity.sourceforge.net/.

- **Recommendation**: Adobe Audition can be purchased for $349. The upgrade costs $99. It's available for Windows at http://www.adobe.com/products/audition/.

- **Alternative**: Sony SoundForge costs $399.95 and is available for Windows at http://www.sonycreativesoftware.com/soundforge/.

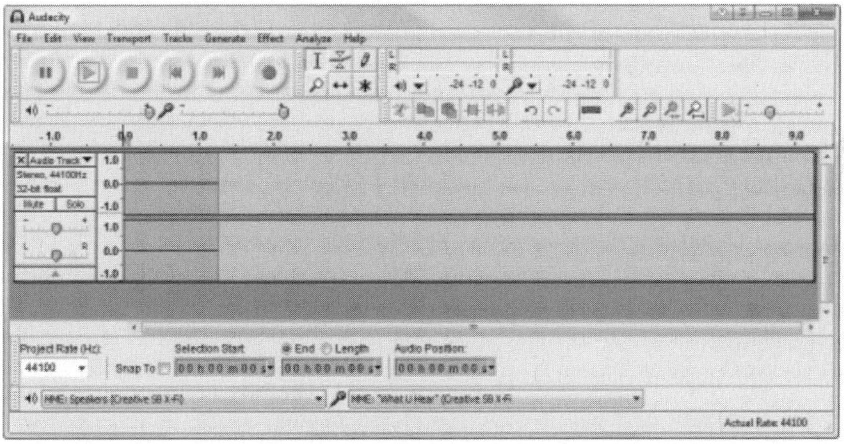

Figure B-14. Audacity is one of the most popular and simple to work with audio editors by professionals.

Web Browser Extensions

The previously mentioned utilities and software products will help you to produce high quality websites, but one area that still needs addressing is the current rise in browser extensions. Especially noteworthy are those made available through Mozilla Firefox. These utilities are almost always free to download, install, and use, and they provide a wealth of additional functionality into the browser that will be useful as you're producing your websites. Hundreds of potentially useful extensions are available through the Firefox add-ons page, but a few which may be of specific use to you have been recommended and listed in the following sections.

LinkED

If you would like to find more potentially useful web development extensions for Mozilla Firefox, you can do so by visiting the following website: https://addons.mozilla.org/en-US/firefox/.

Firebug

Of all the extensions in this list, Firebug is the most well known and beloved (see http://getfirebug.com/). It contains a powerful set of features to help you view, monitor, and debug your website. With HTML, CSS, and JavaScript debugging, editing, and inspection tools, as well as the abilities to log and record errors in your websites and to inspect individual elements to see how they compare against other elements on the page, Firebug really is a Swiss Army knife of epic proportions that no website creator should be without (see Figure B-15).

Figure B-15. Firebug lets you take a peek under the hood of any website.

Codeburner

Codeburner (http://tools.sitepoint.com/codeburner/) is actually an extension of Firebug created by SitePoint. What does it do? Well, it provides added functions to the popular extension in terms of complete documentation of HTML, CSS, and JavaScript, explaining each tag's purpose, providing examples of how it can be used in a website, and noting what browsers contain support for it (see Figure B-16). While Codeburner may not be as well known as Firebug, it gives you some really useful advice when you find yourself at a loss for the meaning behind different pieces of code within your website design. You should think of Codeburner as the same equivalent to one of those pocket reference books you can buy on specific subjects.

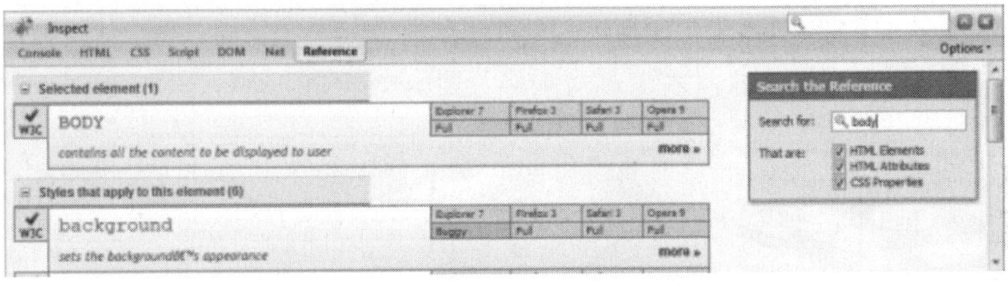

Figure B-16. Codeburner offers reference material for the most commonly used web languages.

Web Developer Options

Have ever wanted to know what would happen to your website if a particular technology was disabled? Or would you like to see where all of the elements and components of your website are located in the page by displaying or outlining them in an easy to view manner? How about running a series of tests on your code or generally just poking around under the hood to determine the causes of problems? If so, Web Developer Options extension is for you (see Figure B-17). It does have some similar functionality to other extensions mentioned in this appendix, it should be noted that its ability to pinpoint and highlight elements of a design are second to none. This add-on for Firefox would be a great addition to your website building utilities. You can find the home page at http://chrispederick.com/work/web-developer/.

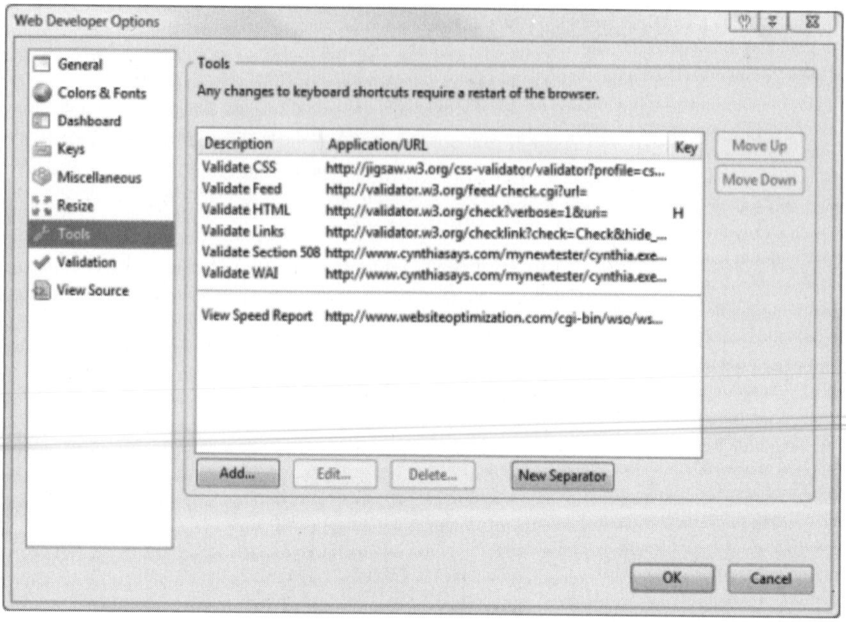

Figure B-17. The Web Developer Options add-on can show you what will happen if a style is disabled.

Firefox Accessibility Extension

The Firefox Accessibility extension shown in Figure B-18 was created by the Illinois Center for Information Technology Accessibility to give people with disabilities an easier browsing experience (see http://firefox.cita.uiuc.edu/). However, this tool is particularly useful for developers when you come to checking how easy the website is to navigate for disabled people. You can produce a series of reports, lists, and validator results that can assist you in both fixing errors in your code and improving the overall accessibility of your websites.

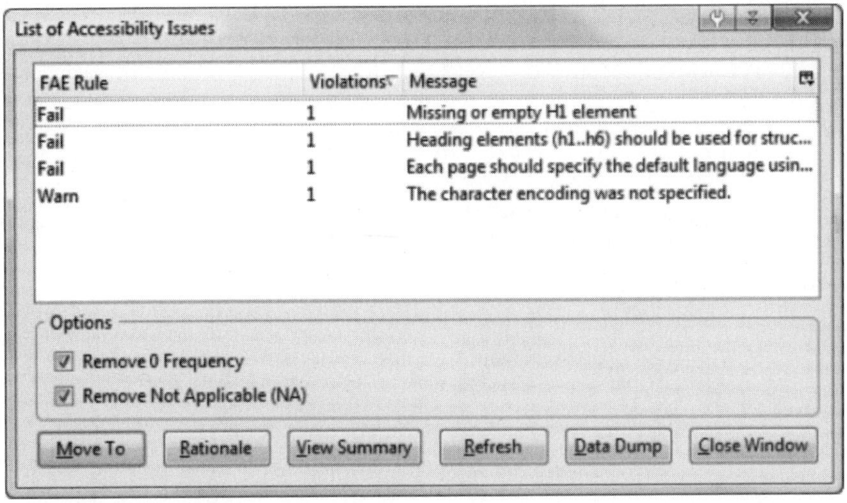

Figure B-18: Reports can be produced using the accessibility extension to help analyze your website.

ColorZilla

A separate color picker may help you produce a palette with ease, but if you are a Firefox user, there may not even be a need for you to purchase or download a separate application because of the powerful little utility known as ColorZilla (see `http://www.colorzilla.com/firefox/`). This add-on (shown in Figure B-19) gives you the ability to mix colors and styles with ease. It comes with an eyedropper tool that lets you select specific colors you see in the browser window and a website analyzer that can extract colors used on the page you are visiting into a custom palette. It even has a color picker that contains a variety of mixers you can use to work out shades, tints, and grab the values for individual choices.

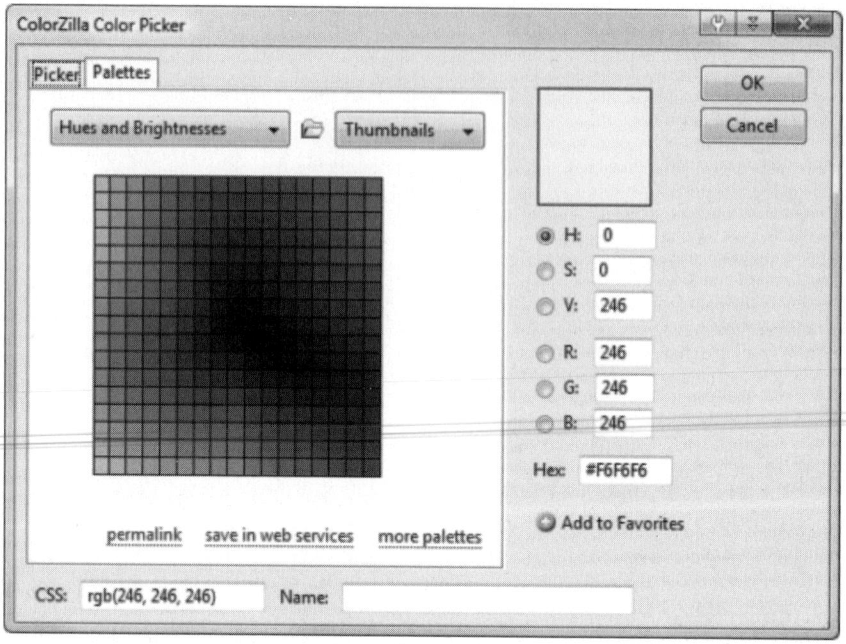

Figure B-19. Produce color schemes based on an existing website with ease using ColorZilla.

Index